Stata Reference Manual
Release 6
Volume 2 H-O

Stata Press
College Station, Texas

Stata Press, 702 University Drive East, College Station, Texas 77840

Title

hadimvo — Identify multivariate outliers

Syntax

`hadimvo` *varlist* [`if` *exp*] [`in` *range*], `generate(`$newvar_1$ [$newvar_2$]`)` [`p(`*#*`)`]

Description

`hadimvo` identifies multiple outliers in multivariate data using the method of Hadi (1992, 1994), creating $newvar_1$ equal to 1 if an observation is an "outlier" and 0 otherwise. Optionally, $newvar_2$ can also be created containing the distances from the basic subset.

Options

`generate(`$newvar_1$ [$newvar_2$]`)` is not optional; it identifies the new variable(s) to be created. Whether you specify two variables or one, however, is optional. $newvar_1$—which is required—will create $newvar_1$ containing 1 if the observation is an outlier in the Hadi sense and 0 otherwise. Specifying `gen(odd)` would call this variable `odd`. $newvar_2$, if specified, will also create $newvar_2$ containing the distances (not the distances squared) from the basic subset. Specifying `gen(odd dist)` creates `odd` and also creates `dist` containing the Hadi distances.

`p(`*#*`)` specifies the "significance" level for outlier cutoff; $0 < \# < 1$. The default is `p(.05)`. Larger numbers identify a larger proportion of the sample as outliers. If # is specified greater than 1, it is interpreted as a percent. Thus, `p(5)` is the same as `p(.05)`.

Remarks

Multivariate analysis techniques are commonly used to analyze data from many fields of study. The data often contains outliers. The search for subsets of the data which, if deleted, would change results markedly is known as the search for outliers. `hadimvo` provides one computer-intensive but practical method for identifying such observations.

Classical outlier detection methods (e.g., Mahalanobis distance and Wilks' test) are powerful when the data contains only one outlier, but the power of these methods decreases drastically when more than one outlying observation is present. The loss of power is usually due to what are known as masking and swamping problems (false negative and false positive decisions) but in addition, these methods often fail simply because they are affected by the very observations they are supposed to identify.

Solutions to these problems often involve an unreasonable amount of calculation and therefore computer time. (Solutions involving hundreds of millions of calculations for samples as small as 30 have been suggested.) The method developed by Hadi (1992, 1994) attempts to surmount these problems and produce an answer, albeit second best, in finite time.

A basic outline of the procedure is as follows: A measure of distance from an observation to a cluster of points is defined. A base cluster of r points is selected and then that cluster is continually redefined by taking the $r + 1$ points "closest" to the cluster as the new base cluster. This continues until some rule stops the redefinition of the cluster.

Ignoring many of the fine details, given k variables, the initial base cluster is defined as $r = k + 1$ points. The distance that is minimized in selecting these $k + 1$ points is a covariance-matrix distance on the variables with their medians removed. (We will use the language loosely; if we were being more precise, we would have said the distance is based on a matrix of second moments, but remember, the medians of the variables have been removed. We would also discuss how the $k + 1$ points must be of full column rank and how they would be expanded to include additional points if they are not.)

Given the base cluster, a more standard mean-based center of the r-observation cluster is defined and the $r + 1$ observations closest in the covariance-matrix sense are chosen as a new base cluster. This is then repeated until the base cluster has $r = \text{int}\big((n + k + 1)/2\big)$ points.

At this point, the method continues in much the same way, except a stopping rule based on the distance of the additional point, and the user-specified $p()$, is introduced.

Simulation results are presented in Hadi (1994).

Examples

```
. hadimvo price weight, gen(odd)
. list if odd                    /* list the outliers           */
. summ price weight if ~odd      /* summary stats for clean data */

. drop odd
. hadimvo price weight, gen(odd D)
. gen id=_n                      /* make an index variable       */
. graph D id                     /* index plot of D              */
. graph price weight [w=D]       /* 2-way scatter, outliers big  */
. graph price weight [w=1/D]     /* same, outliers small         */
. summarize D, detail
. sort D
. list make price weight D odd

. hadimvo price weight mpg, gen(odd2 D2) p(.01)
. regress ... if ~odd2
```

Identifying outliers

You have a theory about $x_1, x_2, \ldots, x_k$ which we will write as $F(x_1, x_2, \ldots, x_k)$. Your theory might be that $x_1, x_2, \ldots, x_k$ are jointly distributed normally, perhaps with a particular mean and covariance matrix; or your theory might be that

$$x_1 = \beta_1 + \beta_2 x_2 + \cdots + \beta_k x_k + u$$

where $u \sim N(0, \sigma^2)$; or your theory might be

$$x_1 = \beta_{10} + \beta_{12} x_2 + \beta_{14} x_4 + u_1$$
$$x_2 = \beta_{20} + \beta_{21} x_1 + \beta_{23} x_3 + u_2$$

or your theory might be anything else—it does not matter. You have some data on $x_1, x_2, \ldots, x_k$, which you will assume is generated by $F(\cdot)$, and from that data you plan to estimate the parameters (if any) of your theory and then test your theory in the sense of how well it explains the observed data.

What if, however, some of your data is generated not by $F(\cdot)$ but by $G(\cdot)$, a different process? For example, you have a theory on how wages are assigned to employees in a firm and, for the bulk of employees, that theory is correct. There are, however, six employees at the top of the hierarchy for whom wages are set by a completely different process. Or, you have a theory on how individuals select different health insurance options except that, for a handful of individuals already diagnosed with serious illness, a different process controls the selection process. Or, you are testing a drug that reduces trauma after surgery except that, for a few patients with a high level of a particular protein, the drug has no effect. Or, in another drug experiment, some of the historical data is simply misrecorded.

The data values generated by $G(\cdot)$ rather than $F(\cdot)$ are called contaminant observations. Of course, the analysis should be based only on the observations generated by $F(\cdot)$, but in practice we do not know which observations those are. In addition, if it happened by chance that some of the observations are within a reasonable distance from the center of $F(\cdot)$, it becomes impossible to determine whether they are contaminants. Accordingly, we adopt the following operational definition: Outliers are observations that do not conform to the pattern suggested by the majority of the observations in a dataset. Accordingly, observations generated by $F(\cdot)$ but located at the tail of $F(\cdot)$ are considered outliers. On the other hand, contaminants that are within a statistically reasonable distance from the center of $F(\cdot)$ are not considered outliers.

It is well worth noting that outliership is strongly related to the completeness of the theory—a grand unified theory would have no outliers because it would explain all processes (including, one supposes, errors in recording the data). Grand unified theories, however, are difficult to come by and are most often developed by synthesizing the results of many special theories.

Theoretical work has tended to focus on one special case: the data contains only one outlier. As mentioned above, the single-outlier techniques often fail to identify multiple outliers, even if applied recursively. One of the classic examples is the star cluster data (a.k.a. Hertzsprung–Russell diagram) shown in the figure below (Rousseeuw and Leroy 1987, 27). For 47 stars, the data contains the (log) light intensity and the (log) effective temperature at the star's surface. (For the sake of illustration, we treat the data here as bivariate data—not as regression data—i.e., the two variables are treated similarly with no distinction between which variable is dependent and which is independent.)

This graph presents a scatter of the data along with two ellipses expected to contain 95% of the data. The larger ellipse is based on the mean and covariance matrix of the full data. All 47 stars are inside the larger ellipse, indicating that classical single-case analysis fails to identify any outliers. The smaller ellipse is based on the mean and covariance matrix of the data without the five stars identified by `hadimvo` as outliers. These observations are located outside the smaller ellipse. The dramatic effects of the outliers can be seen by comparing the two ellipses. The volume of the larger ellipse is much greater than that of the smaller one and the two ellipses have completely different orientations. In fact, their major axes are nearly orthogonal to each other; the larger ellipse indicates a negative correlation ($r = -0.2$) whereas the smaller ellipse indicates a positive correlation ($r = 0.7$). (Theory would suggest a positive correlation: hot things glow.)

(Graph on next page)

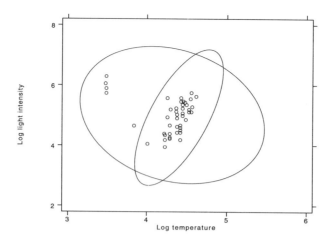

The single-outlier techniques make calculations for each observation under the assumption that it is the only outlier—and the remaining $n - 1$ observations are generated by $F(\cdot)$—producing a statistic for each of the n observations. Thinking about multiple outliers is no more difficult. In the case of two outliers, consider all possible pairs of observations (there are $n(n - 1)/2$ of them) and, for each pair, make a calculation assuming the remaining $n - 2$ observations are generated by $F(\cdot)$. For the three-outlier case, consider all possible triples of observations (there are $n(n - 1)(n - 2)/(3 \times 2)$ of them) and, for each triple, make a calculation assuming the remaining $n - 3$ observations are generated by $F(\cdot)$.

Conceptually, this is easy but practically, it is difficult because of the rapidly increasing number of calculations required (there are also theoretical problems in determining how many outliers to test simultaneously). Techniques designed for detecting multiple outliers, therefore, make various simplifying assumptions to reduce the calculation burden and, along the way, lose some of the theoretical foundation. This loss, however, is no reason for ignoring the problem and the (admittedly second best) solutions available today. It is unreasonable to assume that outliers do not occur in real data.

If outliers exist in the data, they can distort parameter estimation, invalidate test statistics, and lead to incorrect statistical inference. The search for outliers is not merely to improve the estimates of the current model but also to provide valuable insight into the shortcomings of the current model. In addition, outliers themselves can sometimes provide valuable clues as to where more effort should be expended. In a drug experiment, for example, the patients excluded as outliers might well be further researched to understand why they do not fit the theory.

Multivariate, multiple outliers

hadimvo is an example of a multivariate, multiple outlier technique. The multivariate aspect deserves some attention. In the single-equation regression techniques for identifying outliers, such as residuals and leverage, an important distinction is drawn between the dependent and independent variables—the y and the $\mathbf{x}$'s in $y = \mathbf{x}\beta + u$. The notion that the y is a linear function of $\mathbf{x}$ can be exploited and, moreover, the fact that some point $(y_i, \mathbf{x}_i)$ is "far" from the bulk of the other points has different meanings if that "farness" is due to y_i or $\mathbf{x}_i$. A point that is far due to $\mathbf{x}_i$ but, despite that, still close in the y_i given $\mathbf{x}_i$ metric, adds precision to the measurements of the coefficients and may not indicate a problem at all. In fact, if we have the luxury of designing the experiment, which means choosing the values of $\mathbf{x}$ a priori, we attempt to maximize the distance between the $\mathbf{x}$'s (within the bounds of $\mathbf{x}$ we believe are covered by our linear model) to maximize that precision. In that extreme case, the distance of $\mathbf{x}_i$ carries no information as we set it prior to running the experiment. More recently, Hadi and Simonoff (1993) exploit the structure of the linear model and suggest two methods for identifying multiple outliers when the model is fitted to the data (also see [R] **regression diagnostics**).

In the multivariate case, we do not know the structure of the model, so $(y_i, \mathbf{x}_i)$ is just a point and the y is treated no differently from any of the $\mathbf{x}$'s—a fact which we emphasize by writing the point as $(x_{1i}, \mathbf{x}_{2i})$ or simply $(\mathbf{X}_i)$. The technique does assume, however, that the $\mathbf{X}$'s are multivariate normal or at least elliptically symmetric. This leads to a problem if some of the $\mathbf{X}$'s are functionally related to the other $\mathbf{X}$'s, such as the inclusion of x and x^2, interactions such as $x_1 x_2$, or even dummy variables for multiple categories (in which one of the dummies being 1 means the other dummies must be 0). There is no good solution to this problem. One idea, however, is to perform the analysis with and without the functionally related variables and to subject all observations identified for further study (see *What to do with outliers* below).

An implication of `hadimvo` being a multivariate technique is that it would be inappropriate to apply it to $(y, \mathbf{x})$ when $\mathbf{x}$ is the result of experimental design. The technique would know nothing of our design of $\mathbf{x}$ and would inappropriately treat "distance" in the $\mathbf{x}$-metric the same as distance in the y-metric. Even when $\mathbf{x}$ is multivariate normal, unless y and $\mathbf{x}$ are treated similarly it may still be inappropriate to apply `hadimvo` to $(y, \mathbf{x})$ because of the different roles that y and $\mathbf{x}$ play in regression. However, one may apply `hadimvo` on $\mathbf{x}$ to identify outliers which, in this case, are called leverage points. (We should also mention here that if `hadimvo` is applied to $\mathbf{x}$ when it contains constants or any collinear variables, those variables will be correctly ignored, allowing the analysis to continue.)

It is also inappropriate to use `hadimvo` (and other outlier detection techniques) when the sample size is too small. `hadimvo` uses a small-sample correction factor to adjust the covariance matrix of the "clean" subset. Because the quantity $n - (3k + 1)$ appears in the denominator of the correction factor, the sample size must be larger than $3k + 1$. Some authors would require the sample size to be at least $5k$, i.e., at least five observations per variable.

With these warnings, it is difficult to misapply this tool assuming that you do not take the results as more than suggestive. `hadimvo` has a `p()` option that is a "significance level" for the outliers that are chosen. We quote the term significance level because, although great effort has been expended to really make a significance level, approximations are involved and it will not have that interpretation in all cases. It can be thought of as an index between 0 and 1, with increasing values resulting in the labeling of more observations as outliers and with the suggestion that you select a number much as you would a significance level—it is roughly the probability of identifying any given point as an outlier if the data truly were multivariate normal. Nevertheless, the terms significance level or critical values should be taken with a grain of salt. It is suggested that one examine a graphical display (e.g., an index plot) of the distance with perhaps different values of `p()`. The graphs give more information than a simple yes/no answer. For example, the graph may indicate that some of the observations (inliers or outliers) are only marginally so.

What to do with outliers

After a reading of the literature on outlier detection, many people are left with the incorrect impression that once outliers are identified, they should be deleted from the data and analysis continued. Automatic deletion (or even automatic down-weighting) of outliers is not always correct because outliers are not necessarily bad observations. On the contrary, if they are correct, they may be the most informative points in the data. For example, they may indicate that the data did not come from a normally distributed population as is commonly assumed by almost all multivariate techniques.

The proper use of this tool is to label outliers and then subject the outliers to further study, not simply to discard them and continue the analysis with the rest of the data. After further study, it may indeed turn out to be reasonable to discard the outliers, but some mention of the outliers must certainly be made in the presentation of the final results. Other corrective actions may include correction of errors in the data, deletion or down-weighting of outliers, redesigning the experiment or sample survey, collecting more data, etc.

Saved Results

hadimvo saves in r():

Scalars
r(N)   number of outliers remaining

Methods and Formulas

hadimvo is implemented as an ado-file. Formulas are given in Hadi (1992, 1994).

Acknowledgment

We would like to thank Ali S. Hadi of Cornell University for his assistance in writing hadimvo.

References

Gould, W. W. and A. S. Hadi. 1993. smv6: Identifying multivariate outliers. *Stata Technical Bulletin* 11: 28–32. Reprinted in *Stata Technical Bulletin Reprints*, vol. 2, pp. 163–168.

Hadi, A. S. 1992. Identifying multiple outliers in multivariate data. *Journal of the Royal Statistical Society*, Series B 54: 761–771.

——. 1994. A modification of a method for the detection of outliers in multivariate samples. *Journal of the Royal Statistical Society*, Series B 56: 393–396.

Hadi, A. S. and J. S. Simonoff. 1993. Procedures for the identification of multiple outliers in linear models. *Journal of the American Statistical Association* 88: 1264–1272.

Rousseeuw, P. J. and A. M. Leroy. 1987. *Robust Regression and Outlier Detection*. New York: John Wiley & Sons.

Also See

Related: [R] **mvreg**, [R] **regression diagnostics**, [R] **sureg**

Title

> **hausman** — Hausman specification test

Syntax

```
hausman, save

hausman [, { more | less } constant alleqs skipeqs(eqlist) sigmamore ]

hausman, clear
```

Description

hausman performs Hausman's (1978) specification test.

Options

save requests that Stata save the current estimation results. hausman will later compare these results with the estimation results from another model. A model must be saved in this fashion before a test against other models can be performed.

more specifies that the most recently estimated model is the more efficient estimate. This is the default.

less specifies that the most recently estimated model is the less efficient estimate.

constant specifies that the estimated intercept(s) are to be included in the model comparison; by default, they are excluded. The default behavior is appropriate for models where the constant does not have a common interpretation across the two models.

alleqs specifies that all the equations in the model be used to perform the Hausman test; by default, only the first equation is used.

skipeqs(eqlist) specifies in eqlist the names of equations to be excluded from the test. Equation numbers are not allowed in this context as it is the equation names, along with the variable names, that are used to identify common coefficients.

sigmamore allows you to specify that the two covariance matrices used in the test be based on a common estimate of disturbance variance (σ^2)—the variance from the more efficient estimator. This option provides a proper estimate of the contrast variance for so-called tests of exogeneity and over-identification in instrumental variables regression; see Baltagi (1998, 291). Note that this option can only be specified when both estimators save e(sigma) or e(rmse).

clear discards the previously saved estimation results and so frees some memory; it is not necessary to specify hausman, clear before specifying hausman, save.

Remarks

hausman is a general implementation of Hausman's (1978) specification test that compares an estimator that is known to be consistent with an estimator that is efficient under the assumption being tested. The null hypothesis is that the efficient estimator is a consistent and efficient estimator of the true parameters. If it is, there should be no systematic difference between the coefficients of the efficient estimator and a comparison estimator that is known to be consistent for the true parameters. If the two models display a systematic difference in the estimated coefficients, then we have reason to doubt the assumptions on which the efficient estimator is based.

To use hausman, you

. (*estimate the less efficient model*)

. hausman, save

. (*estimate the more efficient model*)

. hausman

Alternatively, you can turn this around:

. (*estimate the more efficient model*)

. hausman, save

. (*estimate the less efficient model*)

. hausman, less

▷ Example

We are studying the factors that affect the wages of young women in the United States between 1970 and 1988 and have a panel-data sample of individual women over that time span.

```
. describe
Contains data from nlswork.dta
    obs:        28,534                          National Longitudinal Survey.
                                                Young Women 14-26 years of age
                                                in 1968
    vars:            6                          23 Aug 1998 10:39
    size:       485,078 (88.4% of memory free)
-------------------------------------------------------------------------------
    1. idcode      int     %8.0g               NLS id
    2. year        byte    %8.0g               interview year
    3. age         byte    %8.0g               age in current year
    4. msp         byte    %8.0g               1 if married, spouse present
    5. ttl_exp     float   %9.0g               total work experience
    6. ln_wage     float   %9.0g               ln(wage/GNP deflator)
-------------------------------------------------------------------------------
Sorted by:  idcode   year
```

We believe that a random-effects specification is appropriate for individual-level effects in our model. We estimate a fixed-effects model that will capture all temporally constant individual-level effects.

```
. xtreg ln_wage age msp ttl_exp, fe
Fixed-effects (within) regression              Number of obs      =     28494
Group variable (i) : idcode                    Number of groups   =      4710

R-sq:  within  = 0.1373                         Obs per group: min =         1
       between = 0.2571                                        avg =       6.0
       overall = 0.1800                                        max =        15

                                               F(3,23781)         =   1262.01
corr(u_i, Xb)  = 0.1476                         Prob > F           =    0.0000
-------------------------------------------------------------------------------
```

```
   ln_wage |     Coef.   Std. Err.       t    P>|t|     [95% Conf. Interval]
-----------+----------------------------------------------------------------
       age |   -.005485    .000837    -6.553   0.000    -.0071256   -.0038443
       msp |   .0033427   .0054868     0.609   0.542    -.0074118    .0140971
   ttl_exp |   .0383604   .0012416    30.895   0.000     .0359268    .0407941
     _cons |   1.593953   .0177538    89.781   0.000     1.559154    1.628752
-----------+----------------------------------------------------------------
   sigma_u |  .37674223
   sigma_e |  .29751014
       rho |  .61591044   (fraction of variance due to u_i)
----------------------------------------------------------------------------
F test that all u_i=0:     F(4709,23781) =      7.76        Prob > F = 0.0000
```

We assume that this model is consistent for the true parameters, and save the results by typing

```
. hausman, save
```

Now, we estimate a random-effects model as a more efficient specification of the individual effects under the assumption that they follow a random-normal distribution. These estimates are then compared to the previously saved results using the hausman command.

```
. xtreg ln_wage age msp ttl_exp, re
Random-effects GLS regression              Number of obs      =      28494
Group variable (i) : idcode                Number of groups   =       4710
R-sq:  within  = 0.1373                    Obs per group: min =          1
       between = 0.2552                                   avg =        6.0
       overall = 0.1797                                   max =         15
Random effects u_i  Gaussian               Wald chi2(3)       =    5100.33
corr(u_i, X)        = 0 (assumed)          Prob > chi2        =     0.0000

----------------------------------------------------------------------------
   ln_wage |     Coef.   Std. Err.       z    P>|z|     [95% Conf. Interval]
-----------+----------------------------------------------------------------
       age |  -.0069749   .0006882   -10.134   0.000    -.0083238   -.0056259
       msp |   .0046594   .0051012     0.913   0.361    -.0053387    .0146575
   ttl_exp |   .0429635   .0010169    42.248   0.000     .0409704    .0449567
     _cons |   1.609916   .0159176   101.141   0.000     1.578718    1.641114
-----------+----------------------------------------------------------------
   sigma_u |  .32648519
   sigma_e |  .29751014
       rho |  .54633481   (fraction of variance due to u_i)
----------------------------------------------------------------------------

. hausman
              ---- Coefficients ----
           |      (b)          (B)          (b-B)     sqrt(diag(V_b-V_B))
           |     Prior       Current      Difference        S.E.
-----------+----------------------------------------------------------------
       age |   -.005485    -.0069749       .0014899         .0004764
       msp |   .0033427     .0046594      -.0013167         .0020206
   ttl_exp |   .0383604     .0429635      -.0046031         .0007124
-----------+----------------------------------------------------------------
             b = less efficient estimates obtained previously from xtreg.
             B = more efficient estimates obtained from xtreg.
    Test:  Ho:  difference in coefficients not systematic
               chi2( 3) = (b-B)´[(V_b-V_B)^(-1)](b-B)
                        =     275.44
               Prob>chi2 =      0.0000
```

Using the current specification, our initial hypothesis that the individual-level effects are adequately modeled by a random-effects model is resoundingly rejected. We realize, of course, that this result is based on the rest of our model specification and that it is entirely possible that random effects might be appropriate for some alternate model of wages.

`hausman` is a generic implementation of the Hausman test and assumes the user knows exactly what they want tested. The test between random- and fixed-effects is so common that Stata provides a special command for use after `xtreg`. We could have obtained the above test, in a slightly different format, by typing

```
. xthaus

Hausman specification test

              ---- Coefficients ----
            |     Fixed        Random
  ln_wage   |    Effects       Effects      Difference
------------+-------------------------------------------
       age  |   -.005485     -.0069749       .0014899
       msp  |   .0033427      .0046594      -.0013167
   ttl_exp  |   .0383604      .0429635      -.0046031

Test:  Ho:  difference in coefficients not systematic

           chi2( 3) = (b-B)´[S^ (-1)](b-B), S = (S_fe - S_re)
                    =    275.44
           Prob>chi2 =     0.0000
```

◁

> ## Example

A stringent assumption of multinomial and conditional logit models is that outcome categories for the model have the property of independence of irrelevant alternatives (IIA). Stated simply, this assumption requires that the inclusion or exclusion of categories does not affect the relative risks associated with the regressors in the remaining categories.

One classic example of a situation where this assumption would be violated involves choice of transportation mode; see McFadden (1974). For simplicity, postulate a transportation model with the four possible outcomes: rides a train to work, takes a bus to work, drives the Ford to work, and drives the Chevrolet to work. Clearly "drives the Ford" is a closer substitute to "drives the Chevrolet" than it is to "rides a train" (at least for most people). This means that excluding "drives the Ford" from the model could be expected to affect the relative risks of the remaining options and the model would not obey the IIA assumption.

Using the same data as presented in [R] **mlogit**, we will use a simplified model to test for IIA. Choice of insurance type among indemnity, prepaid, and uninsured is modeled as a function of age and gender. The indemnity category is allowed to be the base category and the model including all three outcomes is estimated.

```
. mlogit insure age male

Iteration 0:   log likelihood = -555.85446
Iteration 1:   log likelihood = -551.32973
Iteration 2:   log likelihood = -551.32802

Multinomial regression                    Number of obs   =       615
                                          LR chi2(4)      =      9.05
                                          Prob > chi2     =    0.0598
Log likelihood = -551.32802               Pseudo R2       =    0.0081

------------------------------------------------------------------------
   insure  |     Coef.    Std. Err.     z     P>|z|   [95% Conf. Interval]
-----------+------------------------------------------------------------
Prepaid    |
      age  |  -.0100251    .0060181   -1.666   0.096   -.0218204    .0017702
     male  |   .5095747    .1977893    2.576   0.010    .1219148    .8972345
    _cons  |   .2633838    .2787574    0.945   0.345   -.2829708    .8097383
-----------+------------------------------------------------------------
```

```
Uninsure |
     age |   -.0051925    .0113821    -0.456   0.648     -.027501    .017116
    male |    .4748547    .3618446     1.312   0.189    -.2343477   1.184057
   _cons |   -1.756843    .5309591    -3.309   0.001    -2.797504  -.7161824
---------------------------------------------------------------------------

(Outcome insure==Indem is the comparison group)

. hausman, save
```

Under the IIA assumption, we would expect no systematic change in the coefficients if we excluded one of the outcomes from the model. (For an extensive discussion, see Hausman and McFadden, 1984.) We reestimate the model, excluding the uninsured outcome, and perform a Hausman test against the more efficient full model.

```
. mlogit insure age male if insure != "Uninsure":insure

Iteration 0:   log likelihood =  -394.8693
Iteration 1:   log likelihood =  -390.4871
Iteration 2:   log likelihood = -390.48643

Multinomial regression                    Number of obs   =        570
                                          LR chi2(2)      =       8.77
                                          Prob > chi2     =     0.0125
Log likelihood = -390.48643               Pseudo R2       =     0.0111

---------------------------------------------------------------------------
  insure |     Coef.   Std. Err.       z     P>|z|    [95% Conf. Interval]
---------+-----------------------------------------------------------------
Prepaid  |
     age |   -.0101521    .0060049    -1.691   0.091    -.0219214    .0016173
    male |    .5144003    .1981735     2.596   0.009     .1259875    .9028132
   _cons |    .2678043    .2775562     0.965   0.335    -.2761959    .8118046
---------------------------------------------------------------------------

(Outcome insure==Indem is the comparison group)

. hausman, alleqs less constant

              ---- Coefficients ----
         |      (b)          (B)          (b-B)    sqrt(diag(V_b-V_B))
         |    Current       Prior       Difference        S.E.
---------+-----------------------------------------------------------------
     age |   -.0101521    -.0100251    -.0001269            .
    male |    .5144003     .5095747     .0048256         .012334
   _cons |    .2678043     .2633838     .0044205            .
---------+-----------------------------------------------------------------
            b = less efficient estimates obtained from mlogit.
            B = more efficient estimates obtained previously from mlogit.

Test:  Ho:  difference in coefficients not systematic

            chi2(  3) = (b-B)´[(V_b-V_B)^ (-1)](b-B)
                      =        0.08
            Prob>chi2 =      0.9944
```

First, note that the somewhat subtle syntax of the `if` condition on the `mlogit` command was simply used to identify the `"Uninsured"` category using the `insure` value label; see [U] **15.6.3 Value labels**. On examining the output from `hausman`, we see that there is no evidence that the IIA assumption has been violated.

The missing values for the square-root of the diagonal of the covariance matrix of the differences is not comforting but also not surprising. This covariance matrix is guaranteed to be positive definite only asymptotically and assurances are not made about the diagonal elements. Negative values along the diagonal, are possible, and the fourth column of the table is provided more for descriptive than statistical use.

We can also perform the Hausman IIA test against the remaining alternative in the model.

```
. mlogit insure age male if insure != "Prepaid":insure
Iteration 0:    log likelihood = -132.59913
Iteration 1:    log likelihood = -131.78009
Iteration 2:    log likelihood = -131.76808
Iteration 3:    log likelihood = -131.76807
Multinomial regression                          Number of obs    =         338
                                                LR chi2(2)       =        1.66
                                                Prob > chi2      =      0.4356
Log likelihood = -131.76807                     Pseudo R2        =      0.0063
------------------------------------------------------------------------------
    insure |      Coef.   Std. Err.       z    P>|z|     [95% Conf. Interval]
-----------+------------------------------------------------------------------
Uninsure   |
       age |  -.0041055   .0115807    -0.355   0.723    -.0268033    .0185923
      male |   .4591072   .3595663     1.277   0.202    -.2456298    1.163844
     _cons |  -1.801774   .5474476    -3.291   0.001    -2.874752   -.7287968
------------------------------------------------------------------------------
(Outcome insure==Indem is the comparison group)
. hausman, alleqs less constant
             ---- Coefficients ----
           |       (b)          (B)            (b-B)     sqrt(diag(V_b-V_B))
           |     Current       Prior         Difference         S.E.
-----------+------------------------------------------------------------------
       age |   -.0041055    -.0051925          .001087         .0021357
      male |    .4591072     .4748547        -.0157475            .
     _cons |   -1.801774    -1.756843        -.0449311         .1333464
-----------+------------------------------------------------------------------
             b = less efficient estimates obtained from mlogit.
             B = more efficient estimates obtained previously from mlogit.
    Test:  Ho:  difference in coefficients not systematic
             chi2(  3) = (b-B)'[(V_b-V_B)^(-1)](b-B)
                      =      -0.18
             Prob>chi2 =           .
```

In this case, the χ^2 statistic is actually negative. We might interpret this as providing strong evidence that we cannot reject the null hypothesis. Such a result is not an unusual outcome for the Hausman test, particularly when the sample is relatively small—there are only 45 uninsured individuals in this dataset.

Are we surprised by the results of the Hausman test in this example? Not really. Judging from the z-statistics on the original multinomial logit model, we were struggling to identify any structure in the data with the current specification. Even when we were willing to make the assumption of IIA, and estimate the most efficient model under this assumption, few of the effects could be identified as statistically different from those on the base category. Trying to base a Hausman test on a contrast (difference) between two poor estimates is just asking too much of the existing data.

◁

For an example applying the Hausman test to the endogeneity of variables in a simultaneous system, see [R] **ivreg**.

Saved Results

hausman saves in r():

Scalars
    r(chi2) χ^2
    r(df)   degrees of freedom for the statistic
    r(p) p-value for the χ^2

Acknowledgment

Portions of `hausman` are based on an early implementation by Jeroen Weesie, Utrecht University, Netherlands.

Methods and Formulas

`hausman` is implemented as an ado-file.

The Hausman statistic is distributed as χ^2 and is computed as

$$H = (\beta_c - \beta_e)'(V_c - V_e)^{-1}(\beta_c - \beta_e)$$

where

β_c is the coefficient vector from the consistent estimator
β_e is the coefficient vector from the efficient estimator
V_c is the covariance matrix of the coefficients from the consistent estimator
V_e is the covariance matrix of the coefficients from the efficient estimator

In cases where the difference in the variance matrices is not positive definite, a Moore–Penrose generalized inverse is used. As noted in Gourieroux and Monfort (1989, 125–128), choice of generalized inverse is not important asymptotically.

The degrees of freedom for the statistic is the rank of the difference in the variance matrices. When the difference is positive definite, this is the number of common coefficients in the models being compared.

References

Baltagi, B. H. 1998. *Econometrics*. New York: Springer-Verlag.

Gourieroux, H. and A. Monfort. 1989. *Statistics and Econometric Models, Vol. 2*. New York: Springer-Verlag.

Hausman, J. 1978. Specification tests in econometrics. *Econometrica* 46: 1251–1271.

Hausman, J. and D. McFadden. 1984. Specification tests in econometrics. *Econometrica* 52: 1219–1240.

McFadden, D. 1974. Measurement of urban travel demand. *Journal of Public Economics* 3: 303–328.

Also See

Related: [R] **lrtest**, [R] **test**, [R] **xtreg**

Title

heckman — Heckman selection model

Syntax

Basic syntax

> heckman *depvar* [*varlist*] , <u>sel</u>ect(*varlist_s*) [<u>two</u>step]
>
> *or*
>
> heckman *depvar* [*varlist*] , <u>sel</u>ect(*depvar_s* = *varlist_s*) [<u>two</u>step]

Full syntax for maximum likelihood estimates only

> heckman *depvar* [*varlist*] [*weight*] [if *exp*] [in *range*] ,
>
>   <u>sel</u>ect([*depvar_s* =] *varlist_s* [, <u>off</u>set(*varname*) <u>noc</u>onstant])
>
>   [<u>r</u>obust <u>cl</u>uster(*varname*) <u>sc</u>ore(*newvarlist*) <u>ns</u>hazard(*newvarname*)
>
>   <u>mi</u>lls(*newvarname*) <u>off</u>set(*varname*) <u>noc</u>onstant <u>fir</u>st noskip <u>l</u>evel(*#*)
>
>   <u>ite</u>rate(0) *maximize_options*]

Full syntax for Heckman's two-step consistent estimates only

> heckman *depvar* [*varlist*] [if *exp*] [in *range*] , <u>two</u>step
>
>   <u>sel</u>ect([*depvar_s* =] *varlist_s* [, <u>noc</u>onstant])
>
>   [<u>ns</u>hazard(*newvarname*) <u>mi</u>lls(*newvarname*) <u>noc</u>onstant <u>fir</u>st <u>l</u>evel(*#*)]

pweights, aweights, fweights, and iweights are allowed with maximum likelihood estimation; see [U] **14.1.6 weight**. No weights are allowed if twostep is specified.

heckman shares the features of all estimation commands; see [U] **23 Estimation and post-estimation commands**.

Syntax for predict

> predict [*type*] *newvarname* [if *exp*] [in *range*] [, *statistic* <u>nooff</u>set]

where *statistic* is

(Continued on next page)

xb	$x_j b$, fitted values (the default)
ycond	$E(y_j | y_j \text{ observed})$
yexpected	$E(y_j^*)$, y_j taken to be 0 where unobserved
nshazard or mills	nonselection hazard (also called inverse of Mills' ratio)
psel	$P(y_j \text{ observed})$
xbsel	linear prediction for selection equation
stdpsel	standard error of the linear prediction for selection equation
pr(a,b)	$\Pr(y_j | a < y_j < b)$
e(a,b)	$E(y_j | a < y_j < b)$
ystar(a,b)	$E(y_j^*)$, $y_j^* = \max(a, \min(y_j, b))$
stdp	standard error of the prediction
stdf	standard error of the forecast

where a and b may be numbers or variables; a equal to '.' means $-\infty$; b equal to '.' means $+\infty$.

These statistics are available both in and out of sample; type predict ... if e(sample) ... if wanted only for the estimation sample.

Description

heckman estimates regression models with selection using either Heckman's two-step consistent estimator or full maximum-likelihood.

Options

select(...) specifies the variables and options for the selection equation. It is an integral part of specifying a Heckman model and is not optional.

twostep specifies that Heckman's (1979) two-step efficient estimates of the parameters, standard errors, and covariance matrix are to be produced.

robust specifies that the Huber/White/sandwich estimator of the variance is to be used in place of the conventional MLE variance estimator. robust combined with cluster() further allows observations which are not independent within cluster (although they must be independent between clusters).

If you specify pweights, robust is implied. See [U] **23.11 Obtaining robust variance estimates**.

cluster(*varname*) specifies that the observations are independent across groups (clusters) but not necessarily independent within groups. *varname* specifies to which group each observation belongs. cluster() affects the estimated standard errors and variance–covariance matrix of the estimators (VCE), but not the estimated coefficients. cluster() can be used with pweights to produce estimates for unstratified cluster-sampled data.

cluster() implies robust; that is, specifying robust cluster() is equivalent to typing cluster() by itself.

score(*newvarlist*) creates a new variable, or set of new variables, containing the contributions to the scores for each equation and ancillary parameter in the model.

The first new variable specified will contain $u_{1j} = \partial \ln L_j / \partial (\mathbf{x}_j \boldsymbol{\beta})$ for each observation j in the sample, where $\ln L_j$ is the jth observation's contribution to the log likelihood.
The second new variable: $u_{2j} = \partial \ln L_j / \partial (\mathbf{z}_j \boldsymbol{\gamma})$
The third: $u_{3j} = \partial \ln L_j / \partial (\text{atanh } \rho)$
The fourth: $u_{4j} = \partial \ln L_j / \partial (\ln \sigma)$

If only one variable is specified, only the first score is computed; if two variables are specified, the first two scores are computed; and so on.

The jth observation's contribution to the score vector is

$$\left[\partial \ln L_j / \partial \boldsymbol{\beta} \quad \partial \ln L_j / \partial (\boldsymbol{\gamma}) \quad \partial \ln L_j / \partial (\text{atanh } \rho) \quad \partial \ln L_j / \partial (\ln \sigma) \right] = \left[u_{1j}\mathbf{x}_j \quad u_{2j}\mathbf{z}_j \quad u_{3j} \quad u_{4j} \right]$$

The score vector can be obtained by summing over j. See [U] **23.12 Obtaining scores**.

nshazard(*newvarname*) and mills(*newvarname*) are synonyms; either will create a new variable containing the nonselection hazard—what Heckman (1979) referred to as the inverse of the Mills' ratio—from the selection equation. The nonselection hazard is computed from the estimated parameters of the selection equation.

offset(*varname*) is a rarely used option that specifies a variable to be added directly to $\mathbf{Xb}$. This option may be specified on the regression equation, the selection equation, or both.

noconstant omits the constant term from the equations. This option may be specified on the regression equation, the selection equation, or both.

first specifies that the first-step probit estimates of the selection equation be displayed prior to estimation.

noskip specifies that a full maximum-likelihood model with only a constant for the regression equation be estimated. This model is not displayed but is used as the base model to compute a likelihood-ratio test for the model test statistic displayed in the estimation header. By default, the overall model test statistic is an asymptotically equivalent Wald test of all the parameters in the regression equation being zero (except the constant). For many models, this option can significantly increase estimation time.

level(*#*) specifies the confidence level, in percent, for confidence intervals. The default is level(95) or as set by set level; see [U] **23.5 Specifying the width of confidence intervals**.

iterate(0) produces Heckman's (1979) two-step parameter estimates with standard errors computed from the inverse Hessian of the full information matrix at the two-step solution for the parameters. As an alternative, the twostep option computes Heckman's two-step consistent estimates of the standard errors. iterate(*#*) can also be used to restrict the maximum number of iterations during optimization; see [R] **maximize**.

maximize_options control the maximization process; see [R] **maximize**. You will likely never need to specify any of the [R] **maximize** options except for iterate(0) and possibly difficult. If the iteration log shows many "not concave" messages and it is taking many iterations to converge, you may want to try using the difficult option and see if that helps it to converge in fewer steps.

Options for predict

xb the default, calculates the linear prediction $\mathbf{x}_j \mathbf{b}$.

`ycond` calculates the expected value of the dependent variable conditional on the dependent variable being observed, i.e., selected; $E(y_j \mid y_j$ observed$)$.

`yexpected` calculates the expected value of the dependent variable (y_j^*) where that value is taken to be 0 when it is expected to be unobserved; $y_j^* = P(y_j$ observed$)E(y_j \mid y_j$ observed$)$.

The assumption of 0 is valid for many cases where nonselection implies nonparticipation (e.g., unobserved wage levels, insurance claims from those who are uninsured, etc.) but may be inappropriate for some problems (e.g., unobserved disease incidence).

`nshazard` and `mills` are synonyms; either calculates the nonselection hazard—what Heckman (1979) referred to as the inverse of the Mills' ratio—from the selection equation.

`psel` calculates the probability of selection (or being observed):
$$P(y_j \text{ observed}) = \Pr(\mathbf{z}_j \gamma + u_{2j} > 0).$$

`xbsel` calculates the linear prediction for the selection equation.

`stdpsel` calculates the standard error of the linear prediction for the selection equation.

`pr(a,b)` calculates $\Pr(a < \mathbf{x}_j\mathbf{b} + u_1 < b)$, the probability that $y_j|\mathbf{x}_j$ would be observed in the interval (a, b).

a and b may be specified as numbers or variable names; lb and ub are variable names; `pr(20,30)` calculates $\Pr(20 < \mathbf{x}_j\mathbf{b} + u_1 < 30)$; `pr(lb,ub)` calculates $\Pr(lb < \mathbf{x}_j\mathbf{b} + u_1 < ub)$; and `pr(20,ub)` calculates $\Pr(20 < \mathbf{x}_j\mathbf{b} + u_1 < ub)$.

$a = \;.$ means $-\infty$; `pr(.,30)` calculates $\Pr(\mathbf{x}_j\mathbf{b} + u_1 < 30)$;
`pr(lb,30)` calculates $\Pr(\mathbf{x}_j\mathbf{b} + u_1 < 30)$ in observations for which $lb = \;.$
(and calculates $\Pr(lb < \mathbf{x}_j\mathbf{b} + u_1 < 30)$ elsewhere).

$b = \;.$ means $+\infty$; `pr(20,.)` calculates $\Pr(\mathbf{x}_j\mathbf{b} + u_1 > 20)$;
`pr(20,ub)` calculates $\Pr(\mathbf{x}_j\mathbf{b} + u_1 > 20)$ in observations for which $ub = \;.$
(and calculates $\Pr(20 < \mathbf{x}_j\mathbf{b} + u_1 < ub)$ elsewhere).

`e(a,b)` calculates $E(\mathbf{x}_j\mathbf{b} + u_1 \mid a < \mathbf{x}_j\mathbf{b} + u_1 < b)$, the expected value of $y_j|\mathbf{x}_j$ conditional on $y_j|\mathbf{x}_j$ being in the interval (a, b), which is to say, $y_j|\mathbf{x}_j$ is censored.
a and b are specified as they are for `pr()`.

`ystar(a,b)` calculates $E(y_j^*)$ where $y_j^* = a$ if $\mathbf{x}_j\mathbf{b} + u_j \le a$, $y_j^* = b$ if $\mathbf{x}_j\mathbf{b} + u_j \ge b$, and $y_j^* = \mathbf{x}_j\mathbf{b} + u_j$ otherwise, which is to say, y_j^* is truncated. a and b are specified as they are for `pr()`.

`stdp` calculates the standard error of the prediction. It can be thought of as the standard error of the predicted expected value or mean for the observation's covariate pattern. This is also referred to as the standard error of the fitted value.

`stdf` calculates the standard error of the forecast. This is the standard error of the point prediction for a single observation. It is commonly referred to as the standard error of the future or forecast value. By construction, the standard errors produced by `stdf` are always larger than those by `stdp`; see [R] **regress** *Methods and Formulas*.

`nooffset` is relevant only if you specified `offset(`*varname*`)` for `heckman`. It modifies the calculations made by `predict` so that they ignore the offset variable; the linear prediction is treated as $\mathbf{x}_j\mathbf{b}$ rather than $\mathbf{x}_j\mathbf{b} + \text{offset}_j$.

Remarks

The Heckman selection model (Gronau 1974, Lewis 1974, Heckman 1976) assumes that there exists an underlying regression relationship

$$y_j = \mathbf{x}_j\boldsymbol{\beta} + u_{1j} \qquad\qquad regression\ \ equation$$

The dependent variable, however, is not always observed. Rather, the dependent variable for observation j is observed if

$$\mathbf{z}_j\boldsymbol{\gamma} + u_{2j} > 0 \qquad\qquad selection\ \ equation$$

where

$$u_1 \sim N(0, \sigma)$$

$$u_2 \sim N(0, 1)$$

$$\mathrm{corr}(u_1, u_2) = \rho$$

When $\rho \neq 0$, standard regression techniques applied to the first equation yield biased results. heckman provides consistent, asymptotically efficient estimates for all the parameters in such models.

In one classic example, the first equation describes the wages of women. Women choose whether to work and thus, from our point of view as researchers, whether we observe their wages in our data. If women made this decision randomly, we could ignore the fact that not all wages are observed and use ordinary regression to estimate a wage model. Such a random-participation-in-the-labor-force assumption, however, is unlikely to be true; women who would have low wages may be unlikely to choose to work and thus the sample of observed wages is biased upward. In the jargon of economics, women choose not to work when their personal reservation wage is greater than the wage offered by employers. Thus, it is also possible that women who choose not to work could have even higher offer wages than those who do work—they may have high offer wages, but they have even higher reservation wages. One could tell a story that competency is related to wages, but competency is rewarded more at home than in the labor force.

In any case, in this problem—which is the paradigm for most such problems—a solution can be found if there are some variables that strongly affect the chances for observation (the reservation wage) but not the outcome under study (the offer wage). Such a variable might be the number of children in the home. (Actually, one theoretically does not need such identifying variables, but without them, one is depending on functional form to identify the model. It would be difficult for anyone to take such results seriously since the functional-form assumptions have no firm basis in theory.)

▷ Example

In the syntax for heckman, *depvar* and *varlist* are the dependent variable and regressors for the underlying regression model to be estimated ($\mathbf{y} = \mathbf{X}\boldsymbol{\beta}$) and *varlist$_s$* are the variables ($\mathbf{Z}$) thought to determine whether *depvar* is observed or unobserved (selected or not selected). In our female wage example, number of children at home would be included in the second list. By default, heckman will assume that missing values (see [U] **15.2.1 Missing values**) of *depvar* imply that the dependent variable is unobserved (not selected). With some datasets, it is more convenient to specify a binary variable (*depvar$_s$*) that identifies the observations for which the dependent is observed/selected (*depvar$_s \neq$* 0) or not observed (*depvar$_s =$* 0); heckman will accommodate either type of data.

We have a (fictional) dataset on 2,000 women, of whom 1,343 work:

```
. summarize age educ married children wage
    Variable |       Obs        Mean    Std. Dev.       Min        Max
-------------+--------------------------------------------------------
         age |      2000      36.208      8.28656        20         59
        educ |      2000      13.084     3.045912        10         20
     married |      2000       .6705     .4701492         0          1
    children |      2000      1.6445     1.398963         0          5
        wage |      1343    23.69217     6.305374   5.88497   45.80979
```

We will assume that the hourly wage is a function of education and age whereas the likelihood of working (the likelihood of the wage being observed) is a function of marital status, number of children at home, and (implicitly) the wage (via the inclusion of age and education which we think determine the wage):

```
. heckman wage educ age, select(married children educ age)

Iteration 0:   log likelihood =    -5179.2
Iteration 1:   log likelihood =  -5178.307
Iteration 2:   log likelihood = -5178.3045
Iteration 3:   log likelihood = -5178.3045

Heckman selection model                        Number of obs     =       2000
(regression model with sample selection)       Censored obs      =       1343
                                               Uncensored obs    =        657

                                               Wald chi2(2)      =     508.44
Log likelihood = -5178.304                     Prob > chi2       =     0.0000

------------------------------------------------------------------------------
             |      Coef.   Std. Err.      z    P>|z|     [95% Conf. Interval]
-------------+----------------------------------------------------------------
wage         |
        educ |   .9899532   .0532565    18.588   0.000     .8855724    1.094334
         age |   .2131293   .0206031    10.345   0.000      .172748    .2535106
       _cons |   .4857946   1.077038     0.451   0.652    -1.625162    2.596751
-------------+----------------------------------------------------------------
select       |
     married |   .4451714   .0673955     6.605   0.000     .3130787    .5772641
    children |   .4387069   .0277828    15.791   0.000     .3842536    .4931602
        educ |   .0557319   .0107349     5.192   0.000     .0346918    .0767719
         age |   .0365098   .0041533     8.790   0.000     .0283694    .0446502
       _cons |  -2.491015   .1893402   -13.156   0.000    -2.862115   -2.119915
-------------+----------------------------------------------------------------
     /athrho |   .8742051   .1014227     8.619   0.000     .6754203     1.07299
    /lnsigma |   1.792558    .027598    64.953   0.000     1.738467    1.846649
-------------+----------------------------------------------------------------
         rho |   .7035043   .0512267                        .588534     .790585
       sigma |   6.004795   .1657202                       5.688617    6.338545
      lambda |   4.224399    .399228                       3.441926    5.006872
------------------------------------------------------------------------------
LR test of indep. eqns. (rho = 0):   chi2(1) =     61.20   Prob > chi2 = 0.0000
------------------------------------------------------------------------------
```

heckman assumes that wage is the dependent variable and that the first variable list (educ and age) are the determinants of wage. The variables specified in the select() option (married, children, educ, and age) are assumed to determine whether the dependent variable is observed (the selection equation). Thus, we estimated the model

$$\texttt{wage} = \beta_0 + \beta_1 \texttt{educ} + \beta_2 \texttt{age} + u_1$$

and we assumed that wage is observed if

$$\gamma_0 + \gamma_1 \texttt{married} + \gamma_2 \texttt{children} + \gamma_3 \texttt{educ} + \gamma_4 \texttt{age} + u_2 > 0$$

where u_1 and u_2 have correlation ρ.

The reported results for the wage equation are interpreted exactly as though we observed wage data for all women in the sample; the coefficients on age and education level represent the estimated marginal effects of the regressors in the underlying regression equation. The results for the two ancillary parameters require some explanation. heckman does not directly estimate ρ; to constrain ρ within its valid limits, and for numerical stability during optimization, it estimates the inverse hyperbolic tangent of ρ:

$$\text{atanh}\, \rho = \frac{1}{2} \ln\left(\frac{1+\rho}{1-\rho}\right)$$

This estimate is reported as /athrho. In the bottom panel of the output, heckman undoes this transformation for you: the estimated value of ρ is .7035043. The standard error for ρ is computed using the delta method and its confidence intervals are the transformed intervals of /athrho.

Similarly, σ, the standard error of the residual in the wage equation, is not directly estimated; for numerical stability, heckman instead estimates $\ln \sigma$. The untransformed sigma is reported at the end of the output: 6.004795.

Finally, some researchers—especially economists—are used to the selectivity effect summarized not by ρ but by $\lambda = \rho\sigma$. heckman reports this, too, along with an estimate of the standard error and confidence interval.

◁

❑ Technical Note

If each of the equations in the model had contained many regressors, the heckman command could become quite long. An alternate way of specifying our wage model would make use of Stata's global macros. The following lines are an equivalent way of estimating our model.

```
. global wageeq "wage educ age"
. global seleq "married children educ age"
. heckman $wageeq, select($seleq)
```

❑

❑ Technical Note

The reported model χ^2 test is a Wald test of all coefficients in the regression model (except the constant) being 0. heckman is an estimation command, so you can use test, testnl, or lrtest to perform tests against whatever nested alternate model you wish to choose; see [R] test, [R] testnl, and [R] lrtest.

The estimation of ρ and σ in the form atanh ρ and $\ln \sigma$ extends the range of these parameters to infinity in both directions, thus avoiding boundary problems during the maximization. Tests of ρ must be made in the transformed units. However, since atanh$(0) = 0$, the reported test for atanh $\rho = 0$ is equivalent to the test for $\rho = 0$.

The likelihood-ratio test reported at the bottom of the output is an equivalent test for $\rho = 0$ and is computationally the comparison of the joint likelihood of an independent probit model for the selection equation and a regression model on the observed wage data against the heckman model likelihood. The $z = 8.619$ and χ^2 of 61.20, both significantly different from zero, clearly justify the Heckman selection equation with this data.

❑

▷ Example

heckman supports the Huber/White/sandwich estimator of variance under the robust and cluster() options, or when the pweights are used for population weighted data; see [U] **23.11 Obtaining robust variance estimates**. We can obtain robust standard errors for our wage model by specifying clustering on county of residence (the county variable).

```
. heckman wage educ age, select(married children educ age) cluster(county)
Iteration 0:   log likelihood =    -5179.2
Iteration 1:   log likelihood = -5178.307
Iteration 2:   log likelihood = -5178.3045
Iteration 3:   log likelihood = -5178.3045
```

```
Heckman selection model                      Number of obs    =      2000
(regression model with sample selection)     Censored obs     =      1343
                                             Uncensored obs   =       657

                                             Wald chi2(1)     =    272.17
Log likelihood = -5178.304                   Prob > chi2      =    0.0000
```

(standard errors adjusted for clustering on county)

	Coef.	Robust Std. Err.	z	P>|z|	[95% Conf. Interval]
wage						
educ	.9899532	.0600062	16.498	0.000	.8723432	1.107563
age	.2131293	.020995	10.151	0.000	.1719799	.2542787
_cons	.4857946	1.302104	0.373	0.709	-2.066283	3.037872
select						
married	.4451714	.0731473	6.086	0.000	.3018054	.5885375
children	.4387069	.0312386	14.044	0.000	.3774804	.4999334
educ	.0557319	.0110039	5.065	0.000	.0341646	.0772992
age	.0365098	.004038	9.042	0.000	.0285954	.0444241
_cons	-2.491015	.1153302	-21.599	0.000	-2.717058	-2.264972
/athrho	.8742051	.1403338	6.229	0.000	.5991559	1.149254
/lnsigma	1.792558	.0258458	69.356	0.000	1.741901	1.843215
rho	.7035043	.07088			.5364487	.8175069
sigma	6.004795	.1551986			5.708187	6.316814
lambda	4.224399	.5186725			3.20782	5.240979

```
Wald test of indep. eqns. (rho = 0): chi2(1) =    38.81   Prob > chi2 = 0.0000
```

The robust standard errors tend to be a bit larger, but we do not notice any systematic differences. This is not surprising since the data was not constructed to have any county-specific correlations or other characteristics that would deviate from the assumptions of the Heckman model.

◁

▷ Example

The default statistic produced by **predict** after **heckman** is the expected value of the dependent variable from the underlying distribution of the regression model. In our wage model, this is the expected wage rate among all women, regardless of whether they were observed to participate in the labor force.

```
. predict heckwage
(option xb assumed; fitted values)
```

It is instructive to compare these predicted wage values from the Heckman model with an ordinary regression model—a model without the selection adjustment:

```
. regress wage educ age

    Source |       SS       df       MS                  Number of obs =    1343
-----------+------------------------------                F(  2,  1340) =  227.49
     Model | 13524.0337      2  6762.01687               Prob > F      =  0.0000
  Residual | 39830.8609   1340  29.7245231               R-squared     =  0.2535
-----------+------------------------------                Adj R-squared =  0.2524
     Total | 53354.8946   1342  39.7577456               Root MSE      =   5.452

------------------------------------------------------------------------------
      wage |      Coef.   Std. Err.       t    P>|t|     [95% Conf. Interval]
-----------+------------------------------------------------------------------
      educ |   .8965829   .0498061     18.001   0.000     .7988765    .9942893
       age |   .1465739   .0187135      7.833   0.000      .109863    .1832848
     _cons |   6.084875   .8896182      6.840   0.000     4.339679    7.830071
------------------------------------------------------------------------------

. predict regwage
(option xb assumed; fitted values)

. summarize heckwage regwage

  Variable |     Obs        Mean    Std. Dev.      Min         Max
-----------+-----------------------------------------------------
  heckwage |    2000    21.15533    3.839648   14.64791    32.85949
   regwage |    2000    23.12291    3.241911   17.98218    32.66439
```

Since this data was concocted, we know the true coefficients of the wage regression equation to be 1, 0.2, and 1, respectively. We can compute the true mean wage for our sample.

```
. gen truewage = 1 + .2*age + 1*educ

. sum truewage

  Variable |     Obs        Mean    Std. Dev.      Min         Max
-----------+-----------------------------------------------------
  truewage |    2000     21.3256    3.797904         15        32.8
```

Whereas the mean of the predictions from `heckman` is within 18 cents of the true mean wage, ordinary regression yields predictions that are on average about $1.95 per hour too high due to the selection effect. The regression predictions also show somewhat less variation than the true wages.

The coefficients from `heckman` are so close to the true values that they are not worth testing. Conversely, the regression equation is significantly off, but seems to give the right sense. If we relied on the OLS coefficients, would we be led far astray? The effect of age is off by over 5 cents per year of age and the coefficient on education level is off by about 10%. We can test the OLS coefficient on education level against the true value using `test`.

```
. test educ = 1

 ( 1)  educ = 1.0

       F(  1,  1340) =     4.31
            Prob > F =    0.0380
```

Not only is the OLS coefficient on education substantially lower than the true parameter, the difference from the true parameter is statistically significant beyond the 5% level. We can perform a similar test for the OLS age coefficient:

```
. test age = .2

 ( 1)  age = .2

       F(  1,  1340) =     8.15
            Prob > F =    0.0044
```

We find even stronger evidence that the OLS regression results are biased away from the true parameters.

◁

▷ Example

Several other interesting aspects of the Heckman model can be explored with `predict`. Continuing with our wage model, the expected wages for women conditional on participating in the labor force can be obtained with the `ycond` option. Let's get these predictions and compare them with actual wages for women participating in the labor force.

```
. predict hcndwage, ycond
. summarize wage hcndwage if wage ~= .
Variable |    Obs        Mean   Std. Dev.       Min        Max
---------+----------------------------------------------------
    wage |   1343    23.69217    6.305374    5.88497   45.80979
hcndwage |   1343    23.68239    3.335086   16.18338    33.7567
```

We see that the average predictions from `heckman` are very close to the observed levels but do not have exactly the same mean. These conditional wage predictions are available for all observations in the dataset, but can only be directly compared with observed wages where individuals are participating in the labor force.

What if we were interested in making predictions about mean wages for all women? In this case, the expected wage is 0 for those who are not expected to participate in the labor force, with expected participation determined by the selection equation. These values can be obtained with the `yexpected` option of `predict`. For comparison, a variable can be generated where the wage is set to 0 for nonparticipants.

```
. predict hexpwage, yexpected
. gen wage0 = wage
(657 missing values generated)
. replace wage0 = 0 if wage == .
(657 real changes made)
. summarize hexpwage wage0
Variable |    Obs        Mean   Std. Dev.       Min        Max
---------+----------------------------------------------------
hexpwage |   2000    15.92511    5.979337   2.492469   32.45858
   wage0 |   2000    15.90929    12.27081          0   45.80979
```

Again, we note that the predictions from `heckman` are very close to the observed mean hourly wage rate for all women. Why aren't the predictions using `ycond` and `yexpected` exactly equal to their observed sample equivalents? For the Heckman model, unlike linear regression, the sample moments implied by the optimal solution to the model likelihood do not require that these predictions exactly match observed data. Properly accounting for the additional variation from the selection equation requires that the model use more information than just the sample moments of the observed wages.

◁

▷ Example

Stata will also produce Heckman's (1979) two-step efficient estimator of the model with the `twostep` option. Maximum likelihood estimation of the parameters can be time-consuming with large datasets and the two-step estimates may provide a good alternative in such cases. Continuing with the women's wage model, we can obtain the two-step estimates with Heckman's consistent covariance estimates by typing

```
. heckman wage educ age, select(married children educ age) twostep
Heckman selection model -- two-step estimates     Number of obs    =     2000
(regression model with sample selection)          Censored obs     =     1343
                                                  Uncensored obs   =      657

                                                  Wald chi2(4)     =   406.57
                                                  Prob > chi2      =   0.0000
```

	Coef.	Std. Err.	z	P>|z|	[95% Conf. Interval]
wage						
educ	.9825259	.0666283	14.746	0.000	.8519368	1.113115
age	.2118695	.0272552	7.774	0.000	.1584503	.2652887
_cons	.7340391	1.517637	0.484	0.629	-2.240475	3.708553
select						
married	.4308575	.074208	5.806	0.000	.2854125	.5763025
children	.4473249	.0287417	15.564	0.000	.3909922	.5036576
educ	.0583645	.0109742	5.318	0.000	.0368555	.0798735
age	.0347211	.0042293	8.210	0.000	.0264318	.0430105
_cons	-2.467365	.1925635	-12.813	0.000	-2.844782	-2.089948
mills						
lambda	4.001615	.9571839	4.181	0.000	2.12557	5.877661
rho	0.66396					
sigma	6.0269356					
lambda	4.0016155	.9571839				

◁

❑ Technical Note

The Heckman selection model depends strongly on the model being correct; much more so than for ordinary regression. Running a separate probit or logit for sample inclusion followed by a regression, referred to in the literature as the two-part model (Manning, Duan, and Rogers 1987)—not to be confused with Heckman's two-step procedure—is an especially attractive alternative if the regression part of the model arose because of taking a logarithm of zero values. When the goal is to analyze an underlying regression model or predict the value of the dependent variable that would be observed in the absence of selection, however, the Heckman model is more appropriate. When the goal is to predict an actual response, the two-part model is usually the better choice.

The Heckman selection model can be unstable when the model is not properly specified, or if a specific dataset simply does not support the model's assumptions. For example, let's examine the solution to another simulated problem.

```
. heckman yt x1 x2 x3, select(z1 z2)
Iteration 0:   log likelihood = -112.15999
Iteration 1:   log likelihood = -110.90875
Iteration 2:   log likelihood = -109.77375
Iteration 3:   log likelihood = -109.67395  (not concave)
Iteration 4:   log likelihood = -108.30688  (not concave)
  (output omitted)
Iteration 38:  log likelihood = -104.08249  (not concave)
Iteration 39:  log likelihood = -104.08248
```

```
Heckman selection model                      Number of obs   =          150
(regression model with sample selection)     Censored obs    =           63
                                             Uncensored obs  =           87

                                             Wald chi2(3)    = 2199573406.99
Log likelihood = -104.0825                   Prob > chi2     =       0.0000

------------------------------------------------------------------------------
             |      Coef.   Std. Err.      z    P>|z|     [95% Conf. Interval]
-------------+----------------------------------------------------------------
yt           |
          x1 |   .8974192    .000135   6645.324   0.000     .8971545    .8976839
          x2 |  -2.525303   .0000784        .     0.000    -2.525456   -2.525149
          x3 |   2.855786   .0001752        .     0.000     2.855442    2.856129
       _cons |   .6975162   .0799043    8.729     0.000     .5409067    .8541256
-------------+----------------------------------------------------------------
select       |
          z1 |  -.6826319   .0789606   -8.645     0.000    -.8373918   -.5278721
          z2 |   1.003654   .1160931    8.645     0.000     .7761155    1.231192
       _cons |   -.360531   .1108234   -3.253     0.001    -.5777409   -.1433211
-------------+----------------------------------------------------------------
     /athrho |   16.49338   242.6479    0.068     0.946    -459.0877    492.0745
    /lnsigma |  -.5396638   .1156704   -4.666     0.000    -.7663736    -.312954
-------------+----------------------------------------------------------------
         rho |          1   4.58e-12                              -1           1
       sigma |   .5829442   .0674294                         .4646952    .7312835
      lambda |   .5829442   .0674294                         .4507851    .7151033
------------------------------------------------------------------------------
LR test of indep. eqns. (rho = 0):   chi2(1) =    25.67   Prob > chi2 = 0.0000
------------------------------------------------------------------------------
```

The model has converged to a value of ρ that is 1.0—within machine rounding tolerances. Given the form of the likelihood for the Heckman selection model, this implies a division by zero and it is surprising that the model solution turns out as well as it does. Reparameterizing ρ has allowed the estimation to converge, but we clearly have problems with the estimates. Moreover, if this had occurred in a large dataset, waiting over 39 iterations for convergence might take considerable time.

This data was not intentionally developed to cause problems. It is actually generated by a "Heckman process" and when generated starting from different random values can be easily estimated. The luck of the draw in this case merely led to data that, despite its source, did not support the assumptions of the Heckman model.

The two-step model is generally more stable in cases where the data are problematic. It is even tolerant of estimates of ρ less than -1 and greater than 1. For these reasons, the two-step model may be preferred when exploring a large dataset. Still, if the maximum likelihood estimates cannot converge, or converge to a value of ρ that is at the boundary of acceptable values, there is scant support for estimating a Heckman selection model on the data. Heckman (1979) discusses the implications of ρ being exactly 1 or 0, together with the implications of other possible covariance relationships among the model's determinants.

❑

(Continued on next page)

Saved Results

heckman saves in e():

Scalars

e(N)	number of observations	e(selambda)	standard error of λ
e(k)	number of variables	e(rc)	return code
e(k_eq)	number of equations	e(sigma)	sigma
e(k_dv)	number of dependent variables	e(chi2)	χ^2
e(df_m)	model degrees of freedom	e(chi2_c)	χ^2 for comparison test
e(ll)	log likelihood	e(p_c)	p-value for comparison test
e(ll_0)	log likelihood, constant-only model	e(p)	significance of comparison test
	(noskip only)	e(rho)	ρ
e(N_clust)	number of clusters	e(N_cens)	number of censored observations
e(lambda)	λ	e(ic)	number of iterations

Macros

e(cmd)	heckman	e(user)	name of likelihood-evaluator program
e(depvar)	name(s) of dependent variable(s)	e(opt)	type of optimization
e(title)	title in estimation output	e(chi2type)	Wald or LR; type of model χ^2 test
e(title2)	secondary title in estimation output	e(chi2_ct)	Wald or LR; type of model χ^2 test
e(wtype)	weight type		corresponding to e(chi2_c)
e(wexp)	weight expression	e(offset#)	offset for equation #
e(clustvar)	name of cluster variable	e(mills)	variable containing nonselection hazard
			(inverse of Mills')
e(method)	requested estimation method	e(predict)	program used to implement predict
e(vcetype)	covariance estimation method		

Matrices

e(b)	coefficient vector	e(V)	variance–covariance matrix of the
			estimators

Functions

e(sample)	marks estimation sample

Methods and Formulas

heckman is implemented as an ado-file. Greene (1997, 978–981) or Johnston and DiNardo (1997, 446–450) provide an introduction to the Heckman selection model.

Regression estimates using the nonselection hazard (Heckman 1979) provide starting values for maximum likelihood estimation.

The regression equation is

$$y_j = \mathbf{x}_j\boldsymbol{\beta} + u_{1j}$$

The selection equation is

$$\mathbf{z}_j\boldsymbol{\gamma} + u_{2j} > 0$$

where

$$u_1 \sim N(0, \sigma)$$
$$u_2 \sim N(0, 1)$$
$$\mathrm{corr}(u_1, u_2) = \rho$$

The log likelihood for observation j is

$$l_j = \begin{cases} w_j \ln \Phi\left(\dfrac{\mathbf{z}_j\boldsymbol{\gamma} + (y_j - \mathbf{x}_j\boldsymbol{\beta})\rho/\sigma}{\sqrt{1-\rho^2}}\right) - \dfrac{w_j}{2}\left(\dfrac{y_j - \mathbf{x}_j\boldsymbol{\beta}}{\sigma}\right)^2 - w_j\ln(\sqrt{2\pi}\sigma) & y_j \text{ observed} \\[2ex] w_j\ln\Phi(-\mathbf{z}_j\boldsymbol{\gamma}) & y_j \text{ not observed} \end{cases}$$

where $\Phi()$ is the standard cumulative normal and w_j is an optional weight for observation j.

In the maximum likelihood estimation, σ and ρ are not directly estimated. Directly estimated are $\ln\sigma$ and $\text{atanh}\,\rho$:

$$\text{atanh}\,\rho = \frac{1}{2}\ln\left(\frac{1+\rho}{1-\rho}\right)$$

The standard error of $\lambda = \rho\sigma$ is approximated through the propagation of error (delta) method; that is,

$$\text{Var}(\lambda) \approx \mathbf{D}\,\text{Var}\big([\text{atanh}\,\rho \;\; \ln\sigma]\big)\,\mathbf{D}'$$

where $\mathbf{D}$ is the Jacobian of λ with respect to $\text{atanh}\,\rho$ and $\ln\sigma$.

The two-step estimates are computed using Heckman's (1979) procedure.

Probit estimates of the selection equation

$$\text{Pr}(y_j \text{ observed} \mid \mathbf{z}_j) = \Phi(\mathbf{z}_j\boldsymbol{\gamma})$$

are obtained. From these estimates the nonselection hazard, what Heckman (1979) referred to as the inverse of the Mills' ratio, m_j for each observation j is computed as

$$m_j = \frac{\phi(\mathbf{z}_j\widehat{\boldsymbol{\gamma}})}{\Phi(\mathbf{z}_j\widehat{\boldsymbol{\gamma}})}$$

where ϕ is the normal density. We also define

$$\delta_j = m_j(m_j + \widehat{\boldsymbol{\gamma}}\mathbf{z}_j)$$

Following Heckman, the two-step parameter estimates of $\boldsymbol{\beta}$ are obtained by augmenting the regression equation with the nonselection hazard $\mathbf{m}$. Thus, the regressors become $[\,\mathbf{X}\;\;\mathbf{m}\,]$ and we obtain the additional parameter estimate β_m on the variable containing the nonselection hazard.

A consistent estimate of the regression disturbance variance is obtained using the residuals from the augmented regression and the parameter estimate on the nonselection hazard.

$$\widehat{\sigma}^2 = \frac{\mathbf{e}'\mathbf{e} + \beta_m \sum_{j=1}^{N}\delta_j}{N}$$

The two-step estimate of ρ is then

$$\widehat{\rho} = \frac{\beta_m}{\widehat{\sigma}}$$

Heckman derived consistent estimates of the coefficient covariance matrix based on the augmented regression.

Let $\mathbf{W} = [\,\mathbf{X}\ \mathbf{m}\,]$ and $\mathbf{D}$ be a square diagonal matrix of rank N with $(1 - \widehat{\rho}^2 \delta_j)$ on the diagonal elements.

$$\mathbf{V}_{\text{twostep}} = \widehat{\sigma}^2 (\mathbf{W}'\mathbf{W})^{-1} (\mathbf{W}'\mathbf{D}\mathbf{W} + \mathbf{Q})(\mathbf{W}'\mathbf{W})^{-1}$$

where

$$\mathbf{Q} = \widehat{\rho}^2 (\mathbf{W}'\mathbf{D}\mathbf{W}) \mathbf{V}_{\mathbf{p}} (\mathbf{W}'\mathbf{D}\mathbf{W})$$

and $\mathbf{V}_p$ is the variance–covariance estimate from the probit estimation of the selection equation.

References

Greene, W. H. 1997. *Econometric Analysis*. 3d ed. Upper Saddle River, NJ: Prentice–Hall.

Gronau, R. 1974. Wage comparisons: A selectivity bias. *Journal of Political Economy* 82: 1119–1155.

Heckman, J. 1976. The common structure of statistical models of truncation, sample selection, and limited dependent variables and a simple estimator for such models. *The Annals of Economic and Social Measurement* 5: 475–492.

——. 1979. Sample selection bias as a specification error. *Econometrica* 47: 153–161.

Johnston, J. and J. DiNardo. 1997. *Econometric Methods*. 4th ed. New York: McGraw–Hill.

Lewis, H. 1974. Comments on selectivity biases in wage comparisons. *Journal of Political Economy* 82: 1119–1155.

Manning, W. G., N. Duan, and W. H. Rogers. 1987. Monte Carlo evidence on the choice between sample selection and two-part models. *Journal of Econometrics* 35: 59–82.

Also See

Complementary:	[R] **lincom**, [R] **lrtest**, [R] **predict**, [R] **test**, [R] **testnl**, [R] **vce**, [R] **xi**
Related:	[R] **heckprob**, [R] **regress**, [R] **tobit**
Background:	[U] **16.5 Accessing coefficients and standard errors**,
	[U] **23 Estimation and post-estimation commands**,
	[U] **23.11 Obtaining robust variance estimates**,
	[U] **23.12 Obtaining scores**

Title

> **heckprob** — Maximum-likelihood probit estimation with selection

Syntax

heckprob *depvar* $\left[\textit{varlist}\right]$ $\left[\textit{weight}\right]$ $\left[\texttt{if } \textit{exp}\right]$ $\left[\texttt{in } \textit{range}\right]$,

    <u>sel</u>ect($\left[\textit{depvar}_s \ = \ \right]$ *varlist$_s$* $\left[\ , \ \underline{\texttt{off}}\texttt{set}(\textit{varname}) \ \underline{\texttt{nocons}}\texttt{tant} \ \right]$)

    $\left[\ \underline{\texttt{r}}\texttt{obust} \ \underline{\texttt{cl}}\texttt{uster}(\textit{varname}) \ \underline{\texttt{sc}}\texttt{ore}(\textit{newvarlist}) \ \underline{\texttt{fi}}\texttt{rst} \right.$

    $\underline{\texttt{nocons}}\texttt{tant} \ \texttt{noskip} \ \underline{\texttt{l}}\texttt{evel}(\#) \ \underline{\texttt{off}}\texttt{set}(\textit{varname}) \ \textit{maximize\_options} \left. \right]$

iweights, fweights, and pweights are allowed; see [U] **14.1.6 weight**.
heckprob shares the features of all estimation commands; see [U] **23 Estimation and post-estimation commands**.

Syntax for predict

predict $\left[\textit{type}\right]$ *newvarname* $\left[\texttt{if } \textit{exp}\right]$ $\left[\texttt{in } \textit{range}\right]$ $\left[, \ \textit{statistic} \ \underline{\texttt{nooff}}\texttt{set} \right]$

where *statistic* is

<u>pm</u>argin	$\Phi(\mathbf{x}_j\mathbf{b})$, success probability (the default)
p11	$\Phi_2(\mathbf{x}_j\mathbf{b}, \mathbf{z}_j\mathbf{g}, \rho)$, predicted probability $P(y_j^{\text{probit}} = 1, y_j^{\text{select}} = 1)$
p10	$\Phi_2(\mathbf{x}_j\mathbf{b}, -\mathbf{z}_j\mathbf{g}, -\rho)$, predicted probability $P(y_j^{\text{probit}} = 1, y_j^{\text{select}} = 0)$
p01	$\Phi_2(-\mathbf{x}_j\mathbf{b}, \mathbf{z}_j\mathbf{g}, -\rho)$, predicted probability $P(y_j^{\text{probit}} = 0, y_j^{\text{select}} = 1)$
p00	$\Phi_2(-\mathbf{x}_j\mathbf{b}, -\mathbf{z}_j\mathbf{g}, \rho)$, predicted probability $P(y_j^{\text{probit}} = 0, y_j^{\text{select}} = 0)$
psel	$\Phi(\mathbf{z}_j\mathbf{g})$, selection probability
pcond	$\Phi_2(\mathbf{x}_j\mathbf{b}, \mathbf{z}_j\mathbf{g}, \rho)/\Phi(\mathbf{z}_j\mathbf{g})$, probability of success conditional on selection
xb	$\mathbf{x}_j\mathbf{b}$, fitted values
stdp	standard error of fitted values
<u>xbse</u>l	linear prediction for selection equation
stdpsel	standard error of the linear prediction for selection equation

where $\Phi()$ is the standard normal distribution function and $\Phi_2()$ is the bivariate normal distribution function.

These statistics are available both in and out of sample; type predict ... if e(sample) ... if wanted only for the estimation sample.

Description

heckprob estimates maximum-likelihood probit models with sample selection.

Options

select(...) specifies the variables and options for the selection equation. It is an integral part of specifying a selection model and is not optional.

robust specifies that the Huber/White/sandwich estimator of the variance is to be used in place of the conventional MLE variance estimator. robust combined with cluster() further allows observations which are not independent within cluster (although they must be independent between clusters).

If you specify pweights, robust is implied. See [U] **23.11 Obtaining robust variance estimates**.

cluster(*varname*) specifies that the observations are independent across groups (clusters) but not necessarily independent within groups. *varname* specifies to which group each observation belongs. cluster() affects the estimated standard errors and variance–covariance matrix of the estimators (VCE), but not the estimated coefficients. cluster() can be used with pweights to produce estimates for unstratified cluster-sampled data.

cluster() implies robust; that is, specifying robust cluster() is equivalent to typing cluster() by itself.

score(*newvarlist*) creates a new variable, or set of new variables, containing the contributions to the scores for each equation and ancillary parameter in the model.

The first new variable specified will contain $u_{1j} = \partial \ln L_j / \partial(\mathbf{x}_j \boldsymbol{\beta})$ for each observation j in the sample, where $\ln L_j$ is the jth observation's contribution to the log likelihood.
The second new variable: $u_{2j} = \partial \ln L_j / \partial(\mathbf{z}_j \boldsymbol{\gamma})$
The third: $u_{3j} = \partial \ln L_j / \partial(\text{atanh } \rho)$

If only one variable is specified, only the first score is computed; if two variables are specified, the first two scores are computed; and so on.

The jth observation's contribution to the score vector is

$$\left[\, \partial \ln L_j / \partial \boldsymbol{\beta} \;\; \partial \ln L_j / \partial(\boldsymbol{\gamma}) \;\; \partial \ln L_j / \partial(\text{atanh } \rho) \,\right] = \left[\, u_{1j} \mathbf{x}_j \;\; u_{2j} \mathbf{z}_j \;\; u_{3j} \,\right]$$

The score vector can be obtained by summing over j. See [U] **23.12 Obtaining scores**.

first specifies that the first-step probit estimates of the selection equation be displayed prior to estimation.

noconstant omits the constant term from the equation. This option may be specified on the regression equation, the selection equation, or both.

noskip specifies that a full maximum likelihood model with only a constant for the regression equation be estimated. This model is not displayed but is used as the base model to compute a likelihood-ratio test for the model test statistic displayed in the estimation header. By default, the overall model test statistic is an asymptotically equivalent Wald test of all the parameters in the regression equation being zero (except the constant). For many models, this option can significantly increase estimation time.

level(*#*) specifies the confidence level, in percent, for confidence intervals. The default is level(95) or as set by set level; see [U] **23.5 Specifying the width of confidence intervals**.

offset(*varname*) is a rarely used option that specifies a variable to be added directly to **Xb**. This option may be specified on the regression equation, the selection equation, or both.

maximize_options control the maximization process; see [R] **maximize**. With the possible exception of iterate(0) and trace, you should never have to specify them.

Options for predict

pmargin, the default, calculates the univariate (marginal) predicted probability of success $P(y_j^{\text{probit}} = 1)$.

p11 calculates the bivariate predicted probability $P(y_j^{\text{probit}} = 1, y_j^{\text{select}} = 1)$.

p10 calculates the bivariate predicted probability $P(y_j^{\text{probit}} = 1, y_j^{\text{select}} = 0)$.

p01 calculates the bivariate predicted probability $P(y_j^{\text{probit}} = 0, y_j^{\text{select}} = 1)$.

p00 calculates the bivariate predicted probability $P(y_j^{\text{probit}} = 0, y_j^{\text{select}} = 0)$.

psel calculates the univariate (marginal) predicted probability of selection $P(y_j^{\text{select}} = 1)$.

pcond calculates the conditional (on selection) predicted probability of success $P(y_j^{\text{probit}} = 1, y_j^{\text{select}} = 1)/P(y_j^{\text{select}} = 1)$.

xb calculates the probit linear prediction $\mathbf{x}_j\mathbf{b}$.

stdp calculates the standard error of the prediction. It can be thought of as the standard error of the predicted expected value or mean for the observation's covariate pattern. This is also referred to as the standard error of the fitted value.

xbsel calculates the linear prediction for the selection equation.

stdpsel calculates the standard error of the linear prediction for the selection equation.

nooffset is relevant only if you specified offset(*varname*) for heckprob. It modifies the calculations made by predict so that they ignore the offset variable; the linear prediction is treated as $\mathbf{x}_j\mathbf{b}$ rather than $\mathbf{x}_j\mathbf{b} + \text{offset}_j$.

Remarks

The probit model with sample selection (Van de Ven and Van Pragg, 1981) assumes that there exists an underlying relationship

$$y_j^* = \mathbf{x}_j\boldsymbol{\beta} + u_{1j} \qquad\qquad \textit{latent equation}$$

such that we observe only the binary outcome

$$y_j^{\text{probit}} = (y_j^* > 0) \qquad\qquad \textit{probit equation}$$

The dependent variable, however, is not always observed. Rather, the dependent variable for observation j is observed if

$$y_j^{\text{select}} = (\mathbf{z}_j\boldsymbol{\gamma} + u_{2j} > 0) \qquad\qquad \textit{selection equation}$$

where

$$u_1 \sim N(0, 1)$$
$$u_2 \sim N(0, 1)$$
$$\text{corr}(u_1, u_2) = \rho$$

When $\rho \neq 0$, standard probit techniques applied to the first equation yield biased results. heckprob provides consistent, asymptotically efficient estimates for all the parameters in such models.

▷ Example

We use the data from Pindyck and Rubinfeld (1981). In this dataset, the variables are whether children attend private school (priv), number of years the family has been at the present residence (yrs), property tax (ptax), income (inc), and whether one voted for an increase in property taxes (vote).

In this example, we alter the meaning of the data. Here we assume that we observe whether children attend private school only if the family votes for increasing the property taxes. This is not true in the dataset and we make this untrue assumption only to illustrate the use of this command.

We observe whether children attend private school only if the head of household voted for an increase in property taxes. We assume that the vote is affected by the number of years in residence, the current property taxes paid, and the household income. We wish to model whether children are sent to private school based on the number of years spent in the current residence and the current property taxes paid.

```
. heckprob priv yrs ptax, sel(vote=yrs inc ptax)
Fitting probit model:
Iteration 0:   log likelihood = -16.358413
Iteration 1:   log likelihood = -15.536018
Iteration 2:   log likelihood = -15.264342
Iteration 3:   log likelihood = -15.070615
Iteration 4:   log likelihood = -14.982096
Iteration 5:   log likelihood = -14.975069
Iteration 6:   log likelihood = -14.975024

Fitting selection model:
Iteration 0:   log likelihood = -52.387444
Iteration 1:   log likelihood = -45.964207
Iteration 2:   log likelihood = -45.581886
Iteration 3:   log likelihood = -45.576115
Iteration 4:   log likelihood = -45.576114

Comparison:    log likelihood = -60.551138

Fitting full model:
Iteration 0:   log likelihood = -60.551138
Iteration 1:   log likelihood = -60.520931
Iteration 2:   log likelihood = -60.495819
Iteration 3:   log likelihood = -60.495725
Iteration 4:   log likelihood = -60.495725
```

```
Probit model with sample selection          Number of obs    =       80
                                            Censored obs     =       29
                                            Uncensored obs   =       51

                                            Wald chi2(2)     =     1.10
Log likelihood = -60.49573                  Prob > chi2      =   0.5771

------------------------------------------------------------------------------
             |      Coef.   Std. Err.      z    P>|z|     [95% Conf. Interval]
-------------+----------------------------------------------------------------
priv         |
        yrs  |  -.1508048   .1602441    -0.941   0.347    -.4648775    .1632678
       ptax  |   .2507526    1.22814     0.204   0.838    -2.156357    2.657862
      _cons  |  -2.127261   8.327302    -0.255   0.798    -18.44847    14.19395
-------------+----------------------------------------------------------------
vote         |
        yrs  |  -.0082359   .0159395    -0.517   0.605    -.0394767    .023005
        inc  |   1.572097   .5672177     2.772   0.006     .4603703    2.683823
       ptax  |  -2.019357   .7200663    -2.804   0.005    -3.430661   -.6080533
      _cons  |  -1.203783   4.465327    -0.270   0.787    -9.955663    7.548096
------------------------------------------------------------------------------
```

```
/athrho |   -.4722763    1.254447      -0.376   0.707     -2.930946    1.986394
---------+------------------------------------------------------------------------
    rho |   -.4400367    1.011545                          -.9943244    .9630536
---------+------------------------------------------------------------------------

Likelihood ratio test of rho=0:        chi2(1) =   .110826    Pr > chi2 = 0.7392
```

The output shows several iteration logs. The first iteration log corresponds to running the probit model for those observations in the sample where we have observed the outcome. The second iteration log corresponds to running the selection probit model which models whether we observe our outcome of interest. If $\rho = 0$, then the sum of the log likelihoods from these two models will equal the log likelihood of the probit model with sample selection; this sum is printed in the iteration log as the comparison log likelihood.

The final iteration log is for estimating the full probit model with sample selection. A likelihood-ratio test of the log likelihood for this model and the comparison log likelihood is presented at the end of the output. If we had specified the robust option, then this test would be presented as a Wald test instead of a likelihood-ratio test.

◁

▷ Example

In the previous example, we could obtain robust standard errors by specifying the robust option. We also eliminate the iteration logs using the nolog option.

```
. heckprob priv yrs ptax, sel(vote=yrs inc ptax) nolog robust

Probit model with sample selection        Number of obs    =        80
                                          Censored obs     =        29
                                          Uncensored obs   =        51

                                          Wald chi2(2)     =      4.09
Log likelihood = -60.49573                Prob > chi2      =    0.1293

---------------------------------------------------------------------------------
        |                 Robust
        |     Coef.     Std. Err.      z     P>|z|    [95% Conf. Interval]
--------+------------------------------------------------------------------------
priv    |
    yrs |  -.1508048    .0912905    -1.652   0.099     -.329731    .0281213
   ptax |   .2507526    .9603537     0.261   0.794    -1.631506    2.133011
  _cons |  -2.127261    6.184579    -0.344   0.731    -14.24881    9.994292
--------+------------------------------------------------------------------------
vote    |
    yrs |  -.0082359    .0180114    -0.457   0.647     -.0435375   .0270658
    inc |   1.572097     .604663     2.600   0.009      .3869789   2.757214
   ptax |  -2.019357    .6620263    -3.050   0.002     -3.316905  -.7218095
  _cons |  -1.203783    5.278288    -0.228   0.820     -11.54904   9.141471
--------+------------------------------------------------------------------------
/athrho |  -.4722763    1.521202    -0.310   0.756     -3.453777   2.509225
--------+------------------------------------------------------------------------
    rho |  -.4400367    1.226648                        -.9980016   .9868574
---------------------------------------------------------------------------------

Wald test of rho=0:                    chi2(1) =   .096387    Pr > chi2 = 0.7562
```

Regardless of whether we specify the robust option, it is clear that the outcome is not significantly different from the outcome obtained by estimating the probit and selection models separately. This is not surprising since the selection mechanism estimated was invented for the example rather than born from any economic theory.

◁

▷ Example

It is instructive to compare the marginal predicted probabilities with the predicted probabilities we would obtain ignoring the selection mechanism. In order to compare the two approaches, we will synthesize data so that we know the "true" predicted probabilities.

First, we need to generate correlated error terms, which we can do using a standard Cholesky decomposition approach. For our example, we will clear any data from memory and then generate errors that have correlation of .5 using the following commands. Note that we set the seed so that interested readers might type in these same commands and obtain the same results.

```
. clear
. set seed 12309
. set obs 5000
. gen c1 = invnorm(uniform())
. gen c2 = invnorm(uniform())
. matrix P = (1,.5\.5,1)
. matrix A = cholesky(P)
. local fac1 = A[2,1]
. local fac2 = A[2,2]
. gen u1 = c1
. gen u2 = `fac1´*c1 + `fac2´*c2
```

We can check that the errors have the correct correlation using the `corr` command. We will also normalize the errors such that they have a standard deviation of one so that we can generate a bivariate probit model with known coefficients. We do that with the following commands.

```
. summarize u1
. replace u1 = u1/sqrt(r(Var))
. summarize u2
. replace u2 = u2/sqrt(r(Var))
. drop c1 c2
. gen x1 = uniform()-.5
. gen x2 = uniform()+1/3
. gen y1s = 0.5 + 4*x1 + u1
. gen y2s = 3 - 3*x2 + .5*x1 + u2
. gen y1 = (y1s>0)
. gen y2 = (y2s>0)
```

At this point, we have created two dependent variables `y1` and `y2` that are defined by our specified coefficients. We also included error terms for each equation and the error terms are correlated. We run `heckprob` to verify that the data has been correctly generated according to the model

$$y_1 = .5 + 4x_1 + u_1$$
$$y_2 = 3 + .5x_1 - 3x_2 + u_2$$

where we assume that y_1 is observed only if $y_2 = 1$.

```
. heckprob y1 x1, sel(y2 = x1 x2) nolog
Probit model with sample selection              Number of obs    =     5000
                                                Censored obs     =     1790
                                                Uncensored obs   =     3210

                                                Wald chi2(1)     =   941.68
Log likelihood = -3600.854                      Prob > chi2      =   0.0000
```

	Coef.	Std. Err.	z	P>|z|	[95% Conf. Interval]	
y1						
x1	3.985923	.1298904	30.687	0.000	3.731342	4.240503
_cons	.4852946	.0464037	10.458	0.000	.394345	.5762442
y2						
x1	.5998148	.0716655	8.370	0.000	.4593531	.7402765
x2	-3.004937	.0829469	-36.227	0.000	-3.16751	-2.842364
_cons	3.011587	.0782817	38.471	0.000	2.858157	3.165016
/athrho	.5740629	.0860559	6.671	0.000	.4053964	.7427294
rho	.5183368	.062935			.3845568	.6307914

```
Likelihood ratio test of rho=0:      chi2(1) =   46.5767      Pr > chi2 = 0.0000
```

Now that we have verified that we generated data according to a known model, we can obtain and then compare predicted probabilities from the probit model with sample selection and a (usual) probit model.

```
. predict pmarg
. probit y1 x1 if y2==1
```
(*output omitted*)
```
. predict phat
```

Using the (marginal) predicted probabilities from the probit model with sample selection (pmarg) and the predicted probabilities from the (usual) probit model (phat), we can also generate the "true" predicted probabilities from the synthesized y1s variable and then compare the predicted probabilities:

```
. gen ptrue = normprob(y1s)
. summ pmarg ptrue phat
```

Variable	Obs	Mean	Std. Dev.	Min	Max
pmarg	5000	.619436	.3209494	.0658356	.9933942
ptrue	5000	.6090161	.3499095	1.02e-06	1
phat	5000	.6723897	.3063207	.096498	.9971064

Here we see that ignoring the selection mechanism (comparing the phat variable with the true ptrue variable) results in predicted probabilities that are much higher than the true values. Looking at the marginal predicted probabilities from the model with sample selection, however, results in more accurate predictions.

◁

(*Continued on next page*)

Saved Results

`heckprob` saves in `e()`:

Scalars

`e(N)`	number of observations	`e(rc)`	return code
`e(k)`	number of variables	`e(sigma)`	sigma
`e(k_eq)`	number of equations	`e(chi2)`	χ^2
`e(k_dv)`	number of dependent variables	`e(chi2_c)`	χ^2 for comparison test
`e(df_m)`	model degrees of freedom	`e(p_c)`	p-value for comparison test
`e(ll)`	log likelihood	`e(p)`	significance of comparison test
`e(ll_0)`	log likelihood, constant-only model (`noskip` only)	`e(rho)`	ρ
		`e(ic)`	number of iterations
`e(ll_c)`	log likelihood, comparison model	`e(N_cens)`	number of censored observations
`e(N_clust)`	number of clusters		

Macros

`e(cmd)`	`heckprob`	`e(user)`	name of likelihood-evaluator program
`e(depvar)`	name(s) of dependent variable(s)	`e(opt)`	type of optimization
`e(title)`	title in estimation output	`e(method)`	requested estimation method
`e(wtype)`	weight type	`e(chi2type)`	`Wald` or `LR`; type of model χ^2 test
`e(wexp)`	weight expression	`e(chi2_ct)`	type of comparison χ^2 test
`e(clustvar)`	name of cluster variable	`e(offset)`	offset
`e(vcetype)`	covariance estimation method	`e(predict)`	program used to implement `predict`

Matrices

`e(b)`	coefficient vector	`e(V)`	variance–covariance matrix of the estimators

Functions

`e(sample)`	marks estimation sample

Methods and Formulas

`heckprob` is implemented as an ado-file. Van de Ven and Van Pragg (1981) provide an introduction and an explanation of this model.

The probit equation is

$$y_j = (\mathbf{x}_j\boldsymbol{\beta} + u_{1j} > 0)$$

The selection equation is

$$\mathbf{z}_j\boldsymbol{\gamma} + u_{2j} > 0$$

where

$$u_1 \sim N(0, 1)$$
$$u_2 \sim N(0, 1)$$
$$\mathrm{corr}(u_1, u_2) = \rho$$

(Continued on next page)

The log likelihood is

$$L = \sum_{\substack{i \in S \\ y_i \neq 0}} w_i \ln \left[\Phi_2 \left(x_i\beta + \text{offset}_i^\beta, z_i\gamma + \text{offset}_i^\gamma, \rho \right) \right]$$

$$+ \sum_{\substack{i \in S \\ y_i = 0}} w_i \ln \left[\Phi_2 \left(-x_i\beta + \text{offset}_i^\beta, z_i\gamma + \text{offset}_i^\gamma, -\rho \right) \right]$$

$$+ \sum_{i \notin S} w_i \ln \left[1 - \Phi \left(z_i\gamma + \text{offset}_i^\gamma \right) \right]$$

where S is the set of observations for which y_i is observed, $\Phi_2()$ is the cumulative bivariate normal distribution function (with mean $[0\ \ 0]'$), $\Phi()$ is the standard cumulative normal, and w_i is an optional weight for observation i.

In the maximum likelihood estimation, ρ is not directly estimated. Directly estimated is atanh ρ:

$$\text{atanh}\ \rho = \frac{1}{2} \ln \left(\frac{1+\rho}{1-\rho} \right)$$

From the form of the likelihood, it is clear that if $\rho = 0$, then the log likelihood for the probit model with sample selection is equal to the sum of the probit model for the outcome y and the selection model. A likelihood-ratio test may therefore be performed by comparing the likelihood of the full model with the sum of the log likelihoods for the probit and selection models.

References

Greene, W. H. 1997. *Econometric Analysis*. 3d ed. Upper Saddle River, NJ: Prentice–Hall.

Heckman, J. J. 1979. Sample selection bias as a specification error. *Econometrica* 47: 153–161.

Pindyck, R. and D. Rubinfeld. 1981. *Econometric Models and Economic Forecasts*. New York: McGraw–Hill.

Van de Ven, W. P. M. M. and B. M. S. Van Pragg. 1981. The demand for deductibles in private health insurance: A probit model with sample selection. *Journal of Econometrics* 17: 229–252.

Also See

Complementary:	[R] **lincom**, [R] **lrtest**, [R] **predict**, [R] **test**, [R] **testnl**, [R] **vce**, [R] **xi**
Related:	[R] **heckman**, [R] **probit**
Background:	[U] **16.5 Accessing coefficients and standard errors**,
	[U] **23 Estimation and post-estimation commands**,
	[U] **23.11 Obtaining robust variance estimates**,
	[U] **23.12 Obtaining scores**

Title

help — Obtain on-line help

Syntax

Windows and Macintosh: <u>he</u>lp [*command or topic name*]

                          whelp [*command or topic name*]

Unix: {<u>he</u>lp | man} [*command or topic name*]

All: <u>set</u> <u>h</u>elp *filename*

Description

The `help` command displays help information on the specified command or topic. If `help` is not followed by a command or a topic name, a description of how to use the `help` system is displayed. Stata for Unix users may type `help` or `man`—they mean the same thing.

Stata for Windows and Stata for Macintosh users may click on the **Help** menu. They may also type `whelp` *something* to display the help topic for *something* in Stata's Help window.

`set help` specifies the name of the file containing the help information for Stata's built-in commands.

Remarks

See [U] **8 Stata's on-line help and search facilities** for a complete description of how to use `help`.

❑ Technical Note

When you type `help` *something*, Stata first looks along the S_ADO path for *something*`.hlp`; see [U] **20.5 Where does Stata look for ado-files?**. If nothing is found, it then looks in `stata.hlp` for the topic. Unless you have previously given the command `set help` *filename*, the file `stata.hlp` must be in your current directory, somewhere along your path, or in the directory `\stata` (Windows), `/usr/local/stata` (Unix), or `~:Stata` (Macintosh). If it is not, you will see the following when you request help:

```
. help
file stata.hlp not found
r(601);
```

If you store the `stata.hlp` somewhere other than where Stata expects, use the `set help` command to tell Stata where the file is. It is difficult to imagine why you would want to do this.

❑

Also See

Complementary: [R] **search**

Background: [GSM] **3 Help**,
[GSW] **3 Help**,
[U] **8 Stata's on-line help and search facilities**

Title

hetprob — Maximum-likelihood heteroscedastic probit estimation

Syntax

hetprob *depvar* [*indepvars*] [*weight*] [if *exp*] [in *range*] ,

    het(*varlist*, [<u>off</u>set(*varname*)]) [<u>nocon</u>stant <u>l</u>evel(*#*) asis <u>r</u>obust

    <u>cl</u>uster(*varname*) <u>sc</u>ore(*newvar₁* [*newvar₂*]) noskip <u>off</u>set(*varname*)

    maximize_options]

fweights, iweights, and pweights are allowed; see [U] **14.1.6 weight**.
This command shares the features of all estimation commands; see [U] **23 Estimation and post-estimation commands**.
hetprob may be used with sw to perform stepwise estimation; see [R] **sw**.

Syntax for predict

predict [*type*] *newvarname* [if *exp*] [in *range*] [, { p | xb | <u>sigma</u> } <u>nooff</u>set]

These statistics are available both in and out of sample; type predict ... if e(sample) ... if wanted only for
the estimation sample.

Description

hetprob estimates a maximum-likelihood heteroscedastic probit model.

See [R] **logistic** for a list of related estimation commands.

Options

het(*varlist* [, offset(*varname*)]) specifies the independent variables and the offset variable, if
there is one, in the variance function. het() is not optional.

noconstant suppresses the constant term (intercept) in the model.

level(*#*) specifies the confidence level, in percent, for confidence intervals. The default is level(95)
or as set by set level; see [U] **23.5 Specifying the width of confidence intervals**.

asis forces retention of perfect predictor variables and their associated perfectly predicted observations
and may produce instabilities in maximization; see [R] **probit**.

robust specifies that the Huber/White/sandwich estimator of variance is to be used in place of the
traditional calculation; see [U] **23.11 Obtaining robust variance estimates**. robust combined
with cluster() allows observations which are not independent within cluster (although they must
be independent between clusters).

If you specify pweights, robust is implied; see [U] **23.13 Weighted estimation**.

cluster(*varname*) specifies that the observations are independent across groups (clusters) but not necessarily within groups. *varname* specifies to which group each observation belongs; e.g., cluster(personid) in data with repeated observations on individuals. cluster() affects the estimated standard errors and variance–covariance matrix of the estimators (VCE), but not the estimated coefficients; see [U] **23.11 Obtaining robust variance estimates**. cluster() can be used with pweights to produce estimates for unstratified cluster-sampled data, but see the svyprobt command in [R] **svy estimators** for a command designed especially for survey data.

cluster() implies robust; specifying robust cluster() is equivalent to typing cluster() by itself.

score(*newvar*$_1$ [*newvar*$_2$]) creates *newvar*$_1$ containing $u_j = \partial \ln L_j / \partial(\mathbf{x}_j \mathbf{b})$ for each observation j in the sample. The score vector is $\sum \partial \ln L_j / \partial \mathbf{b} = \sum w_j u_j \mathbf{x}_j$; i.e., the product of *newvar* with each covariate summed over observations. The second new variable, *newvar*$_2$, contains $v_j = \partial \ln L_j / \partial(\mathbf{z}_j \boldsymbol{\gamma})$. See [U] **23.12 Obtaining scores**.

noskip requests fitting of the constant-only model and calculation of the corresponding likelihood ratio χ^2 statistic for testing significance of the full model. By default, a Wald χ^2 statistic is computed for testing significance of the full model.

offset(*varname*) specifies that *varname* is to be included in the model with coefficient constrained to be 1.

maximize_options control the maximization process; see [R] **maximize**. You should never have to specify them.

Options for predict

p, the default, calculates the probability of a positive outcome.

xb calculates the linear prediction.

sigma calculates the standard deviation.

nooffset is relevant only if you specified offset(*varname*) for hetprob. It modifies the calculations made by predict so that they ignore the offset variable; the linear prediction is treated as $\mathbf{x}_j \mathbf{b}$ rather than $\mathbf{x}_j \mathbf{b} + \text{offset}_j$.

Remarks

hetprob performs maximum likelihood estimation of the heteroscedastic probit model, a generalization of the probit model. Let y_j, $j = 1, \ldots, N$ be a binary outcome variable taking on the value 0 (failure) or 1 (success). In the probit model, the probability that y_j takes on the value 1 is modeled as a nonlinear function of a linear combination of the k independent variables $\mathbf{x}_j = (x_{1j}, x_{2j}, \ldots, x_{kj})$:

$$\Pr(y_j = 1) = \Phi(\mathbf{x}_j \mathbf{b})$$

in which $\Phi()$ is the cumulative distribution function (CDF) of a standard normal random variable, that is, a normally distributed (Gaussian) random variable with mean 0 and variance 1. The linear combination of the independent variables, $\mathbf{x}_j \mathbf{b}$, is commonly called the *index function* or *index*. Heteroscedastic probit generalizes the probit model by generalizing $\Phi()$ to a normal CDF with a variance no longer fixed at 1 but allowed to vary as a function of the independent variables. hetprob models the variance as a multiplicative function of these m variables $\mathbf{z}_j = (z_{1j}, z_{2j}, \ldots, z_{mj})$, following Harvey (1976):

$$\sigma_j^2 = [\exp(\mathbf{z}_j \boldsymbol{\gamma})]^2$$

Thus the probability of success as a function of all the independent variables is

$$\Pr(y_j = 1) = \Phi\left(\mathbf{x}_j\mathbf{b}/\exp(\mathbf{z}_j\boldsymbol{\gamma})\right)$$

From this expression it is clear that, unlike the index $\mathbf{x}_j\mathbf{b}$, no constant term can be present in $\mathbf{z}_j\boldsymbol{\gamma}$ if the model is to be identifiable.

Suppose the binary outcomes y_j are generated by thresholding an unobserved random variable w which is normally distributed with mean $\mathbf{x}_j\mathbf{b}$ and variance 1 such that

$$y_j = \begin{cases} 1 & \text{if } w_j > 0 \\ 0 & \text{if } w_j \leq 0 \end{cases}$$

This process gives the probit model:

$$\Pr(y_j = 1) = \Pr(w_j > 0) = \Phi(\mathbf{x}_j\mathbf{b})$$

Now suppose that the unobserved w_j are heteroscedastic with variance

$$\sigma_j^2 = [\exp(\mathbf{z}_j\mathbf{b})]^2$$

Relaxing the homoscedastic assumption of the probit model in this manner yields our multiplicative heteroscedastic probit model:

$$\Pr(y_j = 1) = \Phi\left(\mathbf{x}_j\mathbf{b}/\exp(\mathbf{z}_j\boldsymbol{\gamma})\right)$$

▷ Example

For this example, we generate simulated data for a simple heteroscedastic probit model and then estimate the coefficients using hetprob:

```
. set obs 1000
obs was 0, now 1000
. set seed 1234567
. gen x = 1-2*uniform()
. gen xhet = uniform()
. gen sigma = exp(1.5*xhet)
. gen p = normprob((0.3+2*x)/sigma)
. gen y = cond(uniform()<=p,1,0)
. hetprob y x, het(xhet)
Fitting comparison model:
Iteration 0:   log likelihood = -688.53208
Iteration 1:   log likelihood = -592.23614
Iteration 2:   log likelihood = -591.50687
Iteration 3:   log likelihood = -591.50674
Fitting full model:
Iteration 0:   log likelihood = -591.50674
Iteration 1:   log likelihood = -572.12219
Iteration 2:   log likelihood =  -570.7742
Iteration 3:   log likelihood = -569.48921
Iteration 4:   log likelihood = -569.47828
```

```
Iteration 5:    log likelihood = -569.47827
Heteroscedastic probit model:                Number of obs    =       1000
                                             Zero outcomes    =        452
                                             Nonzero outcomes =        548

                                             Wald chi2(1)     =      78.66
Log likelihood = -569.4783                   Prob > chi2      =     0.0000
```

y	Coef.	Std. Err.	z	P>|z|	[95% Conf. Interval]
y					
x	2.228031	.2512073	8.869	0.000	1.735673 2.720388
_cons	.2493822	.0862833	2.890	0.004	.08027 .4184943
lnsigma2					
xhet	1.602537	.2640131	6.070	0.000	1.085081 2.119993

```
Likelihood ratio test of lnsigma2=0: chi2(1) =    44.06   Prob > chi2 = 0.0000
```

In the preceding we created two variables, x and **xhet**, and then simulated the model

$$\Pr(y = 1) = F\Big((\beta_0 + \beta_1 x)/\exp(\gamma_1 \text{xhet})\Big)$$

for $\beta_0 = 0.3$, $\beta_1 = 2$, and $\gamma_1 = 1.5$. As can be seen from **hetprob**'s output, all coefficients are significant and, as we would expect, the Wald test of the full model versus the constant-only model, e.g., the index consisting of $\beta_0 + \beta_1 x$ versus that of just β_0, is significant with $\chi^2(1) = 79$. Likewise the likelihood-ratio test of heteroscedasticity which tests the full model with heteroscedasticity against the full model without is significant with $\chi^2(1) = 44$. See [R] **maximize** for further explanation of the output. Note that for this simple model **hetprob** took five iterations to converge. As stated elsewhere (Greene 1997, 890) this is a difficult model to fit and so it is not uncommon for it to require many iterations or for the optimizer to print out warning and informative messages during the optimization. Slow convergence is especially common for models in which one or more of the independent variables appear in both the index and variance functions.

◁

❑ Technical Note

Stata interprets a value of 0 as a negative outcome (failure) and treats all other values (except missing) as positive outcomes (successes). Thus, if your dependent variable takes on the values 0 and 1, 0 is interpreted as failure and 1 as success. If your dependent variable takes on the values 0, 1, and 2, 0 is still interpreted as failure, but both 1 and 2 are treated as successes.

❑

Robust standard errors

If you specify the **robust** option, **hetprob** reports robust standard errors as described in [U] **23.11 Obtaining robust variance estimates**. To illustrate the effect of this option we will re-estimate our coefficients using the same model and data in our example, only this time adding **robust** to our **hetprob** command:

▷ Example

```
. hetprob y x, het(xhet) robust nolog

Heteroscedastic probit model:                    Number of obs   =       1000
                                                 Zero outcomes   =        452
                                                 Nonzero outcomes =       548

                                                 Wald chi2(1)    =      65.23
Log likelihood = -569.4783                       Prob > chi2     =     0.0000

-------------------------------------------------------------------------------
             |              Robust
           y |    Coef.   Std. Err.      z    P>|z|     [95% Conf. Interval]
-------------+-----------------------------------------------------------------
y            |
           x |  2.228031   .2758597    8.077   0.000    1.687355    2.768705
       _cons |  .2493822   .0843367    2.957   0.003    .0840853    .4146789
-------------+-----------------------------------------------------------------
lnsigma2     |
        xhet |  1.602537   .2671326    5.999   0.000    1.078967    2.126107
-------------------------------------------------------------------------------

Wald test of lnsigma2=0:                  chi2(1) =     35.99   Prob > chi2 = 0.0000
```

The `robust` standard errors for two of the three parameters are larger than the previously reported conventional standard errors. This is to be expected, even though (by construction) we have perfect model specification, since this option trades off efficient estimation of the coefficient variance-covariance matrix for robustness against misspecification.

◁

Specifying the `cluster()` option relaxes the usual assumption of independence between observations to the weaker assumption of independence just between clusters, that is, `hetprob, robust cluster()` is robust with respect to within-cluster correlation. There is a cost in terms of efficiency with this option, since in this case `hetprob` inefficiently sums within cluster for the standard error calculation rather than attempting to exploit what might be assumed about the within-cluster correlation (as do the `xtgee` population-averaged models).

Obtaining predicted values

Once you have estimated a model, you can obtain the predicted probabilities using the `predict` command for both the estimation sample and other samples; see [U] **23 Estimation and post-estimation commands** and [R] **predict**. `predict` without arguments calculates the predicted probability of a positive outcome. With the `xb` option, it calculates the index function combination $x_j b$, where x_j are the independent variables in the jth observation and b is the estimated parameter vector. With the `sigma` option, `predict` calculates the predicted standard deviation $\sigma_j = \exp(z_j \gamma)$.

▷ Example

Returning to our example, we use `predict` to compute the predicted probabilities and standard deviations based on our model in order to compare these with the actual values:

```
. predict phat
(option p assumed; Pr(y))
. gen diff_p = phat - p
```

```
. summ diff_p
    Variable |       Obs        Mean    Std. Dev.        Min         Max
-------------+--------------------------------------------------------
      diff_p |      1000    .0000904    .0833596   -.1628064    .1676046
. predict sigmahat, sigma
. gen diff_s = sigmahat - sigma
. summ diff_s
    Variable |       Obs        Mean    Std. Dev.        Min         Max
-------------+--------------------------------------------------------
      diff_s |      1000    .1558882    .1363698    .0000417    .4819107
```

◁

Saved Results

hetprob saves in e():

Scalars

e(N)	number of observations	e(N_clust)	number of clusters
e(k)	number of variables	e(rc)	return code
e(k_eq)	number of equations	e(chi2)	χ^2
e(k_dv)	number of dependent variables	e(chi2_c)	χ^2 for heteroscedasticity LR test
e(df_m)	model degrees of freedom	e(p_c)	p-value for heteroscedasticity LR test
e(ll)	log likelihood	e(df_m_c)	degrees of freedom for
e(ll_0)	log likelihood, constant-only model		heteroscedasticity LR test
e(ll_c)	log likelihood, comparison model	e(p)	significance
e(N_s)	number of successes	e(ic)	number of iterations
e(N_f)	number of failures		

Macros

e(cmd)	hetprob	e(opt)	type of optimization
e(depvar)	name of dependent variable	e(chi2type)	Wald or LR; type of model χ^2 test
e(title)	title in estimation output	e(chi2_ct)	Wald or LR; type of model χ^2 test
e(clustvar)	name of cluster variable		corresponding to e(chi2_c)
e(vcetype)	covariance estimation method	e(offset#)	offset for equation #
e(user)	name of likelihood-evaluator program	e(predict)	program used to implement predict
e(method)	requested estimation method		

Matrices

e(b)	coefficient vector	e(V)	variance–covariance matrix of the estimators

Functions

e(sample)	marks estimation sample

Methods and Formulas

hetprob is implemented as an ado-file.

The heteroscedastic probit model is a generalization of the probit model since it allows the scale of the inverse link function to vary from observation to observation as a function of the independent variables.

The log-likelihood function for the heteroscedastic probit model is

$$\ln L = \sum_{j \in S} w_j \ln \Phi(\mathbf{x}_j \mathbf{b} / \exp(\mathbf{z}\boldsymbol{\gamma})) + \sum_{j \notin S} w_j \ln \left(1 - \Phi(\mathbf{x}_j \mathbf{b} / \exp(\mathbf{z}\boldsymbol{\gamma}))\right)$$

in which S is the set of all observations j such that $y_j \neq 0$, and w_j denotes the optional weights. $\ln L$ is maximized as described in [R] **maximize**.

References

Greene, W. H. 1997. *Econometric Analysis*. 3d ed. Upper Saddle River, NJ: Prentice–Hall.

Harvey, J. 1976. Estimating regression models with multiplicative heteroscedasticity. *Econometrica* 44: 461–465.

Also See

Complementary:	[R] **lincom**, [R] **linktest**, [R] **lrtest**, [R] **predict**, [R] **sw**, [R] **test**, [R] **testnl**, [R] **vce**, [R] **xi**
Related:	[R] **biprobit**, [R] **clogit**, [R] **cusum**, [R] **glm**, [R] **glogit**, [R] **logistic**, [R] **logit**, [R] **mlogit**, [R] **ologit**, [R] **probit**, [R] **scobit**, [R] **xtprobit**
Background:	[U] **16.5 Accessing coefficients and standard errors**, [U] **23 Estimation and post-estimation commands**, [U] **23.11 Obtaining robust variance estimates**, [U] **23.12 Obtaining scores**, [R] **maximize**

Title

> **hilite** — Highlight a subset of points in a two-way scatterplot

Syntax

> **hilite** *yvar xvar* [**if** *exp*] [**in** *range*], **hi**lite(*exp₂*) [*graph_options*]

Description

> The `hilite` command draws a two-way scatterplot highlighting the observations selected by *exp₂*.

Options

> `hilite(`*exp₂*`)` is not optional. It specifies an expression identifying the observations to be highlighted.
>
> *graph_options* are any of the options allowed with **graph, twoway**; see [G] **graph options**.

Remarks

▷ Example

> You have data on 956 U.S. cities, including average January temperature, average July temperature, and region. The region variable is coded 1, 2, 3, and 4, with 4 standing for the West. You wish to make a graph showing the relationship between January and July temperatures, highlighting the fourth region:
>
> . hilite tempjan tempjuly, hilite(region==4) ylabel xlabel

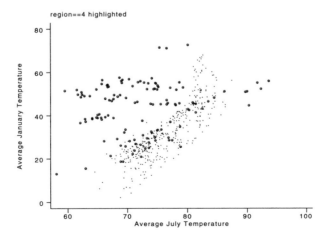

It is possible to use `graph` to product graphs like this, but `hilite` is often more convenient.

◁

❑ Technical Note

By default, `hilite` uses '.' for the plotting symbol and additionally highlights using the o symbol. Its default is equivalent to specifying `symbol(.o)` as one of the *graph_options*. You can vary the symbols used, but you must specify exactly two symbols. The first is used to plot all the data and the second is used for overplotting the highlighted subset.

❑

Methods and Formulas

`hilite` is implemented as an ado-file.

Also See

Background: *Stata Graphics Manual*

Title

hist — Categorical variable histogram

Syntax

hist *varname* [*weight*] [**if** *exp*] [**in** *range*] [, <u>i</u>**ncr**(*#*) *graph_options*]

fweights are allowed; see [U] **14.1.6 weight**.

Description

hist graphs a histogram of *varname*, the result being quite similar to **graph** *varname*, **histogram**. **hist**, however, is intended for use with integer-coded categorical variables.

hist determines the number of bins automatically, the x-axis is automatically labeled, and the labels are centered below the corresponding bar.

hist may only be used with categorical variables with a range of less than 50; i.e., maximum(*varname*) − minimum(*varname*) < 50.

Options

incr(*#*) specifies how the x-axis is to be labeled. **incr**(1), the default if *varname* reflects 25 or fewer categories, labels the minimum, minimum + 1, minimum + 2, ..., maximum. **incr**(2), the default if there are more than 25 categories, would label the minimum, minimum + 2, ..., etc.

graph_options refers to any of the options allowed with **graph**'s **histogram** style excluding **bin()**, **xlabel()**, and **xscale()**. These do include, for instance, **freq**, **ylabel()**, **by()**, **total**, and **saving()**. See [G] **histogram**.

Remarks

▷ Example

You have a categorical variable **rep78** reflecting the repair records of automobiles. It is coded 1 = Poor, 2 = Fair, 3 = Average, 4 = Good, and 5 = Excellent. You could type

(*Continued on next page*)

```
. graph rep78, histogram bin(5)
```

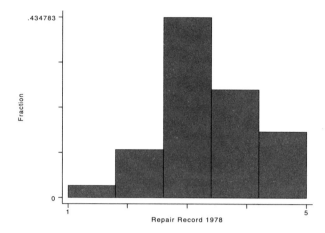

to obtain a histogram. You should specify `bin(5)` because your categorical variable takes on 5 values and you want one bar per value. (You could omit the option in this case, but only because the default value of `bin()` is 5; if you had 4 or 6 bars, you would have to specify it; see [G] **histogram**.) In any case, the resulting graph, while technically correct, is aesthetically displeasing because the numeric code 1 is on the left edge of the first bar while the numeric code 5 is on the right edge of the last bar.

Using `hist` is better:

```
. hist rep78
```

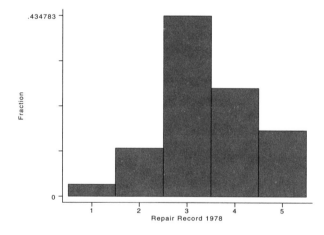

`hist` not only centers the numeric codes underneath the corresponding bar, it also automatically labels all the bars.

You are cautioned: `hist` is not a general replacement for `graph, histogram`. `hist` is intended for use with categorical data only, which is to say, noncontinuous data. If you wanted a histogram of automobile prices, for instance, you would still want to use the `graph, histogram` command.

◁

▷ Example

You may use any of the options you would with **graph, histogram**. Using data collected by Voter Research and Surveys based on questionnaires completed by 15,490 voters from 300 polling places on election day—data originally printed in the *New York Times*, November 5, 1992 and reprinted in Lipset (1993)—you draw the following graph:

```
. hist candi [freq=pop], by(inc) total ylab yline noaxis
                  title(Exit Polling By Family Income)
```

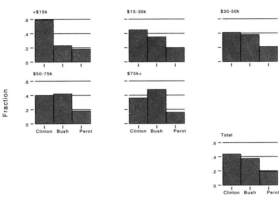

Candidate voted for, 1992
Exit Polling by Family Income

◁

❏ Technical Note

In both of these examples, each bar is labeled; if your categorical variable takes on many values, you may not want to label them all. Typing

```
. hist myvar, incr(2)
```

would label every other bar. Specifying `incr(3)` would label every third bar, and so on.

❏

Methods and Formulas

hist is implemented as an ado-file.

References

Lipset, S. M. 1993. The significance of the 1992 election. *Political Science and Politics* 26(1): 7–16.

Also See

Related:	[G] **histogram**
Background:	*Stata Graphics Manual*

Title

> **hotel** — Hotelling's T-squared generalized means test

Syntax

$\texttt{hotel}$ *varlist* $\bigl[$*weight*$\bigr]$ $\bigl[\texttt{if}\ exp\bigr]$ $\bigl[\texttt{in}\ range\bigr]$ $\bigl[$, $\texttt{by}$(*varname*) $\underline{\texttt{not}}\texttt{able}$ $\bigr]$

$\texttt{aweight}$s and $\texttt{fweight}$s are allowed; see [U] **14.1.6 weight**.

Description

$\texttt{hotel}$ performs Hotelling's T-squared test for testing whether a set of means is zero or, alternatively, equal between two groups.

Options

$\texttt{by}$(*varname*) specifies a variable identifying two groups; the test of equality of means between groups is performed. If $\texttt{by}$() is not specified, a test of means being jointly zero is performed.

$\texttt{notable}$ suppresses printing a table of the means being compared.

Remarks

$\texttt{hotel}$ performs Hotelling's T-squared test of whether a set of means is zero, or two sets of means are equal. It is a multivariate test that reduces to a standard t test if only one variable is specified.

▷ Example

You wish to test whether a new fuel additive improves gas mileage in both stop-and-go and highway situations. Taking twelve cars, you fill them with gas and run them on a highway-style track, recording their gas mileage. You then refill them and run them on a stop-and-go style track. Finally, you repeat the two runs but this time use fuel with the additive. Your data is

```
. describe
Contains data from gasexp.dta
  obs:            12
  vars:            5                          9 Aug 1998 12:45
  size:          288 (99.9% of memory free)
-------------------------------------------------------------------------
  1. id       float  %9.0g                    car id
  2. bmpg1    float  %9.0g                    track1 before additive
  3. ampg1    float  %9.0g                    track1 after additive
  4. bmpg2    float  %9.0g                    track 2 before additive
  5. ampg2    float  %9.0g                    track 2 after additive
-------------------------------------------------------------------------
Sorted by:
```

To perform the statistical test, you jointly test whether the differences in before-and-after results are zero:

```
. gen diff1 = ampg1 - bmpg1
. gen diff2 = ampg2 - bmpg2
. hotel diff1 diff2
Variable |      Obs        Mean    Std. Dev.        Min        Max
---------+-------------------------------------------------------
   diff1 |       12        1.75     2.70101         -3          5
   diff2 |       12    2.083333    2.906367       -3.5        5.5
1-group Hotelling's T-squared = 9.6980676
F test statistic: ((12-2)/(12-1)(2)) x 9.6980676 = 4.4082126

HO: Vector of means is equal to a vector of zeros
             F(2,10) =      4.4082
        Pr > F(2,10) =      0.0424
```

The means are different at the 4.24% significance level.

◁

❏ Technical Note

We used Hotelling's T-squared test because we were testing two differences jointly. Had there been only one difference, we could have used a standard t test; it would have yielded the same results as Hotelling's test:

```
* We could have performed the test like this:
. ttest ampg1 = bmpg1
Paired t test
------------------------------------------------------------------------------
Variable |     Obs        Mean    Std. Err.   Std. Dev.   [95% Conf. Interval]
---------+--------------------------------------------------------------------
   ampg1 |      12       22.75    .9384465    3.250874    20.68449    24.81551
   bmpg1 |      12          21    .7881701    2.730301    19.26525    22.73475
---------+--------------------------------------------------------------------
    diff |      12        1.75    .7797144     2.70101    .0338602     3.46614
------------------------------------------------------------------------------
              Ho: mean(ampg1 - bmpg1) = mean(diff) = 0

Ha: mean(diff) < 0        Ha: mean(diff) ~= 0        Ha: mean(diff) > 0
   t =    2.2444              t =    2.2444              t =    2.2444
 P < t =   0.9768          P > |t| =   0.0463          P > t =   0.0232

* Or like this:
. ttest diff1 = 0
One-sample t test
------------------------------------------------------------------------------
Variable |     Obs        Mean    Std. Err.   Std. Dev.   [95% Conf. Interval]
---------+--------------------------------------------------------------------
   diff1 |      12        1.75    .7797144     2.70101    .0338602     3.46614
------------------------------------------------------------------------------
Degrees of freedom: 11
                     Ho: mean(diff1) = 0

Ha: mean < 0              Ha: mean ~= 0              Ha: mean > 0
   t =    2.2444              t =    2.2444              t =    2.2444
 P < t =   0.9768          P > |t| =   0.0463          P > t =   0.0232
```

```
* Or like this:
. hotel diff1

Variable |      Obs        Mean    Std. Dev.        Min        Max
---------+-----------------------------------------------------------
   diff1 |       12        1.75     2.70101         -3          5

1-group Hotelling's T-squared = 5.0373832
F test statistic: ((12-1)/(12-1)(1)) x 5.0373832 = 5.0373832

H0: Vector of means is equal to a vector of zeros
              F(1,11) =     5.0374
         Pr > F(1,11) =     0.0463
```

❑

▷ Example

Now consider a variation on the experiment: rather than using 12 cars and running each car with and without the fuel additive, you run 24 cars, 12 with the additive and 12 without. You have the following data:

```
. describe

Contains data from gasexp2.dta
  obs:           24
  vars:           4                        9 Aug 1998 12:50
  size:         480 (97.6% of memory free)
-----------------------------------------------------------------------
  1. id        float   %9.0g                   car id
  2. mpg1      float   %9.0g                   track 1
  3. mpg2      float   %9.0g                   track 2
  4. additive  float   %9.0g        yesno      additive?
-----------------------------------------------------------------------
Sorted by:

. tab additive

  additive? |     Freq.       Percent        Cum.
------------+-----------------------------------------
        no  |       12         50.00        50.00
        yes |       12         50.00       100.00
------------+-----------------------------------------
      Total |       24        100.00
```

This is an unpaired experiment because there is no natural pairing of the cars; we want to test that the means of mpg1 are equal for the two groups specified by additive as are the means of mpg2:

```
. hotel mpg1 mpg2, by(additive)
-> additive=        no
Variable |      Obs        Mean    Std. Dev.        Min        Max
---------+-----------------------------------------------------------
    mpg1 |       12          21    2.730301         17         25
    mpg2 |       12    19.91667    2.644319         16         24
-> additive=       yes
Variable |      Obs        Mean    Std. Dev.        Min        Max
---------+-----------------------------------------------------------
    mpg1 |       12       22.75    3.250874         17         28
    mpg2 |       12          22    3.316625       16.5       27.5

2-group Hotelling's T-squared = 7.1347584
F test statistic: ((24-2-1)/(24-2)(2)) x 7.1347584 = 3.4052256

H0: Vectors of means are equal for the two groups
              F(2,21) =     3.4052
         Pr > F(2,21) =     0.0524
```

◁

❑ Technical Note

As in the paired experiment, had there been only one test track, the t test would have yielded the same results as Hotelling's test:

```
. hotel mpg1, by(additive)
-> additive=        no
Variable |        Obs        Mean    Std. Dev.        Min        Max
---------+-----------------------------------------------------------
    mpg1 |         12          21    2.730301         17         25

-> additive=       yes
Variable |        Obs        Mean    Std. Dev.        Min        Max
---------+-----------------------------------------------------------
    mpg1 |         12       22.75    3.250874         17         28

2-group Hotelling's T-squared = 2.0390921
F test statistic: ((24-1-1)/(24-2)(1)) x 2.0390921 = 2.0390921

HO: Vectors of means are equal for the two groups
            F(1,22) =      2.0391
        Pr > F(1,22) =      0.1673

. ttest mpg1, by(additive)
Two-sample t test with equal variances

------------------------------------------------------------------------------
   Group |        Obs        Mean    Std. Err.   Std. Dev.   [95% Conf. Interval]
---------+--------------------------------------------------------------------
      no |         12          21    .7881701    2.730301    19.26525    22.73475
     yes |         12       22.75    .9384465    3.250874    20.68449    24.81551
---------+--------------------------------------------------------------------
combined |         24      21.875    .6264476    3.068954    20.57909    23.17091
---------+--------------------------------------------------------------------
    diff |                   -1.75    1.225518                -4.291568    .7915684
------------------------------------------------------------------------------
Degrees of freedom: 22

                    Ho: mean(no) - mean(yes) = diff = 0

    Ha: diff < 0                 Ha: diff ~= 0                 Ha: diff > 0
       t =  -1.4280                 t =  -1.4280                 t =  -1.4280
    P < t =   0.0837            P > |t| =   0.1673            P > t =   0.9163
```

With more than one pair of means, however, there is no t test equivalent to Hotelling's test although there are other logically (but not practically) equivalent solutions. One is the discriminant function: if the means of mpg1 and mpg2 are different, the discriminant function should separate the groups along that dimension.

```
. regress additive mpg1 mpg2
   Source |        SS       df       MS                 Number of obs =       24
---------+----------------------------               F(  2,    21) =     3.41
    Model | 1.46932917        2  .734664585           Prob > F       =   0.0524
 Residual | 4.53067083       21   .21574623           R-squared      =   0.2449
---------+----------------------------               Adj R-squared  =   0.1730
    Total |       6.00       23  .260869565           Root MSE       =   .46448

------------------------------------------------------------------------------
additive |      Coef.   Std. Err.        t    P>|t|      [95% Conf. Interval]
---------+--------------------------------------------------------------------
    mpg1 |  -.4570407    .2416657    -1.891    0.072     -.959612    .0455306
    mpg2 |   .5014605    .2376762     2.110    0.047     .0071859    .9957352
   _cons |  -.0120115    .7437049    -0.016    0.987     -1.55863    1.534607
------------------------------------------------------------------------------
```

This test would declare the means different at the 5.24% level. Alternatively, we could have estimated this model using logistic regression:

```
. logit additive mpg1 mpg2

Iteration 0:   log likelihood = -16.635532
Iteration 1:   log likelihood = -13.471421
Iteration 2:   log likelihood = -13.371971
Iteration 3:   log likelihood = -13.371143
Iteration 4:   log likelihood = -13.371143

Logit estimates                                 Number of obs   =         24
                                                LR chi2(2)      =       6.53
                                                Prob > chi2     =     0.0382
Log likelihood = -13.371143                     Pseudo R2       =     0.1962

------------------------------------------------------------------------------
additive |     Coef.    Std. Err.       z     P>|z|    [95% Conf. Interval]
---------+--------------------------------------------------------------------
    mpg1 |  -2.306844    1.36139     -1.694   0.090    -4.975119    .3614307
    mpg2 |   2.524477    1.367373     1.846   0.065    -.1555257    5.20448
   _cons |  -2.446527    3.689821    -0.663   0.507    -9.678443    4.78539
------------------------------------------------------------------------------
```

This test would have declared the means different at the 3.82% level.

Are the means different? Hotelling's T-squared and the discriminant function reject equality at the 5.24% level. The logistic regression rejects equality at the 3.82% level.

❏

Saved Results

hotel saves in r():

Scalars

r(N)	number of observations	r(T2)	Hotelling's T-squared
r(k)	number of variables	r(df)	degrees of freedom

Methods and Formulas

hotel is implemented as an ado-file.

See Wilks (1962, 556–561) for a general discussion. The original formulation was by Hotelling (1931) and Mahalanobis (1930, 1936).

For the test of the means of k variables being 0, let $\overline{\mathbf{x}}$ be a $1 \times k$ matrix of the means and $\mathbf{S}$ be the estimated covariance matrix. Then $T^2 = \overline{\mathbf{x}}\mathbf{S}^{-1}\overline{\mathbf{x}}'$.

In the case of two groups, the test of equality is $T^2 = (\overline{\mathbf{x}}_1 - \overline{\mathbf{x}}_2)\mathbf{S}^{-1}(\overline{\mathbf{x}}_1 - \overline{\mathbf{x}}_2)'$.

References

Hotelling, H. 1931. The generalization of Student's ratio. *Annals of Mathematical Statistics* 2: 360–378.

Mahalanobis, P. C. 1930. On tests and measures of group divergence. *Journal Asiatic Society of Bengal* 26: 541–588.

——. 1936. On the generalized distance in statistics. *Proceedings of the National Institute of Science of India* 2: 49–55.

Wilks, S. S. 1962. *Mathematical Statistics*. New York: John Wiley & Sons.

Also See

Related: [R] **regress**, [R] **ttest**

Title

---
if — if programming command

Syntax

```
if exp {
            stata_commands
}
else        stata_command
```

Note that `else` must appear on a separate line from the closing brace (`}`) of the corresponding `if` statement.

Description

The `if` command (not to be confused with the `if` qualifier; see [U] **14.1.3 if exp**) evaluates *exp*. If the result is *true* (nonzero), the commands inside the braces are executed. If the result is *false* (zero), those statements are ignored and the statement (or statements if enclosed in braces) following the `else` is executed.

Remarks

The `if` command is intended for use inside programs and do-files. See [U] **21.3.4 Macros and expressions** for examples of its use.

▷ Example

Do not confuse the `if` command with the `if` qualifier. Typing `if age>21 {summarize age}` will summarize *all* the observations on `age` if the first observation on `age` is greater than 21. Otherwise, it will do nothing. Typing `summarize age if age>21`, on the other hand, summarizes all the observations on `age` that are greater than 21.

◁

▷ Example

`if` is typically used in do-files and programs. For instance, let's write a program to calculate the Tukey (1977, 90–91) "power" function of a variable *x*:

```
. program define power
        if `2'>0 {
                generate z=`1'^`2'
                label variable z "`1'^`2'"
        }
        else if `2'==0 {
                generate z=log(`1')
                label variable z "log(`1')"
        }
        else {
                generate z=-(`1'^(`2'))
                label variable z "-`1'^(`2')"
        }
        end
```

This program takes two arguments. The first argument is the name of an existing variable, x. The second argument is a number, which we will call n. The program creates a new variable **z**. If $n > 0$, **z** is x^n; if $n = 0$, **z** is $\log x$; if $n < 0$, **z** is $-x^n$. No matter which path the program follows through the code, it labels the variable appropriately:

```
. power age 2
. describe z
    7. z              float   %9.0g                age^2
```

◁

❑ Technical Note

If the expression refers to any variables, their values in the first observation are used unless explicit subscripts are specified.

❑

References

Tukey, J. W. 1977. *Exploratory Data Analysis*. Reading, MA: Addison–Wesley Publishing Company.

Also See

Related: [R] **while**

Background: [U] **21 Programming Stata**

Title

> **impute** — Predict missing values

Syntax

> impute *depvar* *varlist* [*weight*] [if *exp*] [in *range*] , <u>g</u>enerate(*newvar₁*)
>
> [<u>varp</u>(*newvar₂*)]

aweights and fweights are allowed; see [U] **14.1.6 weight**.

Description

impute fills in missing values; *depvar* is the variable whose missing values are to be imputed. *varlist* is the list of variables on which the imputations are to be based and *newvar₁* is the new variable to contain the imputations.

impute organizes the cases by patterns of missing data so the missing-value regressions can be conducted efficiently; this necessitates a limit of 31 variables in *varlist*.

Options

generate(*newvar₁*) specifies the name of the new variable to be created and is not optional.

varp(*newvar₂*) specifies the name of a new variable to contain the variance (*not* the standard error) of the prediction.

Remarks

In observations where *depvar* is not equal to missing, *newvar₁* is set equal to *depvar* and *newvar₂* (if specified) is set to zero. Where *depvar* is missing, *newvar₁* is imputed using the prediction from the best available subset of otherwise present data. *newvar₂* (if specified) is set to the variance of the prediction. This variance is in the sense of predict's stdp option, although squared; see [R] **predict**. It is an estimate of how far the prediction of the mean would differ from the actual data point were it known.

This is not the only method for coping with missing data, but it is often much better than deleting cases with any missing data, which is the default. For a discussion of different methods of imputation, see, for example, Little and Rubin (1987).

▷ Example

impute may be used in conjunction with, for instance, regression (or any estimation technique) to avoid the loss of an unacceptable number of cases due to missing data. Bear in mind, however, that the subsequent estimates may be biased because any variable imputed by impute is only an estimate of the unknown, true value. In the case of linear regression, a reasonable bound (in fractional terms) for the bias is given by the ratio of the mean of *newvar₂* to the variance of *newvar₁*. Usually, the bias is toward zero, meaning that the effect of the variable will be underestimated.

You have been hired by the restaurant industry to study expenditures on eating and drinking. You have data on 898 U.S. cities:

```
. describe
Contains data from emd.dta
  obs:             898                          1980 City Data
  vars:              9                          10 Aug 1998 06:30
  size:         34,124 (96.7% of memory free)
-------------------------------------------------------------------------------
  1. fips        long    %10.0g               state/place code
  2. ln_eat      float   %9.0g                ln(Dining sales per capita)
  3. mincpc      int     %8.0g                Per capita money income
  4. ln_rtl      float   %9.0g                ln(retail sales per capita)
  5. jantemp     float   %9.0g                Median January temperature
                                                (Fahrenheit)
  6. precip      float   %9.0g                Annual precipitation (in.)
  7. ln_inc      float   %9.0g                ln(median per capita income)
  8. medage      float   %9.0g                Median age
  9. hhsize      float   %9.0g                Persons per household
-------------------------------------------------------------------------------
Sorted by:
```

You begin by running the regression:

```
. regress ln_eat ln_rtl jantemp precip ln_inc medage hhsize

    Source |       SS       df       MS                  Number of obs =     664
-----------+------------------------------               F(  6,   657) =  212.55
     Model | 87.7285014      6  14.6214169               Prob > F      =  0.0000
  Residual | 45.1948678    657  .068789753               R-squared     =  0.6600
-----------+------------------------------               Adj R-squared =  0.6569
     Total | 132.923369    663  .200487736               Root MSE      =  .26228


    ln_eat |      Coef.   Std. Err.       t    P>|t|     [95% Conf. Interval]
-----------+----------------------------------------------------------------
    ln_rtl |   .6611241   .026623     24.833   0.000     .6088476    .7134006
   jantemp |   .0019624   .0007601     2.582   0.010     .0004698     .003455
    precip |  -.0014311   .0008433    -1.697   0.090    -.0030869    .0002247
    ln_inc |   .1158486   .056352      2.056   0.040     .0051969    .2265003
    medage |  -.0010863   .0002823    -3.847   0.000    -.0016407   -.0005319
    hhsize |  -.0050407   .0004243   -11.880   0.000    -.0058739   -.0042076
     _cons |  -1.377592   .4777641    -2.883   0.004     -2.31572    -.439463
```

Despite having data on 898 cities, your regression was estimated on only 664 cities—74% of the original 898. Some 234 observations were unused due to missing data. In this case, when you type summarize, you discover that each of the independent variables has missing values, so the problem is not that one variable is missing in 26% of the observations, but that each of the variables is missing in some observations. In fact, summarize revealed that each of the variables is missing in roughly 5% of the observations. We lost 26% of our data because, in aggregate, 26% of the observations have one or more missing variables.

Thus, we impute each independent variable on the basis of the other independent variables:

```
. impute ln_rtl  jantemp precip ln_inc medage hhsize, gen(i_ln_rtl)
4.90% (44) observations imputed

. impute jantemp  ln_rtl precip ln_inc medage hhsize, gen(i_jantmp)
5.90% (53) observations imputed

. impute precip  ln_rtl jantemp ln_inc medage hhsize, gen(i_precip)
4.56% (41) observations imputed

. impute ln_inc  ln_rtl jantemp precip medage hhsize, gen(i_ln_inc)
4.34% (39) observations imputed

. impute medage  ln_rtl jantemp precip ln_inc hhsize, gen(i_medage)
4.45% (40) observations imputed
```

```
. impute hhsize  ln_rtl jantemp precip ln_inc medage, gen(i_hhsize)
5.23% (47) observations imputed
```

That done, we can now reestimate the regression on the imputed variables:

```
. regress ln_eat i_ln_rtl i_jantmp i_precip i_ln_inc i_medage i_hhsize

      Source |       SS       df       MS                  Number of obs =     898
-------------+------------------------------                F(  6,   891) =  253.41
       Model |  108.85923      6  18.1432051                Prob > F      =  0.0000
    Residual |  63.7929145    891  .071596986               R-squared     =  0.6305
-------------+------------------------------                Adj R-squared =  0.6280
       Total |  172.652145    897  .192477308               Root MSE      =  .26758

------------------------------------------------------------------------------
      ln_eat |      Coef.   Std. Err.       t    P>|t|     [95% Conf. Interval]
-------------+----------------------------------------------------------------
    i_ln_rtl |   .660906    .0245827     26.885   0.000     .6126593    .7091528
    i_jantmp |   .0021019   .0006932      3.032   0.002     .0007414    .0034625
    i_precip |  -.0013268   .0007646     -1.735   0.083    -.0028275    .0001739
    i_ln_inc |   .095863    .0510231      1.879   0.060    -.0042764    .1960024
    i_medage |  -.0011234   .0002584     -4.348   0.000    -.0016304   -.0006163
    i_hhsize |  -.0052508   .0003953    -13.283   0.000    -.0060267    -.004475
       _cons |  -1.143142   .4304284     -2.656   0.008    -1.987914   -.2983702
------------------------------------------------------------------------------
```

Note that the regression is now estimated on all 898 observations.

◁

▷ Example

impute can also be used with **factor** to extend factor score estimates to cases with missing data. For instance, we have a variant of the automobile data (see [U] **9 Stata's on-line tutorials and sample datasets**) that contains a few additional variables. We will begin by factoring all but the price variable; see [R] **factor**:

```
. factor mpg-foreign, factors(4)
(obs=66)

                (principal factors; 4 factors retained)
    Factor      Eigenvalue     Difference     Proportion     Cumulative
    ----------------------------------------------------------------------
      1          6.99066        5.59538        0.7596         0.7596
      2          1.39528        0.80576        0.1516         0.9112
      3          0.58952        0.29082        0.0640         0.9753
      4          0.29870        0.05618        0.0324         1.0077
      5          0.24252        0.11654        0.0264         1.0341
      6          0.12598        0.08970        0.0137         1.0478
      7          0.03628        0.05085        0.0039         1.0517
      8         -0.01457        0.01275       -0.0016         1.0501
      9         -0.02732        0.02860       -0.0030         1.0472
     10         -0.05591        0.05736       -0.0061         1.0411
     11         -0.11327        0.00564       -0.0123         1.0288
     12         -0.11891        0.02714       -0.0129         1.0159
     13         -0.14605           .          -0.0159         1.0000

                Factor Loadings
    Variable |      1            2            3            4        Uniqueness
    ---------+--------------------------------------------------------------
         mpg |  -0.78200     -0.02985     -0.06546      0.33951      0.26803
       rep78 |  -0.51076      0.68322     -0.11181     -0.01428      0.25963
       rep77 |  -0.27332      0.70653     -0.32005      0.04710      0.32145
      hdroom |   0.56480      0.26549      0.29651      0.16485      0.49542
```

```
   rseat |  0.66134    0.20472    0.36471    0.02062    0.38727
   trunk |  0.72934    0.37094    0.28176    0.12140    0.23633
  weight |  0.95127    0.10135   -0.18056   -0.09179    0.04378
  length |  0.94621    0.19595   -0.05372   -0.10325    0.05274
    turn |  0.88264   -0.05607   -0.08502    0.01169    0.21043
   displ |  0.92199    0.06333   -0.17349   -0.02554    0.11518
  gratio | -0.82782    0.06672    0.24558   -0.10994    0.23787
   order | -0.25907    0.15344    0.01622    0.14668    0.88756
  foreign | -0.75728    0.30756    0.19130   -0.29188    0.21014
```

There appear to be two factors here. Let's pretend that we have given the first two factors an interpretation—we might interpret the first factor as size. We now obtain the factor scores:

```
. score f1 f2
            (based on unrotated factors)
            (2 scorings not used)

            Scoring Coefficients
   Variable |    1          2
 -----------+--------------------
      mpg | -0.02094    0.11106
    rep78 | -0.03224    0.44562
    rep77 | -0.11150    0.27942
   hdroom |  0.05530    0.10017
    rseat |  0.03355    0.02812
    trunk |  0.04603    0.20622
   weight |  0.12250   -0.13040
   length |  0.39996    0.60223
     turn |  0.04562   -0.12825
    displ |  0.19281    0.11611
   gratio | -0.08534    0.03528
    order |  0.00638    0.06433
  foreign | -0.06469    0.28292
```

Although it is not revealed by this output, in 8 cases the scores could not be calculated because of missing values (we would see that if we typed **summarize**). To impute the factor scores to all the observations:

```
. impute f1  mpg-foreign, gen(i_f1)
10.81% (8) observations imputed
. impute f2  mpg-foreign, gen(i_f2)
10.81% (8) observations imputed
```

And we might now run a regression of **price** in terms of the two factors:

```
. regress price i_f1 i_f2
    Source |       SS       df       MS                  Number of obs =      74
 ----------+------------------------------              F( 2,    71) =   11.88
     Model |  159223103       2   79611551.5            Prob > F      =  0.0000
  Residual |  475842293      71   6702004.13            R-squared     =  0.2507
 ----------+------------------------------              Adj R-squared =  0.2296
     Total |  635065396      73   8699525.97            Root MSE      =  2588.8

 ---------------------------------------------------------------------------------
     price |     Coef.    Std. Err.       t      P>|t|     [95% Conf. Interval]
 ----------+----------------------------------------------------------------------
      i_f1 |  1225.347    315.7177      3.881    0.000     595.8234    1854.87
      i_f2 |  911.2878    339.9821      2.680    0.009     233.3827   1589.193
     _cons |  6262.285    301.7093     20.756    0.000     5660.694   6863.877
 ---------------------------------------------------------------------------------
```

◁

Methods and Formulas

`impute` is implemented as an ado-file.

Consider the command `impute` y x_1 x_2 ... x_k, `gen`($\hat{y}$) `varp`($\hat{v}$).

When y is not missing, $\hat{y} = y$ and $\hat{v} = 0$.

Let y_j be an observation for which y is missing. A regressor list is formed from x_1, x_2, ..., x_k containing all x's for which x_{ij} is not missing. If the resulting list is empty, $\hat{y}_j$ and $\hat{v}_j$ are set to missing. Otherwise a regression of y on the list is estimated (see [R] **regress**) and $\hat{y}_j$ is defined as the predicted value of y_j (see [R] **predict**). $\hat{v}_j$ is defined as the square of the standard error of the prediction, as calculated by `predict, stdp`; see [R] **predict**.

References

Goldstein, R. 1996. sed10: Patterns of missing data. *Stata Technical Bulletin* 32: 12–13. Reprinted in *Stata Technical Bulletin Reprints*, vol. 6, p. 115.

——. 1996. sed10.1: Patterns of missing data, update. *Stata Technical Bulletin* 33: 2. Reprinted in *Stata Technical Bulletin Reprints*, vol. 6, pp. 115–116.

Little, R. J. A. and D. B. Rubin. 1987. *Statistical Analysis with Missing Data*. New York: John Wiley & Sons.

Also See

Complementary:	[R] **predict**
Related:	[R] **ipolate**, [R] **regress**

Title

infile — Quick reference for reading data into Stata

Description

This entry provides a quick reference for determining which method to use for reading non-Stata data into memory. See [U] **24 Commands to input data** for another guide that provides more explanation.

Remarks

Summary of the different methods

insheet

- o `insheet` reads text (ASCII) files created by a spreadsheet or a database program.
- o The data must be tab-separated or comma-separated, but not both simultaneously, nor can it be space-separated.
- o A single observation must be on only one line.
- o The first line in the file can optionally contain the names of the variables.

infile (free format)—infile without a dictionary

- o The data can be space-separated, tab-separated, or comma-separated.
- o Strings with embedded spaces or commas must be enclosed in quotes (even if tab- or comma-separated).
- o A single observation can be on more than one line or there can even be multiple observations per line.

infix (fixed format)

- o The data must be in fixed-column format.
- o A single observation can be on more than one line.
- o `infix` has simpler syntax than `infile` (fixed format).

infile (fixed format)—infile with a dictionary

- o The data may be in fixed-column format.
- o A single observation can be on more than one line.
- o `infile` (fixed format) has the most capabilities for reading data.

Examples

▷ Example

```
───────────────────────────────────────── top of examp1.raw ───────────
    1        0        1        John Smith        m
    0        0        1        Paul Lin f        m
    0        1        0        Jan Doe f
    0        0        .        Julie McDonald  f
───────────────────────────────────────── end of examp1.raw ───────────
```

contains tab-separated data. The `type` command with the `showtabs` option shows the tabs:

```
. type examp1.raw, showtabs
1<T>0<T>1<T>John Smith<T>m
0<T>0<T>1<T>Paul Lin<T>m
0<T>1<T>0<T>Jan Doe<T>f
0<T>0<T>.<T>Julie McDonald<T>f
```

It could be read in by

```
. insheet a b c name gender using examp1
```

◁

▷ Example

```
───────────────────────────────────────── top of examp2.raw ───────────
a,b,c,name,gender
1,0,1,John Smith,m
0,0,1,Paul Lin,m
0,1,0,Jan Doe,f
0,0,,Julie McDonald,f
───────────────────────────────────────── end of examp2.raw ───────────
```

could be read in by

```
. insheet using examp2
```

◁

▷ Example

```
───────────────────────────────────────── top of examp3.raw ───────────
    1        0        1        "John Smith"        m
    0        0        1        "Paul Lin"          m
    0        1        0        "Jan Doe"           f
    0        0        .        "Julie McDonald"         f
───────────────────────────────────────── end of examp3.raw ───────────
```

contains tab-separated data with strings in double quotes.

```
. type examp3.raw, showtabs
1<T>0<T>1<T>"John Smith"<T>m
0<T>0<T>1<T>"Paul Lin"<T>m
0<T>1<T>0<T>"Jan Doe"<T>f
0<T>0<T>.<T>"Julie McDonald"<T>f
```

It could be read in by

```
. infile byte (a b c) str15 name str1 gender using examp3
```

or could be read in by

. insheet a b c name gender using examp3

or could be read in by

. infile using dict3

where the dictionary `dict3.dct` contains

── top of dict3.dct ──────────

```
infile dictionary using examp3 {
        byte    a
        byte    b
        byte    c
        str15   name
        str1    gender
}
```

── end of dict3.dct ──────────
                                                                    ◁

▷ Example

── top of examp4.raw ──────────

```
1 0 1 "John Smith" m
0 0 1 "Paul Lin" m
0 1 0 "Jan Doe" f
0 0 . "Julie McDonald" f
```

── end of examp4.raw ──────────

could be read in by

. infile byte (a b c) str15 name str1 gender using examp4

or could be read in by

. infile using dict4

where the dictionary `dict4.dct` contains

── top of dict4.dct ──────────

```
infile dictionary using examp4 {
        byte    a
        byte    b
        byte    c
        str15   name
        str1    gender
}
```

── end of dict4.dct ──────────
                                                                    ◁

▷ Example

── top of examp5.raw ──────────

```
101mJohn Smith
001mPaul Lin
010fJan Doe
00 fJulie McDonald
```

── end of examp5.raw ──────────

could be read in by

. infix a 1 b 2 c 3 str gender 4 str name 5-19 using examp5

or could be read in by

. infix using dict5a

where dict5a.dct contains

```
─────────────────────────────────────────────────────────── top of dict5a.dct ───────
infix dictionary using examp5 {
                a       1
                b       2
                c       3
        str     gender  4
        str     name    5-19
}
─────────────────────────────────────────────────────────── end of dict5a.dct ───────
```

or could be read in by

. infile using dict5b

where dict5b.dct contains

```
─────────────────────────────────────────────────────────── top of dict5b.dct ───────
infile dictionary using examp5 {
        byte    a       %1f
        byte    b       %1f
        byte    c       %1f
        str1    gender  %1s
        str15   name    %15s
}
─────────────────────────────────────────────────────────── end of dict5b.dct ───────
```
◁

▷ Example

```
─────────────────────────────────────────────────────────── top of examp6.raw ───────
line 1 : a heading
There are a total of 4 lines of heading.
The next line contains a useful heading:
----+----1----+----2----+----3----+----4----+-
1       0       1       m       John Smith
0       0       1       m       Paul Lin
0       1       0       f       Jan Doe
0       0               f       Julie McDonald
─────────────────────────────────────────────────────────── end of examp6.raw ───────
```

could be read in by

. infile using dict6a

where dict6a.dct contains

```
─────────────────────────────────────────────────────────── top of dict6a.dct ───────
infile dictionary using examp6 {
_firstline(5)
                byte    a
                byte    b
_column(17)     byte    c       %1f
                str1    gender
_column(33)     str15   name    %15s
}
─────────────────────────────────────────────────────────── end of dict6a.dct ───────
```

or could be read in by

. infix 5 first a 1 b 9 c 17 str gender 25 str name 33-46 using examp6

or could be read in by

. infix using dict6b

where `dict6b.dct` contains

```
─────────────────────────────────────────────────── top of dict6b.dct ───────────
infix dictionary using examp6 {
5 first
                a       1
                b       9
                c       17
        str     gender  25
        str     name    33-46
}
─────────────────────────────────────────────────── end of dict6b.dct ───────────
```
◁

▷ Example

```
─────────────────────────────────────────────────── top of examp7.raw ───────────
a b c gender name
1 0 1
m
John Smith
0 0 1
m
Paul Lin
0 1 0
f
Jan Doe
0 0
f
Julie McDonald
─────────────────────────────────────────────────── end of examp7.raw ───────────
```

could be read in by

. infile using dict7a

where `dict7a.dct` contains

```
─────────────────────────────────────────────────── top of dict7a.dct ───────────
infile dictionary using examp7 {
_firstline(2)
            byte    a
            byte    b
            byte    c
_line(2)
            str1    gender
_line(3)
            str15   name    %15s
}
─────────────────────────────────────────────────── end of dict7a.dct ───────────
```

Or, if you wanted to include variable labels:

. infile using dict7b

where `dict7b.dct` contains

———————————————————————————————— top of dict7b.dct ————————————

```
infile dictionary using examp7 {
_firstline(2)
          byte    a           "Question 1"
          byte    b           "Question 2"
          byte    c           "Question 3"
_line(2)
          str1    gender      "Gender of subject"
_line(3)
          str15   name     %15s
}
```

———————————————————————————————— end of dict7b.dct ————————————

`infix` could also read this data:

`. infix 2 first 3 lines a 1 b 3 c 5 str gender 2:1 str name 3:1-15 using examp7`

or it could be read in by

`. infix using dict7c`

where `dict7c.dct` contains

———————————————————————————————— top of dict7c.dct ————————————

```
infix dictionary using examp7 {
2 first
                a       1
                b       3
                c       5
        str     gender  2:1
        str     name    3:1-15
}
```

———————————————————————————————— end of dict7c.dct ————————————

or it could be read in by

`.infix using dict7d`

where `dict7d.dct` contains

———————————————————————————————— top of dict7d.dct ————————————

```
infix dictionary using examp7 {
2 first
                a       1
                b       3
                c       5
/
        str     gender  1
/
        str     name    1-15
}
```

———————————————————————————————— end of dict7d.dct ————————————

◁

Also See

Complementary:	[R] **edit**, [R] **infile (fixed format)**, [R] **infile (free format)**, [R] **infix (fixed format)**, [R] **input**, [R] **insheet**
Background:	[U] **24 Commands to input data**

Title

---

infile (fixed format) — Read ASCII (text) data in fixed format with a dictionary

---

Syntax

infile using *dfilename* [if *exp*] [in *range*] [, automatic using(*filename*₂) clear]

If *dfilename* is specified without an extension, .dct is assumed.

If *filename*₂ is specified without an extension, .raw is assumed.

The syntax for a dictionary, a file created with an editor or word processor outside of Stata, is

---
——————————————————————————————— top of dictionary file ———————

[infile] dictionary [using *filename*] {
    * *comments may be included freely*
    _lrecl(*#*)
    _firstlineoffile(*#*)
    _lines(*#*)

    _line(*#*)
    _newline[(*#*)]

    _column(*#*)
    _skip[(*#*)]

    [*type*] *varname* [:*lblname*] [% *infmt*] ["*variable label*"]
}
(*your data might appear here*)

——————————————————————————————— end of dictionary file ———————

---

where % *infmt* is { %[*#*[.*#*]]{f|g|e} | %[*#*]s }

If using *filename* is not specified, the data is assumed to begin on the line following the close brace.

If using *filename* is specified, the data is assumed to be located in *filename*. If *filename* is specified without an extension, .raw is assumed.

Description

infile using reads data from a disk dataset that is not in Stata format. infile using does this by first reading *dfilename*, called a dictionary, that describes the format of the data file, and then reads the file containing the data. The dictionary is a file you create in an editor or word processor outside of Stata.

The data may be in the same file as the dictionary or in another file.

Another variation on infile omits the intermediate dictionary; see [R] **infile (free format)**. This variation is easier to use, but will not read fixed-format files. On the other hand, although infile using will read free-format files, the variation is even better at it.

An alternative to infile using for reading fixed-format files is infix; see [R] **infix (fixed format)**. infix provides fewer features than infile using but is easier to use.

Stata has other commands for reading data. If you are not certain that infile using is what you are looking for, see [R] **infile** and [U] **24 Commands to input data**.

Options

automatic causes Stata to create value labels from the nonnumeric data it reads. It also automatically widens the display format to fit the longest label.

using(*filename*₂) specifies the name of a file containing the data. If using() is not specified, the data is assumed to follow the dictionary in *dfilename* or, if the dictionary specifies the name of some other file, that file is assumed to contain the data. If using(*filename*₂) is specified, *filename*₂ is used to obtain the data even if the dictionary itself says otherwise.

clear specifies that it is okay for the new data to replace what is currently in memory. To ensure that you do not lose something important, infile using will refuse to read new data if data is already in memory. clear is one way you can tell infile using that it is okay. The other is to drop the data yourself by typing drop _all before reading new data.

Dictionary directives

* marks comment lines. Wherever you wish to place a comment, begin the line with a *. Comments can appear many times in the same dictionary.

_lrecl(#) is used only when reading datasets that do not have end-of-line delimiters (carriage return, linefeed, or some combination). Such files are often produced by mainframe computers and have been poorly translated from EBCDIC into ASCII. _lrecl() specifies the logical record length. _lrecl() requests that infile act as if a line ends every # characters.

_lrecl() appears only once, and typically not at all, in a dictionary.

_firstlineoffile(#) (abbreviation _first()) is also rarely specified. It states the line of the file where the data begins. _first() is not specified when the data follows the dictionary; Stata can figure that out for itself. _first() is instead specified when reading data from another file and the first line of that file does not contain data because of headers or other markers.

_first() appears only once, and typically not at all, in a dictionary.

_lines(#) states the number of lines per observation in the file. Simple datasets typically have _lines(1). Large datasets often have many lines (sometimes called records) per observation. _lines() is optional even when there is more than one line per observation because infile can sometimes figure it out for itself. Still, if _lines(1) is not right for your data, it is best to specify the directive.

_lines() appears only once in a dictionary.

_line(#) tells infile to jump to line # of the observation. Distinguish _lines() from _line(), and consider a file with _lines(4), meaning four lines per observation. _line(2) says to go to the second line of the observation. _line(4) says to go to the fourth line of the observation. You may jump forward or backward, infile does not care nor is there any inefficiency in going forward to _line(3), reading a few variables, jumping back to _line(1), reading another variable, and jumping forward again to _line(3).

It is not your responsibility to ensure that, at the end of your dictionary, you are on the last line of the observation. infile knows how to get to the next observation because it knows where you are and it knows _lines(), the total number of lines per observation.

_line() may appear, and typically does, many times in a dictionary.

_newline[(#)] is an alternative to _line(). _newline(1), which may be abbreviated _newline, goes forward one line. _newline(2) goes forward two lines. We do not recommend the use of _newline() because _line() is better. If you are currently on line 2 of an observation and want to get to line 6, you could type _newline(4), but your meaning is clearer if you type _line(6).

_newline() may appear many times in a dictionary.

_column(#) jumps to column # on the current line. You may jump forward or backward within a line. _column() may appear many times in a dictionary.

_skip(#) jumps forward # columns on the current line. _skip() is just an alternative to _column(). _skip() may appear many times in a dictionary.

[*type*] *varname* [: *lblname*] [% *infmt*] ["*variable label*"] instructs infile to read a variable. The simplest form of this instruction is the variable name itself: *varname*.

First understand that at all times infile is on some column of some line of an observation. infile starts by being on column 1 of line 1, so pretend that is where we are. Given the simplest directive '*varname*', infile goes through the following logic:

Is the current column blank? If so, skip forward until there is a nonblank column (or until the end of the line). If we just skipped all the way to the end of the line, store a missing value in *varname*. If we skipped to a nonblank column, begin collecting what is there until we come to a blank column or the end of the line. That is the data for *varname*. Now set the current column to wherever we are.

The logic is a bit more complicated. For instance, when skipping forward to find the data, infile might encounter a quote. If so, it then collects the characters for the data by skipping forward until it finds the matching quote. If you specified a % *infmt*, infile skips the skipping-forward step and simply collects the specified number of characters. Nevertheless, the general logic is (optionally) skip, collect, and reset.

Remarks

infile using follows a two-step process to read your data. You type something like infile using descript and

1. infile using reads the file descript.dct, which tells infile about the format of the data; and

2. infile using then reads the data according to the instructions recorded in descript.dct.

descript.dct (the file could be named anything) is called a dictionary and descript.dct is just a text file you create with an editor or word processor outside of Stata.

As for the data themselves, they can be in the same file as the dictionary or in a different file. It does not matter.

Reading free-format files

There is another variation of infile for reading free-format files described in [R] **infile (free format)**. We will refer to the variation as infile without a dictionary. The distinction between the two variations is in the treatment of line breaks. infile without a dictionary does not consider them significant. infile with a dictionary does.

A line, also known as a record, physical record, or physical line (as opposed to observations, or logical records, or logical lines), is a string of characters followed by the line terminator. If you were to type the file, a line is what would appear on your screen if your screen were infinitely wide. Your screen would have to be infinitely wide so that there would be no possibility that a single line could take more than one line of your screen, thus fooling you into thinking there are multiple lines when there is only one.

A logical line, on the other hand, is a sequence of one or more physical lines that represents a single observation of your data. `infile` with a dictionary does not willy-nilly go to new physical lines; it goes to a new line between observations and it goes to a new line when you tell it to, but that is all. `infile` without a dictionary, on the other hand, goes to a new line whenever it needs to, which can be right in the middle of an observation. Thus, consider the following little bit of data which, we will tell you, is for three variables:

```
5 4
1 9 3
2
```

How do you interpret this data?

Here is one interpretation: There are three observations. The first is 5, 4, and missing. The second is 1, 9, and 3. The third is 2, missing, and missing. That is the interpretation that `infile` with a dictionary makes.

Here is another interpretation: There are two observations. The first is 5, 4, and 1. The second is 9, 3, and 2. That is the interpretation that `infile` without a dictionary makes.

Which is right? We would have to ask the person who entered this data. The question is, are the line breaks significant? Do they mean anything? If the line breaks are significant, we use `infile` with a dictionary. If the line breaks are not significant, we use `infile` without a dictionary.

The other distinction between the two `infile`s is that `infile` with a dictionary does not process comma-separated-value format. If your data is comma-separated, see [R] **infile (free format)** or [R] **insheet**.

▷ Example

Outside of Stata you have typed into the file `highway.dct` information on the accident rate per million vehicle miles along a stretch of highway, the speed limit on that highway, and the number of access points (on-ramps and off-ramps) per mile. Your file contains

```
───────────────────────── top of highway.dct, example 1 ──────────
infile dictionary {
        acc_rate  spdlimit acc_pts
}
4.58 55 4.6
2.86  60 4.4
1.61 . 2.2
3.02 60 4.7
───────────────────────── end of highway.dct, example 1 ──────────
```

This file can be read by typing `infile using highway`. Stata displays the dictionary and reads the data:

```
. infile using highway
infile dictionary {
        acc_rate  spdlimit acc_pts
}
(4 observations read)
```

```
. list
        acc_rate   spdlimit    acc_pts
  1.        4.58         55        4.6
  2.        2.86         60        4.4
  3.        1.61          .        2.2
  4.        3.02         60        4.7
```

◁

▷ Example

We can include variable labels in a dictionary so that after we infile the data it will be fully labeled. We could change highway.dct to read

── top of highway.dct, example 2 ──────────

```
infile dictionary {
* This is a comment and will be ignored by Stata
* You might type the source of the data here.
        acc_rate   "Acc. Rate/Million Miles"
        spdlimit   "Speed Limit (mph)"
        acc_pts    "Access Pts/Mile"
}
4.58 55 4.6
2.86  60 4.4
1.61 . 2.2
3.02 60 4.7
```

── end of highway.dct, example 2 ──────────

Now when we type infile using highway, Stata not only reads the data but labels the variables.

◁

▷ Example

We can indicate the variable types in the dictionary. For instance, if we wanted to store acc_rate as a double and spdlimit as a byte, we could change highway.dct to read

── top of highway.dct, example 3 ──────────

```
infile dictionary {
* This is a comment and will be ignored by Stata
* You might type the source of the data here.
 double acc_rate   "Acc. Rate/Million Miles"
 byte   spdlimit   "Speed Limit (mph)"
        acc_pts    "Access Pts/Mile"
}
4.58 55 4.6
2.86  60 4.4
1.61 . 2.2
3.02 60 4.7
```

── end of highway.dct, example 3 ──────────

Since we do not indicate the variable type for acc_pts, it is given the default variable type float (or the type specified by the set type command).

◁

▷ Example

By specifying the types, we can read string variables as well as numeric variables. For instance:

```
——————————————————————————————————— top of emp.dct ———————————
infile dictionary {
* data on employees
  str20 name        "Name"
        age         "Age"
    int sex         "Sex coded 0 male 1 female"
}
"Lisa Gilmore" 25 1
Branton 32 1
'Bill Ross' 27 0
—————————————————————————————————————— end of emp.dct ——————————
```

The strings can be delimited by single or double quotes and quotes may be omitted altogether if the string contains no blanks or other special characters.

◁

❑ Technical Note

You may attach value labels to variables in the dictionary using the colon notation:

```
——————————————————————————————————— top of emp2.dct ———————————
infile dictionary {
* data on name, sex, and age
  str16 name        "Name"
        sex:sexlbl  "Sex"
    int age         "Age"
}
"Arthur Doyle" Male 22
"Mary Hope" Female 37
"Guy Fawkes" Male 48
"Sherry Crooks" Female 25
—————————————————————————————————————— end of emp2.dct ——————————
```

If you wish the value labels to be automatically created, you must specify the `automatic` option on the `infile` command. This data could be read by typing `infile using person2, automatic` assuming the dictionary and data are stored in the file `person2.dct`.

❑

▷ Example

The data need not be in the same file as the dictionary. We might leave the highway data in `highway.raw` and write a dictionary called `highway.dct` describing it:

```
——————————————————————————————————— top of highway.dct, example 4 ———————————
infile dictionary using highway {
* This dictionary reads the file highway.raw.  If the
* file were called highway.txt, the first line would
* read "dictionary using highway.txt"
      acc_rate  "Acc. Rate/Million Miles"
      spdlimit  "Speed Limit (mph)"
      acc_pts   "Access Pts/Mile"
}
—————————————————————————————————————— end of highway.dct, example 4 ——————————
```

◁

▷ Example

The `firstlineoffile()` directive allows you to ignore lines at the top of the file. Consider the following raw dataset:

```
──────────────────────────── top of mydata.raw ────────────
The following data was entered by Marsha Holliday.  It was checked by
Helen Troy.
id income educ sex age
1024 25000 HS Male 28
1025 27000 C Female 24
──────────────────────────── end of mydata.raw ────────────
```

Your dictionary might read

```
──────────────────────────── top of mydata.dct ────────────
infile dictionary using mydata {
        _first(4)
        int id "Identification Number"
        income "Annual income"
        str2 educ "Highest educ level"
        str6 sex
        byte age
}
──────────────────────────── end of mydata.dct ────────────
```
◁

▷ Example

The `_line()` and `_lines()` directives instruct Stata how to read your dataset when there are multiple records per observation. You have the following in `mydata2.raw`:

```
──────────────────────────── top of mydata2.raw ────────────
id income educ sex age
1024 25000 HS
Male
28
1025 27000 C
Female
24
1035 26000 HS
Male
32
1036 25000 C
Female
25
──────────────────────────── end of mydata2.raw ────────────
```

You can read this with a dictionary `mydata2.dct`, which we will just let Stata list as it simultaneously reads the data:

```
. infile using mydata2, clear
```

```
infile dictionary using mydata2 {
    _first(2)                              * Begin reading on line 2
    _lines(3)                              * Each observation takes 3 lines.
    int id "Identification Number"         * Since _line is not specified, Stata
    income "Annual income"                 * assumes that it is 1.
    str2 educ "Highest educ level"
    _line(2)                               * Go to line 2 of the observation.
    str6 sex                               * (values for sex are located on line 2)
    _line(3)                               * Go to line 3 of the observation.
    int age                                * (values for age are located on line 3)
}
(4 observations read)
. list
           id      income       educ        sex      age
    1.    1024       25000         HS       Male       28
    2.    1025       27000          C     Female       24
    3.    1035       26000         HS       Male       32
    4.    1036       25000          C     Female       25
```

Now, here is the really good part: We read these variables in order but that was not necessary. We could just as well have used the dictionary:

─── top of mydata2p.dct ───────────

```
infile dictionary using mydata2 {
    _first(2)
    _lines(3)
    _line(1)    int    id       "Identification number"
                       income   "Annual income"
                str2   educ     "Highest educ level"
    _line(3)    int    age
    _line(2)    str6   sex
}
```

─── end of mydata2p.dct ───────────

We would obtain the same results—and just as quickly—the only difference being that our variables in the final dataset would be in the order specified: id, income, educ, age, and sex.   ◁

❑ Technical Note

You can use _newline to specify where breaks occur, if you prefer:

─── top of highway.dct, example 5 ───────

```
infile dictionary {
            acc_rate   "Acc. Rate/Million Miles"
            spdlimit   "Speed Limit (mph)"
_newline    acc_pts    "Access Pts/Mile"
}
4.58 55
4.6
2.86   60
 4.4
1.61 .
2.2
3.02 60
 4.7
```

─── end of highway.dct, example 5 ───────

The line that reads '1.61 .' could have been read 1.61 (without the period), and the results would have been unchanged. Since dictionaries do not go to new lines automatically, a missing value is assumed for all values not found in the record.   ❑

Reading fixed-format files

Values in formatted data are sometimes packed one against the other with no intervening blanks. For instance, the highway data might appear as

```
───────────────────────────────────── top of highway.raw, example 6 ─────────
  4.58554.6
  2.86604.4
  1.61  2.2
  3.02604.7
───────────────────────────────────── end of highway.raw, example 6 ─────────
```

The first four columns of each record represent the accident rate; the next two columns, the speed limit; and the last three columns, the number of access points per mile.

To read this data, you must specify the % *infmt* in the dictionary. Numeric % *infmt*s are denoted by a leading percent sign (%) followed optionally by a string of the form w or $w.d$, where w and d stand for two integers. The first integer, w, specifies the width of the format. The second integer, d, specifies the number of digits that are to follow the decimal point. Logic requires that d be less than or equal to w. Finally, a character denoting the format type (f, g, or e) is appended. For example, %9.2f specifies an f format that is nine characters wide and has two digits following the decimal point.

Numeric formats

The f format indicates that `infile` is to attempt to read the data as a number. When you do not specify the % *infmt* in the dictionary, `infile` assumes the %f format. The missing width w means that `infile` is to attempt to read the data in free format.

At the start of each observation, `infile` reads a record into its buffer and sets a column pointer to 1, indicating that it is currently on the first column. When `infile` processes a %f format, it moves the column pointer forward through white space. It then collects the characters up to the next occurrence of white space and attempts to interpret those characters as a number. The column pointer is left at the first occurrence of white space following those characters. If the next variable is also free format, the logic repeats.

When you explicitly specify the field width w, as in %wf, `infile` does not skip leading white space. Instead, it collects the next w characters starting at the column pointer and attempts to interpret the result as a number. The column pointer is left at the old value of the column pointer plus w, that is, on the first character following the specified field.

▷ Example

If the data above is stored in `highway.raw`, you could create the following dictionary to read it:

```
───────────────────────────────────── top of highway.dct, example 6 ─────────
  infile dictionary using highway {
          acc_rate   %4f   "Acc. Rate/Million Miles"
          spdlimit   %2f   "Speed Limit (mph)"
          acc_pts    %3f   "Access Pts/Mile
  }
───────────────────────────────────── end of highway.dct, example 6 ─────────
```

When you explicitly indicate the field width, `infile` does not skip intervening characters. The first four columns are used for the variable `acc_rate`, the next two for `spdlimit`, and the last three for `acc_pts`.

◁

❏ **Technical Note**

The d specification in the $\%w.df$ indicates the number of *implied* decimal places in the data. For instance, the string 212 read in a $\%3.2f$ format represents the number 2.12. You should *not* specify d unless your data has elements of this form. The w alone is sufficient to tell `infile` how to read data in which the decimal point is explicitly indicated.

When you specify d, it is taken only as a suggestion. If the decimal point is explicitly indicated in the data, that decimal point always overrides the d specification. Decimal points are also not implied if the data contains an E, e, D, or d, indicating scientific notation.

Fields are right-justified before implying decimal points. Thus, '2 ', ' 2 ', and ' 2' are all read as 0.2 by the $\%3.1f$ format.

❏

❏ **Technical Note**

The g and e formats are the same as the f format. You can specify any of these letters interchangeably. The letters g and e are included as a convenience to those familiar with FORTRAN. In FORTRAN, the e format indicates scientific notation. For example, the number 250 could be indicated as 2.5E+02 or 2.5D+02. FORTRAN programmers would refer to this as an E7.5 format, and in Stata, this format would be indicated as $\%7.5e$. In Stata, however, you need specify only the field width w, so you could read this number using $\%7f$, $\%7g$, or $\%7e$.

The g format is really a FORTRAN output format that indicates a freer format than f. In Stata, the two formats are identical.

Throughout this section, you may freely substitute the g or e formats for the f format.

❏

❏ **Technical Note**

Be careful to distinguish $\%fmts$ and $\%infmts$. $\%fmts$ are also known as *display* formats—they describe how a variable is to look when it is outputted; see [U] **15.5 Formats: controlling how data is displayed**. $\%infmts$ are also known as *input* formats—they describe how a variable looks when it is inputted. For instance, there is an output date format $\%d$, but there is no corresponding input format. (See [U] **27 Commands for dealing with dates** for recommendations on how to read dates.) For the other formats, we have attempted to make the input and output definitions as similar as possible. Thus, we include g, e, and f $\%infmts$, even though they all mean the same thing, since g, e, and f are also $\%fmts$.

❏

String formats

The s format is for reading strings. The syntax is $\%ws$ where the w is optional. If you do not specify the field width, your strings must be enclosed in quotes (single or double) or they must not contain any characters other than letters, numbers, and '_'.

This may surprise you, but the s format can be used for reading numeric variables and the f format can be used for reading string variables! When you specify the field width w in the $\%wf$ format, all embedded blanks in the field are removed before the result is interpreted. They are not removed by the $\%ws$ format.

For instance, the %3f format would read '– 2', '–2 ', or ' –2' as the number −2. The %3s format would not be able to read '– 2' as a number, since the sign is separated from the digit, but it could read ' –2' or '–2 '. The %*w*f format removes blanks; datasets written by some FORTRAN programs separate the sign from the number.

There are, however, some side-effects of this practice. The string '2 2' will be read as 22 by a %3f format. Most FORTRAN compilers would read this number as 202. The %3s format would issue a warning and store a *missing* value.

Now consider reading the string 'a b' into a string variable. Using a %3s format, it will store as it appears: **a b**. Using a %3f format, however, it will be stored as **ab**—the middle blank will be removed.

Examples using the %s format are provided below, right after we discuss specifying column and line numbers.

Specifying column and line numbers

_column() jumps to the specified column. For instance, the documentation of some dataset indicates that the variable **age** is recorded as a 2-digit number in column 47. You could read this by coding

```
_column(47) age %2f
```

After this, you are now at column 49, so if immediately following **age** were a 1-digit number recording **sex** as 0 or 1, you could code

```
_column(47) age %2f
            sex %1f
```

or, if you wanted to be explicit about it:

```
_column(47) age %2f
_column(49) sex %1f
```

It makes no difference. If at column 50 were a 1-digit code for **race**, and you wanted to read it but skip reading the **sex** code, you could code

```
_column(47) age %2f
_column(50) race %1f
```

You could equivalently skip forward using _skip():

```
_column(47) age %2f
_skip(1)    race %1f
```

One advantage of column() over _skip is that it lets you jump forward or backward in a record. If you wanted to read **race** and then **age**, you could code

```
_column(50) race %1f
_column(47) age %2f
```

If the dataset you are reading has multiple lines per observation (sometimes said as multiple records per observation), tell **infile** how many lines per record there are using _lines():

```
_lines(4)
```

_lines() appears only once in a dictionary. Good style says it should be placed near the top of the dictionary, but Stata does not care.

When you want to go to a particular line, include the _line() directive. In our example, let's assume race, sex, and age are recorded on the second line of each observation:

```
_lines(4)
_line(2)
    _column(47) age %2f
    _column(50) race %1f
```

Let's assume id is recorded on line 1.

```
_lines(4)
_line(1)
    _column(1)  id  %4f
_line(2)
    _column(47) age %2f
    _column(50) race %1f
```

_line() works like _column() in that you can jump forward or backward, so this data could just as well be read by

```
_lines(4)
_line(2)
    _column(47) age %2f
    _column(50) race %1f
_line(1)
    _column(1)  id  %4f
```

Remember that this dataset has 4 lines per observation and yet we have never referred to line(3) or line(4). That is okay. Also note that, at the end of our dictionary, we are on line 1, not 4. That is okay, too. infile will still get to the next observation correctly.

❑ Technical Note

Another way to move between records is _newline(). _newline() is to _line() as _skip() is to _column(), which is to say, _newline() can only go forward. There is one difference: _skip() has its uses; _newline() is useful only for backward capability with older versions of Stata.

_skip() has its uses because sometimes one is thinking in terms of columns and sometimes one is thinking in terms of widths. Some data documentation might very well include the sentence "At column 54 are recorded the answers to the 25 questions, one column alloted to each." If we wanted to read the answers to questions 1 and 5, it would indeed be natural to code

```
_column(54) q1 %1f
_skip(3)
            q5 %1f
```

Nobody has ever read data documentation with the statement, "Demographics are recorded on record 2 and, 2 records after that, are the income values." The documentation would instead say, "Record 2 contains the demographic information and record 4, income." The _newline() way of thinking is based on what is convenient for the computer which does, after all, have to eject a certain number of records. That, however, is no reason for making you think that way.

Before that thought occurred to us, Stata users specified _newline() to go forward records. They still can, so their old dictionaries will work. When you use _newline() and do not specify _lines(), it is your responsibility to eject the right number of records so that, at the end of the dictionary, you are on the last record. In this mode, when Stata reexecutes the dictionary to process the next observation, it goes forward one record.

❑

Examples of reading fixed-format files

▷ Example

In this example, each observation occupies two lines. The first two observations in the dataset are

```
John Dunbar                          10001   101 North 42nd Street
1010111111
Sam K. Newey, Jr.                    10002   15663 Roustabout Boulevard
0101000000
```

The first observation tells us that the name of the respondent is John Dunbar; his id is 10001; his address is 101 North 42nd Street; and his answers to questions 1 through 10 are yes, no, yes, no, yes, yes, yes, yes, yes, and yes.

The second observation tells us the name of the respondent is Sam K. Newey, Jr.; his id is 10002; his address is 15663 Roustabout Boulevard; and his answers to questions 1 through 10 were no, yes, no, yes, no, no, no, no, no, and no. (Probably John and Sam are not best friends.)

In order to see the layout within the file, we can temporarily add two rulers to help our eyes see the appropriate columns:

```
----+----1----+----2----+----3----+----4----+----5----+----6----+----7----+----8
John Dunbar                          10001   101 North 42nd Street
1010111111
Sam K. Newey, Jr.                    10002   15663 Roustabout Boulevard
0101000000
----+----1----+----2----+----3----+----4----+----5----+----6----+----7----+----8
```

Each observation in the data appears in two physical lines within our text file. We had to check in our editor to be sure that there really were newline characters (i.e., "hard returns") after the address. This is important because some programs will wrap output for you and a single line may appear as many lines. The two seemingly identical files will differ in that one has a hard return and the other has a soft return added only for display purposes.

In our data, the name occupies columns 1 through 32; a person identifier occupies columns 33 through 37; and the address occupies columns 40 through 80. Our worksheet revealed that the widest address ended in column 80.

The text file containing this data is called **fname.txt**. Our dictionary file looks like this:

```
─────────────────────────────────────────────────── top of fname.dct ───────────
infile dictionary using fname.txt {
*
* Example reading in data where observations extend across more
* than one line.  The next line tells infile there are 2 lines/obs:
*
_lines(2)
*
              str50   name   %32s      "Name of respondent"
_column(33)   long    id     %5f       "Person id"
_skip(2)      str50   addr   %41s      "Address"
_line(2)
_column(1)    byte    q1     %1f       "Question 1"
              byte    q2     %1f       "Question 2"
              byte    q3     %1f       "Question 3"
              byte    q4     %1f       "Question 4"
              byte    q5     %1f       "Question 5"
              byte    q6     %1f       "Question 6"
              byte    q7     %1f       "Question 7"
```

```
              byte    q8      %1f        "Question 8"
              byte    q9      %1f        "Question 9"
              byte    q10     %1f        "Question 10"
      }
```
—— end of fname.dct ————————

Up to five pieces of information may be supplied in the dictionary for each variable: the location of the data, the storage type of the variable, the name of the variable, the input format, and the variable label.

Thus, the str50 line says that the first variable is to be given a storage type of str50, should be called name, and have the variable label "Name of respondent". The %32s is the input format—this tells Stata how to read the data. The s tells Stata not to remove any embedded blanks; the 32 tells Stata to go across 32 columns when reading the data.

The next line says that the second variable is to be assigned a storage type of long, named id, and labeled "Person id". Stata should start reading the information for this variable in column 33. The f tells Stata to remove any embedded blanks, and the 5 says to read across 5 columns.

The third variable is to be given a storage type of str50, called addr, and labeled "Address". The _skip(2) directs Stata to skip 2 columns before beginning to read the data for this variable, and the %41s instructs Stata to read across 41 columns and to not remove embedded blanks.

line(2) instructs Stata to go to line 2 of the observation.

The remainder of the data is 0/1 coded—the answers to the questions. It would be convenient if we could use a shorthand to specify this portion of the dictionary, but we must supply explicit directives.

◁

❑ Technical Note

In the preceding example, there were two pieces of information about location: where the data begins for each variable (the _column(), _skip(), _line()) and how many columns it spans (the %32s, %5f, %41s, %1f). In our dictionary, some of this information was redundant. After reading name, Stata had finished with 32 columns of information. Unless instructed otherwise, Stata would proceed to the next column—column 33—to begin reading information about id. The _column(33) was unnecessary.

The _skip(2) was not, however, unnecessary. Stata had read 37 columns of information and was ready to look at column 38. Although the address information does not begin until column 40, columns 38 and 39 contain blanks. Since these are leading blanks, instead of embedded blanks, Stata would just ignore them. There is no problem so far. The problem is with the %41s. If Stata begins reading the address information from column 38 and reads 41 columns, Stata would stop reading in column 78 ($78 - 41 + 1 = 38$), and the widest address ends in column 80. We could have omitted the _skip(2) if we had specified an input format of %43s.

The _line(2) was necessary although we could have gotten to the second line by coding _newline instead.

The _column(1) could have been omitted. After the _line(), Stata begins in column 1.

See the following example for a dataset where both pieces of location information are required.

❑

▷ Example

The following file contains six variables in a variety of formats. Note that in the dictionary we read the variables `fifth` and `sixth` out of order by forcing the column pointer.

── top of example.dct ────────
```
infile dictionary {
                            first    %3f
                  double    second   %2.1f
                            third    %6f
    _skip(2)      str4      fourth   %4s
    _column(21)             sixth %4.1f
    _column(18)             fifth %2f
}
1.2125.7e+252abcd 1 .232
1.3135.7   52efgh2    5
1.41457    52abcd 3 100.
1.5155.7D+252efgh04 1.7
16 16 .57  52abcd 5 1.71
```
── end of example.dct ────────

Assuming the above is stored in a file called `example.dct`, it can be infiled and listed by typing

```
. infile using example
infile dictionary {
                            first    %3f
                  double    second   %2.1f
                            third    %6f
    _skip(2)      str4      fourth   %4s
    _column(21)             sixth %4.1f
    _column(18)             fifth %2f
}
(5 observations read)

. list
          first   second   third   fourth   sixth   fifth
    1.     1.2      1.2      570     abcd     .232      1
    2.     1.3      1.3      5.7     efgh      .5       2
    3.     1.4      1.4       57     abcd     100       3
    4.     1.5      1.5      570     efgh     1.7       4
    5.     16.      1.6      .57     abcd    1.71       5
```

◁

Reading fixed-block files

❏ Technical Note

The `_lrecl(#)` directive is for use in reading datasets that do not have end-of-line delimiters (carriage return, linefeed, or some combination). Such datasets are typical of IBM mainframes — where they are known as fixed block or FB. The word LRECL is IBM-mainframe jargon for logical record length.

Fixed-block datasets are datasets where each # characters are to be interpreted as a record. For instance, consider the data

```
1 21
2 42
3 63
```

In fixed-block format, this data might be recorded

─── top of mydata.ibm ─────────
```
1 212 423 63
```
─── end of mydata.ibm ─────────

and you would be told, on the side, that the LRECL is 4. If you then pass along that information to `infile`, it will be able to read the data:

─── top of mydata.dct ─────────
```
infile dictionary using mydata.ibm {
        _lrecl(4)
        int     id
        int     age
}
```
─── end of mydata.dct ─────────

When you do not specify the `_lrecl(#)` directive, `infile` assumes that each line ends with the standard ASCII delimiter (which can be linefeed or carriage return or linefeed followed by carriage return or carriage return followed by linefeed). When you do specify `_lrecl(#)`, `infile` reads the data in blocks of # characters and then acts as if that is a line.

A common mistake in processing fixed-block datasets is to be incorrect about the LRECL value, for instance, thinking the LRECL is 160 when it is really 80. To understand what can happen, pretend we thought the LRECL in our data was 6 rather than 4. Taking the characters in groups of 6, the data appears as

```
1 212
423 63
```

Stata has no way of verifying that you have specified the correct LRECL so, if the data appears incorrect, verify you have the correct number.

The maximum LRECL `infile` allows is 18,998 with Stata for Unix, 7,998 with Stata for Windows, and 3,998 with Stata for Macintosh.

❏

References

Gleason, J. R. 1998. dm54: Capturing comments from data dictionaries. *Stata Technical Bulletin* 42: 3–4. Reprinted in *Stata Technical Bulletin Reprints*, vol. 7, pp. 55–57.

Gould, W. W. 1992. dm10: Infiling data: Automatic dictionary creation. *Stata Technical Bulletin* 9: 4–8. Reprinted in *Stata Technical Bulletin Reprints*, vol. 2, pp. 28–34.

Nash, J. D. 1994. dm19: Merging raw data and dictionary files. *Stata Technical Bulletin* 20: 3–5. Reprinted in *Stata Technical Bulletin Reprints*, vol. 4, pp. 22–25.

Also See

Complementary:	[R] **outfile**, [R] **outsheet**, [R] **save**
Related:	[R] **infix (fixed format)**
Background:	[U] **24 Commands to input data**, [R] **infile**

Title

---
infile (free format) — Read unformatted ASCII (text) data

Syntax

<u>inf</u>ile *varlist* [_skip[(#)]] [*varlist* [_skip[(#)] ...]]] using *filename* [if *exp*] [in *range*]

[, <u>a</u>utomatic <u>b</u>yvariable(#) clear]

If *filename* is specified without an extension, .raw is assumed.

Description

infile reads into memory a disk dataset that is *not* in Stata format.

Here we discuss using infile to read free-format data, meaning datasets where the knowledge of the formatting information is not necessary to make sense of them. Another variation on infile allows reading fixed-format data and is discussed in [R] **infile (fixed format)**. Yet another alternative is insheet, which is easier to use if your data is tab- or comma-separated and contains one observation per line. Stata has other commands for reading data, too. If you are not certain that infile is what you are looking for, see [R] **infile** and [U] **24 Commands to input data**.

After the data is read into Stata, the data can be saved as a Stata-format dataset; see [R] **save**.

Options

automatic causes Stata to create value labels from the nonnumeric data it reads. It also automatically widens the display format to fit the longest label.

byvariable(#) specifies that the external data file is organized by variables rather than by observations. All the observations on the first variable appear, followed by all the observations on the second variable, and so on. Time-series datasets sometimes come in this format.

clear specifies that it is okay for the new data to replace what is currently in memory. To ensure that you do not lose something important, infile will refuse to read new data if data is already in memory. clear is one way you can tell infile that it is okay. The other is to drop the data yourself by typing drop _all before reading new data.

Remarks

infile—or, at least, the infile features discussed here—reads data in free or comma-separated-value format.

Remarks are presented under the headings

> *Reading free format data*
> *Reading comma-separated data*
> *Specifying variable types*
> *Reading string variables*
> *Skipping variables*
> *Skipping observations*
> *Reading time-series data*

Reading free format data

In free format, data are separated by one or more white-space characters. White-space characters are blanks, tabs, and newlines (carriage return, linefeed, or carriage-return/linefeed combinations). Thus, a single observation may span any number of lines.

Numeric missing values are indicated by single periods ('.').

▷ Example

In the file `highway.raw`, you have information on the accident rate per million vehicle miles along a stretch of highway, the speed limit on that highway, and the number of access points (on-ramps and off-ramps) per mile. Your file contains

```
─────────────────────────────────── top of highway.raw, example 1 ──────────
4.58 55 4.6
2.86  60 4.4
1.61 . 2.2
3.02 60
4.7
─────────────────────────────────── end of highway.raw, example 1 ──────────
```

You can read this data by typing

```
. infile acc_rate spdlimit acc_pts using highway
(4 observations read)

. list
        acc_rate    spdlimit     acc_pts
  1.        4.58          55         4.6
  2.        2.86          60         4.4
  3.        1.61           .         2.2
  4.        3.02          60         4.7
```

Note that the spacing of the numbers in the original file is irrelevant.

◁

❑ Technical Note

It is not necessary that missing values be indicated by a single period. The third observation on the speed limit is missing in the previous example. The raw data file indicates this by recording a single period. Let's assume that instead the missing value was indicated by the word **unknown**. Thus, the raw data file appears as

```
─────────────────────────────────── top of highway.raw, example 2 ──────────
4.58 55 4.6
2.86  60 4.4
1.61 unknown 2.2
3.02 60
4.7
─────────────────────────────────── end of highway.raw, example 2 ──────────
```

Here is the result of infiling the data:

```
. infile acc_rate spdlimit acc_pts using highway
'unknown' cannot be read as a number for spdlimit[3]
(4 observations read)
```

infile warned us that it did not know what to make of the word unknown, stored a *missing*, and then continued to read the rest of the data. Thus, aside from the warning message, results are unchanged.

Since not all packages indicate missing data in the same way, this feature can be useful when reading data created by them. Whenever infile sees something it does not understand, it warns you, records a *missing*, and continues. If, on the other hand, the missing value were recorded not as unknown but as, say 99, Stata would have no difficulty reading the number, but it would also store 99 rather than missing. To convert such coded missing values to true missing values, see [R] **mvencode**.

❑

Reading comma-separated data

In comma-separated-value format, data are separated by commas. You may intermix comma-separated-value and free format. Missing values are indicated either by single periods or by multiple commas which serve as place holders, or both. As with free format, a single observation may span any number of input lines.

▷ Example

We can modify the format of highway.raw used in the previous example without affecting infile's ability to read it. The data can be read with the same command and the results would be the same if the file instead contains

———————————————————————————— top of highway.raw, example 3 ————————
```
4.58,55 4.6
2.86, 60,4.4
1.61,,2.2
3.02,60
4.7
```
———————————————————————————— end of highway.raw, example 3 ————————

◁

Specifying variable types

The variable names you type following the word infile are new variables. The syntax for a new variable is

$$[type]\ new\_varname\,[\,\underline{:}label\_name\,]$$

A full discussion of this syntax can be found in [U] **14.4 varlists**. As a quick review, new variables are, by default, of type float. This default can be overridden by preceding the variable name with a storage type (byte, int, long, float, double, or str#) or by using the set type command. A list of variables placed in parentheses will be given the same type. For example,

double(*first_var second_var* ... *last_var*)

causes *first_var second_var* ... *last_var* to all be of type double.

There is also a shorthand syntax for variable names with numeric suffixes. The varlist var1-var4 is equivalent to specifying var1 var2 var3 var4.

▷ Example

    In the highway example, we could infile the data acc_rate, spdlimit, and acc_pts and
force the variable spdlimit to be of type int by typing

        . infile acc_rate int spdlimit acc_pts using highway, clear
        (4 observations read)

We could force all variables to be of type double by typing

        . infile double(acc_rate spdlimit acc_pts) using highway, clear
        (4 observations read)

We could call the three variables v1, v2, and v3 and make them all doubles, by typing

        . infile double(v1-v3) using highway, clear
        (4 observations read)   ◁

Reading string variables

    By explicitly specifying the types, we can read string variables as well as numeric variables.

▷ Example

    Typing infile str20 name age sex using myfile would read

    ── top of myfile.raw ─────────
        "Sherri Holliday" 25 1
        Branton 32 1
        "Bill Ross" 27,0
    ── top of myfile.raw ─────────

or even

    ── top of myfile.raw, variation 2 ─────
        ´Sherri Holliday´ 25,1 "Branton" 32
        1,´Bill Ross´, 27,0
    ── end of myfile.raw, variation 2 ─────

Note that the spacing is irrelevant and either single or double quotes may be used to delimit strings.
The quotes do not count when calculating the length of strings. Quotes may be omitted altogether
if the string contains no blanks or other special characters (anything other than letters, numbers, or
underscores).

    Typing

        . infile str20 name age sex using myfile
        (3 observations read)

makes name a str20 and age and sex floats. We might have typed

        . infile str20 name age int sex using myfile
        (3 observations read)

to make sex an int or

        . infile str20 name int(age sex) using myfile
        (3 observations read)

to make both age and sex ints.   ◁

❑ Technical Note

infile can also handle nonnumeric data by using *value labels*. We will briefly review value labels, but you should see [U] **15.6.3 Value labels** for a complete description.

A value label is a mapping from the set of integers to words. For instance, if you had a variable called **sex** in your data that represented the sex of the individual, you might code 0 for male and 1 for female. You could then just remember that every time you see a value of 0 for **sex**, that observation refers to a male, whereas every time you see a value of 1, the observation refers to a female.

Even better, you could inform Stata that 0 represents males and 1 represents females by typing

```
. label define sexfmt 0 "Male" 1 "Female"
```

Then you must tell Stata that this coding scheme is to be associated with the variable **sex**. This is typically done by typing

```
. label values sex sexfmt
```

Thereafter, Stata will print **Male** rather than 0 and **Female** rather than 1 for this variable.

Stata is unique in that it has the ability to turn a value label around. Not only can it go from numeric codes to words like "Male" and "Female", it can go from the words to the numeric code. We tell infile which value label goes with which variable by placing a colon (:) after the variable name and typing the name of the value label. Before we do that, we use the label define command to inform Stata of the coding.

Let's assume that we wish to infile a dataset containing the words **Male** and **Female** and that we wish to store numeric codes rather than the strings themselves. This will result in considerable data compression, especially if we store the numeric code as a **byte**. We have a dataset named **persons.raw** that contains name, sex, and age:

```
───────────────────────────────────── top of persons.raw ───────────
   "Arthur Doyle" Male 22
   "Mary Hope" Female 37
   "Guy Fawkes" Male 48
   "Sherry Crooks" Female 25
───────────────────────────────────── end of persons.raw ───────────
```

Here is how we read and encode it at the same time:

```
. label define sexfmt 0 "Male" 1 "Female"
. infile str16 name sex:sexfmt age using persons
(4 observations read)
. list
               name       sex     age
   1.   Arthur Doyle      Male      22
   2.     Mary Hope     Female      37
   3.    Guy Fawkes       Male      48
   4.  Sherry Crooks    Female      25
```

The **str16** in the infile command applies only to the **name** variable; **sex** is a numeric variable, as we can prove by

```
. list, nolabel
               name       sex     age
   1.   Arthur Doyle        0      22
   2.     Mary Hope         1      37
   3.    Guy Fawkes         0      48
   4.  Sherry Crooks        1      25
```

❑

❑ Technical Note

When infile is directed to use a value label and it finds an entry in the file that does not match any of the codings recorded in the label, it prints a warning message and stores *missing* for the observation. By specifying the automatic option, you can instead have infile automatically add new entries to the value label.

Say you have a dataset containing three variables. The first, region of the country, is a character string; the remaining two variables, which we will just call var1 and var2, contain numbers. You have stored the data in a file called geog.raw:

```
—————————————————————————————————— top of geog.raw ——————————
    "NE"      31.23      87.78
    ´NCntrl´  29.52      98.92
    South     29.62     114.69
    West      28.28     218.92
    NE        17.50      44.33
    NCntrl    22.51      55.21
——————————————————————————————————— end of geog.raw ——————————
```

The easiest way to read this data would be

```
. infile str6 region var1 var2 using geog
```

making region a string variable. You do not want to do this, however, because you are practicing for reading a dataset like this containing 20,000 observations. If region were numerically encoded and stored as a byte, there would be a 5-byte saving per observation, reducing the size of the data by 100,000 bytes. You also do not want to bother first creating the value label. Using the automatic option, infile creates the value label as it encounters new regions automatically.

```
. infile byte region:regfmt var1 var2 using geog, automatic
(6 observations read)
. list
         region      var1       var2
   1.        NE      31.23      87.78
   2.    NCntrl      29.52      98.92
   3.     South      29.62     114.69
   4.      West      28.28     218.92
   5.        NE       17.5      44.33
   6.    NCntrl      22.51      55.21
```

infile automatically created and defined a new value label called regfmt. We can use the label list command to view its contents:

```
. label list regfmt
regfmt:
           1 NE
           2 NCntrl
           3 South
           4 West
```

It is not necessary that the value label be undefined prior to the use of infile with the automatic option. If the value label regfmt had been previously defined as

```
. label define regfmt 2 "West"
```

the result of label list after the infile would have been

```
regfmt:
           2 West
           3 NE
           4 NCntrl
           5 South
```

The `automatic` option is so convenient that you may see no reason for not using it. Here is one. Suppose you had a dataset containing, among other things, an individual's sex. You know that the sex variable is supposed to be coded `male` and `female`. If you read the data using the `automatic` option and if one of the records contains `fmlae`, `infile` will blindly create a third sex rather than print a warning.

❑

Skipping variables

Specifying `_skip` instead of a variable name directs `infile` to ignore the variable in that location. This feature makes it possible to extract manageable subsets from large disk datasets. A number of contiguous variables can be skipped by specifying `_skip(#)` where # is the number of variables to ignore.

▷ Example

In the highway example that started this section, the data file contained three variables: `acc_rate`, `spdlimit`, and `acc_pts`. You can read just the first two variables by typing

    . infile acc_rate spdlimit _skip using highway

You can read the first and last variables by typing

    . infile acc_rate _skip acc_pts using highway, clear

You can read just the first variable by typing

    . infile acc_rate _skip(2) using highway, clear

`_skip` may be specified more than once. If you had a dataset containing four variables, say a, b, c, and d, and you wanted to read just a and c, you could type `infile a _skip c _skip using` *filename*.

◁

Skipping observations

Subsets of observations can be extracted by specifying `if` *exp*, which also makes it possible to extract manageable subsets from large disk datasets. Do not, however, use the *_variable* *_N* in *exp*. Use the `in` *range* modifier to refer to observation numbers within the disk dataset.

▷ Example

Again referring to the highway example, if you type

    . infile acc_rate spdlimit acc_pts if acc_rate>3
    (2 observations read)

only observations for which `acc_rate` is greater than 3 will be infiled. You can type

    . infile acc_rate spdlimit acc_pts in 2/4, clear
    (3 observations read)

to read only the second, third, and fourth observations.

◁

Reading time-series data

If you are dealing with time-series data, you may receive datasets organized by variables rather than by observations. All the observations on the first variable appear, followed by all the observations on the second variable, and so on. The `byvariable(#)` option specifies that the external data file is organized in this way. You specify the number of observations in the parentheses, since `infile` needs to know that number in order to read the data properly. Alternatively, you can mark the end of one variable's data and the beginning of another's by placing a semicolon (';') in the raw data file. You may then specify a number larger than the number of observations in the dataset and leave it to `infile` to determine the actual number of observations. This method can also be used to read unbalanced data.

▷ Example

You have time-series data on four years recorded in the file `time.raw`. The data contains information on year, amount, and cost and is organized by variable:

```
────────────────────────────────────────────────── top of time.raw ──────────
1980 1981 1982 1983
14 17 25 30
120 135 150
180
────────────────────────────────────────────────── end of time.raw ──────────
```

You can read this data by typing

```
. infile year amount cost using time, byvariable(4)
(4 observations read)

. list

        year     amount      cost
1.      1980         14       120
2.      1981         17       135
3.      1982         25       150
4.      1983         30       180
```

If the data instead contained semicolons marking the end of each series and had no information for amount in 1983, the raw data might appear as

```
1980 1981 1982 1983 ;
14 17 25 ;
120 135 150
180 ;
```

You could read this data by typing

```
. infile year amount cost using time, byvariable(100)
(4 observations read)

. list

        year     amount      cost
1.      1980         14       120
2.      1981         17       135
3.      1982         25       150
4.      1983          .       180
```

◁

Also See

Complementary:	[R] **outfile**, [R] **outsheet**, [R] **save**
Related:	[R] **infile (fixed format)**, [R] **input**, [R] **insheet**
Background:	[U] **24 Commands to input data**, [R] **infile**

Title

> **infix (fixed format)** — Read ASCII (text) data in fixed format

Syntax

> infix using *dfilename* [if *exp*] [in *range*] [, using(*filename₂*) clear]

> infix *specification* using *filename* [if *exp*] [in *range*] [, clear]

where *specification* is

> # <u>firstlineoffile</u>
>
> # lines
>
> #<u>:</u>
>
> /
>
> [byte | int | float | long | double | str] *varlist* [#<u>:</u>]#[-#]

and *dfilename*, if it exists, contains

-- top of dictionary file ---------

> infix dictionary [using *filename*] {
>   * comments preceded by asterisk may appear freely
>   specifications
> }
> (*your data might appear here*)

-- end of dictionary file ---------

If *dfilename* is specified without an extension, .dct is assumed.

If *filename₂* or *filename* is specified without an extension, .raw is assumed.

In the first syntax, if using *filename₂* is not specified on the command line and using *filename* is not specified in the dictionary, the data is assumed to begin on the line following the close brace.

Description

infix reads into memory a disk dataset that is *not* in Stata format. infix requires that the data be in fixed-column format.

You have alternatives to infix. infile is one. It can also read data in fixed-format—see [R] **infile (fixed format)**—and it can read data in free format—see [R] **infile (free format)**. Most people think infix is easier to use for reading fixed-format data, but infile has more features. If your data is not fixed-format, another alternative is insheet; see [R] **insheet**. If you are not certain that infix is what you are looking for, see [R] **infile** and [U] **24 Commands to input data**.

In its first syntax, infix reads the data in a two-step process. You first create a disk file describing how the data is recorded. You tell infix to read that file—called a dictionary—and from there infix goes on to read the data. The data can be in the same file as the dictionary or a different file.

In its second syntax, you tell infix how to read the data right on the command line with no intermediate file.

Options

using(*filename₂*) specifies the name of a file containing the data. If using() is not specified, the data is assumed to follow the dictionary in *dfilename* or, if the dictionary specifies the name of some other file, that file is assumed to contain the data. If using(*filename₂*) is specified, *filename₂* is used to obtain the data even if the dictionary itself says otherwise.

clear specifies that it is okay for the new data to replace what is currently in memory. To ensure that you do not lose something important, infix will refuse to read new data if data is already in memory. clear is one way you can tell infix that it is okay. The other is to drop the data yourself by typing drop _all before reading new data.

Specifications

firstlineoffile (abbreviation first) is rarely specified. It states the line of the file where the data begins. first is not specified when the data follows the dictionary; infix can figure that out for itself. first is instead specified when the data appears by itself in a file and the first few lines of that file contain headers or other markers.

first appears only once in the specifications.

lines states the number of lines per observation in the file. Simple datasets typically have '1 lines'. Large datasets often have many lines (sometimes called records) per observation. lines is optional even when there is more than one line per observation because infix can sometimes figure it out for itself. Still, if 1 lines is not right for your data, it is best to specify the directive.

lines appears only once in the specifications.

#: tells infix to jump to line # of the observation. Consider a file with 4 lines, meaning four lines per observation. 2: says to go to the second line of the observation. 4: says to go to the fourth line of the observation. You may jump forward or backward: infix does not care nor is there any inefficiency in going forward to 3:, reading a few variables, jumping back to 1:, reading another variable, and jumping back again to 3:.

It is not your responsibility to ensure that, at the end of your specification, you are on the last line of the observation. infix knows how to get to the next observation because it knows where you are and it knows lines, the total number of lines per observation.

#: may appear, and typically does, many times in the specifications.

/ is an alternative to #:. / goes forward one line. // goes forward two lines. We do not recommend the use of / because #: is better. If you are currently on line 2 of an observation and want to get to line 6, you could type ////, but your meaning is clearer if you type 6:.

/ may appear many times in the specifications.

[byte | int | float | long | double | str] *varlist* [*#:*]*#*[-*#*] instructs infix to read a variable and, sometimes, more than one.

Begin by realizing that the simplest form of this is *varname #*, such as sex 20. That says that variable *varname* is to be read from column # of the current line; variable sex is to be read from column 20 and here, sex is a one-digit number.

varname #-#, such as age 21-23, says to read *varname* from the column range specified; read age from columns 21 through 23 and here, age is a three-digit number.

You can prefix the variable with a storage type. str name 25-44 means to read the string variable name from columns 25 through 44. If you do not specify str, the variable is assumed to be numeric. You can specify the numeric subtype if you wish.

You can specify more than one variable, with or without a type. `byte q1-q5 51-55` means read variables q1, q2, q3, q4, and q5 from columns 51 through 55 and store the five variables as `byte`s.

Finally, you can specify the line on which the variable(s) appear. `age 2:21-23` says that age is to be obtained from the second line, columns 21 through 23. Another way you could say this is by putting together the #: directive with the input-variable directive: `2: age 21-23`. There is a difference, but not with respect to reading the variable `age`. So let's consider two alternatives:

```
1:  str name 25-44    age 2:21-23   q1-q5 51-55
1:  str name 25-44  2: age 21-23    q1-q5 51-55
```

The difference is that the first directive says variables q1 through q5 are on line 1 whereas the second says they are on line 2.

When the colon is put out front, it says on which line variables are to be found when we do not explicitly say otherwise. When the colon is put inside, it applies only to the variable under consideration.

Remarks

There are two ways to use `infix`. One is to type the specifications that describe how to read the fixed-format dataset on the command line:

```
. infix acc_rate 1-4  spdlimit 6-7  acc_pts 9-11  using highway.raw
```

The other is to type the specifications into a file

── top of highway.dct, example 1 ────────

```
infix dictionary using highway.raw {
        acc_rate 1-4
        spdlimit 6-7
        acc_pts  9-11
}
```

── end of highway.dct, example 1 ────────

and then, inside Stata, type

```
. infix using highway.dct
```

Which you use makes no difference to Stata. The first form is more convenient if there are only a few variables and the second form is less prone to error if you are reading a big, complicated file.

The second form allows two variations, the one we just showed—where the data is in another file—and one where the data is in the same file as the dictionary:

── top of highway.dct, example 2 ────────

```
infix dictionary {
        acc_rate 1-4
        spdlimit 6-7
        acc_pts  9-11
}
4.58 55 .46
2.86 60 4.4
1.61    2.2
3.02 60 4.7
```

── end of highway.dct, example 2 ────────

Note that in the first example, the top line of the file read `infix dictionary using highway.raw` whereas in the second the line reads simply `infix dictionary`. When you do not say where the data is, it is implied that the data follows the dictionary.

▷ Example

So let's complete the example we started. You have data on the accident rate per million vehicle miles along a stretch of highway, the speed limit on that highway, and the number of access points per mile. You have created the dictionary file `highway.dct` which contains the dictionary and the data:

─── top of highway.dct, example 2 ─────────

```
infix dictionary {
        acc_rate 1-4
        spdlimit 6-7
        acc_pts  9-11
}
4.58 55 .46
2.86 60 4.4
1.61    2.2
3.02 60 4.7
```

─── end of highway.dct, example 2 ─────────

You created this file outside of Stata using an editor or word processor. Inside Stata, you now read the data. `infix` lists the dictionary so you will know the directives it is following:

```
. infix using highway
infix dictionary {
        acc_rate 1-4
        spdlimit 6-7
        acc_pts  9-11
}
(4 observations read)

. list

        acc_rate   spdlimit    acc_pts
   1.       4.58         55        .46
   2.       2.86         60        4.4
   3.       1.61          .        2.2
   4.       3.02         60        4.7
```

Note that we simply typed `infix using highway` rather than `infix using highway.dct`. When we do not specify the file extension, `infix` assumes we mean `.dct`.

◁

Reading string variables

When you do not say otherwise in your specification—either on the command line or in the dictionary—`infix` assumes variables are numeric. You specify that a variable is a string by placing `str` in front of its name:

```
. infix  id 1-6  str name 7-36  age 38-39  str sex 41  using employee.raw
```

or

─── top of employee.dct ─────────

```
infix dictionary using employee.raw {
        id          1-6
        str name  7-36
        age       38-39
        str sex      40
}
```

─── end of employee.dct ─────────

Reading multiple-lines-per-observation data

When data has multiple lines per observation, sometimes said as multiple records per observation, you specify the number of lines per observation using `lines` and you specify on which line elements appear using #:.

```
. infix  2 lines  1: id 1-6  str name 7-36  2: age 1-2  str sex 4  using emp2.raw
```

or

```
───────────────────────────────────────────── top of emp2.dct ─────────

infix dictionary using emp2.raw {
    2 lines
    1:
        id          1-6
        str name    7-36
    2:
        age         1-2
        str sex     4
}
───────────────────────────────────────────── end of emp2.dct ─────────
```

There are lots of different ways to say the same thing.

▷ Example

Consider the following raw data:

```
────────────────────────────────────────────── top of mydata.raw ──────

id income educ / sex age / rcode, answers to questions 1-5
1024 25000 HS
        Male    28
        1 1 9 5 0 3
1025 27000 C
        Female 24
        0 2 2 1 1 3
1035 26000 HS
        Male    32
        1 1 0 3 2 1
1036 25000 C
        Female 25
        1 3 1 2 3 2
────────────────────────────────────────────── end of mydata.raw ──────
```

This data has 3 lines per observation and the first line is just a comment. One possible set of specifications to read this data is

```
────────────────────────────────────────────── top of mydata1.dct ─────

infix dictionary using mydata {
    2 first
    3 lines
    1:    id      1-4
          income  6-10
          str educ 12-13
    2:    str sex  6-11
          int age  13-14
    3:    rcode    6
          q1-q5    7-16
}
────────────────────────────────────────────── end of mydata1.dct ─────
```

although the one we prefer is

```
                                                  ─── top of mydata2.dct ───
    infix dictionary using mydata {
        2 first
        3 lines
            id          1: 1-4
            income      1: 6-10
            str educ   1:12-13
            str sex     2: 6-11
            age         2:13-14
            rcode       3: 6
            q1-q5       3: 7-16
    }
                                                  ─── end of mydata2.dct ───
```

Either will read this data, so we will use the first and then we will explain why we prefer the second.

```
    . infix using mydata1
    infix dictionary using mydata {
        2 first
        3 lines
        1:      id          1-4
                income      6-10
                str educ  12-13
        2:      str sex    6-11
                int age   13-14
        3:      rcode       6
                q1-q5      7-16
    }
    (4 observations read)

    . list in 1/2

    Observation 1
            id       1024      income      25000      educ      HS
            sex      Male      age            28      rcode      1
            q1          1      q2              9      q3         5
            q4          0      q5              3

    Observation 2
            id       1025      income      27000      educ       C
            sex    Female      age            24      rcode      0
            q1          2      q2              2      q3         1
            q4          1      q5              3
```

Now, what is better about the second? What is better is that the location of each variable is completely documented on each line, in terms of both line number and column. Since infix does not care about the order in which we read the variables, we could take the dictionary, jumble the lines, and it would still work. For instance,

```
                                                  ─── top of mydata3.dct ───
    infix dictionary using mydata {
        2 first
        3 lines
            str sex     2: 6-11
            rcode       3: 6
            str educ   1:12-13
            age         2:13-14
            id          1: 1-4
            q1-q5       3: 7-16
            income      1: 6-10
    }
                                                  ─── end of mydata3.dct ───
```

will also read this data even though, for each observation, we start on line 2, go forward to line 3, jump back to line 1, and at the conclusion, end up on line 1. It is not even inefficient to do this because `infix` does not really jump to record 2, then record 3, then record 1 again, etc. `infix` takes what we say and organizes it efficiently. The order in which we say it makes no difference. Well, it does make one: the order of the variables in the resulting Stata dataset will be the order we specify.

In this case the reordering is senseless but, in real data, reordering variables is often desirable. Moreover, we often construct dictionaries, realize that we omitted a variable, and then go back and modify them. By making each line complete in and of itself, we can add new variables anywhere in the dictionary and not worry that, because of our addition, something occurring later will no longer read correctly.

◁

Reading subsets of observations

If you wanted to read only the males from some raw data file, you might type

```
. infix id 1-6  str name 7-36  age 38-39  str sex 41  using employee.raw if sex=="M"
```

If your specification was instead recorded in a dictionary, you could type

```
. infix using employee.dct if sex=="M"
```

In another dataset, if you wanted to read just the first 100 observations, you could type

```
. infix 2 lines  1: id 1-6  str name 7-36  2: age 1-2  str sex 4  using emp2.raw
> in 1/100
```

Or, if the specification was instead recorded in a dictionary and you wanted observations 101 through 573, you could type

```
. infix using emp2.dct in 101/573
```

Also See

Complementary:	[R] **outfile**, [R] **outsheet**, [R] **save**
Related:	[R] **infile (fixed format)**, [R] **insheet**
Background:	[U] **24 Commands to input data**,
	[R] **infile**

Title

input — Enter data from keyboard

Syntax

in̲p̲ut [*varlist*] [, a̲utomatic l̲abel]

Description

input allows you to type data directly into the dataset in memory. Stata for Windows and Stata for Macintosh users should see [R] **edit** for a better alternative to input.

Options

automatic causes Stata to create value labels from the nonnumeric data it encounters. It also automatically widens the display format to fit the longest label. Specifying automatic implies label even if you do not explicitly type the label option.

label allows you to type the labels (strings) instead of the numeric values for variables associated with value labels. New value labels are not automatically created unless automatic is specified.

Remarks

If there is no data in memory when you type input, you must specify a *varlist*. Stata will then prompt you to enter the new observations until you type end.

▷ Example

You have data on the accident rate per million vehicle miles along a stretch of highway along with the speed limit on that highway. You wish to type this data directly into Stata:

```
. input
nothing to input
r(104);
```

Typing input by itself does not provide enough information about your intentions. Stata needs to know the names of the variables you wish to create:

```
. input acc_rate spdlimit
      acc_rate   spdlimit
  1. 4.58 55
  2. 2.86 60
  3. 1.61 .
  4. end

. _
```

We typed `input acc_rate spdlimit` and Stata responded by repeating the variable names and then prompting us for the first observation. We then typed `4.58` and `55` and pressed *Return*. Stata prompted us for the second observation. We entered it and pressed *Return*. Stata prompted us for the third observation. We knew that the accident rate is 1.61 per million vehicle miles, but we did not know the corresponding speed limit for the highway. We typed the number we knew, 1.61, followed by a period, the missing value indicator. When we pressed *Return*, Stata prompted us for the fourth observation. We were finished entering our data, so we typed `end` in lowercase letters.

We can now `list` the data to verify that we have entered it correctly:

```
. list

     acc_rate    spdlimit
 1.      4.58          55
 2.      2.86          60
 3.      1.61           .
```

◁

If you have data in memory and type `input` without a *varlist*, you will be prompted to enter additional information on *all* the variables. This continues until you type `end`.

▷ Example

You now have an additional observation you wish to add to the dataset. Typing `input` by itself tells Stata that you wish to add new observations:

```
. input

     acc_rate    spdlimit
 4. 3.02 60
 5. end

. _
```

Stata reminded us of the names of our variables and prompted us for the fourth observation. We entered the numbers 3.02 and 60 and pressed *Return*. Stata then prompted us for the fifth observation. We could add as many new observations as we wish. Since we needed to add only one observation, we typed `end`. Our dataset now has four observations.

◁

You may add new variables to the data in memory by typing `input` followed by the names of the new variables. Stata will begin by prompting you for the first observation, then the second, and so on, until either you type `end` or you enter the last observation.

▷ Example

In addition to the accident rate and speed limit, we now obtain data on the number of access points (on-ramps and off-ramps) per mile along each stretch of highway. We wish to enter this new data:

```
. input acc_pts

      acc_pts
 1. 4.6
 2. 4.4
 3. 2.2
 4. 4.7

. _
```

When we typed `input acc_pts`, Stata responded by prompting us for the first observation. There are 4.6 access points per mile for the first highway, so we entered **4.6** and pressed *Return*. Stata then prompted us for the second observation, and so on. We entered each of the numbers. When we entered the final observation, Stata automatically stopped prompting us—we did not have to type **end**. Stata knows that there are four observations in memory, and since we are adding a new variable, it stops automatically.

We can, however, type **end** anytime we wish. If we do so, Stata fills the remaining observations on the new variables with *missing*. To illustrate this, we enter one more variable to our data and then `list` the result:

```
. input junk
          junk
  1. 1
  2. 2
  3. end
. list
         acc_rate   spdlimit    acc_pts      junk
  1.         4.58         55        4.6         1
  2.         2.86         60        4.4         2
  3.         1.61          .        2.2         .
  4.         3.02         60        4.7         .
```

◁

You can input string variables using **input**, but you must remember to explicitly indicate that the variables are strings by specifying the type of the variable before the variable's name.

▷ Example

String variables are indicated by the types **str#**, where *#* represents the storage length, or maximum length, of the variable. For instance, a **str4** variable has maximum length 4, meaning it can contain the strings **a**, **ab**, **abc**, and **abcd** but not **abcde**. Strings shorter than the maximum length can be stored in the variable, but strings longer than the maximum length cannot. You can create variables up to **str80** in Stata.

Since a **str80** variable can store strings shorter than 80 characters, you might wonder why you should not make all your string variables **str80**. You do not want to do this because Stata allocates space for strings based on their *maximum* length. It would waste the computer's memory.

Let's assume that we have no data in memory and wish to enter the following data:

```
. input str16 name age str6 sex
             name           age       sex
  1. "Arthur Doyle" 22 male
  2. "Mary Hope" 37 "female"
  3. Guy Fawkes 48 male
'Fawkes' cannot be read as a number
  3. "Guy Fawkes" 48 male
  4. "Sherry Crooks" 25 female
  5. end

  . _
```

We first typed `input str16 name age str6 sex`, meaning that **name** is to be a **str16** variable and **sex** a **str6** variable. Since we did not specify anything about **age**, Stata made it a numeric variable.

Stata then prompted us to enter our data. On the first line, the name is Arthur Doyle, which we typed in double quotes. The double quotes are not really part of the string; they merely delimit the beginning and end of the string. We followed that with Mr Doyle's age, 22, and his sex, male. We did not bother to type double quotes around the word `male` because it contained no blanks or other special characters. For the second observation, we did type the double quotes around `female`; it changed nothing.

In the third observation we omitted the double quotes around the name, and Stata informed us that Fawkes could not be read as a number and reprompted us for the observation. When we omitted the double quotes, Stata interpreted `Guy` as the name, `Fawkes` as the age, and 48 as the sex. All of this would have been okay with Stata except for one problem: `Fawkes` looks nothing like a number. So Stata complained and gave us another chance. This time, we remembered to put the double quotes around the name.

Stata was satisfied, and we continued. We entered the fourth observation and then typed `end`. Here is our data:

```
. list

                name       age       sex
        1.    Arthur Doyle    22      male
        2.       Mary Hope    37    female
        3.      Guy Fawkes    48      male
        4.   Sherry Crooks    25    female
```

◁

▷ Example

Just as we indicated which variables were strings by placing a storage type in front of the variable name, we can indicate the storage type of our numeric variables as well. Stata has five numeric storage types: `byte`, `int`, `long`, `float`, and `double`. When you do not specify the storage type, Stata assumes the variable is a `float`. You may want to review the definitions of numbers in [U] **15 Data**.

There are two reasons why you might want to explicitly specify the storage type: to induce additional precision or to conserve memory. The default type `float` has plenty of precision for most circumstances because Stata performs all calculations in double precision no matter how the data is stored. If you were storing 9-digit Social Security Numbers, however, you would want to coerce a different storage type or else the last digit would be rounded. `long` would be the best choice; `double` would work equally well, but it would be wasteful of memory.

Sometimes you do not need to store a variable as `float`. If the variable contains only integers between $-32{,}768$ and $32{,}766$, it can be stored as an `int` and it would take only half the space. If a variable contains only integers between -127 and 126, it can be stored as a `byte` which would take only half again as much space. For instance, in the previous example we entered data for `age` without explicitly specifying the storage type; hence, it was a `float`. It would have been better to store it as a `byte`. To do that, we would have typed

```
. input str16 name byte age str6 sex

                name        age       sex
     1. "Arthur Doyle" 22 male
     2. "Mary Hope" 37 "female"
     3. "Guy Fawkes" 48 male
     4. "Sherry Crooks" 25 female
     5. end

   . _
```

Stata understands a number of shorthands. For instance,

```
. input int(a b) c
```

allows you to input three variables, a, b, and c, and makes both a and b ints and c a float. Remember

```
. input int a b c
```

would make a an int but both b and c floats.

```
. input a long b double(c d) e
```

would make a a float, b a long, c and d doubles, and e a float.

Stata has a shorthand for variable names with numeric suffixes. Typing v1-v4 is equivalent to typing v1 v2 v3 v4. Thus,

```
. input int(v1-v4)
```

inputs four variables and stores them as ints.

◁

❏ Technical Note

You may want to stop reading now. The rest of this section deals with using input with value labels. If you are not familiar with value labels, you should first read [U] **15.6.3 Value labels**.

Remember that value labels map numbers into words and vice versa. There are two aspects to the process. First, we must define the association between numbers and words. We might tell Stata that 0 corresponds to male and 1 corresponds to female by typing label define sexlbl 0 "male" 1 "female". The correspondences are named, and in this case we have named the 0↔male 1↔female correspondence sexlbl.

Next, we must associate this value label with a variable. If we had already entered the data and the variable was called sex, we would do this by typing label values sex sexlbl. We would have entered the data by typing 0's and 1's, but at least now when we list the data, we would see the words rather than the underlying numbers.

We can do better than that. After defining the value label, we can associate the value label with the variable at the time we input the data and tell Stata to use the value label to interpret what we type:

```
. label define sexlbl 0 "male" 1 "female"
. input str16 name byte(age sex:sexlbl), label
                 name         age        sex
  1. "Arthur Doyle" 22 male
  2. "Mary Hope" 37 "female"
  3. "Guy Fawkes" 48 male
  4. "Sherry Crooks" 25 female
  5. end

. _
```

After defining the value label, we typed our input command. Two things are noteworthy: We added the label option at the end of the command, and we typed sex:sexlbl for the name of the sex variable. The byte(...) around age and sex:sexlbl was not really necessary: it merely forced both age and sex to be stored as bytes.

Let's first decipher sex:sexlbl. sex is the name of the variable we want to input. The :sexlbl part tells Stata that the new variable is to be associated with the value label named sexlbl. The label option tells Stata that it is to look up any strings we type for labeled variables in their corresponding value label and substitute the number when it stores the data. Thus, when we entered the first observation of our data, we typed `male` for Mr Doyle's sex even though the corresponding variable is numeric. Rather than complaining that ""male" could not be read as a number", Stata accepted what we typed, looked up the number corresponding to `male`, and stored that number in the data.

The fact that Stata has actually stored a number rather than the words `male` or `female` is almost irrelevant. Whenever we `list` the data or make a table, Stata will use the words `male` and `female` just as if those words were actually stored in the data rather than their numeric codings:

```
. list
                    name        age        sex
        1.   Arthur Doyle        22       male
        2.     Mary Hope         37     female
        3.     Guy Fawkes        48       male
        4.  Sherry Crooks        25     female

. tabulate sex
         sex |      Freq.     Percent        Cum.
------------+-----------------------------------
        male |          2       50.00       50.00
      female |          2       50.00      100.00
------------+-----------------------------------
       Total |          4      100.00
```

It is only almost irrelevant since we can make use of the underlying numbers in statistical analyses. For instance, if we were to ask Stata to calculate the mean of `sex` by typing `summarize sex`, Stata would report 0.5. We would interpret that to mean that one-half of our sample is female.

Value labels are permanently associated with variables. Thus, once we associate a value label with a variable, we never have to do so again. If we wanted to add another observation to this data, we could type

```
. input, label
                    name        age        sex
        5. "Mark Esman" 26 male
        6. end

. _
```

❑

❑ Technical Note

The `automatic` option automates the definition of the value label. In the previous example, we informed Stata that `male` corresponds to 0 and `female` corresponds to 1 by typing `label define sexlbl 0 "male" 1 "female"`. It was not necessary to explicitly specify the mapping. Specifying the `automatic` option tells Stata to interpret what we type as follows:

First, see if it is a number. If so, store that number and be done with it. If it is not a number, check the value label associated with the variable in an attempt to interpret it. If an interpretation exists, store the corresponding numeric code. If one does not exist, add a new numeric code corresponding to what was typed. Store that new number and update the value label so that the new correspondence is never forgotten.

We can use these features to reenter our age and sex data. Before reentering the data, we `drop _all` and `label drop _all` to prove that we have nothing up our sleeve:

```
. drop _all
. label drop _all
```

```
. input str16 name byte(age sex:sexlbl), automatic
                  name          age         sex
  1. "Arthur Doyle" 22 male
  2. "Mary Hope" 37 "female"
  3. "Guy Fawkes" 48 male
  4. "Sherry Crooks" 25 female
  5. end

  . _
```

We previously defined the value label `sexlbl` so that `male` corresponded to 0 and `female` corresponded to 1. The label that Stata automatically created is slightly different but just as good:

```
. label list sexlbl
sexlbl:
           1 male
           2 female
```

❑

Also See

Complementary: [R] **save**

Related: [R] **edit**, [R] **infile**

Background: [U] **24 Commands to input data**

Title

---
insheet — Read ASCII (text) data created by a spreadsheet

Syntax

insheet [*varlist*] using *filename* [, <u>d</u>ouble [<u>no</u>]<u>n</u>ames <u>c</u>omma <u>t</u>ab clear]

If *filename* is specified without an extension, .raw is assumed.

Description

insheet reads into memory a disk dataset that is not in Stata format. insheet is intended for reading files created by a spreadsheet or database program. Regardless of the creator, insheet reads text (ASCII) files where there is one observation per line and the values are separated by tabs or commas. In addition, the first line of the file can contain the variable names or not. The best thing about insheet is that if you type

. insheet using *filename*

insheet will read your data; that's all there is to it.

Stata has other commands for reading data. If you are not sure that insheet is what you are looking for, see [R] **infile** and [U] **24 Commands to input data**. If you want to save your data in "spreadsheet-style" format, see [R] **outsheet**.

Options

double forces Stata to store variables as doubles rather than floats; see [U] **15.2.2 Numeric storage types**.

[no]names informs Stata whether variable names are included on the first line of the file. Specifying this option will speed insheet's processing—assuming you are right—but that is all. insheet can determine for itself whether the file includes variable names.

comma tells Stata that the values are comma-separated. Specifying this option will speed insheet's processing—assuming you are right—but that is all. insheet can determine for itself whether the separation character is a comma or a tab.

tab tells Stata the values are tab-separated. Specifying this option will speed insheet's processing—assuming you are right—but that is all. insheet can determine for itself whether the separation character is a tab or a comma.

clear specifies that it is okay for the new data to replace what is currently in memory. To ensure that you do not lose something important, insheet will refuse to read new data if data is already in memory. clear is one way you can tell insheet that it is okay. The other is to drop the data yourself by typing drop _all before reading new data.

Remarks

There is nothing to using `insheet`. You type

```
. insheet using filename
```

and `insheet` will read your data. That is, it will read your data if

1. It can find the file and

2. The file meets `insheet`'s expectations as to the format in which it is written.

Assuring 1 is easy enough; just realize that if you type `infix using myfile`, Stata interprets this as an instruction to read `myfile.raw`. If your file is called `myfile.txt`, type `infix using myfile.txt`.

As for the file's format, most spreadsheets and some database programs write data in the form `insheet` expects. It is easy enough to look—as we will show you—and it is even easier simply to try and see what happens. If typing

```
. insheet using filename
```

does not produce the desired result, you will have to try one of Stata's other `infile` commands; see [R] **infile**.

▷ Example

You have a raw data file on automobiles called `auto.raw`. This file was saved by a spreadsheet and can be read by typing

```
. insheet using auto
(5 vars, 10 obs)

. _
```

That done, we can now look at what we just loaded:

```
. describe
Contains data
  obs:           10
  vars:           5
  size:         290 (99.9% of memory free)
-------------------------------------------------------------------------------
  1. make      str13  %13s
  2. price     int    %8.0g
  3. mpg       byte   %8.0g
  4. rep78     byte   %8.0g
  5. foreign   str8   %9s
-------------------------------------------------------------------------------
Sorted by:
     Note:  dataset has changed since last save
. list
                make    price     mpg    rep78    foreign
   1.    AMC Concord     4099      22        3    Domestic
   2.      AMC Pacer     4749      17        3    Domestic
   3.     AMC Spirit     3799      22        .    Domestic
   4.  Buick Century     4816      20        3    Domestic
   5.  Buick Electra     7827      15        4    Domestic
   6.  Buick LeSabre     5788      18        3    Domestic
   7.     Buick Opel     4453      26        .    Domestic
   8.    Buick Regal     5189      20        3    Domestic
   9.  Buick Riviera    10372      16        3    Domestic
  10.  Buick Skylark     4082      19        3    Domestic
```

Note that this data contains a combination of string and numeric variables. insheet figured all that out by itself.

◁

❏ Technical Note

Now let's back up and look at the auto.raw file. Stata's type command will display files to the screen:

```
. type auto.raw
make      price      mpg      rep78      foreign
AMC Concord      4099      22      3            Domestic
AMC Pacer        4749      17      3            Domestic
AMC Spirit       3799      22                   Domestic
Buick Century    4816      20      3            Domestic
Buick Electra    7827      15      4            Domestic
Buick LeSabre    5788      18      3            Domestic
Buick Opel       4453      26                   Domestic
Buick Regal      5189      20      3            Domestic
Buick Riviera   10372      16      3            Domestic
Buick Skylark    4082      19      3            Domestic
```

This data has tab characters between values. Tab characters are difficult to see since they are invisible and hence indistinguishable from blanks. type's showtabs option makes the tabs visible:

```
. type auto.raw, showtabs
make<T>price<T>mpg<T>rep78<T>foreign
AMC Concord<T>4099<T>22<T>3<T>Domestic
AMC Pacer<T>4749<T>17<T>3<T>Domestic
AMC Spirit<T>3799<T>22<T><T>Domestic
Buick Century<T>4816<T>20<T>3<T>Domestic
Buick Electra<T>7827<T>15<T>4<T>Domestic
Buick LeSabre<T>5788<T>18<T>3<T>Domestic
Buick Opel<T>4453<T>26<T><T>Domestic
Buick Regal<T>5189<T>20<T>3<T>Domestic
Buick Riviera<T>10372<T>16<T>3<T>Domestic
Buick Skylark<T>4082<T>19<T>3<T>Domestic
```

This is an example of the kind of data insheet is willing to read. The first line contains the variable names—although that is not necessary. What is necessary is that the data values have tab characters between them.

insheet would be just as happy if the data values were separated by commas. Here is another variation on auto.raw that insheet can read:

```
. type auto2.raw
make,price,mpg,rep78,foreign
AMC Concord,4099,22,3,Domestic
AMC Pacer,4749,17,3,Domestic
AMC Spirit,3799,22,,Domestic
Buick Century,4816,20,3,Domestic
Buick Electra,7827,15,4,Domestic
Buick LeSabre,5788,18,3,Domestic
Buick Opel,4453,26,,Domestic
Buick Regal,5189,20,3,Domestic
Buick Riviera,10372,16,3,Domestic
Buick Skylark,4082,19,3,Domestic
```

It is easier for us human beings to see the commas rather than the tabs, but computers do not care one way or the other.

❏

▷ Example

The file does not have to contain variable names. Here is another variation on `auto.raw` without the first line and, this time, with commas rather than tabs separating the values:

```
. type auto3.raw
AMC Concord,4099,22,3,Domestic
AMC Pacer,4749,17,3,Domestic
(output omitted)
Buick Skylark,4082,19,3,Domestic
```

Here is what happens when we read it:

```
. insheet using auto3
you must start with an empty dataset
r(18);

. _
```

Oops; we still have the data from the last example in memory.

```
. insheet using auto3, clear
(5 vars, 10 obs)

. describe

Contains data
  obs:           10
  vars:           5
  size:         290 (99.9% of memory free)
-------------------------------------------------------------------------------
    1. v1           str13   %13s
    2. v2           int     %8.0g
    3. v3           byte    %8.0g
    4. v4           byte    %8.0g
    5. v5           str8    %9s
-------------------------------------------------------------------------------
Sorted by:
    Note:  dataset has changed since last save

. list

               v1        v2      v3      v4        v5
  1.    AMC Concord    4099      22       3  Domestic
  2.      AMC Pacer    4749      17       3  Domestic
(output omitted)
10. Buick Skylark    4082      19       3  Domestic
```

The only difference is that rather than the variables being nicely named `make`, `price`, `mpg`, `rep78`, and `foreign`, they are named v1, v2, ..., v5. We could now give our variables nicer names:

```
. rename v1 make

. rename v2 price

. _
```

Another alternative is to specify the variable names when we read the data:

```
. insheet make price mpg rep78 foreign using auto3, clear
(5 vars, 10 obs)

. list

              make    price     mpg    rep78    foreign
  1.    AMC Concord    4099      22       3   Domestic
  2.      AMC Pacer    4749      17       3   Domestic
(output omitted)
10. Buick Skylark    4082      19       3   Domestic
```

If we use this approach, we must not specify too few variables

```
. insheet make price mpg rep78 using auto3, clear
too few variables specified
error in line 1 of file
r(102);
```

or too many.

```
. insheet make price mpg rep78 foreign weight using auto3, clear
too many variables specified
error in line 1 of file
r(103);
```

That is why we recommend

```
. insheet using filename
```

It is not difficult to rename your variables afterwards should that be necessary.

◁

▷ Example

About the only other thing that can go wrong is that the data is not appropriate for reading by insheet. Here is yet another version of the automobile data:

```
. type auto4.raw, showtabs
"AMC Concord"    4099  22  3  Domestic
"AMC Pacer"      4749  17  3  Domestic
"AMC Spirit"     3799  22  .  Domestic
"Buick Century"  4816  20  3  Domestic
"Buick Electra"  7827  15  4  Domestic
"Buick LeSabre"  5788  18  3  Domestic
"Buick Opel"     4453  26  .  Domestic
"Buick Regal"    5189  20  3  Domestic
"Buick Riviera" 10372  16  3  Domestic
"Buick Skylark"  4082  19  3  Domestic
```

Note that we specified type's showtabs option and no tabs are shown. This data is not tab-delimited or comma-delimited and it is not the kind of data insheet is designed to read. Let's try insheet anyway:

```
. insheet using auto4, clear
(1 var, 10 obs)

. describe

Contains data
  obs:            10
  vars:            1
  size:          410 (99.9% of memory free)
-------------------------------------------------------------------------------
  1. v1         str37  %37s
-------------------------------------------------------------------------------
Sorted by:
    Note:  dataset has changed since last save

. list
                               v1
  1. AMC Concord    4099  22  3  Domestic
  2. AMC Pacer      4749  17  3  Domestic
 (output omitted )
 10. Buick Skylark  4082  19  3  Domestic
```

When `insheet` tries to read data that has no tabs or commas, it is fooled into thinking the data contains just one variable. If you had this data, you would have to read it with one of Stata's other commands. `infile` (free format) could read it.

◁

Also See

Complementary:	[R] **outfile**, [R] **outsheet**, [R] **save**
Related:	[R] **infile (free format)**
Background:	[U] **24 Commands to input data**,
	[R] **infile**

Title

> **inspect** — Display simple summary of data's characteristics

Syntax

$\big[$by *varlist*:$\big]$ <u>insp</u>ect $\big[$*varlist*$\big]$ $\big[$if *exp*$\big]$ $\big[$in *range*$\big]$

Description

The `inspect` command provides a quick summary of a numeric variable that differs from that provided by `summarize` or `tabulate`. It reports the number of negative, zero, and positive values; the number of integers and nonintegers; the number of unique values; the number of *missing*; and produces a small histogram. Its purpose is not analytical—instead it allows you to quickly gain familiarity with unknown data.

Remarks

Typing `inspect` by itself produces an inspection for all the variables in the data. If you specify the *varlist*, an inspection of just those variables is presented.

▷ Example

`inspect` is not a replacement or substitute for `summarize` and `tabulate`. It is instead a data management or information tool that lets you quickly gain insight into the values stored in a variable.

For instance, you receive data that purports to be on automobiles, and among the variables in the data is one called `mpg`. Its variable label is `Mileage (mpg)`, which is surely suggestive. You `inspect` the variable:

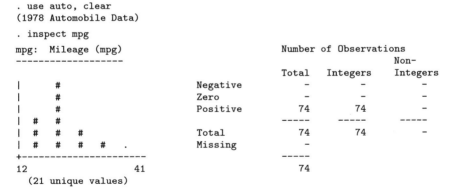

```
. use auto, clear
(1978 Automobile Data)

. inspect mpg

mpg:  Mileage (mpg)                        Number of Observations
--------------------                                        Non-
                                       Total   Integers   Integers
   |      #                 Negative      -         -         -
   |      #                 Zero          -         -         -
   |      #                 Positive     74        74         -
   |   #  #                             -----     -----     -----
   |   #  #  #              Total        74        74         -
   |   #  #  #  #     .     Missing       -
   +----------------------               -----
   12                 41                  74
        (21 unique values)
```

You discover that the variable is never *missing*; all 74 observations in the data have some value for `mpg`. Moreover, the values are all positive and they are all integers as well. Among those 74 observations are 21 unique (different) values. The variable ranges from 12 to 41, and you are provided with a small histogram that suggests the variable appears to be what it claims.

◁

▷ Example

Bob, a co-worker, presents you with some census data. Among the variables in the data is one called `region` which is labeled `Census Region` and is evidently a numeric variable. You `inspect` this variable.

```
. use bobsdata

. inspect region
region:  Census Region                          Number of Observations
----------------------                                         Non-
                                               Total   Integers  Integers
    |         #              Negative             -        -         -
    |         #   #          Zero                 -        -         -
    |     #   #   #          Positive            50       50         -
    |  #  #   #   #                             -----    -----     -----
    |  #  #   #   #          Total               50       50         -
    |  #  #   #   #   .      Missing              -
    +----------------------                      -----
    1                 5                          50
       (5 unique values)
           region is labeled but 1 value is NOT documented in the label.
```

In this data something may be wrong. `region` takes on five unique values. The variable has a value label, however, and one of the observed values is not documented in the label. Perhaps there is a typographical error. A call to Bob would be in order.

◁

▷ Example

You call Bob and there was indeed an error. He fixes it and returns the data to you. Here is what `inspect` produces now:

```
. inspect region
region:  Census Region                          Number of Observations
----------------------                                         Non-
                                               Total   Integers  Integers
    |         #              Negative             -        -         -
    |         #              Zero                 -        -         -
    |     #   #   #          Positive            50       50         -
    |  #  #   #   #                             -----    -----     -----
    |  #  #   #   #          Total               50       50         -
    |  #  #   #   #          Missing              -
    +----------------------                      -----
    1              4                             50
       (4 unique values)
           region is labeled and all values are documented in the label.
```

◁

▷ **Example**

You receive data on the climate in 956 U.S. cities. The variable `tempjan` records the Average January temperature in degrees Fahrenheit. The results of `inspect` are

```
. inspect tempjan
tempjan:  Average January temperature      Number of Observations
------------------------------------                       Non-
                                            Total  Integers  Integers
  |      #                    Negative        -       -         -
  |      #                    Zero            -       -         -
  |      #                    Positive      954      78       876
  |      #   #   #                          -----   -----     -----
  |      #   #   #            Total         954      78       876
  |  .   #   #   #    .       Missing         2
  +----------------------                    -----
  2.2               72.6                     956
  (More than 99 unique values)
```

In two of the 956 observations, `tempjan` is *missing*. Of the 954 cities that have a recorded `tempjan`, all are positive and 78 of them are integer values. `tempjan` varies between 2.2 and 72.6. There are more than 99 unique values of `tempjan` in the data. (Stata gives up counting unique values after 99.)

◁

Saved Results

`inspect` saves in `r()`:

Scalars

`r(N)`	number of observations
`r(N_neg)`	number of negative observations
`r(N_0)`	number of observations equal to 0
`r(N_pos)`	number of positive observations
`r(N_negint)`	number of negative, integer observations
`r(N_posint)`	number of positive, integer observations
`r(N_unique)`	number of unique values or . if more than 99
`r(N_undoc)`	number of undocumented values or . if not labeled

Also See

Related: [R] **codebook**, [R] **compare**, [R] **describe**, [R] **lv**, [R] **summarize**, [R] **table**, [R] **tabsum**, [R] **tabulate**

Title

ipolate — Linearly interpolate (extrapolate) values

Syntax

ipolate *yvar* *xvar*, generate(*newvar*) [by(*varnames*) epolate]

Description

ipolate creates *newvar* = *yvar* where *yvar* is not missing and fills in *newvar* with linearly interpolated (and optionally extrapolated) values of *yvar* where *yvar* is missing.

Options

generate(*newvar*) is not optional; it specifies the name of the new variable to be created.

by(*varnames*) specifies that interpolation (and extrapolation) is to be performed separately for the groups designated by equal values of *varnames*.

epolate specifies values are to be both interpolated and extrapolated. Interpolation only is the default.

Remarks

▷ Example

You have data points on y and x although, in some cases the observations on y are missing. You believe y is a function of x justifying filling in the missing values by linear interpolation:

```
. list
             x          y
  1.         0          .
  2.         1          3
  3.         1.5        .
  4.         2          6
  5.         3          .
  6.         3.5        .
  7.         4          18
. ipolate y x, gen(y1)
(1 missing value generated)
. ipolate y x, gen(y2) epolate
. list
             x          y          y1         y2
  1.         0          .          .          0
  2.         1          3          3          3
  3.         1.5        .          4.5        4.5
  4.         2          6          6          6
  5.         3          .          12         12
  6.         3.5        .          15         15
  7.         4          18         18         18
```

◁

118

▷ Example

You have a dataset of circulation of a magazine from 1970 through 1993. Circulation is recorded in a variable called circ and the year in year. In a few of the years, the circulation is not known so you want to fill it in by linear interpolation:

```
. ipolate circ year, gen(icirc)
```

Now assume you have data on the circulations of 50 magazines; the identity of the magazines is recorded in magazine (which might be a string variable—it does not matter):

```
. ipolate circ year, gen(icirc) by(magazine)
```

If by() is specified, interpolation is performed separately for each group.

◁

▷ Example

You have data on y and x although some of the y values are missing. You wish to smooth $y(x)$ using lowess (see [R] **ksm**) and then fill in missing values of y using interpolated values:

```
. ksm y x, gen(yls) lowess
. ipolate yls x, gen(iyls)
```

◁

Methods and Formulas

ipolate is implemented as an ado-file.

The value y at x is found by finding the closest points (x_0, y_0) and (x_1, y_1), such that $x_0 < x$ and $x_1 > x$, where y_0 and y_1 are observed, and calculating

$$y = \frac{y_1 - y_0}{x_1 - x_0} (x - x_0) + y_0$$

If epolate is specified and if (x_0, y_0) and (x_1, y_1) cannot be found on both sides of x, the two closest points on the same side of x are found and the same formula applied.

Also See

Complementary: [R] **ksm**

Title

> **ivreg** — Instrumental variables and two-stage least squares regression

Syntax

> ivreg *depvar* [*varlist*$_1$] (*varlist*$_2$ = *varlist*$_{iv}$) [*weight*] [if *exp*] [in *range*]
>
>   [, <u>l</u>evel(#) <u>b</u>eta <u>h</u>ascons <u>no</u>constant <u>r</u>obust <u>cl</u>uster(*varname*)
>
>   first <u>noh</u>eader <u>ef</u>orm(*string*) <u>dep</u>name(*varname*) <u>mse</u>1]

aweights, fweights, pweights, and iweights are allowed; see [U] **14.1.6 weight**.

depvar, *varlist*$_1$, *varlist*$_2$, and *varlist*$_{iv}$ may contain time-series operators.

ivreg shares the features of all estimation commands; see [U] **23 Estimation and post-estimation commands**.

Syntax for predict

> predict [*type*] *newvarname* [if *exp*] [in *range*] [, *statistic*]

where *statistic* is

xb	$x_j b$, fitted values (the default)
<u>r</u>esiduals	residuals
<u>p</u>r(*a,b*)	$\Pr(a < y_j < b)$
e(*a,b*)	$E(y_j \mid a < y_j < b)$
<u>y</u>star(*a,b*)	$E(y_j^*)$, $y_j^* = \max(a, \min(y_j, b))$
stdp	standard error of the prediction
stdf	standard error of the forecast

where *a* and *b* may be numbers or variables; *a* equal to '.' means $-\infty$; *b* equal to '.' means $+\infty$.

These statistics are available both in and out of sample; type predict ... if e(sample) ... if wanted only for the estimation sample.

Description

ivreg estimates a linear regression model using instrumental variables (or two-stage least squares) of *depvar* on *varlist*$_1$ and *varlist*$_2$ using *varlist*$_{iv}$ (along with *varlist*$_1$) as instruments for *varlist*$_2$.

In the language of two-stage least squares, *varlist*$_1$ and *varlist*$_{iv}$ are the exogenous variables and *varlist*$_2$ the endogenous variables.

Options

level(*#*) specifies the confidence level, in percent, for confidence intervals. The default is level(95) or as set by set level; see [U] **23.5 Specifying the width of confidence intervals**.

beta asks that normalized beta coefficients be reported instead of confidence intervals.

hascons indicates that a user-defined constant or its equivalent is specified among the independent variables in *varlist*. Some caution is recommended when specifying this option as resulting estimates may not be as accurate as they otherwise would be. See [R] **regress** for more information.

noconstant suppresses the constant term (intercept) in the regression.

robust specifies that the Huber/White/sandwich estimator of variance is to be used in place of the traditional calculation (White, 1980). This alternative variance estimator produces consistent standard errors even if the data is weighted or the residuals are not identically distributed. robust combined with cluster() further allows residuals which are not independent within cluster (although they must be independent between clusters). See [U] **23.11 Obtaining robust variance estimates**.

If you specify pweights, robust is implied; see [U] **23.13 Weighted estimation**.

cluster(*varname*) specifies that the observations are independent across groups (clusters) but not necessarily independent within groups. *varname* specifies to which group each observation belongs; e.g., cluster(personid) in data with repeated observations on individuals. cluster() affects the estimated standard errors and variance–covariance matrix of the estimators (VCE), but not the estimated coefficients; see [U] **23.11 Obtaining robust variance estimates**. cluster() can be used with pweights to produce estimates for unstratified cluster-sampled data, see [U] **23.13 Weighted estimation**, but also see [R] **svy estimators** for a command designed especially for survey data.

cluster() implies robust; specifying robust cluster() is equivalent to typing cluster() by itself.

first requests that the first-stage regression results be displayed.

noheader suppresses the display of the ANOVA table and summary statistics at the top of the output; only the coefficient table is displayed. This option is often used in programs and ado-files.

eform(*string*) is used only in programs and ado-files that employ ivreg to estimate models other than instrumental variable regression. eform() specifies the coefficient table is to be displayed in "exponentiated form" as defined in [R] **maximize** and that *string* is to be used to label the exponentiated coefficients in the table.

depname(*varname*) is used only in programs and ado-files that employ ivreg to estimate models other than instrumental variable regression. depname() may be specified only at estimation time. *varname* is recorded as the identity of the dependent variable even though the estimates are calculated using *depvar*. This affects the labeling of the output—not the results calculated—but could affect subsequent calculations made by predict, where the residual would be calculated as deviations from *varname* rather than *depvar*. depname() is most typically used when *depvar* is a temporary variable (see [R] **macro**) used as a proxy for *varname*.

mse1 is used only in programs and ado-files that employ ivreg to estimate models other than instrumental variables regression. mse1 sets the mean square error to 1 thus forcing the variance–covariance matrix of the estimators to be $(\mathbf{X'DX})^{-1}$ (see [R] **matsize** *Methods and Formulas*) and so affects calculated standard errors. Degrees of freedom for t statistics are calculated as n rather than $n - k$.

Options for predict

xb, the default, calculates the linear prediction.

residuals calculates the residuals; that is, $y_j - x_j b$. These are based on the estimated equation when the observed values of the endogenous variables are used—not the projections of the instruments onto the endogenous variables.

pr(a,b) calculates $\Pr(a < x_j b + u_j < b)$, the probability that $y_j | x_j$ would be observed in the interval (a, b).

> a and b may be specified as numbers or variable names; *lb* and *ub* are variable names;
> pr(20,30) calculates $\Pr(20 < x_j b + u_j < 30)$;
> pr(*lb*,*ub*) calculates $\Pr(lb < x_j b + u_j < ub)$;
> and pr(20,*ub*) calculates $\Pr(20 < x_j b + u_j < ub)$.
>
> $a = .$ means $-\infty$; pr(.,30) calculates $\Pr(x_j b + u_j < 30)$;
> pr(*lb*,30) calculates $\Pr(x_j b + u_j < 30)$ in observations for which $lb = .$
> (and calculates $\Pr(lb < x_j b + u_j < 30)$ elsewhere).
>
> $b = .$ means $+\infty$; pr(20,.) calculates $\Pr(x_j b + u_j > 20)$;
> pr(20,*ub*) calculates $\Pr(x_j b + u_j > 20)$ in observations for which $ub = .$
> (and calculates $\Pr(20 < x_j b + u_j < ub)$ elsewhere).

e(a,b) calculates $E(x_j b + u_j \mid a < x_j b + u_j < b)$, the expected value of $y_j | x_j$ conditional on $y_j | x_j$ being in the interval (a, b), which is to say, $y_j | x_j$ is censored. a and b are specified as they are for pr().

ystar(a,b) calculates $E(y_j^*)$ where $y_j^* = a$ if $x_j b + u_j \leq a$, $y_j^* = b$ if $x_j b + u_j \geq b$, and $y_j^* = x_j b + u_j$ otherwise, which is to say, y_j^* is truncated. a and b are specified as they are for pr().

stdp calculates the standard error of the prediction. It can be thought of as the standard error of the predicted expected value or mean for the observation's covariate pattern. This is also referred to as the standard error of the fitted value.

stdf calculates the standard error of the forecast. This is the standard error of the point prediction for a single observation. It is commonly referred to as the standard error of the future or forecast value. By construction, the standard errors produced by stdf are always larger than those by stdp; see [R] **regress** *Methods and Formulas*.

Remarks

ivreg performs instrumental variables regression (or two-stage least squares), and weighted instrumental variables regression. For a general discussion of two-stage least squares, see Johnston and DiNardo (1997) and Kmenta (1997). While computationally identical, Davidson and MacKinnon (1993, 209–224) present their discussion using instrumental variables terminology. Some of the earliest work on simultaneous systems can be found in Cowles Commission monographs—Koopmans and Marschak (1950) and Koopmans and Hood (1953)—with the first development of two-stage least squares appearing in Theil (1953) and Basmann (1957).

The syntax for ivreg assumes you want to estimate a single equation from a system of equations, or an equation for which you do not want to specify the functional form of the remaining system. If you want to estimate a full system of equations, either using two-stage least squares equation-by-equation or using three-stage least squares, see [R] **reg3**. An advantage of ivreg is that you can estimate a single equation of a multiple-equation system without specifying the functional form of the remaining equations.

▷ Example

Let us assume that you wish to estimate

$$\text{hsngval} = \alpha_0 + \alpha_1\text{faminc} + \alpha_2\text{reg2} + \alpha_3\text{reg3} + \alpha_4\text{reg4} + \epsilon$$

$$\text{rent} = \beta_0 + \beta_1\text{hsngval} + \beta_2\text{pcturban} + \nu$$

You have state data from the 1980 Census. hsngval is the median dollar value of owner-occupied housing, and rent is median monthly gross rent. You postulate that hsngval is a function of family income (faminc) and region of the country (reg2 through reg4). You also postulate that rent is a function of hsngval and the percentage of the population living in urban areas (pcturban).

If you are familiar with multi-equation models, you have probably already noted the triangular structure of our model. This triangular structure is not required. In fact, given the triangular (or recursive) structure of the model, if we were to assume that ϵ and ν were uncorrelated, either of the equations could be consistently estimated by ordinary least squares. This is strictly a characteristic of triangular systems and would not hold if hsngval were assumed to also depend on rent, regardless of assumptions about ϵ and ν. For a more detailed discussion of triangular systems see Kmenta (1997, 719–720).

You tell Stata to estimate the rent equation by specifying the structural equation and the additional exogenous variables in a specific form. The dependent variable appears first and is followed by the exogenous variables in the structural model for rent. These are followed by a group of variables in parentheses separated by an equal sign. The variables to the left of the equal sign are the endogenous regressors in the structural model for rent and those to the right are the additional exogenous variables that will instrument for the endogenous variables. Only the additional exogenous variables need to be specified to the right of the equal sign; those already in the structural model will be automatically included as instruments.

As the following command shows, this is more difficult to describe than to perform. In this example, rent is the endogenous dependent variable, hsngval is an endogenous regressor, and faminc, reg2, reg3, reg4, and pcturban are the exogenous variables.

```
. ivreg rent pcturban (hsngval = faminc reg2-reg4)
Instrumental variables (2SLS) regression
     Source |       SS       df       MS              Number of obs =      50
------------+------------------------------           F(  2,    47) =   42.66
      Model |  36677.4033     2  18338.7017           Prob > F      =  0.0000
   Residual |  24565.7167    47  522.674823           R-squared     =  0.5989
------------+------------------------------           Adj R-squared =  0.5818
      Total |    61243.12    49  1249.85959           Root MSE      =  22.862

------------------------------------------------------------------------------
       rent |      Coef.   Std. Err.       t    P>|t|     [95% Conf. Interval]
------------+-----------------------------------------------------------------
    hsngval |   .0022398   .0003388     6.612   0.000     .0015583    .0029213
   pcturban |    .081516   .3081528     0.265   0.793    -.5384074    .7014394
      _cons |   120.7065   15.70688     7.685   0.000     89.10834    152.3047
------------------------------------------------------------------------------
Instrumented:  hsngval
Instruments:   faminc reg2 reg3 reg4 + pcturban
------------------------------------------------------------------------------
```

◁

▷ **Example**

Given the triangular nature of the estimated system, we might wonder if there is sufficient correlation between the disturbances to warrant estimation by instrumental variables. (We might have a similar question, even if the system were fully simultaneous.) Stata's `hausman` command (see [R] **hausman**) will allow us to test whether there is sufficient difference between the coefficients of the instrumental variables regression and standard OLS to indicate that OLS would be inconsistent for our model. To perform the Hausman test, we use `hausman` to save the `ivreg` estimates, perform an OLS regression, and compare the two using `hausman`.

```
. hausman, save
. regress rent hsngval pcturban

      Source |       SS       df       MS                  Number of obs =      50
-------------+------------------------------                F(  2,    47) =   47.54
       Model |  40983.5269        2  20491.7635            Prob > F      =  0.0000
    Residual |  20259.5931       47  431.055172            R-squared     =  0.6692
-------------+------------------------------                Adj R-squared =  0.6551
       Total |    61243.12       49  1249.85959            Root MSE      =  20.762

-----------------------------------------------------------------------------------
        rent |      Coef.   Std. Err.      t    P>|t|     [95% Conf. Interval]
-------------+---------------------------------------------------------------------
     hsngval |   .0015205   .0002276     6.681   0.000     .0010627    .0019784
    pcturban |   .5248216   .2490782     2.107   0.040     .0237408    1.025902
       _cons |   125.9033   14.18537     8.876   0.000     97.36603    154.4406
-----------------------------------------------------------------------------------

. hausman, constant sigmamore

             ---- Coefficients ----
           |       (b)          (B)            (b-B)     sqrt(diag(V_b-V_B))
           |      Prior        Current       Difference          S.E.
-----------+----------------------------------------------------------------
   hsngval |    .0022398     .0015205        .0007193          .000207
  pcturban |     .081516     .5248216       -.4433056         .1275655
     _cons |    120.7065     125.9033       -5.196801          1.49543
-----------+----------------------------------------------------------------
           b = less efficient estimates obtained previously from ivreg.
           B = more efficient estimates obtained from regress.

Test:  Ho:  difference in coefficients not systematic

            chi2(  3) = (b-B)'[(V_b-V_B)^(-1)](b-B)
                      =      12.08
            Prob>chi2 =     0.0005
```

The Hausman test clearly indicates that OLS is an inconsistent estimator for this equation.

As opposed to a direct test of `hsngval`'s endogeneity, Davidson and MacKinnon (1993, 236–242) have noted that this Hausman test is best interpreted as evaluating whether OLS is a consistent estimator for the model. The null hypothesis is that the model was generated by an OLS process and the test is performed under the assumption that the instrumental variables estimates are consistent. As an alternative to the Hausman test, Davidson and MacKinnon suggest an augmented regression test that is based on the same asymptotic requirements as the Hausman test.

We can easily form the augmented regression by including the predicted values of each endogenous right-hand-side (rhs) variable, as a function of all exogenous variables, in a regression of the original model. For our `hsngval` model, we regress `hsngval` on all exogenous variables and include the prediction from this regression in an OLS regression of the `hsngval` equation.

```
. regress hsngval faminc reg2-reg4 pcturban
  (output omitted )
```

```
. predict hsng_hat
(option xb assumed; fitted values)

. predict hsng_res, res

. regress rent hsngval pcturban hsng_hat
```

Source |	SS	df	MS		Number of obs =	50
---------+					F(3, 46) =	47.05
Model |	46189.152	3	15396.384		Prob > F =	0.0000
Residual |	15053.968	46	327.260173		R-squared =	0.7542
---------+					Adj R-squared =	0.7382
Total |	61243.12	49	1249.85959		Root MSE =	18.09

rent |	Coef.	Std. Err.	t	P>|t|	[95% Conf. Interval]	
---------+						
hsngval |	.0006509	.0002947	2.209	0.032	.0000577	.0012442
pcturban |	.0815159	.2438355	0.334	0.740	-.4092994	.5723313
hsng_hat |	.0015889	.0003984	3.988	0.000	.000787	.0023908
_cons |	120.7065	12.42856	9.712	0.000	95.68912	145.7239

Since we have only a single endogenous rhs variable, our test statistic is just the t statistic for the **hsng_hat** variable. If there were more than one endogenous rhs variable, we would need to perform a joint test of all their predicted value regressors being zero. For this simple case, the **test** statement would be

```
. test hsng_hat

 ( 1)  hsng_hat = 0.0
       F(  1,   46) =   15.91
             Prob > F =    0.0002
```

While the p-value from the augmented regression test is somewhat lower than the p-value from the Hausman test, both tests clearly show that OLS is not indicated for the **rent** equation (under the assumption that the instrumental variables estimator is a consistent estimator for our **rent** model).

◁

▷ Example

Robust standard errors are available with **ivreg**:

```
. ivreg rent pcturban (hsngval = faminc reg2-reg4), robust
```

IV (2SLS) regression with robust standard errors				Number of obs =	50
				F(2, 47) =	21.14
				Prob > F =	0.0000
				R-squared =	0.5989
				Root MSE =	22.862

rent |	Coef.	Robust Std. Err.	t	P>|t|	[95% Conf. Interval]	
---------+						
hsngval |	.0022398	.0006931	3.232	0.002	.0008455	.0036342
pcturban |	.081516	.4585635	0.178	0.860	-.8409949	1.004027
_cons |	120.7065	15.7348	7.671	0.000	89.05217	152.3609

```
Instrumented:  hsngval
Instruments:   faminc reg2 reg3 reg4 + pcturban
```

The robust standard error for the coefficient on housing value is double what was previously estimated.

◁

❑ Technical Note

You may perform weighted two-stage instrumental variables estimation by specifying the [*weight*] qualifier with `ivreg`. You may perform weighted or unweighted two-stage least squares or instrumental variable estimation, suppressing the constant, by specifying the `noconstant` option. In this case, the constant is excluded from *both* the structural equation *and* the instrument list.

❑

Acknowledgments

The robust estimate of variance with instrumental variables was first implemented in Stata by Mead Over, Dean Jolliffe, and Andrew Foster (1996).

Saved Results

`ivreg` saves in `e()`:

Scalars

`e(N)`	number of observations		`e(r2)`	R-squared
`e(df_m)`	model degrees of freedom		`e(F)`	F statistic
`e(df_r)`	residual degrees of freedom		`e(rmse)`	root mean square error
`e(N_clust)`	number of clusters			

Macros

`e(cmd)`	ivreg		`e(clustvar)`	name of cluster variable
`e(depvar)`	name of dependent variable		`e(vcetype)`	covariance estimation method
`e(model)`	iv		`e(instd)`	instrumented variable
`e(wtype)`	weight type		`e(insts)`	instruments
`e(wexp)`	weight expression		`e(predict)`	program used to implement `predict`

Matrices

`e(b)`	coefficient vector		`e(V)`	variance–covariance matrix of the estimators

Functions

`e(sample)`	marks estimation sample

Methods and Formulas

`ivreg` is implemented as an ado-file.

Variables printed in lowercase and not boldfaced (e.g., x) are scalars. Variables printed in lowercase and boldfaced (e.g., $\mathbf{x}$) are column vectors. Variables printed in uppercase and boldfaced (e.g., $\mathbf{X}$) are matrices.

Let $\mathbf{v}$ be a column vector of weights specified by the user. If no weights are specified, then $\mathbf{v} = \mathbf{1}$. Let $\mathbf{w}$ be a column vector of normalized weights. If no weights are specified or if the user specified `fweight`s or `iweight`s, $\mathbf{w} = \mathbf{v}$. Otherwise, $\mathbf{w} = \big(\mathbf{v}/(\mathbf{1'v})\big)(\mathbf{1'1})$.

The *number of observations*, n, is defined as $\mathbf{1'w}$. In the case of `iweight`s, this is truncated to an integer. The *sum of the weights* is $\mathbf{1'v}$. Define $c = 1$ if there is a constant in the regression and zero otherwise. Define k as the number of right-hand-side (rhs) variables (including the constant).

Let $\mathbf{X}$ denote the matrix of observations on the rhs variables, $\mathbf{y}$ the vector of observations on the left-hand-side (lhs) variable, and $\mathbf{Z}$ the matrix of observations on the instruments. In the following formulas, if the user specifies weights, then $\mathbf{X}'\mathbf{X}$, $\mathbf{X}'\mathbf{y}$, $\mathbf{y}'\mathbf{y}$, $\mathbf{Z}'\mathbf{Z}$, $\mathbf{Z}'\mathbf{X}$, and $\mathbf{Z}'\mathbf{y}$ are replaced by $\mathbf{X}'\mathbf{DX}$, $\mathbf{X}'\mathbf{Dy}$, $\mathbf{y}'\mathbf{Dy}$, $\mathbf{Z}'\mathbf{DZ}$, $\mathbf{Z}'\mathbf{DX}$, and $\mathbf{Z}'\mathbf{Dy}$, respectively, where $\mathbf{D}$ is a diagonal matrix whose diagonal elements are the elements of $\mathbf{w}$. We suppress the $\mathbf{D}$ below to simplify the notation.

Define $\mathbf{A}$ as $\mathbf{X}'\mathbf{Z}(\mathbf{Z}'\mathbf{Z})^{-1}(\mathbf{X}'\mathbf{Z})'$ and $\mathbf{a}$ as $\mathbf{X}'\mathbf{Z}(\mathbf{Z}'\mathbf{Z})^{-1}\mathbf{Z}'\mathbf{y}$.

The coefficient vector $\mathbf{b}$ is defined as $\mathbf{A}^{-1}\mathbf{a}$. Although not shown in the notation, unless `hascons` is specified, $\mathbf{A}$ and $\mathbf{a}$ are accumulated in deviation form and the constant calculated separately. This comment applies to all statistics listed below.

The *total sum of squares*, TSS, equals $\mathbf{y}'\mathbf{y}$ if there is no intercept and $\mathbf{y}'\mathbf{y} - \left((\mathbf{1}'\mathbf{y})^2/n\right)$ otherwise. The *degrees of freedom* are $n - c$.

The *error sum of squares*, ESS, is defined as $\mathbf{y}'\mathbf{y} - 2\mathbf{b}\mathbf{X}'\mathbf{y} + \mathbf{b}'\mathbf{X}'\mathbf{Xb}$. The *degrees of freedom* are $n - k$.

The *model sum of squares*, MSS, equals TSS − ESS. The *degrees of freedom* are $k - c$.

The *mean square error*, s^2, is defined as $\text{ESS}/(n - k)$. The *root mean square error* is s, its square root.

If $c = 1$, then F is defined as

$$F = \frac{(\mathbf{b} - \mathbf{c})'\mathbf{A}(\mathbf{b} - \mathbf{c})}{(k - 1)s^2}$$

where $\mathbf{c}$ is a vector of $k - 1$ zeros and kth element $\mathbf{1}'\mathbf{y}/n$. Otherwise, F is defined as *missing*. (In this case, you may use the `test` command to construct any F test you wish.)

The *R-squared*, R^2, is defined as $R^2 = 1 - \text{ESS}/\text{TSS}$.

The *adjusted R-squared*, R_{a}^2, is $1 - (1 - R^2)(n - c)/(n - k)$.

If `robust` is not specified, the conventional estimate of variance is $s^2\mathbf{A}^{-1}$.

For a discussion of robust variance estimates in the context of regression and regression with instrumental variables see [R] **regress**, *Methods and Formulas*. See this same section for a discussion of the formulas for `predict` after `ivreg`.

References

Baltagi, B. H. 1998. *Econometrics*. New York: Springer-Verlag.

Basmann, R. L. 1957. A generalized classical method of linear estimation of coefficients in a structural equation. *Econometrica* 25: 77–83.

Davidson, R. and J. G. MacKinnon. 1993. *Estimation and Inference in Econometrics*. New York: Oxford University Press.

Johnston, J. and J. DiNardo. 1997. *Econometric Methods*. 4th ed. New York: McGraw–Hill.

Kmenta, J. 1997. *Elements of Econometrics*. 2d ed. Ann Arbor: University of Michigan Press.

Koopmans, T. C. and W. C. Hood. 1953. *Studies in Econometric Method*. New York: John Wiley & Sons.

Koopmans, T. C. and J. Marschak. 1950. *Statistical Inference in Dynamic Economic Models*. New York: John Wiley & Sons.

Over, M., D. Jolliffe, and A. Foster. 1996. sg46: Huber correction for two-stage least squares estimates. *Stata Technical Bulletin* 29: 24–25. Reprinted in *Stata Technical Bulletin Reprints*, vol. 5, pp. 140–142.

Theil, H. 1953. *Repeated Least Squares Applied to Complete Equation Systems*. Mimeograph from the Central Planning Bureau, Hague.

White, H. 1980. A heteroskedasticity-consistent covariance matrix estimator and a direct test for heteroskedasticity. *Econometrica* 48: 817–838.

Also See

Complementary:	[R] **lincom**, [R] **linktest**, [R] **predict**, [R] **sw**, [R] **test**, [R] **testnl**, [R] **vce**, [R] **xi**
Related:	[R] **anova**, [R] **areg**, [R] **cnsreg**, [R] **mvreg**, [R] **qreg**, [R] **reg3**, [R] **regress**, [R] **_robust**, [R] **rreg**, [R] **sureg**, [R] **svy estimators**, [R] **xtreg**
Background:	[U] **16.5 Accessing coefficients and standard errors**, [U] **23 Estimation and post-estimation commands**, [U] **23.11 Obtaining robust variance estimates**, [U] **23.13 Weighted estimation**

Title

> **joinby** — Form all pairwise combinations within groups

Syntax

joinby *varlist* using *filename*

Description

joinby joins, within groups formed by *varlist*, observations of the dataset in memory with *filename*, a Stata-format dataset. By join is meant "form all pairwise combinations". *filename* is required to be sorted by *varlist*. If *filename* is specified without an extension, '.dta' is assumed.

Observations unique to one or the other datasets are ignored. Whether one loads one dataset and joins the other or vice versa makes no difference in terms of the number of resulting observations.

If there are variables in common between the two datasets, however, the combined data will contain the values from the master data for those observations.

Remarks

The following, admittedly artificial, example illustrates joinby.

▷ Example

You have two datasets: **child.dta** and **parent.dta**. Both contain a **famid** variable which identifies the people belonging to the same family.

```
. use child
(Data on Children)

. describe

Contains data from child.dta
  obs:            5                          Data on Children
  vars:           4                          20 Jan 1998 11:52
  size:              50 (99.9% of memory free)
-------------------------------------------------------------------------
  1. famid      int    %8.0g                 Family Id Number
  2. childid    byte   %8.0g                 Child Id Number
  3. x1         byte   %8.0g
  4. x2         int    %8.0g
-------------------------------------------------------------------------
Sorted by:  famid

. list

         famid    childid        x1        x2
  1.      1025         3         11       320
  2.      1025         1         12       300
  3.      1025         4         10       275
  4.      1026         2         13       280
  5.      1027         5         15       210
```

129

```
. use parent, clear
(Data on Parents)
. describe
Contains data from parent.dta
  obs:             6                          Data on Parents
  vars:            4                          20 Jan 1998 11:55
  size:          108 (99.9% of memory free)
-------------------------------------------------------------------------------
  1. famid     int    %8.0g                   Family Id Number
  2. parentid  float  %9.0g                   Parent Id Number
  3. x1        float  %9.0g
  4. x3        float  %9.0g
-------------------------------------------------------------------------------
Sorted by:
. list
         famid   parentid      x1        x3
  1.      1030         10      39       600
  2.      1025         11      20       643
  3.      1025         12      27       721
  4.      1026         13      30       760
  5.      1026         14      26       668
  6.      1030         15      32       684
```

You want to "join" the information for the parents and their children. The data on parents is in memory; the data on children on disk. `child.dta` has been sorted by `famid`, but `parent.dta` has not been, so first we `sort` the parents data on `famid`:

```
. sort famid
. joinby famid using child
. describe
Contains data
  obs:             8                          Data on Parents
  vars:            6
  size:          168 (99.8% of memory free)
-------------------------------------------------------------------------------
  1. famid     int    %8.0g                   Family Id Number
  2. parentid  float  %9.0g                   Parent Id Number
  3. x1        float  %9.0g
  4. x3        float  %9.0g
  5. childid   byte   %8.0g                    Child Id Number
  6. x2        int    %8.0g
-------------------------------------------------------------------------------
Sorted by:  famid
. list
         famid   parentid      x1        x3    childid        x2
  1.      1025         12      27       721          3       320
  2.      1025         12      27       721          4       275
  3.      1025         11      20       643          1       300
  4.      1025         11      20       643          3       320
  5.      1025         11      20       643          4       275
  6.      1025         12      27       721          1       300
  7.      1026         13      30       760          2       280
  8.      1026         14      26       668          2       280
```

Notice that

1. `famid` of 1027, which appears only in `child.dta`, and `famid` of 1030, which appears only in `parent.dta`, are not in the combined dataset. Observations for which the matching variable(s) are not in both datasets are omitted.

2. The `x1` variable is in both datasets. Values for this variable in the joined dataset are the values from `parent.dta`—the dataset in memory when we issued the `joinby` command. If we had `child.dta` in memory and `parent.dta` on disk when we requested `joinby`, the values for `x1` would have been from `child.dta`. Values from the dataset in memory take precedence over the dataset on disk.

◁

Methods and Formulas

`joinby` is implemented as an ado-file.

Also See

Complementary:	[R] **save**
Related:	[R] **append**, [R] **cross**, [R] **fillin**, [R] **merge**
Background:	[U] **25 Commands for combining data**

Title

kappa — Interrater agreement

Syntax

kap *varname₁* *varname₂* [*weight*] [if *exp*] [in *range*] [, tab wgt(*wgtid*) absolute]

kapwgt *wgtid* [1 \ # 1 [\ # # 1 ...]]

kap *varname₁* *varname₂* *varname₃* [...] [*weight*] [if *exp*] [in *range*]

kappa *varlist* [if *exp*] [in *range*]

fweights are allowed; see [U] **14.1.6 weight**.

Description

kap (first syntax) calculates the kappa-statistic measure of interrater agreement when there are two unique raters and two or more ratings.

kapwgt defines weights for use by kap in measuring the importance of disagreements.

kap (second syntax) and kappa calculate the kappa-statistic measure in the case of two or more (nonunique) raters and two outcomes, more than two outcomes when the number of raters is fixed, and more than two outcomes when the number of raters varies. kap (second syntax) and kappa produce the same results; they merely differ in how they expect the data to be organized.

kap assumes that each observation is a subject. *varname₁* contains the ratings by the first rater, *varname₂* by the second rater, and so on.

kappa also assumes that each observation is a subject. The variables, however, record the frequencies with which ratings were assigned. The first variable records the number of times the first rating was assigned, the second variable records the number of times the second rating was assigned, and so on.

Options

tab displays a tabulation of the assessments by the two raters.

wgt(*wgtid*) specifies that *wgtid* is to be used to weight disagreements. User-defined weights can be created using kapwgt; in that case, wgt() specifies the name of the user-defined matrix. For instance, you might define

    . kapwgt mine 1 \ .8 1 \ 0 .8 1 \ 0 0 .8 1

and then

    . kap rata ratb, wgt(mine)

132

In addition, two prerecorded weights are available.

wgt(w) specifies weights $1 - |i - j|/(k - 1)$, where i and j index the rows and columns of the ratings by the two raters and k is the maximum number of possible ratings.

wgt(w2) specifies weights $1 - ((i - j)/(k - 1))^2$.

absolute is relevant only if wgt() is also specified; see wgt() above. Option absolute modifies how i, j, and k in the formulas below are defined and how corresponding entries are found in a user-defined weighting matrix. When absolute is not specified, i and j refer to the row and column index, not the ratings themselves. Say the ratings are recorded as $\{0, 1, 1.5, 2\}$. There are 4 ratings; $k = 4$ and i and j are still 1, 2, 3, and 4 in the formulas below. Index 3, for instance, corresponds to rating $= 1.5$. This is convenient but can, with some data, lead to difficulties.

When absolute is specified, all ratings must be integers and they must be coded from the set $\{1, 2, 3, \ldots\}$. Not all values need be used; integer values that do not occur are simply assumed to be unobserved.

Remarks

The kappa-statistic measure of agreement is scaled to be 0 when the amount of agreement is what would be expected to be observed by chance and 1 when there is perfect agreement. For intermediate values, Landis and Koch (1977a, 165) suggest the following interpretations:

below 0.0	Poor
0.00–0.20	Slight
0.21–0.40	Fair
0.41–0.60	Moderate
0.61–0.80	Substantial
0.81–1.00	Almost Perfect

The case of 2 raters

▷ Example

Consider the classification by two radiologists of 85 xeromammograms as normal, benign disease, suspicion of cancer, or cancer (a subset of the data from Boyd et al. 1982 and discussed in the context of kappa in Altman 1991, 403–405).

```
. tabulate rada radb

Radiologist| Radiologist B's assessment
A's        |
assessment |    Normal    benign   suspect    cancer |     Total
-----------+--------------------------------------------+----------
    Normal |        21        12         0         0 |        33
    benign |         4        17         1         0 |        22
   suspect |         3         9        15         2 |        29
    cancer |         0         0         0         1 |         1
-----------+--------------------------------------------+----------
     Total |        28        38        16         3 |        85
```

Our data contains two variables: rada, radiologist A's assessment; radb, radiologist B's assessment. Each observation is a patient.

We can obtain the kappa measure of interrater agreement by typing

```
. kap rada radb
              Expected
Agreement    Agreement     Kappa         Z        Pr>Z
----------------------------------------------------------
  63.53%       30.82%      0.4728       6.81      0.0000
```

Had each radiologist made his determination randomly (but with probabilities equal to the overall proportions), we would expect the two radiologists to agree on 30.8% of the patients. In fact, they agreed on 63.5% of the patients, or 47.3% of the way between random agreement and perfect agreement. The amount of agreement indicates that we can reject that they are making their determinations randomly.

◁

▷ Example

There is a difference between two radiologists disagreeing whether a xeromammogram indicates cancer or the suspicion of cancer and disagreeing whether it indicates cancer or is normal. The weighted kappa attempts to deal with this. `kap` provides two "prerecorded" weights, `w` and `w2`:

```
. kap rada radb, wgt(w)
Ratings weighted by:
    1.0000    0.6667    0.3333    0.0000
    0.6667    1.0000    0.6667    0.3333
    0.3333    0.6667    1.0000    0.6667
    0.0000    0.3333    0.6667    1.0000
              Expected
Agreement    Agreement     Kappa         Z        Pr>Z
----------------------------------------------------------
  86.67%       69.11%      0.5684       7.22      0.0000
```

The `w` weights are given by $1 - |i - j|/(k - 1)$ where i and j index the rows of columns of the ratings by the two raters and k is the maximum number of possible ratings. The weighting matrix is printed above the table. In our case, the rows and columns of the 4×4 matrix correspond to the ratings normal, benign, suspicious, and cancerous.

A weight of 1 indicates an observation should count as perfect agreement. The matrix has 1s down the diagonals—when both radiologists make the same assessment, they are in agreement. A weight of, say, 0.6667 means they are in two-thirds agreement. In our matrix they get that score if they are "one apart"—one radiologist assesses cancer and the other is merely suspicious, or one is suspicious and the other says benign, and so on. An entry of 0.3333 means they are in one-third agreement or, if you prefer, two-thirds disagreement. That is the score attached when they are "two apart". Finally, they are in complete disagreement when the weight is zero, which happens only when they are three apart—one says cancer and the other says normal.

◁

▷ Example

The other prerecorded weight is `w2` where the weights are given by $1 - [(i - j)/(k - 1)]^2$:

```
. kap rada radb, wgt(w2)
Ratings weighted by:
    1.0000    0.8889    0.5556    0.0000
    0.8889    1.0000    0.8889    0.5556
    0.5556    0.8889    1.0000    0.8889
    0.0000    0.5556    0.8889    1.0000
```

Agreement	Expected Agreement	Kappa	Z	Pr>Z
94.77%	84.09%	0.6714	6.22	0.0000

The `w2` weight makes the categories even more alike and is probably inappropriate here.

◁

▷ Example

In addition to prerecorded weights, you can define your own weights with the `kapwgt` command. For instance, you might feel that suspicious and cancerous are reasonably similar, benign and normal reasonably similar, but the suspicious/cancerous group is nothing like the benign/normal group:

```
. kapwgt xm 1 \ .8 1 \ 0 0 1 \ 0 0 .8 1
. kapwgt xm
1.0000
0.8000 1.0000
0.0000 0.0000 1.0000
0.0000 0.0000 0.8000 1.0000
```

You name the weights—we named ours `xm`—and after the weight name, you enter the lower triangle of the weighting matrix, using \ to separate rows. In our example we have four outcomes and so continued entering numbers until we had defined the fourth row of the weighting matrix. If you type `kapwgt` followed by a name and nothing else, it shows you the weights recorded under that name. Satisfied that we have entered them correctly, we now use the weights to recalculate kappa:

```
. kap rada radb, wgt(xm)
Ratings weighted by:
   1.0000   0.8000   0.0000   0.0000
   0.8000   1.0000   0.0000   0.0000
   0.0000   0.0000   1.0000   0.8000
   0.0000   0.0000   0.8000   1.0000
```

Agreement	Expected Agreement	Kappa	Z	Pr>Z
80.47%	52.67%	0.5874	6.79	0.0000

◁

❑ Technical Note

In addition to weights for weighting the differences in categories, you can specify Stata's traditional weights for weighting the data. In the examples above, we have 85 observations in our dataset—one for each patient. If all we knew was the table of outcomes—that there were 21 patients rated normal by both radiologists, etc.—it would be easier to enter the table into Stata and work from it. The easiest way to enter the data is with `tabi`; see [R] **tabulate**.

```
. tabi 21 12 0 0 \ 4 17 1 0 \ 3 9 15 2 \ 0 0 0 1, replace
```

row	col 1	2	3	4	Total
1	21	12	0	0	33
2	4	17	1	0	22
3	3	9	15	2	29
4	0	0	0	1	1
Total	28	38	16	3	85

Pearson chi2(9) =   77.8111   Pr = 0.000

`tabi` felt obligated to tell us the Pearson χ^2 for this table, but we do not care about it. The important thing is that, with the `replace` option, `tabi` left the table in memory:

```
. list in 1/5
         row       col       pop
  1.       1         1        21
  2.       1         2        12
  3.       1         3         0
  4.       1         4         0
  5.       2         1         4
```

The variable `row` is radiologist A's assessment; `col`, radiologist B's assessment; and `pop` the number so assessed by both. Thus,

```
. kap row col [freq=pop]
              Expected
Agreement   Agreement     Kappa        Z        Pr>Z
---------------------------------------------------------
  63.53%      30.82%      0.4728      6.81      0.0000
```

If we are going to keep this data, the names `row` and `col` are not indicative of what the data reflects. We could (see [U] **15.6 Dataset, variable, and value labels**)

```
. rename row rada
. rename col radb
. label var rada "Radiologist A's assessment"
. label var radb "Radiologist B's assessment"
. label define assess 1 normal 2 benign 3 suspect 4 cancer
. label values rada assess
. label values radb assess
. label data "Altman p. 403"
```

`kap`'s `tab` option, which can be used with or without weighted data, shows the table of assessments:

```
. kap rada radb [freq=pop], tab
Radiologist| Radiologist B's assessment
A's        |
assessment |    normal     benign    suspect     cancer |    Total
-----------+--------------------------------------------+----------
    normal |        21         12          0          0 |       33
    benign |         4         17          1          0 |       22
   suspect |         3          9         15          2 |       29
    cancer |         0          0          0          1 |        1
-----------+--------------------------------------------+----------
     Total |        28         38         16          3 |       85
              Expected
Agreement   Agreement     Kappa        Z        Pr>Z
---------------------------------------------------------
  63.53%      30.82%      0.4728      6.81      0.0000
```

❑

❑ Technical Note

You have data on individual patients. There are two raters and the possible ratings are 1, 2, 3, and 4, but neither rater ever used rating 3:

```
. tabulate ratera raterb

           |              raterb
    ratera |         1         2         4 |     Total
-----------+--------------------------------+----------
         1 |         6         4         3 |        13
         2 |         5         3         3 |        11
         4 |         1         1        26 |        28
-----------+--------------------------------+----------
     Total |        12         8        32 |        52
```

In this case, `kap` would determine the ratings are from the set $\{1,2,4\}$ because those were the only values observed. `kap` would expect a user-defined weighting matrix to be 3×3 and, were it not, `kap` would issue an error message. In the formula-based weights, the calculation would be based on $i, j = 1, 2, 3$ corresponding to the three observed ratings $\{1, 2, 4\}$.

Specifying the `absolute` option would make it clear that the ratings are 1, 2, 3, and 4; it just so happens that rating $= 3$ was never assigned. Were a user-defined weighting matrix also specified, `kap` would expect it to be 4×4 or larger (larger because one can think of the ratings being 1, 2, 3, 4, 5, ... and it just so happens that ratings 5, 6, ..., were never observed just as rating $= 3$ was not observed.) In the formula-based weights, the calculation would be based on $i, j = 1, 2, 4$.

```
. kap ratera raterb, wgt(w)

Ratings weighted by:
    1.0000    0.5000    0.0000
    0.5000    1.0000    0.5000
    0.0000    0.5000    1.0000

               Expected
 Agreement    Agreement     Kappa          Z       Pr>Z
-------------------------------------------------------
    79.81%       57.17%     0.5285       4.52     0.0000

. kap ratera raterb, wgt(w) absolute

Ratings weighted by:
    1.0000    0.6667    0.0000
    0.6667    1.0000    0.3333
    0.0000    0.3333    1.0000

               Expected
 Agreement    Agreement     Kappa          Z       Pr>Z
-------------------------------------------------------
    81.41%       55.08%     0.5862       4.85     0.0000
```

If all conceivable ratings are observed in the data, then whether `absolute` is specified makes no difference. For instance, if rater A assigns ratings $\{1, 2, 4\}$ and rater B assigns ratings $\{1, 2, 3, 4\}$, then the complete set of assigned ratings is $\{1, 2, 3, 4\}$, the same as `absolute` would specify. And without `absolute`, it makes no difference whether the ratings are $\{1, 2, 3, 4\}$, $\{0, 1, 2, 3\}$, $\{1, 7, 9, 100\}$, $\{0, 1, 1.5, 2.0\}$, or coded any other way.

❑

The case of more than two raters

In the case of more than two raters, the mathematics are such that the two raters are not considered unique. For instance, if there are three raters, there is no assumption that the three raters who rate the first subject are the same as the three raters that rate the second. Although we call this the more than two raters case, it can be used with two raters when the identities of the two raters vary.

The nonunique rater case can be usefully broken down into three subcases: (a) there are two possible ratings which we will call positive and negative; (b) there are more than two possible ratings but the number of raters per subject is the same for all subjects; and (c) there are more than two possible ratings and the number of raters per subject varies. kappa handles all these cases. To emphasize that there is no assumption of constant identity of raters across subjects, the variables specified contain counts of the number of raters rating the subject into a particular category.

▷ Example

(Two ratings.) Fleiss (1981, 227) offers the following hypothetical ratings by different sets of raters on 25 subjects:

Subject	No. of raters	No. of pos. ratings	Subject	No. of raters	No. of pos. ratings
1	2	2	14	4	3
2	2	0	15	2	0
3	3	2	16	2	2
4	4	3	17	3	1
5	3	3	18	2	1
6	4	1	19	4	1
7	3	0	20	5	4
8	5	0	21	3	2
9	2	0	22	4	0
10	4	4	23	3	0
11	5	5	24	3	3
12	3	3	25	2	2
13	4	4			

We have entered this data into Stata and the variables are called subject, raters, and pos. kappa, however, requires we specify variables containing the number of positive ratings and negative ratings; that is, pos and raters-pos:

```
. gen neg = raters-pos
. kappa pos neg
Two-outcomes, multiple raters:
        Kappa        Z        Pr>Z
      -----------------------------
       0.5415      5.28      0.0000
```

We would have obtained the same results if we had typed kappa neg pos.

◁

▷ Example

(More than two ratings, constant number of raters.) Each of ten subjects is rated into one of three categories by five raters (Fleiss 1981, 230):

```
. list
         subject      cat1      cat2      cat3
  1.        1          1         4         0
  2.        2          2         0         3
  3.        3          0         0         5
  4.        4          4         0         1
  5.        5          3         0         2
  6.        6          1         4         0
  7.        7          5         0         0
  8.        8          0         4         1
  9.        9          1         0         4
 10.       10          3         0         2
```

We obtain the kappa statistic:

```
. kappa cat1-cat3
       Outcome |    Kappa          Z        Pr>Z
---------------+----------------------------------
          cat1 |    0.2917       2.92      0.0018
          cat2 |    0.6710       6.71      0.0000
          cat3 |    0.3490       3.49      0.0002
---------------+----------------------------------
      combined |    0.4179       5.83      0.0000
```

The first part of the output shows the results of calculating kappa for each of the categories separately against an amalgam of the remaining categories. For instance, the cat1 line is the two-rating kappa where positive is cat1 and negative is cat2 or cat3. The test statistic, however, is calculated differently (see *Methods and Formulas*). The combined kappa is the appropriately weighted average of the individual kappas. Note that there is considerably less agreement about the rating of subjects into the first category than there is for the second.

◁

▷ Example

Now suppose that we had the same data as in the previous example, but it is organized differently:

```
. list
       subject     rater1     rater2     rater3     rater4     rater5
  1.         1          1          2          2          2          2
  2.         2          1          1          3          3          3
  3.         3          3          3          3          3          3
  4.         4          1          1          1          1          3
  5.         5          1          1          1          3          3
  6.         6          1          2          2          2          2
  7.         7          1          1          1          1          1
  8.         8          2          2          2          2          3
  9.         9          1          3          3          3          3
 10.        10          1          1          1          3          3
```

In this case, you would use kap rather than kappa:

```
. kap rater1 rater2 rater3 rater4 rater5
There are 5 raters per subject:
       Outcome |    Kappa          Z        Pr>Z
---------------+----------------------------------
             1 |    0.2917       2.92      0.0018
             2 |    0.6711       6.71      0.0000
             3 |    0.3490       3.49      0.0002
---------------+----------------------------------
      combined |    0.4179       5.83      0.0000
```

Note that the information of which rater is which is not exploited when there are more than two raters.

◁

▷ Example

    (More than two ratings, varying number of raters.) In this unfortunate case, kappa can be calculated, but there is no test statistic for testing against $\kappa > 0$. You do nothing differently—**kappa** calculates the total number of raters for each subject and, if it is not a constant, suppresses the calculation of test statistics.

```
. list
          subject       cat1       cat2       cat3
   1.           1          1          3          0
   2.           2          2          0          3
   3.           3          0          0          5
   4.           4          4          0          1
   5.           5          3          0          2
   6.           6          1          4          0
   7.           7          5          0          0
   8.           8          0          4          1
   9.           9          1          0          2
  10.          10          3          0          2

. kappa cat1-cat3
       Outcome |     Kappa           Z        Pr>Z
    -----------+------------------------------------
          cat1 |    0.2685           .           .
          cat2 |    0.6457           .           .
          cat3 |    0.2938           .           .
    -----------+------------------------------------
      combined |    0.3816           .           .

note:  Number of ratings per subject vary; cannot calculate test
       statistics.
```
◁

▷ Example

    This case is similar to the previous example, but the data is organized differently:

```
. list
          subject     rater1     rater2     rater3     rater4     rater5
   1.           1          1          2          2          .          2
   2.           2          1          1          3          3          3
   3.           3          3          3          3          3          3
   4.           4          1          1          1          1          3
   5.           5          1          1          1          3          3
   6.           6          1          2          2          2          2
   7.           7          1          1          1          1          1
   8.           8          2          2          2          2          3
   9.           9          1          3          .          .          3
  10.          10          1          1          1          3          3
```

In this case, we specify **kap**, instead of **kappa**:

```
. kap rater1-rater5
There are between 3 and 5 (median = 5.00) raters per subject:
       Outcome |     Kappa           Z        Pr>Z
    -----------+------------------------------------
            1 |    0.2685           .           .
            2 |    0.6457           .           .
            3 |    0.2938           .           .
    -----------+------------------------------------
      combined |    0.3816           .           .

note:  Number of ratings per subject vary; cannot calculate test
       statistics.
```
◁

Saved Results

kap and kappa save in r():

Scalars

r(N)	number of subjects (kap only)	r(kappa)	kappa
r(prop_o)	observed proportion of agreement (kap only)	r(z)	z statistic
r(prop_e)	expected proportion of agreement (kap only)		

Methods and Formulas

kap, kapwgt, and kappa are implemented as ado-files.

The kappa statistic was first proposed by Cohen (1960). The generalization for weights reflecting the relative seriousness of each possible disagreement is due to Cohen (1968). The analysis-of-variance approach for $k = 2$ and $m \geq 2$ is due to Landis and Koch (1977b). See Altman (1991, 403–409) for an introductory treatment and Fleiss (1981, 212–236) for a more detailed treatment. All formulas below are as presented in Fleiss (1981). Let m be the number of raters and k be the number of rating outcomes.

kap: m = 2

Define w_{ij} $(i = 1, \ldots, k, j = 1, \ldots, k)$ as the weights for agreement and disagreement (wgt()) or, if not weighted, define $w_{ii} = 1$ and $w_{ij} = 0$ for $i \neq j$. If wgt(w) is specified, $w_{ij} = 1 - |i - j|/(k-1)$. If wgt(w2) is specified, $w_{ij} = 1 - \left((i - j)/(k - 1)\right)^2$.

The observed proportion of agreement is

$$p_o = \sum_{i=1}^{k} \sum_{j=1}^{k} w_{ij} p_{ij}$$

where p_{ij} is the fraction of ratings i by the first rater and j by the second. The expected proportion of agreement is

$$p_e = \sum_{i=1}^{k} \sum_{j=1}^{k} w_{ij} p_{i \cdot} p_{\cdot j}$$

where $p_{i \cdot} = \sum_j p_{ij}$ and $p_{\cdot j} = \sum_i p_{ij}$.

Kappa is given by $\widehat{\kappa} = (p_o - p_e)/(1 - p_e)$.

The standard error of $\widehat{\kappa}$ for testing against 0 is

$$\widehat{s}_0 = \frac{1}{(1 - p_e)\sqrt{n}} \sqrt{\left(\sum_i \sum_j p_{i \cdot} p_{\cdot j} [w_{ij} - (\overline{w}_{i \cdot} + \overline{w}_{\cdot j})]^2 \right) - p_e^2}$$

where n is the number of subjects being rated and $\overline{w}_{i \cdot} = \sum_j p_{\cdot j} w_{ij}$ and $\overline{w}_{\cdot j} = \sum_i p_{i \cdot} w_{ij}$. The test statistic $Z = \kappa/s_0$ is assumed to be distributed $N(0, 1)$.

kappa: m > 2, k = 2

Each subject i, $i = 1, \ldots, n$, is found by x_i of m_i raters to be positive (the choice as to what is labeled positive being arbitrary).

The overall proportion of positive ratings is $\bar{p} = \sum_i x_i/(n\bar{m})$, where $\bar{m} = \sum_i m_i/n$. The between-subjects mean square is (approximately)

$$B = \frac{1}{n} \sum_i \frac{(x_i - m_i\bar{p})^2}{m_i}$$

and the within-subject mean square is

$$W = \frac{1}{n(\bar{m} - 1)} \sum_i \frac{x_i(m_i - x_i)}{m_i}$$

Kappa is then defined

$$\widehat{\kappa} = \frac{B - W}{B + (\bar{m} - 1)W}$$

The standard error for testing against 0 (Fleiss and Cuzick 1979) is approximately equal to and calculated as

$$\widehat{s}_0 = \frac{1}{(\bar{m} - 1)\sqrt{n\bar{m}_H}} \sqrt{2(\bar{m}_H - 1) + \frac{(\bar{m} - \bar{m}_H)(1 - 4\bar{p}\bar{q})}{\bar{m}\bar{p}\bar{q}}}$$

where $\bar{m}_H$ is the harmonic mean of m_i and $\bar{q} = 1 - \bar{p}$.

The test statistic $Z = \widehat{\kappa}/\widehat{s}_0$ is assumed to be distributed $N(0, 1)$.

kappa: m > 2, k > 2

Let x_{ij} be the number or ratings on subject i, $i = 1, \ldots, n$, into category j, $j = 1, \ldots, k$. Define $\bar{p}_j$ as the overall proportion of ratings in category j, $\bar{q}_j = 1 - \bar{p}_j$, and let $\widehat{\kappa}_j$ be the kappa statistic given above for $k = 2$ when category j is compared with the amalgam of all other categories. Kappa is (Landis and Koch 1977b)

$$\bar{\kappa} = \frac{\sum_j \bar{p}_j\bar{q}_j\widehat{\kappa}_j}{\sum_j \bar{p}_j\bar{q}_j}$$

In the case where the number of raters per subject $\sum_j x_{ij}$ is a constant m for all i, Fleiss, Nee, and Landis (1979) derived the following formulas for the approximate standard errors. The standard error for testing $\widehat{\kappa}_j$ against 0 is

$$\widehat{s}_j = \sqrt{\frac{2}{nm(m - 1)}}$$

and the standard error for testing $\bar{\kappa}$ is

$$\bar{s} = \frac{\sqrt{2}}{\sum_j \bar{p}_j\bar{q}_j \sqrt{nm(m - 1)}} \sqrt{\left(\sum_j \bar{p}_j\bar{q}_j\right)^2 - \sum_j \bar{p}_j\bar{q}_j(\bar{q}_j - \bar{p}_j)}$$

References

Altman, D. G. 1991. *Practical Statistics for Medical Research*. London: Chapman & Hall.

Boyd, N. F., C. Wolfson, M. Moskowitz, T. Carlile, M. Petitclerc, H. A. Ferri, E. Fishell, A. Gregoire, M. Kiernan, J. D. Longley, I. S. Simor, and A. B. Miller. 1982. Observer variation in the interpretation of xeromammograms. *Journal of the National Cancer Institute* 68: 357–63.

Cohen, J. 1960. A coefficient of agreement for nominal scales. *Educational and Psychological Measurement* 20: 37–46.

——. 1968. Weighted kappa: Nominal scale agreement with provision for scaled disagreement or partial credit. *Psychological Bulletin* 70: 213–220.

Fleiss, J. L. 1981. *Statistical Methods for Rates and Proportions*. 2d ed. New York: John Wiley & Sons.

Fleiss, J. L. and J. Cuzick. 1979. The reliability of dichotomous judgments: unequal numbers of judges per subject. *Applied Psychological Measurement* 3: 537–542.

Fleiss, J. L., J. C. M. Nee, and J. R. Landis. 1979. Large sample variance of kappa in the case of different sets of raters. *Psychological Bulletin* 86: 974–977.

Gould, W. 1997. stata49: Interrater agreement. *Stata Technical Bulletin* 40: 2–8. Reprinted in *Stata Technical Bulletin Reprints*, vol. 7, pp. 20–28.

Landis, J. R. and G. G. Koch. 1977a. The measurement of observer agreement for categorical data. *Biometrics* 33: 159–174.

——. 1977b. A one-way components of variance model for categorical data. *Biometrics* 33: 671–679.

Steichen, T. J. and N. J. Cox. 1998a sg84: Concordance correlation coefficient. *Stata Technical Bulletin* 43: 35–39.

——. 1998b. sg84.1: Concordance correlation coefficient, revisited. *Stata Technical Bulletin* 45: 21–23.

Also See

Related: [R] **tabulate**

Title

---

kdensity — Univariate kernel density estimation

Syntax

kdensity *varname* [*weight*] [if *exp*] [in *range*]

    [, <u>nog</u>raph <u>g</u>enerate(*newvar$_x$ newvar$_{density}$*) n(*#*) <u>w</u>idth(*#*)

        { <u>biw</u>eight | <u>cos</u>ine | <u>epan</u> | <u>gauss</u> | <u>par</u>zen | <u>rec</u>tangle | <u>tria</u>ngle }

        <u>nor</u>mal <u>stud</u>(*#*) at(*var$_x$*) <u>s</u>ymbol(...) <u>c</u>onnect(...) <u>ti</u>tle(*string*)

        graph_options]

fweights and aweights are allowed; see [U] **14.1.6 weight**.

Description

kdensity produces kernel density estimates and graphs the result.

Options

nograph suppresses drawing the graph. This option is often used in combination with the generate() option.

generate(*newvar$_x$ newvar$_{density}$*) stores the results of the estimation. *newvar$_{density}$* will contain the density estimate. *newvar$_x$* will contain the points at which the density is estimated.

n(*#*) specifies the number of points at which the density estimate is to be evaluated. The default is min($N, 50$), where N is the number of observations in memory.

width(*#*) specifies the halfwidth of the kernel, the width of the density window around each point. If w() is not specified, then the "optimal" width is calculated and used. The optimal width is the width that would minimize the mean integrated square error if the data were Gaussian and a Gaussian kernel were used and so is not optimal in any global sense. In fact, for multimodal and highly skewed densities, this width is usually too wide and oversmooths the density (Silverman 1986).

biweight, cosine, epan, gauss, parzen, rectangle, and triangle specify the kernel. By default, epan, specifying the Epanechnikov kernel, is used.

normal requests that a normal density be overlaid on the density estimate for comparison.

stud(*#*) specifies that a Student's t distribution with *#* degrees of freedom be overlaid on the density estimate for comparison.

at(*var$_x$*) specifies a variable that contains the values at which the density should be estimated. This option allows you to more easily obtain density estimates for different variables or different subsamples of a variable and then overlay the estimated densities for comparison.

symbol(...) is graph, twoway's symbol() option for specifying the plotting symbol. The default is symbol(o); see [G] **graph options**.

connect(...) is graph, twoway's connect() option for how points are connected. The default is connect(l), meaning points are connected with straight lines; see [G] **graph options**.

title(*string*) is graph, twoway's title() option for specifying the title. The default title is "Kernel Density Estimate"; see [G] **graph options**.

graph_options are any of the other options allowed with graph, twoway; see [G] **graph options**.

Remarks

Kernel density estimators approximate the density $f(x)$ from observations on x. Histograms do this too, and, in fact, the histogram itself is a kind of kernel density estimate. The data is divided into nonoverlapping intervals and counts of the number of data points within each interval are made. Histograms are bar graphs that depict these frequency counts—the bar is centered at the midpoint of each interval—and its height reflects the average number of data points in the interval.

In more general kernel density estimates, the range is still divided into intervals and estimates of the density at the center of intervals are produced. One difference is that the intervals are allowed to overlap. One can think of sliding the interval—called a window—along the range of the data and collecting the center-point density estimates. The second difference is that, rather than merely counting the number of observations in a window, a weight between 0 and 1 is assigned—based on the distance from the center of the window—and it is the weighted values that are summed. The function that determines these weights is called the kernel.

Kernel density estimates have the advantages of being smooth and of being independent of the choice of origin (corresponding to the location of the bins in a histogram).

See Salgado-Ugarte, Shimizu, and Taniuchi (1993) and Fox (1990) for discussions of kernel density estimators, stressing their use as exploratory data analysis tools.

▷ Example

Goeden (1978) reports data consisting of 316 length observations of coral trout. We wish to investigate the underlying density of the lengths. To begin on familiar ground, we might draw a histogram. In [G] **histogram**, we suggest setting the bins to $\min(\sqrt{n}, 10 \cdot \log_{10} n)$, which for $n = 316$ is roughly 18:

. graph length, xlab ylab bin(18)

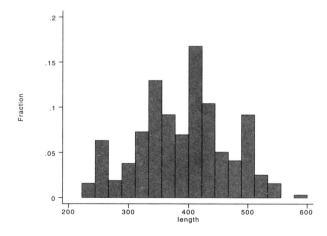

The kernel density estimate, on the other hand, is smooth.

. kdensity length, xlab ylab

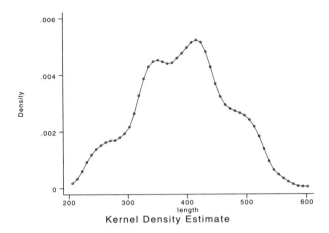

Kernel density estimators are, however, sensitive to an assumption just as are histograms. In histograms, we specify a number of bins. For kernel density estimators, we specify a width. In the graph above, we used the default width. **kdensity** is smarter than **graph, histogram** in that its default width is not a fixed constant, but even so, the default width is not necessarily best.

kdensity saves the width in the return scalar **width**, so typing **display r(width)** reveals it. Doing this, we discover the width is approximately 20.

Widths are similar to the inverse of the number of bins in a histogram; smaller widths mean more detail. The units of the width are the units of x, the variable being analyzed. The width is specified as a halfwidth, meaning the kernel density estimator with halfwidth 20 corresponds to sliding a window of size 40 across the data.

We can specify halfwidths for ourselves using the **width()** option. Smaller widths do not smooth the density as much:

. kdensity length, epan xlab ylab w(10)

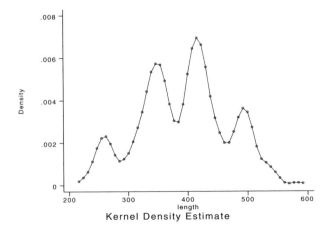

. kdensity length, epan xlab ylab w(15)

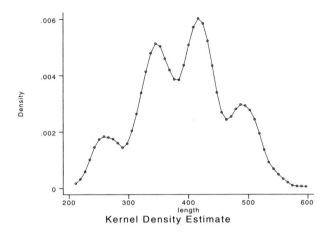

Kernel Density Estimate

◁

▷ Example

Widths held constant, different kernels can produce surprisingly different results. This is really an attribute of the kernel and width combination; for a given width, some kernels are more sensitive than others at identifying peaks in the density estimate.

We can see this using a dataset with lots of peaks. In the automobile data, we characterize the density of weight, the weight of the vehicles. Below, we compare the Epanechnikov and Parzen kernels.

. kdensity weight, epan nogr g(x epan)

. kdensity weight, parzen nogr g(x2 parzen)

. label var epan "Epanechnikov Density Estimate"

. label var parzen "Parzen Density Estimate"

. gr epan parzen x, xlab ylab c(ll)

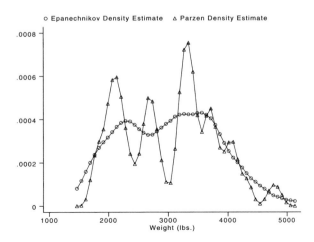

We did not specify a width and so obtained the default width. That width is not a function of the selected kernel, but of data. See the *Methods and Formulas* section for the calculation of the optimal width.

◁

▷ Example

In examining the density estimates, we may wish to overlay a normal density or a Student's *t* density for comparison. Using automobile weights, we can get an idea of the distance from normality with the `normal` option.

```
. kdensity weight, epan normal xlab ylab
```

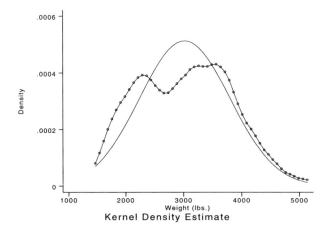

Kernel Density Estimate

◁

▷ Example

Another common desire in examining density estimates is to compare two or more densities. In this example, we will compare the density estimates of the weights for the foreign and domestic cars.

```
. kdensity weight, nogr gen(x fx)
. kdensity weight if foreign==0, nogr gen(fx0) at(x)
. kdensity weight if foreign==1, nogr gen(fx1) at(x)
. label var fx0 "Domestic cars"
. label var fx1 "Foreign cars"
```

(*Continued on next page*)

```
. gr fx0 fx1 x, c(ll) s(TS) xlab ylab
```

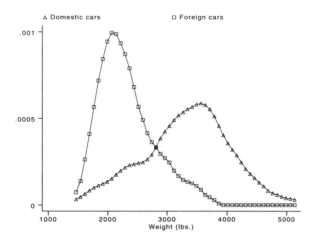

Saved Results

kdensity saves in r():

Scalars
    r(width)   kernel bandwidth
    r(n)   number of points at which the estimate was evaluated
    r(scale)   density bin width

Macros
    r(kernel) name of kernel

Methods and Formulas

kdensity is implemented as an ado-file.

A kernel density estimate is formed by summing the weighted values calculated with the kernel function K as in

$$\widehat{f}_K = \frac{1}{nh} \sum_{i=1}^{n} K\left[\frac{x - X_i}{h}\right]$$

where we may define various kernel functions. kdensity includes seven different kernel functions. The Epanechnikov is the default function if no other kernel is specified and has the property that it is the most efficient in minimizing the mean integrated squared error.

Kernel	Formula	
Biweight	$K[z] = \begin{cases} \frac{15}{16}(1-z^2)^2 \\ 0 \end{cases}$	if $|z| < 1$ otherwise
Cosine	$K[z] = \begin{cases} 1 + \cos(2\pi z) \\ 0 \end{cases}$	if $|z| < 1/2$ otherwise
Epanechnikov	$K[z] = \begin{cases} \frac{3}{4}(1 - \frac{1}{5}z^2)/\sqrt{5} \\ 0 \end{cases}$	if $|z| < \sqrt{5}$ otherwise
Gaussian	$K[z] = \frac{1}{\sqrt{2\pi}} e^{-z^2/2}$	
Parzen	$K[z] = \begin{cases} \frac{4}{3} - 8z^2 + 8|z|^3 \\ 8(1 - |z|)^3/3 \end{cases}$	if $|z| \leq 1/2$ otherwise
Rectangular	$K[z] = \begin{cases} 1/2 \\ 0 \end{cases}$	if $|z| < 1$ otherwise
Triangular	$K[z] = \begin{cases} 1 - |z| \\ 0 \end{cases}$	if $|z| < 1$ otherwise

From the definitions given in the table one can see that the choice of h will drive how many values are included in estimating the density at each point. This value is called the *window width* or *bandwidth*. If the window width is not specified, then it is determined as

$$m = \min\left(\sqrt{\text{variance}_x}, \ \frac{\text{interquartile range}_x}{1.349}\right)$$

$$h = \frac{0.9m}{n^{1/5}}$$

where x is the variable for which we wish to estimate the kernel and n is the number of observations.

Most researchers agree that the choice of kernel is not as important as the choice of bandwidth. There is a great deal of literature on choosing bandwidths under various conditions; see for example Parzen (1962) or Tapia and Thompson (1978). See also Newton (1988) for a comparison with sample spectral density estimation in time-series applications.

Acknowledgments

We gratefully acknowledge the previous work by Isaías H. Salgado-Ugarte of Universidad Nacional Autonoma de Mexico, and Makoto Shimizu and Toru Taniuchi of the University of Tokyo; see Salgado-Ugarte, Shimizu, and Taniuchi (1993). Their article provides the reader with a good overview of the subject of univariate kernel density estimation and presents arguments for its use in exploratory data analysis.

References

Fox, J. 1990. Describing univariate distributions. In *Modern Methods of Data Analysis*, ed. J. Fox and J. S. Long, 58–125. Newbury Park, CA: Sage Publications.

Goeden, G. B. 1978. A monograph of the coral trout, *Plectropomus leopardus* (Lacépède). *Res. Bull. Fish. Serv. Queensl.* 1: 42 p.

Newton, H. J. 1988. *TIMESLAB: A Time Series Analysis Laboratory.* Belmont, CA: Wadsworth & Brooks/Cole.

Parzen, E. 1962. On estimation of a probability density function and mode. *Annals of Mathematical Statistics* 32: 1065–1076.

Salgado-Ugarte, I. H., M. Shimizu, and T. Taniuchi. 1993. snp6: Exploring the shape of univariate data using kernel density estimators. *Stata Technical Bulletin* 16: 8–19. Reprinted in *Stata Technical Bulletin Reprints*, vol. 3, pp. 155–173.

——. 1995. snp6.1: ASH, WARPing, and kernel density estimation for univariate data. *Stata Technical Bulletin* 26: 23–31. Reprinted in *Stata Technical Bulletin Reprints*, vol. 5, pp. 161–172.

——. 1995. snp6.2: Practical rules for bandwidth selection in univariate density estimation. *Stata Technical Bulletin* 27: 5–19. Reprinted in *Stata Technical Bulletin Reprints*, vol. 5, pp. 172–190.

——. 1997. snp13: Nonparametric assessment of multimodality for univariate data. *Stata Technical Bulletin* 38: 27–35. Reprinted in *Stata Technical Bulletin Reprints*, vol. 7, pp. 232–243.

Silverman, B. W. 1986. *Density Estimation for Statistics and Data Analysis.* London: Chapman & Hall.

Tapia, R. A. and J. R. Thompson. 1978. *Nonparametric Probability Density Estimation.* Baltimore: Johns Hopkins University Press.

Also See

Related:	[R] **hist**
Background:	*Stata Graphics Manual*

Title

ksm — Smoothing including lowess

Syntax

ksm *yvar xvar* [if *exp*] [in *range*] [, <u>line</u> <u>we</u>ight <u>low</u>ess <u>bw</u>idth(*#*) <u>logit</u>

<u>ad</u>just gen(*newvar*) <u>no</u>graph *graph_options*]

Description

ksm carries out unweighted and locally weighted smoothing of *yvar* on *xvar*, displays the graph, and optionally saves the smoothed variable. Among **ksm**'s capabilities are lowess (robust locally weighted regression, Cleveland 1979). See Cleveland (1993, 94–101) for a discussion of lowess.

Warning: **ksm** is computationally intensive and may therefore take a long time to run on a slow computer. Lowess calculations on 1,000 observations, for instance, require estimating 1,000 regressions.

Options

line specifies running-line least-squares smoothing; default is running mean.

weight specifies use of Cleveland's (1979) tricube weighting function; default is unweighted.

lowess is equivalent to specifying **line weight** and requests Cleveland's lowess running-line smoother.

bwidth(*#*) specifies the bandwidth. Centered subsets of **bwidth** $\cdot$ N observations are used for calculating smoothed values for each point in the data except for the end points, where smaller, uncentered subsets are used. The greater the **bwidth**, the greater the smoothing. Default is 0.8.

logit transforms the smoothed *yvar* into logits. Predicted values less than .0001 or greater than .9999 are set to $1/N$ and $1 - 1/N$, respectively, before taking logits.

adjust adjusts the mean of the smoothed *yvar* to equal the mean of *yvar* by multiplying by an appropriate factor. This is useful when smoothing binary (0/1) data.

gen(*newvar*) creates *newvar* containing the smoothed values of *yvar* in addition to or instead of displaying the graph.

nograph suppresses displaying the graph.

graph_options are any of the options allowed with **graph, twoway**; see [G] **graph options**.

Remarks

The most common use of **ksm** is to provide lowess—locally weighted scatterplot smoothing. The basic idea is to create a new variable (*newvar*) that, for each *yvar* y_i, contains the corresponding smoothed value. The smoothed values are obtained by running a regression of *yvar* on *xvar* using only the data (x_i, y_i) and a small amount of the data near the point. In lowess, the regression is weighted so that the central point (x_i, y_i) gets the highest weight and points farther away (based on the distance $|x_j - x_i|$) receive less. The estimated regression is then used to predict the smoothed value $\widehat{y}_i$ for y_i only. The procedure is repeated to obtain the remaining smoothed values, which means a separate weighted regression is estimated for every point in the data.

Lowess is a desirable smoother because of its locality—it tends to follow the data. Polynomial smoothing methods, for instance, are global in that what happens on the extreme left of a scatterplot can affect the fitted values on the extreme right.

▷ Example

The amount of smoothing is affected by the **bwidth** and you are warned to experiment with different values. For instance:

. ksm h1 depth, lowess ylab xlab s(Oi)

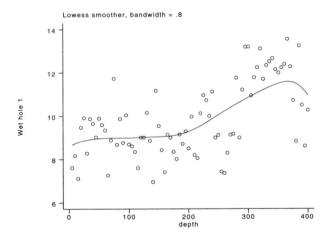

Now compare with

. ksm h1 depth, lowess ylab xlab s(Oi) bwidth(.4)

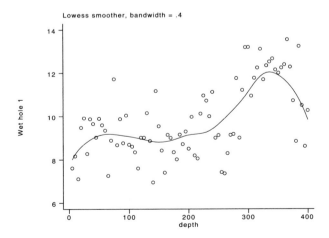

In the first case, the default bandwidth of 0.8 is used, meaning 80% of the data are used in smoothing each point. In the second case, we explicitly specified a bandwidth of 0.4. Smaller bandwidths follow the original data more closely.

◁

▷ Example

Two **ksm** options are especially useful with binary (0/1) data: **adjust** and **logit**. **adjust** adjusts the resulting curve (by multiplication) so that the mean of the smoothed values is equal to the mean of the unsmoothed values. **logit** specifies the smoothed curve is to be in terms of the log of the odds ratio:

```
. ksm foreign mpg, lowess ylab xlab jitter(5) adjust
```

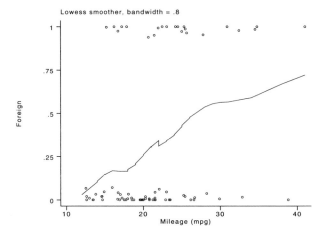

```
. ksm foreign mpg, lowess ylab xlab logit yline(0)
```

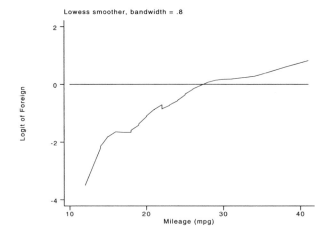

With binary data, if you do not use the **logit** option, it is a good idea to specify **graph**'s **jitter()**

option; see [G] **graph options**. Since the underlying data (whether the car was manufactured outside the United States in this case) takes on only two values, raw data points are more likely to be on top of each other, thus making it impossible to tell how many points there are. graph's jitter() option adds some noise to the data to shift the points around. This noise affects only the location of points on the graph, not the lowess curve.

When you do specify the logit option, the display of the raw data is suppressed.

◁

❏ Technical Note

ksm can be used for other than lowess smoothing. Lowess can be usefully thought of as a combination of two smoothing concepts: the use of predicted values from regression (rather than means) for imputing a smoothed value and the use of the tricube weighting function (rather than a constant weighting function). ksm allows you to combine these concepts freely. You can use line smoothing without weighting (specify line), or mean smoothing without weighting (specify no options), or mean smoothing with tricube weighting (specify weight). Specifying both weight and line is the same as specifying lowess.

❏

Methods and Formulas

ksm is implemented as an ado-file.

Let y_i and x_i be the two variables and assume the data is ordered so that $x_i \leq x_{i+1}$ for $i = 1, \ldots, N - 1$. For each y_i, a smoothed value y_i^s is calculated.

The subset used in calculation of y_i^s are indices $i_- = \max(1, i - k)$ through $i_+ = \min(i + k, N)$, where $k = \lfloor (N \cdot \text{bwidth} - 0.5)/2 \rfloor$. The weights for each of the observations between $j = i_-, \ldots, i_+$ are either 1 (default) or the tricube (weight):

$$w_j = \left(1 - \left(\frac{|x_j - x_i|}{\Delta} \right)^3 \right)^3$$

where $\Delta = 1.0001 \max(x_+ - x_i, x_i - x_-)$. The smoothed value y_i^s is then the (weighted) mean or the (weighted) regression prediction (line).

Acknowledgment

ksm was written by Patrick Royston of the Imperial College School of Medicine, London.

References

Chambers, J. M., W. S. Cleveland, B. Kleiner, and P. A. Tukey. 1983. *Graphical Methods for Data Analysis*. Belmont, CA: Wadsworth International Group.

Cleveland, W. S. 1979. Robust locally weighted regression and smoothing scatterplots. *Journal of the American Statistical Association* 74: 829–836.

——. 1993. *Visualizing Data*. Summit, NJ: Hobart Press.

——. 1994. *The Elements of Graphing Data*. Summit, NJ: Hobart Press.

Goodall, C. 1990. A survey of smoothing techniques. In *Modern Methods of Data Analysis*, ed. J. Fox and J. S. Long, 126–176. Newbury Park, CA: Sage Publications.

Royston, P. 1991. gr6: Lowess smoothing. *Stata Technical Bulletin* 3: 7–9. Reprinted in *Stata Technical Bulletin Reprints*, vol. 1, pp. 41–44.

Salgado-Ugarte, I. H. and M. Shimizu. 1995. snp8: Robust scatterplot smoothing: enhancements to Stata's ksm. *Stata Technical Bulletin* 25: 23–25. Reprinted in *Stata Technical Bulletin Reprints*, vol. 5, pp. 190–194.

Sasieni, P. 1994. snp7: Natural cubic splines. *Stata Technical Bulletin* 22: 19–22. Reprinted in *Stata Technical Bulletin Reprints*, vol. 4, pp. 171–174.

Also See

Related:	[R] **ipolate**, [R] **smooth**
Background:	*Stata Graphics Manual*

Title

> **ksmirnov** — Kolmogorov–Smirnov equality of distributions test

Syntax

ksmirnov *varname* = *exp* [if *exp*] [in *range*]

ksmirnov *varname* [if *exp*] [in *range*] , by(*groupvar*) [e̲xact]

Description

ksmirnov performs one- and two-sample Kolmogorov–Smirnov tests of the equality of distributions. In the first syntax, *varname* is the variable whose distribution is being tested and *exp* must evaluate to the corresponding (theoretical) cumulative. In the second syntax, *groupvar* must take on two distinct values. The distribution of *varname* for the first value of *groupvar* is compared with that of the second value.

When testing for normality, please see [R] **sktest** and [R] **swilk**.

Options

e̲xact specifies the exact p-value is to be computed. This may take a long time if $n > 50$.

Remarks

▷ Example

You have data on x that resulted from two different experiments, labeled as group==1 and group==2. Your data contains

```
. list
          group        x
  1.          2        2
  2.          1        0
  3.          2        3
  4.          1        4
  5.          1        5
  6.          2        8
  7.          2       10
```

You wish to use the two-sample Kolmogorov–Smirnov test to determine if there are any differences in the distribution of x for these two groups:

```
. ksmirnov x, by(group)
Two-sample Kolmogorov-Smirnov test for equality of distribution functions:
Smaller group        D       P-value  Corrected
----------------------------------------------------
1:                0.5000     0.424
2:               -0.1667     0.909
Combined K-S:     0.5000     0.785      0.735
```

157

The first line tests the hypothesis that **x** for group 1 contains *smaller* values than group 2. The largest difference between the distribution functions is 0.5. The approximate p-value for this is 0.424, which is not significant.

The second line tests the hypothesis that **x** for group 1 contains *larger* values than group 2. The largest difference between the distribution functions in this direction is 0.1667. The approximate p-value for this small difference is 0.909.

Finally, the approximate p-value for the combined test is 0.785, corrected to 0.735. The p-values **ksmirnov** calculates are based on the asymptotic distributions derived by Smirnov (1939). These approximations are not very good for small samples ($n < 50$). They are too conservative—real p-values tend to be substantially smaller. We have also included a less conservative approximation for the nondirectional hypothesis based on an empirical continuity correction. That is the 0.734 number reported in the third column.

That number, too, is only an approximation. An exact value can be calculated using the **exact** option:

```
. ksmirnov x, by(group) exact
Two-sample Kolmogorov-Smirnov test for equality of distribution functions:
  Smaller group       D       P-value      Exact
  -------------------------------------------------
  1:                0.5000    0.424
  2:               -0.1667    0.909
  Combined K-S:     0.5000    0.785        0.657
```

◁

▷ Example

Let's now test whether **x** in the example above is distributed normally. Kolmogorov–Smirnov is not a particularly powerful test in testing for normality and we do not endorse such use of it; see [R] **sktest** and [R] **swilk** for better tests.

In any case, we will test against a normal distribution with the same mean and standard deviation:

```
. summarize x
  Variable |    Obs       Mean    Std. Dev.        Min        Max
  ---------+-----------------------------------------------------
         x |      7   4.571429    3.457222          0         10
. ksmirnov x = normprob((x-4.571429)/3.457222)
One-Sample Kolmogorov-Smirnov test against theoretical distribution
          normprob((x-4.571429)/3.457222)

  Smaller group       D       P-value   Corrected
  -------------------------------------------------
  x:                0.1650    0.683
  Cumulative:      -0.1250    0.803
  Combined K-S:     0.1650    0.991        0.978
```

Since Stata has no way of knowing that you based this calculation on the calculated mean and standard deviation of **x**, the test statistics will be slightly conservative in addition to being approximations. Nevertheless, they clearly indicate that the data cannot be distinguished from normally distributed data.

◁

Saved Results

ksmirnov saves in r():

Scalars

r(D_1)	D from line 1	r(D)	combined D
r(p_1)	p-value from line 1	r(p)	combined p-value
r(D_2)	D from line 2	r(p_exact)	combined significance (χ^2 or exact)
r(p_2)	p-value from line 2		

Macros

r(group1)	name of group from line 1	r(group2)	name of group from line 2

Methods and Formulas

ksmirnov is implemented as an ado-file.

In general, the Kolmogorov–Smirnov test (Kolmogorov 1933; Smirnov 1939; also see Conover 1980, "Statistics of the Kolmogorov–Smirnov type", 344–385) is not very powerful against differences in the tails of distributions. In return for this, it is fairly powerful for alternative hypotheses that involve lumpiness or clustering in the data.

The directional hypotheses are evaluated with the statistics

$$D^+ = \max_x \Big(F(x) - G(x) \Big)$$
$$D^- = \min_x \Big(F(x) - G(x) \Big)$$

where $F(x)$ and $G(x)$ are the empirical distribution functions for the sample being compared. The combined statistic is

$$D = \max \Big(|D^+|, |D^-| \Big)$$

The p-value for this statistic may be obtained by evaluating the asymptotic limiting distribution. Let m be the sample size for the first sample, and n be the sample size for the second sample. It was shown by Smirnov (1939) that

$$\lim_{m,n\to\infty} P\Big(\sqrt{mn/(m+n)} D_{m,n} \le z \Big) = 1 - 2 \sum_{i=1}^{\infty} (-1)^{i-1} \exp\big(-2i^2 z^2 \big)$$

The first 5 terms form the approximation P_a used by Stata. The exact p-value is calculated by a counting algorithm; see Gibbons (1971, 127–131). A corrected p-value was obtained by modifying the asymptotic p-value using a numerical approximation technique

$$Z = \Phi^{-1}(P_a) + 1.04/\min(m,n) + 2.09/\max(m,n) - 1.35/\sqrt{mn/(m+n)}$$
$$P = \Phi(Z)$$

where $\Phi()$ is the cumulative normal distribution.

References

Conover, W. J. 1980. *Practical Nonparametric Statistics*. 2d ed. New York: John Wiley & Sons.

Gibbons, J. D. 1971. *Nonparametric Statistical Inference*. New York: McGraw–Hill.

Kolmogorov, A. N. 1933. Sulla determinazione empirica di una legge di distribuzione. *Giornale dell' Istituto Italiano degli Attuari* 4: 83–91.

Smirnov, N. V. 1939. Estimate of deviation between empirical distribution functions in two independent samples (in Russian). *Bulletin Moscow University* 2(2): 3–16.

Also See

Related: [R] **runtest**, [R] **sktest**, [R] **swilk**

Title

kwallis — Kruskal–Wallis equality of populations rank test

Syntax

kwallis *varname* [if *exp*] [in *range*], by(*groupvar*)

Description

kwallis tests the hypothesis that several samples are from the same population. In the syntax diagram above, *varname* refers to the variable recording the outcome and *groupvar* refers to the variable denoting the population. Note that the by() "option" is not optional.

Remarks

▷ Example

You have data on the 50 states. The data contains the median age of the population medage and the region of the country region for each state. You wish to test for the equality of the median age distribution across all four regions simultaneously:

```
. kwallis medage, by(region)
Test: Equality of populations (Kruskal-Wallis Test)
region          _Obs      _RankSum
NE                 9        376.50
N Cntrl           12        294.00
South             16        398.00
West              13        206.50

chi-squared =     17.041 with 3 d.f.
probability =      0.0007
```

From the output we see that we can reject the hypothesis that the populations are the same at any level below 0.07%.

◁

Saved Results

kwallis saves in r():

Scalars

r(df)	degrees of freedom	r(chi2)	χ^2

Methods and Formulas

`kwallis` is implemented as an ado-file.

The Kruskal–Wallis test (Kruskal and Wallis 1952; also see Conover 1980, 229–237 or Altman 1991, 213–215) is a multiple-sample generalization of the two-sample Wilcoxon (also called Mann–Whitney) rank sum test (Wilcoxon 1945; Mann and Whitney 1947). Samples of sizes n_j, $j = 1, \ldots, m$, are combined and ranked in ascending order of magnitude. Tied values are assigned the average ranks. Let n denote the overall sample size and let R_j denote the sum of the ranks for the jth sample. The Kruskal–Wallis one-way analysis-of-variance test H is defined as

$$H = \frac{12}{n(n+1)} \sum_{j=1}^{m} \frac{R_j^2}{n_j} - 3(n+1)$$

The sampling distribution of H is approximately χ^2 with $m - 1$ degrees of freedom.

References

Altman, D. G. 1991. *Practical Statistics for Medical Research*. London: Chapman & Hall.

Conover, W. J. 1980. *Practical Nonparametric Statistics*. 2d ed. New York: John Wiley & Sons.

Kruskal, W. H. and W. A. Wallis. 1952. Use of ranks in one-criterion variance analysis. *Journal of the American Statistical Association* 47: 583–621.

Mann, H. B. and D. R. Whitney. 1947. On a test of whether one of two random variables is stochastically larger than the other. *Annals of Mathematical Statistics* 18: 50–60.

Wilcoxon, F. 1945. Individual comparisons by ranking methods. *Biometrics* 1: 80–83.

Also See

Related: [R] **nptrend**, [R] **oneway**, [R] **runtest**, [R] **signrank**

Title

label — Label manipulation

Syntax

<u>la</u>bel <u>data</u> ["label"]

<u>la</u>bel <u>def</u>ine lblname # "label" [# "label" ...] [, <u>a</u>dd modify nofix]

<u>la</u>bel <u>dir</u>

<u>la</u>bel <u>drop</u> { lblname [lblname ...] | _all }

<u>la</u>bel <u>list</u> [lblname [lblname ...]]

<u>la</u>bel <u>save</u> [lblname [lblname ...]] using filename [, replace]

<u>la</u>bel <u>val</u>ues varname [lblname] [, nofix]

<u>la</u>bel <u>var</u>iable varname ["label"]

Description

label data attaches a label (up to 80 characters) to the data in memory. Dataset labels are displayed when you use the data and when you describe it. If no label is specified, any existing label is removed.

label define defines a list of up to 65,536 (1,000 for Small Stata) associations of integers and text called a value label. The value label is attached to variables by label values.

label dir lists the names of value labels stored in memory.

label drop eliminates value labels.

label list lists the names and contents of value labels stored in memory.

label save saves value labels in a do-file.

label values attaches a value label to a variable. If no value label is specified, any existing value label is detached. The value label, however, is not deleted.

label variable attaches a label (up to 80 characters) to a variable. If no label is specified, any existing variable label is removed.

Options

add allows additional # ↔ label correspondences to be added to lblname. If add is not specified, only new lblnames may be created. If add is specified, you may create new lblnames or add new entries to existing lblnames.

modify allows modification or deletion of existing $\# \leftrightarrow label$ correspondences as well as allowing additional correspondences to be added. Specifying modify implies add even if you do not type the add option.

nofix prevents display formats from being widened according to the maximum length of the value label. Consider label values myvar mylab and pretend that myvar has a %9.0g display format right now. Pretend that the maximum length of the strings in mylab is 12 characters. Then label values would change the format of myvar from %9.0g to %12.0g. nofix prevents this.

nofix is also allowed with label define, but it is relevant only when you are modifying an existing value label. Without the nofix option, label define finds all the variables that use this value label and considers widening their display formats. nofix prevents this.

replace allows *filename* to be replaced even if it already exists.

Remarks

See [U] **15.6 Dataset, variable, and value labels** for a complete description of labels. This entry deals only with details not covered there.

label dir lists the names of all defined value labels. The label list command displays the contents of a value label.

▷ Example

Although describe shows the names of the value labels, those value labels may not exist. Stata does not consider it an error to label the values of a variable with a nonexistent label. When this occurs, Stata still shows the association on describe but otherwise acts as if the variable's values are unlabeled. This way, you can associate a value label name with a variable before creating the corresponding label. Similarly, you can define labels that you have not yet used.

label dir shows you the labels that you actually have defined:

```
. label dir
yesno
sexlbl
```

We have two value labels stored in memory: one called yesno and the other called sexlbl.

We can display the contents of a value label using the label list command:

```
. label list yesno
yesno:
            1 yes
            2 no
```

The value label yesno labels the values 1 as yes and 2 as no.

If you do not specify the name of the value label on the label list command, a listing of all value labels is produced:

```
. label list
yesno:
            1 yes
            2 no
sexlbl:
            0 Male
            1 Female
```

◁

❏ Technical Note

Since Stata can have more value labels stored in memory than are actually used in the data, you may wonder what happens when you **save** the data. In that case, Stata stores with the data only those value labels actually associated with variables.

When you **use** a dataset, Stata eliminates all the value labels stored in memory before loading the data.

❏

You can add new codings to an existing value label using the **add** option with the **label define** command. You can modify existing codings using the **modify** option.

▷ Example

The label **yesno** codes 1 as **yes** and 2 as **no**. Perhaps at some later time you wish to add a third coding: 3 as **maybe**. Typing **label define** without any options results in an error:

```
. label define yesno 3 maybe
label yesno already defined
r(110);
```

If you do not specify the **add** or **modify** options, **label define** can be used only to create *new* value labels. The **add** option lets you add codings to an existing label:

```
. label define yesno 3 maybe, add
. label list yesno
yesno:
          1 yes
          2 no
          3 maybe
```

Perhaps you have accidentally mislabeled a value. For instance, 3 may not mean "maybe" but may instead mean "don't know". **add** will not allow you to change an existing labeling:

```
. label define yesno 3 "don't know", add
invalid attempt to modify label
r(180);
```

Instead, you specify the **modify** option:

```
. label define yesno 3 "don't know", modify
. label list yesno
yesno:
          1 yes
          2 no
          3 don't know
```

In this way, Stata attempts to protect you from yourself. If you type **label define** without any options, you can only create a new value label—you cannot accidentally mutilate an existing one. If you specify the **add** option, you can add new labelings to a label, but you cannot accidentally change one of the existing labelings. If you specify the **modify** option, which you may not abbreviate, you can do whatever you want.

You can even use the **modify** option to eliminate existing labelings. To do this, you map the numeric code to a *null string*, that is, **""**:

```
. label define yesno 3 "", modify
```

```
. label list yesno
yesno:
                1 yes
                2 no
```
◁

You can eliminate entire value labels using the `label drop` command.

▷ Example

We currently have two value labels stored in memory—`sexlbl` and `yesno`. The `label dir` command reports that:

```
. label dir
yesno
sexlbl
```

The data that we have in memory uses only one of the labels—`sexlbl`. `describe` reports that:

```
. describe
Contains data from emp.dta
  obs:           7                     1992 Employee Data
  vars:          4                     10 Aug 1998 12:09
  size:        224 (99.9% of memory free)
-------------------------------------------------------------------------------
    1. name      str16  %16s
    2. empno      float  %9.0g                 Employee number
    3. sex        float  %9.0g      sexlbl     0=male; 1=female
    4. salary     float  %9.0g                 Annual salary, exclusive of
                                               bonus
-------------------------------------------------------------------------------
Sorted by:
```

We can eliminate the `yesno` label by typing `label drop yesno`:

```
. label drop yesno
. label dir
sexlbl
```

We could eliminate *all* the value labels in memory by typing

```
. label drop _all
. label dir
. _
```

Remember that the value label `sexlbl`, which no longer exists, was associated with the variable `sex`. Even after dropping the value label, `sexlbl` is still associated with the variable:

```
. describe
Contains data from emp.dta
  obs:           7                     1992 Employee Data
  vars:          4                     10 Aug 1998 12:09
  size:        224 (99.9% of memory free)
-------------------------------------------------------------------------------
    1. name      str16  %16s
    2. empno      float  %9.0g                 Employee number
    3. sex        float  %9.0g      sexlbl     0=male; 1=female
    4. salary     float  %9.0g                 Annual salary, exclusive of
                                               bonus
-------------------------------------------------------------------------------
Sorted by:
```

As stated earlier, Stata does not mind if a nonexistent value label is associated with a variable. When Stata uses such a variable, it simply acts as if it is not labeled:

```
. list in 1/4
              name      empno       sex     salary
   1.   Hank Rogers      57213         0      24000
   2.     Pat Welch      47229         1      27000
   3. Bob Underhill      57323         0      24000
   4. Richard Doyle      57401         0      24500
```

◁

The `label save` command creates a *do-file* containing `label define` commands for each label you specify. If you do not specify the *lblnames*, all value labels are stored in the file. If you do not specify the extension for *filename*, `.do` is assumed.

▷ Example

Labels are automatically stored with your dataset when you `save` it. Conversely, the `use` command drops all labels before loading the new dataset. You may occasionally wish to move a value label from one dataset to another. The `label save` command allows you to do this.

For example, assume we currently have the value label `yesno` in memory:

```
. label list yesno
yesno:
              1 yes
              2 no
              3 maybe
```

You have a dataset stored on disk called `survey.dta` to which you wish to add this value label. One alternative is to `use survey` and then retype the `label define yesno` command. Retyping the label would not be too tedious in this case, but if the value label in memory mapped, say, the 50 states of the union, retyping it would be irksome. `label save` provides an alternative:

```
. label save yesno using ynfile
file ynfile.do saved
```

Typing `label save yesno using ynfile` caused Stata to create a do-file called `ynfile.do` containing the definition of the `yesno` label.

If we want to see the contents of the file, we can use the Stata `type` command:

```
. type ynfile.do
label define yesno 1 `"yes"´, modify
label define yesno 2 `"no"´, modify
label define yesno 3 `"maybe"´, modify
```

We can now `use` our new dataset, `survey.dta`:

```
. use survey
(Household survey data)
. label dir

. _
```

Using the new dataset causes Stata to eliminate all value labels stored in memory. The label yesno is now gone. Since we saved it in the file ynfile.do, however, we can get it back by typing either do ynfile or run ynfile. If we type do, we will see the commands in the file execute. If we type run, the file will execute silently:

```
. run ynfile
. label dir
yesno
```

The label is now just as if we had typed it from the keyboard.

◁

❑ Technical Note

You can also use the label save command to make editing of value labels easier. You can save a label in a file, leave Stata and use your word processor or editor to edit the label, and then return to Stata. Using do or run, you can load the edited values.

❑

References

Gleason, J. R. 1998. dm56: A labels editor for Windows and Macintosh. *Stata Technical Bulletin* 43: 3–6.

Weesie, J. 1997. dm47: Verifying value label mappings. *Stata Technical Bulletin* 37: 7–8. Reprinted in *Stata Technical Bulletin Reprints*, vol. 7, pp. 39–40.

Also See

Background: [U] **15.6 Dataset, variable, and value labels**

Title

ladder — Ladder of powers

Syntax

ladder *varname* [if *exp*] [in *range*] [, generate(*newvar*) noadjust]

gladder *varname* [if *exp*] [in *range*] [, bin(*#*) *graph_options*]

Description

ladder searches a subset of the ladder of powers (Tukey 1977) for a transform that converts *varname* into a normally distributed variable. sktest is used to test for normality; see [R] **sktest**. Also see [R] **boxcox**.

gladder displays nine histograms of transforms of *varname* according to the ladder of powers.

Options

generate(*newvar*) saves the transformed values corresponding to the minimum chi-squared value from the table. Its use is not, in general, recommended since generate() is quite literal in its interpretation of minimum, thus ignoring nearly equal but perhaps more interpretable transforms.

noadjust is the noadjust option to sktest; see [R] **sktest**.

bin(*#*) specifies the number of bins for the histograms. If not specified, an intelligent choice is made for you (see *Methods and Formulas* below).

graph_options are any of the options allowed with graph, histogram; see [G] **histogram**.

Remarks

▷ Example

You have data on the mileage rating of 74 automobiles and wish to find a transform that makes the variable normally distributed:

```
. ladder mpg
Transformation        formula         Chi-sq(2)    P(Chi-sq)
-----------------------------------------------------------
cube                  mpg^3             43.59        0.000
square                mpg^2             27.03        0.000
raw                   mpg               10.95        0.004
square-root           sqrt(mpg)          4.94        0.084
log                   log(mpg)           0.87        0.647
reciprocal root       1/sqrt(mpg)        0.20        0.905
reciprocal            1/mpg              2.36        0.307
reciprocal square     1/(mpg^2)         11.99        0.002
reciprocal cube       1/(mpg^3)         24.30        0.000
```

Had we typed `ladder mpg, gen(mpgx)`, the variable `mpgx` would have been automatically generated for us containing $1/\sqrt{mpg}$. This is the perfect example of why you should not, in general, specify the `generate()` option. Note that we also cannot reject the hypothesis that the reciprocal of `mpg` is normally distributed and $1/mpg$—gallons per mile—has a better interpretation. It is a measure of energy consumption.

◁

▷ Example

`gladder` explores the same transforms as `ladder` but presents results graphically:

. `gladder mpg`

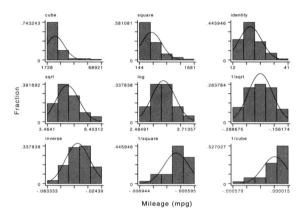

Mileage (mpg)
Histograms by Transformation

◁

❑ Technical Note

`gladder` is useful pedagogically, but some caution must be exercised when using it for research work, especially with large numbers of observations. For instance, consider the following data on the average July temperature in degrees Fahrenheit for 954 U.S. cities:

. `ladder tempjuly`

Transformation	formula	Chi-sq(2)	P(Chi-sq)
cube	tempjuly^3	47.49	0.000
square	tempjuly^2	19.70	0.000
raw	tempjuly	3.83	0.147
square-root	sqrt(tempjuly)	1.83	0.400
log	log(tempjuly)	5.40	0.067
reciprocal root	1/sqrt(tempjuly)	13.72	0.001
reciprocal	1/tempjuly	26.36	0.000
reciprocal square	1/(tempjuly^2)	64.43	0.000
reciprocal cube	1/(tempjuly^3)	.	0.000

The period in the last line indicates that the χ^2 is very large; see [R] **sktest**.

From the table, we see that there is certainly a difference, normality-wise, between the square and square-root transform. If, however, you can see the difference between the transforms in the diagram below, you have better eyes than we do:

. gladder tempjuly

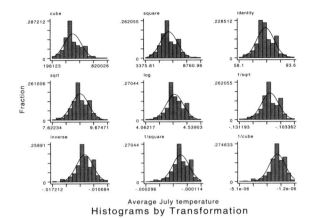

Average July temperature
Histograms by Transformation

A better graph for seeing normality is the quantile-normal graph as produced by qnorm; see [R] **diagplots**. That graph shows that for the square transform, the upper tail, and only the upper tail, diverges from what would be expected. This is detected by sktest as a problem with skewness, as we would learn from using sktest to examine tempjuly squared and square-rooted.

❏

Methods and Formulas

ladder and gladder are implemented as ado-files.

For ladder, results are as reported by sktest; see [R] **sktest**. If generate() is specified, the transform with the minimum χ^2 value is chosen.

gladder sets the number of bins to $\min(\sqrt{n}, 10\log_{10} n)$, rounded to the closest integer, where n is the number of *unique* values of *varname*. See [G] **histogram** for a discussion of the optimal number of bins.

Also see Findley (1990) for a ladder-of-powers variable transformation program that produces one-way graphs with overlaid box plots, in addition to histograms with overlaid normals. Buchner and Findley (1990) discuss ladder-of-powers transformations as one aspect of preliminary data analysis. Also see Hamilton (1992, 18–23).

References

Buchner, D. M. and T. W. Findley. 1990. Research in physical medicine and rehabilitation: viii preliminary data analysis. *American Journal of Physical Medicine and Rehabilitation* 69: 154–169.

Findley, T. W. 1990. sed3: Variable transformation and evaluation. *Stata Technical Bulletin* 2: 15. Reprinted in *Stata Technical Bulletin Reprints*, vol. 1, pp. 85–86.

Hamilton, L. C. 1992. *Regression with Graphics*. Pacific Grove, CA: Brooks/Cole Publishing Company.

Tukey, J. W. 1977. *Exploratory Data Analysis*. Reading, MA: Addison–Wesley Publishing Company.

Also See

Related: [R] **boxcox**, [R] **diagplots**, [R] **lnskew0**, [R] **lv**, [R] **sktest**

Background: *Stata Graphics Manual*

Title

level — Set default confidence level

Syntax

set level #

Description

set level specifies the default confidence level for confidence intervals for all commands that report confidence intervals. The initial value is 95, meaning 95% confidence intervals. # may be between 10 and 99.

Remarks

To change the width of confidence intervals reported by a particular command, it is not necessary to reset the default confidence level. All commands that report confidence intervals have a level(#) option. When you do not specify the option, the confidence intervals are calculated for the default level set by set level or 95% if you have not reset it.

▷ Example

You use the ci command to obtain the confidence interval for the mean of mpg:

```
. ci mpg
Variable |     Obs       Mean    Std. Err.      [95% Conf. Interval]
---------+-----------------------------------------------------------
     mpg |      74    21.2973    .6725511       19.9569    22.63769
```

To obtain 90% confidence intervals, you could type

```
. ci mpg, level(90)
Variable |     Obs       Mean    Std. Err.      [90% Conf. Interval]
---------+-----------------------------------------------------------
     mpg |      74    21.2973    .6725511       20.17683    22.41776
```

or

```
. set level 90
. ci mpg
Variable |     Obs       Mean    Std. Err.      [90% Conf. Interval]
---------+-----------------------------------------------------------
     mpg |      74    21.2973    .6725511       20.17683    22.41776
```

If you opt for the second alternative, the next time you estimate a model (say with regress), 90% confidence intervals will be reported. If you wanted 95% confidence intervals, you could specify level(95) on the estimation command or you could reset the default by typing set level 95.

◁

Also See

Complementary:	[R] **query**
Related:	[R] **ci**
Background:	[U] **23 Estimation and post-estimation commands,**
	[U] **23.5 Specifying the width of confidence intervals**

Title

limits — Quick reference for limits

Description

This entry provides a quick reference for the size limits in Stata. Note that most of these limits are so high that you will never encounter them.

Remarks

Maximum size limits for Small Stata and Intercooled Stata

	Small Stata	Intercooled Stata
Number of observations	about 1,000	2,147,483,647 (1)
Number of variables	99	2,047
Width of a dataset	200	8,192
Value of `matsize`	40	800
Number of characters in a command	1,100	18,648
Number of options for a command	50	50
Number of elements in a `numlist`	1,600	1,600
Number of unique time-series operators in a command	100	100
Number of seasonal suboperators per time-series operator	8	8
Number of dyadic operators in an expression	66	66
Number of numeric literals in an expression	50	50
Number of string literals in an expression	256	256
Length of string in string expression	80	80
Number of sum functions in an expression	5	5
Number of characters in a macro	1,000	18,632
Number of nested do-files	32	32
Number of lines in a program	1,000	3,500
Number of characters in a program	10,000	37,296
Length of variable name	8	8
Length of ado-command name	8	8
Length of global macro name	8	8
Length of local macro name	7	7
Length of a string variable	80	80
Number of conditions in an `if` statement	30	30

(1) limited by memory.

(Continued on next page)

Maximum size limits for specific commands

	Small Stata	Intercooled Stata
anova		
Number of terms in **anova** model **test** statement	8	8
Number of terms in the **repeated()** option	4	4
char		
Maximum length of a single characteristic	1,000	18,632
constraint		
Number of constraints	999	999
encode and **decode**		
Number of unique values for a string variable	1,000	65,536
estimates hold		
Number of stored estimation results	10	10
graph		
(*See Stata Graphics Manual for* **graph** *limits*)		
greigen		
Number of eigenvalues plotted by **greigen**	13	13
grmeanby		
Number of unique values in *varlist*	_N/2	_N/2
hist		
Number of unique values in *varname*	50	50
impute		
Number of variables in *varlist*	31	31

(*Table continued on next page*)

Maximum size limits for specific commands, continued

	Small Stata	Intercooled Stata
infile		
record length without data dictionary	none	none
record length with data dictionary (2)	7,998	7,998
infix		
record length without data dictionary	none	none
record length with data dictionary (2)	7,998	7,998
label		
Length of dataset label	80	80
Length of variable label	80	80
Length of value label	80	80
Length of name of value label	8	8
Number of codings within a single value label	1,000	65,536
matrix		
Size of a single matrix	40×40	800×800
maximize options		
Number of iterations specified with `iterate()`	16,000	16,000
merge		
Number of variables that you can specify in a match-merge	10	10
mlogit		
Number of outcomes in model	20	50
notes		
Maximum length of a single note	1,000	18,632
Number of notes attached to _dta	9,999	9,999
Number of notes attached to each variable	9,999	9,999
numlist		
Number of elements in the numeric list	1,600	1,600
ologit		
Number of outcomes in model	20	50
oprobit		
Number of outcomes in model	20	50

(2) For Stata for Unix, the maximum record length is 19,998.

Maximum size limits for specific commands, continued

	Small Stata	Intercooled Stata
plot		
Number of columns specified with column() option	133	133
Number of lines specified with lines() option	83	83
reg3, **sureg**, and other system estimators		
Number of equations	50	50
set adosize		
Maximum amount of memory that ado-files may consume	500K	500K
sts graph		
Number of by variables (3)	5	5
tabdisp and **table**		
Number of by variables	4	4
Number of margins; that is, the sum of the rows, columns, supercolumns, and by groups	3,000	3,000
tabulate		
Number of rows for a one-way table (4)	500	3,000
Number of rows for a two-way table (4)	160	300
Number of columns for a two-way table	20	20
tabulate, summarize		
Number of cells	376	376
xt estimation commands		
Number of time periods	40	800

(3) May be restricted to fewer depending on other options specified.

(4) For Intercooled Stata for the Macintosh, limits are 2,000 for the number of rows for a one-way table and 180 for number of rows for a two-way table.

Also See

Related: [R] **matsize**, [R] **memory**

Background: [U] **7 Setting the size of memory**

Title

lincom — Linear combinations of estimators

Syntax

lincom *exp* $\left[\,,\underline{\text{level}}(\#)\text{ or hr }\underline{\text{irr}}\ \underline{\text{rrr}}\ \underline{\text{ef}}\text{orm}\,\right]$

exp is any linear combination of coefficients that is valid syntax for **test**; see [R] **test**. Note, however, that *exp* must not contain any additive constants or equal signs.

Description

lincom computes point estimates, standard errors, t or z statistics, p-values, and confidence intervals for a linear combination of coefficients after any estimation command except **anova**. Results can optionally be displayed as odds ratios, hazard ratios, incidence rate ratios, or relative risk ratios.

The **svy** estimation commands for survey data have their own special command **svylc** for estimating linear combinations; see [R] **svylc**.

Options

level(#) specifies the confidence level, in percent, for confidence intervals. The default is **level(95)** or as set by **set level**; see [U] **23.5 Specifying the width of confidence intervals**.

or, **hr**, **irr**, **rrr**, and **eform** all do the same thing; they all report coefficient estimates as $\exp(\widehat{\beta})$ rather than $\widehat{\beta}$. Standard errors and confidence intervals are similarly transformed. Note that **or** is the default after **logistic**. The only difference in these options is how the output is labeled.

Option	Label	Explanation	Example commands
or	Odds Ratio	Odds ratio	logistic, logit
hr	Haz. Ratio	Hazard ratio	stcox, streg
irr	IRR	Incidence Rate Ratio	poisson
rrr	RRR	Relative Rate Ratio	mlogit
eform	exp(b)	Generic label	

Remarks

After fitting a model and obtaining estimates for coefficients $\beta_1, \beta_2, \ldots, \beta_k$, one often wants to view estimates for linear combinations of the β_i, such as $\beta_1 - \beta_2$. lincom can display estimates for any linear combination of the form $c_1\beta_1 + c_2\beta_2 + \cdots + c_k\beta_k$.

lincom works after any estimation command for which **test** works, except **anova**. Any expression that is a valid expression for **test** Syntax 1 (see [R] **test**) is a valid expression for lincom. There is only one exception to this rule: lincom does not allow additive constants; i.e., it cannot display estimates for $c_0 + c_1\beta_1 + \cdots + c_k\beta_k$ when $c_0 \neq 0$.

lincom is useful for viewing odds ratios, hazard ratios, etc., for one group (i.e., one set of covariates) relative to another group (i.e., another set of covariates). See examples below.

▷ Example

We estimate a linear regression

```
. reg y x1 x2 x3

      Source |       SS       df       MS                Number of obs =     148
-------------+------------------------------             F(  3,   144) =   96.12
       Model |  3259.3561        3  1086.45203           Prob > F      =  0.0000
    Residual |  1627.56282     144  11.3025196           R-squared     =  0.6670
-------------+------------------------------             Adj R-squared =  0.6600
       Total |  4886.91892     147  33.2443464           Root MSE      =  3.3619

------------------------------------------------------------------------------
           y |      Coef.   Std. Err.       t    P>|t|     [95% Conf. Interval]
-------------+----------------------------------------------------------------
          x1 |   1.457113    1.07461      1.356   0.177    -.6669339    3.581161
          x2 |   2.221682    .8610358     2.580   0.011     .5197797    3.923583
          x3 |   -.006139    .0005543   -11.076   0.000    -.0072345   -.0050435
       _cons |   36.10135    4.382693     8.237   0.000     27.43863    44.76407
------------------------------------------------------------------------------
```

Suppose that we want to see the difference of the coefficients of x2 and x1. We type

```
. lincom x2 - x1

 ( 1) - x1 + x2 = 0.0

------------------------------------------------------------------------------
           y |      Coef.   Std. Err.       t    P>|t|     [95% Conf. Interval]
-------------+----------------------------------------------------------------
         (1) |   .7645682    .9950282     0.768   0.444     -1.20218    2.731316
------------------------------------------------------------------------------
```

The expression can be any linear combination without a constant.

```
. lincom 3*x1 + 500*x3

 ( 1)   3.0 x1 + 500.0 x3 = 0.0

------------------------------------------------------------------------------
           y |      Coef.   Std. Err.       t    P>|t|     [95% Conf. Interval]
-------------+----------------------------------------------------------------
         (1) |   1.301825    3.396624     0.383   0.702     -5.411858    8.015507
------------------------------------------------------------------------------
```

Expressions with additive constants are not allowed

```
. lincom x1 - 1
additive constant terms not allowed
r(198);
```

nor are nonlinear expressions.

```
. lincom x2/x1
not possible with test
r(131);
```

◁

❑ Technical Note

lincom uses the same shorthands for coefficients as does **test** (see [R] **test**). When you type x1, for instance, lincom knows that you mean the coefficient of x1. The formal syntax for referencing this coefficient is actually _b[x1], or alternatively _coef[x1]. So, more formally, in the last example we could have typed

```
. lincom 3*_b[x1] + 500*_b[x3]
```

❑

Odds ratios and incidence rate ratios

After logistic regression, the `or` option can be specified with `lincom` to display odds ratios for any effect. Incidence rate ratios after commands such as `poisson` can be obtained in a similar fashion—you simply specify the `irr` option.

▷ Example

Consider the low birth weight data from Hosmer and Lemeshow (1989, Table 4.1). We estimate a logistic regression of low birth weight (variable `low`) on the following variables:

Variable	Description	Coding
age	age in years	
black	race black	1 if black, 0 otherwise
other	race other	1 if race other, 0 otherwise
smoke	smoking status	1 if smoker, 0 if nonsmoker
ht	history of hypertension	1 if yes, 0 if no
ui	uterine irritability	1 if yes, 0 if no
lwd	maternal weight before pregnancy	1 if weight < 110 lb., 0 otherwise
ptd	history of premature labor	1 if yes, 0 if no
agelwd	age $\times$ lwd	
smokelwd	smoke $\times$ lwd	

We first estimate a model without the interaction terms `agelwd` and `smokelwd` (Hosmer and Lemeshow 1989, Table 4.8) using `logit`.

```
. logit low age lwd black other smoke ptd ht ui

Iteration 0:  log likelihood =    -117.336
Iteration 1:  log likelihood = -99.431174
Iteration 2:  log likelihood = -98.785718
Iteration 3:  log likelihood =    -98.778
Iteration 4:  log likelihood = -98.777998

Logit estimates                                 Number of obs   =         189
                                                LR chi2(8)      =       37.12
                                                Prob > chi2     =      0.0000
Log likelihood = -98.777998                     Pseudo R2       =      0.1582

------------------------------------------------------------------------------
         low |      Coef.   Std. Err.       z    P>|z|     [95% Conf. Interval]
-------------+----------------------------------------------------------------
         age |  -.0464796   .0373888    -1.243   0.214    -.1197603    .0268011
         lwd |   .8420615   .4055338     2.076   0.038     .0472299    1.636893
       black |   1.073456   .5150752     2.084   0.037     .0639273    2.082985
       other |    .815367   .4452979     1.831   0.067    -.0574008    1.688135
       smoke |   .8071996    .404446     1.996   0.046     .0145001    1.599899
         ptd |   1.281678   .4621157     2.774   0.006     .3759478    2.187408
          ht |   1.435227   .6482699     2.214   0.027     .1646415    2.705813
          ui |   .6576256   .4666192     1.409   0.159    -.2569313    1.572182
       _cons |  -1.216781   .9556797    -1.273   0.203    -3.089878     .656317
------------------------------------------------------------------------------
```

If we want to get the odds ratio for black smokers relative to white nonsmokers (the reference group), we type

```
. lincom black + smoke, or
 ( 1)   black + smoke = 0.0

------------------------------------------------------------------------
   low | Odds Ratio   Std. Err.      z     P>|z|    [95% Conf. Interval]
-------+----------------------------------------------------------------
   (1) |   6.557805    4.744692    2.599   0.009     1.588176    27.07811
------------------------------------------------------------------------
```

lincom computed $\exp(\beta_{\text{black}} + \beta_{\text{smoke}}) = 6.56$. If we want to see the odds ratio for white smokers relative to black nonsmokers, we type

```
. lincom smoke - black, or
 ( 1)   - black + smoke = 0.0

------------------------------------------------------------------------
   low | Odds Ratio   Std. Err.      z     P>|z|    [95% Conf. Interval]
-------+----------------------------------------------------------------
   (1) |   .7662425    .4430176   -0.461   0.645     .2467334    2.379603
------------------------------------------------------------------------
```

Now let's add the interaction terms to the model (Hosmer and Lemeshow 1989, Table 4.10). This time we will use the `logistic` command rather than `logit`. By default, `logistic` displays odds ratios.

```
. logistic low age black other smoke ht ui lwd ptd agelwd smokelwd
Logit estimates                               Number of obs   =        189
                                              LR chi2(10)     =      42.66
                                              Prob > chi2     =     0.0000
Log likelihood =  -96.00616                   Pseudo R2       =     0.1818

------------------------------------------------------------------------
    low | Odds Ratio   Std. Err.      z     P>|z|    [95% Conf. Interval]
--------+---------------------------------------------------------------
    age |   .9194513    .041896    -1.843   0.065     .8408967    1.005344
  black |    2.95383   1.532788     2.087   0.037     1.068277    8.167462
  other |   2.137589   .9919132     1.637   0.102     .8608713    5.307749
  smoke |   3.168096   1.452377     2.515   0.012     1.289956    7.780755
     ht |   3.893141     2.5752     2.055   0.040     1.064768     14.2346
     ui |   2.071284   .9931385     1.519   0.129     .8092928    5.301191
    lwd |   .1772934   .3312383    -0.926   0.354     .0045539    6.902359
    ptd |   3.426633   1.615282     2.613   0.009     1.360252    8.632086
 agelwd |    1.15883     .09602     1.779   0.075     .9851216     1.36317
smokelwd |   .2447849   .2003996    -1.719   0.086     .0491956    1.217988
------------------------------------------------------------------------
```

Hosmer and Lemeshow (1989, Table 4.13) consider the effects of smoking (smoke = 1) and low maternal weight prior to pregnancy (lwd = 1). The effect of smoking among non-low-weight mothers (lwd = 0) is given by the odds ratio 3.17 for `smoke` in the `logistic` output. The effect of smoking among low-weight mothers is given by

```
. lincom smoke + smokelwd
 ( 1)   smoke + smokelwd = 0.0

------------------------------------------------------------------------
   low | Odds Ratio   Std. Err.      z     P>|z|    [95% Conf. Interval]
-------+----------------------------------------------------------------
   (1) |   .7755022    .5749508   -0.343   0.732     .1813465    3.316322
------------------------------------------------------------------------
```

Note that we did not have to specify the `or` option. After `logistic`, `lincom` assumes `or` by default.

The effect of low-weight (lwd = 1) is more complicated since we fit an age × lwd interaction. We must specify the age of mothers for the effect. The effect among 30-year old nonsmokers is given by

```
. lincom lwd + 30*agelwd

 ( 1)   lwd + 30.0 agelwd = 0.0

------------------------------------------------------------------------
     low | Odds Ratio   Std. Err.       z     P>|z|     [95% Conf. Interval]
---------+--------------------------------------------------------------
     (1) |   14.7669    13.56689     2.931    0.003      2.439266    89.39625
------------------------------------------------------------------------
```

lincom computed $\exp(\beta_{\text{lwd}} + 30\beta_{\text{agelwd}}) = 14.8$. It seems a little odd to have entered it as lwd + 30*agelwd, but remember that lwd and agelwd are just lincom's (and test's) shorthand for _b[lwd] and _b[agelwd]. We could have typed

```
. lincom _b[lwd] + 30*_b[agelwd]

 ( 1)   lwd + 30.0 agelwd = 0.0

------------------------------------------------------------------------
     low | Odds Ratio   Std. Err.       z     P>|z|     [95% Conf. Interval]
---------+--------------------------------------------------------------
     (1) |   14.7669    13.56689     2.931    0.003      2.439266    89.39625
------------------------------------------------------------------------
```

◁

Multiple-equation models

lincom also works with multiple-equation models. The only difference is how you refer to the coefficients. Recall that for multiple-equation models, coefficients are referenced using the syntax

[*eqno*] *varname*

where *eqno* is the equation number or equation name and *varname* is the corresponding variable name for the coefficient; see [U] **16.5 Accessing coefficients and standard errors** and [R] **test** for details.

▷ Example

Consider the example from the [R] **mlogit** entry of the manual (Tarlov et al. 1989; Wells et al. 1989).

```
. mlogit insure age male nonwhite site2 site3, nolog
Multinomial regression                     Number of obs   =       615
                                           LR chi2(10)     =     42.99
                                           Prob > chi2     =    0.0000
Log likelihood = -534.36165                Pseudo R2       =    0.0387

------------------------------------------------------------------------
   insure |    Coef.    Std. Err.       z     P>|z|     [95% Conf. Interval]
---------+--------------------------------------------------------------
Prepaid  |
     age |  -.011745    .0061946    -1.896    0.058     -.0238862    .0003962
    male |   .5616934    .2027465     2.770    0.006      .1643175    .9590693
nonwhite |   .9747768    .2363213     4.125    0.000      .5115955    1.437958
   site2 |   .1130359    .2101903     0.538    0.591     -.2989296    .5250013
   site3 |  -.5879879    .2279351    -2.580    0.010     -1.034733   -.1412433
   _cons |   .2697127    .3284422     0.821    0.412     -.3740222    .9134476
```

```
---------+----------------------------------------------------------------
Uninsure |
     age |  -.0077961    .0114418    -0.681   0.496    -.0302217    .0146294
    male |   .4518496    .3674867     1.230   0.219     -.268411     1.17211
nonwhite |   .2170589    .4256361     0.510   0.610    -.6171725     1.05129
   site2 |  -1.211563    .4705127    -2.575   0.010    -2.133751   -.2893747
   site3 |  -.2078123    .3662926    -0.567   0.570    -.9257327     .510108
   _cons |  -1.286943    .5923219    -2.173   0.030    -2.447872   -.1260135
---------+----------------------------------------------------------------
```

(Outcome insure==Indem is the comparison group)

To see the estimate of the sum of the coefficient of `male` and the coefficient of `nonwhite` for the Prepaid outcome, we type

```
. lincom [Prepaid]male + [Prepaid]nonwhite

 ( 1)   [Prepaid]male + [Prepaid]nonwhite = 0.0

------------------------------------------------------------------------
  insure |     Coef.   Std. Err.       z    P>|z|    [95% Conf. Interval]
---------+--------------------------------------------------------------
     (1) |   1.53647   .3272489     4.695   0.000    .8950741    2.177866
------------------------------------------------------------------------
```

To view the estimate as a ratio of relative risks (see [R] **mlogit** for the definition and interpretation), we specify the **rrr** option.

```
. lincom [Prepaid]male + [Prepaid]nonwhite, rrr

 ( 1)   [Prepaid]male + [Prepaid]nonwhite = 0.0

------------------------------------------------------------------------
  insure |       RRR   Std. Err.       z    P>|z|    [95% Conf. Interval]
---------+--------------------------------------------------------------
     (1) |  4.648154   1.521103     4.695   0.000    2.447517    8.827451
------------------------------------------------------------------------
```

◁

Saved Results

lincom saves in `r()`:

Scalars
    r(estimate)   point estimate
    r(se)   estimate of standard error
    r(df)   degrees of freedom

Methods and Formulas

lincom is implemented as an ado-file.

References

Hosmer, D. W., Jr., and S. Lemeshow. 1989. *Applied Logistic Regression*. New York: John Wiley & Sons.

Tarlov, A. R., J. E. Ware, Jr., S. Greenfield, E. C. Nelson, E. Perrin, and M. Zubkoff. 1989. The medical outcomes study. *Journal of the American Medical Association* 262: 925–930.

Wells, K. E., R. D. Hays, M. A. Burnam, W. H. Rogers, S. Greenfield, and J. E. Ware, Jr. 1989. Detection of depressive disorder for patients receiving prepaid or fee-for-service care. *Journal of the American Medical Association* 262: 3298–3302.

Also See

Related: [R] **svylc**, [R] **svytest**, [R] **test**, [R] **testnl**

Background: [U] **16.5 Accessing coefficients and standard errors**,
                     [U] **23 Estimation and post-estimation commands**

Title

linktest — Specification link test for single-equation models

Syntax

linktest [if *exp*] [in *range*] [, *estimation_options*]

When if *exp* and in *range* are not specified, the link test is performed on the same sample as the previous estimation.

Description

linktest performs a link test for model specification after any single-equation estimation command such as logistic, regress, etc.; see [R] **estimation commands**.

Options

estimation_options must be the same options specified with the underlying estimation command.

Remarks

The form of the link test implemented here is based on an idea of Tukey (1949) which was further described by Pregibon (1980), elaborating on work in his unpublished thesis (Pregibon 1979). See *Methods and Formulas* below for more details.

▷ Example

We attempt to explain the mileage ratings of cars in our automobile dataset using the weight, displacement of the engine, and whether the car is manufactured outside the U.S.:

```
. regress mpg weight displ foreign

  Source |       SS       df       MS              Number of obs =      74
---------+------------------------------           F(  3,    70) =   45.88
   Model | 1619.71935      3   539.906448          Prob > F      =  0.0000
Residual | 823.740114     70   11.7677159          R-squared     =  0.6629
---------+------------------------------           Adj R-squared =  0.6484
   Total | 2443.45946     73   33.4720474          Root MSE      =  3.4304

------------------------------------------------------------------------------
     mpg |      Coef.   Std. Err.       t     P>|t|     [95% Conf. Interval]
---------+--------------------------------------------------------------------
  weight |  -.0067745   .0011665     -5.807   0.000    -.0091011   -.0044479
   displ |   .0019286   .0100701      0.192   0.849    -.0181556    .0220129
 foreign |  -1.600631   1.113648     -1.437   0.155    -3.821732    .6204698
   _cons |   41.84795   2.350704     17.802   0.000     37.15962    46.53628
------------------------------------------------------------------------------
```

186

Based on the R^2, we are reasonably pleased with this model.

If our model really is specified correctly, then were we to regress mpg on the prediction and the prediction squared, the prediction squared should have no explanatory power. This is what linktest does:

```
. linktest

  Source |       SS       df       MS                  Number of obs =      74
---------+------------------------------               F(  2,    71) =   76.75
   Model | 1670.71514      2  835.357572               Prob > F      =  0.0000
Residual |  772.744316     71  10.8837228              R-squared     =  0.6837
---------+------------------------------               Adj R-squared =  0.6748
   Total | 2443.45946      73  33.4720474              Root MSE      =   3.299

------------------------------------------------------------------------------
     mpg |      Coef.   Std. Err.       t     P>|t|     [95% Conf. Interval]
---------+--------------------------------------------------------------------
    _hat | -.4127198   .6577736     -0.627   0.532    -1.724283    .8988433
  _hatsq |  .0338198   .015624       2.165   0.034     .0026664    .0649732
   _cons |  14.00705   6.713276      2.086   0.041     .6211545    27.39294
------------------------------------------------------------------------------
```

We find that the prediction squared does have explanatory power, so our specification is not as good as we thought.

Although linktest is formally a test of the specification of the dependent variable, it is often interpreted as a test that, conditional on the specification, the independent variables are specified incorrectly. We will follow that interpretation and now include weight-squared in our model:

```
. gen weight2 = weight*weight

. regress mpg weight weight2 displ foreign

  Source |       SS       df       MS                  Number of obs =      74
---------+------------------------------               F(  4,    69) =   39.37
   Model | 1699.02634      4  424.756584               Prob > F      =  0.0000
Residual |  744.433124     69  10.7888859              R-squared     =  0.6953
---------+------------------------------               Adj R-squared =  0.6777
   Total | 2443.45946      73  33.4720474              Root MSE      =  3.2846

------------------------------------------------------------------------------
     mpg |      Coef.   Std. Err.       t     P>|t|     [95% Conf. Interval]
---------+--------------------------------------------------------------------
  weight | -.0173257   .0040488     -4.279   0.000    -.0254028   -.0092486
 weight2 |  1.87e-06   6.89e-07      2.711   0.008     4.93e-07    3.24e-06
   displ | -.0101625   .0106236     -0.957   0.342    -.031356     .011031
 foreign | -2.560016   1.123506     -2.279   0.026    -4.801349   -.3186833
   _cons |  58.23575   6.449882      9.029   0.000     45.36859    71.10291
------------------------------------------------------------------------------
```

And now we perform the link test on our new model:

```
. linktest

  Source |       SS       df       MS                  Number of obs =      74
---------+------------------------------               F(  2,    71) =   81.08
   Model | 1699.39489      2  849.697445               Prob > F      =  0.0000
Residual |  744.06457      71  10.4797827              R-squared     =  0.6955
---------+------------------------------               Adj R-squared =  0.6869
   Total | 2443.45946      73  33.4720474              Root MSE      =  3.2372
```

```
      mpg |      Coef.   Std. Err.        t    P>|t|     [95% Conf. Interval]
----------+----------------------------------------------------------------
     _hat |   1.141987   .7612218      1.500   0.138    -.3758456     2.65982
   _hatsq |  -.0031916   .0170194     -0.188   0.852    -.0371272    .0307441
    _cons |   -1.50305   8.196444     -0.183   0.855    -17.84629    14.84019
--------------------------------------------------------------------------------
```

We now pass the link test.

◁

▷ Example

Above we followed a standard misinterpretation of the link test—when we discovered a problem, we focused on the explanatory variables of our model. It is at least worth considering varying exactly what the link test tests. The link test told us that our dependent variable was misspecified. For those with an engineering background, mpg is indeed a strange measure. It would make more sense to model energy consumption—gallons per mile—in terms of weight and displacement:

```
. gen gpm = 1/mpg
. regress gpm weight displ foreign

     Source |       SS       df       MS                  Number of obs =      74
------------+------------------------------              F(  3,    70) =   76.33
      Model |  .009157962    3  .003052654              Prob > F      = 0.0000
   Residual |  .002799666   70  .000039995              R-squared     = 0.7659
------------+------------------------------              Adj R-squared = 0.7558
      Total |  .011957628   73  .000163803              Root MSE      = .00632

      gpm |      Coef.   Std. Err.        t    P>|t|     [95% Conf. Interval]
----------+----------------------------------------------------------------
   weight |   .0000144   2.15e-06      6.719   0.000     .0000102    .0000187
    displ |   .0000186   .0000186      1.004   0.319    -.0000184    .0000557
  foreign |   .0066981   .0020531      3.262   0.002     .0026034    .0107928
    _cons |   .0008917   .0043337      0.206   0.838    -.0077515     .009535
--------------------------------------------------------------------------------
```

This model looks every bit as reasonable as our original model.

```
. linktest

     Source |       SS       df       MS                  Number of obs =      74
------------+------------------------------              F(  2,    71) =  117.06
      Model |  .009175219    2  .004587609              Prob > F      = 0.0000
   Residual |  .002782409   71  .000039189              R-squared     = 0.7673
------------+------------------------------              Adj R-squared = 0.7608
      Total |  .011957628   73  .000163803              Root MSE      = .00626

      gpm |      Coef.   Std. Err.        t    P>|t|     [95% Conf. Interval]
----------+----------------------------------------------------------------
     _hat |   .6608413    .515275      1.283   0.204    -.3665877     1.68827
   _hatsq |   3.275857   4.936655      0.664   0.509    -6.567553    13.11927
    _cons |    .008365   .0130468      0.641   0.523    -.0176496    .0343795
--------------------------------------------------------------------------------
```

Specifying the model in terms of gallons-per-mile also solved the specification problem and resulted in a more parsimonious specification.

◁

▷ Example

The link test can be used with any single-equation estimation procedure, not solely regression. Let's turn our problem around and attempt to explain whether a car is manufactured outside the U.S. by its mileage rating and weight. To save paper, we will specify logit's nolog option, which suppresses the iteration log:

```
. logit foreign mpg weight, nolog
Logit estimates                                  Number of obs  =         74
                                                 LR chi2(2)     =      35.72
                                                 Prob > chi2    =     0.0000
Log likelihood = -27.175156                      Pseudo R2      =     0.3966
------------------------------------------------------------------------------
   foreign |     Coef.   Std. Err.       z    P>|z|     [95% Conf. Interval]
-----------+------------------------------------------------------------------
       mpg |  -.1685869   .0919174    -1.834   0.067    -.3487418    .011568
    weight |  -.0039067   .0010116    -3.862   0.000    -.0058894   -.001924
     _cons |   13.70837   4.518707     3.034   0.002     4.851864   22.56487
------------------------------------------------------------------------------
```

When you run linktest after logit, the result is another logit specification:

```
. linktest, nolog
Logit estimates                                  Number of obs  =         74
                                                 LR chi2(2)     =      36.83
                                                 Prob > chi2    =     0.0000
Log likelihood = -26.615714                      Pseudo R2      =     0.4090
------------------------------------------------------------------------------
   foreign |     Coef.   Std. Err.       z    P>|z|     [95% Conf. Interval]
-----------+------------------------------------------------------------------
      _hat |   .8438531   .2738759     3.081   0.002     .3070661    1.38064
    _hatsq |  -.1559115   .1568642    -0.994   0.320    -.4633596    .1515366
     _cons |   .2630557   .4299598     0.612   0.541      -.57965    1.105761
------------------------------------------------------------------------------
```

The link test reveals no problems with our specification.

If there had been a problem, we would have been virtually forced to accept the misinterpretation of the link test—we would have reconsidered our specification of the independent variables. When using logit, we have no control over the specification of the dependent variable other than to change likelihood functions.

We admit to seeing a dataset once where the link test rejected the logit specification. We did change the likelihood function, reestimating the model using probit, and satisfied the link test. Probit has thinner tails than logit. In general, however, you will not be so lucky.

◁

❏ Technical Note

You should specify exactly the same options with linktest as you do with the estimation command, although you do not have to follow this advice as literally as we did in the preceding example. logit's nolog option merely suppresses a part of the output, not what is estimated. We specified nolog both times to save paper.

If you are testing a cox model with censored observations, however, you must specify the dead() option on linktest as well. If you are testing a tobit model, you must specify the censoring points just as you do with the tobit command.

If you are not sure which options are important, duplicate exactly what you specified on the estimation command.

If you do not specify if *exp* or in *range* with `linktest`, Stata will by default perform the link test on the same sample as the previous estimation. Suppose that you omitted some data when performing your estimation, but want to calculate the link test on all the data, which you might do if you believed the model is appropriate for all the data. To do this, you would type 'linktest if e(sample) ~=.'.

❑

Saved Results

`linktest` saves in `r()`:

Scalars
r(t) t statistic on _hatsq   r(df)   degrees of freedom

`linktest` is *not* an estimation command in the sense that it leaves previous estimation results unchanged. For instance, one runs a regression and then performs the link test. Typing `regress` without arguments after the link test still replays the *original* regression.

In terms of integrating an estimation command with `linktest`, `linktest` assumes the name of the estimation command is stored in `e(cmd)` and the name of the dependent variable in `e(depvar)`. After estimation, it assumes the number of degrees of freedom for the t test is given by `e(df_m)` if the macro is defined.

If the estimation command reports Z statistics instead of t statistics, then `linktest` will also report Z statistics. The Z statistic, however, is still returned in `r(t)`; `r(df)` is set to a missing value.

Methods and Formulas

`linktest` is implemented as an ado-file. The link test is based on the idea that if a regression or regression-like equation is properly specified, one should not be able to find any additional independent variables that are significant except by chance. One kind of specification error is called a link error. In regression, this means that the dependent variable needs a transformation or "link" function to properly relate to the independent variables. The idea of a link test is to add an independent variable to the equation that is especially likely to be significant if there is a link error.

Let

$$y = f(\mathbf{X}\beta)$$

be the model and $\widehat{\beta}$ be the parameter estimates. `linktest` calculates

$$\_hat = \mathbf{X}\widehat{\beta}$$

and

$$\_hatsq = \_hat^2$$

The model is then refit with these two variables, and the test is based on the significance of _hatsq. This is the form suggested by Pregibon (1979) based on an idea of Tukey (1949). Pregibon (1980) suggests a slightly different method that has come to be known as "Pregibon's goodness-of-link test". We preferred the older version because it is universally applicable, straightforward, and a good second-order approximation. It is universally applicable in the sense that it can be applied to any single-equation estimation technique whereas Pregibon's more recent tests are estimation-technique specific.

References

Pregibon, D. 1979. *Data Analytic Methods for Generalized Linear Models.* Ph.D. Dissertation. University of Toronto.

——. 1980. Goodness of link tests for generalized linear models. *Applied Statistics* 29: 15–24.

Tukey, J. W. 1949. One degree of freedom for non-additivity. *Biometrics* 5: 232–242.

Also See

Related: [R] **estimation commands**, [R] **lrtest**, [R] **test**, [R] **testnl**

Title

> **list** — List values of variables

Syntax

[by *varlist*:] list [*varlist*] [if *exp*] [in *range*] [, [no]display nolabel noobs]

The second *varlist* may contain time-series operators; see [U] **14.4.3 Time-series varlists**.

Description

list displays the values of variables. If no *varlist* is specified, the values of all the variables are displayed. Windows users should also see **browse** in [R] **edit**.

Options

[no]display forces the format into display or tabular (nodisplay) format. If you do not specify one of these two options, then Stata chooses one based on its judgment of which would be most readable.

nolabel causes the numeric codes rather than the label values (strings) to be displayed.

noobs suppresses printing of the observation numbers.

Remarks

list, typed by itself, lists all the observations and all the variables in the data. If you specify *varlist*, only those variables are listed. Specifying one or both of in *range* and if *exp* limits the observations listed.

▷ Example

list has two output formats, known as tabular and display. The tabular format is suitable for listing a few variables, whereas the display format is suitable for listing an unlimited number of variables. Stata chooses automatically between those two formats:

```
. list in 1/2
Observation 1
         make  AMC Concord       price      4,099         mpg         22
        rep78            3      hdroom        2.5       trunk         11
       weight        2,930      length        186        turn         40
        displ          121      gratio       3.58     foreign   Domestic

Observation 2
         make  AMC Pacer         price      4,749         mpg         17
        rep78            3      hdroom        3.0       trunk         11
       weight        3,350      length        173        turn         40
        displ          258      gratio       2.53     foreign   Domestic
```

```
. list make mpg weight displ rep78 in 1/5
        make                mpg   weight    displ    rep78
 1. AMC Concord             22    2,930      121        3
 2. AMC Pacer               17    3,350      258        3
 3. AMC Spirit              22    2,640      121        .
 4. Buick Century           20    3,250      196        3
 5. Buick Electra           15    4,080      350        4
```

The first case is an example of display format; the second is an example of tabular format. The tabular format is more readable and takes less space, but it is effective only if the variables can fit on a single line across the screen. Stata chose to list all twelve variables in display format, but when the *varlist* was restricted to five variables, Stata chose tabular format.

If you are dissatisfied with Stata's choice, you can make the decision yourself. Specify the display option to force display format and the nodisplay option to force tabular format.

◁

❑ Technical Note

When Stata lists a string variable in tabular output format, it always lists the variable right-justified.

When Stata lists a string variable in display output format, it decides whether to list the variable right-justified or left-justified according to the display format for the string variable; see [U] **15.5 Formats: controlling how data is displayed**. In our previous example, make has a display format of %-18s.

```
. describe make
 1. make      str18  %-18s              Make and Model
```

The negative sign in the %-18s instructs Stata to left-justify this variable. If instead the display format had been %18s, Stata would have right-justified the variable.

Note that it appears from our listing above that foreign is also a string variable, but if we describe it, we see that it is not:

```
. describe foreign
12. foreign   byte
```

foreign is stored as a byte, but it has an associated value label named origin; see [U] **15.6.3 Value labels**. Stata decides whether to right-justify or left-justify a numeric variable with an associated value label using the same rule as Stata uses for string variables: it looks at the display format of the variable. In this case, the display format of %8.0g tells Stata to right-justify the variable. If the display format had been %-8.0g, Stata would have left-justified this variable.

❑

❑ Technical Note

You can list the variables in any order that you desire. When you specify the *varlist*, list makes the display in the order you specify. You may also include variables more than once in the *varlist*.

❑

▷ Example

In some cases, you may wish to suppress the observation numbers. You do this by specifying the noobs option:

```
. list make mpg weight displ foreign in 51/55, noobs
make                 mpg    weight    displ    foreign
Pont. Phoenix         19     3,420      231    Domestic
Pont. Sunbird         24     2,690      151    Domestic
Audi 5000             17     2,830      131     Foreign
Audi Fox              23     2,070       97     Foreign
BMW 320i              25     2,650      121     Foreign
```

◁

❑ Technical Note

You can suppress the use of value labels by specifying the nolabel option. For instance, the variable foreign in the examples above really contains numeric codes, 0 meaning Domestic and 1 meaning Foreign. When you list the variable, however, you see the corresponding value labels rather than the underlying numeric code:

```
. list foreign in 51/55
         foreign
51.    Domestic
52.    Domestic
53.     Foreign
54.     Foreign
55.     Foreign
```

Specifying the nolabel option displays the underlying numeric codes:

```
. list foreign in 51/55, nolabel
         foreign
51.          0
52.          0
53.          1
54.          1
55.          1
```

❑

References

Riley, A. R. 1993. dm15: Interactively list values of variables. *Stata Technical Bulletin* 16: 2–6. Reprinted in *Stata Technical Bulletin Reprints*, vol. 3, pp. 37–41.

Royston, P. and P. Sasieni. 1994. dm16: Compact listing of a single variable. *Stata Technical Bulletin* 17: 7–8. Reprinted in *Stata Technical Bulletin Reprints*, vol. 3, pp. 41–43.

Also See

Related: [R] **display**, [R] **edit**, [R] **tabdisp**

Title

> **lnskew0** — Find zero-skewness log or Box–Cox transform

Syntax

lnskew0 *newvar* = *exp* [if *exp*] [in *range*] [, level(*#*) delta(*#*) zero(*#*)]

bcskew0 *newvar* = *exp* [if *exp*] [in *range*] [, level(*#*) delta(*#*) zero(*#*)]

Description

lnskew0 creates *newvar* = $\ln(\pm exp - k)$, choosing k and the sign of *exp* so that the skewness of *newvar* is zero.

bcskew0 creates *newvar* = $(exp^\lambda - 1)/\lambda$, the Box–Cox power transformation (Box and Cox 1964), choosing λ so that the skewness of *newvar* is zero. *exp* must be strictly positive. Also see [R] **boxcox** for maximum likelihood estimation of λ.

Options

level(*#*) specifies the confidence level for a confidence interval for k (lnskew0) or λ (bcskew0). Unlike usual, the confidence interval is calculated only if level() is specified. As usual, *#* is specified as an integer; 95 means 95% confidence intervals. The level() option is honored only if the number of observations exceeds 7.

delta(*#*) specifies the increment used for calculating the derivative of the skewness function with respect to k (lnskew0) or λ (bcskew0). The default values are 0.02 for lnskew0 and 0.01 for bcskew0.

zero(*#*) specifies a value for skewness to determine convergence that is small enough to be considered zero and is by default 0.001.

Remarks

▷ Example

Using our automobile data (see [U] **9 Stata's on-line tutorials and sample datasets**), we want to generate a new variable equal to $\ln(\text{mpg} - k)$ to be approximately normally distributed. mpg records the miles per gallon for each of our cars. One feature of the normal distribution is that it has skewness 0.

```
. lnskew0 lnmpg = mpg
       Transform |          k     [95% Conf. Interval]       Skewness
----------------+------------------------------------------------------
     ln(mpg-k) |   5.383659      (not calculated)           -7.05e-06
```

This created the new variable $\text{lnmpg} = \ln(\text{mpg} - 5.384)$:

```
. describe lnmpg
   13. lnmpg      float   %9.0g                    ln(mpg-5.3836595)
```

195

Since we did not specify the `level()` option, no confidence interval was calculated. At the outset, we could have typed

```
. lnskew0 lnmpg = mpg, level(95)
       Transform |         k     [95% Conf. Interval]      Skewness
-----------------+----------------------------------------------------
       ln(mpg-k) |  5.383659    -17.12339   9.892416      -7.05e-06
```

The confidence interval is calculated under the assumption that $\ln(\text{mpg} - k)$ really does have a normal distribution. It would be perfectly reasonable to use `lnskew0` even if we did not believe the transformed variable would have a normal distribution—if we literally wanted the zero-skewness transform—although in that case the confidence interval would be an approximation of unknown quality to the true confidence interval. If we now wanted to test the believability of the confidence interval, we could also test our new variable `lnmpg` using `swilk` with the `lnnormal` option.

◁

❑ Technical Note

`lnskew0` (and `bcskew0`) reports the resulting skewness of the variable merely to reassure you of the accuracy of its results. In our above example, `lnskew0` found k such that the resulting skewness was $-7 \cdot 10^{-6}$, a number close enough to zero for all practical purposes. If you wanted to make it even smaller, you could specify the `zero()` option. Typing `lnskew0 new=mpg, zero(1e-8)` changes the estimated k to -5.383552 from -5.383659 and reduces the calculated skewness to $-2 \cdot 10^{-11}$.

When you request a confidence interval, it is possible that `lnskew0` will report the lower confidence interval as '.', which should be taken as indicating the lower confidence limit $k_L = -\infty$. (This cannot happen with `bcskew0`.)

As an example, consider a sample of size n on x and assume the skewness of x is positive, but not significantly so at the desired significance level, say 5%. Then no matter how large and negative you make k_L, there is no value extreme enough to make the skewness of $\ln(x - k_L)$ equal the corresponding percentile (97.5 for a 95% confidence interval) of the distribution of skewness in a normal distribution of the same sample size. You cannot because the distribution of $\ln(x - k_L)$ tends to that of x—apart from location and scale shift—as $x \to \infty$. This "problem" never applies to the upper confidence limit k_U because the skewness of $\ln(x - k_U)$ tends to $-\infty$ as k tends upwards to the minimum value of x.

❑

▷ Example

In the above example, using `lnskew0` with a variable like `mpg` is probably undesirable. `mpg` has a natural zero and we are shifting that zero arbitrarily. On the other hand, use of `lnskew0` with a variable such as temperature measured in Fahrenheit or Celsius would be more appropriate as the zero is indeed arbitrary.

For a variable like `mpg`, it makes more sense to use the Box–Cox power transform (Box and Cox 1964):

$$y^{(\lambda)} = \frac{y^\lambda - 1}{\lambda}$$

λ is free to take on any value, but note that $y^{(1)} = y - 1$, $y^{(0)} = \ln(y)$, and $y^{(-1)} = 1 - 1/y$.

bcskew0 works like lnskew0:

```
. bcskew0 bcmpg = mpg, level(95)
        Transform |          L    [95% Conf. Interval]      Skewness
------------------+-----------------------------------------------------
     (mpg^L-1)/L  |  -.3673283    -1.212752    .4339645       .0001898
```

It is worth noting that the 95% confidence interval includes $\lambda = -1$ (λ is labeled L in the output), which has a rather more pleasing interpretation—gallons per mile—rather than $(\text{mpg}^{-.3673} - 1)/(-.3673)$. The confidence interval, however, is calculated under the assumption that the power transformed variable is normally distributed. It makes perfect sense to use bcskew0 even when one does not believe that the transformed variable will be normally distributed, but in that case the confidence interval is an approximation of unknown quality. If one believes that the transformed data is normally distributed, one can alternatively use boxcox to estimate λ; see [R] **boxcox**.

◁

Saved Results

lnskew0 and bcskew0 save in r():

Scalars

r(gamma)	k (lnskew0)
r(lambda)	λ (bcskew0)
r(lb)	lower bound of confidence interval
r(ub)	upper bound of confidence interval
r(skewness)	resulting skewness of transformed variable

Methods and Formulas

lnskew0 and bcskew0 are implemented as ado-files.

Skewness is as calculated by summarize; see [R] **summarize**. Newton's method with numeric, uncentered derivatives is used to estimate k (lnskew0) and λ (bcskew0). In the case of lnskew0, the initial value is chosen so that the minimum of $x - k$ is 1 and thus $\ln(x - k)$ is 0. bcskew0 starts with $\lambda = 1$.

Acknowledgment

lnskew0 and bcskew0 were written by Patrick Royston of the Imperial College School of Medicine, London.

References

Box, G. E. P. and D. R. Cox. 1964. An analysis of transformations. *Journal of the Royal Statistical Society*, Series B 26: 211–243.

Also See

Related: [R] **boxcox**, [R] **swilk**

Title

> **log** — Echo copy of session to file or device

Syntax

<u>log</u> using *filename* $\left[,\ \underline{\text{nop}}\text{roc append replace} \right]$

<u>log</u> $\left\{ \text{on} \,|\, \underline{\text{off}} \,|\, \underline{\text{c}}\text{lose} \right\}$

<u>set</u> $\left\{ \underline{\text{d}}\text{isplay} \,|\, \underline{\text{log}} \right\}$ $\left\{ \underline{\text{l}}\text{inesize} \,|\, \underline{\text{p}}\text{agesize} \right\}$ #

In addition to the above, Stata for Windows 98/95/NT users may click on the **Open Log** button. Stata for Windows 3.1 users may click on the **Log...** button. Stata for Macintosh users may click on the **Log** button and select **Open Log** from the pop-up menu.

Description

log using opens *filename* and echoes a copy of your session to the file. If *filename* is specified without an extension, .log is assumed.

log close stops logging the session and closes the file. log off temporarily stops logging the session, leaving the file open. log on resumes logging to the file.

set log controls the dimensions of output sent to the log. set display does the same for the terminal.

Options

noproc causes Stata to record only the characters you type. No output of any kind, including error messages, is sent to the file. This option offers a convenient way to create a do-file of your session.

append directs Stata to append to the end of an existing file. append may not be abbreviated.

replace directs Stata to allow overwriting of an existing file. replace may not be abbreviated.

Remarks

For an explanation of the log command, see [U] **18 Printing and preserving output**.

The character width of the lines written to the log file may differ from that of the video monitor. set log linesize allows you to change the maximum width of lines sent to the log. set log pagesize currently has no effect.

set display sets the size of the display rather than the log file. set display pagesize is relevant only for Stata for Unix; it is ignored by Stata for Windows and Stata for Macintosh. set display linesize is relevant only for Stata for Unix and Stata for Macintosh; it is ignored by Stata for Windows.

The linesize parameter indicates the number of characters that can be placed on a line and should be set to 1 less than the full width of the screen. On Unix systems, Stata obtains the value from the /etc/termcap(5) file or /usr/lib/terminfo(4) directory. On certain windowing systems, such as Sunview, the dimension of the window is obtained from the windowing system.

The `pagesize` parameter of `set display` indicates the number of lines that can be displayed before a `--more--` condition. It should be specified as 2 less than the physical number of lines on the screen. On Unix systems, Stata obtains the value from `termcap` or `terminfo` or the windowing system.

Setting the `display pagesize` to zero is the same as making it infinite; `--more--` conditions will never occur, effectively turning off more. `set more off`, however, is preferred; see [R] **more**.

Also See

Complementary: [R] **more**, [R] **query**

Background: [GSM] **16 Logs: Printing and saving output**,
    [GSW] **16 Logs: Printing and saving output**,
    [GSU] **14 Logs: Printing and saving output**,
    [GSU] **fsl**,
    [U] **10 –more– conditions**,
    [U] **14.6 File-naming conventions**,
    [U] **18 Printing and preserving output**

Title

> **logistic** — Logistic regression

Syntax

logistic *depvar varlist* [*weight*] [**if** *exp*] [**in** *range*] [, **l**evel(*#*) **r**obust

cluster(*varname*) **sc**ore(*newvarname*) **asis** **off**set(*varname*) *maximize_options*]

lfit [*depvar*] [*weight*] [**if** *exp*] [**in** *range*] [, **group**(*#*) **t**able **out**sample

all **beta**(*matname*)]

lstat [*depvar*] [*weight*] [**if** *exp*] [**in** *range*] [, **c**utoff(*#*) **all** **beta**(*matname*)]

lroc [*depvar*] [*weight*] [**if** *exp*] [**in** *range*] [, **nog**raph *graph_options*

all **beta**(*matname*)]

lsens [*depvar*] [*weight*] [**if** *exp*] [**in** *range*] [, **nog**raph *graph_options*

genprob(*varname*) **gensens**(*varname*) **genspec**(*varname*) **replace**

all **beta**(*matname*)]

logistic allows **fweights** and **pweights**; **lfit**, **lstat**, **lroc**, and **lsens** allow only **fweights**; see [U] **14.1.6 weight**.
logistic shares the features of all estimation commands; see [U] **23 Estimation and post-estimation commands**.
logistic may be used with **sw** to perform stepwise estimation; see [R] **sw**.

Syntax for predict

predict [*type*] *newvarname* [**if** *exp*] [**in** *range*] [, *statistic* **rule**s **asif** **nooff**set]

where *statistic* is

p	probability of a positive outcome (the default)
xb	$x_j\mathbf{b}$, fitted values
stdp	standard error of the prediction
* dbeta	Pregibon (1981) $\Delta\beta$ influence statistic
* deviance	deviance residual
* dx2	Hosmer and Lemeshow (1989) $\Delta\chi^2$ influence statistic
* ddeviance	Hosmer and Lemeshow (1989) ΔD influence statistic
* hat	Pregibon (1981) leverage
* number	sequential number of the covariate pattern
residuals	Pearson residuals; adjusted for number sharing covariate pattern
* rstandard	standardized Pearson residuals; adjusted for number sharing covariate pattern

Unstarred statistics are available both in and out of sample; type **predict** ... **if e(sample)** ... if wanted only for
the estimation sample. Starred statistics are calculated only for the estimation sample even when **if e(sample)**
is not specified.

200

Description

logistic estimates a logistic regression of *depvar* on *varlist*, where *depvar* is a 0/1 variable (or, more precisely, a 0/non-0 variable). Without arguments, logistic redisplays the last logistic estimates. logistic displays estimates as odds ratios; to view coefficients, type logit after running logistic. To obtain odds ratios for any covariate pattern relative to another, see [R] **lincom**.

lfit displays either the Pearson goodness-of-fit test or the Hosmer–Lemeshow goodness-of-fit test.

lstat displays various summary statistics, including the classification table.

lroc graphs and calculates the area under the ROC curve.

lsens graphs sensitivity and specificity versus probability cutoff and optionally creates new variables containing this data.

lfit, lstat, lroc, and lsens can produce statistics and graphs either for the estimation sample or for any set of observations. However, they always use the estimation sample by default. When weights, if, or in are used with logistic, it is not necessary to repeat them with these commands when you want statistics computed for the estimation sample. Specify if, in, or the all option only when you want statistics computed for a set of observations other than the estimation sample. Specify weights (only fweights are allowed with these commands) only when you want to use a different set of weights.

By default, lfit, lstat, lroc, and lsens use the last model estimated by logistic. Alternatively, the model can be specified by inputting a vector of coefficients with the beta() option and passing the name of the dependent variable *depvar* to the commands.

Here is a list of other estimation commands that may be of interest. See [R] **estimation commands** for a complete list.

(Continued on next page)

blogit	[R] **glogit**	Maximum-likelihood logit regression for grouped data
bprobit	[R] **glogit**	Maximum-likelihood probit regression for grouped data
clogit	[R] **clogit**	Conditional (fixed-effects) logistic regression
cloglog	[R] **cloglog**	Maximum-likelihood complementary log-log estimation
glm	[R] **glm**	Generalized linear models
glogit	[R] **glogit**	Weighted least-squares logit regression for grouped data
gprobit	[R] **glogit**	Weighted least-squares probit regression for grouped data
heckprob	[R] **heckprob**	Maximum-likelihood probit estimation with selection
hetprob	[R] **hetprob**	Maximum-likelihood heteroscedastic probit estimation
logit	[R] **logit**	Maximum-likelihood logit regression
mlogit	[R] **mlogit**	Maximum-likelihood multinomial (polytomous) logistic regression
ologit	[R] **ologit**	Maximum-likelihood ordered logit regression
oprobit	[R] **oprobit**	Maximum-likelihood ordered probit regression
probit	[R] **probit**	Maximum-likelihood probit regression
scobit	[R] **scobit**	Maximum-likelihood skewed logit estimation
svylogit	[R] **svy estimators**	Survey version of `logit`
svymlog	[R] **svy estimators**	Survey version of `mlogit`
svyolog	[R] **svy estimators**	Survey version of `ologit`
svyoprob	[R] **svy estimators**	Survey version of `oprobit`
svyprobt	[R] **svy estimators**	Survey version of `probit`
xtclog	[R] **xtclog**	Random-effects and population-averaged cloglog models
xtlogit	[R] **xtlogit**	Fixed-effects, random-effects, and population-averaged logit models
xtprobit	[R] **xtprobit**	Random-effects and population-averaged probit models
xtgee	[R] **xtgee**	GEE population-averaged generalized linear models

Options

level(*#*) specifies the confidence level, in percent, for confidence intervals. The default is level(95) or as set by set level; see [U] **23.5 Specifying the width of confidence intervals**.

robust specifies that the Huber/White/sandwich estimator of variance is to be used in place of the traditional calculation; see [U] **23.11 Obtaining robust variance estimates**. robust combined with cluster() allows observations which are not independent within cluster (although they must be independent between clusters).

If you specify pweights, robust is implied; see [U] **23.13 Weighted estimation**.

cluster(*varname*) specifies that the observations are independent across groups (clusters) but not necessarily within groups. *varname* specifies to which group each observation belongs; e.g., cluster(personid) in data with repeated observations on individuals. cluster() affects the estimated standard errors and variance–covariance matrix of the estimators (VCE), but not the estimated coefficients; see [U] **23.11 Obtaining robust variance estimates**. cluster() can be used with pweights to produce estimates for unstratified cluster-sampled data, but see the svylogit command in [R] **svy estimators** for a command designed especially for survey data.

cluster() implies robust; specifying robust cluster() is equivalent to typing cluster() by itself.

score(*newvarname*) creates *newvar* containing $u_j = \partial \ln L_j / \partial(\mathbf{x}_j \mathbf{b})$ for each observation j in the sample. The score vector is $\sum \partial \ln L_j / \partial \mathbf{b} = \sum u_j \mathbf{x}_j$; i.e., the product of *newvar* with each covariate summed over observations. See [U] **23.12 Obtaining scores**.

asis forces retention of perfect predictor variables and their associated perfectly predicted observations and may produce instabilities in maximization; see [R] **probit** (*sic*).

offset(*varname*) specifies that *varname* is to be included in the model with coefficient constrained to be 1.

maximize_options control the maximization process; see [R] **maximize**. You should never have to specify them.

group(*#*) specifies the number of quantiles to be used to group the data for the Hosmer–Lemeshow goodness-of-fit test. group(10) is typically specified. If this option is not given, the Pearson goodness-of-fit test is computed using the covariate patterns in the data as groups.

table displays a table of the groups used for the Hosmer–Lemeshow or Pearson goodness-of-fit test with predicted probabilities, observed and expected counts for both outcomes, and totals for each group.

outsample adjusts the degrees of freedom for the Pearson and Hosmer–Lemeshow goodness-of-fit tests for samples outside of the estimation sample. See the section *Samples other than estimation sample* later in this entry.

all requests that the statistic be computed for all observations in the dataset ignoring any if or in restrictions specified with logistic.

beta(*matname*) specifies a row vector containing coefficients for a logistic model. The columns of the row vector must be labeled with the corresponding names of the independent variables in the dataset. The dependent variable *depvar* must be specified immediately after the command name. See the section *Models other than last estimated model* later in this entry.

cutoff(*#*) specifies the value for determining whether an observation has a predicted positive outcome. An observation is classified as positive if its predicted probability is $\geq$ *#*. Default is 0.5.

nograph suppresses graphical output.

graph_options are any of the options allowed with graph, twoway; see [G] **graph options**.

genprob(*varname*), gensens(*varname*), and genspec(*varname*) specify the names of new variables created to contain, respectively, the probability cutoffs and corresponding sensitivity and specificity.

replace requests that if existing variables are specified for genprob(), gensens(), or genspec(), they should be overwritten.

Options for predict

p, the default, calculates the probability of a positive outcome.

xb calculates the linear prediction.

stdp calculates the standard error of the linear prediction.

dbeta calculates the Pregibon (1981) $\Delta\widehat{\beta}$ influence statistic, a standardized measure of the difference in the coefficient vector due to deletion of the observation along with all others that share the same covariate pattern. In Hosmer and Lemeshow (1989) jargon, this statistic is M-asymptotic, that is, adjusted for the number of observations that share the same covariate pattern.

deviance calculates the deviance residual.

dx2 calculates the Hosmer and Lemeshow (1989) $\Delta\chi^2$ influence statistic reflecting the decrease in the Pearson χ^2 due to deletion of the observation and all others that share the same covariate pattern.

ddeviance calculates the Hosmer and Lemeshow (1989) ΔD influence statistic, which is the change in the deviance residual due to deletion of the observation and all others that share the same covariate pattern.

hat calculates the Pregibon (1981) leverage or the diagonal elements of the hat matrix adjusted for the number of observations that share the same covariate pattern.

number numbers the covariate patterns—observations with the same covariate pattern have the same number. Observations not used in estimation have number set to missing. The "first" covariate pattern is numbered 1, the second 2, and so on.

residuals calculates the Pearson residual as given by Hosmer and Lemeshow (1989) and adjusted for the number of observations that share the same covariate pattern.

rstandard calculates the standardized Pearson residual as given by Hosmer and Lemeshow (1989) and adjusted for the number of observations that share the same covariate pattern.

rules requests that Stata use any "rules" that were used to identify the model when making the prediction. By default, Stata calculates missing for excluded observations. See [R] **logit** for an example.

asif requests that Stata ignore the rules and the exclusion criteria, and calculate predictions for all observations possible using the estimated parameter from the model. See [R] **logit** for an example.

nooffset is relevant only if you specified offset(*varname*) for logistic. It modifies the calculations made by predict so that they ignore the offset variable; the linear prediction is treated as $\mathbf{x}_j\mathbf{b}$ rather than $\mathbf{x}_j\mathbf{b} + \text{offset}_j$.

Remarks

Remarks are presented under the headings

> *logistic and logit*
> *Robust estimate of variance*
> *lfit*
> *lstat*
> *lroc*
> *lsens*
> *Samples other than estimation sample*
> *Models other than last estimated model*
> *predict after logistic*

logistic and logit

logistic provides an alternative and preferred way to estimate maximum-likelihood logit models, the other choice being logit described in [R] **logit**.

First, let us dispose of some confusing terminology. We use the words logit and logistic to mean the same thing: maximum likelihood estimation. To some, one or the other of these words connotes transforming the dependent variable and using weighted least squares to estimate the model, but that is not how we use either word here. Thus, the logit and logistic commands produce the same results.

The `logistic` command is generally preferred to `logit` because `logistic` presents the estimates in terms of odds ratios rather than coefficients. To a few, this may seem a disadvantage, but you can type `logit` without arguments after `logistic` to see the underlying coefficients.

Nevertheless, it is still worth reading [R] **logit** because `logistic` shares the same features as `logit`, including omitting variables due to collinearity or one-way causation.

For an introduction to logistic regression, see Lemeshow and Hosmer (1998) or Pagano and Gauvreau (1993, 427–443); for a thorough discussion, see Hosmer and Lemeshow (1989).

▷ Example

Consider the following dataset from a study of risk factors associated with low birth weight described in Hosmer and Lemeshow (1989, appendix 1).

```
. describe
Contains data from lbw.dta
  obs:            189                     Hosmer & Lemeshow data
  vars:            11                     11 Aug 1998 10:56
  size:         3,402 (99.6% of memory free)
-------------------------------------------------------------------------------
   1. id          int     %8.0g           identification code
   2. low         byte    %8.0g           birth weight<2500g
   3. age         byte    %8.0g           age of mother
   4. lwt         int     %8.0g           weight at last menstrual period
   5. race        byte    %8.0g    race   race
   6. smoke       byte    %8.0g           smoked during pregnancy
   7. ptl         byte    %8.0g           premature labor history (count)
   8. ht          byte    %8.0g           has history of hypertension
   9. ui          byte    %8.0g           presence, uterine irritability
  10. ftv         byte    %8.0g           number of visits to physician
                                              during 1st trimester
  11. bwt         int     %8.0g           birth weight (grams)
-------------------------------------------------------------------------------
Sorted by:
```

They want to investigate the causes of low birth weight. In this dataset, `race` is a categorical variable indicating whether a person is white (`race` = 1), black (`race` = 2), or other (`race` = 3). The authors want indicator (dummy) variables for `race` included in the regression. (One of the dummies, of course, must be omitted.) Thus, before we can estimate the model, we must create the race dummy variables.

There are a number of ways we could do this, but the easiest is to let another Stata command, `xi`, do it for us. We type `xi:` in front of our `logistic` command and in our *varlist* include not `race` but `i.race` to indicate we want the indicator variables for this categorical variable; see [R] **xi** for the full details.

(Continued on next page)

```
. xi: logistic low age lwt i.race smoke ptl ht ui
i.race                  Irace_1-3    (naturally coded; Irace_1 omitted)
Logit estimates                          Number of obs   =        189
                                         LR chi2(8)      =      33.22
                                         Prob > chi2     =     0.0001
Log likelihood =   -100.724              Pseudo R2       =     0.1416

--------------------------------------------------------------------------
     low | Odds Ratio   Std. Err.       z     P>|z|    [95% Conf. Interval]
---------+----------------------------------------------------------------
     age |   .9732636    .0354759    -0.743   0.457    .9061578    1.045339
     lwt |   .9849634    .0068217    -2.188   0.029    .9716834    .9984249
 Irace_2 |   3.534767    1.860737     2.399   0.016    1.259736    9.918406
 Irace_3 |   2.368079    1.039949     1.963   0.050    1.001356    5.600207
   smoke |   2.517698    1.00916      2.304   0.021    1.147676    5.523162
     ptl |   1.719161    .5952579     1.565   0.118    .8721455    3.388787
      ht |   6.249602    4.322408     2.650   0.008    1.611152    24.24199
      ui |    2.1351     .9808153     1.651   0.099    .8677528     5.2534
--------------------------------------------------------------------------
```

The odds ratios are for a one-unit change in the variable. If we wanted the odds ratio for `age` to be in terms of 4-year intervals, we would

```
. gen age4 = age/4
. xi: logistic low age4 lwt i.race smoke ptl ht ui
(output omitted)
```

After `logistic`, we can type `logit` to see the model in terms of coefficients and standard errors:

```
. logit
Logit estimates                          Number of obs   =        189
                                         LR chi2(8)      =      33.22
                                         Prob > chi2     =     0.0001
Log likelihood =   -100.724              Pseudo R2       =     0.1416

--------------------------------------------------------------------------
     low |     Coef.    Std. Err.       z     P>|z|    [95% Conf. Interval]
---------+----------------------------------------------------------------
     age | -.0271003    .0364504    -0.743   0.457   -.0985418    .0443412
     lwt | -.0151508    .0069259    -2.188   0.029   -.0287253   -.0015763
 Irace_2 |  1.262647    .5264101     2.399   0.016    .2309024    2.294392
 Irace_3 |  .8620792    .4391531     1.963   0.050    .0013548    1.722804
   smoke |  .9233448    .4008266     2.304   0.021    .1377391    1.708951
     ptl |  .5418366    .346249      1.565   0.118   -.136799     1.220472
      ht |  1.832518    .6916292     2.650   0.008    .4769494    3.188086
      ui |  .7585135    .4593768     1.651   0.099   -.1418484    1.658875
   _cons |  .4612239    1.20459      0.383   0.702   -1.899729    2.822176
--------------------------------------------------------------------------
```

If we wanted to see the `logistic` output again, we would type `logistic` without arguments.

◁

▷ Example

You can specify the confidence interval for the odds ratios with the `level()` option, and you can do this either at estimation time or when you replay the model. For instance, to see our previous models with narrower, 90% confidence intervals:

```
. logistic, level(90)
Logit estimates                              Number of obs   =        189
                                             LR chi2(8)      =      33.22
                                             Prob > chi2     =     0.0001
Log likelihood =    -100.724                 Pseudo R2       =     0.1416
-------------------------------------------------------------------------
     low | Odds Ratio   Std. Err.      z     P>|z|     [90% Conf. Interval]
---------+---------------------------------------------------------------
     age |   .9732636    .0354759   -0.743   0.457     .9166258   1.033401
     lwt |   .9849634    .0068217   -2.188   0.029     .9738063   .9962483
 Irace_2 |   3.534767    1.860737    2.399   0.016     1.487028   8.402379
 Irace_3 |   2.368079    1.039949    1.963   0.050     1.149971   4.876471
   smoke |   2.517698     1.00916    2.304   0.021     1.302185   4.867819
     ptl |   1.719161    .5952579    1.565   0.118     .9726876   3.038505
      ht |   6.249602    4.322408    2.650   0.008     2.003487   19.49478
      ui |     2.1351    .9808153    1.651   0.099      1.00291   4.545424
-------------------------------------------------------------------------
```

◁

Robust estimate of variance

If you specify `robust`, Stata reports the robust estimate of variance described in [U] **23.11 Obtaining robust variance estimates**. Here is the model previously estimated with the robust estimate of variance:

```
. xi: logistic low age lwt i.race smoke ptl ht ui, robust
i.race                  Irace_1-3    (naturally coded; Irace_1 omitted)
Logit estimates                              Number of obs   =        189
                                             Wald chi2(8)    =      29.02
                                             Prob > chi2     =     0.0003
Log likelihood =    -100.724                 Pseudo R2       =     0.1416
-------------------------------------------------------------------------
         |             Robust
     low | Odds Ratio   Std. Err.      z     P>|z|     [95% Conf. Interval]
---------+---------------------------------------------------------------
     age |   .9732636    .0329376   -0.801   0.423     .9108015   1.040009
     lwt |   .9849634    .0070209   -2.126   0.034     .9712984   .9988206
 Irace_2 |   3.534767    1.793616    2.488   0.013     1.307504   9.556051
 Irace_3 |   2.368079    1.026563    1.989   0.047     1.012512   5.538501
   smoke |   2.517698    .9736416    2.388   0.017     1.179852   5.372537
     ptl |   1.719161    .7072902    1.317   0.188     .7675715   3.850476
      ht |   6.249602    4.102026    2.792   0.005     1.726445    22.6231
      ui |     2.1351    1.042775    1.553   0.120     .8197749   5.560858
-------------------------------------------------------------------------
```

Additionally, `robust` allows you to specify `cluster()` and is then able, within cluster, to relax the assumption of independence. To illustrate this, we have made some fictional additions to the low-birth-weight data.

Pretend that this data is not a random sample of mothers but instead is a random sample of mothers from a random sample of hospitals. In fact, that may be true—we do not know the history of this data—but we can pretend in any case.

Hospitals specialize and it would not be too incorrect to say that some hospitals specialize in more difficult cases. We are going to show two extremes. In one, all hospitals are alike but we are going to estimate under the possibility that they might differ. In the other, hospitals are strikingly different. In both cases, we assume patients are drawn from 20 hospitals.

In both examples, we will estimate the same model and we will type the same command to estimate it. Below is the same data we have been using but with a new variable `hospid`, which identifies from which of the 20 hospitals each patient was drawn (and which we have made up):

```
. xi: logistic low age lwt i.race smoke ptl ht ui, robust cluster(hospid)
i.race                  Irace_1-3      (naturally coded; Irace_1 omitted)
```

```
Logit estimates                                   Number of obs   =        189
                                                  Wald chi2(8)    =      76.30
                                                  Prob > chi2     =     0.0000
Log likelihood =     -100.724                     Pseudo R2       =     0.1416
```

```
                          (standard errors adjusted for clustering on hospid)
```

low	Odds Ratio	Robust Std. Err.	z	P>|z|	[95% Conf. Interval]	
age	.9732636	.0249078	-1.059	0.290	.9256494	1.023327
lwt	.9849634	.007971	-1.872	0.061	.9694637	1.000711
Irace_2	3.534767	1.950577	2.288	0.022	1.19852	10.425
Irace_3	2.368079	.7536564	2.709	0.007	1.2691	4.418721
smoke	2.517698	1.087079	2.138	0.032	1.08013	5.868556
ptl	1.719161	.698428	1.334	0.182	.7753659	3.811769
ht	6.249602	4.318176	2.652	0.008	1.613292	24.20984
ui	2.1351	1.062335	1.524	0.127	.8051863	5.661611

The standard errors are quite similar to the standard errors we have previously obtained, whether we used the robust or the conventional estimators. In this example, we invented the hospital ids randomly.

Here are the results of the estimation with the same data but with a different set of hospital ids:

```
. xi: logistic low age lwt i.race smoke ptl ht ui, robust cluster(hospid)
i.race                  Irace_1-3      (naturally coded; Irace_1 omitted)
```

```
Logit estimates                                   Number of obs   =        189
                                                  Wald chi2(8)    =       7.19
                                                  Prob > chi2     =     0.5167
Log likelihood =     -100.724                     Pseudo R2       =     0.1416
```

```
                          (standard errors adjusted for clustering on hospid)
```

low	Odds Ratio	Robust Std. Err.	z	P>|z|	[95% Conf. Interval]	
age	.9732636	.0293064	-0.900	0.368	.9174862	1.032432
lwt	.9849634	.0106123	-1.406	0.160	.9643817	1.005984
Irace_2	3.534767	3.120338	1.430	0.153	.6265521	19.9418
Irace_3	2.368079	1.297738	1.573	0.116	.8089594	6.932114
smoke	2.517698	1.570287	1.480	0.139	.7414969	8.548654
ptl	1.719161	.6799153	1.370	0.171	.7919046	3.732161
ht	6.249602	7.165454	1.598	0.110	.660558	59.12808
ui	2.1351	1.411977	1.147	0.251	.5841231	7.804266

Note the strikingly larger standard errors. What happened? In this data, women most likely to have low-birth-weight babies are sent to certain hospitals and the decision on likeliness is based not just on age, smoking history, etc., but on other things that doctors can see but are not recorded in our data. Thus, merely because a woman is at one of the centers identifies her to be more likely to have a low-birth-weight baby.

So much for our fictional example. The rest of this section uses the real low-birth-weight data. To remind you, the last model we left off with was

```
. xi: logistic low age lwt i.race smoke ptl ht ui
i.race              Irace_1-3    (naturally coded; Irace_1 omitted)
```

```
Logit estimates                         Number of obs   =       189
                                        LR chi2(8)      =     33.22
                                        Prob > chi2     =    0.0001
Log likelihood =   -100.724             Pseudo R2       =    0.1416

------------------------------------------------------------------------------
     low | Odds Ratio   Std. Err.      z    P>|z|     [95% Conf. Interval]
---------+--------------------------------------------------------------------
     age |   .9732636    .0354759    -0.743   0.457     .9061578    1.045339
     lwt |   .9849634    .0068217    -2.188   0.029     .9716834    .9984249
 Irace_2 |   3.534767    1.860737     2.399   0.016     1.259736    9.918406
 Irace_3 |   2.368079    1.039949     1.963   0.050     1.001356    5.600207
   smoke |   2.517698    1.00916      2.304   0.021     1.147676    5.523162
     ptl |   1.719161    .5952579     1.565   0.118     .8721455    3.388787
      ht |   6.249602    4.322408     2.650   0.008     1.611152    24.24199
      ui |    2.1351     .9808153     1.651   0.099     .8677528      5.2534
------------------------------------------------------------------------------
```

lfit

lfit computes goodness-of-fit tests, either the Pearson χ^2 test or the Hosmer–Lemeshow test.

By default, lfit, lstat, lroc, and lsens compute statistics for the estimation sample using the last model estimated by logistic. However, samples other than the estimation sample can be specified; see the section *Samples other than estimation sample* later in this entry. Models other than the last model estimated by logistic can also be specified; see the section *Models other than last estimated model*.

▷ Example

lfit, typed without options, presents the Pearson χ^2 goodness-of-fit test for the estimated model. The Pearson χ^2 goodness-of-fit test is a test of the observed against expected number of responses using cells defined by the covariate patterns; see *predict with the numbers option* below for the definition of covariate patterns.

```
. lfit
Logistic model for low, goodness-of-fit test

      number of observations =        189
number of covariate patterns =        182
          Pearson chi2(173) =     179.24
                Prob > chi2 =     0.3567
```

Our model fits reasonably well. We should note, however, that the number of covariate patterns is close to the number of observations, making the applicability of the Pearson χ^2 test questionable, but not necessarily inappropriate. Hosmer and Lemeshow (1989) suggest regrouping the data by ordering on the predicted probabilities and then forming, say, 10 nearly equal-size groups. lfit with the group() option does this:

```
. lfit, group(10)
Logistic model for low, goodness-of-fit test
(Table collapsed on quantiles of estimated probabilities)
      number of observations =        189
             number of groups =         10
     Hosmer-Lemeshow chi2(8) =       9.65
                  Prob > chi2 =     0.2904
```

Again, we cannot reject our model. If you specify the `table` option, `lfit` displays the groups along with the expected and observed number of positive responses (low-birth-weight babies):

```
. lfit, group(10) table
Logistic model for low, goodness-of-fit test
(Table collapsed on quantiles of estimated probabilities)
_Group    _Prob    _Obs_1    _Exp_1    _Obs_0    _Exp_0    _Total
     1    0.0827         0       1.2        19      17.8        19
     2    0.1276         2       2.0        17      17.0        19
     3    0.2015         6       3.2        13      15.8        19
     4    0.2432         1       4.3        18      14.7        19
     5    0.2792         7       4.9        12      14.1        19
     6    0.3138         7       5.6        12      13.4        19
     7    0.3872         6       6.5        13      12.5        19
     8    0.4828         7       8.2        12      10.8        19
     9    0.5941        10      10.3         9       8.7        19
    10    0.8391        13      12.8         5       5.2        18

             number of observations =       189
                  number of groups =        10
         Hosmer-Lemeshow chi2(8) =          9.65
                   Prob > chi2 =           0.2904
```
◁

❏ Technical Note

`lfit` with the `group()` option puts all observations with the same predicted probabilities into the same group. If, as in the previous example, we request 10 groups, the groups that `lfit` makes are $[p_0, p_{10}]$, $(p_{10}, p_{20}]$, $(p_{20}, p_{30}]$, $\ldots$, $(p_{90}, p_{100}]$, where p_k is the kth percentile of the predicted probabilities, with p_0 the minimum and p_{100} the maximum.

If there are large numbers of ties at the quantile boundaries—as will frequently happen if all independent variables are categorical and there are only a few of them, the sizes of the groups will be uneven. If the totals in some of the groups are small, the χ^2 statistic for the Hosmer–Lemeshow test may be unreliable. In this case, either fewer groups should be specified or the Pearson goodness-of-fit test may be a better choice.

❏

▷ Example

The `table` option can be used without the `group()` option. We would not want to specify this for our current model because there were 182 covariate patterns in the data, caused by the inclusion of the two continuous variables `age` and `lwt` in the model. As an aside, we estimate a simpler model and specify `table` with `lfit`:

```
. logistic low Irace_2 Irace_3 smoke ui
Logit estimates                               Number of obs   =        189
                                              LR chi2(4)      =      18.80
                                              Prob > chi2     =     0.0009
Log likelihood = -107.93404                   Pseudo R2       =     0.0801

---------------------------------------------------------------------------
     low | Odds Ratio  Std. Err.       z     P>|z|    [95% Conf. Interval]
---------+-----------------------------------------------------------------
 Irace_2 |   3.052746   1.498084    2.274    0.023    1.166749     7.987368
 Irace_3 |   2.922593   1.189226    2.636    0.008     1.31646     6.488269
   smoke |   2.945742   1.101835    2.888    0.004     1.41517     6.131701
      ui |   2.419131   1.047358    2.040    0.041     1.03546     5.651783
---------------------------------------------------------------------------
```

```
. lfit, tab
Logistic model for low, goodness-of-fit test
```

_Group	_Prob	_Obs_1	_Exp_1	_Obs_0	_Exp_0	_Total
1	0.1230	3	4.9	37	35.1	40
2	0.2533	1	1.0	3	3.0	4
3	0.2907	16	13.7	31	33.3	47
4	0.2923	15	12.6	28	30.4	43
5	0.2997	3	3.9	10	9.1	13
6	0.4978	4	4.0	4	4.0	8
7	0.4998	4	4.5	5	4.5	9
8	0.5087	2	1.5	1	1.5	3
9	0.5469	2	4.4	6	3.6	8
10	0.5577	6	5.6	4	4.4	10
11	0.7449	3	3.0	1	1.0	4

_Group	_Prob	Irace_2	Irace_3	smoke	ui
1	0.1230	0	0	0	0
2	0.2533	0	0	0	1
3	0.2907	0	1	0	0
4	0.2923	0	0	1	0
5	0.2997	1	0	0	0
6	0.4978	0	1	0	1
7	0.4998	0	0	1	1
8	0.5087	1	0	0	1
9	0.5469	0	1	1	0
10	0.5577	1	0	1	0
11	0.7449	0	1	1	1

```
            number of observations =      189
    number of covariate patterns =       11
              Pearson chi2(6) =        5.71
                 Prob > chi2 =      0.4569
```

◁

❏ Technical Note

logistic and lfit keep track of the estimation sample. If you type logistic ... if x==1, then when you type lfit the statistics will be calculated on the x==1 subsample of the data automatically.

You should specify if or in with lfit only when you wish to calculate statistics for a set of observations other than the estimation sample. See the section *Samples other than estimation sample* later in this entry.

If the logistic model was estimated with fweights, lfit properly accounts for the weights in its calculations. (Note: lfit does not allow pweights.) You do not have to specify the weights when you run lfit. Weights should only be specified with lfit when you wish to use a different set of weights.

❏

(*Continued on next page*)

lstat

▷ Example

lstat presents the classification statistics and classification table after logistic.

```
. lstat
Logistic model for low
                   -------- True --------
Classified |         D              ~D            Total
-----------+----------------------------+-----------
     +     |        21             12   |           33
     -     |        38            118   |          156
-----------+----------------------------+-----------
   Total   |        59            130   |          189
Classified + if predicted Pr(D) >= .5
True D defined as low ~= 0
-----------------------------------------------------
Sensitivity                     Pr( +| D)    35.59%
Specificity                     Pr( -|~D)    90.77%
Positive predictive value       Pr( D| +)    63.64%
Negative predictive value       Pr(~D| -)    75.64%
-----------------------------------------------------
False + rate for true ~D        Pr( +|~D)     9.23%
False - rate for true D         Pr( -| D)    64.41%
False + rate for classified +   Pr(~D| +)    36.36%
False - rate for classified -   Pr( D| -)    24.36%
-----------------------------------------------------
Correctly classified                         73.54%
-----------------------------------------------------
```

By default, lstat uses a cutoff of 0.5, although you can vary this with the cutoff() option. The lsens command can be used to review the potential cutoffs; see lsens below.

◁

lroc

lroc graphs the receiver operating characteristic (ROC) curve—a graph of sensitivity versus one minus specificity as the cutoff c is varied—and calculates the area under it. Sensitivity is the fraction of observed positive-outcome cases that are correctly classified; specificity is the fraction of observed negative-outcome cases that are correctly classified. When the purpose of the analysis is classification, one must choose a cutoff.

The curve starts at $(0, 0)$, corresponding to $c = 1$, and continues to $(1, 1)$, corresponding to $c = 0$. A model with no predictive power would be a $45°$ line. The greater the predictive power, the more bowed the curve, and hence the area beneath the curve is often used as a measure of the predictive power. A model with no predictive power has area 0.5; a perfect model has area 1.

The ROC curve was first discussed in signal detection theory (Peterson, Birdsall, and Fox 1954) and then was quickly introduced into psychology (Tanner and Swets 1954). It has since been applied in other fields, particularly medicine (for instance, Metz 1978). For a classic text on ROC techniques, see Green and Swets (1974).

▷ Example

ROC curves are typically used when the point of the analysis is classification, which it is not in our low-birth-weight model. Nevertheless, the ROC curve is

```
. lroc

Logistic model for low

number of observations =      189
area under ROC curve    =   0.7462
```

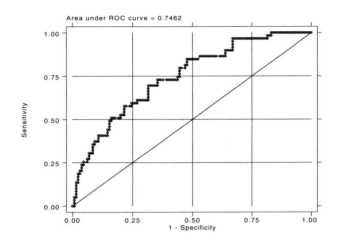

We see that the area under the curve is 0.7462.

◁

lsens

lsens also plots sensitivity and specificity; it plots both sensitivity and specificity versus probability cutoff c. The graph is equivalent to what you would get from lstat if you varied the cutoff probability from 0 to 1.

```
. lsens
```

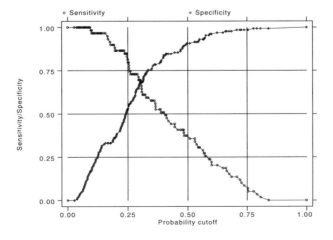

`lsens` will optionally create new variables containing the probability cutoff, sensitivity, and specificity.

```
. lsens, genprob(p) gensens(sens) genspec(spec) nograph
```

Note that the variables created will have $M + 2$ distinct nonmissing values, one for each of the M covariate patterns plus one for $c = 0$ and another for $c = 1$.

Samples other than estimation sample

`lfit`, `lstat`, `lroc`, and `lsens` can be used with samples other than the estimation sample. By default, these commands remember the estimation sample used with the last `logistic` command. To override this, you simply use an `if` or `in` restriction to select another set of observations, or specify the `all` option to force the command to use all the observations in the dataset.

If you use `lfit` with a sample that is completely different from the estimation sample (i.e., no overlap), you should also specify the `outsample` option so that the χ^2 statistic properly adjusts the degrees of freedom upward. For an overlapping sample, the conservative thing to do is to leave the degrees of freedom the same as they are for the estimation sample.

▷ Example

Suppose that we wish to develop a model for predicting low-birth-weight babies. One approach to developing a prediction model would be to divide our data into two groups, a developmental sample and a validation sample. See Lemeshow and Le Gall (1994) and Tilford et al. (1995) for more information on developing prediction models and severity scoring systems.

We will do this with the low-birth-weight data we considered previously. First, we randomly divide the data into two samples.

```
. use lbw, clear
(Hosmer & Lemeshow data)
. set seed 1
. gen r = uniform()
. sort r
. gen group = 1 if _n <= _N/2
(95 missing values generated)
. replace group = 2 if group==.
(95 real changes made)
```

Then we estimate a model using the first sample (group==1), our developmental sample.

```
. xi: logistic low age lwt i.race smoke ptl ht ui if group==1
i.race                  Irace_1-3    (naturally coded; Irace_1 omitted)

Logit estimates                           Number of obs   =        94
                                          LR chi2(8)      =     29.14
                                          Prob > chi2     =    0.0003
Log likelihood = -44.293342               Pseudo R2       =    0.2475
```

```
-------------------------------------------------------------------------------
     low | Odds Ratio   Std. Err.       z      P>|z|     [95% Conf. Interval]
---------+---------------------------------------------------------------------
     age |    .91542    .0553937    -1.460    0.144     .8130414    1.03069
     lwt |   .9744276   .0112295    -2.248    0.025     .9526649   .9966874
 Irace_2 |   5.063678    3.78442     2.170    0.030     1.170327   21.90913
 Irace_3 |   2.606209   1.657608     1.506    0.132     .7492483   9.065522
   smoke |   .909912    .5252898    -0.164    0.870     .2934966   2.820953
     ptl |   3.033543   1.507048     2.234    0.025     1.145718    8.03198
      ht |   21.07656   22.64788     2.837    0.005     2.565304   173.1652
      ui |   .988479    .6699458    -0.017    0.986     .2618557   3.731409
-------------------------------------------------------------------------------
```

To test calibration in the developmental sample, the Hosmer–Lemeshow goodness-of-fit test is calculated using lfit.

```
. lfit, group(10)
Logistic model for low, goodness-of-fit test
(Table collapsed on quantiles of estimated probabilities)
          number of observations =         94
                 number of groups =         10
        Hosmer-Lemeshow chi2(8) =        6.67
                    Prob > chi2 =      0.5721
```

Note that we did not specify an if statement with lfit since we wanted to use the estimation sample. Since the test is nonsignificant, we are satisfied with the fit of our model.

Running lroc gives a measure of the discrimination:

```
. lroc, nograph
Logistic model for low
number of observations =         94
area under ROC curve   =     0.8156
```

Now we test the calibration of our model by performing a goodness-of-fit test on the validation sample. We specify the outsample option so that the degrees of freedom are 10 rather than 8.

```
. lfit if group==2, group(10) table outsample
Logistic model for low, goodness-of-fit test
(Table collapsed on quantiles of estimated probabilities)
_Group     _Prob    _Obs_1    _Exp_1    _Obs_0    _Exp_0    _Total
    1      0.0725       1        0.4        9        9.6       10
    2      0.1202       4        0.8        5        8.2        9
    3      0.1549       3        1.3        7        8.7       10
    4      0.1888       1        1.5        8        7.5        9
    5      0.2609       3        2.2        7        7.8       10
    6      0.3258       4        2.7        5        6.3        9
    7      0.4217       2        3.7        8        6.3       10
    8      0.4915       3        4.1        6        4.9        9
    9      0.6265       4        5.5        6        4.5       10
   10      0.9737       4        7.1        5        1.9        9
          number of observations =         95
                 number of groups =         10
        Hosmer-Lemeshow chi2(10) =       28.03
                    Prob > chi2 =      0.0018
```

We must acknowledge that our model does not fit well on the validation sample. The model's discrimination in the validation sample is appreciably lower as well.

```
. lroc if group==2, nograph
Logistic model for low

number of observations =      95
area under ROC curve   =   0.5839
```

◁

Models other than last estimated model

By default, lfit, lstat, lroc, and lsens use the last model estimated by logistic. One can specify other models using the beta() option.

▷ Example

Suppose that someone publishes the following logistic model of low birth weight:

$$\Pr(\texttt{low} = 1) = F(-0.02\,\texttt{age} - 0.01\,\texttt{lwt} + 1.3\,\texttt{black} + 1.1\,\texttt{smoke} + 0.5\,\texttt{ptl} + 1.8\,\texttt{ht} + 0.8\,\texttt{ui} + 0.5)$$

where F is the cumulative logistic distribution. Note that these coefficients are not odds ratios; they are the equivalent of what logit produces.

We can see whether this model fits our data. First, we enter the coefficients as a row vector and label its columns with the names of the independent variables plus _cons for the constant (see [R] **matrix define** and [R] **matrix rowname**).

```
. matrix input b = (-.02 -.01 1.3 1.1 .5 1.8 .8 .5)
. matrix colnames b = age lwt black smoke ptl ht ui _cons
```

We run lfit using the beta() option to specify b. The dependent variable is entered right after the command name, and the outsample option gives the proper degrees of freedom.

```
. lfit low, beta(b) group(10) outsample
Logistic model for low, goodness-of-fit test
(Table collapsed on quantiles of estimated probabilities)
        number of observations =      189
             number of groups =       10
    Hosmer-Lemeshow chi2(10) =      27.33
                 Prob > chi2 =     0.0023
```

Although the fit of the model is poor, lroc shows that it does exhibit some predictive ability.

```
. lroc low, beta(b) nograph
Logistic model for low

number of observations =     189
area under ROC curve   =   0.7275
```

◁

predict after logistic

`predict` is used after `logistic` to obtain predicted probabilities, residuals, and influence statistics for the estimation sample. The suggested diagnostic graphs below are from Hosmer and Lemeshow (1989), where they are more elaborately explained. Also see Collett (1991, 120–160) for a thorough discussion of model checking.

predict without options

Typing `predict p` after estimation calculates the predicted probability of a positive outcome.

We previously ran the model `logistic low age lwt Irace_2 Irace_3 smoke ptl ht ui`. We obtain the predicted probabilities of a positive outcome by typing

```
. predict p
(option p assumed; Pr(low))

. summarize p low

Variable |    Obs        Mean    Std. Dev.       Min        Max
---------+-----------------------------------------------------
       p |    189    .3121693    .1913915    .0272559    .8391283
     low |    189    .3121693    .4646093           0           1
```

predict with the xb and stdp options

`predict` with the `xb` option calculates the linear combination $x_j\mathbf{b}$, where x_j are the independent variables in the jth observation and $\mathbf{b}$ is the estimated parameter vector. This is sometimes known as the index function since the cumulative density indexed at this value is the probability of a positive outcome.

With the `stdp` option, `predict` calculates the standard error of the prediction, which is *not* adjusted for replicated covariate patterns in the data. The influence statistics described below are adjusted for replicated covariate patterns in the data.

predict with the residuals option

`predict` can calculate more than predicted probabilities. The Pearson residual is defined as the square root of the contribution of the covariate pattern to the Pearson χ^2 goodness-of-fit statistic, signed according to whether the observed number of positive responses within the covariate pattern is less or greater than expected. For instance,

```
. predict r, residuals

. summarize r, detail

                          Pearson residual
-------------------------------------------------------------
        Percentiles      Smallest
  1%     -1.750923      -2.283885
  5%     -1.129907      -1.750923
 10%      -.9581174     -1.636279     Obs               189
 25%      -.6545911     -1.636279     Sum of Wgt.       189

 50%      -.3806923                   Mean         -.0242299
                         Largest      Std. Dev.     .9970949
 75%       .8162894      2.23879
 90%      1.510355       2.317558     Variance      .9941981
 95%      1.747948       3.002206     Skewness      .8618271
 99%      3.002206       3.126763     Kurtosis      3.038448
```

We notice the prevalence of a few, large positive residuals:

```
. sort r
. list id r low p age race in -5/l
            id          r     low           p     age      race
185.        33   2.224501       1    .1681123      19     white
186.        57    2.23879       1     .166329      15     white
187.        16   2.317558       1    .1569594      27     other
188.        77   3.002206       1    .0998678      26     white
189.        36   3.126763       1    .0927932      24     white
```

predict with the number option

Covariate patterns play an important role in logistic regression. Two observations are said to share the same covariate pattern if the independent variables for the two observations are identical. Although one thinks of having individual observations, the statistical information in the sample can be summarized by the covariate patterns, the number of observations with that covariate pattern, and the number of positive outcomes within the pattern. Depending on the model, the number of covariate patterns can approach or be equal to the number of observations or it can be considerably less.

All the residual and diagnostic statistics calculated by Stata are in terms of covariate patterns, not observations. That is, all observations with the same covariate pattern are given the same residual and diagnostic statistics. Hosmer and Lemeshow (1989) argue that such "M-asymptotic" statistics are more useful than "N-asymptotic" statistics.

To understand the difference, think of an observed positive outcome with predicted probability of 0.8. Taking the observation in isolation, the "residual" must be positive—we expected 0.8 positive responses and observed 1. This may indeed be the "correct" residual, but not necessarily. Under the M-asymptotic definition, we ask how many successes we observed across all observations with this covariate pattern. If that number were, say, 6, and there were a total of 10 observations with this covariate pattern, then the residual is negative for the covariate pattern—we expected 8 positive outcomes but observed 6. predict makes this kind of calculation and then attaches the same residual to all observations in the covariate pattern.

Thus, there may be occasions when you want to find all observations sharing a covariate pattern. number allows you to do this:

```
. predict pattern, number
. summarize pattern
Variable |     Obs       Mean    Std. Dev.       Min        Max
---------+--------------------------------------------------------
 pattern |     189    89.2328    53.16573          1        182
```

We previously estimated the model logistic low age lwt Irace_2 Irace_3 smoke ptl ht ui over 189 observations. There are 182 covariate patterns in our data.

predict with the deviance option

The deviance residual is defined as the square root of the contribution to the likelihood-ratio test statistic of a saturated model versus the fitted model. It has slightly different properties from the Pearson residual (see Hosmer and Lemeshow, 1989):

```
. predict d, deviance
```

```
. summarize d, detail
                         deviance residual
-------------------------------------------------------------
      Percentiles      Smallest
 1%    -1.843472       -1.911621
 5%     -1.33477       -1.843472
10%    -1.148316       -1.843472      Obs                 189
25%    -.8445325       -1.674869      Sum of Wgt.         189

50%    -.5202702                      Mean          -.1228811
                        Largest       Std. Dev.      1.049237
75%     .9129041        1.894089
90%     1.541558        1.924457      Variance       1.100898
95%     1.673338        2.146583      Skewness       .6598857
99%     2.146583        2.180542      Kurtosis       2.036938
```

predict with the rstandard option

Pearson residuals do not have a standard deviation equal to 1, a fine point. `rstandard` generates Pearson residuals normalized to have *expected* standard deviation equal to 1.

```
. predict rs, rstandard
. summarize r rs
Variable |    Obs       Mean   Std. Dev.       Min        Max
---------+--------------------------------------------------
       r |    189  -.0242299   .9970949  -2.283885   3.126763
      rs |    189  -.0279135   1.026406    -2.4478   3.149081
. correlate r rs
(obs=189)
         |      r        rs
---------+------------------
       r |  1.0000
      rs |  0.9998   1.0000
```

Remember that we previously created r containing the (unstandardized) Pearson residuals. In this data, whether you use standardized or unstandardized residuals does not much matter.

predict with the hat option

`hat` calculates the leverage of a covariate pattern—a scaled measure of distance in terms of the independent variables. Large values indicate covariate patterns "far" from the average covariate pattern—patterns that can have a large effect on the estimated model even if the corresponding residual is small. This suggests the following:

(Continued on next page)

```
. predict h, hat
. graph h r, border yline(0) ylab xlab
```

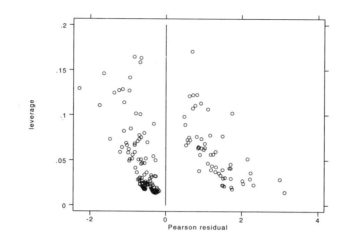

The points to the left of the vertical line are observed negative outcomes; in this case, our data contains almost as many covariate patterns as observations, so most covariate patterns are unique. In such unique patterns, we observe either 0 or 1 success and expect p, thus forcing the sign of the residual. If we had fewer covariate patterns, which is to say, if we did not have continuous variables in our model, there would be no such interpretation and we would not have drawn the vertical line at 0.

Points on the left and right edges of the graph represent large residuals — covariate patterns that are not fitted well by our model. Points at the top of our graph represent high leverage patterns. When analyzing the influence of observations on the model, we are most interested in patterns with high leverage and small residuals — patterns that might otherwise escape our attention.

predict with the dx2 option

There are many ways to measure influence of which **hat** is one example. **dx2** measures the decrease in the Pearson χ^2 goodness-of-fit statistic that would be caused by deleting an observation (and all others sharing the covariate pattern):

(Continued on next page)

```
. predict dx2, dx2
. graph dx2 p, border ylab xlab
```

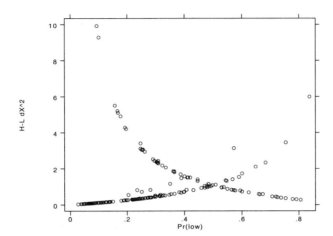

Paraphrasing Hosmer and Lemeshow (1989), the points going from the top left to the bottom right correspond to covariate patterns with the number of positive outcomes equal to the number in the group; the points on the other curve correspond to 0 positive outcomes. In our data, most of the covariate patterns are unique, so the points tend to lie along one or the other curves; the points that are off the curves correspond to the few repeated covariate patterns in our data in which all the outcomes are not the same.

We examine this graph for large values of dx2—there are two at the top left.

predict with the ddeviance option

Another measure of influence is the change in the deviance residuals due to deletion of a covariate pattern:

```
. predict dd, ddeviance
```

As with dx2, one typically graphs ddeviance against the probability of a positive outcome. We direct you to Hosmer and Lemeshow (1989) for an example and the interpretation of this graph.

predict with the dbeta option

One of the more direct measures of influence of interest to model fitters is the Pregibon (1981) dbeta measure, a measure of the change in the coefficient vector that would be caused by deleting an observation (and all others sharing the covariate pattern):

(Continued on next page)

```
. predict db, dbeta
. graph db p, border ylab xlab
```

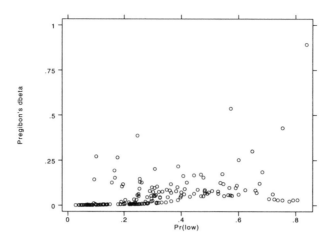

One observation has a large effect on the estimated coefficients. We can easily find this point:

```
. sort db
. list in 1
Observation 189
```

id	188	low	0	age	25
lwt	95	race	white	smoke	1
ptl	3	ht	0	ui	1
ftv	0	bwt	3637	Irace_2	0
Irace_3	0	p	.8391283	r	-2.283885
pattern	117	d	-1.911621	rs	-2.4478
h	.1294439	dx2	5.991726	dd	4.197658
db	.8909163

Hosmer and Lemeshow (1989) suggest a graph that combines two of the influence measures:

```
. graph dx2 p [w=db], border ylab xlab t1("Symbol size proportional to dBeta")
```

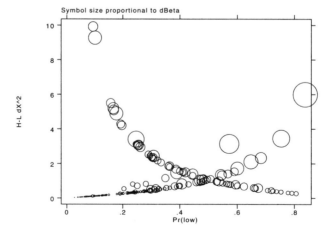

We can easily spot the most influential points by the **dbeta** and **dx2** measures.

Saved Results

`logistic` saves in `e()`:

Scalars

`e(N)`	number of observations	`e(ll_0)`	log likelihood, constant-only model
`e(df_m)`	model degrees of freedom	`e(N_clust)`	number of clusters
`e(r2_p)`	pseudo R-squared	`e(chi2)`	χ^2
`e(ll)`	log likelihood		

Macros

`e(cmd)`	`logistic`	`e(clustvar)`	name of cluster variable
`e(depvar)`	name of dependent variable	`e(vcetype)`	covariance estimation method
`e(wtype)`	weight type	`e(chi2type)`	Wald or LR; type of model χ^2 test
`e(wexp)`	weight expression	`e(predict)`	program used to implement `predict`
`e(offset)`	offset		

Matrices

`e(b)`	coefficient vector	`e(V)`	variance–covariance matrix of the estimators

Functions

`e(sample)`	marks estimation sample

`lfit` saves in `r()`:

Scalars

`r(N)`	number of observations	`r(df)`	degrees of freedom
`r(m)`	number of covariate patterns or groups	`r(chi2)`	χ^2

`lstat` saves in `r()`:

Scalars

`r(P_corr)`	percent correctly classified	`r(P_1p)`	positive predictive value
`r(P_p1)`	sensitivity	`r(P_1n)`	negative predictive value
`r(P_n0)`	specificity	`r(P_0p)`	false positive rate given classified positive
`r(P_p0)`	false positive rate given true negative	`r(P_0n)`	false negative rate given classified negative
`r(P_n1)`	false negative rate given true positive		

`lroc` saves in `r()`:

Scalars

`r(N)`	number of observations	`r(area)`	area under the ROC curve

`lsens` saves in `r()`:

Scalars

`r(N)`	number of observations

Methods and Formulas

`logistic`, `lfit`, `lstat`, `lroc`, and `lsens` are implemented as ado-files.

Define $\mathbf{x}_j$ as the (row) vector of independent variables, augmented by 1, and $\mathbf{b}$ as the corresponding estimated parameter (column) vector. The logistic regression model is estimated by `logit`; see [R] **logit** for details of estimation.

The odds ratio corresponding to the ith coefficient is $\psi_i = \exp(b_i)$. The standard error of the odds ratio is $s_i^\psi = \psi_i s_i$, where s_i is the standard error of b_i estimated by `logit`.

Define $I_j = \mathbf{x}_j \mathbf{b}$ as the predicted index of the jth observation. The predicted probability of a positive outcome is

$$p_j = \frac{\exp(I_j)}{1 + \exp(I_j)}$$

lfit

Let M be the total number of covariate patterns among the N observations. View the data as collapsed on covariate patterns $j = 1, 2, \ldots, M$ and define m_j as the total number of observations having covariate pattern j and y_j as the total number of positive responses among observations with covariate pattern j. Define p_j as the predicted probability of a positive outcome in covariate pattern j.

The Pearson χ^2 goodness-of-fit statistic is

$$\chi^2 = \sum_{j=1}^{M} \frac{(y_j - m_j p_j)^2}{m_j p_j (1 - p_j)}$$

This χ^2 statistic has approximately $M - k$ degrees of freedom for the estimation sample, where k is the number of independent variables including the constant. For a sample outside of the estimation sample, the statistic has M degrees of freedom.

The Hosmer–Lemeshow goodness-of-fit χ^2 (Hosmer and Lemeshow 1980; Lemeshow and Hosmer 1982; Hosmer, Lemeshow, and Klar 1988) is calculated similarly, except rather than using the M covariate patterns as the group definition, the quantiles of the predicted probabilities are used to form groups. Let $G = \#$ be the number of quantiles requested with `group(#)`. The smallest index $1 \leq q(i) \leq M$ such that

$$W_{q(i)} = \sum_{j=1}^{q(i)} m_j \geq \frac{N}{G}$$

gives $p_{q(i)}$ as the upper boundary of the ith quantile for $i = 1, 2, \ldots, G$. Let $q(0) = 1$ denote the first index.

The groups are then

$$\left[p_{q(0)}, p_{q(1)} \right], \left(p_{q(1)}, p_{q(2)} \right], \ldots, \left(p_{q(G-1)}, p_{q(G)} \right]$$

If the `table` option is given, the upper boundaries $p_{q(1)}, \ldots, p_{q(G)}$ of the groups appear next to the group number on the output.

The resulting χ^2 statistic has approximately $G - 2$ degrees of freedom for the estimation sample. For a sample outside of the estimation sample, the statistic has G degrees of freedom.

predict after logistic

Index j will now be used to index observations, not covariate patterns. Redefine m_j for each observation as the total number of observations sharing j's covariate pattern. Redefine y_j as the total number of positive responses among observations sharing j's covariate pattern.

The Pearson residual for the jth observation is defined

$$r_j = \frac{y_j - m_j p_j}{\sqrt{m_j p_j (1 - p_j)}}$$

For $m_j > 1$, the deviance residual d_j is defined

$$d_j = \pm \sqrt{2 \left[y_j \ln \left(\frac{y_j}{m_j p_j} \right) + (m_j - y_j) \ln \left(\frac{m_j - y_j}{m_j (1 - p_j)} \right) \right]}$$

where the sign is the same as the sign of $(y_j - m_j p_j)$. In the limiting cases, the deviance residual is given by

$$d_j = \begin{cases} -\sqrt{2 m_j |\ln(1 - p_j)|} & \text{if } y_j = 0 \\ \sqrt{2 m_j |\ln p_j|} & \text{if } y_j = m_j \end{cases}$$

The *unadjusted* diagonal elements of the hat matrix h_{Uj} are given by $h_{Uj} = (\mathbf{X V X'})_{jj}$, where V is the estimated covariance matrix of parameters. The adjusted diagonal elements h_j created by `hat` are then $h_j = m_j p_j (1 - p_j) h_{Uj}$.

The standardized Pearson residual r_{Sj} is $r_j / \sqrt{1 - h_j}$.

The Pregibon (1981) $\Delta \widehat{\beta}_j$ influence statistic is

$$\Delta \widehat{\beta}_j = \frac{r_j^2 h_j}{(1 - h_j)^2}$$

The corresponding change in the Pearson χ^2 is r_{Sj}^2. The corresponding change in the deviance residual is $\Delta D_j = d_j / (1 - h_j)$.

lstat and lsens

Again, let j index observations. Define c as the `cutoff()` specified by the user or, if not specified, as 0.5. Let p_j be the predicted probability of a positive outcome and y_j be the actual outcome, which we will treat as 0 or 1, although Stata treats it as 0 and non-0, excluding missing observations.

A prediction is classified as *positive* if $p_j \geq c$ and otherwise is classified as *negative*. The classification is *correct* if it is *positive* and $y_j = 1$ or if it is *negative* and $y_j = 0$.

Sensitivity is the fraction of $y_j = 1$ observations that are correctly classified. *Specificity* is the percent of $y_j = 0$ observations that are correctly classified.

lroc

The ROC curve is a graph of *specificity* against $(1 - sensitivity)$. This is guaranteed to be a monotone nondecreasing function, since the number of correctly predicted successes increases, and the number of correctly predicted failures decreases, as the classification cutoff c decreases.

The area under the ROC curve is the area on the bottom of this graph, and is determined by integrating the curve. The vertices of the curve are determined by sorting the data according to the predicted index, and the integral is computed using the trapezoidal rule.

References

Brady, A. R. 1998. sbe21: Adjusted population attributable fractions from logistic regression. *Stata Technical Bulletin* 42: 8–12. Reprinted in *Stata Technical Bulletin Reprints*, vol. 7, pp. 137–143.

Collett, D. 1991. *Modelling Binary Data*. London: Chapman & Hall.

Garrett, J. M. 1997. sbe14: Odds ratios and confidence intervals for logistic regression models with effect modification. *Stata Technical Bulletin* 36: 15–22. Reprinted in *Stata Technical Bulletin Reprints*, vol. 6, pp. 104–114.

Green, D. M. and J. A. Swets. 1974. *Signal Detection Theory and Psychophysics*. rev. ed. Huntington, NY: Krieger.

Hilbe, J. 1997. sg63: Logistic regression: standardized coefficients and partial correlations. *Stata Technical Bulletin* 35: 21–22. Reprinted in *Stata Technical Bulletin Reprints*, vol. 6, pp. 162–163.

Hosmer, D. W., Jr., and S. Lemeshow. 1980. Goodness-of-fit tests for the multiple logistic regression model. *Communications in Statistics* A9: 1043–1069.

——. 1989. *Applied Logistic Regression*. New York: John Wiley & Sons.

Hosmer, D. W., Jr., S. Lemeshow, and J. Klar. 1988. Goodness-of-fit testing for the logistic regression model when the estimated probabilities are small. *Biometric Journal* 30: 911–924.

Lemeshow, S. and D. W. Hosmer, Jr. 1982. A review of goodness of fit statistics for use in the development of logistic regression models. *American Journal of Epidemiology* 115: 92–106.

——. 1998. Logistic regression. In *Encyclopedia of Biostatistics*, ed. P. Armitage and T. Colton, 2316–2327. New York: John Wiley & Sons.

Lemeshow, S. and J.-R. Le Gall. 1994. Modeling the severity of illness of ICU patients: a systems update. *Journal of the American Medical Association* 272: 1049–1055.

Metz, C. E. 1978. Basic principles of ROC analysis. *Seminars in Nuclear Medicine* 8: 283–298.

Pagano, M. and K. Gauvreau. 1993. *Principles of Biostatistics*. Belmont, CA: Duxbury Press.

Paul, C. 1998. sg92: Logistic regression for data including multiple imputations. *Stata Technical Bulletin* 45: 28–30.

Peterson, W. W., T. G. Birdsall, and W. C. Fox. 1954. The theory of signal detection. *Trans. IRE Professional Group on Information Theory*, PGIT-4: 171–212.

Pregibon, D. 1981. Logistic regression diagnostics. *Annals of Statistics* 9: 705–724.

Tanner, W. P., Jr., and J. A. Swets. 1954. A decision-making theory of visual detection. *Psychological Review* 61: 401–409.

Tilford, J. M., P. K. Roberson, and D. H. Fiser. 1995. sbe12: Using lfit and lroc to evaluate mortality prediction models. *Stata Technical Bulletin* 28: 14–18. Reprinted in *Stata Technical Bulletin Reprints*, vol. 5, pp. 77–81.

Tobias, A. and M. J. Campbell. 1998. sg90: Akaike's information criterion and Schwarz's criterion. *Stata Technical Bulletin* 45: 23–25.

Weesie, J. 1998. sg87: Windmeijer's goodness-of-fit test for logistic regression. *Stata Technical Bulletin* 44: 22–27.

Also See

Complementary:	[R] **adjust**, [R] **lincom**, [R] **linktest**, [R] **lrtest**, [R] **predict**, [R] **sw**, [R] **test**, [R] **testnl**, [R] **vce**, [R] **xi**
Related:	[R] **brier**, [R] **clogit**, [R] **cloglog**, [R] **cusum**, [R] **glm**, [R] **glogit**, [R] **logit**, [R] **probit**, [R] **scobit**, [R] svy estimators
Background:	[U] **16.5 Accessing coefficients and standard errors**, [U] **23 Estimation and post-estimation commands**, [U] **23.11 Obtaining robust variance estimates**, [U] **23.12 Obtaining scores**, [R] **maximize**

Title

---
logit — Maximum-likelihood logit estimation

Syntax

$$\left[\text{by } varlist:\right] \quad \underline{\text{logit}} \quad depvar \left[indepvars\right] \left[weight\right] \left[\text{if } exp\right] \left[\text{in } range\right]$$

$$\left[\, , \underline{\text{level}}(\#) \text{ nocoef } \underline{\text{nocon}}\text{stant or } \underline{\text{r}}\text{obust } \underline{\text{cl}}\text{uster}(varname) \underline{\text{sc}}\text{ore}(newvarname)\right.$$

$$\underline{\text{off}}\text{set}(varname) \text{ asis } maximize\_options \left.\right]$$

fweights, iweights, and pweights are allowed; see [U] **14.1.6 weight**.

logit shares the features of all estimation commands; see [U] **23 Estimation and post-estimation commands**.

logit may be used with sw to perform stepwise estimation; see [R] **sw**.

Syntax for predict

$$\text{predict } \left[type\right] newvarname \left[\text{if } exp\right] \left[\text{in } range\right] \left[\, , statistic \underline{\text{rules}} \text{ asif } \underline{\text{nooff}}\text{set} \right]$$

where *statistic* is

p	probability of a positive outcome (the default)
xb	$\mathbf{x}_j\mathbf{b}$, fitted values
stdp	standard error of the prediction
* <u>dbeta</u>	Pregibon (1991) $\Delta\beta$ influence statistic
* <u>deviance</u>	deviance residual
* <u>dx2</u>	Hosmer and Lemeshow (1989) $\Delta\chi^2$ influence statistic
* <u>ddeviance</u>	Hosmer and Lemeshow (1989) ΔD influence statistic
* <u>hat</u>	Pregibon (1981) leverage
* <u>number</u>	sequential number of the covariate pattern
residuals	Pearson residuals; adjusted for number sharing covariate pattern
* <u>rstandard</u>	standardized Pearson residuals; adjusted for number sharing covariate pattern

Unstarred statistics are available both in and out of sample; type predict ... if e(sample) ... if wanted only for the estimation sample. Starred statistics are calculated only for the estimation sample even when if e(sample) is not specified.

Description

logit estimates a maximum-likelihood logit model.

Also see [R] **logistic**; logistic displays estimates as odds ratios. A number of auxiliary commands that can be run after either logit estimation or logistic estimation are described in [R] **logistic**. A list of related estimation commands is given in [R] **logistic**.

Options

level(#) specifies the confidence level, in percent, for confidence intervals. The default is level(95) or as set by set level; see [U] **23.5 Specifying the width of confidence intervals**.

nocoef specifies that the coefficient table is not to be displayed. This option is sometimes used by program writers but is of no use interactively.

noconstant suppresses the constant term (intercept) in the logit model.

or reports the estimated coefficients transformed to odds ratios, i.e., e^b rather than b. Standard errors and confidence intervals are similarly transformed. This option affects how results are displayed, not how they are estimated. or may be specified at estimation or when replaying previously estimated results.

robust specifies that the Huber/White/sandwich estimator of variance is to be used in place of the traditional calculation; see [U] **23.11 Obtaining robust variance estimates**. robust combined with cluster() allows observations which are not independent within cluster (although they must be independent between clusters).

If you specify pweights, robust is implied; see [U] **23.13 Weighted estimation**.

See [R] **logistic** for examples using this option.

cluster(varname) specifies that the observations are independent across groups (clusters) but not necessarily within groups. varname specifies to which group each observation belongs; e.g., cluster(personid) in data with repeated observations on individuals. cluster() affects the estimated standard errors and variance–covariance matrix of the estimators (VCE), but not the estimated coefficients; see [U] **23.11 Obtaining robust variance estimates**. cluster() can be used with pweights to produce estimates for unstratified cluster-sampled data, but see the svylogit command in [R] **svy estimators** for a command designed especially for survey data.

cluster() implies robust; specifying robust cluster() is equivalent to typing cluster() by itself.

See [R] **logistic** for examples using this option.

score(newvarname) creates newvar containing $u_j = \partial \ln L_j / \partial(\mathbf{x}_j \mathbf{b})$ for each observation j in the sample. The score vector is $\sum \partial \ln L_j / \partial \mathbf{b} = \sum u_j \mathbf{x}_j$; i.e., the product of newvar with each covariate summed over observations. See [U] **23.12 Obtaining scores**.

offset(varname) specifies that varname is to be included in the model with coefficient constrained to be 1.

asis forces retention of perfect predictor variables and their associated perfectly predicted observations and may produce instabilities in maximization; see [R] **probit**.

maximize_options control the maximization process; see [R] **maximize**. You should never have to specify them.

Options for predict

p, the default, calculates the probability of a positive outcome.

xb calculates the linear prediction.

stdp calculates the standard error of the linear prediction.

dbeta calculates the Pregibon (1981) $\Delta\widehat{\beta}$ influence statistic, a standardized measure of the difference in the coefficient vector due to deletion of the observation along with all others that share the same covariate pattern. In Hosmer and Lemeshow (1989) jargon, this statistic is M-asymptotic, that is, adjusted for the number of observations that share the same covariate pattern.

deviance calculates the deviance residual.

dx2 calculates the Hosmer and Lemeshow (1989) $\Delta\chi^2$ influence statistic reflecting the decrease in the Pearson χ^2 due to deletion of the observation and all others that share the same covariate pattern.

ddeviance calculates the Hosmer and Lemeshow (1989) ΔD influence statistic, which is the change in the deviance residual due to deletion of the observation and all others that share the same covariate pattern.

hat calculates the Pregibon (1981) leverage or the diagonal elements of the hat matrix adjusted for the number of observations that share the same covariate pattern.

number numbers the covariate patterns—observations with the same covariate pattern have the same **number**. Observations not used in estimation have **number** set to missing. The "first" covariate pattern is numbered 1, the second 2, and so on.

residuals calculates the Pearson residual as given by Hosmer and Lemeshow (1989) and adjusted for the number of observations that share the same covariate pattern.

rstandard calculates the standardized Pearson residual as given by Hosmer and Lemeshow (1989) and adjusted for the number of observations that share the same covariate pattern.

rules requests that Stata use any "rules" that were used to identify the model when making the prediction. By default, Stata calculates missing for excluded observations.

asif requests that Stata ignore the rules and the exclusion criteria, and calculate predictions for all observations possible using the estimated parameter from the model.

nooffset is relevant only if you specified **offset**(*varname*) for **logistic**. It modifies the calculations made by **predict** so that they ignore the offset variable; the linear prediction is treated as $\mathbf{x}_j\mathbf{b}$ rather than $\mathbf{x}_j\mathbf{b} + \text{offset}_j$.

Remarks

logit performs maximum likelihood estimation of models with dichotomous dependent (left-hand-side) variables coded as 0/1 (or, more precisely, coded as 0 and not-0).

▷ Example

You have data on the make, weight, and mileage rating of 22 foreign and 52 domestic automobiles. You wish to estimate a logit model explaining whether a car is foreign based on its weight and mileage. Here is an overview of your data:

```
. describe

Contains data from auto.dta
  obs:            74                          1978 Automobile Data
  vars:            4                          11 Sep 1998 10:08
  size:         1,998 (99.9% of memory free)
------------------------------------------------------------------------
  1. make        str18  %-18s                 Make and Model
  2. mpg         int    %8.0g                 Mileage (mpg)
  3. weight      int    %8.0gc                Weight (lbs.)
  4. foreign     byte   %8.0g      origin     Car type
------------------------------------------------------------------------
Sorted by:  foreign
     Note:  dataset has changed since last saved

. inspect foreign

foreign:  Car type                      Number of Observations
------------------                                   Non-
                                    Total   Integers  Integers
   |  #                 Negative      -        -         -
   |  #                 Zero         52       52         -
   |  #                 Positive     22       22         -
   |  #                              -----    -----     -----
   |  #    #            Total        74       74         -
   |  #    #            Missing       -
   +---------------------            -----
   0                    1            74
     (2 unique values)

     foreign is labeled and all values are documented in the label.
```

The variable **foreign** takes on two unique values, 0 and 1. The value 0 denotes a domestic car and 1 denotes a foreign car.

The model you wish to estimate is

$$\Pr(\texttt{foreign} = 1) = F(\beta_0 + \beta_1 \texttt{weight} + \beta_2 \texttt{mpg})$$

where $F(z) = e^z/(1 + e^z)$ is the cumulative logistic distribution.

To estimate this model, you type

```
. logit foreign weight mpg
Iteration 0:   log likelihood =  -45.03321
Iteration 1:   log likelihood = -29.898968
Iteration 2:   log likelihood = -27.495771
Iteration 3:   log likelihood = -27.184006
Iteration 4:   log likelihood = -27.175166
Iteration 5:   log likelihood = -27.175156

Logit estimates                               Number of obs   =         74
                                              LR chi2(2)      =      35.72
                                              Prob > chi2     =     0.0000
Log likelihood = -27.175156                   Pseudo R2       =     0.3966

------------------------------------------------------------------------
  foreign |     Coef.   Std. Err.      z     P>|z|    [95% Conf. Interval]
----------+-------------------------------------------------------------
   weight |  -.0039067   .0010116   -3.862   0.000   -.0058894   -.001924
      mpg |  -.1685869   .0919174   -1.834   0.067   -.3487418    .011568
    _cons |   13.70837   4.518707    3.034   0.002    4.851864   22.56487
------------------------------------------------------------------------
```

You find that heavier cars are less likely to be foreign and that cars yielding better gas mileage are also less likely to be foreign, at least holding the weight of the car constant.

See [R] **maximize** for an explanation of the output.

◁

❑ Technical Note

Stata interprets a value of 0 as a negative outcome (failure) and treats all other values (except missing) as positive outcomes (successes). Thus, if your dependent variable takes on the values 0 and 1, 0 is interpreted as failure and 1 as success. If your dependent variable takes on the values 0, 1, and 2, 0 is still interpreted as failure, but both 1 and 2 are treated as successes.

If you prefer a more formal mathematical statement, when you type logit y x, Stata estimates the model

$$\Pr(y_j \neq 0 \mid \mathbf{x}_j) = \frac{\exp(\mathbf{x}_j\boldsymbol{\beta})}{1 + \exp(\mathbf{x}_j\boldsymbol{\beta})}$$

❑

Model identification

The logit command has one more feature, and it is probably the most useful. logit will automatically check the model for identification and, if it is underidentified, drop whatever variables and observations are necessary for estimation to proceed.

▷ Example

Have you ever estimated a logit model where one or more of your independent variables perfectly predicted one or the other outcome?

For instance, consider the following small amount of data:

Outcome y	Independent Variable x
0	1
0	1
0	0
1	0

Let's imagine we wish to predict the outcome on the basis of the independent variable. Notice that the outcome is always zero whenever the independent variable is one. In our data $\Pr(y = 0 \mid x = 1) = 1$, which in turn means that the logit coefficient on x must be minus infinity with a corresponding infinite standard error. At this point, you may suspect we have a problem.

Unfortunately, not all such problems are so easily detected, especially if you have a lot of independent variables in your model. If you have ever had such difficulties, then you have experienced one of the more unpleasant aspects of computer optimization. The computer has no idea that it is trying to solve for an infinite coefficient as it begins its iterative process. All it knows is that, at each step, making the coefficient a little bigger, or a little smaller, works wonders. It continues on its merry way until either (1) the whole thing comes crashing to the ground when a numerical overflow error occurs or (2) it reaches some predetermined cutoff that stops the process. Meantime, you have been waiting. In addition, the estimates that you finally receive, if you receive any at all, may be nothing more than numerical roundoff.

Stata watches for these sorts of problems, alerts you, fixes them, and properly estimates the model.

Let's return to our automobile data. Among the variables we have in the data is one called `repair` that takes on three values. A value of 1 indicates that the car has a poor repair record, 2 indicates an average record, and 3 indicates a better-than-average record. Here is a tabulation of our data:

```
. tabulate foreign repair

           |             repair
   foreign |         1          2          3 |     Total
-----------+---------------------------------+----------
  Domestic |        10         27          9 |        46
   Foreign |         0          3          9 |        12
-----------+---------------------------------+----------
     Total |        10         30         18 |        58
```

Notice that all the cars with poor repair records (`repair==1`) are domestic. If we were to attempt to predict `foreign` on the basis of the repair records, the predicted probability for the `repair==1` category would have to be zero. This in turn means that the logit coefficient must be minus infinity, and that would set most computer programs buzzing.

Let's try Stata on this problem. First, we make up two new variables, `rep_is_1` and `rep_is_2`, that indicate the `repair` category.

```
. generate rep_is_1 = (repair==1)

. generate rep_is_2 = (repair==2)
```

The statement `generate rep_is_1 = (repair==1)` creates a new variable, `rep_is_1`, that takes on the value 1 when `repair` is 1 and zero otherwise. Similarly, the next `generate` statement creates `rep_is_2` that takes on the value 1 when `repair` is 2 and zero otherwise. We are now ready to estimate our logit model. See [R] **probit** for the corresponding probit model.

```
. logit for rep_is_1 rep_is_2
Note: rep_is_1~=0 predicts failure perfectly
      rep_is_1 dropped and 10 obs not used
Iteration 0:   log likelihood = -26.992087
Iteration 1:   log likelihood = -22.483187
Iteration 2:   log likelihood = -22.230498
Iteration 3:   log likelihood = -22.229139
Iteration 4:   log likelihood = -22.229138
Iteration 5:   log likelihood = -22.229138
Iteration 6:   log likelihood = -22.229138
Iteration 7:   log likelihood = -22.229138

Logit estimates                               Number of obs   =         48
                                              LR chi2(1)      =       9.53
                                              Prob > chi2     =     0.0020
Log likelihood = -22.229138                   Pseudo R2       =     0.1765

------------------------------------------------------------------------------
   foreign |      Coef.   Std. Err.       z    P>|z|     [95% Conf. Interval]
-----------+------------------------------------------------------------------
  rep_is_2 |  -2.197225   .7698004    -2.854   0.004    -3.706006   -.6884436
     _cons |   7.47e-16   .4714045     0.000   1.000    -.9239359    .9239359
------------------------------------------------------------------------------
```

Remember that all the cars with poor repair records (`rep_is_1`) are domestic, so the model cannot be estimated, or at least it cannot be estimated if we restrict ourselves to finite coefficients. Stata noted that fact. It said, "Note: rep_is_1~=0 predicts failure perfectly". This is Stata's mathematically precise way of saying what we said in English. When `rep_is_1` is not equal to 0, the car is domestic.

Stata then went on to say, "rep_is_1 dropped and 10 obs not used". This is Stata eliminating the problem. First, the variable rep_is_1 had to be removed from the model because it would have an infinite coefficient. Then, the 10 observations that led to the problem had to be eliminated as well so as not to bias the remaining coefficients in the model. The 10 observations that are not used are the 10 domestic cars that have poor repair records.

Finally, Stata estimated what was left of the model, which is all that can be estimated.

◁

❑ Technical Note

Stata is pretty smart about catching problems of these sorts. It will catch "one-way causation by a dummy variable", as we demonstrated above.

Stata also watches for "two-way causation"; that is, a variable that perfectly determines the outcome, both successes and failures. In this case Stata says, "so-and-so predicts outcome perfectly" and stops. Statistics dictates that no model can be estimated.

Stata also checks your data for collinear variables; it will say "so-and-so dropped due to collinearity". No observations need to be eliminated in this case, and model estimation will proceed without the offending variable.

It will also catch a subtle problem that can arise with continuous data. For instance, if we were estimating the chances of surviving the first year after an operation, and if we included in our model age, and if all the persons over 65 died within the year, Stata will say, "age > 65 predicts failure perfectly". It will then inform us about the fixup it takes and estimate what can be estimated of our model.

logit (and logistic and probit) will also occasionally display messages such as

```
Note: 4 failures and 0 successes completely determined.
```

There are two causes for a message like this. Let us deal with the most unlikely case first. This case occurs when a continuous variable (or a combination of a continuous variable with other continuous or dummy variables) is simply a great predictor of the dependent variable. Consider Stata's auto.dta dataset with 6 observations removed.

```
. use auto
(1978 Automobile Data)

. drop if foreign==0 & gratio>3.1
(6 observations deleted)

. logit foreign mpg weight gratio, nolog
Logit estimates                              Number of obs   =         68
                                             LR chi2(3)      =      72.64
                                             Prob > chi2     =     0.0000
Log likelihood = -6.4874814                  Pseudo R2       =     0.8484

------------------------------------------------------------------------------
  foreign |     Coef.    Std. Err.       z     P>|z|    [95% Conf. Interval]
----------+-------------------------------------------------------------------
      mpg | -.4944907    .2655508    -1.862    0.063   -1.014961     .0259792
   weight | -.0060919    .003101     -1.964    0.049   -.0121698    -.000014
   gratio |  15.70509    8.166234     1.923    0.054   -.3004359     31.71061
    _cons | -21.39527    25.41486    -0.842    0.400   -71.20747     28.41694
------------------------------------------------------------------------------
Note: 4 failures and 0 successes completely determined.
```

Note that there are no missing standard errors in the output. If you receive the "completely determined" message and have one or more missing standard errors in your output, see the second case discussed below.

What's happening here is simply that `gratio` is a great predictor of `foreign`. Note `gratio`'s large coefficient. `logit` thought that the 4 observations with the smallest predicted probabilities were essentially predicted perfectly.

```
. predict p
(option p assumed; Pr(foreign))
. sort p
. list p in 1/4

            p
  1.  1.34e-10
  2.  6.26e-09
  3.  7.84e-09
  4.  1.49e-08
```

If this happens to you, there is no need to do anything. Computationally, the model is sound. It is the second case discussed below that requires careful examination.

The second case occurs when the independent terms are all dummy variables or continuous ones with repeated values (e.g., age). In this case, one or more of the estimated coefficients will have missing standard errors. For example, consider this dataset consisting of 5 observations.

```
. list

         y        x1        x2
  1.     0         0         0
  2.     0         1         0
  3.     1         1         0
  4.     0         0         1
  5.     1         0         1

. logit y x1 x2, nolog
```

Logit estimates

Number of obs	= 5
LR chi2(2)	= 1.18
Prob > chi2	= 0.5530
Pseudo R2	= 0.1761

Log likelihood = -2.7725887

y	Coef.	Std. Err.	z	P>|z|	[95% Conf. Interval]
x1	18.26157	2	9.131	0.000	14.34164 22.1815
x2	18.26157	.	.	.	. .
_cons	-18.26157	1.414214	-12.913	0.000	-21.03338 -15.48976

Note: 1 failure and 0 successes completely determined.

```
. predict p
(option p assumed; Pr(y))
. list

         y        x1        x2          p
  1.     0         0         0    1.17e-08
  2.     0         1         0         .5
  3.     1         1         0         .5
  4.     0         0         1         .5
  5.     1         0         1         .5
```

Two things are happening here. The first is that `logit` is able to fit the outcome ($y = 0$) for the covariate pattern $x1 = 0$ and $x2 = 0$ (i.e., the first observation) perfectly. It is this observation that is the "1 failure ... completely determined". The second thing to note is that if this observation is dropped, then $x1$, $x2$, and the constant are collinear.

This is the cause of the message "completely determined" and the missing standard errors. It happens when you have a covariate pattern (or patterns) with only one outcome, and there is collinearity when the observations corresponding to this covariate pattern are dropped.

If this happens to you, confirm the causes. First identify the covariate pattern with only one outcome. (For your data, replace x1 and x2 with the independent variables of your model.)

```
. egen pattern = group(x1 x2)

. quietly logit y x1 x2

. predict p

. summarize p

Variable |     Obs        Mean    Std. Dev.       Min        Max
---------+------------------------------------------------------
       p |       5          .4    .2236068    1.17e-08         .5
```

If successes were completely determined, that means there are predicted probabilities that are almost 1. If failures were completely determined, that means there are predicted probabilities that are almost 0. The latter is the case here. So we locate the corresponding value of **pattern**:

```
. tab pattern if p < 1e-7

group(x1 x2)|      Freq.     Percent        Cum.
------------+-----------------------------------
          1 |          1      100.00      100.00
------------+-----------------------------------
      Total |          1      100.00
```

Once we omit this covariate pattern from the estimation sample, `logit` can deal with the collinearity:

```
. logit y x1 x2 if pattern~=1, nolog
Note: x2 dropped due to collinearity.

Logit estimates                            Number of obs   =          4
                                           LR chi2(1)      =       0.00
                                           Prob > chi2     =     1.0000
Log likelihood = -2.7725887                Pseudo R2       =     0.0000

------------------------------------------------------------------------
       y |      Coef.   Std. Err.       z    P>|z|     [95% Conf. Interval]
---------+--------------------------------------------------------------
      x1 |          0           2    0.000   1.000     -3.919928   3.919928
   _cons |          0    1.414214    0.000   1.000     -2.771808   2.771808
------------------------------------------------------------------------
```

We omit the collinear variable. Then we must decide whether to include or to omit the observations with **pattern** = 1. We could include them:

```
. logit y x1, nolog

Logit estimates                            Number of obs   =          5
                                           LR chi2(1)      =       0.14
                                           Prob > chi2     =     0.7098
Log likelihood = -3.2958369                Pseudo R2       =     0.0206

------------------------------------------------------------------------
       y |      Coef.   Std. Err.       z    P>|z|     [95% Conf. Interval]
---------+--------------------------------------------------------------
      x1 |   .6931472    1.870827    0.371   0.711     -2.973605     4.3599
   _cons |  -.6931472    1.224742   -0.566   0.571     -3.093597   1.707302
------------------------------------------------------------------------
```

Or exclude them:

```
. logit y x1 if pattern~=1, nolog
```

```
Logit estimates                                 Number of obs  =          4
                                                LR chi2(1)     =       0.00
                                                Prob > chi2    =     1.0000
Log likelihood = -2.7725887                     Pseudo R2      =     0.0000
```

y	Coef.	Std. Err.	z	P>|z|	[95% Conf. Interval]
x1	0	2	0.000	1.000	-3.919928 3.919928
_cons	0	1.414214	0.000	1.000	-2.771808 2.771808

If the covariate pattern that predicts outcome perfectly is meaningful, you may want to exclude these observations from the model. In this case, one would report covariate pattern such and such predicted outcome perfectly and that the best model for the rest of the data is .... But, more likely, the perfect prediction was simply the result of having too many predictors in the model. In this case, one would omit the extraneous variable(s) from further consideration and report the best model for all the data.

❑

Obtaining predicted values

Once you have estimated a logit model, you can obtain the predicted probabilities using the predict command for both the estimation sample and other samples; see [U] **23 Estimation and post-estimation commands** and [R] **predict**. Here we will make only a few additional comments.

predict without arguments calculates the predicted probability of a positive outcome; i.e., $\Pr(y_j = 1) = F(\mathbf{x}_j\mathbf{b})$. With the **xb** option, it calculates the linear combination $\mathbf{x}_j\mathbf{b}$, where $\mathbf{x}_j$ are the independent variables in the jth observation and $\mathbf{b}$ is the estimated parameter vector. This is sometimes known as the index function since the cumulative density indexed at this value is the probability of a positive outcome.

In both cases, Stata remembers any "rules" used to identify the model and calculates missing for excluded observations unless **rules** or **asif** is specified. This is covered in the following example.

For information about the other statistics available after predict, see [R] **logistic**.

▷ Example

In the previous example, we estimated the logit model logit foreign rep_is_1 rep_is_2. To obtain predicted probabilities:

```
. predict p
(10 missing values generated)
. summarize foreign p
```

Variable	Obs	Mean	Std. Dev.	Min	Max
foreign	58	.2068966	.4086186	0	1
p	48	.25	.1956984	.1	.5

Stata remembers any "rules" used to identify the model and sets predictions to missing for any excluded observations. In the previous example, logit dropped the variable rep_is_1 from our model and excluded 10 observations. Thus, when we typed predict p, those same 10 observations were again excluded and their predictions set to missing.

predict's rules option will use the rules in the prediction. During estimation, we were told "rep_is_1~=0 predicts failure perfectly", so the rule is that when rep_is_1 is not zero, one should predict 0 probability of success or a positive outcome:

```
. predict p2, rules

. summarize foreign p p2
```

Variable	Obs	Mean	Std. Dev.	Min	Max
foreign	58	.2068966	.4086186	0	1
p	48	.25	.1956984	.1	.5
p2	58	.2068966	.2016268	0	.5

predict's asif option will ignore the rules and the exclusion criteria, and calculate predictions for all observations possible using the estimated parameters from the model:

```
. predict p3, asif

. summarize for p p2 p3
```

Variable	Obs	Mean	Std. Dev.	Min	Max
foreign	58	.2068966	.4086186	0	1
p	48	.25	.1956984	.1	.5
p2	58	.2068966	.2016268	0	.5
p3	58	.2931034	.2016268	.1	.5

Which is right? What predict does by default is the most conservative approach. If a large number of observations had been excluded due to a simple rule, one could be reasonably certain that the rules prediction is correct. The asif prediction is only correct if the exclusion is a fluke and you would be willing to exclude the variable from the analysis anyway. In that case, however, you should reestimate the model to include the excluded observations.

◁

Saved Results

logit saves in e():

Scalars

e(N)	number of observations	e(ll)	log likelihood
e(df_m)	model degrees of freedom	e(ll_0)	log likelihood, constant-only model
e(r2_p)	pseudo R-squared	e(chi2)	χ^2
e(N_clust)	number of clusters		

Macros

e(cmd)	logit	e(vcetype)	covariance estimation method
e(depvar)	name of dependent variable	e(chi2type)	Wald or LR; type of model χ^2 test
e(wtype)	weight type	e(offset)	offset
e(wexp)	weight expression	e(predict)	program used to implement predict
e(clustvar)	name of cluster variable		

Matrices

e(b)	coefficient vector	e(V)	variance–covariance matrix of the estimators

Functions

e(sample)	marks estimation sample

Methods and Formulas

The word logit is due to Berkson (1944) and is by analogy with the word probit. For an introduction to logit and probit, see, for example, Aldrich and Nelson (1984) or Hamilton (1992).

The likelihood function for logit is

$$\ln L = \sum_{j \in S} w_j \ln F(\mathbf{x}_j \mathbf{b}) + \sum_{j \notin S} w_j \ln\big[1 - F(\mathbf{x}_j \mathbf{b})\big]$$

where S is the set of all observations j such that $y_j \neq 0$, $F(z) = e^z/(1 + e^z)$, and w_j denotes the optional weights. $\ln L$ is maximized as described in [R] **maximize**.

If robust standard errors are requested, the calculation described in *Methods and Formulas* of [R] **regress** is carried forward with $\mathbf{u}_j = [1 - F(\mathbf{x}_j \mathbf{b})]\mathbf{x}_j$ for the positive outcomes and $-F(\mathbf{x}_j \mathbf{b})\mathbf{x}_j$ for the negative outcomes. q_c is given by its asymptotic-like formula.

References

Aldrich, J. H. and F. D. Nelson. 1984. *Linear Probability, Logit, and Probit Models.* Newbury Park, CA: Sage Publications.

Berkson, J. 1944. Application of the logistic function to bio-assay. *Journal of the American Statistical Association* 39: 357–365.

Hamilton, L. C. 1992. *Regression with Graphics.* Pacific Grove, CA: Brooks/Cole Publishing Company.

Hosmer, D. W., Jr., and S. Lemeshow. 1989. *Applied Logistic Regression.* New York: John Wiley & Sons.

Johnston, J. and J. DiNardo. 1997. *Econometric Methods.* 4th ed. New York: McGraw–Hill.

Judge, G. G., W. E. Griffiths, R. C. Hill, H. Lütkepohl, and T.-C. Lee. 1985. *The Theory and Practice of Econometrics.* 2d ed. New York: John Wiley & Sons.

Pregibon, D. 1981. Logistic regression diagnostics. *Annals of Statistics* 9: 705–724.

Also See

Complementary:	[R] **adjust**, [R] **lincom**, [R] **linktest**, [R] **lrtest**, [R] **predict**, [R] **sw**, [R] **test**, [R] **testnl**, [R] **vce**, [R] **xi**
Related:	[R] **clogit**, [R] **cloglog**, [R] **cusum**, [R] **glm**, [R] **glogit**, [R] **logistic**, [R] **probit**, [R] **scobit**, [R] **svy estimators**, [R] **xtclog**, [R] **xtgee**, [R] **xtlogit**, [R] **xtprobit**
Background:	[U] **16.5 Accessing coefficients and standard errors**, [U] **23 Estimation and post-estimation commands**, [U] **23.11 Obtaining robust variance estimates**, [U] **23.12 Obtaining scores**, [R] **maximize**

Title

loneway — Large one-way ANOVA, random effects, and reliability

Syntax

loneway *response_var group_var* [*weight*] [**if** *exp*] [**in** *range*] [, **mean** **median** **exact**]

aweights are allowed; see [U] **14.1.6 weight**.

Description

loneway estimates one-way analysis-of-variance (ANOVA) models on datasets with a large number of levels of *group_var* and presents different ancillary statistics from **oneway** (see [R] **oneway**):

Feature	oneway	loneway
Estimate one-way model	x	x
on fewer than 376 levels	x	x
on more than 376 levels		x
Bartlett's test for equal variance	x	
Multiple-comparison tests	x	
Intragroup correlation and S.E.		x
Intragroup correlation confidence interval		x
Est. reliability of group-averaged score		x
Est. S.D. of group effect		x
Est. S.D. within group		x

Options

mean specifies that the expected value of the $F_{k-1, N-k}$ distribution be used as the reference point F_m in the estimation of ρ instead of the default value of 1.

median specifies that the median of the $F_{k-1, N-k}$ distribution be used as the reference point F_m in the estimation of ρ instead of the default value of 1.

exact requests that exact confidence intervals be computed, as opposed to the default asymptotic confidence intervals. This option is allowed only if the groups are equal in size and weights are not used.

Remarks

▷ Example

loneway's output looks like that of **oneway** except that, at the end, additional information is presented. Using our automobile data (see [U] **9 Stata's on-line tutorials and sample datasets**), we have created a (numeric) variable called **manu** identifying the manufacturer of each car and within each manufacturer we have retained a maximum of four models, selecting those with the lowest mpg. We can compute the intraclass correlation of mpg for all manufacturers with at least four models as follows:

```
. loneway mpg manu if nummod == 4
                One Way Analysis of Variance for mpg: Mileage (mpg)
                                              Number of obs =         36
                                              R-squared    =     0.5228

        Source            SS          df       MS              F      Prob > F
--------------------------------------------------------------------------------
Between manu          621.88889        8     77.736111         3.70     0.0049
Within manu           567.75          27     21.027778
--------------------------------------------------------------------------------
Total                1189.6389        35     33.989683

        Intraclass         Asy.
        correlation        S.E.          [95% Conf. Interval]
------------------------------------------------------------------
          0.40270        0.18770          0.03481      0.77060

        Estimated SD of manu effect               3.765247
        Estimated SD within manu                  4.585605
        Est. reliability of a manu mean           .7294979
                (evaluated at n=4.00)
```

◁

In addition to the standard one-way ANOVA output, loneway produces the R-squared, estimated standard deviation of the group effect, and estimated standard deviation within group, the intragroup correlation, the estimated reliability of the group-averaged mean, and, in the case of unweighted data, the asymptotic standard error and confidence interval for the intragroup correlation.

R-squared

The R-squared is, of course, simply the underlying R^2 for a regression of *response_var* on the levels of *group_var*, or mpg on the various manufacturers in this case.

The random effects ANOVA model

loneway assumes we observe a variable y_{ij} measured for n_i elements within k groups or classes such that

$$y_{ij} = \mu + \alpha_i + \epsilon_{ij}, \quad i = 1, 2, \ldots, k, \quad j = 1, 2, \ldots, n_i$$

and α_i and ϵ_{ij} are independent zero-mean random variables with variance σ_α^2 and σ_ϵ^2, respectively. This is the random effects ANOVA model, also known as the components of variance model, in which it is typically assumed that the y_{ij} are normally distributed.

The interpretation with respect to our example is that the observed value of our response variable, mpg, is created in two steps. First, the ith manufacturer is chosen and a value α_i is determined—the typical mpg for that manufacturer less the overall mpg μ. Then a deviation, ϵ_{ij}, is chosen for the jth model within this manufacturer. This is how much that particular automobile differs from the typical mpg value for models from this manufacturer.

For our sample of 36 car models, the estimated standard deviations are $\sigma_\alpha = 3.8$ and $\sigma_\epsilon = 4.6$. Thus, a little more than half of the variation in mpg between cars is attributable to the car model with the rest attributable to differences between manufacturers. These standard deviations differ from those that would be produced by a (standard) fixed-effects regression in that the regression would require the sum within each manufacturer of the ϵ_{ij}, $\epsilon_{i.}$ for the ith manufacturer, to be zero while these estimates merely impose the constraint that the sum is *expected* to be zero.

Intraclass correlation

There are various estimators of the intraclass correlation, such as the pairwise estimator, which is defined as the Pearson product-moment correlation computed over all possible pairs of observations that can be constructed within groups. For a discussion of various estimators see Donner (1986). loneway computes what is termed the analysis of variance, or ANOVA, estimator. This intraclass correlation is the theoretical upper bound on the variation in *response_var* that is explainable by *group_var*, of which R-squared is an overestimate because of the serendipity of fitting. Note, this correlation is comparable to an R-squared—you do not have to square it.

In our example, the intra-manu correlation, the correlation of mpg within manufacturer, is 0.40. Since aweights weren't used and the default correlation was computed, i.e., the mean and median options were not specified, loneway also provided the asymptotic confidence interval and standard error of the intraclass correlation estimate.

Estimated reliability of the group-averaged score

The estimated reliability of the group-averaged score or mean has an interpretation similar to that of the intragroup correlation; it is a comparable number if we average *response_var* by *group_var*, or mpg by manu in our example. It is the theoretical upper bound of a regression of manufacturer-averaged mpg on characteristics of manufacturers. Why would we want to collapse our 36-observation data into a 9-observation dataset of manufacturer averages? Because the 36 observations might be a mirage. When General Motors builds cars, do they sometimes put a Pontiac label and sometimes a Chevrolet label on them, so that it appears in our data as if we have two cars when we really have only one, replicated? If that were the case, and if it were the case for many other manufacturers, then we would be forced to admit that we do not have data on 36 cars; we have data on 9 manufacturer-averaged characteristics.

Saved Results

loneway saves in r():

Scalars

r(N)	number of observations	r(rho_t)	estimated reliability
r(rho)	intraclass correlation	r(se)	asymp. SE of intraclass correlation
r(lb)	lower bound of 95% CI for rho	r(sd_w)	estimated SD within group
r(ub)	upper bound of 95% CI for rho	r(sd_b)	estimated SD of group effect

Methods and Formulas

loneway is implemented as an ado-file.

The mean squares in the loneway's ANOVA table are computed as follows:

$$MS_\alpha = \sum_i w_{i\cdot}(\bar{y}_{i\cdot} - \bar{y}_{\cdot\cdot})^2 / (k-1)$$

and

$$MS_\epsilon = \sum_i \sum_j w_{ij}(y_{ij} - \bar{y}_{i\cdot})^2 / (N-k)$$

in which

$$w_{i\cdot} = \sum_j w_{ij}, \quad w_{\cdot\cdot} = \sum_i w_{i\cdot}, \quad \bar{y}_{i\cdot} = \sum_j w_{ij} y_{ij} / w_{i\cdot}, \quad \text{and} \quad \bar{y}_{\cdot\cdot} = \sum_i w_{i\cdot} \bar{y}_{i\cdot} / w_{\cdot\cdot}$$

The corresponding expected values of these mean squares are

$$E(MS_\alpha) = \sigma_\epsilon^2 + g\sigma_\alpha^2 \quad \text{and} \quad E(MS_\epsilon) = \sigma_\epsilon^2$$

in which

$$g = \frac{w_{\cdot\cdot} - \sum_i w_{i\cdot}^2 / w_{\cdot\cdot}}{k - 1}$$

Note that in the unweighted case, we get

$$g = \frac{N - \sum_i n_i^2 / N}{k - 1}$$

As expected, $g = m$ for the case of no weights and equal group sizes in the data, i.e., $n_i = m$ for all i. Replacing the expected values with the observed values and solving yields the ANOVA estimates of σ_α^2 and σ_ϵ^2. Substituting these into the definition of the intraclass correlation

$$\rho = \frac{\sigma_\alpha^2}{\sigma_\alpha^2 + \sigma_\epsilon^2}$$

yields the ANOVA estimator of the intraclass correlation:

$$\rho_A = \frac{F_{obs} - 1}{F_{obs} - 1 + g}$$

Note that F_{obs} is the observed value of the F statistic from the ANOVA table. For the case of no weights and equal n_i, ρ_A = roh, the intragroup correlation defined by Kish (1965). Two slightly different estimators are available through the **mean** and **median** options (Gleason 1997). If either of these options is specified the estimate of ρ becomes

$$\rho = \frac{F_{obs} - F_m}{F_{obs} + (g - 1)F_m}$$

For the **mean** option, $F_m = E(F_{k-1,N-K}) = (N - k)/(N - k - 2)$, i.e., the expected value of the ANOVA table's F statistic. For the **median** option, F_m is simply the median of the F statistic. Note that setting F_m to 1 gives ρ_A so for large samples these different point estimators are essentially the same. Also, since the intraclass correlation of the random effects model is by definition nonnegative, for any of the three possible point estimators ρ is truncated to zero if F_{obs} is less than F_m.

For the case of no weighting, interval estimators for ρ_A are computed. If the groups are equal-sized (all n_i equal) and the **exact** option is specified, the following exact (under the assumption that the y_{ij} are normally distributed) $100(1 - \alpha)\%$ confidence interval is computed:

$$\left[\frac{F_{obs} - F_m F_u}{F_{obs} + (g - 1)F_m F_u}, \frac{F_{obs} - F_m F_l}{F_{obs} + (g - 1)F_m F_l} \right]$$

with $F_m = 1$, $F_l = F_{\alpha/2,k-1,N-k}$, and $F_u = F_{1-\alpha/2,k-1,N-k}$, $F_{\cdot,k-1,N-k}$ being the cumulative distribution function for the F distribution with $k-1$ and $N-k$ degrees of freedom. Note that if **mean** or **median** is specified, F_m is defined as above. If the groups are equal-sized and **exact** is not specified then the following asymptotic $100(1-\alpha)\%$ confidence interval for ρ_A is computed: $[\rho_A - z_{\alpha/2}V(\rho_A), \rho_A + z_{\alpha/2}V(\rho_A)]$ where $z_{\alpha/2}$ is the $100(1-\alpha/2)$ percentile of the standard normal distribution and $V(\rho_A)$ is the asymptotic standard error of ρ defined below. Note that this confidence interval is also available for the case of unequal groups. It is not applicable, and therefore not computed, for the estimates of ρ provided by the **mean** and **median** options. Again, since the intraclass coefficient is nonnegative, if the lower bound is negative for either confidence interval, it is truncated to zero. As might be expected, the coverage probability of a truncated interval is higher than its nominal value.

The asymptotic standard error of ρ_A, assuming the y_{ij} are normally distributed, is also computed when appropriate, namely for unweighted data and when ρ_A is computed (neither the **mean** nor the **median** options are specified):

$$V(\rho_A) = \frac{2(1-\rho)^2}{g^2}(A+B+C)$$

with

$$A = \frac{[1+\rho(g-1)]^2}{N-k}$$

$$B = \frac{(1-\rho)[1+\rho(2g-1)]}{k-1}$$

$$C = \frac{\rho^2[\sum n_i^2 - 2N^{-1}\sum n_i^3 + N^{-2}(\sum n_i^2)^2]}{(k-1)^2}$$

and ρ_A is substituted for ρ (Donner 1986).

The estimated reliability of the group-averaged score, known as the *Spearman–Brown prediction formula* in the psychometric literature (Winer, Brown, and Michels 1991, 1014), is

$$\rho_t = \frac{t\rho}{1+(t-1)\rho}$$

for group size t. **loneway** computes ρ_t for $t = g$.

The estimated standard deviation of the group effect is $\sigma_\alpha = \sqrt{(MS_\alpha - MS_\epsilon)/g}$. This comes from the assumption that an observation is derived by adding a group effect to a within-group effect.

The estimated standard deviation within group is the square root of the mean square due to error, or $\sqrt{MS_\epsilon}$.

Acknowledgment

We would like to thank John Gleason of Syracuse University for his contributions to this improved version of **loneway**.

References

Donner, A. 1986. A review of inference procedures for the intraclass correlation coefficient in the one-way random effects model. *International Statistical Review* 54: 67–82.

Gleason, J. R. 1997. sg65: Computing intraclass correlations and large ANOVAs. *Stata Technical Bulletin* 35: 25–31. Reprinted in *Stata Technical Bulletin Reprints*, vol. 6, pp. 167–176.

Kish, L. 1965. *Survey Sampling*. New York: John Wiley & Sons.

Winer, B. J., D. R. Brown, and K. M. Michels. 1991. *Statistical Principles in Experimental Design*. 3d ed. New York: McGraw–Hill.

Also See

Related: [R] **oneway**

Title

lrtest — Likelihood-ratio test after model estimation

Syntax

lrtest [, saving(*name*) using(*name*) model(*name*) df(*#*)]

where *name* may be a name or a number but may not exceed 4 characters.

Description

lrtest saves information about and performs likelihood-ratio tests between pairs of maximum likelihood models such as those estimated by cox, logit, logistic, poisson, etc. lrtest may be used with any estimation command that reports a log-likelihood value or, equivalently, displays output like that described in [R] **maximize**.

lrtest, typed without arguments, performs a likelihood-ratio test of the most recently estimated model against the model previously saved by lrtest, saving(0). It is your responsibility to ensure that the most recently estimated model is nested within the previously saved model.

lrtest provides an important alternative to test for maximum likelihood models.

Options

saving(*name*) specifies that the summary statistics associated with the most recently estimated model are to be saved as *name*. If no other options are specified, the statistics are saved and no test is performed. The larger model is typically saved by typing lrtest, saving(0).

using(*name*) specifies the name of the larger model against which a model is to be tested. If this option is not specified, using(0) is assumed.

model(*name*) specifies the name of the nested model (a constrained model) to be tested. If not specified, the most recently estimated model is used.

df(*#*) is seldom specified; it overrides the automatic degrees-of-freedom calculation.

Remarks

The standard use of lrtest is

1. Estimate the larger model using one of Stata's estimation commands and then type lrtest, saving(0).

2. Estimate an alternative, nested model (a constrained model) and then type lrtest.

▷ Example

You have data on infants born with low birth weights along with characteristics of the mother (Hosmer and Lemeshow 1989 and more fully described in [R] **logistic**). You estimate the following model:

```
. logistic low age lwt race2 race3 smoke ptl ht ui
Logit estimates                                  Number of obs   =        189
                                                 LR chi2(8)      =      33.22
                                                 Prob > chi2     =     0.0001
Log likelihood =    -100.724                     Pseudo R2       =     0.1416

--------------------------------------------------------------------------
     low | Odds Ratio  Std. Err.      z     P>|z|    [95% Conf. Interval]
---------+----------------------------------------------------------------
     age |  .9732636   .0354759    -0.743   0.457    .9061578    1.045339
     lwt |  .9849634   .0068217    -2.188   0.029    .9716834    .9984249
   race2 |  3.534767   1.860737     2.399   0.016    1.259736    9.918406
   race3 |  2.368079   1.039949     1.963   0.050    1.001356    5.600207
   smoke |  2.517698   1.00916      2.304   0.021    1.147676    5.523162
     ptl |  1.719161   .5952579     1.565   0.118    .8721455    3.388787
      ht |  6.249602   4.322408     2.650   0.008    1.611152    24.24199
      ui |   2.1351    .9808153     1.651   0.099    .8677528     5.2534
--------------------------------------------------------------------------
```

You now wish to test the constraint that the coefficients on `age`, `lwt`, `ptl`, and `ht` are all zero (or equivalently in this case, that the odds ratios are all 1). One solution is

```
. test age lwt ptl ht
 ( 1)   age = 0.0
 ( 2)   lwt = 0.0
 ( 3)   ptl = 0.0
 ( 4)   ht = 0.0
          chi2( 4) =    12.38
        Prob > chi2 =     0.0147
```

This test is based on the inverse of the information matrix and is therefore based on a quadratic approximation to the likelihood function; see [R] **test**. A more precise test would be to reestimate the model, applying the proposed constraints, and then calculate the likelihood-ratio test. `lrtest` assists you in doing this.

You first save the statistics associated with the current model:

```
. lrtest, saving(0)
```

The "name" 0 was not chosen arbitrarily, although we could have chosen any name. Why we chose 0 will become clear shortly. Having saved the information on the current model, we now estimate the constrained model, which in this case is the model omitting `age`, `lwt`, `ptl`, and `ht`:

```
. logistic low race2 race3 smoke ui
Logit estimates                                  Number of obs   =        189
                                                 LR chi2(4)      =      18.80
                                                 Prob > chi2     =     0.0009
Log likelihood = -107.93404                      Pseudo R2       =     0.0801

--------------------------------------------------------------------------
     low | Odds Ratio  Std. Err.      z     P>|z|    [95% Conf. Interval]
---------+----------------------------------------------------------------
   race2 |  3.052746   1.498084     2.274   0.023    1.166749    7.987368
   race3 |  2.922593   1.189226     2.636   0.008    1.31646     6.488269
   smoke |  2.945742   1.101835     2.888   0.004    1.41517     6.131701
      ui |  2.419131   1.047358     2.040   0.041    1.03546     5.651783
--------------------------------------------------------------------------
```

That done, typing `lrtest` will compare this model with the model we previously saved:

```
. lrtest
Logistic:  likelihood-ratio test            chi2(4)     =      14.42
                                            Prob > chi2 =     0.0061
```

The more precise syntax for the test is `lrtest, using(0)`, meaning that the current model is to be compared with the model saved as 0. The name 0, as we previously said, is special—when you do not specify the name of the `using()` model, `using(0)` is assumed. Thus, saving the original model as 0 saved us some typing when we performed the test.

Comparing results, `test` reported that `age`, `lwt`, `ptl`, and `ht` were jointly significant at the 1.5% level; `lrtest` reports they are significant at the 0.6% level. `lrtest`'s results should be viewed as more accurate.

◁

▷ Example

Typing `lrtest, saving(0)` and later `lrtest` by itself is the way `lrtest` is most commonly used, although here is how we might use the other options:

. logit chd age age2 sex	*estimate full model*
. lrtest, saving(0)	*save results*
. logit chd age sex	*estimate simpler model*
. lrtest	*obtain test*
. lrtest, saving(1)	*save logit results as 1*
. logit chd sex	*estimate simplest model*
. lrtest	*compare with full model*
. lrtest, using(1)	*compare with model 1*
. lrtest, model(1)	*repeat against full model test*

◁

▷ Example

Returning to the low birth weight data in the first example, you now wish to test that the coefficient on `race2` is equal to that on `race3`. The base model is still stored in 0, so you need only estimate the constrained model and perform the test. Letting z be the index of the logit, the base model is

$$z = \beta_0 + \beta_1 \texttt{age} + \beta_2 \texttt{lwt} + \beta_3 \texttt{race2} + \beta_4 \texttt{race3} + \cdots$$

If $\beta_3 = \beta_4$, this can be written

$$z = \beta_0 + \beta_1 \texttt{age} + \beta_2 \texttt{lwt} + \beta_3 (\texttt{race2} + \texttt{race3}) + \cdots$$

To estimate the constrained model, we create a variable equal to the sum of `race2` and `race3` and estimate the model including that variable in their place:

(Continued on next page)

```
. gen race23 = race2 + race3
. logistic low age lwt race23 smoke ptl ht ui
Logit estimates                               Number of obs   =        189
                                              LR chi2(7)      =      32.67
                                              Prob > chi2     =     0.0000
Log likelihood =  -100.9997                   Pseudo R2       =     0.1392

------------------------------------------------------------------------------
     low | Odds Ratio   Std. Err.       z    P>|z|     [95% Conf. Interval]
---------+--------------------------------------------------------------------
     age |  .9716799    .0352638    -0.792   0.429     .9049649    1.043313
     lwt |  .9864971    .0064627    -2.075   0.038     .9739114    .9992453
  race23 |  2.728186    1.080206     2.535   0.011     1.255586    5.927907
   smoke |  2.664498    1.052379     2.481   0.013     1.228633    5.778414
     ptl |  1.709129    .5924775     1.546   0.122     .8663666    3.371691
      ht |  6.116391    4.215585     2.628   0.009      1.58425    23.61385
      ui |   2.09936    .9699702     1.605   0.108     .8487997    5.192407
------------------------------------------------------------------------------
```

Comparing this model with our original model, we obtain

```
. lrtest
Logistic:  likelihood-ratio test               chi2(1)    =        0.55
                                               Prob > chi2 =      0.4577
```

By comparison, typing `test race2=race3` after estimating our base model results in a significance level of .4572.

◁

Saved Results

lrtest saves in r():

Scalars
    r(p)   two-sided p-value   r(chi2) χ^2
    r(df)   degrees of freedom

Programmers desiring that an estimation command be compatible with lrtest should note that it requires the following macros to be defined:

e(cmd)   name of estimation command
e(ll)   log-likelihood value
e(df_m)   model degrees of freedom
e(N)   number of observations

Methods and Formulas

lrtest is implemented as an ado-file.

Let L_0 and L_1 be the log-likelihood values associated with the full and constrained models, respectively. Then $\chi^2 = -2(L_1 - L_0)$ with $d_0 - d_1$ degrees of freedom, where d_0 and d_1 are the model degrees of freedom associated with the full and constrained models (Judge et al. 1985, 216–217).

References

Hosmer, D. W., Jr., and S. Lemeshow. 1989. *Applied Logistic Regression.* New York: John Wiley & Sons.

Judge, G. G., W. E. Griffiths, R. C. Hill, H. Lütkepohl, and T.-C. Lee. 1985. *The Theory and Practice of Econometrics.* 2d ed. New York: John Wiley & Sons.

Also See

Related: [R] **estimation commands**, [R] **linktest**, [R] **test**, [R] **testnl**

Title

> **ltable** — Life tables for survival data

Syntax

> ltable *timevar* [*deadvar*] [*weight*] [if *exp*] [in *range*] [, by(*groupvar*) level(#)
>
> survival failure hazard intervals(*interval*) test tvid(*varname*) noadjust
>
> notab graph *graph_options* noconf]

where *interval* is { w | # | #,#,... }

fweights are allowed; see [U] **14.1.6 weight**.

Description

ltable displays and graphs life tables for individual-level or aggregate data and optionally presents the likelihood-ratio and log-rank tests for equivalence of groups. ltable also allows examining the empirical hazard function through aggregation. Also see [R] **st sts** for alternative commands.

timevar specifies the time of failure or censoring. If *deadvar* is not specified, all values of *timevar* are interpreted as failure times; otherwise, *timevar* is interpreted as a failure time where *deadvar* ≠ 0 and as a censoring time otherwise. Observations with *timevar* or *deadvar* equal to missing are ignored.

Note carefully that *deadvar* does *not* specify the *number* of failures. An observation with *deadvar* equal to 1 or 50 has the same interpretation—the observation records one failure. Specify frequency weights for aggregated data (e.g., ltable time [freq=number]).

Options

by(*groupvar*) creates separate tables (or graphs within the same image) for each value of *groupvar*. *groupvar* may be string or numeric.

level(#) specifies the confidence level, in percent, for confidence intervals. The default is level(95) or as set by set level; see [R] **level**.

survival, failure, and hazard indicate the table to be displayed. If not specified, the default is the survival table. Specifying failure would display the cumulative failure table. Specifying survival failure would display both the survival and the cumulative failure table. If graph is specified, multiple tables may not be requested.

intervals(*interval*) specifies the time intervals into which the data are to be aggregated for tabular presentation. A single numeric argument is interpreted as the width of the interval. For instance, interval(2) aggregates data into the time intervals $0 \le t < 2$, $2 \le t < 4$, and so on. Not specifying interval() is equivalent to specifying interval(1). Since in most data failure times are recorded as integers, this amounts to no aggregation except that implied by the recording of the time variable and so produces Kaplan–Meier product-limit estimates of the survival curve (with an actuarial adjustment; see the noadjust option below). Also see [R] **st sts list**. Although it is possible to examine survival and failure without aggregation, some form of aggregation is almost always required for examining the hazard.

When more than one argument is specified, time intervals are aggregated as specified. For instance, interval(0,2,8,16) aggregates data into the intervals $0 \leq t < 2$, $2 \leq t < 8$, $8 \leq t < 16$, and (if necessary) the open-ended interval $t \geq 16$.

interval(w) is equivalent to interval(0,7,15,30,60,90,180,360,540,720), corresponding to one week, (roughly) two weeks, one month, two months, three months, six months, 1 year, 1.5 years, and 2 years when failure times are recorded in days. The w is meant to suggest widening intervals.

test presents two χ^2 measures of the differences between groups when by() is specified. test does nothing if by() is not specified.

tvid(*varname*) is for use with longitudinal data with time-varying parameters as processed by cox; see [R] **cox**. Each subject appears in the data more than once and equal values of *varname* identify observations referring to the same subject. When tvid() is specified, only the last observation on each subject is used in making the table. The order of the data does not matter, and "last" here means the last observation chronologically.

noadjust suppresses the actuarial adjustment for deaths and censored observations. The default is to consider the adjusted number at risk at the start of the interval as the total at the start minus (the number dead or censored)/2. If noadjust is specified, the number at risk is simply the total at the start, corresponding to the standard Kaplan and Meier assumption. noadjust should be specified when using ltable to list results corresponding to those produced by sts list; see [R] **st sts list**.

notab suppresses displaying the table. This option is often used with graph.

graph requests that the table be presented graphically as well as in tabular form; when notab is also specified, only the graph is presented. When specifying graph, only one table can be calculated and graphed at a time; see survival, failure, and hazard above.

graph_options are any of the options allowed with graph, twoway; see [G] **graph options**. When noconf is specified, twoway's connect() and symbol() may be specified with one argument; the default is connect(l) symbol(O).

When noconf is not specified, the connect() and symbol() options may be specified with one or three arguments. The default is connect(l||) and symbol(Oii), drawing the confidence band as vertical lines at each point. When you specify one argument, you modify the first argument of the default. When you specify three, you completely control the graph. Thus, connect(lll) would draw the confidence band as a separate curve around the survival, failure, or hazard.

noconf suppresses graphing the confidence intervals around survival, failure, or hazard.

Remarks

Life tables date back to the seventeenth century; Edmund Halley (1693) is often credited with their development. ltable is for use with "cohort" data and, although one often thinks of such tables as following a population from the "birth" of the first member to the "death" of the last, more generally, such tables can be thought of as a reasonable way to list any kind of survival data. For an introductory discussion of life tables, see Pagano and Gauvreau (1993, 446–451); for an intermediate discussion, see, for example, Armitage and Berry (1987, 421–435) or Selvin (1996, 311–355); and for a more complete discussion, see Chiang (1984).

▷ Example

In Pike (1966), two groups of rats were exposed to a carcinogen and the number of days to death from vaginal cancer recorded (reprinted in Kalbfleisch and Prentice 1980, 2):

Group 1	143	164	188	188	190	192	206	209	213	216
	220	227	230	234	246	265	304	216*	244*	
Group 2	142	156	163	198	205	232	232	233	233	233
	233	239	240	261	280	280	296	296	323	204*
	344*									

The '*' on a few of the entries indicate that the observation was censored—as of the recorded day, the rat had still not died due to vaginal cancer but was withdrawn from the experiment for other reasons.

Having entered this data into Stata, the first few observations are

```
. list in 1/5
        group        t      died
1.          1      143         1
2.          1      164         1
3.          1      188         1
4.          1      188         1
5.          1      190         1
```

That is, the first observation records a rat from group 1 that died on the 143rd day. The variable died records whether that rat died or was withdrawn (censored):

```
. list if died==0
        group        t      died
18.         1      216         0
19.         1      244         0
39.         2      204         0
40.         2      344         0
```

Four rats, two from each group, did not die but were withdrawn.

The survival table for group 1 is

```
. ltable t died if group==1
```

Interval		Beg. Total	Deaths	Lost	Survival	Std. Error	[95% Conf. Int.]	
143	144	19	1	0	0.9474	0.0512	0.6812	0.9924
164	165	18	1	0	0.8947	0.0704	0.6408	0.9726
188	189	17	2	0	0.7895	0.0935	0.5319	0.9153
190	191	15	1	0	0.7368	0.1010	0.4789	0.8810
192	193	14	1	0	0.6842	0.1066	0.4279	0.8439
206	207	13	1	0	0.6316	0.1107	0.3790	0.8044
209	210	12	1	0	0.5789	0.1133	0.3321	0.7626
213	214	11	1	0	0.5263	0.1145	0.2872	0.7188
216	217	10	1	1	0.4709	0.1151	0.2410	0.6712
220	221	8	1	0	0.4120	0.1148	0.1937	0.6194
227	228	7	1	0	0.3532	0.1125	0.1502	0.5648
230	231	6	1	0	0.2943	0.1080	0.1105	0.5070
234	235	5	1	0	0.2354	0.1012	0.0750	0.4459
244	245	4	0	1	0.2354	0.1012	0.0750	0.4459
246	247	3	1	0	0.1570	0.0930	0.0312	0.3721
265	266	2	1	0	0.0785	0.0724	0.0056	0.2864
304	305	1	1	0	0.0000	.	.	.

The reported survival rates are the survival rates at the end of the interval. Thus, 94.7% of rats survived 144 days or more.

◁

❑ Technical Note

If you compare the table just printed with the corresponding table in Kalbfleisch and Prentice (1980, 14), you will notice that the survival estimates differ beginning with the interval 216–217, the first interval containing a censored observation. ltable treats censored observations as if they were withdrawn half-way through the interval. The table printed in Kalbfleisch and Prentice treated censored observations as if they were withdrawn at the end of the interval even through Kalbfleisch and Prentice (1980, 15) mention how results could be adjusted for censoring.

In this case, the same results as printed in Kalbfleisch and Prentice could be obtained by incrementing the time of withdrawal by 1 for the four censored observations. We say "in this case" because there were no deaths on the incremented dates. For instance, one of the rats was withdrawn on the 216th day, a day on which there was also a real death. There were no deaths on day 217, however, so moving the withdrawal forward one day is equivalent to assuming the withdrawal occurred at the end of the day 216–217 interval. If the adjustments are made and ltable used to calculate survival in both groups, results are as printed in Kalbfleisch and Prentice except that, for group 2 in the interval 240–241, they report the survival as .345 when they mean .354.

In any case, the one-half adjustment for withdrawals is generally accepted but it is important to remember that it is only a crude adjustment and one that becomes cruder the wider the intervals.

❑

▷ Example

When you do not specify the intervals, ltable uses unit intervals. The only aggregation performed on the data was aggregation due to deaths or withdrawals occurring on the same "day". If we wanted to see the table aggregated into 30-day intervals, we would type

```
. ltable t died if group==1, interval(30)
```

Interval		Beg. Total	Deaths	Lost	Survival	Std. Error	[95% Conf. Int.]	
120	150	19	1	0	0.9474	0.0512	0.6812	0.9924
150	180	18	1	0	0.8947	0.0704	0.6408	0.9726
180	210	17	6	0	0.5789	0.1133	0.3321	0.7626
210	240	11	6	1	0.2481	0.1009	0.0847	0.4552
240	270	4	2	1	0.1063	0.0786	0.0139	0.3090
300	330	1	1	0	0.0000	.	.	.

The interval printed 120 150 means the interval including 120, and up to but not including 150. The reported survival rate is the survival rate just after the close of the interval.

When you specify more than one number as the argument to interval(), you specify not the widths but the cutoff points themselves.

```
. ltable t died if group==1, interval(120,180,210,240,330)
```

Interval		Beg. Total	Deaths	Lost	Survival	Std. Error	[95% Conf. Int.]	
120	180	19	2	0	0.8947	0.0704	0.6408	0.9726
180	210	17	6	0	0.5789	0.1133	0.3321	0.7626
210	240	11	6	1	0.2481	0.1009	0.0847	0.4552
240	330	4	3	1	0.0354	0.0486	0.0006	0.2245

If any of the underlying failure or censoring times are larger than the last cutoff specified, they are treated as being in the open-ended interval:

```
. ltable t died if group==1, interval(120,180,210,240)
```

Interval		Beg. Total	Deaths	Lost	Survival	Std. Error	[95% Conf. Int.]	
120	180	19	2	0	0.8947	0.0704	0.6408	0.9726
180	210	17	6	0	0.5789	0.1133	0.3321	0.7626
210	240	11	6	1	0.2481	0.1009	0.0847	0.4552
240	.	4	3	1	0.0354	0.0486	0.0006	0.2245

Whether the last interval is treated as open-ended or not makes no difference for survival and failure tables, but does affect hazard tables. If the interval is open-ended, the hazard is not calculated for it.

◁

▷ Example

The by(*varname*) option specifies that separate tables are to be presented for each value of *varname*. Remember that our rat data contains two groups:

```
. ltable t died, by(group) interval(30)
```

Interval		Beg. Total	Deaths	Lost	Survival	Std. Error	[95% Conf. Int.]	
group 1								
120	150	19	1	0	0.9474	0.0512	0.6812	0.9924
150	180	18	1	0	0.8947	0.0704	0.6408	0.9726
180	210	17	6	0	0.5789	0.1133	0.3321	0.7626
210	240	11	6	1	0.2481	0.1009	0.0847	0.4552
240	270	4	2	1	0.1063	0.0786	0.0139	0.3090
300	330	1	1	0	0.0000	.	.	.
group 2								
120	150	21	1	0	0.9524	0.0465	0.7072	0.9932
150	180	20	2	0	0.8571	0.0764	0.6197	0.9516
180	210	18	2	1	0.7592	0.0939	0.5146	0.8920
210	240	15	7	0	0.4049	0.1099	0.1963	0.6053
240	270	8	2	0	0.3037	0.1031	0.1245	0.5057
270	300	6	4	0	0.1012	0.0678	0.0172	0.2749
300	330	2	1	0	0.0506	0.0493	0.0035	0.2073
330	360	1	0	1	0.0506	0.0493	0.0035	0.2073

◁

▷ Example

A failure table is simply a different way of looking at a survival table; failure is $1 -$ survival:

```
. ltable t died if group==1, interval(30) failure
```

Interval		Beg. Total	Deaths	Lost	Cum. Failure	Std. Error	[95% Conf. Int.]	
120	150	19	1	0	0.0526	0.0512	0.0076	0.3188
150	180	18	1	0	0.1053	0.0704	0.0274	0.3592
180	210	17	6	0	0.4210	0.1133	0.2374	0.6679
210	240	11	6	1	0.7519	0.1009	0.5448	0.9153
240	270	4	2	1	0.8937	0.0786	0.6910	0.9861
300	330	1	1	0	1.0000	.	.	.

◁

▷ Example

Selvin (1996, 332) presents follow-up data from Cutler and Ederer (1958) on six cohorts of kidney cancer patients. The goal is to estimate the 5-year survival probability.

Year	Interval	Alive	Deaths	Lost	With- drawn	Year	Interval	Alive	Deaths	Lost	With- drawn
1946	0-1	9	4	1		1948	0-1	21	11	0	
	1-2	4	0	0			1-2	10	1	2	
	2-3	4	0	0			2-3	7	0	0	
	3-4	4	0	0			3-4	7	0	0	7
	4-5	4	0	0		1949	0-1	34	12	0	
	5-6	4	0	0	4		1-2	22	3	3	
1947	0-1	18	7	0			2-3	16	1	0	15
	1-2	11	0	0		1950	0-1	19	5	1	
	2-3	11	1	0			1-2	13	1	1	11
	3-4	10	2	2		1951	0-1	25	8	2	15
	4-5	6	0	0	6						

The following is the Stata dataset corresponding to the table:

```
. list
        year      t      died      pop
1.      1946     .5        1         4
2.      1946     .5        0         1
3.      1946    5.5        0         4
4.      1947     .5        1         7
5.      1947    2.5        1         1
etc.
```

As summary data may often come in the form shown above, it is worth understanding exactly how the data was translated for use with ltable. t records the time of death or censoring (lost to follow-up or withdrawal). died contains 1 if the observation records a death and 0 if it instead records lost or withdrawn patients. pop records the number of patients in the category. The first line of the table stated that, in the 1946 cohort, there were 9 patients at the start of the interval 0-1, and during the interval, 4 died, and 1 was lost to follow-up. Thus, we entered in observation 1 that at $t = .5$, 4 patients died and, in observation 2, that at $t = .5$, 1 patient was censored. We ignored the information on the total population because ltable will figure that out for itself.

The second line of the table indicated that in the interval 1–2, 4 patients were still alive at the beginning of the interval and, during the interval, 0 died or were lost to follow-up. Since no patients died or were censored, we entered nothing into our data. Similarly, we entered nothing for lines 3, 4, and 5 of the table. The last line for 1946 stated that, in the interval 5–6, 4 patients were alive at the beginning of the interval and that those 4 patients were withdrawn. In observation 3, we entered that there were 4 censorings at $t = 5.5$.

The fact that we chose to record the times of deaths or censoring as midpoints of intervals does not matter; we could just as well have recorded the times as 0.8 and 5.8. By default, ltable will form intervals 0–1, 1–2, and so on, and place observations into the intervals to which they belong. We suggest using 0.5 and 5.5 because those numbers correspond to the underlying assumptions made by ltable in making its calculations. Using midpoints reminds you of the assumptions.

To obtain the survival rates, we type

```
. ltable t died [freq=pop]
```

Interval	Beg. Total	Deaths	Lost	Survival	Std. Error	[95% Conf. Int.]	
0 1	126	47	19	0.5966	0.0454	0.5017	0.6792
1 2	60	5	17	0.5386	0.0478	0.4405	0.6269
2 3	38	2	15	0.5033	0.0508	0.4002	0.5977
3 4	21	2	9	0.4423	0.0602	0.3225	0.5554
4 5	10	0	6	0.4423	0.0602	0.3225	0.5554
5 6	4	0	4	0.4423	0.0602	0.3225	0.5554

We estimate the 5-year survival rate as .4423 and the 95% confidence interval as .3225 to .5554.

Selvin (1996, 336), in presenting these results, lists the survival in the interval 0–1 as 1, in 1–2 as .597, in 2–3 as .539, and so on. That is, relative to us, he shifted the rates down one row and inserted a 1 in the first row. In his table, the survival rate is the survival rate at the *start* of the interval. In our table, the survival rate is the survival rate at the *end* of the interval (or, equivalently, at the start of the next interval). This is, of course, simply a difference in the way the numbers are presented and not in the numbers themselves.

◁

▷ Example

The discrete hazard function is the rate of failure—the number of failures occurring within a time interval divided by the width of the interval (assuming there are no censored observations). While the survival and failure tables are meaningful at the "individual" level—with intervals so narrow that each contains only a single failure—that is not true for the discrete hazard. If all intervals contained one death and if all intervals were of equal width, the hazard function would be $1/\Delta t$ and so appear to be a constant!

The empirically determined discrete hazard function can only be revealed by aggregation. Gross and Clark (1975, 37) print data on malignant melanoma at the M. D. Anderson Tumor Clinic between 1944 and 1960. The interval is the time from initial diagnosis:

Interval (years)	Number lost to follow-up	Number withdrawn alive	Number dying
0–1	19	77	312
1–2	3	71	96
2–3	4	58	45
3–4	3	27	29
4–5	5	35	7
5–6	1	36	9
6–7	0	17	3
7–8	2	10	1
8–9	0	8	3
9+	0	0	32

For our statistical purposes, there is no difference between the number lost to follow-up (patients who disappeared) and the number withdrawn alive (patients dropped by the researchers)—both are censored. We have entered the data into Stata; here is a small amount of it:

```
. list in 1/6

          t       d       pop
1.       .5       1       312
2.       .5       0        19
3.       .5       0        77
4.      1.5       1        96
5.      1.5       0         3
6.      1.5       0        71
```

We entered each group's time of death or censoring as the midpoint of the intervals and entered the numbers of the table, recording d as 1 for deaths and 0 for censoring. The hazard table is

```
. ltable t d [freq=pop], hazard interval(0,1,2,3,4,5,6,7,8,9)
```

Interval		Beg. Total	Cum. Failure	Std. Error	Hazard	Std. Error	[95% Conf. Int.]	
0	1	913	0.3607	0.0163	0.4401	0.0243	0.3924	0.4877
1	2	505	0.4918	0.0176	0.2286	0.0232	0.1831	0.2740
2	3	335	0.5671	0.0182	0.1599	0.0238	0.1133	0.2064
3	4	228	0.6260	0.0188	0.1461	0.0271	0.0931	0.1991
4	5	169	0.6436	0.0190	0.0481	0.0182	0.0125	0.0837
5	6	122	0.6746	0.0200	0.0909	0.0303	0.0316	0.1502
6	7	76	0.6890	0.0208	0.0455	0.0262	0.0000	0.0969
7	8	56	0.6952	0.0213	0.0202	0.0202	0.0000	0.0598
8	9	43	0.7187	0.0235	0.0800	0.0462	0.0000	0.1705
9	.	32	1.0000	.	.	.	.	.

We specified the interval() option as we did and not as interval(1) (or omitting the option altogether) to force the last interval to be open-ended. Had we not, and if we had recorded t as 9.5 for observations in that interval (as we did), ltable would have calculated a hazard rate for the "interval". In this case, the result of that calculation would have been 2, but no matter what the result, it would have been meaningless since we do not know the width of the interval.

You are not limited to merely examining a column of numbers. With the graph option, you can see the result graphically:

```
. ltable t d [freq=pop], hazard i(0,1,2,3,4,5,6,7,8,9) graph notab
> xlab(0,2,4,6,8,10) border
```

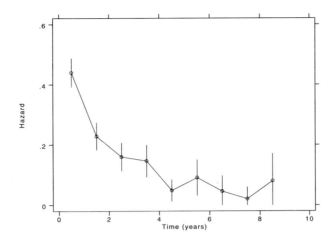

The vertical lines in the graph represent the 95% confidence intervals for the hazard; specifying noconf would have suppressed them. Among the options we did specify, although it is not required, notab suppressed printing the table, saving us some paper. xlab() and border were passed through to the graph command (see [G] **graph options**) and were similarly unnecessary, but made the graph look better.

◁

▷ Example

You can graph the survival function the same way you graph the hazard function: just omit the hazard option.

◁

Methods and Formulas

ltable is implemented as an ado-file.

Let τ_i be the individual failure or censoring times. The data is aggregated into intervals given by t_j, $j = 1, \ldots, J$, and $t_{J+1} = \infty$ with each interval containing counts for $t_j \leq \tau < t_{j+1}$. Let d_j and m_j be the number of failures and censored observations during the interval and N_j the number alive at the start of the interval. Define $n_j = N_j - m_j/2$ as the adjusted number at risk at the start of the interval. If the noadjust option is specified, $n_j = N_j$.

The product-limit estimate of the survivor function is

$$S_j = \prod_{k=1}^{j} \frac{n_k - d_k}{n_k}$$

(Kalbfleisch and Prentice 1980, 12, 15). Greenwood's formula for the asymptotic standard error of S_j is

$$s_j = S_j \sqrt{\sum_{k=1}^{j} \frac{d_k}{n_k(n_k - d_k)}}$$

(Greenwood 1926; Kalbfleisch and Prentice 1980, 14, 15). s_j is reported as the standard deviation of survival but is not used in generating the confidence intervals since it can produce intervals outside 0 and 1. The "natural" units for the survival function are $\log(-\log S_j)$ and the asymptotic standard error of that quantity is

$$\widehat{s}_j = \sqrt{\frac{\sum d_k / \left(n_k(n_k - d_k)\right)}{\left[\sum \log\left((n_k - d_k)/n_k\right)\right]^2}}$$

(Kalbfleisch and Prentice 1980, 15). The corresponding confidence intervals are $S_j^{\exp(\pm z_{1-\alpha/2}\,\widehat{s}_j)}$.

The cumulative failure time is defined as $G_j = 1 - S_j$ and thus the variance is the same as for S_j and the confidence intervals are $1 - S_j^{\exp(\pm z_{1-\alpha/2}\,\widehat{s}_j)}$.

For purposes of graphing, both S_j and G_j are graphed against t_{j+1}.

Define the within-interval failure rate as $f_j = d_j/n_j$. The maximum likelihood estimate of the (within-interval) hazard is then

$$\lambda_j = \frac{f_j}{(1 - f_j/2)(t_{j+1} - t_j)}$$

The standard error of λ_j is

$$s_{\lambda_j} = \lambda_j \sqrt{\frac{1 - [(t_{j+1} - t_j)\lambda_j/2]^2}{d_j}}$$

from which a confidence interval is calculated. For graphing purposes, λ_j is graphed against $(t_j + t_{j+1})/2$.

If the noadjust option is specified, the estimate of the hazard is

$$\lambda_j = \frac{f_j}{t_{j+1} - t_j}$$

and its standard error is

$$s_{\lambda_j} = \frac{\lambda_j}{\sqrt{d_j}}$$

The confidence interval is

$$\left[\frac{\lambda_j}{2d_j}\chi^2_{2d_j,\alpha/2}\,,\ \frac{\lambda_j}{2d_j}\chi^2_{2d_j,1-\alpha/2}\right]$$

where $\chi^2_{2d_j,q}$ is the qth quantile of the χ^2 distribution with $2d_j$ degrees of freedom (Cox and Oakes 1984, 53–54, 38–40).

For the likelihood-ratio test for homogeneity, let d_g be the total number of deaths in the gth group. Define $T_g = \sum_{i \in g} \tau_i$, where i indexes the individual failure or censoring times. The χ^2 value with $G - 1$ degrees of freedom (where G is the total number of groups) is

$$\chi^2 = 2\left[\left(\sum d_g\right)\log\left(\frac{\sum T_g}{\sum d_g}\right) - \sum d_g \log\left(\frac{T_g}{d_g}\right)\right]$$

(Lawless 1982, 113).

The log-rank test for homogeneity is the test presented by sts test; see [R] st sts.

Acknowledgments

ltable is based on the lftbl command by Henry Krakauer and John Stewart (1991). We also thank Michel Henry-Amar, Centre Regional Francois Baclesse, Caen, France for his comments.

References

Armitage, P. and G. Berry. 1987. *Statistical Methods in Medical Research*. 2d ed. Oxford: Blackwell Scientific Publications.

Chiang, C. L. 1984. *The Life Table and Its Applications*. Malabar, FL: Krieger.

Cox, D. R. and D. Oakes. 1984. *Analysis of Survival Data*. London: Chapman and Hall.

Cutler, S. J. and E. Ederer. 1958. Maximum utilization of the life table method in analyzing survival. *Journal of Chronic Diseases* 8: 699–712.

Greenwood, M. 1926. The natural duration of cancer. *Reports on Public Health and Medical Subjects* 33: 1–26. London: His Majesty's Stationery Office.

Gross, A. J. and V. A. Clark. 1975. *Survival Distributions: Reliability Applications in the Biomedical Sciences*. New York: John Wiley & Sons.

Halley, E. 1693. An estimate of the degrees of mortality of mankind, drawn from curious tables of the births and funerals at the city of Breslau, with an attempt to ascertain the price of annuities on lives. *Philosophical Transactions* 17: 596–610. London: The Royal Society.

Kahn, H. A. and C. T. Sempos. 1989. *Statistical Methods in Epidemiology*. New York: Oxford University Press.

Kalbfleisch, J. D. and R. L. Prentice. 1980. *The Statistical Analysis of Failure Time Data*. New York: John Wiley & Sons.

Krakauer, H. and J. Stewart. 1991. ssa1: Actuarial or life-table analysis of time-to-event data. *Stata Technical Bulletin* 1: 23–25. Reprinted in *Stata Technical Bulletin Reprints*, vol. 1, pp. 200–202.

Lawless, J. F. 1982. *Statistical Models and Methods for Lifetime Data*. New York: John Wiley & Sons.

Pagano, M. and K. Gauvreau. 1993. *Principles of Biostatistics*. Belmont, CA: Duxbury Press.

Pike, M. C. 1966. A method of analysis of a certain class of experiments in carcinogenesis. *Biometrics* 22: 142–161.

Selvin, S. 1996. *Statistical Analysis of Epidemiologic Data*. 2d ed. New York: Oxford University Press.

Also See

Related:	[R] **cox**, [R] **st**, [R] **weibull**
Background:	*Stata Graphics Manual*

lv — Letter-value displays

Syntax

lv [*varlist*] [if *exp*] [in *range*] [, generate t̲ail(*#*)]

Description

lv shows a letter-value display (Tukey 1977, 44–49; Hoaglin 1983) for each variable in *varlist*. If no variables are specified, letter-value displays are shown for each numeric variable in the data.

Options

generate adds four new variables to the data: _mid, containing the midsummaries; _spread, containing the spreads; _psigma, containing the pseudosigmas; and _z2, containing the squared values from a $N(0, 1)$ corresponding to the particular letter value. If the variables _mid, _spread, _psigma, and _z2 already exist, their contents are replaced. At most, only the first 11 observations of each variable are used; the remaining observations contain missing. If *varlist* specifies more than one variable, the newly created variables contain results for the last variable specified.

tail(*#*) indicates the inverse of the tail density through which letter values are to be displayed. 2 corresponds to the median (meaning half in each tail), 4 to the fourths (roughly the 25th and 75th percentiles), 8 to the eighths, and so on. *#* may be specified as 4, 8, 16, 32, 64, 128, 256, 512, or 1,024 and defaults to a value of *#* that has corresponding depth just greater than 1. The default is taken as 1,024 if the calculation results in a number larger than 1,024. Given the intelligent default, this option is rarely specified.

Remarks

Letter-value displays are a collection of observations drawn systematically from the data, focusing especially on the tails rather than the middle of the distribution. The displays are called letter-value displays because letters have been (almost arbitrarily) assigned to tail densities:

Letter	Tail Area	Letter	Tail Area
M	1/2	B	1/64
F	1/4	A	1/128
E	1/8	Z	1/256
D	1/16	Y	1/512
C	1/32	X	1/1024

▷ Example

You have data on the mileage ratings of 74 automobiles. To obtain a letter-value display:

```
. lv mpg
```

```
#      74                    Mileage (mpg)
               ----------------------------------------
M    37.5 |                     20              |  spread  pseudosigma
F    19   |       18         21.5      25 |           7     5.216359
E    10   |       15         21.5      28 |          13     5.771728
D     5.5 |       14         22.25     30.5 |        16.5    5.576303
C     3   |       14         24.5      35 |          21     5.831039
B     2   |       12         23.5      35 |          23     5.732448
A     1.5 |       12         25        38 |          26     6.040635
      1   |       12         26.5      41 |          29     6.16562

          |                                 |  # below     # above
inner fence |     7.5                35.5 |       0           1
outer fence |     -3                   46 |       0           0
```

The decimal points can be made to line up and thus the output made more readable by specifying a display format for the variable; see [U] **15.5 Formats: controlling how data is displayed**.

```
. format mpg %9.2f

. lv mpg
#      74                    Mileage (mpg)
               ----------------------------------------
M    37.5 |                    20.00            |  spread  pseudosigma
F    19   |       18.00       21.50     25.00 |      7.00         5.22
E    10   |       15.00       21.50     28.00 |     13.00         5.77
D     5.5 |       14.00       22.25     30.50 |     16.50         5.58
C     3   |       14.00       24.50     35.00 |     21.00         5.83
B     2   |       12.00       23.50     35.00 |     23.00         5.73
A     1.5 |       12.00       25.00     38.00 |     26.00         6.04
      1   |       12.00       26.50     41.00 |     29.00         6.17

          |                                     |  # below     # above
inner fence |     7.50                  35.50 |       0           1
outer fence |     -3.00                 46.00 |       0           0
```

At the top, the number of observations is indicated as 74. The first line shows the statistics associated with M, the letter value that puts half the density in each tail, or the median. The median has *depth* 37.5 (that is, in the ordered data, M is 37.5 observations in from the extremes) and has value 20. The next line shows the statistics associated with F or the fourths. The fourths have depth 19 (that is, in the ordered data, the lower fourth is observation 19 and the upper fourth is observation $74 - 19 + 1$), and the values of the lower and upper fourths are 18 and 25. The number in the middle is the point halfway between the fourths—called a midsummary. If the distribution were perfectly symmetric, the midsummary would equal the median. The spread is the difference between the lower and upper summaries ($25 - 18 = 7$). For fourths, half the data lies within a 7-mpg band. The pseudosigma is a calculation of the standard deviation using only the lower and upper summaries and assuming that the variable is normally distributed. If the data really were normally distributed, all the pseudosigmas would be roughly equal.

After the letter values, the line labeled with depth 1 reports the minimum and maximum values. In this case, the halfway point between the extremes is 26.5, which is greater than the median, indicating that 41 is more extreme than 12, at least relative to the median. Also note that, with each letter value, the midsummaries are increasing—our data is skewed. The pseudosigmas are also increasing, indicating that the data is spreading out relative to a normal distribution although, given the evident skewness, this elongation may be an artifact of the skewness.

At the end is an attempt to identify outliers, although the points so identified are merely outside some predetermined cutoff. Points outside the inner fence are called *outside values* or *mild outliers*. Points outside the outer fence are called *severe outliers*. The inner fence is defined as $(3/2)$IQR and the outer fence as 3IQR above and below the F summaries, where the IQR is the spread of the fourths.

◁

❑ Technical Note

The form of the letter-value display has varied slightly with different authors. `lv` displays appear as described by Hoaglin (1983) but as modified by Emerson and Stoto (1983), where they included the midpoint of each of the spreads. This format was later adopted by Hoaglin (1985). If the distribution is symmetric, the midpoints will all be roughly equal. On the other hand, if the midpoints vary systematically, the distribution is skewed.

The pseudosigmas are obtained from the lower and upper summaries for each letter value. For each letter value, they are the standard deviation a normal distribution would have if its spread for the given letter value were to equal the observed spread. If the pseudosigmas are all roughly equal, the data is said to have *neutral elongation*. If the pseudosigmas increase systematically, the data is said to be more elongated than a normal; i.e., have thicker tails. If the pseudosigmas decrease systematically, the data is said to be less elongated than a normal; i.e., have thinner tails.

Interpretation of the number of mild and severe outliers is more problematic. The following discussion is drawn from Hamilton (1991):

Obviously, the presence of any such outliers does not rule out that the data has been drawn from a normal; in large datasets, there will most certainly be observations outside $(3/2)$IQR and 3IQR. Severe outliers, however, comprise about two per million (.0002%) of a normal population. In samples, they lie far enough out to have substantial effects on means, standard deviations, and other classical statistics. The .0002%, however, should be interpreted carefully; outliers appear more often in small samples than one might expect from population proportions due to sampling variation in estimated quartiles. Monte Carlo simulation by Hoaglin, Iglewicz, and Tukey (1986) obtained these results on the percentages and numbers of outliers in random samples from a normal population:

n	percentage		number	
	any outliers	severe	any outliers	severe
10	2.83	.362	.283	.0362
20	1.66	.074	.332	.0148
50	1.15	.011	.575	.0055
100	.95	.002	.95	.002
200	.79	.001	1.58	.002
300	.75	.001	2.25	.003
∞	.70	.0002	∞	∞

Thus, the presence of any severe outliers in samples of less than 300 is sufficient to reject normality. Hoaglin, Iglewicz, and Tukey (1981) suggested the approximation $.00698 + .4/n$ for the fraction of mild outliers in a sample of size n or, equivalently, $.00698n + .4$ for the number of outliers.

❑

▷ Example

The generate option adds the variables _mid, _spread, _psigma, and _z2 to your data, making possible many of the diagnostic graphs suggested by Hoaglin (1985).

```
. lv mpg, generate
(output omitted)
. list _mid _spread _psigma _z2 in 1/12
            _mid    _spread    _psigma         _z2
  1.          20          .          .           0
  2.        21.5          7   5.216359    .4501955
  3.        21.5         13   5.771728     1.26828
  4.       22.25       16.5   5.576303    2.188846
  5.        24.5         21   5.831039     3.24255
  6.        23.5         23   5.732448    4.024532
  7.          25         26   6.040635    4.631499
  8.           .          .          .           .
  9.           .          .          .           .
 10.           .          .          .           .
 11.        26.5         29    6.16562     5.53073
 12.           .          .          .           .
```

Observations 12 through the end are missing for these new variables. The definition of the observations is always the same. The first observation contains the M summary, the second the F, the third the E, and so on. Observation 11 always contains the summary for depth 1. Observations 8 through 10—corresponding to letter values Z, Y, and X—contain missing because these statistics were not calculated. We have only 74 observations and their depth would be 1.

Hoaglin (1985) suggests graphing the midsummary against z^2. If the distribution is not skewed, the points in the resulting graph will be along a horizontal line:

```
. graph _mid _z2, border ylabel xlabel
```

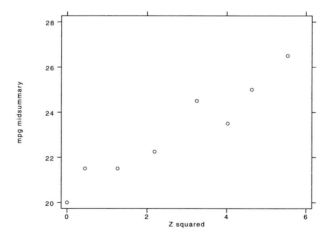

The graph clearly indicates the skewness of the distribution. One might also graph _psigma against _z2 to examine elongation.

◁

Saved Results

lv saves in r():

Scalars

r(N)	number of observations	r(u_C)	upper 32nd
r(min)	minimum	r(l_B)	lower 64th
r(max)	maximum	r(u_B)	upper 64th
r(median)	median	r(l_A)	lower 128th
r(l_F)	lower 4th	r(u_A)	upper 128th
r(u_F)	upper 4th	r(l_Z)	lower 256th
r(l_E)	lower 8th	r(u_Z)	upper 256th
r(u_E)	upper 8th	r(l_Y)	lower 512th
r(l_D)	lower 16th	r(u_Y)	upper 512th
r(u_D)	upper 16th	r(l_X)	lower 1024th
r(l_C)	lower 32nd	r(u_X)	upper 1024th

The lower/upper 8ths, 16ths, ..., 1024ths will be defined only if there is sufficient data.

Methods and Formulas

lv is implemented as an ado-file.

Let N be the number of (nonmissing) observations on x, and let $x_{(i)}$ refer to the ordered data when i is an integer. Define $x_{(i+.5)} = (x_{(i)} + x_{(i+1)})/2$; the median is defined as $x_{((N+1)/2)}$.

Define $x_{[d]}$ as the pair of numbers $x_{(d)}$ and $x_{(N+1-d)}$ where d is called the *depth*. Thus, $x_{[1]}$ refers to the minimum and maximum of the data. Define $m = (N+1)/2$ as the depth of the median, $f = (\lfloor m \rfloor + 1)/2$ as the depth of the fourths, $e = (\lfloor f \rfloor + 1)/2$ as the depth of the eighths, and so on. Depths are reported on the far left of the letter-value display. The corresponding fourths of the data are $x_{[f]}$, the eighths $x_{[e]}$, and so on. These values are reported inside the display. The middle value is defined as the corresponding midpoint of $x_{[\cdot]}$. The spreads are defined as the difference in $x_{[\cdot]}$.

The corresponding point z_i on a standard normal distribution is obtained as (Hoaglin 1985, 456–457)

$$z_i = \begin{cases} F^{-1}\big[(d_i - 1/3)/(N + 1/3)\big] & \text{if } d_i > 1 \\ F^{-1}\big[0.695/(N + 0.390)\big] & \text{otherwise} \end{cases}$$

where d_i is the depth of the letter value. The corresponding pseudosigma is obtained as the ratio of the spread to $-2z_i$ (Hoaglin 1985, 431).

Define $(F_l, F_u) = x_{[f]}$. The inner fence has cutoffs $F_l - \frac{3}{2}(F_u - F_l)$ and $F_u + \frac{3}{2}(F_u - F_l)$. The outer fence has cutoffs $F_l - 3(F_u - F_l)$ and $F_u + 3(F_u - F_l)$.

The inner fence values reported by lv are almost exactly equal to those used by **graph, box** to identify outside points. The only difference is that **graph** uses a slightly different definition of fourths: namely, the 25th and 75th percentiles as defined by **summarize**.

References

Emerson, J. D. and M. A. Stoto. 1983. Transforming data. In *Understanding Robust and Exploratory Data Analysis*, ed. D. C. Hoaglin, F. Mosteller, and J. W. Tukey, 97–128. New York: John Wiley & Sons.

Fox, J. 1990. Describing univariate distributions. In *Modern Methods of Data Analysis*, ed. J. Fox and J. S. Long, 58–125. Newbury Park, CA: Sage Publications.

Hamilton, L. C. 1991. sed4: Resistant normality check and outlier identification. *Stata Technical Bulletin* 3: 15–18. Reprinted in *Stata Technical Bulletin Reprints*, vol. 1, pp. 86–90.

Hoaglin, D. C. 1983. Letter values: a set of selected order statistics. In *Understanding Robust and Exploratory Data Analysis*, ed. D. C. Hoaglin, F. Mosteller, and J. W. Tukey, 33–57. New York: John Wiley & Sons.

——. 1985. Using quantiles to study shape. In *Exploring Data Tables, Trends, and Shapes*, ed. D. C. Hoaglin, F. Mosteller, and J. W. Tukey, 417–460. New York: John Wiley & Sons.

Hoaglin, D. C., B. Iglewicz, and J. W. Tukey. 1981. Small-sample performance of a resistant rule for outlier detection. *1980 Proceedings of the Statistical Computing Section*, 144–152. Washington, DC: American Statistical Association.

——. 1986. Performance of some resistant rules for outlier labeling. *Journal of the American Statistical Association* 81: 991–999.

Tukey, J. W. 1977. *Exploratory Data Analysis*. Reading, MA: Addison–Wesley Publishing Company.

Also See

Related: [R] **diagplots**, [R] **stem**, [R] **summarize**

Title

> **macro** — Macro definition and manipulation

Syntax

<u>g</u>lobal *mname* [=*exp* | :*extended_fcn* | "[*string*]" | `"[*string*]"´]

<u>loc</u>al *lclname* [=*exp* | :*extended_fcn* | "[*string*]" | `"[*string*]"´]

tempvar *lclname* [*lclname* [...]]

tempname *lclname* [*lclname* [...]]

tempfile *lclname* [*lclname* [...]]

<u>ma</u>cro <u>dir</u>

<u>ma</u>cro <u>drop</u> { *mname* [*mname* [...]] | *mname** | _all }

<u>ma</u>cro <u>l</u>ist [*mname* [*mname* [...]] | _all]

<u>ma</u>cro <u>s</u>hift [#]

where *extended_fcn* is any of

  { <u>type</u> | <u>format</u> | <u>val</u>ue <u>label</u> | <u>var</u>iable <u>label</u> } *varname*

  <u>label</u> { *valuelabelname* | (*varname*) } { maxlength | # [#] }

  data <u>label</u>

  <u>sorted</u>by

  set { adosize | beep | display linesize | display pagesize | graphics | level |

      log linesize | log pagesize | matsize | more | rmsg | textsize | trace |

      type | virtual }

  log [on]

  sysdir [STATA | UPDATES | BASE | SITE | STBPLUS | PERSONAL | *dirname*]

  <u>env</u>ironment *name*

  <u>di</u>splay ...   (see [R] **display**)

  { <u>rown</u>ames | <u>coln</u>ames | <u>rowe</u>q | <u>cole</u>q | <u>rowf</u>ullnames | <u>colf</u>ullnames } *matrixname*

  word { count | # of } *string*

  piece # # of { "[*string*]" | `"[*string*]"´ }

  subinstr { <u>g</u>lobal *mname2* | <u>loc</u>al *lclname2* } { "from" | `"from"´ }

    { "to" | `"to"´ } [, all <u>c</u>ount({ <u>g</u>lobal *mname3* | <u>loc</u>al *lclname3* }) <u>w</u>ord]

  tempvar | tempfile

268

Description

global assigns strings to specified global macro names (*mnames*). local assigns strings to local macro names (*lclnames*). Both regular quotes (" and ") and compound double quotes (` " and " ´) are allowed; see [U] **21.3.5 Double quotes**. If the *string* has embedded quotes, then compound double quotes are needed.

tempvar assigns names to the specified local macro names that may be used as temporary variable names in the dataset. When the program or do-file concludes, any variables in the dataset with these assigned names are dropped.

tempname assigns names to the specified local macro names that may be used as temporary scalar or matrix names. When the program or do-file concludes, any scalars or matrices in the dataset with these assigned names are dropped.

tempfile assigns names to the specified local macro names that may be used as names for temporary files. When the program or do-file concludes, any datasets created with these assigned names are erased.

macro manipulates global and local macros.

Remarks

Remarks are presented under the headings

> Formal definition of a macro
> Global and local macro names
> Macro assignment
> Macro extended functions for extracting data attributes
> Macro extended functions for accessing Stata system parameters
> Macro extended functions for accessing operating-system parameters
> Macro extended functions for formatting results
> Macro extended functions related to matrices
> Macro extended functions for parsing
> The tempvar, tempname, and tempfile commands
> Temporary variables
> Temporary scalars and matrices
> Temporary files
> Manipulation of macros
> Macros as arguments: macro shift

Macros are a tool used in programming Stata and this entry assumes you have read [U] **21 Programming Stata** and especially [U] **21.3 Macros**. This entry concerns advanced issues not previously covered. Also, for your convenience, a table of the predefined system macros can be found in [R] **macro system**.

Formal definition of a macro

A *macro* has a *macro name* and *macro contents*. Everywhere a punctuated macro name appears in a command—punctuation is defined below—the macro contents are substituted for the macro name.

Macros come in two types, called global and local macros. Macro names are up to 8 characters long for global macros and 7 characters long for local macros. The contents of global macros are defined with the global command and local macros with the local command. Global macros are just that. Local macros exist solely within the program or do-file in which they are defined. If that program or do-file calls another program or do-file, the local macros previously defined temporarily cease to exist and their existence is reestablished when the calling program regains control. When a program or do-file ends, its local macros are permanently deleted.

To substitute the macro contents of a global macro name, the macro name is typed (punctuated) with a dollar sign ($) in front. To substitute the macro contents of a local macro name, the macro name is typed (punctuated) with surrounding left and right single quotes (` ´). In either case, braces ({ }) can be used to clarify meaning and form nested constructions. When the contents of an undefined macro are substituted, the macro name (and punctuation) are removed and nothing is substituted in its place.

For example:

The input . . .	Means the same as . . .
```global a "myvar"```	
```gen $a = oldvar```	```gen myvar = oldvar```
```gen a = oldvar```	```gen a = oldvar```
```local a "myvar"```	
```gen `a´ = oldvar```	```gen myvar = oldvar```
```gen a = oldvar```	```gen a = oldvar```
```global a "newvar"```	
```global i = 2```	
```gen ai = oldvar```	```gen newvar2 = oldvar```
```local a "newvar"```	
```local i = 2```	
```gen `a´`i´ = oldvar```	```gen newvar2 = oldvar```
```global b1 "newvar"```	
```global i=1```	
```gen ${b$i} = oldvar```	```gen newvar = oldvar```
```local b1 "newvar"```	
```local i=1```	
```gen `b`i´´ = oldvar```	```gen newvar = oldvar```
```global b1 "newvar"```	
```global a "b"```	
```global i = 1```	
```gen ${$a$i} = oldvar```	```gen newvar = oldvar```
```local b1 "newvar"```	
```local a "b"```	
```local i = 1```	
```gen ``a´`i´´ = oldvar```	```gen newvar = oldvar```

Global and local macro names

What we next say is an exceedingly fine point: Global macro names that begin with an underscore are really local macros; this is why local macro names can have only 7 characters. The command `local` is formally defined as equivalent to `global _`. Thus, the following are equivalent:

```
local x                   global _x
local i=1                 global _i=1
local name "Bill"         global _name "Bill"
local fmt : format myvar  global _fmt : format myvar
local 3 `2´               global _3 $_2
```

`tempvar` is formally defined as equivalent to `local` *name* `: tempvar` for each name specified after `tempvar`. Thus,

```
tempvar a b c
```

is equivalent to

```
local a : tempvar
local b : tempvar
local c : tempvar
```

which in turn is equivalent to

```
global _a : tempvar
global _b : tempvar
global _c : tempvar
```

`tempfile` is defined similarly.

Macro assignment

When you type

```
. local name "something"
```

or

```
. local name `"something"´
```

that *something* becomes the contents of the macro. The compound double quotes (`` `" `` and `` "´ ``) are needed when *something* contains quotation marks. When you type

```
. local name = something
```

that *something* is evaluated as an expression and the result becomes the contents of the macro. Note the presence and lack of the equals sign. That is, if you type

```
. local problem "2+2"
. local result = 2+2
```

then `problem` contains 2+2 whereas `result` contains 4.

Finally, when you type

```
. local name : something
```

that *something* is interpreted as an extended macro function. (Note the colon rather than nothing or the equals sign.) Of course, all of this applies to `global` as well as `local`.

Macro extended functions for extracting data attributes

The macro extended functions `type`, `format`, `value label`, `variable label`, `data label`, `sortedby`, and `label` obtain attributes from the dataset in memory.

▷ Example

We demonstrate these macros interactively so you can see what it is they return. These functions, and macros in general, become useful when used in programs.

```
. describe
```

```
Contains data from emp1.dta
  obs:            1                        Employee Data
  vars:           3                        16 Jul 1998 11:38
  size:          30 (99.9% of memory free)
-------------------------------------------------------------------------
  1. name      str18   %18s                Employee name
  2. sex       float   %9.0g     sexlbl
  3. age       float   %9.0g
-------------------------------------------------------------------------
Sorted by:
. global tofname : type name
. display "$tofname"
str18
. local fmt : format age
. display "`fmt'"
%9.0g
. local vl : value label sex
. display "`vl'"
sexlbl
. local lbl : variable label name
. display "`lbl'"
Employee name
. sort name age
. local sl : sortedby
. display "`sl'"
name age
. local dl : data label
. display "`dl'"
Employee Data
```
◁

The macro extended function `value label` returns the name of a value label associated with a variable.

▷ Example

In this example, variable q2 is associated with the value label named `yesno`. Variable `age` has no associated value label. Variable `vote` is associated with the value label named `party`. We begin by listing the defined value labels:

```
. label list
party:
             1 Democrat
             2 Republican
             3 Socialist
yesno:
             0 no
             1 yes
. local vname1 : value label q2
. local vname2 : value label age
. local vname3 : value label vote
. display "vname1 is |`vname1'|, vname2 is |`vname2'|, vname3 is |`vname3'|"
vname1 is |yesno|, vname2 is ||, vname3 is |party|
```

Notice that in the case of `age`, macro `vname2` contains `""`; variable `age` has no associated value label.
◁

The macro extended function `label` returns information about the label values associated with a variable or a label value definition. The label for a particular value may be obtained. You can also specify that the label be trimmed to a certain number of characters. The length of the longest label can also be obtained.

▷ Example

We continue with our previous example:

```
. local x : label yesno 0
. display "`x'"
no
. local y : label (q2) 1
. display "`y'"
yes
. local z : label yesno 5
. display "`z'"
5
```

If parentheses are used, the name is taken to be a variable name. Without parentheses the name is assumed to be a value label definition name. Since the label `yesno` does not map 5, the 5 itself was returned in the last case. We now show that the labels can be trimmed and that the maximum length of the labels can be obtained.

```
. local a : label party 1
. display "`a'"
Democrat
. local b : label party 1 3
. display "`b'"
Dem
. local c : label (vote) maxlength
. display "`c'"
10
```
◁

Macro extended functions for accessing Stata system parameters

The `set` macro extended function obtains current settings (the ones set by `set` and shown by `query`). For instance, we could obtain the current value of `matsize`:

```
. local x : set matsize
. display "`x'"
40
```

The `log on` and `log` functions return the current logging status.

▷ Example

```
. local x : log on
. display "`x'"
off
. log using myfile
. local x : log on
```

```
. display "`x'"
on
. local fn : log
. display "`fn'"
C:\data\myfile.log
```

◁

The `sysdir` macro extended function returns various Stata system directory path names.

▷ Example

We wish to obtain the name of the `STATA` system directory. From a Windows computer we get

```
. local sdir : sysdir STATA
. display "`sdir'"
C:\STATA/
```

The forward slash at the end may look strange but it works and protects us in case we ever try to say something like "``sdir'$myfile`" or "``sdir'`myfile'`". If we had used a backslash instead of a forward slash at the end of `sdir`, the result would not be correct since the backslash acts as an escape character and would change the meaning of the $ or ` that follow it.

From a Macintosh computer we have

```
. local sdir : sysdir STATA
. display "`sdir'"
:Macintosh HD:Stata:
```

and from within a Unix operating system we obtain

```
. local sdir : sysdir STATA
. display "`sdir'"
/usr/local/stata/
```

◁

Macro extended functions for accessing operating-system parameters

The Windows and Unix operating systems have the concept of environment variables. The macro extended function `environment` imports their contents into Stata's macros.

▷ Example

Here is an example from Windows:

```
. local x: environment TEMP
. display "`x'"
C:\TEMP
```

And here is one from Unix:

```
. local x: environment HOME
. display "`x'"
/home/wwg
```

◁

Macro extended functions for formatting results

The `display` command allows you to display formatted output; see [R] **display (for programmers)**. The `display` extended function is the `display` command except that the output is rerouted, not appearing on the screen, but being placed into the contents of a macro. Using `display`, you can format things appearing in macros.

▷ Example

```
. local x = sqrt(2)
. display "`x'"                      /* as string to see entire contents */
1.414213562373095
. display %9.4f sqrt(2)              /* since you can do this */
   1.4142
. local y : display %9.4f sqrt(2)    /* you can do this, too */
. display "`y'"
   1.4142
. local z : display "sqrt(2) = " _col(14) %9.4f sqrt(2)
. display "`z'"
sqrt(2) =      1.4142
```

◁

You can use all the features of `display` that make sense, which is to say, you may not set the colors with `in` *color* because macros do not have colors, you may not use `_continue` to suppress going to a new line on the real display (it is not being displayed), you may not use `_newline` (for the same reason), and you may not use `_request` to obtain input from the console (because input and output have nothing to do with macro definition). With those exceptions, everything else works. See [R] **display (for programmers)**.

Macro extended functions related to matrices

The functions `rownames`, `colnames`, `roweq`, `coleq`, `rowfullnames`, and `colfullnames` obtain the specified information about the specified matrix; see [R] **matrix define**.

Macro extended functions for parsing

`word count` counts the number of tokens in a string. `word # of` extracts the #th token from the string. A token is a word (characters separated by spaces) or set of words enclosed in quotes.

▷ Example

```
. local n : word count this is a test
. display "n = `n'"
n = 4
. local n : word count "this is" "a second" test
. display "n = `n'"
n = 3
. local first : word 1 of "this is" "a second" test
. display "The first token is: `first'"
The first token is: this is
```

```
. local n : word count `"and "this is a" third test"´
. display "n = `n´"
n = 1
. local phrase `"and "this is a" third test"´
. local n : word count `phrase´
. display "n = `n´"
n = 4
. local second : word 2 of `phrase´
. display "The second token is: `second´"
The second token is: this is a
```

We draw your attention to the subtle difference between using a string literal (such as: `` `"and
"this is a" third test"´ ``) and using a macro (such as: `` `phrase´ ``). See [U] **21.3.5 Double quotes**.
◁

The `piece` macro extended function provides a smart method of breaking a string into pieces of
roughly the specified length. The first number following the word `piece` indicates which piece to
obtain. The second number indicates the maximum length of each piece. Each piece is built trying
to fill to the maximum length without breaking in the middle of a word. However, when a word is
longer than the specified length the word will be split. Some examples illustrate.

▷ Example

```
. local str "Four score and seven years ago"
. local part1 : piece 1 12 of "`str´"
. local part2 : piece 2 12 of "`str´"
. local part3 : piece 3 12 of "`str´"
. display "`part1´" _newline "`part2´" _newline "`part3´"
Four score
and seven
years ago
. local str "extraordinary, a rare find"
. local part1 : piece 1 9 of "`str´"
. local part2 : piece 2 9 of "`str´"
. local part3 : piece 3 9 of "`str´"
. display "`part1´" _newline "`part2´" _newline "`part3´"
extraordi
nary, a
rare find
. local part4 : piece 4 9 of "`str´"
. display "|`part4´|"
||
```
◁

The `subinstr` macro extended function performs string substitutions. The `all` option causes the
substitution to occur as many times as the *from* string occurs. Without the `all` option only the first
occurrence of *from* has *to* substituted. The `word` option indicates that substitutions are allowed only
on space-separated tokens (words). In this case, a token at the beginning or end of a macro also
counts as being space-separated. The `count` option places the number of substitutions that occur into
the named macro. Here are examples:

▷ Example

```
. local str "a or b or c or d"

. global newstr : subinstr local str "c" "sand"

. display "$newstr"
a or b or sand or d

. local str2 : subinstr global newstr "or" "and", all count(local n)

. display "`str2'"
a and b and sand and d

. display "`n'"
3

. local str3: subinstr local str2 "and" "x", all word

. display "`str3'"
a x b x sand x d
```

Notice that the "and" in "sand" did not get replaced by "x" since the word option was specified.

◁

The tempvar, tempname, and tempfile commands

The tempvar, tempname, and tempfile commands generate names that may be used for temporary variables, temporary scalars and matrices, and temporary files. A temporary something is a something that exists while the program or do-file is running but, once it concludes, automatically ceases to exist.

Temporary variables

You are writing a program and, in the middle of it, you need to calculate a new variable equal to $var1^2 + var2^2$ for use in the calculation. You might be tempted to write

```
( code omitted )
gen sumsq = var1^2 + var2^2
( code continues )
( code uses sumsq in subsequent calculations )
drop sumsq
```

This would be a poor idea. First, users of your program might already have a variable called sumsq and if they did, your program will break at the generate statement with the error "sumsq already defined". Second, your program in the subsequent code might call some other program, and perhaps that program (poorly) also attempts to create a variable sumsq. Third, even if nothing goes wrong, if users press *Break* after your code had executed the generate but before the drop, you would leave behind the sumsq variable, confusing them.

The way around these problems is to use temporary variables. Your code should read:

```
( code omitted )
tempvar sumsq
gen `sumsq' = var1^2 + var2^2
( code continues )
( code uses `sumsq' in subsequent calculations )
( you do not bother to drop `sumsq' )
```

The `tempvar sumsq` command created a local macro called `sumsq` and stored in it a name that is different from any name currently in the data. Subsequently, you then use `` `sumsq´ `` with single quotes around it rather than `sumsq` in your calculation, so that rather than calling your temporary variable `sumsq`, you are calling it whatever Stata wants you to call it. With that small change, your program works just as before.

Another advantage to temporary variables is that you do not have to drop them—Stata will do that for you when your program terminates and Stata will do that regardless of the reason for your program terminating. So, if users press *Break* after the `generate`, your program is stopped, the temporary variables dropped, and things really are just as if the user had never run your program in the first place.

❑ Technical Note

So what do these temporary variable names assigned by Stata look like? It should not matter to you; however they look, they are guaranteed to be unique (`tempvar` will not hand out the same name to more than one program concurrently executing). Nevertheless, to satisfy your curiosity:

```
. tempvar var1 var2
. display "`var1´ `var2´"
__000009 __00000A
```

Although we reveal the style of the names created by `tempvar`, you should not depend on this style. All that is important is

1. The names are unique; they differ from one call to the next.

2. You should assume that they are so long that you cannot prefix or suffix them with additional characters and make use of them.

3. Stata keeps track of any names created by `tempvar` and, when the program or do-file ends, searches the data for those names. Any variables found with those names are automatically dropped. This happens regardless of whether your program ends with an error.

❑

Temporary scalars and matrices

`tempname` is the equivalent of `tempvar` for obtaining names for scalars and matrices. This use is explained, with examples, in [R] **scalar**.

❑ Technical Note

The temporary names created by `tempname` look just like those created by `tempvar`. The same cautions and features apply to `tempname` as `tempvar`:

1. The names are unique; they differ from one call to the next.

2. You should assume that they are so long that you cannot prefix or suffix them with additional characters and make use of them.

3. Stata keeps track of any names created by `tempname` and, when the program or do-file ends, searches for scalars or matrices with those names. Any scalars or matrices so found are automatically dropped; see [R] **scalar**. This happens regardless of whether your program ends with an error.

❑

Temporary files

`tempfile` is the equivalent of `tempvar` for obtaining names for disk files. Before getting into that, let us discuss how you should not use `tempfile`. Sometimes, in the midst of your program, you will find it necessary to destroy the user's data to obtain your desired result. You do not want to change the data, but it cannot be helped, and therefore you would like to arrange things so that the user's original data is restored at the conclusion of your program.

In such a case, you might be tempted to save the user's data in a (temporary) file, do your damage, and then restore the data. You can do this, but it is complicated because you then have to worry about the user pressing *Break* after you have stored the data, done the damage, but have not yet restored it. Working with `capture` (see [R] **capture**), you can program all of this, but you do not have to. Stata's `preserve` command (see [R] **preserve**) will handle saving the user's data and, however your program concludes, restoring it.

Still, there may be times when you need temporary files. As our example:

```
( code omitted )
preserve                        /* preserve user's data */
keep var1 var2 xvar
save master, replace
drop var2
save part1, replace
use master, clear
drop var1
rename var2 var1
append using part1
erase master.dta
erase part1.dta
( code continues )
```

This is poor code even though it does use `preserve` so that, no matter how this code concludes, the user's original data will be brought back. It is poor because datasets called `master.dta` and `part1.dta` might already exist and, if they do, this program will replace the user's (assumedly valuable) data. It is also poor because, if the user presses *Break* before both (temporary) datasets are erased, they will be left behind consuming (assumedly valuable) disk space.

Here is how the code should read:

```
( code omitted )
preserve                        /* preserve user's data */
keep var1 var2 xvar
tempfile master part1           /* declare temporary files */
save `master'
drop var2
save `part1'
use `master', clear
drop var1
rename var2 var1
append using `part1'
( code continues, temporary files are not erased )
```

In this draft, Stata was asked to provide the names of temporary files in local macros named `master` and `part1`. We then put single quotes around `master` and `part1` wherever we referred to them so that, rather than using the names `master` and `part1`, we used the names Stata handed us. At the end of our program, we no longer bother to erase the temporary files. Since Stata gave us the temporary filenames, it knows they are temporary and will erase them for us and it will do this whether our program completes, has an error, or the user presses *Break*.

❑ Technical Note

So what do the temporary filenames look like? Again, it should not matter to you, but for the curious:

```
. tempfile file1 file2
. display "`file1´ `file2´"
/tmp/St13310.0001 /tmp/St13310.0002
```

We were using the Unix version of Stata; had we been using the Windows version, the last line might read:

```
. display "`file1´ `file2´"
C:\WIN\TEMP\__000003.tmp C:\WIN\TEMP\__000004.tmp
```

Under Windows, Stata uses the environment variable TEMP to determine where temporary files are to be located. This variable is typically set in your autoexec.bat file. Ours is set to C:\WIN\TEMP. If the variable is not defined, Stata locates temporary files in your current directory.

Under Unix, Stata uses the environment variable TMPDIR to determine where temporary files are to be located. If the variable is not defined, Stata locates temporary files in /tmp.

Although we reveal the style of the names created by tempfile, just as with tempvar, you should not depend on it. tempfile produces names the operating system finds pleasing and all that is important is

1. The names are unique; they differ from one call to the next.

2. You should assume that they are so long that you cannot prefix or suffix them with additional characters and make use of them.

3. Stata keeps track of any names created by tempfile and, when your program or do-file ends, looks for files with those names. Any files found are automatically erased. This happens regardless of whether your program ends with an error.

Actually, item 3 is true only for version 3.1 and above. If you set the version to a lower number (see [R] **version**), then item 3 should read: "You, as the programmer, are responsible for removing any temporary files—they are not automatically deleted". We turn off this feature in case some old, user-written programs depended on files being left around.   ❑

Manipulation of macros

macro dir and macro list list the names and contents of all defined macros; both do the same thing:

```
. macro list
_file2:    /tmp/St13310.0002
_file1:    /tmp/St13310.0001
_var2:     __00000A
_var1:     __000009
S_FN:      auto.dta
_lbl:      Employee name
_vl:       sexlbl
_fmt:      %9.0g
tofname:   str18
F1:        help
F2:        #review;
F3:        describe;
F7:        save
```

```
F8:        use
S_ADO:     UPDATES;BASE;SITE;.;PERSONAL;STBPLUS;~/ado/
S_FLAVOR:  Intercooled
S_OS:      Unix
S_MACH:    Sun Solaris
S_level:   95
```

`macro drop` eliminates macros from memory, although it is rarely used since typically most macros are local and automatically disappear when the program ends. Macros can also be eliminated by defining their contents to be nothing using `global` or `local`, but `macro drop` is more convenient.

Typing `macro drop` *base*∗ drops all global macros whose names begin with *base*.

Typing `macro drop _all` eliminates all macros except system macros—macros that begin with an "S_".

Typing `macro drop S_*` does not drop all system macros that begin with S_. It leaves certain macros in place that should not be casually deleted.

▷ Example

```
. macro drop _var* _lbl tofname _fmt
. macro list
_file2:    /tmp/St13310.0002
_file1:    /tmp/St13310.0001
S_FN:      auto.dta
_v1:       sexlbl
F1:        help
F2:        #review;
F3:        describe;
F7:        save
F8:        use
S_ADO:     UPDATES;BASE;SITE;.;PERSONAL;STBPLUS;~/ado/
S_FLAVOR:  Intercooled
S_OS:      Unix
S_MACH:    Sun Solaris
S_level:   95
. macro drop _all
. macro list
S_FN:      auto.dta
S_ADO:     UPDATES;BASE;SITE;.;PERSONAL;STBPLUS;~/ado/
S_FLAVOR:  Intercooled
S_OS:      Unix
S_MACH:    Sun Solaris
S_level:   95
. macro drop S_*
. macro list
S_ADO:     UPDATES;BASE;SITE;.;PERSONAL;STBPLUS;~/ado/
S_FLAVOR:  Intercooled
S_OS:      Unix
S_MACH:    Sun Solaris
S_level:   95
```

◁

❏ Technical Note

Stata usually requires you explicitly to drop something before redefining it. For instance, before redefining a value label with the `label define` command or redefining a program with the `program define` command, you must type `label drop` or `program drop`. This way you are protected from accidentally replacing something that might require considerable effort to reproduce.

Macros, however, may be redefined freely. It is *not* necessary to `drop` a macro before redefining it. Macros typically consist of short strings that could be easily reproduced if necessary. The inconvenience of the protection is not justified by the small benefit.

❏

Macros as arguments: macro shift

It sometimes occur in programs that you have in a macro a list of things—numbers, variable names, etc.—that you wish to access one at a time. For instance, after parsing (see [U] **21.4 Program arguments**), you might have in the local macro `` `varlist´ `` a list of variable names. The `tokenize` command (see [R] **tokenize**) will take any macro containing a list and assign the elements to local macros named `` `1´ ``, `` `2´ ``, and so on. That is, if `` `varlist´ `` contained "mpg weight displ", then coding

```
tokenize `varlist´
```

will make `` `1´ `` contain "mpg", `` `2´ `` contain "weight", `` `3´ `` contain "displ", and `` `4´ `` contain "" (nothing). The empty fourth macro marks the end of the list.

`macro shift` is often used to work through these elements one at a time in constructs like

```
while "`1´" ~= "" {
        do something based on `1´
        macro shift
}
```

`macro shift` discards `` `1´ ``, shifts `` `2´ `` to `` `1´ ``, `` `3´ `` to `` `2´ ``, and so on. For instance, in our example, after the first `macro shift`, `` `1´ `` will contain "weight", `` `2´ `` will contain "displ", and `` `3´ `` will contain "" (nothing).

Some programmers prefer to avoid `macro shift` and instead code

```
local i = 1
while "``i´´" ~= "" {
        do something based on ``i´´
        local i = `i´ + 1
}
```

Either form is equally acceptable; the second has the advantage that what is in `` `1´ ``, `` `2´ ``, ..., remains unchanged so that one can pass through the list multiple times without resetting it (coding "`tokenize `varlist´`" again).

`macro shift #` performs multiple macro shifts or, if # is 0, none at all. That is, `macro shift 2` is equivalent to two `macro shift` commands. `macro shift 0` does nothing.

Also See

Complementary:	[R] **char**, [R] **gettoken**, [R] **numlist**, [R] **return**, [R] **syntax**, [R] **tokenize**
Related:	[R] **matrix define**, [R] **preserve**, [R] **scalar**
Background:	[U] **15.8 Characteristics**, [U] **21 Programming Stata**, [U] **21.3 Macros**, [R] **macro system**

Title

> **macro system** — Quick reference for system macros

Description

This entry provides a quick reference for system macros. See [U] **21.3.10 Built-in global system macros** for details on the system macros.

Remarks

See [U] **21.3 Macros** for an introduction to macros.

See [R] **macro** for advanced issues not covered in [U] **21.3 Macros**.

Macros that begin with the characters S_ are called *system macros* and some are predefined for you:

System macro	Definition
S_ADO	path over which Stata looks for its ado-files
S_DATE	11-character string expressing the current date
S_FLAVOR	"Small" or "Intercooled"
S_FN	filename last specified with a use or save
S_FNDATE	date and time the file in S_FN was last saved
S_level	significance level for confidence intervals
S_MACH	type of computer
S_MODE	(Unix only) indicates if in batch mode
S_OS	name of operating system
S_OSDTL	level of operating system, if significant
S_TIME	8-character string expressing current time

Also See

Related: [R] **macro**, [R] **return**

Background: [U] **21.3 Macros**

Title

> **mark** — Mark observations for inclusion

Syntax

> marksample *lmacname* $\left[\right.$, <u>nova</u>rlist <u>s</u>trok <u>zero</u>weight$\left.\right]$
>
> mark *newmarkvar* $\left[weight\right]$ $\left[\text{if } exp\right]$ $\left[\text{in } range\right]$ $\left[\right.$, <u>zero</u>weight$\left.\right]$
>
> markout *markvar* $\left[varlist\right]$ $\left[\right.$, <u>s</u>trok $\left.\right]$

aweights, fweights, pweights, and iweights are allowed; see [U] **14.1.6 weight**.

varlist may contain time-series operators; see [U] **14.4.3 Time-series varlists**.

Description

marksample, mark, and markout are for use in Stata programs. They create a 0/1 variable recording which observations are to be used in subsequent code. The idea is to determine the relevant sample early in code:

```
program define ...
        (parse the arguments)
        (determine which observations are to be used)
        rest of code ... if to be used
end
```

marksample, mark, and markout assist in this.

```
program define ...
        (parse the arguments)
        (use mark* to create temporary variable `touse´ containing 0 or 1)
        rest of code ... if `touse´
end
```

marksample is for use in programs where the arguments are parsed using the syntax command; see [R] **syntax**. marksample creates a temporary byte variable, stores the name of the temporary variable in *lmacname*, and fills in the temporary variable with 0s and 1s according to whether the observation should be used. This determination is made by accessing information stored by syntax concerning the *varlist*, if *exp*, etc., allowed by the program. It is typically used as

```
program define ...
        syntax ...
        marksample touse
        rest of code ... if `touse´
end
```

mark starts with an already created temporary variable name. It fills in *newmarkvar* with 0s and 1s according to whether the observation should be used according to the *weight*, if *exp*, and in *range* specified. markout modifies the variable created by mark by resetting it to contain 0 in observations that have missing value recorded for any of the variables in *varlist*. These commands are usually used as

285

```
          program define ...
               (parse the arguments)
               tempvar touse
               mark `touse' ...
               markout `touse' ...
               rest of code ... if `touse'
          end
```

marksample is better than **mark** because there is less chance of your forgetting to include some part of the sample restriction. **markout** can be used after **mark** or **marksample** when there are variables other than the varlist and observations that contain missing values of those variables are also to be excluded. For instance, the following code is common:

```
          program define ...
               syntax ... [, Denom(varname) ... ]
               marksample touse
               markout `touse' `denom'
               rest of code ... if `touse'
          end
```

Regardless of whether you use **mark** or **marksample**, followed or not by **markout**, the following rules are applied:

1. The marker variable is set to 0 in observations for which *weight* is 0 (but see option **zeroweight**).

2. The appropriate error message is issued and all stops if *weight* is invalid (such as being less than 0 in some observation, or being a noninteger in the case of frequency weights, etc.).

3. The marker variable is set to 0 in observations for which the **if** *exp* is not satisfied.

4. The marker variable is set to 0 in observations outside of the **in** *range*.

5. The marker variable is set to 0 in observations for which any of the numeric variables in *varlist* contain numeric missing value.

6. The marker variable is set to 0 in *all* observations if any of the variables in *varlist* are strings, but see option **strok**.

7. The marker variable is set to 1 in the remaining observations.

Options

novarlist is for use with **marksample**. It specifies that missing values among variables in *varlist* are not to cause the marker variable to be set to 0. Specify **novarlist** if you previously specified

```
          syntax newvarlist ...
```

   or

```
          syntax newvarname ...
```

In addition, specify **novarlist** in instances where missing values are not to cause observations to be excluded (perhaps you are analyzing the pattern of missing values).

strok is for use with **marksample** or **markout**. Specify this option if string variables in *varlist* are to be allowed. **strok** changes Rule 6 above to read

"The marker variable is set to 0 in observations for which any of the string variables in *varlist* contain "".""

zeroweight is for use with **marksample** or **mark**. It deletes Rules 1 above, meaning that observations will not be excluded because the weight is zero.

Remarks

By far the most common programming error—made by us at StataCorp and others—is to use different samples at different parts of a Stata program. We strongly recommend that programmers identify the sample at the outset. This is easy with `marksample` (or alternatively, `mark` and `markout`). Consider a Stata program that begins

```
program define myprog
        version 6.0
        syntax varlist [if] [in]
        . . .
end
```

Pretend this program makes a statistical calculation based on the observations specified in *varlist* that do not contain missing values (such as a linear regression). The program must identify the observations that it is to use. Moreover, since the user can specify if *exp* or in *range*, these restrictions, too, must be taken into account. `marksample` makes this easy:

```
        version 6.0
        syntax varlist [if] [in]
        marksample touse
        . . .
end
```

Or to produce the same result, we could create the temporary variable `touse` and then use `mark` and `markout` as follows:

```
program define myprog
        version 6.0
        syntax varlist [if] [in]
        tempvar touse
        mark `touse´ `if´ `in´
        markout `touse´ `varlist´
        . . .
end
```

The result will be the same.

The `mark` command creates temporary variable `` `touse´ `` (temporary because of the preceding `tempvar`; see [R] **macro**) based on the if *exp* and in *range*. If there is no if *exp* or in *range*, `` `touse´ `` will contain 1 for every observation in the data. If `if price>1000` was specified by the user, only observations for which `price` is greater than 1,000 will have `touse` set to 1; the remaining will have `touse` set to zero.

The `markout` command updates the `` `touse´ `` marker created by `mark`. For observations for which `` `touse´ `` is 1—observations that might potentially be used—the variables in *varlist* are checked for missing values. If such an observation has any of the variables equal to missing, the observation's `` `touse´ `` value is reset to 0.

Thus, observations to be used all have `` `touse´ `` set to 1; including if `` `touse´ `` at the end of statistical or data-management commands will restrict the command to operate on the appropriate sample.

▷ Example

Let's write a program to do the same thing as `summarize` except that our program will engage in casewise deletion—if an observation has a missing value in any of the variables, it is to be excluded from all the calculations.

```
program define cwsumm
        version 6.0
        syntax [varlist(ts)] [if] [in] [aweight fweight] [, Detail noFormat]
        marksample touse
        summarize `varlist' [`weight'`exp'] if `touse', `detail' `format'
end
```

◁

Also See

Complementary: [R] **syntax**

Background: [U] **21 Programming Stata**

Title

> **matrix** — Introduction to matrix commands

Description

An introduction to matrices in Stata is found in [U] **17 Matrix expressions**. This entry provides an overview of the `matrix` commands and provides additional background information on matrices in Stata.

Remarks

An overview of the `matrix` commands is presented below. This is followed by information on matrices not covered elsewhere.

Overview of matrix commands

Documentation on matrices in Stata are grouped below into three categories—Basics, Programming, and Specialized. We recommend that you begin with [U] **17 Matrix expressions** and then read [R] **matrix define**. After that, feel free to skip around.

Basics

[U] **17 Matrix expressions**	Introduction to matrices in Stata
[R] **matrix define**	Matrix definition, operators, and functions
[R] **matrix utility**	Listing, renaming, and dropping matrices

Programming

[R] **matrix accum**	Forming cross-product matrices
[R] **ml**	Maximum likelihood estimation
[R] **estimates**	Posting and redisplaying estimation results
[R] **matrix rowname**	Naming rows and columns
[R] **matrix score**	Scoring data from coefficient vectors

Specialized

[R] **matrix constraint**	Constrained estimation
[R] **matrix mkmat**	Convert variables to matrix and vice versa
[R] **matrix svd**	Singular value decomposition
[R] **matrix symeigen**	Eigenvalues and vectors of symmetric matrices
[R] **matrix get**	Accessing system matrices

Creating and replacing matrices

In general, matrices do not have to be preallocated or dimensioned prior to creation, but the exception is when you want to create an $r \times c$ matrix and then fill in each element one-by-one; see the description of the J() function in [R] **matrix define**. Matrices are typically created by `matrix define` or `matrix accum`; see [R] **matrix accum**.

Stata takes a high-handed approach to redefining matrices. You know that, when dealing with data, you must distinguish between creating a new variable or replacing the contents of an existing variable — Stata has two commands: `generate` and `replace`. For matrices, there is no such distinction. If you define a new matrix, it is created. If you give the same command and the matrix already exists, the currently existing matrix is destroyed and then the new one defined. This treatment is the same as that given to macros and scalars.

Name space

The term "name space" refers to how names are interpreted. For instance, the variables in your data occupy one name space — other things, such as value labels, macros, and scalars, can have the same name and there is no confusion.

Macros are something else that have their own name space; macros can have the same names as other things and Stata can still tell by context when you are referring to a macro because of the punctuation. When you type `gen newvar=myname`, `myname` must refer to a variable. When you type `gen newvar=`myname`` — note the single quotes around `myname` — `myname` must refer to a local macro. When you type `gen newvar=$myname`, `myname` must refer to a global macro.

Scalars and matrices share the same name space, which is to say, scalars and matrices may have the same names as variables in the data, etc., but they cannot have the same names as each other. Thus, when you define a matrix called, say, `myres`, if a scalar by that name already exists, it is destroyed and the matrix replaces it. Correspondingly, if you define a scalar called `myres`, if a matrix by that name exists, it is destroyed and the scalar replaces it.

Naming conventions in programs

If you are writing Stata programs or ado-files using matrices, you may have some matrices you wish to leave behind for other programs to build upon, but you will certainly have other matrices which are nothing more than leftovers in making the calculation. Such matrices are called *temporary*. You should use Stata's `tempname` facility (see [R] **macro**) to name such matrices. These matrices will be automatically discarded when your program ends. For example, a piece of your program might read

```
tempname YXX XX
matrix accum `YXX` = price weight mpg
matrix `XX` = `YXX`[2...,2...]
```

Note the single quotes around the names after they are obtained from `tempname`; see [U] **21.3 Macros**.

❏ Technical Note

Let us consider writing a regression program in Stata. (There is actually no need for such a program since Stata already has the `regress` command.) A well-written estimation command would allow the `level()` option for specifying the width of confidence intervals and it would replay results when the command is typed without arguments. Here is a well-written version:

```
program define myreg, eclass
        version 6.0
        if ~replay() {
                syntax varlist(min=2 numeric) [if] [in] [, Level(integer $S_level)]

                marksample touse        /* mark the sample */

                tokenize "`varlist'"   /* put varlist into numbered arguments */

                tempname YXX XX Xy b hat V

                /* compute cross products YXX = (Y'Y , Y'X \ X'Y , X'X) */
                quietly matrix accum `YXX' = `varlist' if `touse'
                local nobs = r(N)
                local df = `nobs' - (rowsof(`YXX') - 1)
                matrix `XX' = `YXX'[2...,2...]
                matrix `Xy' = `YXX'[1,2...]

                /* compute the beta vector */
                matrix `b' = `Xy' * syminv(`XX')

                /* compute the covariance matrix */
                matrix `hat' = `b' * `Xy''
                matrix `V' = syminv(`XX') * (`YXX'[1,1] - `hat'[1,1])/`df'

                /* post the beta vector and covariance matrix */
                estimates post `b' `V', dof(`df') obs(`nobs') depname(`1') /*
                                     */ esample(`touse')

                /* save estimation information */
                est local depvar "`1'"
                est local cmd "myreg"
        }
        else {  /* replay */
                syntax [, Level(integer $S_level)]
        }

        if "`e(cmd)'"~="myreg" { error 301 }
        if `level' < 10 | `level' > 99 {
                di in red "level() must be between 10 and 99 inclusive"
                exit 198
        }

        /* print the regression table */
        estimates display, level(`level')
end
```

The syntax of our new command is

$$\texttt{myreg } \textit{depvar indepvars } [\texttt{if } \textit{exp}] \; [\texttt{in } \textit{range}] \; [, \; \texttt{level}(\#) \;]$$

and myreg, typed without arguments, redisplays the output of the last myreg command. After estimation with myreg, the user may use correlate to display the covariance matrix of the estimators, predict to obtain predicted values or standard errors of the prediction, and test to test linear hypotheses about the estimated coefficients. The command is indistinguishable from any other Stata estimation command.

Despite the excellence of our work, we do have some criticisms:

1. myreg does not display the ANOVA table, R^2, etc.; it should and could be made to, although we would have to insert our own display statements before the estimates display instruction.

2. The program makes copious use of matrices with different names, resulting in extra memory use while the estimation is being made; the code could be made more economical, if less readable, by reusing matrices.

3. `myreg` makes the least-squares calculation using the absolute cross-product matrix, an invitation to numerical problems if the data is not consistently scaled. Stata's own `regress` command is more careful and we could be, too: `matrix accum` does have an option for forming the cross-product matrix in deviation form, but its use would complicate this program. This does not overly concern us, although we should make a note of it when we document `myreg`. Nowadays, users expect to be protected in linear regression, but have no such expectations for more complicated estimation schemes because avoiding the problem can be difficult to nearly impossible.

There is one nice feature of our program that did not occur to us when we wrote it. We use `syminv()` to form the inverse of the cross-product matrix and `syminv()` can handle singular matrices. If there is a collinearity problem, `myreg` behaves just like `regress`: it drops the offending variables and notes they are dropped when it displays the output (at the `estimates display` step).

❏

❏ Technical Note

Our linear regression program is quite a bit longer than one might have written in an exclusively matrix programming language. After all, the coefficients can be obtained from $(\mathbf{X}'\mathbf{X})^{-1}\mathbf{X}'\mathbf{y}$ and in a dedicated matrix language, one would type nearly that, and obtaining the standard errors would require only a couple more matrix calculations. In fact, we did type nearly that to make the calculation; the extra lines in our program have mostly to do with syntax issues and linking to the rest of Stata. In writing your own programs, you might be tempted not to bother linking to the rest of Stata. Fight the temptation.

Linking to the rest of Stata pays off: in this case, we do not merely display the numerical results, we display them in a readable form, complete with variable names. We made a command that is indistinguishable from Stata's other estimation commands. If the user wants to test `_b[denver]=_b[la]`, the user types literally that; there is no need to remember the matrix equation and to count variables (such as constrain the third minus the fifteenth variable to sum to zero).

❏

Also See

Related: [R] **estimates**, [R] **matrix define**, [R] **ml**

Background: [U] **17 Matrix expressions**,
                  [U] **21 Programming Stata**

Title

matrix accum — Form cross-product matrices

Syntax

matrix <u>ac</u>cum **A** = *varlist* $\left[weight\right]$ $\left[if\ exp\right]$ $\left[in\ range\right]$ $\left[,\ \underline{\text{no}}\text{constant}\right.$

   <u>deviations</u> <u>means</u>(m) $\left.\right]$

matrix <u>gls</u>accum **A** = *varlist* $\left[weight\right]$ $\left[if\ exp\right]$ $\left[in\ range\right]$, <u>group</u>(*groupvar*)

   <u>gls</u>mat($\left\{\mathbf{W}\,|\,stringvarname\right\}$) <u>row</u>(*rowvar*) $\left[\underline{\text{no}}\text{constant}\right]$

matrix <u>vec</u>accum **a** = *varlist* $\left[weight\right]$ $\left[if\ exp\right]$ $\left[in\ range\right]$ $\left[,\ \underline{\text{no}}\text{constant}\ \right]$

aweights, fweights, iweights, and pweights are allowed; see [U] **14.1.6 weight**.

varlist may contain time-series operators; see [U] **14.4.3 Time-series varlists**.

Description

matrix accum accumulates cross-product matrices from the data to form $\mathbf{A} = \mathbf{X}'\mathbf{X}$.

matrix glsaccum accumulates cross-product matrices from the data using a specified inner weight matrix to form $\mathbf{A} = \mathbf{X}'\mathbf{B}\mathbf{X}$ where $\mathbf{B}$ is a block diagonal matrix.

matrix vecaccum accumulates the first variable against remaining variables in *varlist* to form a row vector of accumulated inner products to form $\mathbf{a} = \mathbf{x}_1'\mathbf{X}$ where $\mathbf{X} = (\mathbf{x}_2, \mathbf{x}_3, \ldots)$.

Options

noconstant suppresses the addition of a "constant" to the $\mathbf{X}$ matrix. If noconstant is not specified, it is as if a column of 1s is added to $\mathbf{X}$ before the accumulation begins. For instance, in the case of accum without noconstant, $\mathbf{X}'\mathbf{X}$ is really $(\mathbf{X}, \mathbf{1})'(\mathbf{X}, \mathbf{1})$, resulting in

$$\begin{pmatrix} \mathbf{X}'\mathbf{X} & \mathbf{X}'\mathbf{1} \\ \mathbf{1}'\mathbf{X} & \mathbf{1}'\mathbf{1} \end{pmatrix}$$

Thus, the last row and column contain the sums of the columns of $\mathbf{X}$ and the element in the last row and column contains the number of observations. If p variables are specified in the *varlist*, the resulting matrix is $(p+1) \times (p+1)$. Specifying noconstant suppresses the addition of this row and column (or just column in the case of vecaccum).

deviations, allowed only with matrix accum, causes the accumulation to be performed in terms of deviations from the mean. If noconstant is not specified, the accumulation of $\mathbf{X}$ is done in terms of deviations, but the added row and column of sums are *not* in deviation format (in which case they would be zeros). With noconstant specified, the resulting matrix divided through by $N - 1$, where N is the number of observations, is a covariance matrix.

means(**m**), allowed only with accum, creates matrix **m**: $1 \times (p+1)$ or $1 \times p$ (depending whether noconstant is also specified) containing the means of **X**.

group(*groupvar*), required with glsaccum and not allowed otherwise, specifies the name of a variable that identifies the groups of observations to be individually weighted by glsmat(). The data must be sorted by *groupvar*.

glsmat($\{$**W** | *stringvarname*$\}$), required with glsaccum and not allowed otherwise, specifies the name of the matrix or the name of a string variable in the data that contains the name of the matrix which is to be used to weight the observations in the group(). *stringvarname* must be str8 or less.

row(*rowvar*), required with glsaccum and not allowed otherwise, specifies the name of a numeric variable containing the row numbers that specify the row and column of the glsmat() matrix to use in the inner-product calculation.

Remarks

accum

matrix accum is a straightforward command that accumulates a single matrix that holds $\mathbf{X'X}$ and $\mathbf{X'y}$, which is typically used in $\mathbf{b} = (\mathbf{X'X})^{-1}\mathbf{X'y}$. Say we wish to run a regression of the variable price on mpg and weight. We can begin by accumulating the full cross-product matrix for all three variables:

```
. matrix accum A = price weight mpg
(obs=74)

. matrix list A

symmetric A[4,4]
                price      weight         mpg       _cons
price  3.448e+09
weight 1.468e+09   7.188e+08
   mpg   9132716     4493720       36008
 _cons    456229      223440        1576          74
```

In our accumulation, accum automatically added a constant; we specified three variables and got back a 4×4 matrix. The constant term is always added last. In terms of our regression model, the matrix we just accumulated has $\mathbf{y} = $ price and $\mathbf{X} = $ (weight, mpg, _cons), and can be written:

$$\mathbf{A} = (\mathbf{y}, \mathbf{X})'(\mathbf{y}, \mathbf{X}) = \begin{pmatrix} \mathbf{y'y} & \mathbf{y'X} \\ \mathbf{X'y} & \mathbf{X'X} \end{pmatrix}$$

Thus, we can extract $\mathbf{X'X}$ from the submatrix of $\mathbf{A}$ beginning at the second row and column and we can extract $\mathbf{X'y}$ from the first column of $\mathbf{A}$, omitting the first row:

```
. matrix XX = A[2...,2...]
. matrix list XX

symmetric XX[3,3]
               weight         mpg       _cons
weight  7.188e+08
   mpg    4493720       36008
 _cons     223440        1576          74
```

```
. matrix Xy = A[2...,1]
. matrix list Xy
Xy[3,1]
                 price
weight   1.468e+09
   mpg     9132716
 _cons      456229
```

We can now calculate $\mathbf{b} = (\mathbf{X}'\mathbf{X})^{-1}\mathbf{X}'\mathbf{y}$:

```
. matrix b = syminv(XX)*Xy
. matrix list b
b[3,1]
                 price
weight   1.7465592
   mpg  -49.512221
 _cons   1946.0687
```

The same result could have been obtained directly from $\mathbf{A}$:

```
. matrix b = syminv(A[2...,2...])*A[2...,1]
```

❑ Technical Note

matrix accum, with the deviations and noconstant options, can also be used to obtain covariance matrices. The covariance between variables x_i and x_j is defined as

$$C_{ij} = \frac{\sum_{k=1}^{n}(x_{ik} - \overline{x}_i)(x_{jk} - \overline{x}_j)}{n - 1}$$

Without the deviations option, matrix accum calculates a matrix with elements

$$R_{ij} = \sum_{k=1}^{n} x_{ik}x_{jk}$$

and with the deviations option:

$$A_{ij} = \sum_{k=1}^{n}(x_{ik} - \overline{x}_i)(x_{jk} - \overline{x}_j)$$

Thus, the covariance matrix $\mathbf{C} = \mathbf{A}/(n - 1)$.

```
. matrix accum Cov = price weight mpg, deviations noconstant
(obs=74)
. matrix Cov = Cov/(r(N)-1)
. matrix list Cov
symmetric Cov[3,3]
               price      weight         mpg
price        8699526
weight     1234674.8   604029.84
   mpg    -7996.2829  -3629.4261   33.472047
```

In addition to calculating the cross-product matrix, matrix accum records the number of observations in $r(N)$, a feature we use in calculating the normalizing factor. With the corr() matrix function defined in [R] **matrix define**, we can convert the covariance matrix into a correlation matrix:

```
. matrix P = corr(Cov)
. matrix list P

symmetric P[3,3]
              price       weight         mpg
  price           1
 weight    .53861146            1
    mpg   -.46859669   -.80717486          1
```

◁

glsaccum

`matrix glsaccum` is a generalization of `matrix accum` useful in producing GLS-style weighted accumulations. Whereas `matrix accum` produces matrices of the form $\mathbf{X}'\mathbf{X}$, `glsaccum` produces matrices of the form $\mathbf{X}'\mathbf{BX}$, where

$$
B = \begin{pmatrix} \mathbf{W}_1 & 0 & \cdots & 0 \\ 0 & \mathbf{W}_2 & \cdots & 0 \\ \vdots & \vdots & \ddots & \vdots \\ 0 & 0 & \cdots & \mathbf{W}_K \end{pmatrix}
$$

The matrices $\mathbf{W}_k$, $k = 1, \ldots, K$, are called the weighting matrices for observation group k. In the above, each of the $\mathbf{W}_k$ matrices is square but there is no assumption that they are all the same dimension. Note that by writing

$$
\mathbf{X} = \begin{pmatrix} \mathbf{X}_1 \\ \mathbf{X}_2 \\ \vdots \\ \mathbf{X}_K \end{pmatrix}
$$

the accumulation made by `glsaccum` can be written as

$$
\mathbf{X}'\mathbf{BX} = \mathbf{X}_1'\mathbf{W}_1\mathbf{X}_1 + \mathbf{X}_2'\mathbf{W}_2\mathbf{X}_2 + \cdots + \mathbf{X}_K'\mathbf{W}_K\mathbf{X}_K
$$

`glsaccum` requires you to specify three options: group(*groupvar*), glsmat(*matname*) or glsmat(*matvar*), and row(*rowvar*). Observations sharing the same value of *groupvar* are said to be in the same observation group—this specifies the group k in which they are to be accumulated. How $\mathbf{W}_k$ is assembled is the subject of the other two options.

Think of there being a super weighting matrix for the group, which we will call $\mathbf{V}_k$. $\mathbf{V}_k$ is specified by glsmat()—the same super matrix can be used for all observations by specifying a *matname* as the argument to glsmat or, if a variable name is specified, different super matrices can be specified—the contents of the variable will be used to obtain the particular name of the super matrix. (More correctly, the contents of the variable for the first observation in the group will be used: super matrices can vary across groups, but must be the same within group.)

Weighting matrix $\mathbf{W}_k$ is made from the super matrix $\mathbf{V}_k$ by selecting the rows and columns specified in row(*rowvar*). In the simple case, $\mathbf{W}_k = \mathbf{V}_k$. This happens when there are m observations in the group and the first observation in the group has *rowvar* = 1, the second *rowvar* = 2, and so on. To fix ideas, let $m = 3$ and write

$$
\mathbf{V}_1 = \begin{pmatrix} v_{11} & v_{12} & v_{13} \\ v_{21} & v_{22} & v_{23} \\ v_{31} & v_{32} & v_{33} \end{pmatrix}
$$

V need not be symmetric. Let's pretend the first four observations in our data contain

obs. no.	*groupvar*	*rowvar*
1	1	1
2	1	2
3	1	3
4	2	...

In this data, the first three observations are in the first group because they share an equal *groupvar*. It is not important that *groupvar* happens to equal 1; it is important that the values are equal. The *rowvars* are, in order, 1, 2, and 3, so $\mathbf{W}_1$ is formed by selecting the first row and column of $\mathbf{V}_1$, then the second row and column of $\mathbf{V}_1$, and finally the third row and column of $\mathbf{V}_1$; to wit,

$$\mathbf{W}_1 = \begin{pmatrix} v_{11} & v_{12} & v_{13} \\ v_{21} & v_{22} & v_{23} \\ v_{31} & v_{32} & v_{33} \end{pmatrix}$$

or $\mathbf{W}_1 = \mathbf{V}_1$. Now, consider the same data, but reordered:

obs. no.	*groupvar*	*rowvar*
1	1	2
2	1	1
3	1	3
4	2	...

$\mathbf{W}_1$ is now formed by selecting the second row and column, then the first row and column, and finally the third row and column of $\mathbf{V}_1$. These steps can be performed sequentially, reordering first the rows and then the columns; the result is

$$\mathbf{W}_1 = \begin{pmatrix} v_{22} & v_{21} & v_{23} \\ v_{12} & v_{11} & v_{13} \\ v_{32} & v_{31} & v_{33} \end{pmatrix}$$

This reorganization of the $\mathbf{W}_1$ matrix exactly undoes the reorganization of the $\mathbf{X}_1$ matrix, so $\mathbf{X}_1'\mathbf{W}_1\mathbf{X}_1$ remains unchanged. Given how $\mathbf{W}_k$ is assembled from $\mathbf{V}_k$, the order of the row numbers in the data does not matter.

`glsaccum` is willing to carry this concept even further. Consider the data:

obs. no.	*groupvar*	*rowvar*
1	1	1
2	1	3
3	1	3
4	2	...

Note that now *rowvar* equals 1 followed by 3 twice, so the first row and column of $\mathbf{V}_1$ are selected, followed by the third row and column twice; the second column is never selected. The resulting weighting matrix is

$$\mathbf{W}_1 = \begin{pmatrix} v_{11} & v_{13} & v_{13} \\ v_{31} & v_{33} & v_{33} \\ v_{31} & v_{33} & v_{33} \end{pmatrix}$$

Such odd weighting would not occur in, say, time-series analysis where the matrix might be weighting lags and leads. It could very well occur in an analysis of individuals in families, where 1 might indicate head of household, 2 a spouse, and 3 a child. In fact, such a case could be handled with a 3×3 super weighting matrix V even if the family became quite large: the appropriate weighting matrix $\mathbf{W}_k$ would be assembled, on a group-by-group (family-by-family) basis, from the underlying super matrix.

vecaccum

The first variable in the *varlist* is treated differently from the others by vecaccum. Think of the first variable as specifying a vector $\mathbf{y}$ and the remaining variables as specifying matrix $\mathbf{X}$. vecaccum makes the accumulation $\mathbf{y'X}$ to return a row vector with elements

$$a_i = \sum_{k=1}^{n} y_k x_{ki}$$

Like accum, vecaccum adds a constant _cons to $\mathbf{X}$ unless noconstant is specified.

vecaccum serves two purposes. First, terms like $\mathbf{y'X}$ often occur in calculating derivatives of likelihood functions; vecaccum provides a fast way of calculating them. Second, it is useful in time-series accumulations of the form:

$$\mathbf{C} = \sum_{t=1}^{T} \sum_{\delta=-k}^{k} \mathbf{x}'_{t-\delta} \mathbf{x}_t W_\delta r_{t-\delta} r_t$$

In this calculation, $\mathbf{X}$ is an observation matrix with elements x_{tj} with t indexing time (observations) and j variables, $t = 1, \ldots, T$ and $j = 1, \ldots, p$. $\mathbf{x}_t$ $(1 \times p)$ refers to the tth row of this matrix. Thus, $\mathbf{C}$ is a $p \times p$ matrix.

The Newey–West covariance matrix uses the definition $W_\delta = 1 - |\delta|/(k+1)$ for $\delta \leq k$. To make the calculation, the user (programmer) cycles through each of the j variables, forming

$$z_{tj} = \sum_{\delta=-k}^{k} x_{(t-\delta)j} W_\delta r_{t-\delta} r_t$$

Writing $\mathbf{z}_j = (z_{1j}, z_{2j}, \ldots, z_{Tj})'$, $\mathbf{C}$ is then

$$\mathbf{C} = \sum_{j=1}^{p} \mathbf{z}'_j \mathbf{X}$$

In this derivation, the user must decide in advance the maximum lag length k such that observations that are far apart in time must have increasingly small covariances in order to establish the convergence results.

The Newey–West estimator is in the class of generalized methods of moments (GMM) estimators. The choice of a maximum lag length k is a reflection of the length in time beyond which the autocorrelation becomes negligible for the purposes of estimating the variance matrix. The code fragment given below is merely for illustration of the matrix commands as Stata includes estimation with the Newey–West covariance matrix in the newey command. See [R] **newey** or Greene (1997, 506) for details on this estimator.

Note that it is calculations like $\mathbf{z}'_j \mathbf{X}$ that are made by vecaccum. Also note that $\mathbf{z}_j$ can be treated as a temporary variable in the data.

```
assume `1´,`2´, etc. contain the x's including constant
assume `r´ contains the r variable
assume `k´ contains the k range
tempname C factor t c
tempvar z
```

```
local p : word count `*´
matrix `C´ = J(`p´,`p´,0)
gen double `z´ = 0
local d = 0
while `d´ <= `k´ {
        if `d´ > 0 { scalar `factor´ = 1 } /* Add each submatrix twice */
        else scalar `factor´ = 0.5          /* except for the lag=0 case */
        local w = (1 - `d´/(`k´+1))
        capture mat drop `t´
        local j = 1
        while `j´ <= `p´ {
                replace `z´ = ``j´´[_n-`d´]*`w´*`r´[_n-`d´]*`r´
                mat vecaccum `c´ = `z´ `*´, nocons
                mat `t´ = `t´ \ `c´
                local j = `j´+1
        }
        mat `C´ = `C´ + (`t´ + `t´´)*`factor´
        local d = `d´+1
}
local `p´ = "_cons"                      /* Rename last var to _cons */
mat rownames `C´ = `*´
mat colnames `C´ = `*´
```
assume inverse and scaling for standard error reports

Treatment of user-specified weights

accum, glsaccum, and vecaccum all allow weights. Here is how they are treated:

All three commands can be thought of as returning something of the form $X_1' B X_2$. In the case of accum, $X_1 = X_2$ and $B = I$; in the case of glsaccum, $X_1 = X_2$; in the case of vecaccum, $B = I$, X_1 is a column vector, and X_2 is a matrix.

In point of fact, the commands really calculate $X_1' W^{1/2} B W^{1/2} X_2$, where W is a diagonal matrix. If no weights are specified, $W = I$. Now assume weights are specified and let v: $1 \times n$ be the specified weights. If fweights or pweights are specified, then $W = \text{diag}(v)$. If aweights are specified, then $W = \text{diag}[v/(1'v)(1'1)]$, which is to say, the weights are normalized to sum to the number of observations. If iweights are specified, they are treated like fweights except that the elements of v are not restricted to be positive integers.

Saved Results

matrix accum, glsaccum, and vecaccum save the number of observations in r(N). glsaccum (with aweights) and vecaccum also stores the sum of the weight in r(sum_w), but accum does not.

References

Greene, W. H. 1997. *Econometric Analysis*. 3d ed. Upper Saddle River, NJ: Prentice–Hall.

Also See

Complementary:	[R] **ml**
Background:	[U] **17 Matrix expressions**,
	[R] **matrix**

Title

matrix constraint — Constrained estimation

Syntax

matrix makeCns [*clist*]

matrix dispCns

matcproc **T a C**

where *clist* is a list of constraint numbers, separated by commas or dashes. 1,2,3 would refer to constraints 1, 2, and 3, as would 1-3. 1-3,9 would refer to constraints 1, 2, 3, and 9.

T, **a**, and **C** are names of new or existing matrices.

Description

matrix makeCns makes a constraint matrix; the matrix can be obtained by the matrix get(Cns) function (see [R] **matrix get**). matrix dispCns displays the system-stored constraint matrix in readable form. matcproc returns matrices helpful for performing constrained estimation including the constraint matrix.

Remarks

Users of estimation commands that allow constrained estimation define constraints using the constraint command; they indicate which constraints they want to use by specifying the constraints(*clist*) option to the estimation command. This entry concerns programming such sophisticated estimators. Before reading it, you should be familiar with constraints from a user's perspective; see [R] **constraint**. You should also be familiar with programming estimation commands that do not include constraints; see [R] **estimates** and [R] **ml**.

Overview

You have an estimation command and wish to allow a set of linear constraints to be specified for the parameters by the user and then to produce estimates subject to those constraints. Stata will do most of the work for you. First, it will collect the constraints—all you have to do is add an option to your estimation command to allow the user to specify which constraints to use. Second, it will process those constraints, converting them from algebraic form (such as group1=group2) to a constraint matrix. Third, it will convert the constraint matrix into two, almost magical matrices that will, in the case of maximum likelihood estimation, allow you to write your routine almost as if there were no constraints.

There will be a "reduced-form" parameter vector b_c which your likelihood-calculation routine will receive. That vector, multiplied by one of the almost magical matrices and then added to the other, can be converted into a regular parameter vector with the constraints applied, so, other than the few extra matrix calculations, you can calculate the likelihood function as if there were no constraints. You can do the same thing with respect to the first and second derivatives (if you are calculating them) except that, after getting them, you will need to perform another matrix multiplication or two to convert them into the reduced form.

Once the optimum is found, you will have reduced-form parameter vector $\mathbf{b}_c$ along with variance–covariance matrix $\mathbf{V}_c$. Both can be easily converted into full-form-but-constrained $\mathbf{b}$ and $\mathbf{V}$.

Finally, you will post the results along with the constraint matrix Stata made up for you in the first place. You can, with a few lines of program code, arrange it so that, every time results are replayed, the constraints under which they were produced are redisplayed and in standard algebraic format.

Mathematics

Let $\mathbf{R}\mathbf{b}' = \mathbf{r}$ be the constraint, for $\mathbf{R}$ a $c \times p$ constraint matrix imposing c constraints on p parameters, $\mathbf{b}$ a $1 \times p$ parameter vector, and $\mathbf{r}$ a $c \times 1$ vector of constraint values.

We wish to construct a $p \times k$ matrix $\mathbf{T}$ that takes $\mathbf{b}$ into a reduced-rank form, where $k = p - c$. There are obviously lots of $\mathbf{T}$ matrices that will do this; we choose one with properties that

$$\mathbf{b}_c = \mathbf{b}_0\mathbf{T}$$
$$\mathbf{b} = \mathbf{b}_c\mathbf{T}' + \mathbf{a}$$

where $\mathbf{b}_c$ is a reduced-form projection of any solution $\mathbf{b}_0$, i.e., $\mathbf{b}_c$ is a vector of lesser dimension ($1 \times k$ rather than $1 \times p$) that can be treated as if it were unconstrained. The second equation says that $\mathbf{b}_c$ can be mapped back into a higher-dimensioned, properly constrained $\mathbf{b}$; $1 \times p$ vector $\mathbf{a}$ is a constant that depends only on $\mathbf{R}$ and $\mathbf{r}$.

With such a $\mathbf{T}$ matrix and $\mathbf{a}$ vector, one can engage in unconstrained optimization of $\mathbf{b}_c$. If ultimately the estimate $\mathbf{b}_c$ with variance–covariance matrix $\mathbf{V}_c$ is produced, it can be mapped back into $\mathbf{b} = \mathbf{b}_c\mathbf{T}' + \mathbf{a}$ and $\mathbf{V} = \mathbf{T}\mathbf{V}_c\mathbf{T}'$. The resulting $\mathbf{b}$ and $\mathbf{V}$ can then be posted.

❑ Technical Note

So how did we get so lucky? This happy solution arises if

$$\mathbf{T} = \text{first } k \text{ eigenvectors of } \mathbf{I} - \mathbf{R}'(\mathbf{R}\mathbf{R}')^{-1}\mathbf{R} \qquad (p \times k)$$
$$\mathbf{L} = \text{last } c \text{ eigenvectors of } \mathbf{I} - \mathbf{R}'(\mathbf{R}\mathbf{R}')^{-1}\mathbf{R} \qquad (p \times c)$$
$$\mathbf{a} = \mathbf{r}'(\mathbf{L}'\mathbf{R}')^{-1}\mathbf{L}'$$

because

$$(\mathbf{b}_c, \mathbf{r}') = \mathbf{b}(\mathbf{T}, \mathbf{R}')$$

If $\mathbf{R}$ consists of a set of consistent constraints, then it is guaranteed to have rank c. Thus, $\mathbf{R}\mathbf{R}'$ is a $c \times c$ invertible matrix.

We will now show that $\mathbf{R}\mathbf{T} = 0$ and $\mathbf{R}(\mathbf{L}\mathbf{L}') = \mathbf{R}$.

Since $\mathbf{R}$: $c \times p$ is assumed to be of rank c, the first k eigenvalues of $\mathbf{P} = \mathbf{I} - \mathbf{R}'(\mathbf{R}\mathbf{R}')^{-1}\mathbf{R}$ are positive and the last c are zero. Break $\mathbf{R}$ into a basis spanned by these components. If $\mathbf{R}$ had any components in the first k, they could not be annihilated by $\mathbf{P}$, contradicting

$$\mathbf{R}\mathbf{P} = \mathbf{R} - \mathbf{R}\mathbf{R}'(\mathbf{R}\mathbf{R}')^{-1}\mathbf{R} = 0$$

Therefore, $\mathbf{T}$ and $\mathbf{R}$ are orthogonal to each other. Since $(\mathbf{T}, \mathbf{L})$ is an orthonormal basis, $(\mathbf{T}, \mathbf{L})'$ is its inverse, so $(\mathbf{T}, \mathbf{L})(\mathbf{T}, \mathbf{L})' = \mathbf{I}$. Thus,

$$\mathbf{T}\mathbf{T}' + \mathbf{L}\mathbf{L}' = \mathbf{I}$$
$$(\mathbf{T}\mathbf{T}' + \mathbf{L}\mathbf{L}')\mathbf{R}' = \mathbf{R}'$$
$$(\mathbf{L}\mathbf{L}')\mathbf{R}' = \mathbf{R}'$$

So, we conclude $\mathbf{r} = \mathbf{bR}(\mathbf{LL}')$. $\mathbf{RL}$ is an invertible $c \times c$ matrix, so

$$\left(\mathbf{b}_c, \mathbf{r}'(\mathbf{L}'\mathbf{R})^{-1}\right) = \mathbf{b}\left(\mathbf{T}, \mathbf{L}\right)$$

Remember, $(\mathbf{T}, \mathbf{L})$ is a set of eigenvectors, meaning $(\mathbf{T}, \mathbf{L})^{-1} = (\mathbf{T}, \mathbf{L})'$, so $\mathbf{b} = \mathbf{b}_c\mathbf{T}' + \mathbf{r}'(\mathbf{L}'\mathbf{R}')^{-1}\mathbf{L}'$.

❏

If a solution is being found by likelihood methods, the reduced form parameter vector will be passed to the maximizer and from there to the program that has to compute a likelihood value from it. In order to find the likelihood value, the inner routines can compute $\mathbf{b} = \mathbf{b}_c\mathbf{T}' + \mathbf{a}$. The routine may then go on to produce a set of $1 \times p$ first derivatives $\mathbf{d}$ and $p \times p$ second derivatives $\mathbf{H}$ even though the problem is of lesser dimension. These matrices can be reduced to the k-dimensional space via

$$\mathbf{d}_c = \mathbf{dT}$$
$$\mathbf{H}_c = \mathbf{T}'\mathbf{HT}$$

❏ Technical Note

Alternatively, if a solution were to be found by direct matrix methods, then the programmer must derive a new solution based on $\mathbf{b} = \mathbf{b}_c\mathbf{T}' + \mathbf{a}$. For example, the least-squares normal equations come from differentiating $(\mathbf{y} - \mathbf{Xb})^2$. Setting the derivative with respect to $\mathbf{b}$ to zero results in

$$\mathbf{T}'\mathbf{X}'\left(\mathbf{y} - \mathbf{X}(\mathbf{Tb}_c' + \mathbf{a}')\right) = 0$$

yielding

$$\mathbf{b}_c' = (\mathbf{T}'\mathbf{X}'\mathbf{XT})^{-1}[\mathbf{T}'\mathbf{X}'\mathbf{y} - \mathbf{T}'\mathbf{X}'\mathbf{Xa}']$$
$$\mathbf{b}' = \mathbf{T}\left[(\mathbf{T}'\mathbf{X}'\mathbf{XT})^{-1}[\mathbf{T}'\mathbf{X}'\mathbf{y} - \mathbf{T}'\mathbf{X}'\mathbf{Xa}']\right] + \mathbf{a}'$$

Using the matrices $\mathbf{T}$ and $\mathbf{a}$, the solution is not merely to constrain the $\mathbf{b}'$ obtained from an unconstrained solution $(\mathbf{X}'\mathbf{X})^{-1}\mathbf{X}'\mathbf{y}$ even though you might know that, in this case, with further substitutions this could be reduced to

$$\mathbf{b}' = (\mathbf{X}'\mathbf{X})^{-1}\mathbf{X}'\mathbf{y} + (\mathbf{X}'\mathbf{X})^{-1}\mathbf{R}'[\mathbf{R}(\mathbf{X}'\mathbf{X})^{-1}\mathbf{R}']^{-1}(\mathbf{r} - \mathbf{R}(\mathbf{X}'\mathbf{X})^{-1}\mathbf{X}'\mathbf{y})$$

❏

Linkage of the mathematics to Stata

Users define constraints using the `constraint` command; see [R] **constraint**. The constraints are numbered and Stata stores them in algebraic format—the same format in which the user typed them. Stata does this because, until the estimation problem is defined, it cannot know how to interpret the constraint. Think of the constraint _b[group1]=_b[group2], meaning two coefficients are to be constrained to equality, along with the constraint _b[group3]=2. The constraint matrices $\mathbf{R}$ and $\mathbf{r}$ are defined so that $\mathbf{Rb}' = \mathbf{r}$ imposes the constraint. The matrices *might* be

$$
\begin{pmatrix} 0 & 0 & 1 & -1 & 0 & 0 \\ 0 & 0 & 0 & 0 & 1 & 0 \end{pmatrix}
\begin{pmatrix} b_1 \\ b_2 \\ b_3 \\ b_4 \\ b_5 \\ b_6 \end{pmatrix}
= \begin{pmatrix} 0 \\ 2 \end{pmatrix}
$$

if it just so happened that the third and fourth coefficients corresponded to `group1` and `group2`, and the fifth corresponded to `group3`. Then again, it might look differently if the coefficients were organized differently.

Therefore, Stata must wait until estimation begins to define the $\mathbf{R}$ and $\mathbf{r}$ matrices. Stata learns about the organization of a problem from the names bordering the coefficient vector and variance–covariance matrix. Therefore, Stata requires you to `post` a dummy estimation result that has the correct names. Based on that, it can now determine the organization of the constraint matrix and make it for you. Once a (dummy) estimation result has been posted, `makeCns` can make the constraint matrices and, once they are built, you can obtain copies of them using `matrix` *mname*=`get(Cns)`. Stata stores the constraint matrices $\mathbf{R}$ and $\mathbf{r}$ as a single, $c \times (p+1)$ matrix $\mathbf{C} = (\mathbf{R}, \mathbf{r})$. Putting them together makes it easier to pass them to subroutines.

The second step in the process is to convert the constrained problem to a reduced-form problem. We outlined the mathematics above; the `matcproc` command will produce the $\mathbf{T}$ and $\mathbf{a}$ matrices. If you are performing maximum likelihood, your likelihood, gradient, and Hessian calculation subroutines can still work in the full metric by using the same $\mathbf{T}$ and $\mathbf{a}$ matrices to translate the reduced-format parameter vector back to the original metric. If you do this, and if you are calculating gradients or Hessians, you must remember to compress them to reduced form using the $\mathbf{T}$ and $\mathbf{a}$ matrices.

When you have a reduced-form solution, you translate this back to a constrained solution using $\mathbf{T}$ and $\mathbf{a}$. You then `post` the constrained solutions, along with the original `Cns` matrix, and use `estimates display` to display the results.

Thus, the outline of a program to perform constrained estimation is

```
program define myest, eclass
        version 6.0
        if ~replay() {
                #delimit ;
                syntax whatever [, whatever Constraints(numlist)
                        Level(integer $S_level)];
                #delimit cr
                any other parsing of the user's estimation request
                tempname b V C T a bc Vc
                local p=number of parameters
                define the model ( set the row and column names) in `b´
                if "`constra´"~="" {
                        matrix `V´=`b´´*`b´
                        estimates post `b´ `V´             /* a dummy solution */
                        matrix makeCns `constra´
                        matrix dispCns                     /* display constraints */
                        local shown "yes"
                        matcproc `T´ `a´ `C´
                        obtain solution in `bc´ and `Vc´
                        matrix `b´ = `bc´*`T´ + `a´
                        matrix `V´ = `T´*`Vc´*`T´´   /* note prime */
                        estimates post `b´ `V´ `C´, options
                }
```

```
                        else {
                                obtain standard solution in `b´ and `V´
                                estimates post `b´ `V´, options
                        }
                        store whatever else you want in e()
                        est local cmd "myest"
                }
                else {    /* replay */
                        if "`e(cmd)´"~="myest" { error 301 }
                        syntax [, Level(integer $S_level)]
                }
                if `level´<10 | `level´>99 {
                        di in red "level() must be between 10 and 99 inclusive"
                        exit 198
                }
                if "`shown´"~="yes" {
                        matrix dispCns  /* display any constraints on replay */
                }
                output any header above the coefficient table
                estimates display, level(`level´)
        end
```

There is one point that might escape your attention: Immediately after obtaining the constraint, we display the constraints even before we undertake the estimation. This way, a user who has made a mistake may press *Break* rather than waiting until the estimation is complete to discover the error.

Our code also redisplays the constraints every time the problem output is repeated (by typing *myest* without arguments). So that the constraints are not shown twice at the time of estimation, we set the local macro shown to contain yes. If the output is ever repeated, the local macro shown will never be defined (and so will not contain yes) and we will redisplay the constraints along with the results of our estimation.

Also See

Complementary:	[R] **constraint**, [R] **estimates**, [R] **ml**
Related:	[R] **cnsreg**
Background:	[U] **17 Matrix expressions**,
	[U] **21 Programming Stata**,
	[U] **23 Estimation and post-estimation commands**,
	[R] **matrix**

Title

---

matrix define — Matrix definition, operators, and functions

Syntax

matrix [define] *matname* = *matrix_expression*

matrix [input] *matname* = (# [,# ...] [\ # [, # ...] [\ [...]]])

Description

matrix define performs matrix computations. The word define may be omitted.

matrix input provides a method of inputting matrices. The word input may be omitted (see discussion that follows).

For an introduction and overview of matrices in Stata, see [U] **17 Matrix expressions**.

Remarks

matrix define calculates matrix results from other matrices. For instance,

    . matrix define D = A + B + C

creates D containing the sum of A, B, and C. The word define may be omitted,

    . matrix D = A + B + C

and the command may be further abbreviated:

    . mat D=A+B+C

The same matrix may appear on both the left and the right of the equals sign in all contexts and Stata will not become confused. Complicated matrix expressions are allowed.

With matrix input you define the matrix elements rowwise; commas are used to separate elements within a row and backslashes are used to separate the rows. Spacing does not matter.

    . matrix input A = (1,2\3,4)

The above would also work if you omitted the input subcommand.

    . matrix A = (1,2\3,4)

There is a subtle difference: The first method uses the matrix input command; the second uses the matrix expression parser. Omitting input allows expressions in the command. For instance,

    . matrix X = (1+1, 2*3/4 \ 5/2, 3)

is understood but

```
. matrix input X = (1+1, 2*3/4 \ 5/2, 3)
```

would produce an error.

matrix input, however, has two advantages. First, it allows input of very large matrices. (The expression parser is limited because it must "compile" the expressions and, if the result is too long, will produce an error.) Second, **matrix input** allows you to omit the commas.

Further remarks are presented under the headings

> *Inputting matrices by hand*
> *Matrix operators*
> *Matrix functions*
> *Matrix functions returning scalars*
> *Subscripting and element-by-element definition*
> *Name conflicts in expressions (name spaces)*
> *Macro extended functions*

Inputting matrices by hand

Before turning to operations on matrices, let's examine how matrices are created. Typically, at least in programming situations, you obtain matrices by accessing one of Stata's internal matrices (e(b) and e(V) or see [R] **matrix get**) or accumulating it from the data (see [R] **matrix accum**). Nevertheless, the easiest way to create a matrix is to enter it using **matrix input**—this may not be the normal way one creates matrices, but it is useful for performing small, experimental calculations.

▷ Example

To create the matrix

$$A = \begin{pmatrix} 1 & 2 \\ 3 & 4 \end{pmatrix}$$

you type

```
. matrix A = (1,2 \ 3,4)
```

The spacing does not matter. To define the matrix

$$B = \begin{pmatrix} 1 & 2 & 3 \\ 4 & 5 & 6 \end{pmatrix}$$

you type

```
. matrix B = (1,2,3 \ 4,5,6)
```

To define the matrix

$$C = \begin{pmatrix} 1 & 2 \\ 3 & 4 \\ 5 & 6 \end{pmatrix}$$

you type

```
. matrix C = (1,2 \ 3,4 \ 5,6)
```

If you need more than one line and are working interactively, you merely keep typing; Stata will wrap the line around the screen. If you are working in a do- or ado-file, see [U] **19.1.3 Long lines in do-files**.

So how do you create vectors? You enter the elements, separating them either by commas or by backslashes. To create the row vector

$$\mathbf{D} = (\,1 \quad 2 \quad 3\,)$$

you type

         . matrix D = (1,2,3)

To create the column vector

$$\mathbf{E} = \begin{pmatrix} 1 \\ 2 \\ 3 \end{pmatrix}$$

you type

         . matrix E = (1\2\3)

To create the 1×1 matrix $\mathbf{F} = (\,2\,)$ you type

         . matrix F = (2)

In these examples we have omitted the `input` subcommand. They would work either way.

◁

Matrix operators

In what follows, uppercase letters $\mathbf{A}$, $\mathbf{B}$, ..., stand for matrix names. The matrix operators are

+ meaning addition. `matrix C=A+B`, $\mathbf{A}$: $r \times c$ and $\mathbf{B}$: $r \times c$, creates $\mathbf{C}$: $r \times c$ containing the elementwise addition $\mathbf{A} + \mathbf{B}$. An error is issued if the matrices are not conformable. Row and column names are obtained from $\mathbf{B}$.

− meaning subtraction or negation. `matrix C=A-B`, $\mathbf{A}$: $r \times c$ and $\mathbf{B}$: $r \times c$, creates $\mathbf{C}$ containing the elementwise subtraction $\mathbf{A} - \mathbf{B}$. An error is issued if the matrices are not conformable. `matrix C=-A` creates $\mathbf{C}$ containing the elementwise negation of $\mathbf{A}$. Row and column names are obtained from $\mathbf{B}$.

∗ meaning multiplication. `matrix C=A*B`, $\mathbf{A}$: $a \times b$ and $\mathbf{B}$: $b \times c$, returns $\mathbf{C}$: $a \times c$ containing the matrix product $\mathbf{AB}$; an error is issued if $\mathbf{A}$ and $\mathbf{B}$ are not conformable. The row names of $\mathbf{C}$ are obtained from the row names of $\mathbf{A}$, and the column names of $\mathbf{C}$ from the column names of $\mathbf{B}$.

`matrix C=A*s` or `matrix C=s*A`, $\mathbf{A}$: $a \times b$ and s a Stata scalar (see [R] **scalar**) or a literal number, returns $\mathbf{C}$: $a \times b$ containing the elements of $\mathbf{A}$ each multiplied by s. The row and column names of $\mathbf{C}$ are obtained from $\mathbf{A}$. For example, `matrix VC=MYMAT*2.5` multiplies each element of `MYMAT` by 2.5 and stores the result in `VC`.

/ meaning matrix division by scalar. `matrix C=A/s`, $\mathbf{A}$: $a \times b$ and s a Stata scalar (see [R] **scalar**) or a literal number, returns $\mathbf{C}$: $a \times b$ containing the elements of $\mathbf{A}$ each divided by s. The row and column names of $\mathbf{C}$ are obtained from $\mathbf{A}$.

meaning Kronecker product. `matrix C=A#B`, $\mathbf{A}$: $a \times b$ and $\mathbf{B}$: $c \times d$, returns $\mathbf{C}$: $ac \times bd$ containing the Kronecker product $\mathbf{A} \otimes \mathbf{B}$, all elementwise products of $\mathbf{A}$ and $\mathbf{B}$. The upper-left submatrix of $\mathbf{C}$ is the product $A_{1,1}\mathbf{B}$; the submatrix to the right is $A_{1,2}\mathbf{B}$; and so on. Row and column names are obtained by using the subnames of $\mathbf{A}$ as resulting equation names and the subnames of $\mathbf{B}$ for the subnames of $\mathbf{C}$ in each submatrix.

Nothing meaning copy. `matrix B=A` copies $\mathbf{A}$ into $\mathbf{B}$. The row and column names of $\mathbf{B}$ are obtained from $\mathbf{A}$. The `matrix rename` command (see [R] **matrix utility**) will rename instead of copy a matrix.

´ meaning transpose. `matrix B=A´`, $\mathbf{A}$: $r \times c$, creates $\mathbf{B}$: $c \times r$ containing the transpose of $\mathbf{A}$. The row names of $\mathbf{B}$ are obtained from the column names of $\mathbf{A}$ and the column names of $\mathbf{B}$ from the row names of $\mathbf{A}$.

, meaning join columns by row. `matrix C=A,B`, $\mathbf{A}$: $a \times b$ and $\mathbf{B}$: $a \times c$, returns $\mathbf{C}$: $a \times (b+c)$ containing $\mathbf{A}$ in columns 1 through b and $\mathbf{B}$ in columns $b+1$ through $b+c$ (the columns of $\mathbf{B}$ are appended to the columns of $\mathbf{A}$). An error is issued if the matrices are not conformable. The row names of $\mathbf{C}$ are obtained from $\mathbf{A}$. The column names are obtained from $\mathbf{A}$ and $\mathbf{B}$.

\ meaning join rows by column. `matrix C=A\B`, $\mathbf{A}$: $a \times b$ and $\mathbf{B}$: $c \times b$, returns $\mathbf{C}$: $(a+c) \times b$ containing $\mathbf{A}$ in rows 1 through a and $\mathbf{B}$ in rows $a+1$ through $a+c$ (the rows of $\mathbf{B}$ are appended to the rows of $\mathbf{A}$). An error is issued if the matrices are not conformable. The column names of $\mathbf{C}$ are obtained from $\mathbf{A}$. The row names are obtained from $\mathbf{A}$ and $\mathbf{B}$.

`matrix define` allows complicated matrix expressions. Parentheses may be used to control order of evaluation. The default order of precedence for the matrix operators is (from highest to lowest)

Matrix operator precedence

Operator	symbol
parentheses	()
transpose	´
negation	–
Kronecker product	#
division by scalar	/
multiplication	*
subtraction	–
addition	+
column join	,
row join	\

▷ Example

The following examples are artificial but informative:

```
. matrix A = (1,2\3,4)
. matrix B = (5,7\9,2)
. matrix C = A+B
. matrix list C
C[2,2]
      c1   c2
r1    6    9
r2    12   6
. matrix B = A-B
. matrix list B
B[2,2]
      c1   c2
r1    -4   -5
r2    -6    2
. matrix X = (1,1\2,5\8,0\4,5)
. matrix C = 3*X*A´*B
```

```
. matrix list C

C[4,2]
         c1     c2
r1     -162     -3
r2     -612    -24
r3     -528     24
r4     -744    -18

. matrix D = (X´*X - A´*A)/4

. matrix rownames D = dog cat        /* see [R] matrix rowname */

. matrix colnames D = bark meow      /* see [R] matrix rowname */

. matrix list D

symmetric D[2,2]
         bark    meow
dog     18.75
cat      4.25    7.75

. matrix rownames A = aa bb          /* see [R] matrix rowname */

. matrix colnames A = alpha beta     /* see [R] matrix rowname */

. matrix list A

A[2,2]
        alpha    beta
aa          1       2
bb          3       4

. matrix D=A#D

. matrix list D

D[4,4]
          alpha:   alpha:    beta:    beta:
           bark     meow     bark     meow
aa:dog    18.75     4.25     37.5      8.5
aa:cat     4.25     7.75      8.5     15.5
bb:dog    56.25    12.75       75       17
bb:cat    12.75    23.25       17       31

. matrix G=A,B\D

. matrix list G

G[6,4]
         alpha    beta      c1       c2
    aa       1       2      -4       -5
    bb       3       4      -6        2
aa:dog   18.75    4.25    37.5      8.5
aa:cat    4.25    7.75     8.5     15.5
bb:dog   56.25   12.75      75       17
bb:cat   12.75   23.25      17       31

. matrix Z = (B - A)´*(B + A´*-B)/4  /* complex expressions ok */

. matrix list Z

Z[2,2]
          c1      c2
alpha    -81    -1.5
 beta  -44.5     8.5
```

◁

❑ Technical Note

Programmers: Watch out for confusion when combining ´ meaning transpose with local macros, where ´ is one of the characters that enclose macro names: `` `mname´ ``. Stata will not become confused, but you might. Compare

```
. matrix `new1´ = `old´
. matrix `new2´ = `old´´
```

Note that matrix `new2´ contains matrix `old´, transposed. Stata will become confused if you type

```
. matrix `C´ = `A´\`B´
```

because the backslash in front of the `B´ makes the macro processor take the left quote literally. No substitution is ever made for `B´. Even worse, the macro processor assumes the backslash was meant for it and so removes the character! Pretend `A´ contained a, `B´ contained b, and `C´ contained c. After substitution, the line would read

```
. matrix c = a`B´
```

which is not at all what was intended. To make your meaning clear, put a space after the backslash:

```
. matrix `C´ = `A´\ `B´
```

which would then be expanded to read

```
. matrix c = a\ b
```

❑

Matrix functions

In addition to matrix operators, Stata has matrix functions. The matrix functions allow expressions to be passed as arguments. The following matrix functions are provided:

matrix **A**=I(*dim*) defines **A** as the *dim* × *dim* identity matrix where *dim* is a scalar expression and will be rounded to the nearest integer. matrix **A**=I(3) defines **A** as the 3 × 3 identity matrix.

matrix **A**=J(*r*,*c*,*z*) defines **A** as an *r* × *c* matrix containing elements *z*. *r*, *c*, and *z* are scalar expressions with *r* and *c* rounded to the nearest integer. matrix **A**=J(2,3,0) returns a 2 × 3 matrix containing 0 for each element.

matrix **L**=cholesky(*mexp*) performs Cholesky decomposition. An error is issued if the matrix expression *mexp* does not evaluate to a square, symmetric matrix. matrix **L**=cholesky(**A**) produces the lower-triangular (square root) matrix **L** such that $LL' = A$. Row and column names of **L** are obtained from **A**.

matrix **B**=syminv(*mexp*), for *mexp* evaluating to a square, symmetric, and positive definite matrix, returns the inverse. If *mexp* does not evaluate to a positive definite matrix, rows will be inverted until the diagonal terms are zero or negative; the rows and columns corresponding to these terms will be set to 0, producing a g2 inverse. Row names of **B** are obtained from the column names of *mexp* and column names of **B** are obtained from the row names of *mexp*.

matrix **B**=inv(*mexp*), for *mexp* evaluating to a square but not necessarily symmetric or positive definite matrix, returns the inverse. A singular matrix will result in an error. Row names of **B** are obtained from the column names of *mexp* and column names of **B** are obtained from the row names of *mexp*. syminv() should be used in preference to inv(), which is less accurate, whenever possible. (Also see [R] **matrix svd** for singular value decomposition.)

matrix **B**=sweep(*mexp*,*n*) applies the sweep operator to the *n*th row and column of the square matrix resulting from the matrix expression *mexp*. *n* is a scalar expression and will be rounded to the nearest integer. The names of **B** are obtained from *mexp* except that the *n*th row and column names are interchanged. For **A**: $n \times n$, $B = \text{sweep}(A, k)$ produces **B**: $n \times n$ defined as

$$B_{kk} = \frac{1}{A_{kk}}$$

$$B_{ik} = -\frac{A_{ik}}{A_{kk}}, \qquad i \neq k \qquad (kth\ column)$$

$$B_{kj} = \frac{A_{ij}}{A_{kk}}, \qquad j \neq k \qquad (jth\ row)$$

$$B_{ij} = A_{ij} - \frac{A_{ik}A_{kj}}{A_{kk}}, \qquad i \neq k, j \neq k$$

matrix B=corr(*mexp*), for *mexp* evaluating to a covariance matrix, stores the corresponding correlation matrix in **B**. Row and column names are obtained from *mexp*.

matrix B=diag(*mexp*), for *mexp* evaluating to a row or column vector ($1 \times c$ or $c \times 1$), creates **B**: $c \times c$ with diagonal elements from *mexp* and off-diagonal elements 0. Row and column names are obtained from the column names of *mexp* if *mexp* is a row vector or the row names if *mexp* is a column vector.

matrix B=vecdiag(*mexp*), for *mexp* evaluating to a square $c \times c$ matrix, creates **B**: $1 \times c$ containing the diagonal elements from *mexp*. **vecdiag()** is the opposite of **diag()**. The row name is set to **r1**. The column names are obtained from the column names of *mexp*.

nullmat(B) may only be used with the row-join (,) and column-join (\) operators and informs Stata that **B** might not exist. If **B** does not exist then the row-join or column-join operator simply returns the other matrix operator argument. An example of the use of **nullmat()** is given in [U] **17.8.1 Matrix functions returning matrices**.

matrix B=get(*systemname*) returns in **B** a copy of the Stata internal matrix *systemname*; see [R] **matrix get**. You can obtain the coefficient vector and variance–covariance matrix after an estimation command either with **matrix get** or by reference to **e(b)** and **e(V)**.

▷ Example

The examples are, once again, artificial but informative.

```
. matrix myid = I(3)
. matrix list myid
symmetric myid[3,3]
     c1   c2   c3
r1    1
r2    0    1
r3    0    0    1
. matrix new = J(2,3,0)
. matrix list new
new[2,3]
     c1   c2   c3
r1    0    0    0
r2    0    0    0
. matrix A = (1,2\2,5)
. matrix Ainv = syminv(A)
. matrix list Ainv
symmetric Ainv[2,2]
     r1   r2
c1    5
c2   -2    1
```

```
. matrix L = cholesky(4*I(2) + A´*A)

. matrix list L

L[2,2]
           c1          c2
c1          3           0
c2          4   4.1231056

. matrix B = (1,5,9\2,1,7\3,5,1)

. matrix Binv = inv(B)

. matrix list Binv

Binv[3,3]
            r1          r2          r3
c1  -.27419355   .32258065   .20967742
c2   .15322581  -.20967742   .08870968
c3   .05645161   .08064516  -.07258065

. matrix C = sweep(B,1)

. matrix list C

C[3,3]
     r1   c2   c3
c1    1    5    9
r2   -2   -9  -11
r3   -3  -10  -26

. matrix C = sweep(C,1)

. matrix list C

C[3,3]
     c1  c2  c3
r1    1   5   9
r2    2   1   7
r3    3   5   1

. matrix Cov = (36.6598,-3596.48\-3596.48,604030)

. matrix R = corr(Cov)

. matrix list R

symmetric R[2,2]
           c1          c2
r1          1
r2  -.7642815            1

. matrix d = (1,2,3)

. matrix D = diag(d)

. matrix list D

symmetric D[3,3]
     c1  c2  c3
c1    1
c2    0   2
c3    0   0   3

. matrix e = vecdiag(D)

. matrix list e

e[1,3]
     c1  c2  c3
r1    1   2   3

. * matrix function arguments can be other matrix functions and expressions
. matrix F = diag(inv(B) * vecdiag(diag(d) + 4*sweep(B+J(3,3,10),2)´*I(3))´)
```

```
. matrix list F
symmetric F[3,3]
            c1          c2          c3
c1  -3.2170088
c2          0   -7.686217
c3          0           0    2.3548387
```

◁

Matrix functions returning scalars

In addition to the above functions used with `matrix define`, functions that can be described as matrix functions returning matrices, there are matrix functions that return mathematical scalars. The list of functions that follow should be viewed as a continuation of [U] **16.3 Functions**. If the functions listed below are used in a scalar context (for example used with `display` or `generate`) then **A**, **B**, ..., below stand for matrix names (possibly as a string literal or string variable name—details later). If the functions below are used in a matrix context (in `matrix define` for instance) then **A**, **B**, ..., may also stand for matrix expressions.

`rowsof(A)` and `colsof(A)` return the number of rows or columns of **A**.

`rownumb(A, string)` and `colnumb(A, string)` return the row or column number associated with the name specified by *string*. For instance, `rownumb(MYMAT,"price")` returns the row number (say, 3) in `MYMAT` that has name `price` (subname `price` and equation name blank). `colnumb(MYMAT,"out2:price")` returns the column number associated with name `out2:price` (subname `price` and equation name `out2`). If row or column name is not found, missing is returned.

`rownumb()` and `colnumb()` can also return the first row or column number associated with an equation name. For example, `colnumb(MYMAT,"out2:")` returns the first column number in `MYMAT` that has equation name `out2`. Missing is returned if the equation name `out2` is not found.

`trace(A)` returns the sum of the diagonal elements of square matrix **A**. If **A** is not square, missing is returned.

`det(A)` returns the determinant of square matrix **A**. The determinant is the volume of the $p-1$ dimensional manifold described by the matrix in p-dimensional space. If **A** is not square, missing is returned.

`diag0cnt(A)` returns the number of zeros on the diagonal of the square matrix **A**. If **A** is not square, missing is returned.

`mreldif(A,B)` returns the relative difference of matrix **A** and **B**. If **A** and **B** do not have the same dimensions, missing is returned. The matrix relative difference is defined as:

$$\max_{i,j}\left(\frac{|\mathbf{A}[i,j]-\mathbf{B}[i,j]|}{|\mathbf{B}[i,j]|+1}\right)$$

`el(A,i,j)` and `A[i,j]` return the i,j element of **A**. In most cases, either construct may be used; `el(MYMAT,2,3)` and `MYMAT[2,3]` are equivalent although `MYMAT[2,3]` is more readable. In the case of the second construct, however, **A** must be a matrix name—it cannot be a string literal or string variable. The first construct allows **A** to be a matrix name, string literal, or string variable. For instance, assume `mymat` (as opposed to `MYMAT`) is a string variable in the data containing matrix names. `mymat[2,3]` refers to the $(2,3)$ element of the matrix named `mymat`, a matrix which probably does not exist and so produces an error. `el(mymat,2,3)` refers to the data variable mymat; the contents of that variable will be taken to obtain the matrix name and el() will then return the $(2, 3)$ element of that matrix. If that matrix does not exist, Stata will not issue an error; because you referred to it indirectly, the el() function will return missing.

In either construct, i and j may be any expression (an *exp*) evaluating to a real. MYMAT[2,3+1] returns the $(2, 4)$ element. In programs that loop, you might refer to MYMAT[`i´,`j´+1].

In a matrix context (like matrix define), the first argument of el() may be a matrix expression. For instance matrix A = $B*$el$(B-C,1,1)$ is allowed but display el$(B-C,1,1)$ would be an error since display is in a scalar context.

The matrix functions returning scalars defined above can be used in any context that allows an expression—what is abbreviated *exp* in the syntax diagrams throughout this manual. For instance, trace() returns the (scalar) trace of a matrix. Say you have a matrix called MYX. You could type

```
. generate tr = trace(MYX)
```

although this would be a silly thing to do. It would be silly because it would force Stata to evaluate the trace of the matrix many times, once for each observation in the data, and it would then store that same result over and over again in the new data variable tr. But you could do it because, if you examine the syntax diagram for generate (see [R] **generate**), generate allows an *exp*.

If you just wanted to see the trace of MYX, you could type

```
. display trace(MYX)
```

because the syntax diagram for display also allows an *exp*; see [R] **display**. More usefully, you could do either of the following:

```
. local tr = trace(MYX)
. scalar tr = trace(MYX)
```

This is more useful because it will evaluate the trace only once and then store the result. In the first case, the result will be stored in a local macro (see [R] **macro**); in the second, it will be stored in a Stata scalar (see [R] **scalar**).

▷ Example

Storing the number as a scalar is better for two reasons: it is more accurate (scalars are stored in double precision) and it is faster (macros are stored as printable characters and this conversion is a time-consuming operation). Not too much should be made of the accuracy issue; macros are stored with at least 13 digits, but it can make a difference in some cases.

In any case, let us demonstrate that both methods work with the simple trace function:

```
. matrix A = (1,6\8,4)
. local tr = trace(A)
. display `tr´
5
. scalar sctr = trace(A)
. scalar list sctr
      sctr =          5
```

◁

❑ Technical Note

The use of a matrix function returning scalar with **generate** does not have to be silly because, instead of specifying a matrix name, you may specify a string variable in the data. If you do, in each observation the contents of the string variable will be taken as a matrix name and the function applied to that matrix for that observation. If there is no such matrix, missing will be returned. Thus, if your data contained

```
. list

        matname
    1.       X1
    2.       X2
    3.        Z
```

You could type

```
. generate tr = trace(matname)
(1 missing value generated)

. list

        matname        tr
    1.       X1         5
    2.       X2         .
    3.        Z        16
```

Evidently, we have no matrix called **X2** stored. All the matrix functions returning scalars allow you to specify either a matrix name directly or a string variable that indirectly specifies the matrix name. When you indirectly specify the matrix and the matrix does not exist—as happened above—the function evaluates to missing. When you directly specify the matrix and it does not exist, you get an error:

```
. display trace(X2)
X2 not found
r(111);
```

This is true not only for **trace()**, but for every matrix function that returns a scalar described above.

❑

Subscripting and element-by-element definition

matrix B=A$[r_1,r_2]$, for range expressions r_1 and r_2 (defined below), extracts a submatrix from **A** and stores it in **B**. Row and column names of **B** are obtained from the extracted rows and columns of **A**. In what follows, assume **A** is $a \times b$.

A range expression can be a literal number. **matrix B=A[1,2]** would return a 1×1 matrix containing $A_{1,2}$.

A range expression can be a number followed by two periods followed by another number, meaning the rows or columns from the first number to the second. **matrix B=A[2..4,1..5]** would return a 3×5 matrix containing the second through fourth rows and the first through fifth columns of **A**.

A range expression can be a number followed by three periods, meaning all the remaining rows or columns from that number. **matrix B=A[3,4...]** would return a $1 \times b - 3$ matrix (row vector) containing the fourth through last elements of the third row of **A**.

A range expression can be a quoted string, in which case it refers to the row or column with the specified name. matrix **B**=**A**["price","mpg"] returns a 1×1 matrix containing the element whose row name is price and column name mpg, which would be the same as matrix **B**=**A**[2,3] if the second row were named price and the third column mpg. matrix **B**=**A**["price",1...] would return the $1 \times b$ vector corresponding to the row named price. In either case, if there is no matrix row or column with the specified name, an error is issued and the return code set to 111. If the row and/or column names include both an equation name and a subname, the fully qualified name must be specified, as in matrix **B**=**A**["eq1:price",1...].

A range expression can be a quoted string containing only an equation name, in which case it refers to all rows or columns with the specified equation name. matrix **B**=**A**["eq1:","eq1:"] would return the submatrix of rows and columns that have equation names eq1.

A range expression containing a quoted string referring to an element (not to an entire equation) can be combined with the .. and ... syntaxes above: matrix **B**=**A**["price"...,"price"...] would define **B** as the submatrix of **A** beginning with the rows and columns corresponding to price. matrix **B**=**A**["price".."mpg","price".."mpg"] would define **B** as the submatrix of **A** starting at rows and columns corresponding to price and continuing through the rows and columns corresponding to mpg.

A range expression can be mixed. matrix **B**=**A**[1.."price",2] defines **B** as the column vector extracted from the second column of **A** containing the first element through the element corresponding to price.

Scalar expressions may be used in place of literal numbers. The resulting number will be rounded to the nearest integer. Subscripting with scalar expressions may be used in any expression context (such as generate, replace, etc.). Subscripting with row and column names may only be used in a matrix expression context. This is really not a constraint; see the rownumb() and colnumb() functions discussed previously in the section titled *Matrix functions returning scalars*.

matrix **A**[*r,c*]=*exp* changes the *r,c* element of **A** to contain the result of the evaluated scalar expression, as defined in [U] **16 Functions and expressions** and as further defined in *Matrix functions returning scalars*. *r* and *c* may be scalar expressions and will be rounded to the nearest integer. The matrix **A** must already exist; the matrix function J() can be used to achieve this.

matrix **A**[*r,c*]=*mexp* places the matrix resulting from the *mexp* matrix expression into the already existing matrix **A** with the upper left corner of the *mexp* matrix located at the *r,c* element of **A**. If there is not enough room to place the *mexp* matrix at that location a conformability error will be issued and the return code set to 503. *r* and *c* may be scalar expressions and will be rounded to the nearest integer.

▷ Example

Continuing with our artificial but informative examples:

```
. matrix A = (1,2,3,4\5,6,7,8\9,10,11,12\13,14,15,16)
. matrix rownames A = mercury venus earth mars
. matrix colnames A = poor average good exc
. matrix list A

A[4,4]
            poor   average     good     exc
mercury        1         2        3       4
  venus        5         6        7       8
  earth        9        10       11      12
   mars       13        14       15      16
. matrix b = A[1,2..3]
```

```
. matrix list b
b[1,2]
          average      good
mercury       2         3
. matrix b = A[2...,1..3]
. matrix list b
b[3,3]
          poor   average    good
venus       5       6         7
earth       9      10        11
 mars      13      14        15
. matrix b = A["venus".."earth","average"...]
. matrix list b
b[2,3]
        average     good      exc
venus       6        7         8
earth      10       11        12
. matrix b = A["mars",2...]
. matrix list b
b[1,3]
        average     good      exc
mars       14       15        16
. matrix b = A[sqrt(9)+1..substr("xmars",2,4),2.8..2*2]  /* strange but valid */
. mat list b
b[1,2]
      good    exc
mars   15      16
. matrix rownames A = eq1:alpha eq1:beta eq2:alpha eq2:beta
. matrix colnames A = eq1:one eq1:two eq2:one eq2:two
. matrix list A
A[4,4]
            eq1:   eq1:   eq2:   eq2:
            one    two    one    two
eq1:alpha    1      2      3      4
 eq1:beta    5      6      7      8
eq2:alpha    9     10     11     12
 eq2:beta   13     14     15     16
. matrix b = A["eq1:","eq2:"]
. matrix list b
b[2,2]
            eq2:   eq2:
            one    two
eq1:alpha    3      4
 eq1:beta    7      8
. matrix A[3,2] = sqrt(9)
. matrix list A
A[4,4]
            eq1:   eq1:   eq2:   eq2:
            one    two    one    two
eq1:alpha    1      2      3      4
 eq1:beta    5      6      7      8
eq2:alpha    9      3     11     12
 eq2:beta   13     14     15     16
. matrix X = (-3,0\-1,-6)
```

```
. matrix A[1,3] = X
. matrix list A

A[4,4]
            eq1:   eq1:   eq2:   eq2:
            one    two    one    two
eq1:alpha     1      2     -3      0
 eq1:beta     5      6     -1     -6
eq2:alpha     9      3     11     12
 eq2:beta    13     14     15     16
```

◁

❑ Technical Note

matrix $\mathbf{A}[i,j]$=*exp* can be used to implement matrix formulas that perhaps Stata does not have built in. Let's pretend Stata could not multiply matrices. We could still multiply matrices, and after some work, we could do so conveniently. Given two matrices $\mathbf{A}$: $a \times b$ and $\mathbf{B}$: $b \times c$, the (i,j) element of $\mathbf{C} = \mathbf{AB}$, $\mathbf{C}$: $a \times c$, is defined as

$$C_{ij} = \sum_{k=1}^{b} A_{ik}B_{kj}$$

Here is a Stata program to make that calculation:

```
program define matmult                    /* arguments A B C, creates C=A*B     */
        version 6.0
        args A B C                        /* unload arguments into better names */
        if colsof(`A')~=rowsof(`B') {     /* check conformability               */
                error 503
        }
        local a = rowsof(`A')             /* obtain dimensioning information     */
        local b = colsof(`A')             /*     see Matrix functions returning  */
        local c = colsof(`B')             /*     scalars above                   */
        matrix `C' = J(`a',`c',0)         /* create result containing 0s         */
        local i=1
        while `i'<=`a' {
                local j=1
                while `j'<=`c' {
                        local k=1
                        while `k'<=`b' {
                                matrix `C'[`i',`j'] = `C'[`i',`j'] + /*
                                */ `A'[`i',`k']*`B'[`k',`j']
                                local k=`k'+1
                        }
                        local j=`j'+1
                }
                local i=`i'+1
        }
end
```

Now, if in some other program, we needed to multiply matrix **XXI** by **Xy** to form result **beta**, we could type **matmult XXI Xy beta** and never use Stata's built-in method for multiplying matrices (**matrix beta=XXI*Xy**). If we typed the program **matmult** into a file named **matmult.ado**, we would not even have to bother to load **matmult** before using it—it would be loaded automatically; see [U] **20 Ado-files**.

❑

Name conflicts in expressions (name spaces)

See [R] **matrix** for a description of name spaces. A matrix might have the same name as a variable in the data and, if it does, Stata might appear confused when evaluating an expression (an *exp*). When the names conflict, Stata uses the rule that it always takes the data-variable interpretation. You can override this.

First, when working interactively, you can avoid the problem by simply naming your matrices differently from your variables.

Second, when writing programs, you can avoid name conflicts by obtaining names for matrices from `tempname`; see [R] **macro**.

Third, whether working interactively or writing programs, when using names that might conflict, you can use the `matrix()` pseudo-function to force Stata to take the matrix name interpretation.

`matrix(`*name*`)` says that *name* is to be interpreted as a matrix name. For instance, consider the statement `local new=trace(xx)`. This might work and it might not. If `xx` is a matrix and there is no variable named `xx` in your data, it will work. If there is also a numeric variable named `xx` in your data, it will not. Typing the statement will produce a type-mismatch error—Stata assumes when you type `xx` you are referring to the data variable `xx` because there is a data variable `xx`. Typing `local new=trace(matrix(xx))` will produce the desired result in that case. When writing programs using matrix names not obtained from `tempname`, you are strongly advised to state explicitly that all matrix names are matrix names by using the `matrix()` function.

The only exception to this recommendation has to do with the construct $A[i, j]$. The two subscripts key Stata that A must be a matrix name and not an attempt to subscript a variable and so `matrix()` is not needed. This exception applies only to $A[i,j]$; it does not apply to `el(`A,i,j`)` which would be more safely written `el(matrix(`A`),`i,j`)`.

❑ Technical Note

The `matrix()` and `scalar()` pseudo-functions (see [R] **scalar**) are really the same function, but you do not need to understand this fine point to program Stata successfully. Understanding might, however, lead to producing more readable code. The formal definition is this:

`scalar(`*exp*`)` (and therefore `matrix(`*exp*`)`) evaluates *exp*, but restricts Stata to interpreting all names in *exp* as scalar or matrix names. Recall that scalars and matrices share the same name space.

Ergo, since `scalar()` and `matrix()` are the same function, you can type `trace(matrix(xx))` or `trace(scalar(xx))`: both do the same thing even though the second looks wrong. Since `scalar()` and `matrix()` allow an *exp*, you could also type `scalar(trace(xx))` and achieve the same result. `scalar()` evaluates the *exp* inside the parentheses: it merely restricts how names are interpreted, so now `trace(xx)` clearly means the trace of the matrix named `xx`.

How can you make your code more readable? Pretend you wanted to calculate the trace plus the determinant of matrix `xx` and store it in the Stata scalar named `tpd` (no, there is no reason you would ever want to make such a silly calculation). You are writing a program and so want to protect yourself from `xx` also existing in the data. One solution would be

```
scalar tpd = trace(matrix(xx)) + det(matrix(xx))
```

Knowing the full interpretation rule, however, you realize you can shorten this to

```
scalar tpd = matrix(trace(xx) + det(xx))
```

and then, to make it more readable, you substitute `scalar()` for `matrix()`:

```
scalar tpd = scalar(trace(xx) + det(xx))
```

❑

Macro extended functions

The following macro extended functions (see [R] **macro**) are also defined:

rownames **A** and colnames **A** return the list of all the row or column subnames (with time-series operators if applicable) of **A**, separated by single blanks. Note that the equation names, even if present, are not included.

roweq **A** and coleq **A** return the list of all row equation names or column equation names of **A**, separated by single blanks, and with each name appearing however many times it appears in the matrix.

rowfullnames **A** and colfullnames **A** return the list of all the row or column names including equation names of **A**, separated by single blanks.

▷ Example

These functions are provided as macro functions and standard expression functions because Stata's expression evaluator is limited to working with strings of no more than 80 characters in length, something not true of Stata's macro parser. A matrix with many rows or columns can produce an exceedingly long list of names.

In sophisticated programming situations, you sometimes want to process the matrices by row and column names rather than by row and column number. For instance, assume you are programming and have two matrices, **xx** and **yy**. You know they contain the same column names but they might be in a different order. You want to reorganize **yy** to be in the same order as **xx**. The following code fragment will create `newyy´ (a matrix name obtained from tempname) containing **yy** in the same order as **xx**:

```
tempname newyy newcol
local names : colfullnames(xx)
local name : word 1 of `names´
local i=1
while "`name´"~="" {
        local j = colnumb(yy,"`name´")
        if `j´==. {
                display in red "column for `name´ not found"
                exit 111
        }
        matrix `newcol´ = yy[1...,`j´]
        matrix `newyy´ = nullmat(`newyy´),`newcol´
        local i=`i´+1
        local name : word `i´ of `names´
}
```

◁

References

Weesie, J. 1997. dm49: Some new matrix commands. *Stata Technical Bulletin* 39: 17–20. Reprinted in *Stata Technical Bulletin Reprints*, vol. 7, pp. 43–48.

Also See

Complementary:	[R] **macro**, [R] **matrix get**, [R] **matrix utility**, [R] **scalar**
Background:	[U] **16.3 Functions**,
	[U] **17 Matrix expressions**,
	[R] **matrix**

Title

matrix get — Access system matrices

Syntax

<u>matrix</u> [<u>def</u>ine] *matname* = get(*internal_Stata_matrix_name*)

where *internal_Stata_matrix_name* is

_b	coefficients after any estimation command
VCE	covariance matrix of estimators after any estimation command
Rr	constraint matrix after `test`
Cns	constraint matrix after any estimation command
Ld	factor loadings after `factor`
Ev	eigenvalues after `factor`
Psi	uniquenesses after `factor`
Co	correlation matrix after `factor`
SD	standard deviations after `factor`
Mean	means after `factor`

Description

The get() matrix function obtains a copy of an internal Stata system matrix. Some system matrices can also be obtained more easily by directly referring to the returned result after a command. In particular the coefficient vector can be referred to as e(b) and the variance–covariance matrix of estimators as e(V) after an estimation command.

Remarks

get() obtains copies of matrices containing coefficients and the covariance matrix of the estimators after estimation commands (such as regress, probit, etc.) and obtains copies of matrices left behind by other Stata commands. The other side of get() is estimates post, which allows ado-file estimation commands to post results to Stata's internal areas; see [R] **estimates**.

▷ Example

After any model estimation command the coefficients are available in _b and the variance–covariance matrix of the estimators in VCE.

```
. regress price weight mpg
(output omitted)
```

In this case we can directly use e(b) and e(V) to obtain the matrices.

```
. matrix list e(b)
e(b)[1,3]
          weight        mpg      _cons
y1     1.7465592  -49.512221  1946.0687
```

```
. matrix list e(V)

symmetric e(V)[3,3]
               weight         mpg        _cons
weight    .41133468
   mpg    44.601659      7422.863
 _cons  -2191.9032   -292759.82     12938766
```

We can also use the **matrix get** command to obtain these matrices.

```
. matrix b = get(_b)

. matrix V = get(VCE)

. matrix list b

b[1,3]
          weight         mpg        _cons
y1     1.7465592   -49.512221    1946.0687

. matrix list V

symmetric V[3,3]
               weight         mpg        _cons
weight    .41133468
   mpg    44.601659      7422.863
 _cons  -2191.9032   -292759.82     12938766
```

Note that the columns of **b** and both dimensions of **V** are properly labeled.

◁

▷ Example

After **test**, the restriction matrix is available in **Rr**. Having just estimated a regression of **price** on **weight** and **mpg**, we will run a test and then get the restriction matrix:

```
. test weight=1, notest

 ( 1)   weight = 1.0

. test mpg=40, accum

 ( 1)   weight = 1.0
 ( 2)   mpg = 40.0

        F(  2,    71) =    6.29
              Prob > F =   0.0030

. matrix rxtr=get(Rr)

. matrix list rxtr

rxtr[2,4]
      c1   c2   c3   c4
r1     1    0    0    1
r2     0    1    0   40
```

◁

Also See

Background: [U] **16.5 Accessing coefficients and standard errors,**
                    [U] **17 Matrix expressions,**
                    [R] **matrix**

Title

matrix mkmat — Convert variables to matrix and vice versa

Syntax

mkmat *varlist* $\big[$if *exp*$\big]$ $\big[$in *range*$\big]$ $\big[$, ma̲trix(*matname*) $\big]$

svmat $\big[$*type*$\big]$ **A** $\big[$, n̲ames({col|eqcol|matcol|*string*}) $\big]$

matname **A** *namelist* $\big[$, r̲ows(*range*) c̲olumns(*range*) e̲xplicit $\big]$

where **A** is the name of an existing matrix, *type* is a storage type for the new variables, and *namelist* is one of (1) a *varlist*, i.e., names of existing variables possibly abbreviated; (2) _cons and the names of existing variables possibly abbreviated; (3) arbitrary names when the explicit option is specified.

Description

mkmat stores the variables listed in *varlist* in column vectors of the same name; that is, $N \times 1$ matrices where $N =$ _N, the number of observations in the dataset. Or, optionally, they can be stored as a $N \times k$ matrix, where k is the number of variables in *varlist*.

svmat takes a matrix and stores its columns as new variables. It is the reverse of the mkmat command which creates a matrix from existing variables.

matname renames the rows and columns of a matrix. matname differs from the matrix rownames and matrix colnames commands in that matname expands varlist abbreviations and also allows a restricted range for the rows or columns. See [R] **matrix rowname**.

Options

matrix() requests that the vectors be combined in a matrix, instead of creating the column vectors.

names({col|eqcol|matcol|*string*}) specifies how the new variables are to be named.
  names(col) uses the column names of the matrix to name the variables.
  names(eqcol) uses the equation names prefixed to the column names.
  names(matcol) uses the matrix name prefixed to the column names.
  names(*string*) names the variables *string*1, *string*2, ..., *string*n, where *string* is a user-specified *string* and *n* is the number of columns of the matrix.
  If names() is not specified, the variables are named **A**1, **A**2, ..., **A**n, where **A** is the name of the matrix. If necessary, names will be truncated to 8 characters; if these names are not unique, an error message will be returned.

rows(*range*) and columns(*range*) specify the rows and columns of the matrix to rename. The number of rows or columns specified must be equal to the number of names in *namelist*. If both rows() and columns() are given, then the specified rows are named *namelist* and the specified columns are also named *namelist*. The range must be given in one of the following forms:

```
rows(.)      renames all the rows;
rows(2..8)   renames rows 2 through 8;
rows(3)      renames only row 3;
rows(4...)   renames row 4 to the last row.
```

If neither `rows()` nor `columns()` is given, then `rows(.) columns(.)` is the default. That is, the matrix must be square, and both the rows and the columns are named *namelist*.

`explicit` suppresses the expansion of varlist abbreviations and omits the verification that the names are those of existing variables. That is, the names in *namelist* are used explicitly and can be any valid row or column names.

Remarks

mkmat

Although cross-products of variables can be loaded into a matrix using the `matrix accum` command, in some instances, programmers may find it more convenient to work with the variables in their datasets as vectors instead of as cross products. `mkmat` allows the user a simple way to load specific variables into matrices in Stata's memory.

▷ Example

`mkmat` uses the variable name to name the single column in the vector. This feature guarantees that the variable name will be carried along in any additional matrix calculations. This feature is also useful when vectors are combined in a general matrix.

```
. describe
Contains data from test.dta
  obs:           10
  vars:           3                        19 Jul 1998 08:52
  size:         160 (99.9% of memory free)
-------------------------------------------------------------------
  1. x         float  %9.0g
  2. y         float  %9.0g
  3. z         float  %9.0g
-------------------------------------------------------------------
Sorted by:
. list

             x          y          z
  1.         1         10          2
  2.         2          9          4
  3.         3          8          3
  4.         4          7          5
  5.         5          6          7
  6.         6          5          6
  7.         7          4          8
  8.         8          3         10
  9.         9          2          1
 10.        10          1          9
. mkmat x y z, matrix(xyzmat)
. matrix dir
        xyzmat[10,3]
```

```
. matrix list xyzmat

xyzmat[10,3]
        x    y    z
  r1    1   10    2
  r2    2    9    4
  r3    3    8    3
  r4    4    7    5
  r5    5    6    7
  r6    6    5    6
  r7    7    4    8
  r8    8    3   10
  r9    9    2    1
 r10   10    1    9
```

If any of the variables has missing values, you will receive an error message and no matrices will be created.

```
. matrix drop _all

. replace y = . in 5
(1 real change made, 1 to missing)

. mkmat x y z
matrix y would have missing values
r(504);

. matrix dir

.
```

This problem can be taken care of by restricting the matrix to nonmissing values.

◁

❏ Technical Note

mkmat provides a useful addition to Stata's matrix commands, but it will work only with small dataset sizes.

Stata limits matrices to being no more than matsize × matsize which, by default, means 40 × 40, and, even with Intercooled Stata, this can be increased to a maximum of 800 × 800. Such limits appear to contradict Stata's claims of being able to process large datasets. By limiting Stata's matrix capabilities to matsize × matsize, has not Stata's matrix language itself been limited to datasets no larger than matsize? It would certainly appear so; in the simple matrix calculation for regression coefficients $(\mathbf{X}'\mathbf{X})^{-1}\mathbf{X}'\mathbf{y}$, $\mathbf{X}$ is an $n \times k$ matrix (n being the number of observations and k the number of variables) and, given the matsize constraint, n must certainly be less than 800.

Our answer is as follows: Yes, $\mathbf{X}$ is limited in the way stated but note that $\mathbf{X}'\mathbf{X}$ is a mere $k \times k$ matrix and, similarly, $\mathbf{X}'\mathbf{y}$ only $k \times 1$. Both these matrices are well within Stata's matrix-handling capabilities and Stata's matrix accum command (see [R] **matrix accum**) can directly create both of them.

Moreover, even if Stata could hold the $n \times k$ matrix $\mathbf{X}$, it would still be more efficient to use matrix accum to form $\mathbf{X}'\mathbf{X}$. $\mathbf{X}'\mathbf{X}$, interpreted literally, says to load a copy of the data, transpose it, load a second copy of the data, and then form the matrix product. Thus, two copies of the data occupy memory in addition to the original copy Stata already had available (and from which matrix accum could directly form the result with no additional memory use). For small n, the inefficiency is not important but, for large n, the inefficiency could make the calculation infeasible. For instance, with $n = 12{,}000$ and $k = 6$, the additional memory use is 1,125K bytes.

More generally, matrices in statistical applications tend to have dimension $k \times k$, $n \times k$, and $n \times n$, with k small and n large. Terms dealing with the data are of the generic form $\mathbf{X}'_{k_1 \times n} \mathbf{W}_{n \times n} \mathbf{Z}_{n \times k_2}$. ($\mathbf{X}'\mathbf{X}$ fits the generic form with $\mathbf{X} = \mathbf{X}$, $\mathbf{W} = \mathbf{I}$, and $\mathbf{Z} = \mathbf{X}$.) Matrix programming languages are not capable of dealing with the deceivingly simple calculation $\mathbf{X}'\mathbf{W}\mathbf{Z}$ because of the staggering size of the $\mathbf{W}$ matrix. For $n = 12{,}000$, storing $\mathbf{W}$ requires a little more than a gigabyte of memory. In statistical formulas, however, $\mathbf{W}$ is given by formula and, in fact, never needs to be stored in its entirety. Exploitation of this fact is all that is needed to resurrect the use of a matrix programming language in statistical applications. Matrix programming languages may be inefficient because of copious memory use, but in statistical applications, the inefficiency is minor for matrices of size $k \times k$ or smaller. Our design of the various `matrix accum` commands allow calculating terms of the form $\mathbf{X}'\mathbf{W}\mathbf{Z}$ and this one feature, we have found, is all that is necessary to allow efficient and robust use of matrix languages.

Programs for creating data matrices such as that offered by `mkmat` are useful for pedagogical purposes and, in addition, for a specific application where Stata's matsize constraint is not binding; it seems so natural. On the other hand, it is important that general tools not be implemented by forming data matrices because such tools will be drastically limited in terms of the dataset size. Coding the problem in terms of the various `matrix accum` commands (see [R] **matrix accum**) is admittedly more tedious but, by abolishing data matrices from your programs, you will produce tools suitable for use on large datasets.

❑

svmat

▷ Example

Let us get the vector of coefficients from a regression and use `svmat` to save the vector as a new variable, save the dataset, load the dataset back into memory, use `mkmat` to create a vector from the variable, and finally, use `matname` to rename the columns of the row vector.

```
. quietly regress mpg weight gratio foreign
. matrix b = e(b)
. matrix list b

b[1,4]
        weight      gratio     foreign       _cons
y1   -.00613903   1.4571134  -2.2216815   36.101353
. matrix c = b´
. svmat double c, name(bvector)
. list bvector1 in 1/5

        bvector1
  1.  -.00613903
  2.   1.4571134
  3.  -2.2216815
  4.   36.101353
  5.           .
. save example
file example.dta saved
. use example
. mkmat bvector1 if bvector1~=.
```

```
. matrix list bvector1
bvector1[4,1]
        bvector1
r1   -.00613903
r2    1.4571134
r3   -2.2216815
r4    36.101353
. matrix d = bvector1´
. matname d wei gr for _cons, c(.)
. matrix list d
d[1,4]
                weight       gratio      foreign       _cons
bvector1    -.00613903    1.4571134   -2.2216815    36.101353
```

◁

Methods and Formulas

mkmat, svmat, and matname are implemented as ado-files.

Acknowledgment

mkmat was written by Ken Heinecke of CIMCO, Madison, Wisconsin.

References

Gould, W. W. 1994. ip6.1: Data and matrices. *Stata Technical Bulletin* 20: 10. Reprinted in *Stata Technical Bulletin Reprints*, vol. 4, pp. 70–71.

Heinecke, K. 1994. ip6: Storing variables in vectors and matrices. *Stata Technical Bulletin* 20: 8–9. Reprinted in *Stata Technical Bulletin Reprints*, vol. 4, pp. 68–70.

Sribney, W. M. 1995. ip6.2: Storing matrices as variables. *Stata Technical Bulletin* 24: 9–10. Reprinted in *Stata Technical Bulletin Reprints*, vol. 4, pp. 71–73.

Also See

Related:	[R] **matrix accum**
Background:	[U] **17 Matrix expressions**,
	[R] **matrix**

Title

matrix rowname — Name rows and columns

Syntax

matrix rownames **A** = *name(s)*

matrix colnames **A** = *name(s)*

matrix roweq **A** = *name(s)*

matrix coleq **A** = *name(s)*

Description

matrix **rownames** and **colnames** reset the row and column names of an already existing matrix. Row and column names may have three parts: *equation_name:ts_operator.subname*. Here, *name* can be: *subname*, *ts_operator.subname*, *equation_name:*, *equation_name:subname*, or *equation_name:ts_operator.subname*.

matrix **roweq** and **coleq** also reset the row and column names of an already existing matrix but, if a simple name is specified (a name without a colon), it is interpreted as an equation name.

In either case, the part of the name not specified is left unchanged.

Remarks

See [U] **17.2 Row and column names** for a description of the row and column names bordering a matrix.

▷ Example

In general, the names bordering matrices are set correctly by Stata due to the tracking of the matrix algebra and you will not need to reset them. Nevertheless, imagine you have formed $X'X$ in the matrix named **XX** and that it corresponds to the underlying variables price, weight, and mpg:

```
. matrix list XX
symmetric XX[3,3]
           c1          c2          c3
r1   3.448e+09
r2   1.468e+09   7.188e+08
r3     9132716     4493720       36008
```

You did not form this matrix with matrix **accum** because, had you done so, the rows and columns would already be correctly named. However you formed it, you now want to reset the names:

```
. matrix rownames XX = price weight mpg

. matrix colnames XX = price weight mpg

. matrix list XX
symmetric XX[3,3]
             price      weight         mpg
 price   3.448e+09
weight   1.468e+09   7.188e+08
   mpg     9132716     4493720       36008
```

                                                                                                ◁

▷ Example

We now demonstrate setting the equation names, time-series operator, and subnames.

```
. matrix list AA
symmetric AA[4,4]
            c1          c2          c3          c4
r1     .2967663
r2    .03682017    .57644416
r3   -.87052852    .32713601    20.274957
r4    -1.572579   -.63830843   -12.150097    26.099582

. matrix rownames AA = length L3D2.length mpg L.mpg

. matrix colnames AA = length L3D2.length mpg L.mpg

. matrix roweq AA = eq1 eq1 eq2 eq2

. matrix coleq AA = eq1 eq1 eq2 eq2

. matrix list AA
symmetric AA[4,4]
                         eq1:          eq1:         eq2:        eq2:
                                      L3D2.                       L.
                       length        length          mpg         mpg
   eq1:length        .2967663
eq1:L3D2.length      .03682017    .57644416
       eq2:mpg      -.87052852    .32713601    20.274957
     eq2:L.mpg       -1.572579   -.63830843   -12.150097   26.099582
```

                                                                                                ◁

❑ Technical Note

matrix rownames and colnames behave in some situations in ways that may surprise you. Among the surprises are

1. If your list of names includes no colons—does not mention the equation names—whatever equation names are in place are left in place; they are not changed.

2. If your list of names has every name ending in a colon—so that it mentions only the equation names and not the subnames—whatever subnames are in place are left in place; they are not changed.

3. If your list of names has fewer names than are required to label all the rows or columns, the last name in the list is replicated. (If you specify too many names, you will get the conformability error message and no names are changed.)

These surprises have their uses but, if you make a mistake, the result really may surprise you. For instance, rule 3, by itself, is just odd. Combined with rule 2, however, rule 3 allows you to set all the equation names in a matrix easily. If you type 'matrix rownames XX = myeq:', all the equation names in the row are reset while the subnames are left unchanged:

```
. matrix rownames XX = myeq:

. matrix list XX

symmetric XX[3,3]
                      price        weight          mpg
  myeq:price   3.448e+09
 myeq:weight   1.468e+09   7.188e+08
    myeq:mpg     9132716     4493720         36008
```

Setting equation names is often done before forming a partitioned matrix so that, when the components are assembled, each has the correct equation name.

Thus, to review, to get the result above, we could have typed

```
. matrix rownames XX = myeq:price myeq:weight myeq:mpg
```

or

```
. matrix rownames XX = price weight mpg

. matrix rownames XX = myeq:
```

or even

```
. matrix rownames XX = myeq:

. matrix rownames XX = price weight mpg
```

All would have resulted in the same outcome. The real surprise comes, however, when you make a mistake:

```
. matrix rownames XX = myeq:

. matrix rownames XX = price weight

. matrix list XX

symmetric XX[3,3]
                      price        weight          mpg
  myeq:price   3.448e+09
 myeq:weight   1.468e+09   7.188e+08
 myeq:weight     9132716     4493720         36008
```

Our mistake above is that we listed only two names for the subnames of the rows of **XX** and **matrix rownames** then labeled both of the last rows with the subname **weight**.

❑

❑ Technical Note

The equation name _: by itself is special; it means the null equation name. For instance, as of the last technical note, we were left with the result:

```
. matrix list XX

symmetric XX[3,3]
                      price        weight          mpg
  myeq:price   3.448e+09
 myeq:weight   1.468e+09   7.188e+08
 myeq:weight     9132716     4493720         36008
```

Let's fix it:

```
. matrix rownames XX = price weight mpg
. matrix rownames XX = _:
. matrix list XX

symmetric XX[3,3]
               price       weight         mpg
 price   3.448e+09
weight   1.468e+09    7.188e+08
   mpg     9132716      4493720       36008
```

❑

❑ Technical Note

matrix roweq and coleq are really the same commands as matrix rownames and colnames. They differ in only one respect: If a specified name does not contain a colon, roweq and coleq interpret that name as if it did end in a colon.

matrix rownames, colnames, roweq, and coleq are often used in conjunction with the rowfullnames, colfullnames, rownames, colnames, roweq, and coleq macro extended functions introduced in [R] **matrix define**. It is important to remember that the rownames and colnames extended macro functions return only the subname and, if present, the time-series operator:

```
. matrix list AA
symmetric AA[4,4]
                           eq1:         eq1:         eq2:         eq2:
                                        L3D2.                      L.
                         length       length          mpg          mpg
   eq1:length         .2967663
eq1:L3D2.length        .03682017    .57644416
      eq2:mpg         -.87052852     .32713601    20.274957
    eq2:L.mpg          -1.572579    -.63830843   -12.150097    26.099582
. local rsubs : rownames AA

. display "The row subnames of AA are -- `rsubs´ --"
The row subnames of AA are -- length L3D2.length mpg L.mpg --
```

Similarly, the roweq extended macro function returns only the equation names and without the trailing colon:

```
. local reqs : roweq AA
. display "The row equations of AA are -- `reqs´ --"
The row equations of AA are -- eq1 eq1 eq2 eq2 --
```

Thus, now consider the problem that you have two matrices named A and B which have the same number of rows. A is correctly labeled and includes equation names. You want to copy the names of A to B. You might be tempted to type

```
. local names : rownames A
. matrix rownames B = `names´
```

This is not adequate. You will have copied the subnames but not the equation names. To copy both parts of the names, you can type

```
. local subs : rownames A
. local eqs : roweq A
. matrix rownames B = `subs´
. matrix roweq B = `eqs´
```

This method can be used even when there might not be equation names. The equation name _ is special: not only does setting an equation to that name remove the equation name but, when there is no equation name, the `roweq` and `coleq` macro extended functions return that name.

A better way to copy the names is using the `rowfullnames` and `colfullnames` extended macro functions (see [R] **matrix define** and [R] **macro**). You can more compactly type

```
. local rname : rowfullnames A
. matrix rownames B = `rname´
```

❑

Also See

Complementary:　　[R] **macro**, [R] **matrix define**

Background:　　[U] **17 Matrix expressions**,
　　　　　　　　[R] **matrix**

Title

> **matrix score** — Score data from coefficient vectors

Syntax

$\underline{\text{mat}}\text{rix}\ \underline{\text{sco}}\text{re}\ \left[type\right]\ newvar = \mathbf{b}\ \left[\text{if}\ exp\right]\ \left[\text{in}\ range\right]\ \left[\ ,\ \left\{\ \text{eq}(\#\#)\ |\ \text{eq}(eqname)\ \right\}\right.$

$\underline{\text{m}}\text{issval}(\#)\ \text{replace}\ \big]$

where **b** is a $1 \times p$ matrix.

Description

matrix score creates $newvar_j = \mathbf{x}_j \mathbf{b}'$ (**b** a row vector) where $\mathbf{x}_j$ is the row vector of values of the variables specified by the column names of **b**. The name _cons is treated as a variable equal to 1.

Options

eq(##) or **eq**(*eqname*) specify the equation—by either number or name—for selecting coefficients from **b** to use in scoring. See [U] **17.2 Row and column names** and [R] **matrix rowname** for more on equation labels with matrices.

missval(*#*) specifies the value to be assumed if any values are missing from the variables referenced by the coefficient vector. By default, this value is taken to be missing (.) and any missing value among the variables produces a missing score.

replace specifies that *newvar* already exists. In this case, observations not included by **if** *exp* and **in** *range* are left unchanged; that is, they are not changed to missing. Be warned that **replace** does not promote the storage type of the existing variable; if the variable was stored as an **int**, the calculated scores would be truncated to integers when stored.

Remarks

Scoring refers to forming linear combinations of variables in the data with respect to a coefficient vector. For instance, consider the vector **coefs**:

```
. matrix list coefs

coefs[1,3]
          weight         mpg       _cons
y1     1.7465592   -49.512221   1946.0687
```

Scoring the data with this vector would create a new variable equal to the linear combination:

$$1.7465592\,\text{weight} - 49.512221\,\text{mpg} + 1946.0687$$

The vector is interpreted as coefficients; the corresponding names of the variables are obtained from the column names (row names if **coefs** were a column vector). To form this linear combination, we type

```
. matrix score lc = coefs
```

```
. summarize lc
Variable |      Obs        Mean    Std. Dev.       Min        Max
---------+-----------------------------------------------------------
      lc |       74    6165.257    1597.606    3406.46   9805.269
```

If the coefficient vector has equation names, matrix score with the eq() option selects the appropriate coefficients for scoring. eq(#1) is assumed if no eq() option is specified.

```
. matrix list coefs
coefs[1,5]
         price:       price:       price:      displ:      displ:
         weight          mpg        _cons      weight       _cons
y1    1.7358275   -51.298249    2016.5101   .10574552  -121.99702
. matrix score lcnoeq = coefs
. matrix score lca = coefs , eq(price)
. matrix score lc1 = coefs , eq(#1)
. matrix score lcb = coefs , eq(displ)
. matrix score lc2 = coefs , eq(#2)
. summarize lcnoeq lca lc1 lcb lc2
Variable |      Obs        Mean    Std. Dev.       Min        Max
---------+-----------------------------------------------------------
  lcnoeq |       74    6165.257    1598.264   3396.859   9802.336
     lca |       74    6165.257    1598.264   3396.859   9802.336
     lc1 |       74    6165.257    1598.264   3396.859   9802.336
     lcb |       74    197.2973    82.18474    64.1151   389.8113
     lc2 |       74    197.2973    82.18474    64.1151   389.8113
```

❏ Technical Note

If the same equation name is scattered in different sections of the coefficient vector then the results may not be what you expect.

```
. matrix list bad
bad[1,5]
         price:       price:      displ:       price:      displ:
         weight          mpg      weight        _cons       _cons
y1    1.7358275   -51.298249   .10574552    2016.5101  -121.99702
. matrix score badnoeq = bad
. matrix score bada = bad , eq(price)
. matrix score bad1 = bad , eq(#1)
. matrix score badb = bad , eq(displ)
. matrix score bad2 = bad , eq(#2)
. matrix score bad3 = bad , eq(#3)
. matrix score bad4 = bad , eq(#4)
. summarize badnoeq bada bad1 badb bad2 bad3 bad4
Variable |      Obs        Mean    Std. Dev.       Min        Max
---------+-----------------------------------------------------------
 badnoeq |       74    4148.747    1598.264   1380.349   7785.826
    bada |       74    4148.747    1598.264   1380.349   7785.826
    bad1 |       74    4148.747    1598.264   1380.349   7785.826
    badb |       74    319.2943    82.18474   186.1121   511.8083
    bad2 |       74    319.2943    82.18474   186.1121   511.8083
    bad3 |       74     2016.51           0    2016.51    2016.51
    bad4 |       74    -121.997           0   -121.997   -121.997
```

Coefficient vectors created by Stata estimation commands will have equation names together.   ❏

Also See

Background: [U] **17 Matrix expressions**,
                   [R] **matrix**

Title

Syntax

<u>matrix</u> <u>svd</u> **U w V** = **A**

where **U**, **w**, and **V** are matrix names (the matrices may exist or not) and **A** is the name of an existing $m \times n, m \geq n$ matrix.

Description

The **svd** matrix command produces the singular value decomposition (SVD) of **A**.

Remarks

The singular value decomposition of $m \times n$ matrix **A**, $m \geq n$, is defined as

$$\mathbf{A} = \mathbf{U}\,\mathrm{diag}(\mathbf{w})\mathbf{V}'$$

U: $m \times n$, **w**: $1 \times n$ (diag(**w**): $n \times n$), and **V**: $n \times n$, where **U** is column orthogonal ($\mathbf{U}'\mathbf{U} = \mathbf{I}$ if $m = n$), all the elements of **w** are positive or zero, and $\mathbf{V}'\mathbf{V} = \mathbf{I}$.

Singular value decomposition can be used to obtain a g2-inverse of **A** (**A***: $n \times m$, such that $\mathbf{A}\mathbf{A}^*\mathbf{A} = \mathbf{A}$ and $\mathbf{A}^*\mathbf{A}\mathbf{A}^* = \mathbf{A}^*$—the first two Moore–Penrose conditions) via $\mathbf{A}^* = \mathbf{V}[\mathrm{diag}(1/w_j)]\mathbf{U}'$ where $1/w_j$ refers to individually taking the reciprocal of the elements of **w** and substituting 0 if $w_j = 0$ or is small. If **A** is square and of full rank, $\mathbf{A}^* = \mathbf{A}^{-1}$.

▷ Example

Singular value decomposition is used to obtain accurate inverses of nearly singular matrices and to obtain g2-inverses of matrices which are singular, to construct orthonormal bases, and to develop approximation matrices. Our example will merely prove that **matrix svd** works:

```
. matrix A = (1,2,9\2,7,5\2,4,18)

. matrix svd U w V = A

. matrix list U
U[3,3]
             c1          c2          c3
r1   -.42313293    .89442719   -.1447706
r2    -.3237169   -6.016e-17    .94615399
r3   -.84626585    -.4472136   -.2895412

. matrix list w
w[1,3]
           c1          c2          c3
r1   21.832726    2.612e-16   5.5975071
```

```
. matrix list V

V[3,3]
             c1          c2          c3
c1  -.12655765  -.96974658    .2087456
c2  -.29759672   .23786237   .92458514
c3  -.94626601   .05489132  -.31869671

. matrix newA = U*diag(w)*V´

. matrix list newA

newA[3,3]
    c1  c2  c3
r1   1   2   9
r2   2   7   5
r3   2   4  18
```

As claimed **newA** is equal to our original **A**.

The g2-inverse of **A** is computed below. The second element of **w** is small, so we decide to set the corresponding element of $\mathrm{diag}(1/w_j)$ to zero. We then show that the resulting **Ainv** matrix has the properties of a g2-inverse for **A**.

```
. matrix Winv = J(3,3,0)

. matrix Winv[1,1] = 1/w[1,1]

. matrix Winv[3,3] = 1/w[1,3]

. matrix Ainv = V*Winv*U´

. matrix list Ainv

Ainv[3,3]
             r1          r2          r3
c1  -.0029461   .03716103  -.0058922
c2  -.0181453   .16069635  -.03629059
c3   .02658185  -.0398393    .05316371

. matrix AAiA = A*Ainv*A

. matrix list AAiA

AAiA[3,3]
    c1  c2  c3
r1   1   2   9
r2   2   7   5
r3   2   4  18

. matrix AiAAi = Ainv*A*Ainv

. matrix list AiAAi

AiAAi[3,3]
             r1          r2          r3
c1  -.0029461   .03716103  -.0058922
c2  -.0181453   .16069635  -.03629059
c3   .02658185  -.0398393    .05316371
```

◁

Also See

Complementary: [R] **matrix define**

Background: [U] **17 Matrix expressions**,
                       [R] **matrix**

Title

matrix symeigen — Eigenvalues and vectors of symmetric matrices

Syntax

matrix symeigen **X** **v** = **A**

Description

Given an $n \times n$ symmetric matrix **A**, **matrix symeigen** returns the eigenvectors in the columns of **X**: $n \times n$ and the corresponding eigenvalues in **v**: $1 \times n$. The eigenvalues are sorted; **v**[1,1] contains the largest eigenvalue (and **X**[1...,1] its corresponding eigenvector) and **v**[1,n] contains the smallest eigenvalue (and **X**[1...,n] its corresponding eigenvector).

Remarks

Typing **matrix symeigen** **X** **v** = **A** for **A** $n \times n$ returns

$$\mathbf{v} = \left(\lambda_1, \lambda_2, \ldots, \lambda_n \right)$$
$$\mathbf{X} = \left(\mathbf{x}_1, \mathbf{x}_2, \ldots, \mathbf{x}_n \right)$$

where $\lambda_1 \geq \lambda_2 \geq \ldots \geq \lambda_n$. Each $\mathbf{x}_i$ and λ_i is a solution to

$$\mathbf{A}\mathbf{x}_i = \lambda_i \mathbf{x}_i$$

or, more compactly,

$$\mathbf{A}\mathbf{X} = \mathbf{X}\,\mathrm{diag}(\mathbf{v})$$

▷ Example

Eigenvalues and eigenvectors have many uses. We will merely demonstrate that **symeigen** returns matrices meeting the definition:

```
. matrix list A
symmetric A[3,3]
            weight          mpg       length
weight    44094178
   mpg  -264948.11    2443.4595
length   1195077.3   -7483.5135    36192.662
. matrix symeigen X lambda = A
. matrix list lambda
lambda[1,3]
            e1           e2           e3
r1    44128163    3830.4869    820.73955
. matrix list X
X[3,3]
                 e1           e2           e3
weight    .99961482   -.02756261    .00324179
   mpg   -.00600667    -.1008305    .99488549
length    .02709477    .99452175    .10095722
```

338

```
. matrix AX = A*X

. matrix XLambda = X*diag(lambda)

. matrix list AX

AX[3,3]
                 e1           e2           e3
weight     44111166   -105.57823    2.6606641
   mpg    -265063.5   -386.22991    816.54187
length   1195642.6    3809.5025    82.859585

. matrix list XLambda

XLambda[3,3]
                 e1           e2           e3
weight     44111166   -105.57823    2.6606641
   mpg    -265063.5   -386.22991    816.54187
length   1195642.6    3809.5025    82.859585
```

◁

Methods and Formulas

Stata's internal eigenvalue and eigenvector extraction routines are translations of the public domain EISPACK routines, Smith et al. (1976), which are in turn based on Wilkinson and Reinsch (1971). EISPACK was developed under contract for the Office of Scientific and Technical Information, U.S. Department of Energy, by Argonne National Laboratory and supported by funds provided by the Nuclear Regulatory Commission. Stata's use of these routines is by permission of the National Energy Software Center of the Argonne National Laboratory. A brief but excellent introduction to the techniques employed by these routines can be found in Press et al. (1992, 456–495).

References

Press, W. H., S. A. Teukolsky, W. T. Vetterling, and B. P. Flannery. 1992. *Numerical Recipes in C: The Art of Scientific Computing.* 2d ed. Cambridge University Press.

Smith, B. T., et al. 1976. *Matrix Eigen System Routines—EISPACK Guide.* 2d ed. vol. 6 of Lecture Notes in Computer Science. New York: Springer-Verlag.

Wilkinson, J. H. and C. Reinsch. 1971. *Linear Algebra,* vol. 2 of *Handbook for Automatic Computation.* New York: Springer-Verlag.

Also See

Background: [U] **17 Matrix expressions,**
                    [R] **matrix**

Title

> **matrix utility** — List, rename, and drop matrices

Syntax

matrix <u>d</u>ir

matrix <u>l</u>ist *mname* $\Big[$, <u>nob</u>lank <u>noh</u>alf <u>noh</u>eader <u>non</u>ames <u>f</u>ormat(*%fmt*) <u>t</u>itle(*string*) $\Big]$

matrix <u>ren</u>ame *oldname newname*

matrix drop $\Big\{$ _all | *mname(s)* $\Big\}$

Description

matrix dir lists the names of currently existing matrices. matrix list lists the contents of a matrix. matrix rename changes the name of a matrix. matrix drop eliminates a matrix.

Options

noblank suppresses printing a blank line before printing the matrix. This is useful in programs.

nohalf specifies that, even if the matrix is symmetric, the full matrix is to be printed. The default is to print only the lower triangle in such cases.

noheader suppresses the display of the matrix name and dimension before the matrix itself. This is useful in programs.

nonames suppresses the display of the bordering names around the matrix.

format(*%fmt*) specifies the format to be used to display the individual elements of the matrix. The default is format(%10.0g).

title(*string*) adds the specified title *string* to the header displayed before the matrix itself. If noheader is specified, title() does nothing because displaying the header is suppressed.

Remarks

▷ Example

Little needs to be said by way of introduction. In the example below, however, note that matrix list normally displays only the lower half of symmetric matrices; nohalf prevents this.

```
. matrix dir
            a[2,2]
            b[3,3]
. matrix rename a z
. matrix dir
            z[2,2]
            b[3,3]
```

```
. matrix list b
symmetric b[3,3]
      c1  c2  c3
r1   2
r2   5   8
r3   4   6   3
. matrix list b, nohalf
symmetric b[3,3]
      c1  c2  c3
r1   2   5   4
r2   5   8   6
r3   4   6   3
. matrix drop b
. matrix dir
          z[2,2]
. matrix drop _all
. matrix dir
```

◁

❏ Technical Note

When writing programs and using matrix names obtained through `tempname` (see [R] **macro**), it is not necessary to explicitly drop matrices; the matrices are removed automatically at the conclusion of the program.

```
. program define example
  1.          tempname a
  2.          matrix `a´ = (1,2\3,4)              /* this is temporary  */
  3.          matrix b = (5,6\7,8)                /* and this permanent */
  4.          display "The temporary matrix a contains:"
  5.          matrix list `a´, noheader
  6. end
. example
The temporary matrix a contains
      c1  c2
r1   1   2
r2   3   4
. matrix dir
          b[2,2]
```

Nevertheless, dropping matrices with temporary names in programs when they are no longer needed is recommended unless the program is about to exit (when they will be dropped anyway). Matrices consume memory; dropping them frees memory.

❏

Also See

Background: [U] **17 Matrix expressions**,
               [R] **matrix**

Title

> **matsize** — Set the maximum number of variables in a model

Syntax

> set matsize #

where $10 \leq \# \leq 800$

Description

> set matsize sets the maximum number of variables that can be included in any of Stata's model-estimation commands. The command may not be used with Small Stata; matsize is permanently frozen at 40. For Intercooled Stata, the initial value is 40, but it may be changed upward or downward. The upper limit is 800.

Remarks

> set matsize affects the internal size of matrices that Stata uses. The default of 40, for instance, means that linear regression models are limited to 38 independent variables—38 because the constant uses one position and the dependent variable another, making a total of 40.
>
> Under Stata for Windows 3.1 and Stata for Macintosh, there must be no data in memory when you change matsize and increasing matsize decreases the amount of memory available for data. Under Stata for Windows 98/95/NT and Stata for Unix, you may change matsize with data in memory, but increasing matsize increases the amount of memory consumed by Stata, increasing the probability of page faults and thus of making Stata run more slowly.

▷ Example

> You wish to estimate a model of y on the variables x1 through x100. Without thinking, you type
>
> ```
> . regress y x1-x100
> matsize too small; type -help matsize-
> r(908);
> ```
>
> You realize that you need to increase matsize; you are using Intercooled Stata and type
>
> ```
> . set matsize 150
> no; data in memory would be lost
> r(4);
> ```
>
> You are using Stata for Windows 3.1 or Stata for Macintosh. You must
>
> ```
> . save mydata
> file mydata.dta saved
> . drop _all
> . set matsize 150
> . use mydata
> . regress y x1-x100
>   (output omitted )
> ```

Under Stata for Windows 98/95/NT or Stata for Unix, you do not have to go to that trouble:

```
. regress y x1-x100
matsize too small; type -help matsize-
r(908);
. set matsize 150
. regress y x1-x100
  (output omitted )
```

◁

Also See

Background: [U] **7 Setting the size of memory**

Title

> **maximize** — Details of iterative maximization

Syntax

mle_cmd ... [, [no]log trace gradient hessian showstep iterate(#)

tolerance(#) ltolerance(#) gtolerance(#) difficult from(init_specs)]

where *init_specs* is one of

matname [, skip copy]

{ [*eqname*:]*name* = # | /*eqname* = # } [...]

[# ...], copy

Description

Stata has two maximum likelihood optimizers: one is used by internally coded commands and the other is the **ml** command used by estimators implemented as ado-files. Both optimizers use the Newton–Raphson method with step halving (to avoid downhill steps) and special fixups when nonconcave regions of the likelihood are encountered. The two optimizers are similar, but differ in the details of their implementation. For information on programming maximum likelihood estimators in ado-files, see [R] **ml** and *Maximum Likelihood Estimation with Stata* (Gould and Sribney 1999).

Options

log and nolog specify whether an iteration log showing the progress of the log likelihood is to be displayed. For most commands, the log is displayed by default and nolog suppresses it. For a few commands (such as the svy maximum likelihood estimators), it is the opposite; you must specify log to see the log.

trace adds to the iteration log a display of the current parameter vector.

gradient (ml-programmed estimators only) adds to the iteration log a display of the current gradient vector.

hessian (ml-programmed estimators only) adds to the iteration log a display of the current negative Hessian matrix.

showstep (ml-programmed estimators only) adds to the iteration log a report on the steps within an iteration. This option was added so that developers at Stata could view the stepping when they were improving the ml optimizer code. At this point, it mainly provides entertainment.

iterate(#) specifies the maximum number of iterations. When the number of iterations equals iterate(), the optimizer stops and presents the current results. If convergence is declared before this threshold is reached, it will stop when convergence is declared. Specifying iterate(0) is useful for viewing results evaluated at the initial value of the coefficient vector. iterate(0) and from() specified together will allow one to view results evaluated at a specified coefficient vector; note, however, that only a few commands allow the from() option. iterate(16000) is the default for both estimators programmed internally and estimators programmed with ml.

tolerance(#) specifies the tolerance for the coefficient vector. When the relative change in the coefficient vector from one iteration to the next is less than or equal to tolerance(), estimates are declared to have converged. If this criterion is satisfied, convergence is declared regardless of the status of the likelihood tolerance ltolerance().

tolerance(1e-4) is the default for estimators programmed internally in Stata.

tolerance(1e-6) is the default for estimators programmed with ml.

ltolerance(#) specifies the tolerance for the log likelihood. When the relative change in the log likelihood from one iteration to the next is less than or equal to ltolerance(), estimates are declared to have converged. If this criterion is satisfied, convergence is declared regardless of the status of the coefficient vector tolerance tolerance().

ltolerance(0) is the default for estimators programmed internally in Stata.

ltolerance(1e-7) is the default for estimators programmed with ml.

gtolerance(#) (ml-programmed estimators only) specifies an optional tolerance for the gradient relative to the coefficients. When $|g_i\, b_i| \leq$ gtolerance() for all parameters b_i and the corresponding elements of the gradient g_i, then the gradient tolerance criterion is met. Unlike tolerance() and ltolerance(), the gtolerance() criterion must be met in addition to any other tolerance. That is, convergence is declared when gtolerance() is met and tolerance() or ltolerance() is met. The gtolerance() option is provided for particularly deceptive likelihood functions that may trigger premature declarations of convergence. The option must be specified for gradient checking to be activated; by default the gradient is not checked.

difficult (ml-programmed estimators only) specifies that the likelihood function is likely to be difficult to maximize due to nonconcave regions. When the message "not concave" appears repeatedly, ml's standard stepping algorithm may not be working well. difficult specifies that a different stepping algorithm is to be used in nonconcave regions. There is no guarantee that difficult will work better than the default; sometimes it is better, sometimes it is worse. The difficult option should only be attempted when the default stepper declares convergence and the last iteration is "not concave", or when the default stepper is repeatedly issuing "not concave" messages and only producing tiny improvements in the log likelihood.

from() specifies initial values for the coefficients. Note that only a few estimators in Stata currently support this option. The initial values can be specified in one of three ways: (1) by specifying the name of a vector containing the initial values (e.g., from(b0) where b0 is a properly labeled vector), (2) by specifying coefficient names with the values (e.g., from(age=2.1 /sigma=7.4)), or by specifying a list of values (e.g., from(2.1 7.4, copy)). from() is intended for use when doing bootstraps (see [R] **bstrap**) and in other special situations (e.g., used with iterate(0)). Even when the values specified in from() are close to the values that maximize the likelihood, only a couple of iterations may be saved. Poor values in from() may lead to convergence problems.

skip specifies that any parameters found in the specified initialization vector that are not also found in the model are to be ignored. The default action is to issue an error message.

copy specifies that the list of numbers or the initialization vector is to be copied into the initial-value vector by position rather than by name.

Remarks

Only in rare circumstances would a user ever need to specify any of the these options, with the exception of nolog. nolog is useful for reducing the amount of output appearing in log files.

The following is an example of an iteration log:

```
Iteration 0:    log likelihood = -3791.0251
Iteration 1:    log likelihood =  -3761.738
Iteration 2:    log likelihood = -3758.0632  (not concave)
Iteration 3:    log likelihood = -3758.0447
Iteration 4:    log likelihood = -3757.5861
Iteration 5:    log likelihood =  -3757.474
Iteration 6:    log likelihood = -3757.4613
Iteration 7:    log likelihood = -3757.4606
Iteration 8:    log likelihood = -3757.4606
     (table of results omitted)
```

At iteration 8, the model converged. The only notable thing about this iteration log is the message "not concave" at the second iteration. This example was produced using the `heckman` command; its likelihood is not globally concave, so it is not surprising that this message sometimes appears. The other message that is occasionally seen is "backed up". Neither of these messages should be of any concern *unless* they appear at the final iteration.

If a "not concave" message appears at the last step, then there are two possibilities. One is that it is a "valid" result, but there is collinearity in the model that the command did not catch. Stata checks for obvious collinearity among the independent variables prior to performing the maximization, but strange collinearities or near collinearities can sometimes arise between coefficients and ancillary parameters. The second cause for a "not concave" message at the final step is that the optimizer entered a very flat region of the likelihood, and prematurely declared convergence.

If a "backed up" message appears at the last step, then there are also two possibilities. One is that it found a perfect maximum and it could not step to a better point; if this is the case, all is fine—but this is a highly unlikely occurrence. The second is that the optimizer worked itself into a bad concave spot, where the computed gradient and Hessian gave a bad direction for stepping.

If either of these messages appear at the last step, do maximization again with the `gradient` option. If the gradient goes to zero, the optimizer has found a maximum—it may not be unique, but it is a maximum. From the standpoint of maximum likelihood estimation, it is a valid result. If the gradient is not zero, it is not a valid result, and you should try the following: Try tightening up the convergence criterion. Try `ltol(0)` `tol(1e-7)` or else try `gtol(0.1)` (with the default `ltol()` `tol()`) and see if the optimizer can work its way out of the bad region.

If you get repeated "not concave" steps with little progress being made at each step, try specifying the `difficult` option. Sometimes `difficult` works wonderfully, reducing the number of iterations and producing convergence at a good (i.e., concave) point. Other times, `difficult` works poorly, taking much longer to converge than the default stepper.

Saved Results

Maximum likelihood estimators save in `e()`:

Scalars

`e(N)`	number of observations	always saved
`e(df_m)`	model degrees of freedom	always saved
`e(r2_p)`	pseudo R-squared	sometimes saved
`e(ll)`	log likelihood	always saved
`e(ll_0)`	log likelihood, constant-only model	usually saved
`e(chi2)`	χ^2	usually saved
`e(N_clust)`	number of clusters	saved when `cluster` specified; see [U] **23.11 Obtaining robust variance estimates**

Macros

e(cmd)	name of command	always saved
e(depvar)	name(s) of dependent variable(s)	usually saved
e(clustvar)	name of cluster variable	saved when cluster specified; see [U] **23.11 Obtaining robust variance estimates**
e(vcetype)	covariance estimation method	saved when robust is specified or implied; see [U] **23.11 Obtaining robust variance estimates**
e(chi2type)	Wald or LR; type of model χ^2 test	usually saved
e(wtype)	weight type	saved when weights are specified or implied
e(wexp)	weight expression	saved when weights are specified or implied
e(predict)	program used to implement predict	usually saved

Matrices

e(b)	coefficient vector	always saved
e(V)	variance–covariance matrix of the estimators	always saved

Functions

e(sample)	marks estimation sample	

See the *Saved Results* section in the manual entry for any maximum likelihood estimator for a complete list of returned results.

Methods and Formulas

Let L_1 be the log likelihood of the full model (i.e., the log-likelihood value shown on the output), and let L_0 be the log likelihood of the "constant-only" model. The likelihood-ratio χ^2 model test is defined as $2(L_1 - L_0)$. The pseudo R^2 (Judge et al. 1985) is defined as $1 - L_1/L_0$. This is simply the log likelihood on a scale where 0 corresponds to the "constant-only" model and 1 corresponds to perfect prediction for discrete models; i.e., predicted probabilities are all 1 and the overall log likelihood is 0.

By default, Stata's maximum likelihood estimators display standard errors based on variance estimates given by the inverse of the negative Hessian (second derivatives) matrix. If robust, cluster(), or pweights are specified, then standard errors are based on the robust variance estimator (see [U] **23.11 Obtaining robust variance estimates**); in this case, likelihood-ratio tests are not appropriate (see [U] **30 Overview of survey estimation**), and the model χ^2 is a Wald test.

Some maximum likelihood routines have the ability to report coefficients in an exponentiated form; e.g., odds ratios in logistic. Let b be the unexponentiated coefficient, s its standard error, and b_0 and b_1 the reported confidence interval for b. In exponentiated form, the point estimate is e^b, the standard error $e^b s$, and the confidence interval e^{b_0} and e^{b_1}. The displayed Z statistics and p-values are the same as those for the unexponentiated results. This is justified since $e^b = 1$ and $b = 0$ are equivalent hypotheses, and normality is more likely to hold in the b metric.

References

Gould, W. and W. Sribney. 1999. *Maximum Likelihood Estimation with Stata*. College Station, TX: Stata Press.

Judge, G. G., W. E. Griffiths, R. C. Hill, H. Lütkepohl, and T.-C. Lee. 1985. *The Theory and Practice of Econometrics*. 2d ed. New York: John Wiley & Sons.

Also See

Complementary:	[R] **lrtest**, [R] **ml**
Background:	[U] **23 Estimation and post-estimation commands**

Title

```
means — Arithmetic, geometric, and harmonic means
```

Syntax

means [*varlist*] [*weight*] [if *exp*] [in *range*] [, <u>a</u>dd(*#*) <u>o</u>nly <u>l</u>evel(*#*)]

aweights and fweights are allowed; see [U] **14.1.6 weight**.

Description

means computes the arithmetic, geometric, and harmonic means, and corresponding confidence intervals, for each variable in *varlist* or for all the variables in the data if *varlist* is not specified. If you simply want arithmetic means and corresponding confidence intervals, see [R] **ci**.

Options

add(*#*) adds the value *#* to each variable in *varlist* before computing the means and confidence intervals. This is useful when analyzing variables with nonpositive values.

only modifies the action of the add(*#*) option. If specified, the add(*#*) option only adds *#* to variables with at least one nonpositive value.

level(*#*) specifies the confidence level, in percent, for confidence intervals. The default is level(95) or as set by set level; see [U] **23.5 Specifying the width of confidence intervals**.

Remarks

▷ Example

You have a dataset containing 8 observations on a variable named x. The eight values are 5, 4, −4, −5, 0, 0, *missing*, and 7.

```
. means x
Variable |    Type      Obs      Mean     [95% Conf. Interval]
---------+-------------------------------------------------------
       x | Arithmetic    7         1     -3.204405   5.204405
         | Geometric     3   5.192494     2.57899   10.45448
         | Harmonic      3   5.060241    3.023008    15.5179
---------+-------------------------------------------------------

. means x, add(5)
Variable |    Type      Obs      Mean     [95% Conf. Interval]
---------+-------------------------------------------------------
       x | Arithmetic    7         6     1.795595    10.2044 *
         | Geometric     6   5.477226     2.1096   14.22071 *
         | Harmonic      6   3.540984         .          . *
---------+-------------------------------------------------------
(*) 5 was added to the variable(s) prior to calculating the results.
Missing values in confidence interval(s) for harmonic mean indicate
confidence interval undefined for corresponding variable(s).
Consult Reference Manual for details.
```

The number of observations displayed for the arithmetic mean is the number of nonmissing observations. The number of observations displayed for the geometric and harmonic means is the number of nonmissing, positive observations. Specifying the add(5) option results in 3 additional positive observations. Note that the confidence interval for the harmonic mean is not reported; see *Methods and Formulas* below.

◁

Saved Results

means saves in r():

Scalars

r(N)	number of nonmissing observations; used for arithmetic mean
r(N_pos)	number of nonmissing positive observations; used for geometric & harmonic means
r(mean)	arithmetic mean
r(lb)	lower bound of confidence interval for arithmetic mean
r(ub)	upper bound of confidence interval for arithmetic mean
r(Var)	variance of untransformed data
r(mean_g)	geometric mean
r(lb_g)	lower bound of confidence interval for geometric mean
r(ub_g)	upper bound of confidence interval for geometric mean
r(Var_g)	variance of $\ln x_i$
r(mean_h)	harmonic mean
r(lb_h)	lower bound of confidence interval for harmonic mean
r(ub_h)	upper bound of confidence interval for harmonic mean
r(Var_h)	variance of $1/x_i$

Methods and Formulas

means is implemented as an ado-file.

See, for example, Armitage and Berry (1987) or Snedecor and Cochran (1989). For a history of the concept of the mean, see Plackett (1958).

When restricted to the same set of values (i.e., to positive values), the arithmetic mean ($\overline{x}$) is greater than or equal to the geometric mean which in turn is greater than or equal to the harmonic mean. Exact equality holds only if all values within a sample are equal to a positive constant.

The arithmetic mean and its confidence interval are identical to those provided by ci; see [R] **ci**.

To compute the geometric mean, means first creates $u_j = \ln x_j$ for all positive x_j. The arithmetic mean of the u_j and its confidence interval are then computed as in ci. Let $\overline{u}$ be the resulting mean, and $[L, U]$ the corresponding confidence interval. The geometric mean is then $\exp(\overline{u})$ and its confidence interval is $[\exp(L), \exp(U)]$.

The same procedure is followed for the harmonic mean, except in this case $u_j = 1/x_j$. The harmonic mean is then $1/\overline{u}$ and its confidence interval is $[1/U, 1/L]$ if L is greater than zero. If L is not greater than zero, then this confidence interval is not defined and missing values are reported.

When weights are specified, means applies the weights to the transformed values, $u_j = \ln x_j$ and $u_j = 1/x_j$ respectively, when computing the geometric and harmonic means. For details on how the weights are used to compute the mean and variance of the u_j, see [R] **summarize**. Without weights, the formula for the geometric mean reduces to

$$\exp\!\left(\frac{1}{n}\sum_j \ln(x_j)\right)$$

Without weights, the formula for the harmonic mean is

$$\frac{n}{\sum_j \dfrac{1}{x_j}}$$

Acknowledgments

This improved version of **means** is based on the **gmci** command (Carlin, Vidmar, and Ramalheira 1998) and was written by John Carlin, University of Melbourne, Australia; Suzanna Vidmar, University of Melbourne, Australia; and Carlos Ramalheira, Coimbra University Hospital, Portugal.

References

Armitage, P. and G. Berry. 1987. *Statistical Methods in Medical Research.* 2d ed. Oxford: Blackwell Scientific Publications.

Carlin, J., S. Vidmar, and C. Ramalheira. 1998. sg75: Geometric means and confidence intervals. *Stata Technical Bulletin* 41: 23–25. Reprinted in *Stata Technical Bulletin Reprints,* vol. 7, pp. 197–199.

Kotz, S. and N. L. Johnson. ed. 1985. *Encyclopedia of Statistical Sciences,* vol. 1, vol. 3. New York: John Wiley & Sons.

Plackett, R. L. 1958. The principle of the arithmetic mean. *Biometrika* 45: 130–135.

Snedecor, G. W. and W. G. Cochran. 1989. *Statistical Methods.* 8th ed. Ames, IA: Iowa State University Press.

Also See

Related: [R] **ci**, [R] **summarize**

Title

> **memory** — Memory size considerations

Syntax

set <u>mem</u>ory #[k | m]

memory

set <u>vir</u>tual { on | off }

where # is specified in terms of kilobytes or megabytes.

Description

set memory, memory, and set virtual are relevant only if you are using Intercooled Stata.

set memory allows you to increase or decrease the amount of memory allocated to Stata while Stata is running. Increases are obtained from the operating system; decreases are returned to the operating system. set memory can be specified only if you are using Stata for Windows 98/95/NT or Stata for Unix.

Stata for Windows 3.1 and Stata for Macintosh users must instead set the amount of memory at the time they invoke Stata; see [GSW] **B.6 Specifying the amount of memory allocated** (Windows 3.1) or [GSM] **A.5 Specifying the amount of memory allocated** (Macintosh).

memory displays a report on Stata's memory usage. memory is available on all Intercooled Statas regardless of platform.

set virtual controls whether Stata should perform extra work to arrange its memory to keep objects close together. By default, virtual is set off. set virtual is available on all Intercooled Statas regardless of platform.

Remarks

Remarks are presented under the headings

> *Resetting the amount of memory*
> *Obtaining the memory report and how Stata uses memory*
> *Using virtual memory*

If you use Stata for Windows 3.1 or Stata for Macintosh, skip the first heading.

Resetting the amount of memory

If you use Stata for Windows 98/95/NT or any flavor of Stata for Unix, you can change the amount of memory Stata has allocated while Stata is running:

```
. set memory 4m
no; data in memory would be lost
r(4);
```

You can change the amount of memory, but only when there is no data in memory:

```
. drop _all
. set memory 4m
(4096k)
```

You can increase it

```
. set memory 32m
(32768k)
```

or decrease it:

```
. set memory 1m
(1024k)
```

If you ask for more than your operating system can provide, you will be told so:

```
. set memory 128m
op. sys. refuses to provide memory
r(909);
```

The number you type can be specified in megabytes or kilobytes. When you suffix numbers with **m** it means megabytes. When you suffix numbers with **k** (or nothing) it means kilobytes.

```
. set memory 4000k
(4000k)
. set memory 1000
(1000k)
```

❏ Technical Note

(This note is relevant only if you use Stata for Unix.) There is a detail in the operating system's handling of returned memory that we have glossed over. You probably think that the checking out and returning of memory from the operating system is handled like the checking out and returning of a book at a library. With some operating systems, it is handled that way, but others have a variation. Operating systems handle returned memory in one of three ways:

1. The instant memory is returned, it is marked as returned and is available for other programs to check out.

2. When memory is returned it is put in a special bin and, five or ten minutes from now, it will be marked as returned for other programs to check out. In the meantime, you could check it out again if you want, but no other program can.

3. When memory is returned it is put in the special bin and never moved from there. You can have the memory back, but no other program can ever have that memory.

Windows 98/95/NT follow policy 1. The various flavors of Unix differ on which policy they follow and this has implications.

Let's imagine you are pushing your Unix computer to its limits and have allocated lots of memory to Stata. You suddenly want to jump out of Stata and do something in Unix, so you use Stata's **shell** command to obtain a new shell:

```
. shell
op. sys. refused to start new process
r(702);
```

This can happen if there is no free memory. This reminds you that Stata has all the memory but you no longer need it, so you return most of it:

```
. set memory 4m
(4096k)
```

Now you try the `shell` command again. What will happen?

1. If your system follows policy 1, `shell` will work.

2. If your system follows policy 2, `shell` will not work, but five or ten minutes from now, it will start working again.

3. If your system follows policy 3, `shell` will not work.

The result hinges on whether the operating system really takes back, and when, the memory Stata returns. If your operating system follows policy 3, you must `exit` and restart Stata. If your operating system follows policy 2 and you are in a hurry, you can `exit` and restart, too.

❑

Obtaining the memory report and how Stata uses memory

Type `memory` and Stata will give you a memory report. Below, we just started Stata:

```
. memory
Total memory                1,048,576 bytes    100.00%
overhead (pointers)                 0             0.00%
data                                0             0.00%
                           ------------
data + overhead                     0             0.00%
programs, saved results, etc.     368             0.04%
                           ------------
Total                             368             0.04%
Free                        1,048,208            99.96%
```

If you perform this experiment on your computer, you will probably see different numbers. Here is our memory report after we load the automobile data that comes with Stata:

```
. use auto
(1978 Automobile Data)

. memory
Total memory                1,048,576 bytes    100.00%
overhead (pointers)               296             0.03%
data                            3,182             0.30%
                           ------------
data + overhead                 3,478             0.33%
programs, saved results, etc.   1,040             0.10%
                           ------------
Total                           4,518             0.43%
Free                        1,044,058            99.57%
```

Total memory refers to the total amount of memory Stata has allocated to its data areas—the number that can be specified at start-up time or reset by `set memory`. Well, almost. If you use Stata for Macintosh, total memory refers to a number somewhat smaller than that because Stata has to carve an area out of the total for another purpose. Stata for Macintosh users: just accept that the number is smaller than the number you specified and know that the larger the number you specify at start-up time, the larger the total memory will be; see the technical note below.

Overhead, data, and data + overhead refer to the amount of memory necessary to hold the data currently in memory. Start with the middle number.

3,182 bytes is the total amount of memory necessary to hold the automobile data and you could work this out for yourself from a `describe, detail`. The automobile data has 74 observations and each observation requires 43 bytes (called the width), and $74 \times 43 = 3{,}182$.

296 bytes is the pointer overhead associated with this data. Stata needs something called a pointer to keep track of where each observation is stored in memory. On this computer pointers are 4 bytes—but that varies—and the data has 74 observations, so $4 \times 74 = 296$.

Data + overhead is just the sum of the two numbers: $296 + 3{,}182 = 3{,}478$ is the total amount of memory Stata needs to store and keep track of this data.

Programs, saved results, etc., is the total amount of memory Stata has used to store just what it says: Stata's programs (ado-files), macros, matrices, value labels, and all sorts of other things. This is sometimes referred to as Stata's dynamic memory. The report shows 960 bytes this instant but the number changes frequently.

Here is a memory report from another session in which we have loaded a dataset with 69,515 observations on 23 variables and are in the midst of analyzing it using `xtgee`:

```
. memory
    Total memory                  6,291,456 bytes     100.00%

    overhead (pointers)             278,060             4.42%
    data                          2,572,055            40.88%
                                  ------------
    data + overhead               2,850,115            45.30%

    programs, saved results, etc.    43,936             0.70%
                                  ------------
    Total                         2,894,051            46.00%
    Free                          3,397,405            54.00%
```

❑ **Technical Note**

Stata for Macintosh. The total amount of memory shown by `memory` is less than the amount you tell your Macintosh to allocate because we need to use some of that memory for other purposes. How much we need is given by $88\,\mathtt{matsize}^2 + 8\,\mathtt{matsize} + k$, where k is a constant for you (but varies slightly across Macintoshes). Thus, you will see total memory rise and fall according to the value to which you `set matsize`.

Let's compare `matsize` $= 40$ with 80. For `matsize` $= 80$, we need $88 \cdot 80^2 + 8 \cdot 80 + k = 563{,}840 + k$. For `matsize` $= 40$, we need $88 \cdot 40^2 + 8 \cdot 40 + k = 141{,}120 + k$. The difference is then 422,720. Conclusion: if `matsize` was 40 and you `set matsize 80`, `memory` will report that total memory declines by 422,720 bytes. Since it is in "total memory" that Stata stores your data, reducing the value of `matsize` is one way of reallocating your memory.

❑

Using virtual memory

Virtual memory refers to using more memory than is physically present on your computer. This is a feature provided by the operating system, not Stata, and one that you as a Stata user may find yourself sometimes exploiting.

Virtual memory is slow. You will be unhappy if you need to use virtual memory on a daily basis. On the other hand, virtual memory can get you out of a bind and that is the right way to use it with Stata.

You do *NOT* need to `set virtual on` for Stata to use virtual memory. All `set virtual on` does is maybe make Stata run a little faster when the operating system is paging a lot. `set virtual on` will not make Stata run fast, just faster.

Virtual memory is most efficient (which is not to say efficient) when the program being executed exhibits something called locality of reference. This is the idea that if the program accesses one location in memory, subsequent memory references will be to a location near that. If you `set virtual on` Stata's memory-management routines will go to extra work to arrange things so that the idea is true more often. Hence, Stata will run a little faster. If Stata is not using virtual memory, setting `virtual on` will make Stata run a little slower because Stata will be going to extra work for no good reason.

You `set virtual on` by typing the command

```
. set virtual on
```

You can check whether `virtual` is on or off using `query`:

```
. query
-------------------------------------------------------- Status
       type | float      display linesize | 79
    virtual | off                 pagesize | 23
       more | on           log linesize | 79
       beep | off                 pagesize | 0
       rmsg | off                    trace | off
    matsize | 40                  textsize | 100
    adosize | 65                     level | 95
   graphics | on
-------------------------------------------------------- Files
        log | closed
       help | C:\STATA\stata.hlp
```

`virtual` is reported on the second line of the left column. To `set virtual off`, type the command

```
. set virtual off
```

Saved Results

`memory` saves in `r()`:

Scalars
`r(k)`	number of variables
`r(width)`	width of dataset
`r(N_cur)`	maximum observations (current partition)
`r(N_curmax)`	max. max. observations (current partition)
`r(k_cur)`	maximum variables (current partition)
`r(w_cur)`	maximum width (current partition)
`r(M_total)`	total memory allocated to Stata (bytes)
`r(M_data)`	total memory available to data (bytes)
`r(M_dyn)`	total programs, saved results, etc. (bytes)
`r(size_ptr)`	size of memory pointer (bytes)
`r(matsize)`	matsize
`r(adosize)`	adosize

Note that there are four saved results that refer to the current partition. At any instant Stata has partitioned the memory into observations and variables. The characteristics of the partition can change at any time including right in the middle of a command, so the first four numbers are really of little interest in that they do not reflect any real constraint. What they do reflect is efficiency. If something should occur that violates any of those limits, Stata will have to silently go to work to reform the partition, something it is able to do reasonably efficiently and without any disk accesses. Also note that the description of r(N_curmax) is not a typographical error. It records the maximum number of observations in the current partition if the size of total programs, saved results, etc. (what is recorded in r(M_dyn)) were zero. When Stata is faced with a request that violates the current partition's limits, it considers the possibility of discarding memory copies of ado-files that have not been used recently. Ado-files are loaded automatically on an as-needed basis and so how long they are kept in memory is only an efficiency issue. Stata considers reducing the memory requirement as an alternative to repartitioning.

The output produced by memory can be calculated from the saved results by

$$\text{total memory} = \texttt{r(M\_data)}$$

$$\text{overhead (pointers)} = \texttt{\_N} \times \texttt{r(size\_ptr)}$$

$$\text{data} = \texttt{\_N} \times \texttt{r(width)}$$

$$\text{programs, saved results, etc.} = \texttt{r(M\_dyn)}$$

References

Sasieni, P. 1997. ip20: Checking for sufficient memory to add variables. *Stata Technical Bulletin* 40: 13. Reprinted in *Stata Technical Bulletin Reprints*, vol. 7, p. 86.

Also See

Complementary:	[R] **query**
Background:	[U] **7 Setting the size of memory**

Title

merge — Merge datasets

Syntax

<u>merge</u> [*varlist*] **using** *filename* [, <u>nol</u>abel **update replace** <u>nok</u>eep _merge(*varname*)]

If *filename* is specified without an extension, **.dta** is assumed.

Description

merge joins corresponding observations from the dataset currently in memory (called the master dataset) with those from the Stata-format dataset stored as *filename* (called the using dataset) into single observations.

Options

nolabel prevents Stata from copying the value label definitions from the disk dataset into the dataset in memory. Even if you do not specify this option, in no event do label definitions from the disk dataset replace label definitions already in memory.

update varies the action **merge** takes when an observation is matched. By default, the master data is held inviolate—values from the master data are retained when variables are found in both datasets. If **update** is specified, however, the values from the using dataset are retained in cases where the master data contains missing.

replace, allowed with **update** only, specifies that even in the case when the master data contains nonmissing values, they are to be replaced with corresponding values from the using data when the corresponding values are not equal. A nonmissing value, however, will never be replaced with a missing value.

nokeep causes **merge** to ignore observations in the using data that have no corresponding observation in the master. The default is to add these observations to the merged result and mark such observations with _merge = 2.

_merge(*varname*) specifies the name of the variable that is to be created that will mark the source of the resulting observation. The default is _merge(_merge); that is, if you do not specify this option, the new variable will be named _merge. See *The two kinds of merges* below for details.

Remarks

Remarks are presented under the headings

> *The two kinds of merges*
> *One-to-one merge*
> *Match merge*
> *Updating data*

357

Distinguish carefully between merging and appending datasets, and the corresponding Stata commands `merge` and `append`. Appending refers to the addition of new observations on existing variables. If one thinks of data as a rectangle with observations going down and variables going across, appending increases the dataset's length. Merging adds new variables to existing observations, increasing the dataset's width.

Say you have data in which each observation records the characteristics of a particular automobile such as the car's price, weight, etc. If you have two such datasets, one for domestic and another for imported cars, and you wish to combine them into a single dataset, you are reading the wrong entry; see [R] **append**.

On the other hand, if you have two datasets, one recording price and ther other weight, mileage, etc., and you wish to combine them into a single set, continue reading; `merge` does this.

In addition to `merge`, another command, `joinby`, forms all pairwise combinations of observations within group. Say you have one dataset on mothers and fathers and another on their children. If you wish to combine them so that each parent is matched with every one of their children (each child is matched with both parents), so that a 2-parent, 3-child family results in $2 \times 3 = 6$ observations, see [R] **joinby**.

The two kinds of merges

`merge` joins the observations stored in memory with the observations stored in *filename*. The disk dataset must be a Stata-format dataset; that is, it must have been created with the **save** command.

Stata performs two kinds of merges. If no *varlist* is specified, Stata performs a *one-to-one* merge. In a one-to-one merge, the first observation of one dataset is joined with the first observation of the other dataset, the second observation is joined with the second, and so on. If a *varlist* is specified, however, Stata uses those variables to perform a *match* merge. In a match merge, observations are joined only if the values of the variables in the specified *varlist* match.

Regardless of the style of merge being performed, `merge` always adds a new variable called (by default) _**merge** to the dataset. This variable takes on the values 1, 2, or 3 to mark the source of the resulting observation. The coding is

1. The observation occurred only in the master dataset.

2. The observation occurred only in the using dataset.

3. The observation is the result of joining an observation from the master dataset with one from the using dataset.

When you use the `update` option, this coding is extended to include

4. Same as 3 except that missing values in the master were updated with values from the using.

5. Same as 3 except that some values in the master disagree with values in the using.

One-to-one merge

In a one-to-one merge, the first observation in the master dataset is joined with the first observation in the using dataset, the second observation is joined with the second, and so on. If variables with the same name occur in both the master and the using datasets, the joined observation retains those variables' *original* values, the values of the variables in the master dataset. When the master and using datasets contain different numbers of observations, missing values are joined with the remaining observations from the longer dataset.

▷ Example

You have two datasets stored on disk that you wish to merge into a single dataset. The first dataset, called `odd.dta`, contains the first five positive odd numbers. The second dataset, called `even.dta`, contains the fifth through eighth positive even numbers. (Our example is admittedly not realistic, but it does illustrate the concept.) We show you each of the datasets below:

```
. use odd
(First five odd numbers)

. list

       number      odd
  1.        1        1
  2.        2        3
  3.        3        5
  4.        4        7
  5.        5        9

. use even
(5th through 8th even numbers)

. list

       number     even
  1.        5       10
  2.        6       12
  3.        7       14
  4.        8       16
```

We will join these two datasets using a one-to-one merge. Since the even data is already in memory (we just used it above), we type `merge using odd`. The result is

```
. merge using odd
number was int now float

. list

       number     even      odd    _merge
  1.        5       10        1        3
  2.        6       12        3        3
  3.        7       14        5        3
  4.        8       16        7        3
  5.        5        .        9        2
```

The first thing you will notice is the new variable `_merge`. Every time Stata merges two datasets, it creates this variable and assigns the value of 1, 2, or 3 to each observation. The value 1 indicates that the resulting observation occurred only in the master dataset, 2 indicates the observation occurred only in the using dataset, and 3 indicates the observation occurred in both datasets and is thus the result of joining an observation from the master dataset with an observation from the using dataset.

In this case, the first four observations are marked by `_merge` equal to 3, and the last observation by `_merge` equal to 2. The first four observations are the result of joining observations from the two datasets, and the last observation is a result of adding a new observation from the using data. These values reflect the fact that the original data in memory had four observations, and the odd data stored on disk had five observations. The new last observation is from the odd data exclusively: `number` is 5, `odd` is 9, and `even` has been filled in with *missing*.

Notice that `number` takes on the values 5 through 8 for the first four observations. Those are the values of `number` from the original data in memory—the even data—and conflict with the value of `number` stored in the first four observations of the odd data. `number` in that dataset took on the values 1 through 4, and those values were lost during the merge process. When Stata joins observations and there is a conflict between the value of a variable in memory and the value stored in the using data, Stata by default retains the value stored in memory.

When the command `merge using odd` was issued, Stata responded with "number was int now float". Let's `describe` the datasets in this example:

```
. describe using odd
Contains data                                    First five odd numbers
    obs:           5                             8 Jun 1998 14:32
   vars:           2
   size:          60
-------------------------------------------------------------------------------
    1. number    float  %9.0g
    2. odd       float  %9.0g                     Odd numbers
-------------------------------------------------------------------------------
Sorted by:
. describe using even
Contains data                                    5th through 8th even numbers
    obs:           4                             12 Aug 1998 10:35
   vars:           2
   size:          40
-------------------------------------------------------------------------------
    1. number    int    %8.0g
    2. even      float  %9.0g                     Even numbers
-------------------------------------------------------------------------------
Sorted by:
```

Note that `number` is stored as a `float` in `odd.dta`, but is stored as an `int` in `even.dta`; see [U] **15.2.2 Numeric storage types**. When you `merge` two datasets, Stata engages in automatic variable promotion; that is, if there are conflicts in numeric storage types, the more precise storage type will be used. The resulting dataset, therefore, will have `number` stored as a `float`, and Stata told you this when it said "number was int now float".

◁

Match merge

In a match merge, observations are joined if the values of the variables in the *varlist* are the same. Since the values must be the same, obviously the variables in the *varlist* must appear in both the master and the using datasets.

A match merge proceeds by taking an observation from the master dataset and one from the using dataset and comparing the values of the variables in the *varlist*. If the *varlist* values match, then the observations are joined. If the *varlist* values do not match, the observation from the *earlier* dataset (the dataset whose *varlist* value comes first in the sort order) is joined with a pseudo-observation from the *later* dataset (the other dataset). All the variables in the pseudo-observation contain missing values. The actual observation from the later dataset is retained and compared with the next observation in the earlier dataset, and the process repeats.

▷ Example

The result is not nearly so incomprehensible as the explanation. Let's return to the data used in the previous example and `merge` the two datasets on variable `number`. We first `use` the even data and then type `merge number using odd`:

```
. use even
(5th through 8th even numbers)
. merge number using odd
master data not sorted
r(5);
```

Rather than the data being merged, we suffer the error message "master data not sorted". Match merges require that the data be sorted in the order of the *varlist*, which in this case means ascending order of number. If you look at the previous example, you will observe that the data is in such an order, so the message is more than a little confusing. Before Stata can merge two datasets, however, the data must not only be sorted but Stata must *know* that they are sorted.

The basis of Stata's knowledge is the internal information it keeps on the sort order, and Stata reveals the extent of its knowledge whenever you describe the data:

```
. describe
Contains data from even.dta
  obs:            4                          5th through 8th even numbers
  vars:           2                          12 Aug 1998 10:35
  size:          40 (99.9% of memory free)
-------------------------------------------------------------------------------
  1. number     int    %8.0g
  2. even       float  %9.0g                 Even numbers
-------------------------------------------------------------------------------
Sorted by:
```

The last line of the description shows that the data is "Sorted by:" nothing. We tell Stata to sort the data (or to learn that it is already sorted) with the sort command:

```
. sort number
. describe
Contains data from even.dta
  obs:            4                          5th through 8th even numbers
  vars:           2                          12 Aug 1998 10:35
  size:          40 (99.9% of memory free)
-------------------------------------------------------------------------------
  1. number     int    %8.0g
  2. even       float  %9.0g                 Even numbers
-------------------------------------------------------------------------------
Sorted by:  number
```

Now when we describe the data, Stata informs us that the data is sorted by number. Now that Stata knows the data is sorted, let's try again:

```
. merge number using odd
using data not sorted
r(5);
```

Stata still refuses to carry out our request, this time complaining that the *using* data is not sorted. Both datasets, the master and the using, must be in ascending order of number before Stata can perform a merge.

As before, if you look at the previous example you will discover that odd.dta is in ascending order of number, but as before, Stata does not know this yet. We need to save the data we just sorted, use the odd data, sort it, and re-save it:

```
. save even, replace
file even.dta saved
. use odd
(First 5 odd numbers)
. sort number
. save odd, replace
file odd.dta saved
```

Now we should be able to merge the two datasets:

```
. use even
(5th through 8th even numbers)
. merge number using odd
number was int now float
. list
        number      even       odd     _merge
   1.        5        10         9         3
   2.        6        12         .         1
   3.        7        14         .         1
   4.        8        16         .         1
   5.        1         .         1         2
   6.        2         .         3         2
   7.        3         .         5         2
   8.        4         .         7         2
```

It worked! Let's understand what happened. Even though both datasets were sorted by number, we immediately discern that the result is no longer in ascending order of number. It will be easier to understand what happened if we re-sort the data and then list it again:

```
. sort number
. list
        number      even       odd     _merge
   1.        1         .         1         2
   2.        2         .         3         2
   3.        3         .         5         2
   4.        4         .         7         2
   5.        5        10         9         3
   6.        6        12         .         1
   7.        7        14         .         1
   8.        8        16         .         1
```

Notice that number now goes from 1 to 8, with no repeated values and no values left out of the sequence. Recall that the odd data defined observations for number between 1 and 5, whereas the even data defined observations between 5 and 8. Thus, the variable odd is defined for number equal to 1 through 5, and even is defined for number equal to 5 through 8.

For instance, in the first observation number is 1, even is *missing*, and odd is 1. The value of _merge, 2, indicates that this observation came from the using dataset—odd.dta. In the last observation number is 8, even is 16, and odd is *missing*. The value of _merge, 1, indicates that this observation came from the master dataset—even.dta.

The fifth observation is worth comment. number is 5, even is 10, and odd is 9. Both even and odd are defined, since both the even and the odd datasets had information for number equal to 5. The value of _merge, 3, also tells us that both datasets contributed to the formation of the observation.

◁

▷ Example

Although the previous example demonstrated, in glorious detail, how the match-merging process works, it was not a practical example of how you will ordinarily employ it. Here is a more realistic application.

You have two datasets containing information on automobiles. The identifying variable in each dataset is make, a string variable containing the manufacturer and the model. By *identifying* variable, we mean a variable that is unique for every observation in the data. Values for make—for instance, Honda Accord—are sufficient for identifying each observation.

One dataset, called `autotech.dta`, also contains `mpg`, `weight`, and `length`. The other dataset, called `autocost.dta`, contains `price` and `rep78`, the 1978 repair record.

```
. describe using autotech
Contains data                              1978 Automobile Data
  obs:            74                        11 Aug 1998 18:31
  vars:            4
  size:        2,072
-------------------------------------------------------------------------------
  1. make        str18   %18s              Make and Model
  2. mpg         int     %8.0g             Mileage (mpg)
  3. weight      int     %8.0g             Weight (lbs.)
  4. length      int     %8.0g             Length (in.)
-------------------------------------------------------------------------------
Sorted by:  make

. describe using autocost
Contains data                              1978 Automobile Data
  obs:            74                        11 Aug 1998 18:31
  vars:            3
  size:        1,924
-------------------------------------------------------------------------------
  1. make        str18   %18s              Make and Model
  2. price       int     %8.0g             Price
  3. rep78       int     %8.0g             Repair Record 1978
-------------------------------------------------------------------------------
Sorted by:  make
```

You desire, we assume, to merge these two datasets into a single dataset:

```
. use autotech
(Automobile Models)

. merge make using autocost
```

Let's now examine the result:

```
. describe
Contains data from autotech.dta
  obs:            74                        1978 Automobile Data
  vars:            7                        11 Aug 1998 18:31
  size:        2,442 (99.7% of memory free)
-------------------------------------------------------------------------------
  1. make        str18   %18s              Make and Model
  2. mpg         int     %8.0g             Mileage (mpg)
  3. weight      int     %8.0g             Weight (lbs.)
  4. length      int     %8.0g             Length (in.)
  5. price       int     %8.0g             Price
  6. rep78       int     %8.0g             Repair Record 1978
  7. _merge      byte    %8.0g
-------------------------------------------------------------------------------
Sorted by:
     Note:  dataset has changed since last saved
```

We have a single dataset containing all the information from the two original datasets—or at least it appears that we do. Before accepting that conclusion, we need to verify the result. We think that we entered data for the same cars in each dataset, so every variable should be defined for every car. Although we know it is unlikely, we recognize the possibility that we made a mistake and accidentally left some cars out of one or the other dataset. We can reassure ourselves of our infallibility by tabulating _merge:

```
. tabulate _merge
    _merge |      Freq.     Percent        Cum.
-----------+-----------------------------------
         3 |         74      100.00      100.00
-----------+-----------------------------------
     Total |         74      100.00
```

We see that _merge is 3 for every observation in the data. We made no mistake—for every observation in `autocost.dta`, there was an observation in `autotech.dta` and vice versa.

Now pretend that we have another dataset containing additional information on these automobiles—`automore.dta`—and we want to merge that data as well. Before we can do so, we must **sort** the data we have in memory by `make` since after a **merge** the sort order may have changed:

```
. sort make
. merge make using automore
_merge already defined
r(110);
```

After sorting the data, Stata refused to merge the new dataset, complaining instead that _merge is already defined. Every time Stata merges datasets it wants to create a variable called _merge (or *varname* if the _merge(*varname*) option was specified). In this case, there is an _merge variable left over from the last time we merged. We have three choices: We can **rename** the _merge variable, we can **drop** it, or we can specify a different variable name with the _merge() option. In this case _merge contains no useful information—we already verified that the previous merge went as expected—so we **drop** it and try again:

```
. drop _merge
. merge make using automore
```

Stata performed our request; whatever new variables were contained in `automore.dta` are now contained in our single, master dataset—perhaps. One should not jump to conclusions. After a match merge, you should *always* **tabulate** _merge to verify that the expected actually happened, as we do below:

```
. tabulate _merge
    _merge |      Freq.     Percent        Cum.
-----------+-----------------------------------
         1 |          1        1.33        1.33
         2 |          1        1.33        2.67
         3 |         73       97.33      100.00
-----------+-----------------------------------
     Total |         75      100.00
```

Surprise! In this case something strange did happen. Some 73 of the observations merged as we anticipated. However, the new data `automore.dta` added one new car to the dataset (identified by _merge equal to 2) and failed to define new variables for another car in our original dataset (identified by _merge equal to 1). Perhaps this is what should happen, but it is more likely that we have a mistake in `automore.dta`. We probably misidentified one car so that to Stata it appeared as data on a new car, resulting in one new observation and missing data on another.

If this happened to us, we would now figure out why it happened. We would type `list make if _merge==1` to learn the identity of the car that did not appear in `automore.dta`, and we would type `list make if _merge==2` to learn the identity of the car that `automore.dta` added to our data.

◁

❑ Technical Note

It is difficult to overemphasize the importance of tabulating _merge no matter how sure you are that you have no errors. It takes only a second and can save you hours of grief. Along the same lines, one-to-one merges are a bad idea. In the example above, we could have performed all the merges as one-to-one merges and saved a small amount of typing. Let's examine what would have happened.

We first merged autotech.dta with autocost.dta by typing merge make using autocost. We could perform a one-to-one merge by typing merge using autocost. The result would be the same; the datasets line up and are in the same sort order, so sequentially matching the observations from the two datasets would have resulted in a perfectly matched dataset.

In the second case, we merged the data in memory with automore.dta by typing merge make using automore. A one-to-one merge would have led to disaster, and we would never have known it! If we type merge using automore, Stata would sequentially, and blindly, join observations. Since there are the same number of observations in each dataset, everything would appear to merge perfectly.

We speculated in the previous example that we had an error in automore.dta. Remember that automore.dta included data on one new car and lacked data on an existing car. Even if there is no error, things have gone awry. No matter what, the data in memory and automore.dta do not match. For instance, assume that this new car is the first observation of automore.dta and that it is some (perhaps mistaken) model of Ford. Assume that the first observation of the data in memory is on a Chevrolet. Stata could and would silently join data on the Chevrolet with data on the Ford, and thereafter data on a Volvo with data on a Saab, and even data on a Volkswagen with data on a Cadillac. And you would never know.

Every dataset should carry a variable or a set of variables that *uniquely* identifies each observation, and then you should always use those variables when merging data. Ignore this advice at your own peril.

❑

❑ Technical Note

Circumstances may arise when you will merge two datasets knowing there will be mismatches. Say you have an analysis dataset on patients from the cancer ward of a particular hospital and you have just received another dataset containing their demographic information. Actually, this other dataset contains not just their demographic information but the demographic information on every patient in the hospital during the year. You could,

```
. merge patid using demog
. drop if _merge==2
```

Equivalently, you could

```
. merge patid using demog, nokeep
```

The nokeep option tells merge not to store observations from the using data that do not appear in the master. There is an advantage in this. When we merged and dropped, we stored the irrelevant observations and then discarded them, so the data in memory temporarily grew. When we merge with the nokeep option, the data never grows beyond what was absolutely necessary.

❑

❑ Technical Note

In our automobile example, we had a single identifying variable. Sometimes you will have identifying variables, variables that, taken together, are unique for every observation.

Let's imagine that, rather than having a single variable called **make**, we had two variables: **manuf** and **model**. **manuf** contains the manufacturer and **model** contains the model. Rather than having a single variable recording, say, "Honda Accord", we have two variables, one recording "Honda" and another recording "Accord". Stata can deal with data like this. You can go back through our previous example and substitute **manuf model** everywhere you see **make**. For instance, rather than typing **merge make using autocost**, we would have typed **merge manuf model using autocost**.

Now let's make one more change in our assumptions. Let's assume that **manuf** and **model** are not string variables but are instead numerically coded variables. Perhaps the number 15 stands for Honda in the **manuf** variable and the number 2 stands for Accord in the **model** variable. We do not have to remember our numeric codes because we have smartly created value labels telling Stata what number stands for what string of characters. We now go back to the step where we merged **autotech.dta** with **autocost.dta**:

```
. use autotech
(Automobile models)

. merge manuf model using autocost
(label manuf already defined)
(label model already defined)
```

Stata makes two minor comments but otherwise carries out our request. It notes that the labels **manuf** and **model** are already defined. The messages refer to the *value labels* named **manuf** and **model**.

Both datasets contain value label definitions that turn the numeric codes for manufacturer and model into words. When Stata merged the two datasets, it already had one set of definitions in memory (obtained when we typed **use autotech**) and thus ignored the second set of definitions contained in **autocost.dta**. Stata felt obliged to mention the second set of definitions while otherwise ignoring them since they *might* contain different codings. In this case, we know they are the same since we created them. (*Hint:* You should never give the same name to value labels containing different codings.)

❑

When one is performing a match merge, the master and/or using datasets may have multiple observations with the same *varlist* value. These multiple observations are joined sequentially, as in a one-to-one merge. If the datasets have an unequal number of observations with the same *varlist* value, the last such observation in the *shorter* dataset is replicated until the number of observations is equal.

▷ Example

The process of replicating the observation from the shorter dataset is known as *spreading* and can be put to practical use. Suppose you have two datasets. **dollars.dta** contains the dollar sales and costs of your firm, by region, for the last year:

```
. use dollars
(Regional Sales & Costs)
. list
            region      sales        cost
    1.          NE      360523      138097
    2.      N Cntrl     419472      227677
    3.       South      532399      330499
    4.        West      310565      165348
```

sforce.dta contains the names of the individuals in your sales force along with the region in which they operate:

```
. use sforce
(Sales Force)
. list
            region        name
    1.          NE      Ecklund
    2.          NE       Franks
    3.      N Cntrl      Krantz
    4.      N Cntrl       Phipps
    5.      N Cntrl       Willis
    6.       South      Anderson
    7.       South       Dubnoff
    8.       South          Lee
    9.       South       McNiel
   10.        West       Charles
   11.        West         Grant
   12.        West          Cobb
```

You now wish to merge these two datasets by region, spreading the sales and cost information across all observations for which it is relevant; that is, you want to add the variables sales and costs to the sales force data. The variable sales will assume the value $360,523 for the first two observations, $419,472 for the next three observations, and so on.

```
. merge region using dollars
(label region already defined)
. list
            region        name       sales        cost    _merge
    1.          NE      Ecklund      360523      138097         3
    2.          NE       Franks      360523      138097         3
    3.      N Cntrl      Krantz      419472      227677         3
    4.      N Cntrl       Phipps      419472      227677         3
    5.      N Cntrl       Willis      419472      227677         3
    6.       South      Anderson     532399      330499         3
    7.       South       Dubnoff     532399      330499         3
    8.       South          Lee      532399      330499         3
    9.       South       McNiel      532399      330499         3
   10.        West       Charles     310565      165348         3
   11.        West         Grant     310565      165348         3
   12.        West          Cobb     310565      165348         3
```

Even though there are 12 observations in the sales force data and only 4 observations in the sales and cost data, all the records merged. The dollars.dta contained one observation for the NE region. The sforce.dta contained two observations for the same region. Thus, the single observation in dollars.dta was matched to both the observations in sforce.dta. In technical jargon, the single record in dollars.dta was replicated, or *spread*, across the observations in sforce.dta.

◁

Updating data

merge with the update option varies merge's actions when an observation in the master is matched with an observation in the using data. Without the update option, merge leaves the values in the master data alone and adds the data for the new variables. With the update option, merge adds the new variables, but it also replaces missing values in the master observation with corresponding values from the using. (Missing values means numeric missing (.) and empty strings ("").)

The values for _merge are extended:

_merge	meaning
1	obs. from master data
2	obs. from using data
3	obs. from both, master agrees with using
4	obs. from both, missing in master updated
5	obs. from both, master disagrees with using

In the case of _merge == 5, the master values are retained unless replace is specified, in which case the master values are updated just as if they had been missing.

Pretend dataset 1 contains variables id, a, and b; dataset 2 contains id, a, and x. You merge the two datasets by id, dataset 1 being the master data in memory and dataset 2 the using data on disk. Consider two observations that match and call the values from the first dataset id_1, etc., and those from the second id_2, etc. The resulting dataset will have variables id, a, b, x, and _merge. merge's typical logic is

1. The fact that the observations match means $id_1 = id_2$. Set $id = id_1$.

2. Variable a occurs in both datasets. Ignore a_2 and set $a = a_1$.

3. Variable b occurs in only dataset 1. Set $b = b_1$.

4. Variable x occurs in only dataset 2. Set $x = x_2$.

5. Set _merge $= 3$.

With update, the logic is modified:

1. (unchanged.) Since the observations match, $id_1 = id_2$. Set $id = id_1$.

2. Variable a occurs in both datasets:

   a. If $a_1 = a_2$, set $a = a_1$ and set _merge $= 3$.

   b. If a_1 contains missing and a_2 is nonmissing, set $a = a_2$ and set _merge $= 4$, indicating an update was made.

   c. If a_2 contains missing, set $a = a_1$ and set _merge $= 3$ (indicating no update).

   d. If $a_1 \neq a_2$ and both contain nonmissing, set $a = a_1$ or, if replace was specified, $a = a_2$ but, regardless, set _merge $= 5$, indicating a disagreement.

Rules 3 and 4 remain unchanged.

▷ Example

In original.dta you have data on some cars including the make, price, and mileage rating. In updates.dta you have some updated data on these cars along with a new variable recording engine displacement. The datasets contain

```
. use original, clear
(original data)
. list
        make              price      mpg
1. Chev. Chevette         3,299       29
2. Chev. Malibu           4,504        .
3. Datsun 510             5,079       24
4. Merc. XR-7             6,303        .
5. Olds Cutlass           4,733       19
6. Renault Le Car         3,895       26
7. VW Dasher              7,140       23

. use updates, clear
(updates, mpg and displ)
. list
        make               mpg      displ
1. Chev. Chevette            .        231
2. Chev. Malibu             22        200
3. Datsun 510               24        119
4. Merc. XR-7               14        302
5. Olds Cutlass            19        231
6. Renault Le Car           25         79
7. VW Dasher                23         97
```

Updating our data, we obtain

```
. use original, clear
(original data)
. merge make using updates, update
. list
        make              price      mpg    displ    _merge
1. Chev. Chevette         3,299       29      231         3
2. Chev. Malibu           4,504       22      200         4
3. Datsun 510             5,079       24      119         3
4. Merc. XR-7             6,303       14      302         4
5. Olds Cutlass           4,733       19      231         3
6. Renault Le Car         3,895       26       79         5
7. VW Dasher              7,140       23       97         3
```

All observations merged because all have _merge $\geq$ 3. The observations having _merge = 3 have mpg just as it was recorded in the original data. In observation 1, mpg is 29 because the updated data had mpg = .; in observation 3, mpg remains 24 because the updated data also stated that mpg is 24.

The observations having _merge = 4 have had their mpg data updated. The mpg variable was missing in observations 2 and 4 and new values were obtained from the update data.

The observation having _merge = 5 has its mpg just as it was recorded in the original data, just as do the _merge = 3 observations, but there is an important difference. There is a disagreement about the value of mpg; the original claims it is 26 and the updated, 25. Had we specified the replace option, mpg would now contain the updated 25 but the observation would still be marked _merge = 5. replace affects only which value is retained in the case of disagreement.

◁

References

Nash, J. D. 1994. dm19: Merging raw data and dictionary files. *Stata Technical Bulletin* 20: 3–5. Reprinted in *Stata Technical Bulletin Reprints*, vol. 4, pp. 22–25.

Also See

Complementary:	[R] **save**, [R] **sort**
Related:	[R] **append**, [R] **cross**, [R] **joinby**
Background:	[U] **25 Commands for combining data**

Title

meta — Meta analysis

Remarks

Stata should have a meta-analysis command, but as of the date that this manual was written, Stata does not. Stata users, however, have developed an excellent suite of commands for performing meta-analysis, many of which have been published in the *Stata Technical Bulletin* (STB).

Issue	insert	author(s)	command	description
STB-38	sbe16	S. Sharp, J. Sterne	meta	meta-analysis for an outcome of two exposures or two treatment regimens
STB-42	sbe16.1	S. Sharp, J. Sterne	meta	update of sbe16
STB-43	sbe16.2	S. Sharp, J. Sterne	meta	update; *install this version*
STB-41	sbe19	T. Steichen	metabias	performs the Begg and Mazumdar (1994) adjusted rank correlation test for publication bias and the Egger et al. (1997) regression asymmetry test for publication bias
STB-44	sbe19.1	T. Steichen, M. Egger, J. Sterne	metabias	update; *install this version*
STB-41	sbe20	A. Tobias	galbr	performs the Galbraith plot (1988) which is useful for investigating heterogeneity in meta-analysis
STB-42	sbe22	J. Sterne	metacum	performs cumulative meta-analysis using fixed- or random-effects models, and graphs the result
STB-42	sbe23	S. Sharp	metareg	extends a random-effects meta-analysis to estimate the extent to which one or more covariates, with values defined for each study in the analysis, explains heterogeneity in the treatment effects
STB-44	sbe24	M. J. Bradburn, J. J. Deeks, D. G. Altman	metan, funnel, labbe	meta-analysis of studies with two groups funnel plot of precision versus treatment effect L'Abbe plot
STB-45	sbe24.1	M. J. Bradburn, J. J. Deeks, D. G. Altman	funnel	*install this version*

Additional commands may be available; enter Stata and type `search meta analysis`.

To download and install from the Internet the Sharp and Stern `meta` command, for instance, Stata for Windows and Stata for Macintosh users could

1. Pull down **Help** and select **STB and User-written Programs**.

2. Click on *http://www.stata.com*.

3. Click on *stb*.

4. Click on *stb42*.

5. Click on *sbe16.2*.

6. Click on *click here to install*.

or they, along with Stata for Unix users, could instead type commands:

1. Navigate to the appropriate STB issue:
    a. Type `net from http://www.stata.com`
       Type `net cd stb`
       Type `net cd stb42`

    or

    b. Type `net from http://www.stata.com/stb/stb42`

2. Type `net describe sbe16.2`

3. Type `net install sbe16.2`

If you are not connected to the Internet, you must install the inserts above from an STB diskette; see [U] **20.8 How do I obtain and install STB updates?**.

References

Begg, C. B. and M. Mazumdar. 1994. Operating characteristics of a rank correlation test for publication bias. *Biometrics* 50: 1088–1101.

Bradburn, M. J., J. J. Deeks, and D. G. Altman. 1998. sbe24: metan—an alternative meta-analysis command. *Stata Technical Bulletin* 44: 4–15.

Egger, M., G. D. Smith, M. Schneider, and C. Minder. 1997. Bias in meta-analysis detected by a simple, graphical test. *British Medical Journal* 315: 629–634.

Galbraith, R. F. 1988. A note on graphical presentation estimated odds ratios from several clinical trials. *Statistics in Medicine* 7: 889–894.

L'Abbé, K. A., A. S. Detsky, and K. O'Rourke. 1987. Meta-analysis in clinical research. *Annals of Internal Medicine* 107: 224–233.

Sharp, S. 1998. sbe23: Meta-analysis regression. *Stata Technical Bulletin* 42: 16–22. Reprinted in *Stata Technical Bulletin Reprints*, vol. 7, pp. 148–155.

Sharp, S. and J. Sterne. 1997. sbe16: Meta-analysis. *Stata Technical Bulletin* 38: 9–14. Reprinted in *Stata Technical Bulletin Reprints*, vol. 7, pp. 100–106.

——. 1998a. sbe16.1: New syntax and output for the meta-analysis command. *Stata Technical Bulletin* 42: 6–8. Reprinted in *Stata Technical Bulletin Reprints*, vol. 7, pp. 106–108.

——. 1998b. sbe16.2: Corrections to the meta-analysis command. *Stata Technical Bulletin* 43: 15.

Steichen, T. J. 1998. sbe19: Tests for publication bias in meta-analysis. *Stata Technical Bulletin* 41: 9–15. Reprinted in *Stata Technical Bulletin Reprints*, vol. 7, pp. 125–133.

Steichen, T. J., M. Egger, and J. Sterne. 1998. sbe19.1: Tests for publication bias in meta-analysis. *Stata Technical Bulletin* 44: 3–4.

Sterne, J. 1998. sbe22: Cumulative meta-analysis. 1998 *Stata Technical Bulletin* 42: 13–16. Reprinted in *Stata Technical Bulletin Reprints*, vol. 7, pp. 143–147.

Tobias, A. 1997. sbe20: Assessing heterogeneity in meta-analysis: the Galbraith plot. *Stata Technical Bulletin* 41: 15–17. Reprinted in *Stata Technical Bulletin Reprints*, vol. 7, pp. 133–136.

Title

mkdir — Create directory

Syntax

mkdir *directory-name* [, pub̲lic]

Double quotes may be used to enclose the directory name and the quotes must be used if the directory contains embedded blanks.

Description

mkdir creates a new directory (folder).

Options

public specifies that *directory-name* is to be readable by everyone; otherwise, the directory will be created according to the default permissions you have set with your operating system.

Remarks

Examples:

Windows

. mkdir myproj
. mkdir c:\projects\myproj
. mkdir "c:\My Projects\Project 1"

Unix

. mkdir myproj
. mkdir ~/projects/myproj

Macintosh

. mkdir myproj
. mkdir :hdisk:projects:project1
. mkdir ":Hard Disk:My Projects:Project 1"

Also See

Related: [R] **cd**, [R] **copy**, [R] **dir**, [R] **erase**, [R] **shell**, [R] **type**

Background: [U] **14.6 File-naming conventions**

Title

mkspline — Linear spline construction

Syntax

mkspline *newvar*$_1$ #$_1$ [*newvar*$_2$ #$_2$ [...]] *newvar*$_k$ = *oldvar* [if *exp*] [in *range*]

[, m̲arginal]

mkspline *stubname* # = *oldvar* [if *exp*] [in *range*] [, m̲arginal p̲ctile]

Description

mkspline creates variables containing a linear spline of *oldvar*.

In the first syntax, mkspline creates *newvar*$_1$, ..., *newvar*$_k$ containing a linear spline of *oldvar* with knots at the specified #$_1$, ..., #$_{k-1}$.

In the second syntax, mkspline creates # variables named *stubname*1, ..., *stubname*# containing a linear spline of *oldvar*. The knots are equally spaced over the range of *oldvar* or are placed at the percentiles of *oldvar*.

Options

marginal specifies that the new variables are to be constructed so that, when used in estimation, the coefficients represent the change in the slope from the preceding interval. The default is to construct the variables so that, when used in estimation, the coefficients will measure the slopes for the interval.

pctile is allowed only with the second syntax. It specifies that the knots are to be placed at percentiles of the data rather than equally spaced based on the range.

Remarks

Linear splines allow estimating the relationship between y and x as a piecewise linear function. A piecewise linear function is just that: it is a function composed of linear segments—straight lines. One linear segment represents the function for values of x below x_0. Another linear segment handles values between x_0 and x_1, and so on. The linear segments are arranged so that they join at x_0, x_1, ..., which are called the knots. An example of a piecewise linear function is shown below.

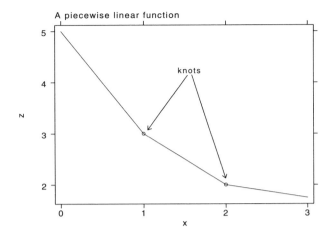

A piecewise linear function

▷ Example

You wish to estimate a model of log income on education and age using a piecewise linear function for age:

$$\text{lninc} = b_0 + b_1 \, \text{educ} + f(\text{age}) + u$$

The knots are to be at ten-year intervals: 20, 30, 40, 50, and 60.

```
. mkspline age1 20 age2 30 age3 40 age4 50 age5 60 age6 = age, marginal
. regress lninc educ age1-age6
  (output omitted )
```

Since you specified the `marginal` option, you could test whether the age effect is the same in the 30–40 and 40–50 intervals by asking whether the **age4** coefficient were zero. With the `marginal` option, coefficients measure the change in slope from the preceding group. Specifying `marginal` changes only the interpretation of the coefficients; the same model is estimated in either case. That is, without the `marginal` option, the interpretation of the coefficients would have been

$$\frac{dy}{d\text{age}} = \begin{cases} a_1 & \text{if age} < 20 \\ a_2 & \text{if } 20 \leq \text{age} < 30 \\ a_3 & \text{if } 30 \leq \text{age} < 40 \\ a_4 & \text{if } 40 \leq \text{age} < 50 \\ a_5 & \text{if } 50 \leq \text{age} < 60 \\ a_6 & \text{otherwise.} \end{cases}$$

With the `marginal` option specified, the interpretation is

$$\frac{dy}{d\text{age}} = \begin{cases} a_1 & \text{if age} < 20 \\ a_1 + a_2 & \text{if } 20 \leq \text{age} < 30 \\ a_1 + a_2 + a_3 & \text{if } 30 \leq \text{age} < 40 \\ a_1 + a_2 + a_3 + a_4 & \text{if } 40 \leq \text{age} < 50 \\ a_1 + a_2 + a_3 + a_4 + a_5 & \text{if } 50 \leq \text{age} < 60 \\ a_1 + a_2 + a_3 + a_4 + a_5 + a_6 & \text{otherwise.} \end{cases}$$

◁

▷ Example

As a second example, pretend you have a binary outcome variable called outcome. You are beginning an analysis and wish to parameterize the effect of dosage on outcome. You wish to divide the data into five equal-width groups of dosage for the piecewise linear function.

```
. mkspline dose 5 = dosage
. logistic outcome dose1-dose5
  (output omitted )
```

mkspline dose 5 = dosage creates five variables, dose1, dose2, ..., dose5, equally spacing the knots over the range of dosage. If dosage varied between 0 and 100, mkspline dose 5 = dosage has the same effect as typing

```
. mkspline dose1 20 dose2 40 dose3 60 dose4 80 dose5 = dosage
```

The pctile option sets the knots to divide the data into five equal sample-size groups rather than five equal-width ranges. Typing

```
. mkspline dose 5 = dosage, pctile
```

places the knots at the 20th, 40th, 60th, and 80th percentiles of the data.

◁

Methods and Formulas

mkspline is implemented as an ado-file.

Let V_i, $i = 1, \ldots, n$, be the variables to be created, k_i, $i = 1, \ldots, n-1$ be the corresponding knots, and $\mathcal{V}$ be the original variable (the command is mkspline V_1 k_1 V_2 k_2 ... V_n = $\mathcal{V}$). Then

$$V_1 = \min(\mathcal{V}, k_1)$$

$$V_i = \max\left(\min(\mathcal{V}, k_i), k_{i-1}\right) - k_{i-1} \quad i = 2, \ldots, n$$

If the marginal option is specified, the definitions are

$$V_1 = \mathcal{V}$$

$$V_i = \max(0, \mathcal{V} - k_{i-1}) \quad i = 2, \ldots, n$$

In the second syntax, mkspline *stubname* # = $\mathcal{V}$, let m and M be the minimum and maximum of $\mathcal{V}$. Without the pctile option, knots are set at $m + (M - m)(i/n)$ for $i = 1, \ldots, n-1$. If pctile is specified, knots are set at the $100(i/n)$ percentiles, for $i = 1, \ldots, n-1$. Percentiles are calculated by egen's pctile() function.

References

Gould, W. W. 1993. sg19: Linear splines and piecewise linear functions. *Stata Technical Bulletin* 15: 13–17. Reprinted in *Stata Technical Bulletin Reprints*, vol. 3, pp. 98–104.

Greene, W. H. 1997. *Econometric Analysis*. 3d ed. Upper Saddle River, NJ: Prentice–Hall.

Panis, C. 1994. sg24: The piecewise linear spline transformation. *Stata Technical Bulletin* 18: 27–29. Reprinted in *Stata Technical Bulletin Reprints*, vol. 3, pp. 146–149.

Also See

Related: [R] **fracpoly**

Title

> **ml** — Maximum likelihood estimation

Syntax

ml clear

ml <u>mod</u>el   *method progname eq* $\begin{bmatrix} eq \ldots \end{bmatrix}$ $\begin{bmatrix} weight \end{bmatrix}$ $\begin{bmatrix} \text{if } exp \end{bmatrix}$ $\begin{bmatrix} \text{in } range \end{bmatrix}$ $\Big[,$
                             <u>rob</u>ust <u>cl</u>uster(*varname*) <u>t</u>itle(*string*) <u>no</u>preserve
                             <u>coll</u>inear <u>miss</u>ing lf0($\#_k$ $\#_{ll}$) <u>cont</u>inue <u>wald</u>test(*#*)
                             obs(*#*) noscvars $\Big]$

ml <u>q</u>uery

ml check

ml <u>sea</u>rch $\begin{bmatrix} \begin{bmatrix} / \end{bmatrix} eqname \begin{bmatrix} : \end{bmatrix} \#_{lb} \ \#_{ub} \end{bmatrix}$ $\begin{bmatrix} \ldots \end{bmatrix}$
                     $\Big[,$ <u>r</u>epeat(*#*) <u>no</u>log <u>trace</u> <u>rest</u>art <u>no</u>rescale $\Big]$

ml <u>p</u>lot $\begin{bmatrix} eqname: \end{bmatrix} name$ $\begin{bmatrix} \# \begin{bmatrix} \# \begin{bmatrix} \# \end{bmatrix} \end{bmatrix} \end{bmatrix}$ $\Big[,$ <u>sav</u>ing(*filename*$\begin{bmatrix} , \text{ replace} \end{bmatrix}$) $\Big]$

ml init $\Big\{ \begin{bmatrix} eqname: \end{bmatrix} name\text{=}\# \ | \ /eqname\text{=}\# \Big\}$ $\begin{bmatrix} \ldots \end{bmatrix}$
ml init   *#* $\begin{bmatrix} \# \ \ldots \end{bmatrix}$, copy
ml init   *matname* $\begin{bmatrix} , \text{ skip copy} \end{bmatrix}$

ml <u>re</u>port

ml trace $\Big\{ \text{on} \ | \ \text{off} \Big\}$

ml count $\begin{bmatrix} \text{clear} \ | \ \text{on} \ | \ \text{off} \end{bmatrix}$

ml <u>max</u>imize $\Big[,$ <u>dif</u>ficult <u>no</u>log <u>trace</u> <u>grad</u>ient <u>hess</u>ian showstep
                  <u>iter</u>ate(*#*) <u>lt</u>olerance(*#*) <u>tol</u>erance(*#*) <u>nowarn</u>ing novce
                  <u>sc</u>ore(*newvarnames*) <u>noout</u>put <u>l</u>evel(*#*) <u>ef</u>orm(*string*) noclear $\Big]$

ml <u>graph</u> $\begin{bmatrix} \# \end{bmatrix}$ $\Big[,$ <u>sav</u>ing(*filename*$\begin{bmatrix} , \text{ replace} \end{bmatrix}$) $\Big]$

ml <u>d</u>isplay $\Big[,$ <u>no</u>header <u>ef</u>orm(*string*) <u>first</u> neq(*#*) <u>plus</u> <u>l</u>evel(*#*) $\Big]$

where *method* is { lf | d0 | d1 | d1debug | d2 | d2debug }

and *eq* is the equation to be estimated, enclosed in parentheses, and optionally with a name to be given to the equation, preceded by a colon:

([*eqname*:] [*varnames* =] [*varnames*] [, *eq_options*])

or *eq* is the name of a parameter such as sigma with a slash in front

/*eqname*   which is equivalent to   (*eqname*:)

and *eq_options* are

<u>nocons</u>tant <u>off</u>set(*varname*) <u>expo</u>sure(*varname*)

---

fweights, pweights, aweights, and iweights are allowed, see [U] **14.1.6 weight**. With all but method lf, you must write your likelihood-evaluation program a certain way if pweights are to be specified, and pweights may not be specified with method d0.

ml shares the features of all estimation commands; see [U] **23 Estimation and post-estimation commands**. To redisplay results, type ml display.

Syntax of ml model in noninteractive mode

ml <u>mod</u>el *method progname eq* [*eq* ...] [*weight*] [if *exp*] [in *range*], <u>maximize</u>

[<u>robust</u> <u>cluster</u>(*varname*) <u>title</u>(*string*) <u>nopreserve</u> <u>collinear</u>

<u>missing</u> lf0(#*k* #*ll*) <u>contin</u>ue <u>wald</u>test(#) obs(#) noscvars

<u>init</u>(*ml_init_args*) <u>sear</u>ch(on | quietly | off) <u>repeat</u>(#)

<u>bounds</u>(*ml_search_bounds*) <u>diff</u>icult <u>nolog</u> <u>trace</u> <u>gradient</u>

<u>hessian</u> showstep <u>iterate</u>(#) <u>ltol</u>erance(#) <u>tol</u>erance(#)

<u>nowarn</u>ing novce <u>score</u>(*newvarlist*)]

Noninteractive mode is invoked by specifying option maximize. Use maximize when ml is to be used as a subroutine of another ado-file or program and you want to carry forth the problem, from definition to posting of final results, in one command.

Syntax of subroutines for use by method d0, d1, and d2 evaluators

mleval   *newvarname* = *vecname* [, eq(#)]

mleval   *scalarname* = *vecname*, scalar [eq(#)]

mlsum   *scalarname*$_{\text{lnf}}$ = *exp* [if *exp*] [, <u>nowei</u>ght]

mlvecsum   *scalarname*$_{\text{lnf}}$ *rowvecname* = *exp* [if *exp*] [, eq(#)]

mlmatsum   *scalarname*$_{\text{lnf}}$ *matrixname* = *exp* [if *exp*] [, eq(#[,#])]

Syntax of user-written evaluator

Summary of notation

The log-likelihood function is $\ln L(\theta_{1j}, \theta_{2j}, \ldots, \theta_{Ej})$ where $\theta_{ij} = \mathbf{x}_{ij}\mathbf{b}_i$ and $j = 1, \ldots, N$ indexes observations and $i = 1, \ldots, E$ indexes the linear equations defined by `ml model`. If the likelihood satisfies the linear-form restrictions, it can be decomposed as $\ln L = \sum_{j=1}^{N} \ln \ell(\theta_{1j}, \theta_{2j}, \ldots, \theta_{Ej})$.

Method lf evaluators:

```
program define progname
        version 6
        args lnf theta1 [theta2 ... ]
        /* if you need to create any intermediate results: */
        tempvar tmp1 tmp2 ...
        quietly gen double `tmp1´ = ...
        ...
        quietly replace `lnf´ = ...
end
```

where

`lnf´	variable to be filled in with observation-by-observation values of $\ln \ell_j$
`theta1´	variable containing evaluation of 1st equation $\theta_{1j}=\mathbf{x}_{1j}\mathbf{b}_1$
`theta2´	variable containing evaluation of 2nd equation $\theta_{2j}=\mathbf{x}_{2j}\mathbf{b}_2$

Method d0 evaluators:

```
program define progname
        version 6
        args todo b lnf

        tempvar theta1 theta2 ...
        mleval `theta1´ = `b´, eq(1)
        mleval `theta2´ = `b´, eq(2) /* if there is a θ₂ */
        ...

        /* if you need to create any intermediate results: */
        tempvar tmp1 tmp2 ...
        gen double `tmp1´ = ...
        ...

        mlsum `lnf´ = ...
end
```

where

`todo´	always contains 1 (may be ignored)
`b´	full parameter row vector $\mathbf{b}=(\mathbf{b}_1,\mathbf{b}_2,\ldots,\mathbf{b}_E)$
`lnf´	scalar to be filled in with overall $\ln L$

Method d1 evaluators:

```
program define progname
        version 6
        args todo b lnf g [negH g1 [g2 ... ] ]

        tempvar theta1 theta2 ...
        mleval `theta1´ = `b´, eq(1)
        mleval `theta2´ = `b´, eq(2) /* if there is a θ₂ */
        ...

        /* if you need to create any intermediate results: */
        tempvar tmp1 tmp2 ...
        gen double `tmp1´ = ...
        ...
```

```
        mlsum `lnf´ = ...
        if `todo´==0 | `lnf´==. { exit }

        tempname d1 d2 ...
        mlvecsum `lnf´ `d1´ = formula for ∂ ln ℓⱼ/∂θ₁ⱼ, eq(1)
        mlvecsum `lnf´ `d2´ = formula for ∂ ln ℓⱼ/∂θ₂ⱼ, eq(2)
        ...
        matrix `g´ = (`d1´,`d2´, ... )
end
```

where

`todo´	contains 0 or 1
	0⇒`lnf´to be filled in; 1⇒`lnf´ and `g´ to be filled in
`b´	full parameter row vector **b**=(**b**₁,**b**₂,...,**b**ₑ)
`lnf´	scalar to be filled in with overall ln L
`g´	row vector to be filled in with overall **g**=∂ ln L/∂**b**
`negH´	argument to be ignored
`g1´	variable optionally to be filled in with ∂ ln ℓⱼ/∂**b**₁
`g2´	variable optionally to be filled in with ∂ ln ℓⱼ/∂**b**₂
...	

Method d2 evaluators:

```
program define progname
        version 6
        args todo b lnf g negH [g1 [g2 ... ] ]
        tempvar theta1 theta2 ...
        mleval `theta1´ = `b´, eq(1)
        mleval `theta2´ = `b´, eq(2) /* if there is a θ₂ */
        ...

        /* if you need to create any intermediate results: */
        tempvar tmp1 tmp2 ...
        gen double `tmp1´ = ...
        ...

        mlsum `lnf´ = ...
        if `todo´==0 | `lnf´==. { exit }

        tempname d1 d2 ...
        mlvecsum `lnf´ `d1´ = formula for ∂ ln ℓⱼ/∂θ₁ⱼ, eq(1)
        mlvecsum `lnf´ `d2´ = formula for ∂ ln ℓⱼ/∂θ₂ⱼ, eq(2)
        ...
        matrix `g´ = (`d1´,`d2´, ... )
        if `todo´==1 | `lnf´==. { exit }

        tempname d11 d12 d22 ...
        mlmatsum `lnf´ `d11´ = formula for −∂² ln ℓⱼ/∂θ₁ⱼ², eq(1)
        mlmatsum `lnf´ `d12´ = formula for −∂² ln ℓⱼ/∂θ₁ⱼ∂θ₂ⱼ, eq(1,2)
        mlmatsum `lnf´ `d22´ = formula for −∂² ln ℓⱼ/∂θ₂ⱼ², eq(2)
        ...
        matrix `negH´ = (`d11´,`d12´, ... \ `d12´´,`d22´, ... )
end
```

where

`todo´	contains 0, 1, or 2
	0⇒`lnf´ to be filled in; 1⇒`lnf´ and `g´ to be filled in;
	2⇒`lnf´, `g´, and `negH´ to be filled in
`b´	full parameter row vector **b**=(**b**₁,**b**₂,...,**b**ₑ)
`lnf´	scalar to be filled in with overall ln L
`g´	row vector to be filled in with overall **g**=∂ ln L/∂**b**
`negH´	matrix to be filled in with overall negative Hessian −**H**=−∂² ln L/∂**b**∂**b**′
`g1´	variable optionally to be filled in with ∂ ln ℓⱼ/∂**b**₁
`g2´	variable optionally to be filled in with ∂ ln ℓⱼ/∂**b**₂
...	

Global macros for use by all evaluators

$ML_y1	name of first dependent variable
$ML_y2	name of second dependent variable, if any
...	
$ML_samp	variable containing 1 if observation to be used; 0 otherwise
$ML_w	variable containing weight associated with observation or 1 if no weights specified

Method lf evaluators can ignore $ML_samp, but restricting calculations to the $ML_samp==1 subsample will speed execution. Method lf evaluators must ignore $ML_w; application of weights is handled by the method itself.

Method d0, d1, and d2 can ignore $ML_samp as long as ml model's nopreserve option is not specified. Method d0, d1, and d2 will run more quickly if nopreserve is specified. Method d0, d1, and d2 evaluators can ignore $ML_w only if they use mlsum, mlvecsum, and mlmatsum to produce final results.

Description

ml clear clears the current problem definition. This command is rarely if ever used because, when you type ml model, any previous problem is automatically cleared.

ml model defines the current problem.

ml query displays a description of the current problem.

ml check verifies that the log-likelihood evaluator you have written seems to work. We strongly urge the use of this command.

ml search searches for (better) initial values. We recommend use of this command.

ml plot provides a graphical way of searching for (better) initial values.

ml init provides of a way of setting initial values to user-specified values.

ml report reports the values of $\ln L$, its gradient, and its negative Hessian at the initial values or current parameter estimates $\mathbf{b}_0$.

ml trace traces the execution of the user-defined log-likelihood evaluation program.

ml count counts the number of times the user-defined log-likelihood evaluation program is called. It was intended as a debugging tool for those developing ml and now it serves little use besides entertainment. ml count clear clears the counter. ml count on turns on the counter. ml count without arguments reports the current values of the counters. ml count off stops counting calls.

ml maximize maximizes the likelihood function and reports final results. Once ml maximize has successfully completed, the previously mentioned ml commands may no longer be used—ml graph and ml display may be used.

ml graph graphs the log-likelihood values against the iteration number.

ml display redisplays final results.

progname is the name of a program you write to evaluate the log-likelihood function. In this documentation, it is referred to as the user-written evaluator or sometimes simply as the evaluator. The program you write is written in the style required by the method you choose. The methods are lf, d0, d1, and d2. Thus, if you choose to use method lf, your program is called a method lf evaluator. Method lf evaluators are required to evaluate the observation-by-observation log likelihood $\ln \ell_j$, $j = 1, \ldots, N$. Method d0 evaluators are required to evaluate the overall log likelihood $\ln L$. Method d1 evaluators are required to evaluate the overall log likelihood and its gradient vector $\mathbf{g} = \partial \ln L / \partial \mathbf{b}$. Method d2 evaluators are required to evaluate the overall log likelihood, its gradient, and its negative Hessian matrix $-H = -\partial^2 \ln L / \partial \mathbf{b} \partial \mathbf{b}'$.

mleval is a subroutine for use by method d0, d1, and d2 evaluators to evaluate the coefficient vector **b** that they are passed.

mlsum is a subroutine for use by method d0, d1, and d2 evaluators to define the value $\ln L$ that is to be returned.

mlvecsum is a subroutine for use by method d1 and d2 evaluators to define the gradient vector **g** that is to be returned. It is suitable for use only when the likelihood function meets the linear-form restrictions.

mlmatsum is a subroutine for use by method d2 evaluators to define the negative Hessian $-\mathbf{H}$ matrix that is to be returned. It is suitable for use only when the likelihood function meets the linear-form restrictions.

Options for use with ml model in interactive or noninteractive mode

robust and cluster(*varname*) specify the robust variance estimator, as does specifying pweights.

> If you have written a method lf evaluator, robust, cluster(), and pweights will work. There is nothing to do except specify the options.

> If you have written a method d0 evaluator, robust, cluster(), and pweights will not work. Specifying these options will result in an error message.

> If you have written a method d1 or d2 evaluator and the likelihood function satisfies the linear-form restrictions, robust, cluster(), and pweights will work only if you fill in the equation scores; otherwise, specifying these options will result in an error message.

title(*string*) specifies the title to be placed on the estimation output when results are complete.

nopreserve specifies that it is not necessary for ml to ensure that only the estimation subsample is in memory when the user-written likelihood evaluator is called. nopreserve is irrelevant when using method lf.

> For the other methods, if nopreserve is not specified, then ml saves the dataset in a file (preserves the original dataset) and drops the irrelevant observations before calling the user-written evaluator. This way, even if the evaluator does not restrict its attentions to the $ML\_samp==1$ subsample, results will still be correct. Later, ml automatically restores the original data.

> ml need not go through these machinations in the case of method lf because the user-written evaluator calculates observation-by-observation values and it is ml itself that sums the components.

> ml goes through these machinations if and only if the estimation sample is a subsample of the data in memory. If the estimation sample includes every observation in memory, ml does not preserve the original data. Thus, programmers must not damage the original data unless they preserve the data themselves.

> We recommend interactive users of ml not specify nopreserve; the speed gain is not worth the chances of incorrect results.

> We recommend programmers do specify nopreserve, but only after verifying that their evaluator really does restrict its attentions solely to the $ML\_samp==1$ subsample.

collinear specifies that ml is not to remove the collinear variables within equations. There is no reason one would want to leave collinear variables in place, but this option is of interest to programmers who, in their code, have already removed collinear variables and thus do not want ml to waste computer time checking again.

missing specifies that observations containing variables with missing values are not to be eliminated from the estimation sample. There are two reasons one might want to specify missing.

Programmers may wish to specify `missing` because, in other parts of their code, they have already eliminated observations with missing values and thus do not want `ml` to waste computer time looking again.

All users may wish to specify `missing` if their model explicitly deals with missing values. Stata's `heckman` command is a good example of this. In such cases, there will be observations where missing values are allowed and other observations where they are not—where their presence should cause the observation to be eliminated. If you specify `missing`, it is your responsibility to specify an `if` *exp* that eliminates the irrelevant observations.

`lf0(#_k #_{ll})` is typically used by programmers. It specifies the number of parameters and log-likelihood value of the "constant-only" model so that `ml` can report a likelihood-ratio test rather than a Wald test. These values were, perhaps, analytically determined, or they may have been determined by a previous estimation of the constant-only model on the estimation sample.

Also see the `continue` option directly below.

If you specify `lf0()`, it must be safe for you to specify the `missing` option, too, else how did you calculate the log likelihood for the constant-only model on the same sample? You must have identified the estimation sample, and done so correctly, so there is no reason for `ml` to waste time rechecking your results. Which is to say, do not specify `lf0()` unless you are certain your code identifies the estimation sample correctly.

`lf0()`, even if specified, is ignored if `robust`, `cluster()`, or `pweights` are specified because in that case a likelihood-ratio test would be inappropriate.

`continue` is typically specified by programmers. It does two things:

First, it specifies that a model has just been estimated, by either `ml` or some other estimation command such as `logit`, and that the likelihood value stored in `e(ll)` and the number of parameters stored in `e(b)` as of this instant are the relevant values of the constant-only model. The current value of the log likelihood is used to present a likelihood-ratio test unless `robust`, `cluster()`, or `pweights` are specified because, in that case, a likelihood-ratio test would be inappropriate.

Second, `continue` sets the initial values $\mathbf{b}_0$ for the model about to be estimated according to the `e(b)` currently stored.

The comments made about specifying `missing` with `lf0()` apply equally well in this case.

`waldtest(#)` is typically specified by programmers. By default, `ml` presents a Wald test, but that is overridden if options `lf0()` or `continue` are specified, and that is overridden again (so we are back to the Wald test) if `robust`, `cluster()`, or `pweights` are specified.

`waldtest(0)` prevents even the Wald test from being reported.

`waldtest(-1)` is the default. It specifies that a Wald test is to be performed, if it is performed, by constraining all coefficients except for the intercept to 0 in the first equation. Remaining equations are to be unconstrained. The logic as to whether a Wald test is performed is the standard: perform the Wald test if neither `lf0()` nor `continue` were specified, but force a Wald test if `robust`, `cluster`, or `pweights` were specified.

`waldtest(k)` for $k \leq -1$ specifies that a Wald test is to be performed, if it is performed, by constraining all coefficients except for intercepts to 0 in the first $|k|$ equations; remaining equations are to be unconstrained. The logic as to whether a Wald test is performed is the standard.

`waldtest(k)` for $k \geq 1$ works like the above except that it forces a Wald test to be reported even if the information to perform the likelihood-ratio test is available and even if none of `robust`, `cluster`, or `pweights` were specified. `waldtest(k)`, $k \geq 1$, may not be specified with `lf0()`.

obs(*#*) is used mostly by programmers. It specifies that the number of observations reported, and ultimately stored in e(N), is to be *#*. Ordinarily, ml works that out for itself, and correctly. Programmers may want to specify this option when, in order for the likelihood-evaluator to work for N observations, they first had to modify the data so that it contained a different number of observations.

noscvars is used mostly by programmers. It specifies that method d0, d1, or d2 is being used but that the likelihood evaluation program does not calculate nor use arguments `g1´, `g2´, etc., which are the score vectors. Thus, ml can save a little time by not generating and passing those arguments.

Options for use with ml model in noninteractive mode

In addition to the above options, the following options are for use with ml model in noninteractive mode. Noninteractive mode is for programmers who use ml as a subroutine and want to issue a single command that will carry forth the estimation from start to finish.

maximize is not optional. It specifies noninteractive mode.

init(*ml_init_args*) sets the initial values b_0. *ml_init_args* are whatever you would type after the ml init command.

search(on | quietly | off) specifies whether ml search is to be used to improve the initial values. search(on) is the default and is equivalent to running separately ml search, repeat(0). search(quietly) is the same as search(on) except that it suppresses ml search's output. search(off) prevents the calling of ml search altogether.

repeat(*#*) is ml search's repeat() option and is relevant only if search(off) is not specified. repeat(0) is the default.

bounds(*ml_search_bounds*) is relevant only if search(off) is not specified. The command ml model issues is 'ml search *ml_search_bounds*, repeat(*#*)'. Specifying search bounds is optional.

difficult, nolog, trace, gradient, hessian, showstep, iterate(), ltolerance(), tolerance(), nowarning, novce, and score() are ml maximize's equivalent options.

Options for use when specifying equations

noconstant specifies that the equation is not to include an intercept.

offset(*varname*) specifies that the equation is to be $xb + varname$; that the equation is to include *varname* with coefficient constrained to be 1.

exposure(*varname*) is an alternative to offset(*varname*); it specifies that the equation is to be $xb + \ln(varname)$. The equation is to include $\ln(varname)$ with coefficient constrained to be 1.

Options for use with ml search

repeat(*#*) specifies the number of random attempts that are to be made to find a better initial-value vector. The default is repeat(10).

repeat(0) specifies that no random attempts are to be made. More correctly, repeat(0) specifies that no random attempts are to be made if the initial initial-value vector is a feasible starting point. If it is not, ml search will make random attempts even if you specify repeat(0) because it has no alternative. The repeat() option refers to the number of random attempts to be made to improve the initial values. When the initial starting value vector is not feasible, `ml search` will make up to 1,000 random attempts to find starting values. It stops the instant it finds one set of values that works and then moves into its improve-initial-values logic.

`repeat(k)`, $k > 0$, specifies the number of random attempts to be made to improve the initial values.

`nolog` specifies that no output is to appear while `ml search` looks for better starting values. If you specify `nolog` and the initial starting-value vector is not feasible, `ml search` will ignore the fact that you specified the `nolog` option. If `ml search` must take drastic action to find starting values, it feels you should know about this even if you attempted to suppress its usual output.

`trace` specifies that you want more detailed output about `ml search`'s actions than it would usually provide. This is more entertaining than useful. `ml search` prints a period each time it evaluates the likelihood function without obtaining a better result and a plus when it does.

`restart` specifies that random actions are to be taken to obtain starting values and that the resulting starting values are not to be a deterministic function of the current values. Users should not specify this option mainly because, with `restart`, `ml search` intentionally does not produce as good a set of starting values as it could. `restart` is included for use by the optimizer when it gets into serious trouble. The random actions are to ensure that the actions of the optimizer and `ml search`, working together, do not result in a long, endless loop.

`restart` implies `norescale`, which is why we recommend you do not specify `restart`. In testing, cases were discovered where `rescale` worked so well that, even after randomization, the rescaler would bring the starting values right back to where they had been the first time and so defeated the intended randomization.

`norescale` specifies that `ml search` is not to engage in its rescaling actions to improve the parameter vector. We do not recommend specifying this option because rescaling tends to work so well.

Options for use with ml plot

`saving(`*filename*`[, replace])` specifies that the graph is to be saved in *filename*.`gph`.

Options for use with ml init

`skip` specifies that any parameters found in the specified initialization vector that are not also found in the model are to be ignored. The default action is to issue an error message.

`copy` specifies that the list of numbers or the initialization vector is to be copied into the initial-value vector by position rather than by name.

Options for use with ml maximize

`difficult` specifies that the likelihood function is likely to be difficult to maximize. In particular, `difficult` states that there may be regions where $-\mathbf{H}$ is not invertible and that, in those regions, `ml`'s standard fixup may not work well. `difficult` specifies that a different fixup requiring substantially more computer time is to be used. For the majority of likelihood functions, `difficult` is likely to increase execution times unnecessarily. For other likelihood functions, specifying `difficult` is of great importance.

`nolog`, `trace`, `gradient`, `hessian`, and `showstep` control the display of the iteration log.

nolog suppresses reporting of the iteration log.

trace adds to the iteration log a report on the current parameter vector.

gradient adds to the iteration log a report on the current gradient vector.

hessian adds to the iteration log a report on the current negative Hessian matrix.

showstep adds to the iteration log a report on the steps within iteration.

iterate(#), ltolerance(#), and tolerance(#) specify the definition of convergence.

iterate(16000) tolerance(1e-6) ltolerance(1e-7) are the default.

Convergence is declared when

$$\text{mreldif}(\mathbf{b}_{i+1}, \mathbf{b}_i) \leq \text{tolerance}()$$

$$\mathbf{or} \quad \text{reldif}(\ln L(\mathbf{b}_{i+1}), \ln L(\mathbf{b}_i)) \leq \text{ltolerance}()$$

In addition, iteration stops when $i = $ iterate(); in that case, results along with the message "convergence not achieved" are presented. The return code is still set to 0.

nowarning is allowed only with iterate(0). nowarning suppresses the "convergence not achieved" message. Programmers might specify iterate(0) nowarning when they have a vector **b** already containing what are the final estimates and want ml to calculate the variance matrix and post final estimation results. In that case, specify 'init(b) search(off) iterate(0) nowarning nolog'.

novce is allowed only with iterate(0). novce substitutes the zero matrix for the variance matrix which in effect posts estimation results as fixed constants.

score(*newvarlist*) specifies that the equation scores are to be stored in the specified new variables. Either specify one new variable name per equation or specify a short name suffixed with a *. E.g., score(sc*) would be taken as specifying sc1 if there were one equation and sc1 and sc2 if there were two equations. In order to specify score(), either you must be using method lf or the estimation subsample must be the entire data in memory or you must have specified the nopreserve option.

nooutput suppresses display of the final results. This is different from prefixing ml maximize with quietly in that the iteration log is still displayed (assuming nolog is not specified).

level(#) is the standard confidence-level option. It specifies the confidence level, in percent, for confidence intervals of the coefficients. The default is level(95) or as set by set level; see [U] **23.5 Specifying the width of confidence intervals**.

eform(*string*) is ml display's eform() option.

noclear specifies that after the model has converged, the ml problem definition is not to be cleared. Perhaps you are having convergence problems and intend to run the model to convergence, then use ml search to see if those values can be improved, and then start the estimation again.

Options for use with ml graph

saving(*filename*[, replace]) specifies that the graph is to be saved in *filename*.gph.

Options for use with ml display

noheader suppresses display of the header above the coefficient table that displays the final log-likelihood value, the number of observations, and the model significance test.

eform(*string*) displays the coefficient table in exponentiated form: for each coefficient, $\exp(b)$ rather than b is displayed and standard errors and confidence intervals are transformed. Display of the intercept, if any, is suppressed. *string* is the table header that will be displayed above the transformed coefficients and must be 11 characters or less in length, for example, eform("Odds ratio")

first displays a coefficient table reporting results for the first equation only, and the report makes it appear that the first equation is the only equation. This is used by programmers who estimate ancillary parameters in the second and subsequent equations and will report the values of such parameters themselves.

neq(#) is an alternative to first. neq(#) displays a coefficient table reporting results for the first # equations. This is used by programmers who estimate ancillary parameters in the $# + 1$ and subsequent equations and will report the values of such parameters themselves.

plus displays the coefficient table just as it would be ordinarily, but then, rather than ending the table in a line of dashes, ends it in dashes–plus-sign–dashes. This is so that programmers can write additional display code to add more results to the table and make it appear as if the combined result is one table. Programmers typically specify plus with options first or neq().

level(#) is the standard confidence-level option. It specifies the confidence level, in percent, for confidence intervals of the coefficients. The default is level(95) or as set by set level; see [U] **23.5 Specifying the width of confidence intervals**.

Options for use with mleval

eq(#) specifies the equation number i for which $\theta_{ij} = \mathbf{x}_{ij}\mathbf{b}_i$ is to be evaluated. eq(1) is assumed if eq() is not specified.

scalar asserts that the ith equation is known to evaluate to a constant; the equation was specified as (), (*name*:), or /*name* on the ml model statement. If you specify this option, the new variable created is created as a scalar. If the ith equation does not evaluate to a scalar, an error message is issued.

Options for use with mlsum

noweight specifies that weights ($ML_w) are to be ignored when summing the likelihood function.

Options for use with mlvecsum

eq(#) specifies the equation for which a gradient vector $\partial \ln L / \partial \mathbf{b}_i$ is to be constructed. The default is eq(1).

Options for use with mlmatsum

eq($\#[,\#]$) specifies the equations for which the negative Hessian matrix is to be constructed. The default is eq(1), which means the same as eq(1,1), which means $-\partial^2 \ln L/\partial \mathbf{b}_1 \partial \mathbf{b}_1'$. Specifying eq($i,j$) results in $-\partial^2 \ln L/\partial \mathbf{b}_i \partial \mathbf{b}_j'$.

Remarks

For a thorough discussion of ml, see *Maximum Likelihood Estimation with Stata* (Gould and Sribney, 1999). The book provides a tutorial introduction to ml, notes on advanced programming issues, as well as a discourse on maximum likelihood estimation both from theoretical and practical standpoints.

ml requires that you write a program that evaluates the log-likelihood function and, possibly, its first and second derivatives. The style of the program you write depends upon the method chosen; method lf and d0 require your program evaluate the log likelihood only; method d1 requires your program evaluate the log likelihood and gradient; method d2 requires your program evaluate the log likelihood, gradient, and negative Hessian. Method lf and d0 differ form each other in that, with method lf, your program is required to produce observation-by-observation log-likelihood values $\ln \ell_j$ and it is assumed that $\ln L = \sum_j \ln \ell_j$; with method d0, your program is required to produce the overall value $\ln L$.

Once you have written the program—called an evaluator—you define a model to be estimated using ml model and obtain estimates using ml maximize. You might type

```
. ml model ...
. ml maximize
```

but we recommend that you type

```
. ml model ...
. ml check
. ml search
. ml maximize
```

ml check will verify your evaluator has no obvious errors, and ml search will find better initial values.

You fill in the ml model statement with (1) the method you are using, (2) the name of your program, and (3) the "equations". You write your evaluator in terms of θ_1, θ_2, $\ldots$, each of which has a linear equation associated with it. That linear equation might be as simple as $\theta_i = b_0$, or it might be $\theta_i = b_1\text{mpg} + b_2\text{weight} + b_3$, or it might omit the intercept b_3. The equations are specified in parentheses on the ml model line.

Suppose you are using method lf and the name of your evaluator program is myprog. The following statement

```
. ml model lf myprog (mpg weight)
```

would specify a single equation with $\theta_i = b_1\text{mpg} + b_2\text{weight} + b_3$. If you wanted to omit b_3, you would type

```
. ml model lf myprog (mpg weight, nocons)
```

and if all you wanted was $\theta_i = b_0$, you would type

```
. ml model lf myprog ()
```

With multiple equations, you list the equations one after the other; so if you typed

```
. ml model lf myprog (mpg weight) ()
```

you would be specifying $\theta_1 = b_1\text{mpg} + b_2\text{weight} + b_3$ and $\theta_2 = b_4$. You would write your likelihood in terms of θ_1 and θ_2. If the model was linear regression, θ_1 might be the **xb** part and θ_2 the variance of the residuals.

When you specify the equations, you also specify any dependent variables. If you type

```
. ml model lf myprog (price = mpg weight) ()
```

price would be the one and only dependent variable, and that would be passed to your program in **$ML_y1**. If your model had two dependent variables, you could type

```
. ml model lf myprog (price displ = mpg weight) ()
```

and then **$ML_y1** would be **price** and **$ML_y2** would be **displ**. You can specify however many dependent variables are necessary and specify them on any equation. It does not matter on which equation you specify them; the first one specified is placed in **$ML_y1**, the second in **$ML_y2**, and so on.

▷ Example

Using method lf, we are to produce observation-by-observation values of the log likelihood. The probit log-likelihood function is

$$\ln \ell_j = \begin{cases} \ln \Phi(\theta_{1j}) & \text{if } y_j = 1 \\ \ln \Phi(-\theta_{1j}) & \text{if } y_j = 0 \end{cases}$$

$$\theta_{1j} = \mathbf{x}_j \mathbf{b}_1$$

The following is the method lf evaluator for this likelihood function:

```
program define myprobit
        version 6.0
        args lnf theta1
        quietly replace `lnf' = ln(normprob(`theta1')) if $ML_y1==1
        quietly replace `lnf' = ln(normprob(-`theta1')) if $ML_y1==0
end
```

If we wanted to estimate a model of **foreign** on **mpg** and **weight**, we would type

```
. ml model lf myprobit (foreign = mpg weight)
. ml maximize
```

The 'foreign =' part specifies that y is **foreign**. The 'mpg weight' part specifies that $\theta_{1j} = b_1\text{mpg}_j + b_2\text{weight}_j + b_3$. The result of running this is

```
. ml model lf myprobit (foreign = mpg weight)
```

```
. ml maximize
initial:        log likelihood = -51.292891
alternative:    log likelihood = -45.055272
rescale:        log likelihood = -45.055272
Iteration 0:    log likelihood = -45.055272
Iteration 1:    log likelihood = -27.904114
Iteration 2:    log likelihood =  -26.85781
Iteration 3:    log likelihood = -26.844198
Iteration 4:    log likelihood = -26.844189
Iteration 5:    log likelihood = -26.844189
```

```
                                         Number of obs   =          74
                                         Wald chi2(2)    =       20.75
Log likelihood = -26.844189              Prob > chi2     =      0.0000

------------------------------------------------------------------------
 foreign |     Coef.   Std. Err.      z    P>|z|     [95% Conf. Interval]
---------+--------------------------------------------------------------
     mpg | -.1039503   .0515689    -2.016   0.044    -.2050235   -.0028772
  weight | -.0023355   .0005661    -4.126   0.000     -.003445   -.0012261
   _cons |  8.275464   2.554142     3.240   0.001     3.269438    13.28149
------------------------------------------------------------------------
```

◁

▷ Example

A two-equation, two-dependent variable model is little different. Rather than receiving one theta, our program will receive two. Rather than there being one dependent variable in ML_y1, there will be dependent variables in ML_y1 and ML_y2. For instance, the Weibull regression log-likelihood function is

$$\ln \ell_j = (t_j e^{\theta_{1j}})^{\exp(\theta_{2j})} + d_j [\theta_{2j} - \theta_{1j} + (e^{\theta_{2j}} - 1)(\ln t_j - \theta_{1j})]$$

$$\theta_{1j} = \mathbf{x}_j \mathbf{b}_1$$

$$\theta_{2j} = s$$

where t_j is the time of failure or censoring and $d_j = 1$ if failure and 0 if censored. We can make the log likelihood a little easier to program by introducing some extra variables:

$$p_j = \exp(\theta_{2j})$$

$$M_j = t_j \exp(-\theta_{1j})^{p_j}$$

$$R_j = \ln t_j - \theta_{1j}$$

$$\ln \ell_j = -M_j + d_j [\theta_{2j} - \theta_{1j} + (p_j - 1)R_j]$$

The method lf evaluator for this is

```
program define myweib
        version 6.0
        args lnf theta1 theta2

        tempvar p M R
        quietly gen double `p' = exp(`theta2')
        quietly gen double `M' = ($ML_y1*exp(-`theta1'))^`p'
        quietly gen double `R' = ln($ML_y1)-`theta1'

        quietly replace `lnf' = -`M' + $ML_y2*(`theta2'-`theta1' + (`p'-1)*`R')
end
```

We can estimate a model by typing

```
. ml model lf myweib (studytim died = drug2 drug3 age) ()
. ml maximize
```

Note that we specified '()' for the second equation. The second equation corresponds to the Weibull shape parameter s and the linear combination we want for s contains just an intercept. Alternatively, we could type

```
. ml model lf myweib (studytim died = drug2 drug3 age) /s
```

Typing /s means the same thing as typing (s:) and both really mean the same thing as (). The s, either after a slash or in parentheses before a colon, labels the equation. It makes the output look prettier and that is all:

```
. ml model lf myweib (studytim died = drug2 drug3 age) /s

. ml max

initial:       log likelihood =       -744
alternative:   log likelihood = -356.14276
rescale:       log likelihood = -200.80201
rescale eq:    log likelihood = -136.69232
Iteration 0:   log likelihood = -136.69232  (not concave)
Iteration 1:   log likelihood = -124.11744
Iteration 2:   log likelihood = -113.88918
Iteration 3:   log likelihood = -110.30382
Iteration 4:   log likelihood = -110.26747
Iteration 5:   log likelihood = -110.26736
Iteration 6:   log likelihood = -110.26736

                                          Number of obs   =         48
                                          Wald chi2(3)    =      35.25
Log likelihood = -110.26736               Prob > chi2     =     0.0000

------------------------------------------------------------------------------
             |      Coef.   Std. Err.       z    P>|z|     [95% Conf. Interval]
---------+--------------------------------------------------------------------
eq1          |
     drug2   |   1.012966   .2903917     3.488   0.000     .4438086    1.582123
     drug3   |    1.45917   .2821195     5.172   0.000     .9062261    2.012114
       age   |  -.0671728   .0205688    -3.266   0.001    -.1074868   -.0268587
     _cons   |   6.060723   1.152845     5.257   0.000     3.801188    8.320259
---------+--------------------------------------------------------------------
s            |
     _cons   |   .5573333   .1402154     3.975   0.000     .2825162     .8321504
------------------------------------------------------------------------------
```

◁

▷ Example

Method d0 evaluators receive $\mathbf{b} = (\mathbf{b_1}, \mathbf{b_2}, \ldots, \mathbf{b_E})$, the coefficient vector, rather than the already evaluated $\theta_1, \theta_2, \ldots, \theta_E$, and they are required to evaluate the overall log-likelihood $\ln L$ rather than $\ln \ell_j, \; j = 1, \ldots, N$.

Use `mleval` to produce the thetas from the coefficient vector.

Use `mlsum` to sum the components that enter into $\ln L$.

In the case of Weibull, $\ln L = \sum \ln \ell_j$, and our method d0 evaluator is

```
program define weib0
        version 6.0
        args todo b lnf

        tempvar theta1 theta2
        mleval `theta1' = `b', eq(1)
        mleval `theta2' = `b', eq(2)

        local t "$ML_y1"             /* this is just for readability */
        local d "$ML_y2"

        tempvar p M R
        quietly gen double `p' = exp(`theta2')
        quietly gen double `M' = (`t'*exp(-`theta1'))^`p'
        quietly gen double `R' = ln(`t')-`theta1'

        mlsum `lnf' = -`M' + `d'*(`theta2'-`theta1' + (`p'-1)*`R')
end
```

To estimate our model using this evaluator, we would type

```
. ml model d0 weib0 (studytim died = drug2 drug3 age) /s
. ml maximize
```

◁

❑ Technical Note

Method d0 does not require $\ln L = \sum_j \ln \ell_j$, $j = 1, \ldots, N$, as method lf does. Your likelihood function might have independent components only for groups of observations. Panel data estimators have a log-likelihood value $\ln L = \sum_i \ln L_i$ where i indexes the panels, each of which contains multiple observations. Conditional logistic regression has $\ln L = \sum_k \ln L_k$ where k indexes the risk pools. Cox regression has $\ln L = \sum_{(t)} \ln L_{(t)}$ where (t) denotes the ordered failure times.

To evaluate such likelihood functions, first calculate the within-group log-likelihood contributions. This usually involves **generate** and **replace** statements prefixed with **by**, as in

```
tempvar sumd
by group: gen double `sumd' = sum($ML_y1)
```

Structure your code so that the log-likelihood contributions are recorded in the last observation of each group. Let's pretend that variable is named `cont'. To sum the contributions, code

```
tempvar last
quietly by group: gen byte `last' = (_n==_N)
mlsum `lnf' = `cont' if `last'
```

It is of great importance that you inform **mlsum** as to the observations that contain log-likelihood values to be summed. First, you do not want to include intermediate results in the sum. Second, **mlsum** does not skip missing values. Rather, if **mlsum** sees a missing value among the contributions, it sets the overall result `lnf' to missing. That is how ml **maximize** is informed that the likelihood function could not be evaluated at the particular value of **b**. ml **maximize** will then take action to escape from what it thinks is an infeasible area of the likelihood function.

When the likelihood function violates the linear-form restriction $\ln L = \sum_j \ln \ell_j$, $j = 1, \ldots, N$, with $\ln \ell_j$ being a function solely of values within the jth observation, use method d0. In the following examples we will demonstrate methods d1 and d2 with likelihood functions that meet this linear-form restriction. The d1 and d2 methods themselves do not require the linear-form restriction, but use of the utility routines **mlvecsum** and **mlmatsum** do. Using method d1 or d2 when the restriction is violated is a difficult programming exercise.

❑

▷ Example

Method d1 evaluators are required to produce the gradient vector $\mathbf{g} = \partial \ln L / \partial \mathbf{b}$ as well as the overall log-likelihood value. Using `mlvecsum`, we can obtain $\partial \ln L / \partial \mathbf{b}$ from $\partial \ln L / \partial \theta_i$, $i = 1, \ldots, E$. The derivatives of the Weibull log-likelihood function are

$$\frac{\partial \ln \ell_j}{\partial \theta_{1j}} = p_j (M_j - d_j)$$

$$\frac{\partial \ln \ell_j}{\partial \theta_{2j}} = d_j - R_j p_j (M_j - d_j)$$

The method d1 evaluator for this is

```
program define weib1
        version 6
        args todo b lnf g                                    /* g is new */

        tempvar t1 t2
        mleval `t1´ = `b´, eq(1)
        mleval `t2´ = `b´, eq(2)

        local t "$ML_y1"
        local d "$ML_y2"

        tempvar p M R
        quietly gen double `p´ = exp(`t2´)
        quietly gen double `M´ = (`t´*exp(-`t1´))^^`p´
        quietly gen double `R´ = ln(`t´)-`t1´

        mlsum `lnf´ = -`M´ + `d´*(`t2´-`t1´ + (`p´-1)*`R´)
        if `todo´==0 | `lnf´==. { exit }                     /* <-- new */
                                                             /* <-- new */
        tempname d1 d2                                       /* <-- new */
        mlvecsum `lnf´ `d1´ = `p´*(`M´-`d´), eq(1)           /* <-- new */
        mlvecsum `lnf´ `d2´ = `d´ - `R´*`p´*(`M´-`d´), eq(2) /* <-- new */
        matrix `g´ = (`d1´,`d2´)                             /* <-- new */
end
```

We obtained this code by starting with our method d0 evaluator and then adding the extra lines method d1 requires. To estimate our model using this evaluator, we could type

```
. ml model d1 weib1 (studytim died = drug2 drug3 age) /s
. ml maximize
```

but we recommend you first substitute method d1debug for method d1 and type

```
. ml model d1debug weib1 (studytim died = drug2 drug3 age) /s
. ml maximize
```

Method d1debug will compare the derivatives we calculate with numerical derivatives and thus verify that our program is correct.

◁

▷ Example

Method d2 evaluators are required to produce $-\mathbf{H} = \partial^2 \ln L / \partial \mathbf{b} \partial \mathbf{b}'$, the negative Hessian matrix, as well as the gradient and log-likelihood value. `mlmatsum` will help calculate $\partial^2 \ln L / \partial \mathbf{b} \partial \mathbf{b}'$ from the negative second derivatives with respect to theta. For the Weibull model, these negative second derivatives are

$$-\frac{\partial^2 \ln \ell_j}{\partial \theta_{1j}^2} = p_j^2 M_j$$

$$-\frac{\partial^2 \ln \ell_j}{\partial \theta_{1j} \partial \theta_{2j}} = -p_j (M_j - d_j + R_j p_j M_j)$$

$$-\frac{\partial^2 \ln \ell_j}{\partial \theta_{2j}^2} = p_j R_j (R_j p_j M_j + M_j - d_j)$$

The method d2 evaluator is

```
program define weib2
        version 6
        args todo b lnf g negH                          /* negH added */
        tempvar t1 t2
        mleval `t1' = `b', eq(1)
        mleval `t2' = `b', eq(2)
        local t "$ML_y1"
        local d "$ML_y2"
        tempvar p M R
        quietly gen double `p' = exp(`t2')
        quietly gen double `M' = (`t'*exp(-`t1'))^`p'
        quietly gen double `R' = ln(`t')-`t1'
        mlsum `lnf' = -`M' + `d'*(`t2'-`t1' + (`p'-1)*`R')
        if `todo'==0 | `lnf'==. { exit }
        tempname d1 d2
        mlvecsum `lnf' `d1' = `p'*(`M'-`d'), eq(1)
        mlvecsum `lnf' `d2' = `d' - `R'*`p'*(`M'-`d'), eq(2)
        matrix `g' = (`d1',`d2')
        if `todo'==1 | `lnf'==. { exit }                /* new from here down */
        tempname d11 d12 d22
        mlmatsum `lnf' `d11' = `p'^2 * `M', eq(1)
        mlmatsum `lnf' `d12' = -`p'*(`M'-`d' + `R'*`p'*`M'), eq(1,2)
        mlmatsum `lnf' `d22' = `p'*`R'*(`R'*`p'*`M' + `M' - `d') , eq(2)
        matrix `negH' = (`d11',`d12' \ `d12'',`d22')
end
```

We started with our previous method d1 evaluator and added the lines that method d2 requires. We could now estimate a model by typing

```
. ml model d2 weib2 (studytim died = drug2 drug3 age) /s
. ml maximize
```

but we would recommend you first substitute method d2debug for method d2 and type

```
. ml model d2debug weib2 (studytim died = drug2 drug3 age) /s
. ml maximize
```

Method d2debug will compare the first and second derivatives we calculate with numerical derivatives and thus verify that our program is correct.

◁

As we stated earlier, to produce the robust variance estimator with method lf, there is nothing to do except specify robust, cluster(), and/or pweights. For method d0, these options do not work. For methods d1 and d2, these options will work if your likelihood function meets the linear-form restrictions and you fill in the equation scores. The equation scores are defined as

$$\frac{\partial \ln \ell_j}{\partial \theta_{1j}}, \quad \frac{\partial \ln \ell_j}{\partial \theta_{2j}}, \quad \cdots$$

Your evaluator will be passed variables, one for each equation, which you fill in with the equation scores. For *both* method d1 and d2, these variables are passed in the sixth and subsequent positions of the argument list. That is, you must process the arguments as

```
args todo b lnf g negH g1 g2 ...
```

Note that for method d1, the `negH` argument is not used; it is merely a place holder.

▷ Example

If you have used `mlvecsum` in your method d1 or d2 evaluator, it is easy to turn it in a program that allows the computation of the robust variance estimator. The expression that you specified on the right-hand side of `mlvecsum` is the equation score.

Here we turn the program that we gave earlier in the method d1 example into one that allows `robust`, `cluster()`, and/or `pweights`.

```
program define weib1
        version 6
        args todo b lnf g negH g1 g2        /* negH, g1, and g2 are new */

        tempvar t1 t2
        mleval `t1´ = `b´, eq(1)
        mleval `t2´ = `b´, eq(2)

        local t "$ML_y1"
        local d "$ML_y2"

        tempvar p M R
        quietly gen double `p´ = exp(`t2´)
        quietly gen double `M´ = (`t´*exp(-`t1´))^`p´
        quietly gen double `R´ = ln(`t´)-`t1´

        mlsum `lnf´ = -`M´ + `d´*(`t2´-`t1´ + (`p´-1)*`R´)
        if `todo´==0 | `lnf´==. { exit }

        tempname d1 d2
        quietly replace `g1´ = `p´*(`M´-`d´)              /* <-- new     */
        quietly replace `g2´ = `d´ - `R´*`p´*(`M´-`d´)    /* <-- new     */
        mlvecsum `lnf´ `d1´  = `g1´, eq(1)                /* <-- changed */
        mlvecsum `lnf´ `d2´  = `g2´, eq(2)                /* <-- changed */
        matrix `g´ = (`d1´,`d2´)
end
```

To estimate our model and get the robust variance estimates, we type

```
. ml model d1 weib1 (studytim died = drug2 drug3 age) /s, robust
. ml maximize
```

◁

(Continued on next page)

Saved Results

ml saves in e():

Scalars

e(N)	number of observations	e(ll_0)	log likelihood, constant-only model (if LR
e(k)	number of parameters		saved by e(chi2type)
e(k_eq)	number of equations	e(N_clust)	number of clusters
e(k_dv)	number of dependent variables	e(rc)	return code
e(df_m)	model degrees of freedom	e(chi2)	χ^2
e(ll)	log likelihood	e(ic)	number of iterations

Macros

e(cmd)	ml	e(vcetype)	covariance estimation method
e(depvar)	name of dependent variable	e(user)	name of likelihood-evaluator program
e(wtype)	weight type	e(opt)	type of optimization
e(wexp)	weight expression	e(chi2type)	Wald or LR; type of model χ^2 test
e(clustvar)	name of cluster variable		

Matrices

e(b)	coefficient vector	e(ilog)	iteration log (up to 20 iterations)
e(V)	variance–covariance matrix of the estimators		

Functions

e(sample)	marks estimation sample

References

Gould, W. and W. Sribney. 1999. *Maximum Likelihood Estimation with Stata*. College Station, TX: Stata Press.

Also See

Complementary: [R] **estimates**, [R] **matrix**, [R] **maximize**, [R] **nl**

Title

> **mlogit** — Maximum-likelihood multinomial (polytomous) logistic regression

Syntax

$$\left[\text{by } \textit{varlist}:\right] \underline{\text{mlog}}\text{it} \left[\textit{depvar indepvars} \left[\textit{weight}\right] \left[\text{if } \textit{exp}\right] \left[\text{in } \textit{range}\right]\right]$$

$$\left[, \underline{\text{basecategory}}(\#) \underline{\text{constraints}}(\textit{clist}) \underline{\text{robust}} \underline{\text{cl}}\text{uster}(\textit{varname}) \underline{\text{sc}}\text{ore}(\textit{newvarlist})\right.$$

$$\left.\underline{\text{level}}(\#) \underline{\text{rrr}} \underline{\text{no}}\text{constant } \textit{maximize\_options}\right]$$

where *clist* is of the form $\#\left[-\#\right]\left[, \#\left[-\#\right] \ldots\right]$

fweights, pweights, and iweights are allowed; see [U] **14.1.6 weight**.
mlogit shares the features of all estimation commands; see [U] **23 Estimation and post-estimation commands**.

Syntax for predict

$$\text{predict } \left[\textit{type}\right] \textit{newvarname}(s) \left[\text{if } \textit{exp}\right] \left[\text{in } \textit{range}\right] \left[, \left\{ \text{ p } | \text{ xb } | \text{ stdp } | \text{ stddp } \right\}\right.$$

$$\left.\underline{\text{out}}\text{come}(\textit{outcome}) \right]$$

Note that you specify one new variable with xb, stdp, and stddp and specify either one or k new variables with p.
These statistics are available both in and out of sample; type predict ... if e(sample) ... if wanted only for
the estimation sample.

Description

mlogit estimates maximum-likelihood multinomial logit models, also known as polytomous
logistic regression. Constraints may be defined to perform constrained estimation. Some people refer
to conditional logistic regression as multinomial logit. If you are one of them, see [R] **clogit**.

See [R] **logistic** for a list of related estimation commands.

A maximum of 50 categories can be estimated with Intercooled Stata; 20 categories with Small
Stata.

Options

basecategory(#) specifies the value of *depvar* that is to be treated as the base category. The default
is to choose the most frequent category.

constraints(*clist*) specifies the linear constraints to be applied during estimation. The default is
to perform unconstrained estimation. Constraints are defined with the constraint command;
see [R] **constraint**. constraints(1) specifies that the model is to be constrained according
to constraint 1; constraints(1-4) specifies constraints 1 through 4; constraints(1-4,8)
specifies constraints 1 through 4 and 8. It is not considered an error to specify nonexistent
constraints so long as some of the constraints exist. Thus, constraint(1-999) would specify
that all defined constraints be applied.

`robust` specifies that the Huber/White/sandwich estimator of variance is to be used in place of the traditional calculation; see [U] **23.11 Obtaining robust variance estimates**. `robust` combined with `cluster()` allows observations which are not independent within cluster (although they must be independent between clusters).

If you specify `pweights`, `robust` is implied; see [U] **23.13 Weighted estimation**.

`cluster(`*varname*`)` specifies that the observations are independent across groups (clusters) but not necessarily within groups. *varname* specifies to which group each observation belongs; e.g., `cluster(personid)` in data with repeated observations on individuals. `cluster()` affects the estimated standard errors and variance–covariance matrix of the estimators (VCE), but not the estimated coefficients; see [U] **23.11 Obtaining robust variance estimates**. `cluster()` can be used with `pweights` to produce estimates for unstratified cluster-sampled data, but see the `svymlog` command in [R] **svy estimators** for a command designed especially for survey data.

`cluster()` implies `robust`; specifying `robust cluster()` is equivalent to typing `cluster()` by itself.

`score(`*newvarlist*`)` creates $k - 1$ new variables, where k is the number of observed outcomes. The first variable contains $\partial \ln L_j / \partial (\mathbf{x}_j \mathbf{b}_1)$; the second variable contains $\partial \ln L_j / \partial (\mathbf{x}_j \mathbf{b}_2)$; and so on. Note that if you were to specify the option `score(sc*)`, Stata would create the appropriate number of new variables and they would be named `sc1`, `sc2`, ... `sc`$(k - 1)$.

`level(`*#*`)` specifies the confidence level, in percent, for confidence intervals. The default is `level(95)` or as set by `set level`; see [U] **23.5 Specifying the width of confidence intervals**.

`rrr` reports the estimated coefficients transformed to relative risk ratios, i.e., e^b rather than b; see *Description of model* below for an explanation of this concept. Standard errors and confidence intervals are similarly transformed. This option affects how results are displayed, not how they are estimated. `rrr` may be specified at estimation or when replaying previously estimated results.

`noconstant` suppresses the constant term in the model.

maximize_options control the maximization process; see [R] **maximize**. You should never have to specify them.

Options for predict

`p`, the default, calculates the probability of a positive outcome conditional on one positive outcome within group.

If you do not also specify the `outcome(`*outcome*`)` option, you must specify k new variables. For instance, say you estimated your model by typing `mlogit insure age male` and that `insure` takes on three values. Then you could type `predict p1 p2 p3, pr` to obtain all three predicted probabilities. It does not matter which category `mlogit` chose as the base category; `predict` will calculate all three probabilities correctly.

If you also specify the `outcome(`*outcome*`)` option, then you specify one new variable. Say that `insure` took on values 1, 2, and 3. Then typing `predict p1, pr outcome(1)` would produce the same p1 as above, `predict p2, pr outcome(2)` the same p2 as above, etc. If `insure` took on values 7, 22, and 93, you would specify `outcome(7)`, `outcome(22)`, and `outcome(93)`.

`xb` calculates the linear prediction. You must also specify the `outcome(`*outcome*`)` option.

`stdp` calculates the standard error of the linear prediction. You must also specify the `outcome(`*outcome*`)` option.

`stddp` calculates the standard error of the difference in two linear predictions. You must specify option `outcome(`*outcome*`)` and in this case you specify the two particular outcomes of interest inside the parentheses; for example, `predict sed, stddp outcome(1,3)`.

`outcome(`*outcome*`)` specifies for which outcome the statistic is to be calculated. `equation()` is a synonym for `outcome()`: it does not matter which you use, and the standard rules for specifying an `equation()` apply.

Remarks

Remarks are presented under the headings

> *Description of model*
> *Estimating unconstrained models*
> *Obtaining predicted values*
> *Testing hypotheses about coefficients*
> *Estimating constrained models*

`mlogit` performs maximum likelihood estimation of models with discrete dependent (left-hand-side) variables. It is intended for use when the dependent variable takes on more than two outcomes and the outcomes have no natural ordering. If the dependent variable takes on only two outcomes, estimates are identical to those produced by `logistic` or `logit`; see [R] **logistic** and [R] **logit**. If the outcomes are ordered, see [R] **ologit**.

Description of model

For an introduction to multinomial logit models, see, for instance, Aldrich and Nelson (1984, 73–77), Greene (1997, chapter 19), Hosmer and Lemeshow (1989, 216–238), and Long (1997, chapter 6). For a description with an emphasis on the difference in assumptions and data requirements for conditional and multinomial logit, see Judge et al. (1985, 768–772).

Consider the outcomes 1, 2, 3, ..., m recorded in y, and the explanatory variables X. For expositional purposes, assume there are $m = 3$ outcomes. Think of these three outcomes as "buy an American car", "buy a Japanese car", and "buy a European car". The values of y are then said to be "unordered". Even though the outcomes are coded 1, 2, and 3, the numerical values are arbitrary in the sense that $1 < 2 < 3$ does not imply that outcome 1 (buy American) is less than outcome 2 (buy Japanese) is less than outcome 3 (buy European). It is this unordered categorical property of y that distinguishes the use of `mlogit` from `regress` (which is appropriate for a continuous dependent variable), from `ologit` (which is appropriate for ordered categorical data), and from `logit` (which is appropriate for two outcomes and which can therefore be thought of as ordered).

In the multinomial logit model, we estimate a set of coefficients $\beta^{(1)}$, $\beta^{(2)}$, and $\beta^{(3)}$ corresponding to each outcome category:

$$\Pr(y = 1) = \frac{e^{X\beta^{(1)}}}{e^{X\beta^{(1)}} + e^{X\beta^{(2)}} + e^{X\beta^{(3)}}}$$

$$\Pr(y = 2) = \frac{e^{X\beta^{(2)}}}{e^{X\beta^{(1)}} + e^{X\beta^{(2)}} + e^{X\beta^{(3)}}}$$

$$\Pr(y = 3) = \frac{e^{X\beta^{(3)}}}{e^{X\beta^{(1)}} + e^{X\beta^{(2)}} + e^{X\beta^{(3)}}}$$

The model, however, is unidentified in the sense that there is more than one solution to $\beta^{(1)}$, $\beta^{(2)}$, and $\beta^{(3)}$ that leads to the same probabilities for $y = 1$, $y = 2$, and $y = 3$. To identify the model, one of $\beta^{(1)}$, $\beta^{(2)}$, or $\beta^{(3)}$ is arbitrarily set to 0—it does not matter which. That is, if we arbitrarily set $\beta^{(1)} = 0$, the remaining coefficients $\beta^{(2)}$ and $\beta^{(3)}$ would measure the change relative to the $y = 1$ group. If we instead set $\beta^{(2)} = 0$, the remaining coefficients $\beta^{(1)}$ and $\beta^{(3)}$ would measure the change relative to the $y = 2$ group. The coefficients would differ because they have different interpretations, but the predicted probabilities for $y = 1$, 2, and 3 would still be the same. Thus, either parameterization would be a solution to the same underlying model.

Setting $\beta^{(1)} = 0$, the equations become

$$\Pr(y = 1) = \frac{1}{1 + e^{X\beta^{(2)}} + e^{X\beta^{(3)}}}$$

$$\Pr(y = 2) = \frac{e^{X\beta^{(2)}}}{1 + e^{X\beta^{(2)}} + e^{X\beta^{(3)}}}$$

$$\Pr(y = 3) = \frac{e^{X\beta^{(3)}}}{1 + e^{X\beta^{(2)}} + e^{X\beta^{(3)}}}$$

The relative probability of $y = 2$ to the base category is

$$\frac{\Pr(y = 2)}{\Pr(y = 1)} = e^{X\beta^{(2)}}$$

Let us call this ratio the relative risk and let us further assume that X and $\beta_k^{(2)}$ are vectors equal to $(x_1, x_2, \ldots, x_k)$ and $(\beta_1^{(2)}, \beta_2^{(2)}, \ldots, \beta_k^{(2)})'$, respectively. The ratio of the relative risk for a one-unit change in x_i is then

$$\frac{e^{\beta_1^{(2)} x_1 + \cdots + \beta_i^{(2)}(x_i + 1) + \cdots + \beta_k^{(2)} x_k}}{e^{\beta_1^{(2)} x_1 + \cdots + \beta_i^{(2)} x_i + \cdots + \beta_k^{(2)} x_k}} = e^{\beta_i^{(2)}}$$

Thus, the exponentiated value of a coefficient is the relative risk ratio for a one unit change in the corresponding variable, it being understood that risk is measured as the risk of the category relative to the base category.

Estimating unconstrained models

▷ Example

You have data on the type of health insurance available to 616 psychologically depressed subjects in the U.S. (Tarlov et al. 1989; Wells et al. 1989). The insurance is categorized as being either an indemnity plan (i.e., regular fee-for-service insurance which may have a deductible or coinsurance rate) or a prepaid plan (a fixed up-front payment allowing subsequent unlimited use as provided, for instance, by an HMO). The third possibility is that the subject has no insurance whatsoever. You wish to explore the demographic factors associated with each subject's insurance choice. As an introduction to the data, one of the demographic factors is the race of the participant, coded as white or nonwhite:

```
. tabulate insure nonwhite, chi2 col
```

```
            | nonwhite
   insure |         0          1 |     Total
----------+----------------------+----------
    Indem |       251         43 |       294
          |     50.71      35.54 |     47.73
----------+----------------------+----------
   Prepaid |       208         69 |       277
          |     42.02      57.02 |     44.97
----------+----------------------+----------
  Uninsure |        36          9 |        45
          |      7.27       7.44 |      7.31
----------+----------------------+----------
    Total |       495        121 |       616
          |    100.00     100.00 |    100.00

        Pearson chi2(2) =   9.5599   Pr = 0.008
```

Although `insure` appears to take on the values Indem, Prepaid, and Uninsure, it actually takes on the values 1, 2, and 3. The words appear because a value label has been associated with the numeric variable `insure`; see [U] **15.6.3 Value labels**.

When you estimate a multinomial logit model, you can tell `mlogit` which group to use as the base category or you can let `mlogit` choose. To estimate a model of `insure` on `nonwhite`, letting `mlogit` choose the base category, we type

```
. mlogit insure nonwhite
Iteration 0:   log likelihood = -556.59502
Iteration 1:   log likelihood = -551.78935
Iteration 2:   log likelihood = -551.78348
Iteration 3:   log likelihood = -551.78348

Multinomial regression                           Number of obs   =        616
                                                 LR chi2(2)      =       9.62
                                                 Prob > chi2     =     0.0081
Log likelihood = -551.78348                      Pseudo R2       =     0.0086

------------------------------------------------------------------------------
    insure |      Coef.   Std. Err.      z    P>|z|     [95% Conf. Interval]
-----------+------------------------------------------------------------------
Prepaid    |
  nonwhite |   .6608212   .2157321     3.063   0.002     .2379942    1.083648
     _cons |  -.1879149   .0937644    -2.004   0.045    -.3716896   -.0041401
-----------+------------------------------------------------------------------
Uninsure   |
  nonwhite |   .3779585    .407589     0.927   0.354    -.4209012    1.176818
     _cons |  -1.941934   .1782185   -10.896   0.000    -2.291236   -1.592632
------------------------------------------------------------------------------
(Outcome insure==Indem is the comparison group)
```

`mlogit` chose the indemnity group as the base or comparison group and presented coefficients for the outcomes prepaid and uninsured. According to the model, the probability of prepaid for whites (`nonwhite = 0`) is

$$\Pr(\text{insure} = \text{Prepaid}) = \frac{e^{-.188}}{1 + e^{-.188} + e^{-1.942}} = 0.420$$

Similarly, for nonwhites, the probability of prepaid is

$$\Pr(\text{insure} = \text{Prepaid}) = \frac{e^{-.188+.661}}{1 + e^{-.188+.661} + e^{-1.942+.378}} = 0.570$$

These results agree with the column percentages presented by `tabulate` since the `mlogit` model is fully saturated. That is, there are enough terms in the model to fully explain the column percentage in each cell. Note that the model chi-squared and the `tabulate` chi-squared are in almost perfect agreement; both are testing that the column percentages of `insure` are the same for both values of `nonwhite`.

◁

▷ Example

By specifying the `basecategory()` option, you can control which category of the outcome variable is treated as the comparison group. Left to its own, `mlogit` chose to make category 1, indemnity, the base category. If we wanted to make category 2, prepaid, the base, we type

```
. mlogit insure nonwhite, base(2)
Iteration 0:   log likelihood = -556.59502
Iteration 1:   log likelihood = -551.78935
Iteration 2:   log likelihood = -551.78348
Iteration 3:   log likelihood = -551.78348

Multinomial regression                          Number of obs   =        616
                                                LR chi2(2)      =       9.62
                                                Prob > chi2     =     0.0081
Log likelihood = -551.78348                     Pseudo R2       =     0.0086

------------------------------------------------------------------------------
    insure |     Coef.   Std. Err.      z    P>|z|     [95% Conf. Interval]
-----------+------------------------------------------------------------------
Indem      |
  nonwhite |  -.6608212   .2157321    -3.063   0.002    -1.083648   -.2379942
     _cons |   .1879149   .0937644     2.004   0.045     .0041401    .3716896
-----------+------------------------------------------------------------------
Uninsure   |
  nonwhite |  -.2828628   .3977302    -0.711   0.477      -1.0624    .4966741
     _cons |  -1.754019   .1805145    -9.717   0.000    -2.107821   -1.400217
------------------------------------------------------------------------------
(Outcome insure==Prepaid is the comparison group)
```

The `basecategory()` option requires that we specify the numeric value of the category, so we could not type `base(Prepaid)`.

Although the coefficients now appear to be different, note that the summary statistics reported at the top are identical. With this parameterization, the probability of prepaid insurance for whites is

$$\Pr(\text{insure} = \text{Prepaid}) = \frac{1}{1 + e^{.188} + e^{-1.754}} = 0.420$$

This is the same answer we obtained previously.

◁

▷ Example

By specifying `rrr`, which we can do at estimation time or when we redisplay results, we see the model in terms of relative risk ratios:

```
. mlogit, rrr
Multinomial regression                          Number of obs   =        616
                                                LR chi2(2)      =       9.62
                                                Prob > chi2     =     0.0081
Log likelihood = -551.78348                     Pseudo R2       =     0.0086

------------------------------------------------------------------------------
    insure |       RRR    Std. Err.       z     P>|z|     [95% Conf. Interval]
-----------+------------------------------------------------------------------
Indem      |
  nonwhite |   .516427    .1114099     -3.063   0.002     .3383588     .7882073
-----------+------------------------------------------------------------------
Uninsure   |
  nonwhite |  .7536232    .2997387     -0.711   0.477     .3456254     1.643247
------------------------------------------------------------------------------
(Outcome insure==Prepaid is the comparison group)
```

Looked at this way, the relative risk of choosing an indemnity over a prepaid plan is 0.52 for nonwhites relative to whites.

◁

▷ Example

One of the advantages of `mlogit` over `tabulate` is that continuous variables can be included in the model and you can include multiple categorical variables. In examining the data on insurance choice, you decide you want to control for age, gender, and site of study (the study was conducted in three sites):

```
. mlogit insure age male nonwhite site2 site3
Iteration 0:  log likelihood = -555.85446
Iteration 1:  log likelihood = -534.72983
Iteration 2:  log likelihood = -534.36536
Iteration 3:  log likelihood = -534.36165
Iteration 4:  log likelihood = -534.36165
Multinomial regression                          Number of obs   =        615
                                                LR chi2(10)     =      42.99
                                                Prob > chi2     =     0.0000
Log likelihood = -534.36165                     Pseudo R2       =     0.0387

------------------------------------------------------------------------------
    insure |     Coef.    Std. Err.       z     P>|z|     [95% Conf. Interval]
-----------+------------------------------------------------------------------
Prepaid    |
       age |  -.011745    .0061946     -1.896   0.058    -.0238862     .0003962
      male |  .5616934    .2027465      2.770   0.006     .1643175     .9590693
  nonwhite |  .9747768    .2363213      4.125   0.000     .5115955     1.437958
     site2 |  .1130359    .2101903      0.538   0.591    -.2989296     .5250013
     site3 | -.5879879    .2279351     -2.580   0.010    -1.034733    -.1412433
     _cons |  .2697127    .3284422      0.821   0.412    -.3740222     .9134476
-----------+------------------------------------------------------------------
Uninsure   |
       age | -.0077961    .0114418     -0.681   0.496    -.0302217     .0146294
      male |  .4518496    .3674867      1.230   0.219    -.268411      1.17211
  nonwhite |  .2170589    .4256361      0.510   0.610    -.6171725     1.05129
     site2 | -1.211563    .4705127     -2.575   0.010    -2.133751    -.2893747
     site3 | -.2078123    .3662926     -0.567   0.570    -.9257327     .510108
     _cons | -1.286943    .5923219     -2.173   0.030    -2.447872    -.1260135
------------------------------------------------------------------------------
(Outcome insure==Indem is the comparison group)
```

These results suggest that the inclination of nonwhites to choose prepaid care is even stronger than it was without controlling. We also see that subjects in site 2 are less likely to be uninsured.

◁

Obtaining predicted values

▷ Example

After estimation, `predict` can be used to obtain predicted probabilities, index values, and standard errors of the index, or differences in the index. For instance, in the preceding example we estimated a model of insurance-choice on various characteristics. We can obtain the predicted probabilities for outcome 1 by typing

```
. predict p1 if e(sample), outcome(1)
(option p assumed; predicted probability)
(29 missing values generated)

. summarize p1

Variable |    Obs       Mean   Std. Dev.       Min        Max
---------+----------------------------------------------------
      p1 |    615   .4764228   .1032279   .1698142     .71939
```

Note that we included `if e(sample)` to restrict the calculation to the estimation sample. If you look back at the previous example, the multinomial logit model was estimated on 615 observations; there must be missing values in our dataset.

Although we typed `outcome(1)`, specifying 1 for the indemnity category, we could have typed `outcome(Indem)`. For instance, to obtain the probabilities for prepaid, we could type

```
. predict p2 if e(sample), outcome(prepaid)
(option p assumed; predicted probability)
equation prepaid not found
r(303);

. predict p2 if e(sample), outcome(Prepaid)
(option p assumed; predicted probability)
(29 missing values generated)

. summarize p2

Variable |    Obs       Mean   Std. Dev.       Min        Max
---------+----------------------------------------------------
      p2 |    615   .4504065   .1125962   .1964103   .7885724
```

When specifying the label, it must be specified exactly as it appears in the underlying value label (or how it appears in the `mlogit` output), and that includes capitalization.

Here, we have used `predict` to obtain probabilities for the same sample on which we estimated. That is not necessary. We could use another dataset that had the independent variables defined (in our example, `age`, `male`, `nonwhite`, `site2`, and `site3`) and use `predict` to obtain predicted probabilities; in this case, we would not specify `if e(sample)`.

◁

❏ Technical Note

predict can also be used to obtain the "index" values—the $\sum x_i \widehat{\beta}_i^{(k)}$—as well as the probabilities:

```
. predict idx1, outcome(Indem) xb
(1 missing value generated)

. summarize idx1
Variable |      Obs      Mean    Std. Dev.      Min         Max
---------+----------------------------------------------------------
    idx1 |      643         0           0        0           0
```

The indemnity category was our base category—the category for which all the coefficients were set to 0—and so the index is always 0. For the prepaid and uninsured categories:

```
. predict idx2, outcome(Prepaid) xb
(1 missing value generated)

. predict idx3, outcome(Uninsure) xb
(1 missing value generated)

. summarize idx2 idx3
Variable |      Obs      Mean    Std. Dev.      Min         Max
---------+----------------------------------------------------------
    idx2 |      643  -.0566113   .4962973  -1.298198    1.700719
    idx3 |      643  -1.980747   .6018139  -3.112741   -.8258458
```

We can obtain the standard error of the index by specifying the **stdp** option:

```
. predict se2, outcome(Prepaid) stdp
(1 missing value generated)

. list p2 idx2 se2 in 1/5

            p2         idx2          se2
  1.   .3709022   -.4831167    .2437772
  2.   .4977667     .055111    .1694686
  3.   .4113073   -.1712106    .1793498
  4.   .5424927    .3788345    .2513701
  5.   .4623673   -.0925817    .1452616
```

(We obtained the probability **p2** in the previous example.)

Finally, predict can calculate the standard error of the difference in the index values between two outcomes with the **stddp** option:

```
. predict se_2_3, outcome(Prepaid,Uninsure) stddp
(1 missing value generated)

. list idx2 idx3 se_2_3 in 1/5

          idx2         idx3       se_2_3
  1. -.4831167   -3.073253    .5469354
  2.   .055111   -2.715986    .4331917
  3. -.1712106   -1.579621    .3053815
  4.  .3788345   -1.462007    .4492552
  5. -.0925817   -2.814022    .4024784
```

In the first observation, the difference in the indexes is $-.483 - (-3.073) = 2.59$. The standard error of that difference is .547.

❏

▷ Example

It is more difficult to interpret the results from `mlogit` than `clogit` or `logit` since there are multiple equations. For example, suppose one of the independent variables in your model takes on the values 0 and 1 and you are attempting to understand the effect of this variable. Assume the coefficient on this variable for the second outcome, $\beta^{(2)}$, is positive. You might then be tempted to reason that the probability of the second outcome is higher if the variable is 1 rather than 0. Most of the time, that will be true; occasionally, you will be surprised. It could be that the probability of some other category will increase even more (say $\beta^{(3)} > \beta^{(2)}$) and thus the probability of outcome 2 actually falls relative to that outcome.

Prediction can be used to aid interpretation.

Continuing with our previously estimated insurance-choice model, we wish to describe the model's predictions by race. For this purpose, we can use the "method of recycled predictions", in which we vary characteristics of interest across the whole dataset and average the predictions. That is, we have data on both whites and nonwhites, and our individuals have other characteristics as well. We will first pretend that all the people in our data are white but hold their other characteristics constant. We then calculate the probabilities of each outcome. Next we will pretend that all the people in our data are nonwhite, still holding their other characteristics constant. Again we calculate the probabilities of each outcome. The difference in those two sets of calculated probabilities, then, is the difference due to race, holding other characteristics constant.

```
. gen byte nonwhold = nonwhite          /* save real race       */
. replace nonwhite = 0                  /* make everyone white  */
(126 real changes made)
. predict wpind, outcome(Indem)         /* predict probabilities */
(option p assumed; predicted probability)
(1 missing value generated)
. predict wpp, outcome(Prepaid)
(option p assumed; predicted probability)
(1 missing value generated)
. predict wpnoi, outcome(Uninsure)
(option p assumed; predicted probability)
(1 missing value generated)
. replace nonwhite=1                     /* make everyone nonwhite */
(644 real changes made)
. predict nwpind, outcome(Indem)
(option p assumed; predicted probability)
(1 missing value generated)
. predict nwpp, outcome(Prepaid)
(option p assumed; predicted probability)
(1 missing value generated)
. predict nwpnoi, outcome(Uninsure)
(option p assumed; predicted probability)
(1 missing value generated)
. replace nonwhite=nonwhold              /* restore real race    */
(518 real changes made)
. summarize wpind wpp wpnoi nwpind nwpp nwpnoi
```

Variable	Obs	Mean	Std. Dev.	Min	Max
wpind	643	.5141673	.0872679	.3092903	.71939
wpp	643	.4082052	.0993286	.1964103	.6502247
wpnoi	643	.0776275	.0360283	.0273596	.1302816
nwpind	643	.3112809	.0817693	.1511329	.535021
nwpp	643	.630078	.0979976	.3871782	.8278881
nwpnoi	643	.0586411	.0287185	.0209648	.0933874

Earlier in this entry we presented a cross-tabulation of insurance type and race. Those values were unadjusted. The means reported above are the values adjusted for age, sex, and site. Combining the results gives

	Unadjusted white	Unadjusted nonwhite	Adjusted white	Adjusted nonwhite
Indemnity	.51	.36	.52	.31
Prepaid	.42	.57	.41	.63
Uninsured	.07	.07	.08	.06

We find, for instance, that while 57% of nonwhites in our data had prepaid plans, after adjusting for age, sex, and site, 63% of nonwhites choose prepaid plans.

◁

❏ Technical Note

Classification of predicted values followed by comparison of the classifications with the observed outcomes is a second way predicted values can help interpret a multinomial logit model. This is a variation on the notions of sensitivity and specificity for logistic regression. Here, we will adopt a three-part classification with respect to indemnity and prepaid: definitely predicting indemnity, definitely predicting prepaid, and ambiguous.

```
. predict indem, outcome(Indem) xb              /* obtain indexes       */
(1 missing value generated)
. predict prepaid, outcome(Prepaid) xb
(1 missing value generated)
. gen diff = prepaid-indem                       /* obtain difference    */
(1 missing value generated)
. predict sediff, outcome(Indem,Prepaid) stddp   /* and its standard error */
(1 missing value generated)
. gen type = 1 if diff/sediff < -1.96            /* definitely indemnity  */
(504 missing values generated)
. replace type = 3 if diff/sediff > 1.96         /* definitely prepaid    */
(100 real changes made)
. replace type = 2 if type==. & diff/sediff!=.   /* ambiguous             */
(404 real changes made)
. label def type 1 "Def Ind" 2 "Ambig" 3 "Def Prep"
. label values type type                         /* label results         */
. tabulate insure type
```

		type		
insure	Def Ind	Ambig	Def Prep	Total
Indem	78	183	33	294
Prepaid	44	177	56	277
Uninsure	12	28	5	45
Total	134	388	94	616

One substantive point learned by this exercise is that the predictive power of this model is modest. There are a substantial number of misclassifications in both directions, though there are more correctly classified observations than misclassified observations.

A second interesting point is that the uninsured look overwhelmingly as though they might have come from the indemnity system rather than the prepaid system.

❏

Testing hypotheses about coefficients

▷ Example

Hypotheses about the coefficients are tested with `test` just as they are after any estimation command; see [R] **test**. The only important point to note is `test`'s syntax for dealing with multiple equation models. You are warned that `test` bases its results on the estimated covariance matrix and that a likelihood-ratio test may be preferred; see *Estimating constrained models* below for an example of `lrtest`.

If one simply lists variables after the `test` command, one is testing that the corresponding coefficients are zero across all equations:

```
. test site2 site3

 ( 1)   [Prepaid]site2 = 0.0
 ( 2)   [Uninsure]site2 = 0.0
 ( 3)   [Prepaid]site3 = 0.0
 ( 4)   [Uninsure]site3 = 0.0

           chi2(  4) =    19.74
         Prob > chi2 =     0.0006
```

One can test that all the coefficients (except the constant) in a single equation are zero by simply typing the outcome in square brackets:

```
. test [Uninsure]

 ( 1)   [Uninsure]age = 0.0
 ( 2)   [Uninsure]male = 0.0
 ( 3)   [Uninsure]nonwhite = 0.0
 ( 4)   [Uninsure]site2 = 0.0
 ( 5)   [Uninsure]site3 = 0.0

           chi2(  5) =     9.31
         Prob > chi2 =     0.0973
```

Specification of the outcome is just as with `predict`; you can specify the label if the outcome variable is labeled, or you can specify the numeric value of the outcome. We would have obtained the same test as above had we typed `test [3]`, since 3 is the value of `insure` for the outcome uninsured.

The two syntaxes can be combined. To test that the coefficients on the site variables are 0 in the equation corresponding to the outcome prepaid, we can type

```
. test [Prepaid]: site2 site3

 ( 1)   [Prepaid]site2 = 0.0
 ( 2)   [Prepaid]site3 = 0.0

           chi2(  2) =    10.78
         Prob > chi2 =     0.0046
```

We specified the outcome and then followed that with a colon and the variables we wanted to test.

We can also test that coefficients are equal across equations. To test that all coefficients except the constant are equal for the prepaid and uninsured outcomes:

```
. test [Prepaid=Uninsure]

 ( 1)   [Prepaid]age - [Uninsure]age = 0.0
 ( 2)   [Prepaid]male - [Uninsure]male = 0.0
 ( 3)   [Prepaid]nonwhite - [Uninsure]nonwhite = 0.0
 ( 4)   [Prepaid]site2 - [Uninsure]site2 = 0.0
 ( 5)   [Prepaid]site3 - [Uninsure]site3 = 0.0

           chi2(  5) =    13.80
         Prob > chi2 =     0.0169
```

To test that only the site variables are equal:

```
. test [Prepaid=Uninsure]: site2 site3
 ( 1)   [Prepaid]site2 - [Uninsure]site2 = 0.0
 ( 2)   [Prepaid]site3 - [Uninsure]site3 = 0.0
           chi2(  2) =   12.68
         Prob > chi2 =    0.0018
```

Finally, we can test any arbitrary constraint by simply entering the equation, specifying the coefficients as described in [U] **16.5 Accessing coefficients and standard errors**. The following hypothesis is senseless but illustrates the point:

```
. test ([Prepaid]age+[Uninsure]site2)/2 = 2-[Uninsure]nonwhite
 ( 1)   .5 [Prepaid]age + [Uninsure]nonwhite + .5 [Uninsure]site2 = 2.0
           chi2(  1) =   22.45
         Prob > chi2 =    0.0000
```

Please see [R] **test** for more information on **test**. All that is said about combining hypotheses across **test** commands (the **accum** option) is relevant after **mlogit**.

◁

Estimating constrained models

mlogit can estimate models with subsets of coefficients constrained to be zero, subsets of coefficients constrained to be equal both within and across equations, and with subsets of coefficients arbitrarily constrained to equal linear combinations of other estimated coefficients.

Before estimating a constrained model, you define the constraints using the **constraint** command; see [R] **constraint**. Constraints are numbered and the syntax for specifying a constraint is exactly the same as the syntax for testing constraints; see *Testing hypotheses about coefficients* above. Once the constraints are defined, you estimate using **mlogit**, specifying the **constraint()** option. Typing **constraint(4)** would use the constraint you previously saved as 4. Typing **constraint(1,4,6)** would use the previously stored constraints 1, 4, and 6. Typing **constraint(1-4,6)** would use the previously stored constraints 1, 2, 3, 4, and 6.

Sometimes, you will not be able to specify the constraints without knowledge of the omitted group. In such cases, assume the omitted group is whatever group is convenient for you and include the **basecategory()** option when you type the **mlogit** command.

▷ Example

Among other things, constraints can be used as a means of hypothesis testing. In our insurance-choice model, we previously tested the hypothesis that there is no distinction between having indemnity insurance and being uninsured. This we did with the **test** command. Indemnity-style insurance was the omitted group, so we typed

```
. test [Uninsure]
 ( 1)   [Uninsure]age = 0.0
 ( 2)   [Uninsure]male = 0.0
 ( 3)   [Uninsure]nonwhite = 0.0
 ( 4)   [Uninsure]site2 = 0.0
 ( 5)   [Uninsure]site3 = 0.0
           chi2(  5) =    9.31
         Prob > chi2 =    0.0973
```

(Had indemnity not been the omitted group, we would have typed `test [Uninsure=Indem]`.)

The results produced by `test` are based on the estimated covariance matrix of the coefficients and so are an approximation. Since the probability of being uninsured is quite low, the log likelihood may be nonlinear for the uninsured. Conventional statistical wisdom is not to trust the asymptotic answer under these circumstances, but to perform a likelihood-ratio test instead.

Stata has a `lrtest` likelihood-ratio test command; to use it we must estimate both the unconstrained and the constrained models. The unconstrained model is what we have previously estimated. Following the instruction in [R] **lrtest**, we first save the unconstrained model results:

```
. lrtest, saving(0)
```

To estimate the constrained model, we must reestimate our model with all the coefficients except the constant set to 0 in the `Uninsure` equation. We define the constraint and then reestimate:

```
. constraint define 1 [Uninsure]
. mlogit insure age male nonwhite site2 site3, constr(1)

 ( 1)   [Uninsure]age = 0.0
 ( 2)   [Uninsure]male = 0.0
 ( 3)   [Uninsure]nonwhite = 0.0
 ( 4)   [Uninsure]site2 = 0.0
 ( 5)   [Uninsure]site3 = 0.0
Iteration 0:   log likelihood = -555.85446
Iteration 1:   log likelihood = -539.80523
Iteration 2:   log likelihood = -539.75644
Iteration 3:   log likelihood = -539.75643
```

```
Multinomial regression                        Number of obs   =       615
                                              LR chi2(5)      =     32.20
                                              Prob > chi2     =    0.0000
Log likelihood = -539.75643                   Pseudo R2       =    0.0290

------------------------------------------------------------------------------
   insure |      Coef.   Std. Err.      z    P>|z|     [95% Conf. Interval]
----------+-------------------------------------------------------------------
Prepaid   |
      age |  -.0107025   .0060039    -1.783   0.075    -.0224699    .0010649
     male |   .4963616   .1939683     2.559   0.010     .1161908    .8765324
 nonwhite |    .942137   .2252094     4.183   0.000     .5007347    1.383539
    site2 |   .2530912   .2029465     1.247   0.212    -.1446767    .6508591
    site3 |  -.5521774   .2187237    -2.525   0.012    -.9808678   -.1234869
    _cons |   .1792752   .3171372     0.565   0.572    -.4423023    .8008527
----------+-------------------------------------------------------------------
Uninsure  |
      age |  (dropped)
     male |  (dropped)
 nonwhite |  (dropped)
    site2 |  (dropped)
    site3 |  (dropped)
    _cons |   -1.87351   .1601099   -11.701   0.000     -2.18732     -1.5597
------------------------------------------------------------------------------
(Outcome insure==Indem is the comparison group)
```

We can now perform the likelihood-ratio test:

```
. lrtest
Mlogit:  likelihood-ratio test                   chi2(5)    =     10.79
                                                 Prob > chi2 =    0.0557
```

The likelihood-ratio chi-squared is 10.79 with 5 degrees of freedom—just slightly greater than the magic $p = .05$ level. Thus, we should not call this difference significant.

◁

❏ Technical Note

In certain circumstances, a multinomial logit model should be estimated with conditional logit; see [R] **clogit**. With substantial data manipulation, clogit is capable of handling the same class of models with some interesting additions. For example, if we had available the price and deductible of the most competitive insurance plan of each type, this information could not be used by mlogit but could be incorporated by clogit.

❏

Saved Results

mlogit saves in e():

Scalars

e(N)	number of observations	e(ll_0)	log likelihood, constant-only model
e(k_cat)	number of categories	e(N_clust)	number of clusters
e(df_m)	model degrees of freedom	e(chi2)	χ^2
e(r2_p)	pseudo R-squared	e(ibasecat)	base category number
e(ll)	log likelihood	e(basecat)	the value of *depvar* that is to be treated as the base category

Macros

e(cmd)	mlogit	e(clustvar)	name of cluster variable
e(depvar)	name of dependent variable	e(vcetype)	covariance estimation method
e(wtype)	weight type	e(chi2type)	Wald or LR; type of model χ^2 test
e(wexp)	weight expression	e(predict)	program used to implement predict

Matrices

e(b)	coefficient vector	e(V)	variance–covariance matrix of the estimators
e(cat)	category values		

Functions

e(sample)	marks estimation sample

Methods and Formulas

The model for multinomial logit is

$$\Pr(Y_i = k) = \frac{\exp\left(\sum\limits_{j=0}^{p} x_{ij}\beta_{jk}\right)}{\sum\limits_{m=1}^{r} \exp\left(\sum\limits_{j=0}^{p} x_{ij}\beta_{jm}\right)}$$

This model is described in Greene (1997, chapter 19).

Newton–Raphson maximum likelihood is used; see [R] **maximize**.

In the case of constrained equations, the set of constraints is orthogonalized and a subset of maximizable parameters is selected. For example, a parameter that is constrained to zero is not a maximizable parameter. If two parameters are constrained to be equal to each other, only one is a maximizable parameter.

Let $\mathbf{r}$ be the vector of maximizable parameters. Note that $\mathbf{r}$ is physically a subset of the solution parameters $\mathbf{b}$. A matrix $\mathbf{T}$ and a vector $\mathbf{m}$ are defined

$$\mathbf{b} = \mathbf{Tr} + \mathbf{m}$$

with the consequence that

$$\frac{df}{d\mathbf{b}} = \frac{df}{d\mathbf{r}}\mathbf{T}'$$

$$\frac{d^2 f}{d\mathbf{b}^2} = \mathbf{T}\frac{d^2 f}{d\mathbf{r}^2}\mathbf{T}'$$

$\mathbf{T}$ consists of a block form in which one block is a permutation of the identity matrix and the other part describes how to calculate the constrained parameters from the maximizable parameters.

References

Aldrich, J. H. and F. D. Nelson. 1984. *Linear Probability, Logit, and Probit Models.* Newbury Park, CA: Sage Publications.

Greene, W. H. 1997. *Econometric Analysis.* 3d ed. Upper Saddle River, NJ: Prentice–Hall.

Hamilton, L. C. 1993. sqv8: Interpreting multinomial logistic regression. *Stata Technical Bulletin* 13: 24–28. Reprinted in *Stata Technical Bulletin Reprints*, vol. 3, pp. 176–181.

Hosmer, D. W., Jr., and S. Lemeshow. 1989. *Applied Logistic Regression.* New York: John Wiley & Sons.

Judge, G. G., W. E. Griffiths, R. C. Hill, H. Lütkepohl, and T.-C. Lee. 1985. *The Theory and Practice of Econometrics.* 2d ed. New York: John Wiley & Sons.

Long, J. S. 1997. *Regression Models for Categorical and Limited Dependent Variables.* Thousand Oaks, CA: Sage Publications.

Tarlov, A. R., J. E. Ware, Jr., S. Greenfield, E. C. Nelson, E. Perrin, and M. Zubkoff. 1989. The medical outcomes study. *Journal of the American Medical Association* 262: 925–930.

Wells, K. E., R. D. Hays, M. A. Burnam, W. H. Rogers, S. Greenfield, and J. E. Ware, Jr. 1989. Detection of depressive disorder for patients receiving prepaid or fee-for-service care. *Journal of the American Medical Association* 262: 3298–3302.

Also See

Complementary:	[R] **constraint**, [R] **lincom**, [R] **lrtest**, [R] **predict**, [R] **test**, [R] **testnl**, [R] **xi**
Related:	[R] **clogit**, [R] **logistic**, [R] **ologit**, [R] **svy estimators**
Background:	[U] **16.5 Accessing coefficients and standard errors**, [U] **23 Estimation and post-estimation commands**, [U] **23.11 Obtaining robust variance estimates**, [U] **23.12 Obtaining scores**, [R] **maximize**

Title

> **more** — Pause until key is depressed

Syntax

<u>more</u>

<u>set</u> <u>more</u> { on | off }

Description

<u>more</u> causes Stata to display --more-- and pause until any key is depressed.

<u>set</u> <u>more</u> on, which is the default, tells Stata that when a --more-- message is displayed, wait until a key is depressed before continuing.

<u>set</u> <u>more</u> off tells Stata not to display the --more-- message, and, therefore, don't pause.

Remarks

When you see --more-- at the bottom of the screen

Press ...	and Stata...
letter *l* or *Enter*	displays the next line
letter *q*	acts as if you pressed *Break*
space bar or any other key	displays the next screen

In addition, Stata for Windows and Stata for Macintosh users can press the **More** button to display the next screen.

--more-- is Stata's way of telling you it has something more to show you, but showing you that something more will cause the information on the screen to scroll off.

If you type set more off, --more-- conditions will never arise—Stata's output will scroll by at full speed.

If you type set more on, --more-- conditions will be restored at the appropriate places.

Programmers: Do-file writers sometimes include set more off in their do-files because they do not care to interactively review the output. They want Stata to proceed at full speed because they plan on making a log of the output which they will review later.

Do-file writers need not bother to set more on at the end of their do-file. Stata automatically restores the previous set more when the do-file (or program) concludes.

413

The more programming command

Ado-file programmers need take no special action to have --more-- conditions arise when the screen is full. Stata handles that automatically.

If, however, you wish to force a --more-- condition early, you can include the more command in your program. The syntax of more is

    more

more takes no arguments.

Also See

Complementary: [R] **query**

Background: [U] **10 –more– conditions**

Title

mvencode — Change missing to coded missing value and vice versa

Syntax

mvencode *varlist* [if *exp*] [in *range*] , <u>mv</u>(*#*) [<u>o</u>verride]

mvdecode *varlist* [if *exp*] [in *range*] , <u>mv</u>(*#*)

Description

mvencode changes all occurrences of missing to *#* in the specified *varlist*.

mvdecode changes all occurrences of *#* to missing in the specified *varlist*.

Options

mv(*#*) specifies the numeric value to which or from which missing is to be changed and is not optional.

override specifies that the protection provided by mvencode is to be overridden. Without this option, mvencode refuses to make the requested change if *#* is already used in the data.

Remarks

One occasionally reads datasets where missing (e.g., failed to answer a survey question, or the data was not collected, or whatever) is coded with a special numeric value. Popular codings are 9, 99, −9, −99, and the like. If missing were encoded as −99,

```
. mvdecode _all, mv(-99)
```

would translate the special code to the Stata missing value '.'. Use this command cautiously since, even if −99 were not a special code, all −99's in the data would be changed to missing.

Conversely, one occasionally needs to export a dataset to software that does not understand that '.' means missing value, so one codes missing with a special numeric value. To change all missings to −99:

```
. mvencode _all, mv(-99)
```

mvencode is smart: it will automatically recast variables upward if necessary, so even if a variable is stored as a byte, its missing values can be recoded to, say, 999. In addition, mvencode refuses to make the change if *#* (−99 in this case) is already used in the data, so you can be certain that your coding is unique. You can override this feature by including the override option.

▷ Example

Our automobile data (described in [U] **9 Stata's on-line tutorials and sample datasets**) contains 74 observations and 12 variables. Let us first attempt to translate whatever missing values there are in the data to 1:

```
. mvencode _all, mv(1)
make:    string variable ignored
rep78:   already 1 in    2 observations
foreign: already 1 in   22 observations
no action taken
r(9);
```

Our attempt failed. mvencode first informed us that make is a string variable—this is not a problem but is reported merely for our information. String variables are ignored by mvencode. It next informed us that rep78 already was coded 1 in 2 observations and that foreign was already coded 1 in 22 observations. Thus, 1 would be a poor choice for encoding missing values because, after encoding, you could not tell a real 1 from a coded missing value 1.

We could force mvencode to encode the data with 1 anyway by typing mvencode _all, mv(1) override and that would be appropriate if the 1s in our data already represented missing data. They do not however, and we will code missing as 999:

```
. mvencode _all, mv(999)
make:    string variable ignored
rep78:   5 missing values
```

This worked, and we are informed that the only changes necessary were to 5 observations of rep78.

◁

▷ Example

Let us now pretend that we just read in the automobile data from some raw dataset where all the missing values were coded 999. We can convert the 999's to real missings by typing

```
. mvdecode _all, mv(999)
make:    string variable ignored
rep78:   5 missing values
```

We are informed that make is a string variable and so was ignored and that rep78 contained 5 observations with 999. Those observations have now been changed to contain missing.

◁

Methods and Formulas

mvencode and mvdecode are implemented as ado-files.

Also See

Related: [R] **generate**, [R] **recode**

Title

> **mvreg** — Multivariate regression

Syntax

> mvreg *depvarlist* = *varlist* [*weight*] [if *exp*] [in *range*] [, <u>nocons</u> <u>corr</u> <u>noh</u>eader
>
> <u>not</u>able <u>l</u>evel(*#*)]

aweights and fweights are allowed; see [U] **14.1.6 weight**.

mvreg shares the features of all estimation commands; see [U] **23 Estimation and post-estimation commands**.

Syntax for predict

> predict [*type*] *newvarname* [if *exp*] [in *range*] [, <u>eq</u>uation(*eqno* [,*eqno*])
>
> { xb | stdp | <u>res</u>iduals | <u>dif</u>ference | <u>stddp</u> }]

These statistics are available both in and out of sample; type predict ... if e(sample) ... if wanted only for the estimation sample.

Description

mvreg estimates multivariate regression models.

Options

nocons omits the constant term from the estimation.

corr displays the correlation matrix of the residuals between the equations.

noheader suppresses display of the table reporting F statistics, R-squared, and root mean square error above the coefficient table.

notable suppresses display of the coefficient table.

level(*#*) specifies the confidence level, in percent, for confidence intervals. The default is level(95) or as set by set level; see [U] **23.5 Specifying the width of confidence intervals**.

Options for predict

equation(*eqno*[,*eqno*]) specifies to which equation you are referring.

equation() is filled in with one *eqno* for options xb, stdp, and residuals. equation(#1) would mean the calculation is to be made for the first equation, equation(#2) would mean the second, and so on. Alternatively, you could refer to the equations by their names. equation(income) would refer to the equation named income and equation(hours) to the equation named hours.

If you do not specify equation(), results are as if you specified equation(#1).

difference and stddp refer to between-equation concepts. To use these options, you must specify two equations; e.g., equation(#1,#2) or equation(income,hours). When two equations must be specified, equation() is not optional. With equation(#1,#2), difference computes the prediction of equation(#1) minus the prediction of equation(#2).

xb, the default, calculates the fitted values—the prediction of $x_j b$ for the specified equation.

stdp calculates the standard error of the prediction for the specified equation. It can be thought of as the standard error of the predicted expected value or mean for the observation's covariate pattern. This is also referred to as the standard error of the fitted value.

residuals calculates the residuals.

difference calculates the difference between the linear predictions of two equations in the system.

stddp is allowed only after you have previously estimated a multiple-equation model. The standard error of the difference in linear predictions $(x_{1j} b - x_{2j} b)$ between equations 1 and 2 is calculated.

For more information on using predict after multiple-equation estimation commands, see [R] **predict**.

Remarks

Multivariate regression differs from multiple regression in that *several* dependent variables are jointly regressed on the same independent variables. Multivariate regression is related to Zellner's seemingly unrelated regression (see [R] **sureg**) but, since the same set of independent variables is used for each dependent variable, the syntax is simpler and the calculations faster.

The individual coefficients and standard errors produced by mvreg are identical to those that would be produced by regress estimating each equation separately. The difference is that mvreg, being a joint estimator, also estimates the between-equation covariances, so you can test coefficients across equations and, in fact, the test syntax makes such tests more convenient.

▷ Example

Using the automobile data, we estimate a multivariate regression for "space" variables (hdroom, trunk, and turn) in terms of a set of other variables including three "performance variables" (displ, gratio, and mpg):

```
. mvreg hdroom trunk turn = price mpg displ gratio length weight
Equation      Obs   Parms      RMSE    "R-sq"           F         P
------------------------------------------------------------------------
hdroom         74      7    .7390205   0.2996    4.777213   0.0004
trunk          74      7    3.052314   0.5326     12.7265   0.0000
turn           74      7    2.132377   0.7844    40.62042   0.0000


             |      Coef.   Std. Err.       t    P>|t|     [95% Conf. Interval]
-------------+----------------------------------------------------------------
hdroom       |
       price |  -.0000528     .000038    -1.392   0.168    -.0001286     .0000229
         mpg |  -.0093774    .0260463    -0.360   0.720     -.061366     .0426112
       displ |   .0031025    .0024999     1.241   0.219    -.0018873     .0080922
      gratio |   .2108071    .3539588     0.596   0.553    -.4956975     .9173118
      length |    .015886     .012944     1.227   0.224    -.0099504     .0417223
      weight |  -.0000868    .0004724    -0.184   0.855    -.0010296     .0008561
       _cons |  -.4525117    2.170073    -0.209   0.835    -4.783995     3.878972
-------------+----------------------------------------------------------------
trunk        |
       price |   .0000445    .0001567     0.284   0.778    -.0002684     .0003573
         mpg |  -.0220919    .1075767    -0.205   0.838    -.2368159     .1926322
       displ |   .0032118    .0103251     0.311   0.757    -.0173971     .0238207
      gratio |  -.2271321    1.461926    -0.155   0.877    -3.145149     2.690884
      length |    .170811    .0534615     3.195   0.002     .0641014     .2775206
      weight |  -.0015944     .001951    -0.817   0.417    -.0054885     .0022997
       _cons |  -13.28253    8.962868    -1.482   0.143    -31.17249     4.607428
```

```
---------+-----------------------------------------------------------------------
  turn   |
   price |   -.0002647     .0001095    -2.418   0.018     -.0004833    -.0000462
     mpg |   -.0492948     .0751542    -0.656   0.514     -.1993031     .1007136
   displ |    .0036977     .0072132     0.513   0.610     -.0106999     .0180953
  gratio |   -.1048432     1.021316    -0.103   0.919     -2.143399     1.933712
  length |     .072128     .0373487     1.931   0.058     -.0024204     .1466764
  weight |    .0027059      .001363     1.985   0.051     -.0000145     .0054264
   _cons |    20.19157     6.261549     3.225   0.002      7.693467     32.68967
---------+-----------------------------------------------------------------------
```

We should have specified the `corr` option so that we would also see the correlations between the residuals of the equations. We can correct our omission because `mvreg`—like all estimation commands—typed without arguments redisplays results. The `noheader` and `notable` (read no-table) options suppress redisplaying the output we have already seen:

```
. mvreg, notable noheader corr

Correlation matrix of residuals:

          hdroom     trunk      turn
hdroom    1.0000
 trunk    0.4986    1.0000
  turn   -0.1090   -0.0628    1.0000

Breusch-Pagan test of independence: chi2(3) =     19.566, Pr = 0.0002
```

The Breusch–Pagan test is significant, so the residuals of these three space variables are not independent of each other.

The three performance variables among our independent variables are `mpg`, `displ`, and `gratio`. We can jointly test the significance of these three variables, in all the equations, by typing

```
. test mpg displ gratio

 ( 1)   [hdroom]mpg = 0.0
 ( 2)   [trunk]mpg = 0.0
 ( 3)   [turn]mpg = 0.0
 ( 4)   [hdroom]displ = 0.0
 ( 5)   [trunk]displ = 0.0
 ( 6)   [turn]displ = 0.0
 ( 7)   [hdroom]gratio = 0.0
 ( 8)   [trunk]gratio = 0.0
 ( 9)   [turn]gratio = 0.0

       F(  9,     67) =      0.33
            Prob > F =    0.9622
```

These three variables are not, as a group, significant. We might have suspected this from their individual significance in the individual regressions, but this multivariate test provides an overall assessment with a single p-value.

We can also perform a test for the joint significance of all three equations:

```
. test [hdroom]
(output omitted )

. test [trunk], accum
(output omitted )

. test [turn], accum

 ( 1)   [hdroom]price = 0.0
 ( 2)   [hdroom]mpg = 0.0
 ( 3)   [hdroom]displ = 0.0
 ( 4)   [hdroom]gratio = 0.0
```

```
( 5)  [hdroom]length = 0.0
( 6)  [hdroom]weight = 0.0
( 7)  [trunk]price = 0.0
( 8)  [trunk]mpg = 0.0
( 9)  [trunk]displ = 0.0
(10)  [trunk]gratio = 0.0
(11)  [trunk]length = 0.0
(12)  [trunk]weight = 0.0
(13)  [turn]price = 0.0
(14)  [turn]mpg = 0.0
(15)  [turn]displ = 0.0
(16)  [turn]gratio = 0.0
(17)  [turn]length = 0.0
(18)  [turn]weight = 0.0
        F( 18,    67) =    19.34
           Prob > F =     0.0000
```

The set of variables as a whole is strongly significant. We might have suspected this, too, from the individual equations.

◁

❏ Technical Note

The `mvreg` command provides a good way to deal with multiple comparisons. If we wanted to assess the effect of `length`, we might be dissuaded from interpreting any of its coefficients except that in the `trunk` equation. `[trunk]length`—the coefficient on `length` in the `trunk` equation—has a p-value of .002, but in the remaining two equations, it has p-values of only .224 and .058.

A conservative statistician might argue that there are 18 tests of significance in `mvreg`'s output (not counting those for the intercept), so p-values above $.05/18 = .0028$ should be declared insignificant at the 5% level. A more aggressive but, in our opinion, reasonable approach would be to first note that the three equations are jointly significant, so we are justified in making some interpretation. Then, we would work through the individual variables using `test`, possibly using $.05/6 = .0083$ (6 because there are 6 independent variables) for the 5% significance level. For instance, examining `length`:

```
. test length
( 1)  [hdroom]length = 0.0
( 2)  [trunk]length = 0.0
( 3)  [turn]length = 0.0
        F( 3,    67) =     4.94
           Prob > F =     0.0037
```

The reported significance level of .0037 is less than .0083, so we will declare this variable significant. `[trunk]length` is certainly significant with its p-value of .002, but what about in the remaining two equations with p-values .224 and .058? Performing a joint test:

```
. test [hdroom]length [turn]length
( 1)  [hdroom]length = 0.0
( 2)  [turn]length = 0.0
        F( 2,    67) =     2.91
           Prob > F =     0.0613
```

At this point, reasonable statisticians could disagree. The .06 significance value suggests no interpretation but these were the two least-significant values out of three, so one would expect the p-value to be a little high. Perhaps an equivocal statement is warranted: there seems to be an effect, but chance cannot be excluded.

❏

Saved Results

mvreg saves in e():

Scalars

e(N)	number of observations
e(k)	number of parameters (including constant)
e(k_eq)	number of equations
e(df_r)	residual degrees of freedom
e(chi2)	Breusch–Pagan χ^2 (corr only)
e(df_chi2)	degrees of freedom for Breusch–Pagan χ^2 (corr only)

Macros

e(cmd)	mvreg
e(eqnames)	names of equations
e(r2)	R-squared for each equation
e(rmse)	RMSE for each equation
e(F)	F statistic for each equation
e(p_F)	significance of F for each equation
e(predict)	program used to implement predict

Matrices

e(b)	coefficient vector
e(V)	variance–covariance matrix of the estimators
e(Sigma)	$\widehat{\mathbf{\Sigma}}$ matrix

Functions

e(sample)	marks estimation sample

Methods and Formulas

mvreg is implemented as an ado-file.

Given q equations and p independent variables (including the constant), the parameter estimates are given by the $p \times q$ matrix

$$\mathbf{B} = (\mathbf{X'WX})^{-1}\mathbf{X'WY}$$

where $\mathbf{Y}$ is a $n \times q$ matrix of dependent variables and $\mathbf{X}$ is a $n \times p$ matrix of independent variables. $\mathbf{W}$ is a weighting matrix equal to $\mathbf{I}$ if no weights are specified. If weights are specified, let $\mathbf{v}: 1 \times n$ be the specified weights. If fweight frequency weights are specified, $\mathbf{W} = \text{diag}(\mathbf{v})$. If aweight analytic weights are specified, $\mathbf{W} = \text{diag}[\mathbf{v}/(\mathbf{1'v})(\mathbf{1'1})]$, which is to say, the weights are normalized to sum to the number of observations.

The residual covariance matrix is

$$\mathbf{R} = (\mathbf{Y'WY} - \mathbf{B'}(\mathbf{X'WX})\mathbf{B})/(n - p)$$

The estimated covariance matrix of the estimates is $\mathbf{R} \otimes (\mathbf{X'WX})^{-1}$. These results are identical to those produced by sureg when the same list of independent variables is specified repeatedly; see [R] **sureg**.

The Breusch and Pagan (1980) χ^2 statistic—a Lagrange multiplier statistic—is given by

$$\lambda = n \sum_{i=1}^{q} \sum_{j=1}^{i-1} r_{ij}^2$$

where r_{ij} is the estimated correlation between the residuals of the equations and n is the number of observations. It is distributed as χ^2 with $q(q-1)/2$ degrees of freedom.

References

Breusch, T. and A. Pagan. 1980. The LM test and its applications to model specification in econometrics. *Review of Economic Studies* 47: 239–254.

Also See

Complementary:	[R] **lincom**, [R] **predict**, [R] **test**, [R] **testnl**, [R] **vce**
Related:	[R] **reg3**, [R] **regress**, [R] **regression diagnostics**, [R] **sureg**
Background:	[U] **16.5 Accessing coefficients and standard errors**,
	[U] **23 Estimation and post-estimation commands**

Title

> **nbreg** — Negative binomial regression

Syntax

nbreg *depvar* [*indepvars*] [*weight*] [if *exp*] [in *range*] [, level(*#*) irr

    exposure(*varname*) offset(*varname*) robust cluster(*varname*) score(*newvars*)

    noconstant nolrtest *maximize_options*]

gnbreg *depvar* [*indepvars*] [*weight*] [if *exp*] [in *range*] [, lnalpha(*varlist*) level(*#*) irr

    exposure(*varname*) offset(*varname*) robust cluster(*varname*) score(*newvars*)

    noconstant nolrtest *maximize_options*]

fweights, iweights, pweights, and aweights are allowed; see [U] **14.1.6 weight**. Note that although aweights are allowed, they are not recommended; see Rogers (1991).

These commands share the features of all estimation commands; see [U] **23 Estimation and post-estimation commands**.

Syntax for predict

predict [*type*] *newvarname* [if *exp*] [in *range*] [, *statistic* nooffset]

where *statistic* is

n	predicted number of events (the default)
ir	incidence rate (equivalent to predict ..., n nooffset)
xb	linear prediction
stdp	standard error of the prediction

and in addition, relevant only after **gnbreg**,

alpha	predicted values of alpha
lnalpha	predicted values of ln(alpha)
stdplna	standard error of predicted ln(alpha)

These statistics are available both in and out of sample; type predict ... if e(sample) ... if wanted only for the estimation sample.

Description

nbreg estimates a negative binomial maximum-likelihood regression of *depvar* on *varlist*, where *depvar* is a nonnegative count variable. In this model, the count variable is believed to be generated by a Poisson-like process, except that the variation is greater than that of a true Poisson. This extra variation is referred to as overdispersion. See [R] **poisson** before reading this entry.

gnbreg is a generalized negative binomial regression; the shape parameter alpha may also be parameterized.

Persons who have panel datasets should see [R] **xtnbreg**.

Options

level(#) specifies the confidence level, in percent, for confidence intervals. The default is level(95) or as set by set level; see [U] **23.5 Specifying the width of confidence intervals**.

irr reports estimated coefficients transformed to incidence rate ratios, i.e., e^b rather than b. Standard errors and confidence intervals are similarly transformed. This option affects how results are displayed, not how they are estimated or stored. irr may be specified at estimation or when replaying previously estimated results.

exposure(*varname*) and offset(*varname*) are different ways of specifying the same thing. exposure() specifies a variable that reflects the amount of exposure over which the *depvar* events were observed for each observation; ln(*varname*) with coefficient constrained to be 1 is entered into the log-link function. offset() specifies a variable that is to be entered directly into the log-link function with coefficient constrained to be 1; thus exposure is assumed to be $e^{varname}$.

robust specifies that the Huber/White/sandwich estimator of variance is to be used in place of the traditional calculation; see [U] **23.11 Obtaining robust variance estimates**. robust combined with cluster() allows observations which are not independent within cluster (although they must be independent between clusters).

If you specify pweights, robust is implied; see [U] **23.13 Weighted estimation**.

cluster(*varname*) specifies that the observations are independent across groups (clusters) but not necessarily within groups. *varname* specifies to which group each observation belongs; e.g., cluster(personid) in data with repeated observations on individuals. cluster() affects the estimated standard errors and variance–covariance matrix of the estimators (VCE), but not the estimated coefficients; see [U] **23.11 Obtaining robust variance estimates**.

cluster() implies robust; specifying robust cluster() is equivalent to typing cluster() by itself.

score(*newvars*) creates *newvar* containing $u_j = \partial \ln L_j / \partial(\mathbf{x}_j \mathbf{b})$ for each observation j in the sample. The score vector is $\sum \partial \ln L_j / \partial \mathbf{b} = \sum u_j \mathbf{x}_j$; i.e., the product of *newvar* with each covariate summed over observations. If two *newvars* are specified, then the score from the ancillary parameter equation is also saved. See [U] **23.12 Obtaining scores**.

noconstant suppresses the constant term (intercept) in the regression.

nolrtest suppresses fitting the Poisson model. Without this option, the Poisson model is fit and the likelihood used in a likelihood-ratio test of the alpha parameter.

maximize_options control the maximization process; see [R] **maximize**. You should never have to specify them, although we often recommend specifying trace.

lnalpha(*varlist*) is allowed only with gnbreg. If this option is not specified, gnbreg and nbreg will produce the same results because the shape parameter will be parameterized as a constant. lnalpha() allows specifying a linear equation for ln(alpha). Specifying lnalpha(male old) means $\ln(\text{alpha}) = a_0 + a_1 \text{male} + a_2 \text{old}$, where a_0, a_1, and a_2 are parameters to be fitted along with the other model coefficients.

Options for predict

n, the default, calculates the predicted number of events, which is $\exp(\mathbf{x}_j\mathbf{b})$ if neither off-set(*varname*) nor exposure(*varname*) was specified when the model was estimated; or $\exp(\mathbf{x}_j\mathbf{b} + \text{offset})$ if offset(*varname*) was specified; or $\exp(\mathbf{x}_j\mathbf{b}) * \text{exposure}$ if expo-sure(*varname*) was specified.

ir calculates the incidence rate $\exp(\mathbf{x}_j\mathbf{b})$, the predicted number of events when exposure is 1. This is equivalent to n when neither offset(*varname*) nor exposure(*varname*) was specified when the model was estimated.

xb calculates the linear prediction.

stdp calculates the standard error of the linear prediction.

alpha, lnalpha, and stdplna are relevant after gnbreg estimation only; they produce the predicted values of alpha or ln(alpha) and the standard error of the predicted ln(alpha), respectively.

nooffset is relevant only if you specified offset(*varname*) or exposure(*varname*) when you estimated the model. It modifies the calculations made by predict so that they ignore the offset or exposure variable; the linear prediction is treated as $\mathbf{x}_j\mathbf{b}$ rather than $\mathbf{x}_j\mathbf{b} + \text{offset}_j$, and specifying predict ... is equivalent to specifying predict ... , nooffset ir.

Remarks

See Long (1997, chapter 8) for an introduction to the negative binomial regression model and for a discussion of other regression models for count data.

Negative binomial regression is used to estimate models of the number of occurrences (counts) of an event when the event has extra-Poisson variation; that is, it has overdispersion. The Poisson regression model is

$$y_i \sim \text{Poisson}(\mu_i)$$

where

$$\mu_i = \exp(\mathbf{x}_i\boldsymbol{\beta} + \text{offset}_i)$$

for observed counts y_i with covariates $\mathbf{x}_i$ for the ith observation. One derivation of the negative binomial is that individual units follow a Poisson regression model, but there is an omitted variable u_i such that e^{u_i} follows a gamma distribution with mean 1 and variance α:

$$y_i \sim \text{Poisson}(\mu_i^*)$$

where

$$\mu_i^* = \exp(\mathbf{x}_i\boldsymbol{\beta} + \text{offset}_i + u_i)$$

and

$$e^{u_i} \sim \text{gamma}(1/\alpha, 1/\alpha)$$

(Note that the scale (i.e., the second) parameter for the gamma(a, λ) distribution is sometimes parameterized as $1/\lambda$; see the *Methods and Formulas* section for the explicit definition of the distribution.)

We refer to α as the overdispersion parameter. The larger α is, the greater the overdispersion. The Poisson model corresponds to $\alpha = 0$. nbreg parameterizes α as $\ln\alpha$. gnbreg allows $\ln\alpha$ to be modeled as $\ln\alpha_i = \mathbf{z}_i\boldsymbol{\gamma}$, a linear combination of covariates $\mathbf{z}_i$.

nbreg

It is not uncommon to posit a Poisson regression model and observe a lack of model fit. The following data appeared in Rodríguez (1993):

```
. list

        cohort   age_mos    deaths    exposure
  1.         1       0.5       168       278.4
  2.         1       2.0        48       538.8
  3.         1       4.5        63       794.4
  4.         1       9.0        89     1,550.8
  5.         1      18.0       102     3,006.0
  6.         1      42.0        81     8,743.5
  7.         1      90.0        40    14,270.0
  8.         2       0.5       197       403.2
  9.         2       2.0        48       786.0
 10.         2       4.5        62     1,165.3
 11.         2       9.0        81     2,294.8
 12.         2      18.0        97     4,500.5
 13.         2      42.0       103    13,201.5
 14.         2      90.0        39    19,525.0
 15.         3       0.5       195       495.3
 16.         3       2.0        55       956.7
 17.         3       4.5        58     1,381.4
 18.         3       9.0        85     2,604.5
 19.         3      18.0        87     4,618.5
 20.         3      42.0        70     9,814.5
 21.         3      90.0        10     5,802.5

. gen logexp = ln(exposure)

. quietly tab cohort, gen(coh)

. poisson deaths coh2 coh3, offset(logexp)

Iteration 0:    log likelihood = -2544.9221
Iteration 1:    log likelihood = -2160.0921
Iteration 2:    log likelihood = -2159.5162
Iteration 3:    log likelihood = -2159.5159
Iteration 4:    log likelihood = -2159.5159

Poisson regression                              Number of obs   =         21
                                                LR chi2(2)      =      49.16
Log likelihood = -2159.5159                     Prob > chi2     =     0.0000

------------------------------------------------------------------------------
      deaths |      Coef.   Std. Err.      z    P>|z|     [95% Conf. Interval]
-------------+----------------------------------------------------------------
        coh2 |  -.3020405   .0573319    -5.268   0.000    -.4144089   -.1896721
        coh3 |   .0742143   .0589726     1.258   0.208    -.0413698    .1897983
       _cons |  -3.899488   .0411345   -94.798   0.000     -3.98011   -3.818866
      logexp |  (offset)
------------------------------------------------------------------------------

. poisgof

        Goodness of fit chi-2 =   4190.689
        Prob > chi2(18)       =     0.0000
```

The extreme significance of the goodness-of-fit χ^2 indicates the Poisson regression model is inappropriate — suggesting to us that we should try a negative binomial model:

```
. nbreg deaths coh2 coh3, offset(logexp) nolog
Negative binomial regression                      Number of obs  =        21
                                                  LR chi2(2)     =      0.40
Log likelihood =  -131.3799                       Prob > chi2    =    0.8171

------------------------------------------------------------------------------
  deaths |     Coef.   Std. Err.       z    P>|z|    [95% Conf. Interval]
---------+--------------------------------------------------------------------
    coh2 | -.2676187   .7237203    -0.370   0.712   -1.686084    1.150847
    coh3 | -.4573957   .7236651    -0.632   0.527   -1.875753    .9609618
   _cons | -2.086731    .511856    -4.077   0.000    -3.08995   -1.083511
  logexp |  (offset)
---------+--------------------------------------------------------------------
 /lnalpha|  .5939963   .2583615     2.299   0.021    .0876171    1.100376
---------+--------------------------------------------------------------------
   alpha |  1.811212   .4679475                       1.09157    3.005295
------------------------------------------------------------------------------
Likelihood ratio test of alpha=0:   chi2(1) =   4056.27   Prob > chi2 = 0.0000
```

Our original Poisson model is a special case of the negative binomial—it corresponds to $\alpha = 0$. nbreg, however, estimates α indirectly, estimating instead $\ln \alpha$. In our model, $\ln \alpha = 0.594$, meaning that $\alpha = 1.81$ (nbreg undoes the transformation for us at the bottom of the output).

The Z statistic printed in the table for $\ln \alpha$ is a test of $\ln \alpha = 0$, which is equivalent to $\alpha = 1$. This test, however, is not very meaningful.

In order to test $\alpha = 0$ (equivalent to $\ln \alpha = -\infty$), nbreg performs a likelihood-ratio test. The staggering χ^2 value of 4,056 asserts that the probability that we would observe this data conditional on $\alpha = 0$, i.e., conditional on the process being Poisson, is virtually zero. The data is not Poisson. It is not accidental that this χ^2 value is quite close to the goodness-of-fit statistic from the Poisson regression itself.

❑ Technical Note

The negative binomial model deals with cases where there is more variation than would be expected were the process Poisson. The negative binomial model is not helpful if there is less than Poisson variation—if the variance of the count variable is less than its mean. But underdispersion is uncommon. Poisson models arise because of independently generated events. Overdispersion comes about if some of the parameters (causes) of the Poisson processes are unknown. To obtain underdispersion, the sequence of events would have to somehow be regulated; that is, events would not be independent, but controlled based on past occurrences.

❑

gnbreg

gnbreg is a generalization of nbreg. Whereas in nbreg a single $\ln \alpha$ is estimated, gnbreg allows $\ln \alpha$ to vary observation by observation as a linear combination of another set of covariates: $\ln \alpha_i = \mathbf{z}_i \gamma$.

We will assume the number of deaths is a function of age whereas the $\ln \alpha$ parameter is a function of cohort. To estimate the model, we type

```
. gnbreg deaths age_mos, lnalpha(coh2 coh3) offset(logexp)
Fitting comparison model:

Iteration 0:   log likelihood = -794.3501
Iteration 1:   log likelihood = -674.76807
Iteration 2:   log likelihood = -671.99707
Iteration 3:   log likelihood = -671.99463
Iteration 4:   log likelihood = -671.99512
Iteration 5:   log likelihood = -671.99463

Fitting constant-only model:

Iteration 0:   log likelihood =   -187.067
Iteration 1:   log likelihood = -134.87712
Iteration 2:   log likelihood = -131.59045
Iteration 3:   log likelihood = -131.57949
Iteration 4:   log likelihood = -131.57948

Fitting full model:

Iteration 0:   log likelihood = -123.73088
Iteration 1:   log likelihood =  -117.6703
Iteration 2:   log likelihood = -117.56306
Iteration 3:   log likelihood = -117.56164
Iteration 4:   log likelihood = -117.56164
```

Generalized negative binomial regression		Number of obs	=	21
		LR chi2(1)	=	28.04
Log likelihood = -117.56164		Prob > chi2	=	0.0000

deaths	Coef.	Std. Err.	z	P>|z|	[95% Conf. Interval]	
deaths						
age_mos	-.0516657	.0051747	-9.984	0.000	-.061808	-.0415233
_cons	-1.867225	.2227944	-8.381	0.000	-2.303894	-1.430556
logexp	(offset)					
lnalpha						
coh2	.0939546	.7187747	0.131	0.896	-1.314818	1.502727
coh3	.0815279	.7365476	0.111	0.912	-1.362079	1.525135
_cons	-.4759581	.5156502	-0.923	0.356	-1.486614	.5346978

```
Likelihood ratio test of alpha=0:   chi2(3) =  1108.87     Pr > chi2 = 0.0000
```

We find that age is a significant determinant of the number of deaths. The standard errors for the variables in the $\ln \alpha$ equation suggest that the overdispersion parameter does not vary across cohorts. We can test this by typing

```
. test coh2 coh3

 ( 1)  [lnalpha]coh2 = 0.0
 ( 2)  [lnalpha]coh3 = 0.0

        chi2(  2) =     0.02
      Prob > chi2 =     0.9904
```

There is no evidence of variation by cohort in this data.

Predicted values

After **nbreg** and **gnbreg**, **predict** returns the predicted number of events:

```
. nbreg deaths coh2 coh3, nolog
Negative binomial regression                   Number of obs   =         21
                                               LR chi2(2)      =       0.14
Log likelihood = -108.48841                    Prob > chi2     =     0.9307

------------------------------------------------------------------------------
      deaths |      Coef.   Std. Err.      z    P>|z|     [95% Conf. Interval]
-------------+----------------------------------------------------------------
        coh2 |   .0591305   .2978419     0.199   0.843    -.5246289     .64289
        coh3 |  -.0538792   .2981621    -0.181   0.857    -.6382662   .5305077
       _cons |   4.435906   .2107213    21.051   0.000      4.0229   4.848912
-------------+----------------------------------------------------------------
     /lnalpha |  -1.207379   .3108622    -3.884   0.000    -1.816657  -.5980999
-------------+----------------------------------------------------------------
       alpha |     .29898   .0929416                       .1625683   .5498555
------------------------------------------------------------------------------
Likelihood ratio test of alpha=0:   chi2(1) =    434.62   Prob > chi2 = 0.0000

. predict count
(option n assumed; predicted number of events)

. summarize deaths count

    Variable |     Obs        Mean   Std. Dev.       Min        Max
-------------+--------------------------------------------------------
      deaths |      21    84.66667    48.84192        10        197
       count |      21    84.66667     4.00773        80   89.57143
```

Saved Results

nbreg and **gnbreg** save in **e()**:

Scalars

e(N)	number of observations	e(ll_c)	log likelihood, comparison model
e(k)	number of variables	e(rc)	return code
e(k_eq)	number of equations	e(chi2)	χ^2
e(k_dv)	number of dependent variables	e(chi2_c)	χ^2 for comparison test
e(df_m)	model degrees of freedom	e(p)	significance
e(ll)	log likelihood	e(ic)	number of iterations
e(ll_0)	log likelihood, constant-only model	e(N_clust)	number of clusters

Macros

e(cmd)	nbreg or gnbreg	e(chi2type)	Wald or LR; type of model χ^2 test
e(depvar)	name of dependent variable	e(chi2_ct)	Wald or LR; type of model χ^2 test
e(title)	title in estimation output		corresponding to e(chi2_c)
e(wtype)	weight type	e(user)	name of likelihood-evaluator program
e(wexp)	weight expression	e(opt)	type of optimization
e(clustvar)	name of cluster variable	e(offset#)	offset for equation #
e(vcetype)	covariance estimation method	e(predict)	program used to implement predict

Matrices

e(b)	coefficient vector	e(V)	variance–covariance matrix of the estimators

Functions

e(sample)	marks estimation sample

Methods and Formulas

nbreg and gnbreg are implemented as ado-files.

See [R] **poisson** and Feller (1968, 156–164) for an introduction to the Poisson distribution.

A negative binomial distribution can be regarded as a gamma mixture of Poisson random variables. The number of times something occurs, y_i, is distributed as $\text{Poisson}(\nu_i \mu_i)$. That is, its conditional likelihood is

$$f(y_i \mid \nu_i) = \frac{(\nu_i \mu_i)^{y_i} e^{-\nu_i \mu_i}}{\Gamma(y_i + 1)}$$

where $\mu_i = \exp(\mathbf{x}_i \boldsymbol{\beta} + \text{offset}_i)$ and ν_i is an unobserved parameter with a $\text{gamma}(1/\alpha, 1/\alpha)$ density:

$$g(\nu) = \frac{\nu^{(1-\alpha)/\alpha} e^{-\nu/\alpha}}{\alpha^{1/\alpha} \Gamma(1/\alpha)}$$

This gamma distribution has mean 1 and variance α, where α is our ancillary parameter. (Note that the scale (i.e., the second) parameter for the $\text{gamma}(a, \lambda)$ distribution is sometimes parameterized as $1/\lambda$; the above density defines how it has been parameterized here.)

The unconditional likelihood for the ith observation is therefore

$$f(y_i) = \int_0^\infty f(y_i \mid \nu) g(\nu) \, d\nu$$

$$= \frac{\Gamma(m + y_i)}{\Gamma(y_i + 1)\Gamma(m)} p_i^m (1 - p_i)^{y_i}$$

where $p_i = 1/(1 + \alpha \mu_i)$ and $m = 1/\alpha$. Solutions for α are handled by searching for $\ln \alpha$ since α is required to be greater than zero.

The scores and log-likelihood (with weights and offsets) are given by

$$\psi(z) = \text{digamma function evaluated at } z$$
$$\psi'(z) = \text{trigamma function evaluated at } z$$
$$\alpha = \exp(\tau) \qquad m = 1/\alpha \qquad p_i = 1/(1 + \alpha \mu_i) \qquad \mu_i = \exp(x_i \beta + \text{offset}_i)$$
$$\mathcal{L} = \sum_{i=1}^{n} \Big[w_i \ln(\Gamma(m + y_i)) - w_i \ln(\Gamma(y_i + 1)) -$$
$$w_i \ln(\Gamma(m)) + w_i m \ln(p_i) + w_i y_i \ln(1 - p_i) \Big]$$
$$\text{score}(\beta)_i = p_i(y_i - \mu_i)$$
$$\text{score}(\tau)_i = -m \left[\frac{\alpha(\mu_i - y_i)}{1 + \alpha \mu_i} - \ln(1 + \alpha \mu_i) + \psi(y_i + m) - \psi(m) \right]$$

In the case of **gnbreg**, α is allowed to vary across the observations according to the parameterization $\ln \alpha_i = \mathbf{z}_i \boldsymbol{\gamma}$.

Maximization for **gnbreg** is via the lf linear-form method and for **nbreg** is via the d2 method described in [R] **ml**.

References

Feller, W. 1968. *An Introduction to Probability Theory and Its Applications*, vol. 1. 3d ed. New York: John Wiley & Sons.

Hilbe, J. 1998. sg91: Robust variance estimators for MLE Poisson and negative binomial regression. *Stata Technical Bulletin* 45: 26–28.

Long, J. S. 1997. *Regression Models for Categorical and Limited Dependent Variables*. Thousand Oaks, CA: Sage Publications.

Rodríguez, G. 1993. sbe10: An improvement to poisson. *Stata Technical Bulletin* 11: 11–14. Reprinted in *Stata Technical Bulletin Reprints*, vol. 2, pp. 94–98.

Rogers, W. H. 1991. sbe1: Poisson regression with rates. *Stata Technical Bulletin* 1: 11–12. Reprinted in *Stata Technical Bulletin Reprints*, vol. 1, pp. 62–64.

——. 1993. sg16.4: Comparison of nbreg and glm for negative binomial. *Stata Technical Bulletin* 16: 7. Reprinted in *Stata Technical Bulletin Reprints*, vol. 3, pp. 82–84.

Also See

Complementary:	[R] **lincom**, [R] **linktest**, [R] **lrtest**, [R] **predict**, [R] **test**, [R] **testnl**, [R] **vce**, [R] **xi**
Related:	[R] **glm**, [R] **poisson**, [R] **xtnbreg**, [R] **zip**
Background:	[U] **16.5 Accessing coefficients and standard errors**, [U] **23 Estimation and post-estimation commands**, [U] **23.11 Obtaining robust variance estimates**, [U] **23.12 Obtaining scores**, [R] **maximize**

Title

net — Install and manage user-written additions from the net

Syntax

```
net from        directory_or_url

net cd          path_or_url

net link        linkname

net

net describe    pkgname

net set ado     dirname
net set other   dirname
net query

net install     pkgname      [, all replace]

net get         pkgname      [, all replace]

ado                          [, find(string) from(dirname)]

ado dir         [pkgid]      [, find(string) from(dirname)]

ado describe    [pkgid]      [, find(string) from(dirname)]

ado uninstall   pkgid        [, from(dirname)]
```

where

    pkgname is   name of package

    pkgid is   name of a package
       or   a number in square brackets: [#]

    dirname is   a directory name
       or   STBPLUS   (default)
       or   PERSONAL
       or   SITE

Description

net fetches and installs additions to Stata. The additions can be obtained from the Internet or from diskette. The additions can be ado-files (new commands), help files, or even datasets. Collections of files are bound together into *packages*. For instance, the package named zz49 might add the xyz command to Stata. At a minimum such a package would contain xyz.ado and xyz.hlp, the code to implement the new command and the on-line help to describe it. That the package contains two files is a detail: you use net to fetch the package zz49—however many files there are.

ado manages the packages you have installed using net. The ado command allows you to list packages you have previously installed and to uninstall them.

Stata for Windows and Stata for Macintosh users can also access the features of net and ado by pulling down **Help** and selecting **STB and User-written Programs**.

Options

all is for use with net install and net get. Typed with either one, it makes the command equivalent to typing net install followed by net get.

replace is for use with net install and net get. It specifies that the fetched files are to replace already existing files if any of the files already exist.

find(*string*) is for use with ado, ado dir, and ado describe. It specifies that the descriptions of the packages installed on your computer are to be searched and the package descriptions containing *string* are to be listed.

from(*dirname*) is for use with ado. It specifies where the packages are installed. The default is from(STBPLUS). STBPLUS is a codeword that Stata understands to correspond to a particular directory on your computer that was set at installation time. On Windows computers, STBPLUS probably means the directory c:\ado\stbplus, but it might mean something else. You can find out what it means by typing sysdir. What it means is irrelevant if you use the defaults.

Remarks

For an introduction to the use of net and ado, see [U] **32 Using the Internet to keep up to date**. The purpose of this documentation is

1. To briefly but accurately describe net and ado and all their features.

2. To provide documentation to those who wish to set up their own sites to distribute additions to Stata.

Remarks are presented under the headings

> Definition of a package
> The purpose of the net and ado commands
> Content pages
> Package-description pages
> Where packages are installed
> A summary of the net command
> A summary of the ado command
> Relationship of net and ado to the point-and-click interface
> Creating your own site
> Format of content and package-description files
> Example 1
> Example 2
> Metacharacters in content and package-description files
> Error-free file delivery

Definition of a package

A *package* is a collection of files—typically .ado and .hlp files—that provides a new feature in Stata. Packages contain additions that you wish were part of Stata at the outset. We write such additions and so do other users.

One source of these additions is the *Stata Technical Bulletin* (STB). The STB is a printed journal and corresponding software. If you want the journal, you must subscribe, but the software is available for free from our web site. If you do not have Internet access, you may purchase the STB disk from StataCorp.

The purpose of the net and ado commands

The purpose of the **net** command is to make distribution and installation of packages easy. The goal is to get you quickly to a package description page that summarizes the addition:

```
. net describe rte_stat
--------------------------------------------------------------------------
package rte_stat from http://www.wemakeitupaswego.edu/faculty/sgazer/
--------------------------------------------------------------------------
TITLE
        rte_stat.  The robust-to-everything statistic; update.
DESCRIPTION/AUTHOR(S)
        S. Gazer, Dept. of Applied Theoretical Mathematics, WMIUAWG Univ.
        Aleph-0 100% confidence intervals proved too conservative for some
        applications; Aleph-1 confidence intervals have been substituted.
        The new robust-to-everything supplants the previous robust-to-
        everything-conceivable statistic.  See "Inference in the absence
        of data" (forthcoming).  After installation, see help rte.
INSTALLATION FILES                                (type net install rte_stat)
        rte.ado
        rte.hlp
        nullset.ado
        random.ado
--------------------------------------------------------------------------
```

Should you decide the addition might prove useful, **net** makes it easy to install it:

```
. net install rte_stat
checking rte_stat consistency and verifying not already installed...
installing into C:\ado\stbplus\ ...
installation complete.
```

The purpose of the **ado** command is to help you manage packages installed with **net**. Perhaps you remember that you installed a package that calculates the robust-to-everything statistic but cannot remember the name of the corresponding command. You could use **ado** to look over what you have previously installed and so find the **rte** command:

```
. ado
[1] package dm55 from http://www.stata.com/stb/stb43
        STB-43 dm55.  Generating sequences and patterns of numeric data.
  (output omitted )
[15] package rte_stat from http://www.wemakeitupaswego.edu/faculty/sgazer
        rte_stat.  The robust-to-everything statistic; update.
  (output omitted )
[27] package snp13 from http://www.stata.com/stb/stb38
        STB-38 snp13.  Sequences of integers.
```

Or you might type,

```
. ado, find("robust-to-everything")
[15] package rte_stat from http://www.wemakeitupaswego.edu/faculty/sgazer
        rte_stat.  The robust-to-everything statistic; update.
```

Perhaps you decide that **rte**, despite the author's claims, is not worth the disk space it occupies. You can use **ado** to erase it:

```
. ado uninstall rte_stat
package rte_stat from http://www.wemakeitupaswego.edu/faculty/sgazer
        rte_stat.  The robust-to-everything statistic; update.

(package uninstalled)
```

`ado uninstall` is easier than erasing the files by hand because `ado uninstall` will erase every file associated with the package and, moreover, `ado` knows where on your computer `rte_stat` is installed; you would have to hunt for the files.

Content pages

There are two types of pages displayed by `net`: content pages and package-description pages. When you type `net from`, `net cd`, `net link`, or `net` without arguments, Stata goes to the directed place and displays the content page:

```
. net from http://www.stata.com
--------------------------------------------------------------------------------
http://www.stata.com/
STB and other user-written additions for use with Stata
--------------------------------------------------------------------------------

Welcome to Stata Corporation.

Below we provide additions to Stata that were published in the STB or
mentioned on Statalist.  These are NOT THE OFFICIAL UPDATES; you fetch and
install the official updates by typing -update-.

DIRECTORIES you could -net cd- to:
    stb             materials published in the Stata Technical Bulletin
    users           materials by various people including StataCorp employees
    links           other locations providing additions to Stata
--------------------------------------------------------------------------------
```

A content page tells you about other content pages and/or package-description pages. The above example lists other content pages only. Below we follow one of the links:

```
. net cd stb
--------------------------------------------------------------------------------
http://www.stata.com/stb/
The Stata Technical Bulletin
--------------------------------------------------------------------------------

PLACES you could -net link- to:
    stata           StataCorp web site
DIRECTORIES you could -net cd- to:
  (output omitted )
    stb46           STB-46, Nov     1998
    stb45           STB-45, Sept    1998
    stb44           STB-44, July    1998
    stb43           STB-43, May     1998
    stb42           STB-42, March   1998
    stb41           STB-41, January 1998
  (output omitted )
--------------------------------------------------------------------------------

. net cd stb43
--------------------------------------------------------------------------------
http://www.stata.com/stb/stb43/
STB-43 May 1998
--------------------------------------------------------------------------------

DIRECTORIES you could -net cd- to:
    ..              Other STBs
PACKAGES you could -net describe-:
    dm55            Generating sequences and patterns of numeric data
    dm56            A labels editor for Windows and Macintosh
    dm57            A notes editor for Windows and Macintosh
    dm58            A package for the analysis of husband-wife data
    ip25            Parameterized Monte Carlo simulations
```

```
            sbe16_2              Corrections to the meta-analysis command
            sg33_1               Enhancements for calc. of adj. means and proportions
            sg81                 Multivariable fractional polynomials
            sg82                 Fractional polynomials for st data
            sg83                 Parameter estimation for the Gumbel distribution
            sg84                 Concordance correlation coefficient
        --------------------------------------------------------------------------------
```

dm55, dm56, . . . , sg84 are links to package-description pages.

1. When you type **net from**, you follow that with a location and the content page at the location is displayed.

    a. The location could be a URL such as *http://www.stata.com*. The content page at that location would then be listed.

    b. The location could be **a:** on a Windows computer or **:diskette:** on a Macintosh computer. The content page on that source would be listed. That would work if you had a special diskette obtained from StataCorp (an STB diskette) or a special diskette prepared by another user.

    c. The location could even be a directory on your computer, but that would work only if that directory had the right kind of files in it.

2. Once you have specified a location, typing **net cd** will take you into subdirectories of that location, if there are any. Typing

    ```
    . net from http://www.stata.com
    . net cd stb
    ```

    has the same effect as typing

    ```
    . net from http://www.stata.com/stb
    ```

    The result of typing **net cd** is to display the content page from that location.

3. Typing **net** without arguments redisplays the current content page. The current content page is the content page last displayed.

4. **net link** is similar in effect to **net cd** in that the result is to change the location, but rather than changing to subdirectories of the current location, **net link** jumps to another location:

    ```
    . net from http://www.bimmer.org
    --------------------------------------------------------------------------------
    http://www.bimmer.org/
    bimmer.org
    --------------------------------------------------------------------------------

    Welcome to www.bimmer.org.
    No, we don´t use statistical software, but we rather like one of the
    employees at StataCorp so we agreed to put four files on our web site
    so you could see how a user site might look and see that having Stata
    materials does not interfere with the other HTML files.

    By the way, if you are a BMW enthusiast, visit our homepage sometime.
    It is http://www.bimmer.org.

    PLACES you could -net link- to:
        stata            StataCorp´s main page

    PACKAGES you could -net describe-:
        bimmer           A sample package
    --------------------------------------------------------------------------------
    ```

Typing `net link stata` would jump to *http://www.stata.com*:

```
. net link stata
--------------------------------------------------------------------------------
http://www.stata.com/
STB and other user-written additions for use with Stata
--------------------------------------------------------------------------------
Welcome to Stata Corporation.
  (output omitted )
--------------------------------------------------------------------------------
```

Package-description pages

Package-description pages describe what you might install:

```
. net from http://www.stata.com/stb/stb43
  (output omitted )
. net describe sg84
--------------------------------------------------------------------------------
package sg84 from http://www.stata.com/stb/stb43
--------------------------------------------------------------------------------
TITLE
      STB-43 sg84.  Concordance correlation coefficient.

DESCRIPTION/AUTHOR(S)
      STB insert by
      Thomas J. Steichen, RJRT,
      Nicholas J. Cox, University of Durham, UK.
      After installation, see help concord.

INSTALLATION FILES                              (type net install sg84)
      sg84/concord.ado
      sg84/concord.hlp
ANCILLARY FILES                                 (type net get sg84)
      sg84/atkinson.dta
      sg84/blalt.dta
--------------------------------------------------------------------------------
```

A package-description page describes the package and tells you how to install the component files. Package-description pages potentially describe two types of files:

1. Installation files: Files you type `net install` to install and which are required to make the addition work.

2. Ancillary files: Additional files you might want to install—you type `net get` to install them— but which you can ignore. Ancillary files are typically datasets that are useful for demonstration purposes. Ancillary files are not really installed in the sense of being copied to an official place for use by Stata itself. They are merely copied into the current directory so that you may use them if you wish.

You install the official files by typing `net install` followed by the package name:

```
. net install sg84
checking sg84 consistency and verifying not already installed...
installing into C:\ado\stbplus\ ...
installation complete.
```

You get the ancillary files—if there are any and if you want them—by typing `net get` followed by the package name:

```
. net get sg84
checking sg84 consistency and verifying not already installed...

copying into current directory...
        copying  atkinson.dta
        copying  blalt.dta
ancillary files successfully copied.
```

Most users ignore the ancillary files.

Once you have installed a package—typed `net install`—`ado` can redisplay the package-description page whenever you wish:

```
. ado describe sg84
-------------------------------------------------------------------------------
[28] package sg84 from http://www.stata.com/stb/stb43
-------------------------------------------------------------------------------
TITLE
        STB-43 sg84.  Concordance correlation coefficient.
DESCRIPTION/AUTHOR(S)
        STB insert by
        Thomas J. Steichen, RJRT,
        Nicholas J. Cox, University of Durham, UK.
        After installation, see help concord.
INSTALLATION FILES
        c\concord.ado
        c\concord.hlp
INSTALLED ON
        5 Oct 1999
-------------------------------------------------------------------------------
```

Note that the package-description page shown by `ado` says from where we got the package and the date on which we installed it. Also note that it does not mention the ancillary files that were originally part of this package. Ancillary files are not tracked by `ado`.

Where packages are installed

Packages should be installed in STBPLUS or SITE. STBPLUS and SITE are codewords that Stata understands and that correspond to some real directory on your computer. Typing `sysdir` will tell you where these places are, if you care.

```
. sysdir
   STATA:  C:\STATA\
 UPDATES:  C:\STATA\ado\updates\
    BASE:  C:\STATA\ado\base\
    SITE:  C:\STATA\ado\site\
 STBPLUS:  C:\ado\stbplus\
PERSONAL:  C:\ado\personal\
OLDPLACE:  C:\ado\
```

If you type `sysdir`, you may obtain different results.

By default, `net` installs in the STBPLUS directory and `ado` tells you about what is installed there. If you are on a multiple-user system, you may wish to install some packages in the SITE directory. This way, they will be available to all users of Stata and not just you. To do that, before using `net install`, type

```
. net set ado SITE
```

and when reviewing what is installed or removing packages, redirect `ado` to that directory:

```
. ado ..., from(SITE)
```

In both cases, you literally type "SITE" because Stata will understand that `SITE` means the site ado-directory as defined by `sysdir`. In order to install into `SITE`, you must have write access to that directory.

If you reset where `net` installs and then, in the same session, wish to install into your private ado-directory, type

```
. net set ado STBPLUS
```

That is how things were originally. If you are confused as to where you are, type `net query`.

A summary of the net command

The purpose of the `net` command is to display content pages and package-description pages. Such pages are provided over the Internet and most users get them there. We recommend you start at *http://www.stata.com* and work out from there.

You do not need Internet access to use `net`. The additions published in the STB are also available on diskette which can be obtained from StataCorp; see [R] **stb**. There is a charge for the diskette.

`net from` is how you jump to a location. The location's content page is displayed.

`net cd` and `net link` change from there to other locations. `net cd` enters subdirectories of the original location. `net link` jumps from one place to another, where the location is being determined by what the content-provider coded on their content page.

`net describe` lists a package-description page. Packages are named, and you type `net describe` *pkgname*.

`net install` installs a package into your copy of Stata. `net get` copies any additional files (ancillary files) to your current directory.

A summary of the ado command

The purpose of the `ado` command is to list the package descriptions of packages you have previously installed.

Typing `ado` without arguments is the same as typing `ado dir`. They list the names and titles of the packages you have installed.

`ado describe` lists full package-description pages.

`ado uninstall` removes packages from your computer.

Since you can install packages from a variety of sources, there is no guarantee that the package names are unique. Thus, the packages installed on your computer are numbered sequentially and you may refer to them by name or by number. For instance, say you wanted to get rid of the robust-to-everything statistic command you previously installed:

```
. ado, find("robust-to-everything")
[15] package rte_stat from http://www.wemakeitupaswego.edu/faculty/sgazer
        rte_stat.  The robust-to-everything statistic; update.
```

You could type

```
. ado uninstall rte_stat
```

or you could type

```
. ado uninstall [15]
```

Typing "`ado uninstall rte_stat`" would work only if the name `rte_stat` were unique; otherwise `ado` would refuse and you would have to type the number.

The `find()` option is allowed with `ado dir` and `ado describe`. It searches the package description for the word or phrase you specify, ignoring case (`alpha` matches `Alpha`). The complete package description is searched, including the author's name and the name of the files. Thus, if `rte` was the name of a command you wanted to eliminate but you could not remember the name of the package, you could type

```
. ado, find(rte)
[15] package rte_stat from http://www.wemakeitupaswego.edu/faculty/sgazer
        rte_stat.  The robust-to-everything statistic; update.
```

Relationship of net and ado to the point-and-click interface

Stata for Windows users and Macintosh users may instead pull down **Help** and select **STB and User-written Programs**. There are advantages and disadvantages:

1. Flipping through content and package-description pages is easier; it is much like a browser. See Chapter 19 in the *Getting Started* manual.

2. When browsing at a product-description page note that the `.hlp` files are highlighted. You may click on `.hlp` files to review them before installing the package.

3. You may not redirect from where `ado` searches for files.

Creating your own site

The rest of this entry concerns how to create your own site to distribute additions to Stata. The idea is that you have written additions for use with Stata—say `xyz.ado` and `xyz.hlp`—and you wish to put them out so that coworkers or researchers at other institutions can easily install them. Or perhaps you just have a dataset that you and others want to share.

In any case, all you need is a homepage. You place the files you want to distribute on your homepage (or in a subdirectory), and you add two more files—a content file and a package description file—and you are done.

Format of content and package-description files

The content file describes the content page. It must be named `stata.toc`:

```
――――――――――――――――――――――――――――――――――――――― top of stata.toc ――――――――
OFF                                      (to make site unavailable temporarily)
* lines starting with * are comments; they are ignored

* blank lines are ignored, too

* d lines display description text
* the first d line is the title and the remaining ones are text.
* blank d lines display a blank line
```

```
d  title
d  text
d  text
d
...
*  l  lines display links
l  word-to-show  path-or-url  [ description]
l  word-to-show  path-or-url  [ description]
...
*  t  lines display other directories within the site
t  path  [description]
t  path  [description]
...
*  p  lines display packages
p  pkgname  [description]
p  pkgname  [description]
...
```
—— end of stata.toc ————————

Package files describe packages and are named *pkgname*.`pkg`:

———————————————————————————————————— top of *pkgname*.pkg ————————

```
*  lines starting with  *  are comments; they are ignored

*  blank lines are ignored, too

*  d  lines display package description text
*  the first  d  line is the title and the remaining ones are text.
*  blank  d  lines display a blank line
d  title
d  text
d  text
d
...
*  f  identifies the component files
f  [path/]filename  [description]
f  [path/]filename  [description]

*  e  line is optional; it means stop reading
e
```
———————————————————————————————————— end of *pkgname*.pkg ————————

Example 1

Say we want the user to see the following:

```
. net from http://www.university.edu/~me
---------------------------------------------------------------------------
http://www.university.edu/~me
Chris Farrar, Uni University
---------------------------------------------------------------------------

PACKAGES you could -net describe-:
    xyz                interval-truncated survival
```

```
. net describe xyz
-------------------------------------------------------------------------------
package xyz from http://www.university.edu/~me
-------------------------------------------------------------------------------
TITLE
      xyz.  interval-truncated survival.
DESCRIPTION/AUTHOR(S)
      C. Farrar, Uni University.
INSTALLATION FILES                                 (type net install xyz)
      xyz.ado
      xyz.hlp
ANCILLARY FILES                                    (type net get xyz)
      sample.dta
-------------------------------------------------------------------------------
```

The files to do this would be

```
-------------------------------------------------- top of stata.toc ----------
d Chris Farrar, Uni University
p xyz interval-truncated survival
-------------------------------------------------- end of stata.toc ----------
```

```
-------------------------------------------------- top of xyz.pkg ----------
d xyz.  interval-truncated survival.
d C. Farrar, Uni University.
p xyz.ado
p xyz.hlp
p sample.dta
-------------------------------------------------- end of xyz.pkg ----------
```

On his homepage, Chris would place the files

```
            stata.toc    (shown above)
            xyz.pkg      (shown above)
            xyz.ado      file to be delivered (for use by net install)
            xyz.hlp      file to be delivered (for use by net install)
            sample.dta   file to be delivered (for use by net get)
```

Note that Chris does nothing to distinguish ancillary files from installation files.

Example 2

S. Gazer wants to create a more complex site:

```
. net from http://www.wemakeitupaswego.edu/faculty/sgazer
-------------------------------------------------------------------------------
http://www.wemakeitupaswego.edu/faculty/sgazer
Data-free inference materials
-------------------------------------------------------------------------------
S. Gazer, Department of Applied Theoretical Mathematics
Also see my homepage for the preprint of "Irrefutable inference".
PLACES you could -net link- to:
    stata           StataCorp web site
DIRECTORIES you could -net cd- to:
    ir              irrefutable inference programs (work in progress)
PACKAGES you could -net describe-:
    rtec            Robust-to-everything-conceivable statistic
    rte             Robust-to-everything statistic
```

```
. net describe rte
-------------------------------------------------------------------------------
package rte from http://www.wemakeitupaswego.edu/faculty/sgazer/
-------------------------------------------------------------------------------

TITLE
      rte.  The robust-to-everything statistic; update.

DESCRIPTION/AUTHOR(S)
      S. Gazer, Dept. of Applied Theoretical Mathematics, WMIUAWG Univ.
      Aleph-0 100% confidence intervals proved too conservative for some
      applications; Aleph-1 confidence intervals have been substituted.
      The new robust-to-everything supplants the previous robust-to-
      everything-conceivable statistic.  See "Inference in the absence
      of data" (forthcoming).  After installation, see help rte.

      Support:  email sgazer@wemakeitupaswego.edu

INSTALLATION FILES                             (type net install rte)
      rte.ado
      rte.hlp
      nullset.ado
      random.ado

ANCILLARY FILES                                (type net get rte)
      empty.dta
-------------------------------------------------------------------------------
```

The files to do this would be

```
                                                 ———— top of stata.toc ————
  d Data-free inference materials
  d S. Gazer, Department of Applied Theoretical Mathematics
  d
  d Also see my homepage for the preprint of "Irrefutable inference".
  l stata http://www.stata.com
  d ir irrefutable inference programs (work in progress)
  p rtec Robust-to-everything-conceivable statistic
  p rte  Robust-to-everything statistic
                                                 ———— end of stata.toc ————
```

```
                                                 ———— top of rte.pkg ————
  d rte.  The robust-to-everything statistic; update.
  d S. Gazer, Dept. of Applied Theoretical Mathematics, WMIUAWG Univ.
  d Aleph-0 100% confidence intervals proved too conservative for some
  d applications; Aleph-1 confidence intervals have been substituted.
  d The new robust-to-everything supplants the previous robust-to-
  d everything-conceivable statistic.  See "Inference in the absence
  d of data" (forthcoming).  After installation, see help rte.
  d
  d Support:  email sgazer@@wemakeitupaswego.edu
  f rte.ado
  f rte.hlp
  f nullset.ado
  f random.ado
  f empty.dta
                                                 ———— end of rte.pkg ————
```

On his homepage, Mr Gazer would place the files:

stata.toc	(shown above)
rte.pkg	(shown above)
rte.ado	(file to be delivered)
rte.hlp	(file to be delivered)
nullset.ado	(file to be delivered)
random.ado	(file to be delivered)
empty.dta	(file to be delivered)
rtec.pkg	the other package referred to in stata.toc
rtec.ado	the corresponding files to be delivered
rtec.hlp	
ir/stata.toc	the contents file for when the user types net cd ir
ir/...	whatever other .pkg files are referred to
ir/...	whatever other files are to be delivered

For complex sites, a different structure may prove more convenient:

stata.toc	(shown above)
rte.pkg	(shown above)
rtec.pkg	the other package referred to in stata.toc
rte/	directory containing rte files to be delivered:
rte/rte.ado	(file to be delivered)
rte/rte.hlp	(file to be delivered)
rte/nullset.ado	(file to be delivered)
rte/random.ado	(file to be delivered)
rte/empty.dta	(file to be delivered)
rtec/	directory containing rtec files to be delivered:
rtec/...	(files to be delivered)
ir/stata.toc	the contents file for when the user types net cd ir
ir/*.pkg	whatever other package files are referred to
ir/*/...	whatever other files are to be delivered

If you prefer this structure, it is simply a matter of changing the bottom of the **rte.pkg** from reading

```
f rte.ado
f rte.hlp
f nullset.ado
f random.ado
f empty.dta
```

to reading

```
f rte/rte.ado
f rte/rte.hlp
f rte/nullset.ado
f rte/random.ado
f rte/empty.dta
```

Note that in writing paths and files, the directory separator forward slash (/) is used regardless of operating system. That is because forward slash is what the Internet uses.

Also note that it does not matter whether the files you put out are in DOS/Windows, Macintosh, or Unix format (how lines end is recorded differently). When Stata reads the files over the Internet, it will figure out the file format on its own and it will automatically translate the files to what is appropriate for the receiver.

Metacharacters in content and package-description files

The text listed on the second and subsequent d lines in both `stata.toc` and *pkgname*.pkg may contain the standard Stata help metacharacters:

`^this^`	displays **this** in boldface
`^^`	displays a single caret
`@this@`	displays *this* as a link to `this.hlp`
`@@`	displays a single at sign
`@this!text for link@`	displays *text for link* as a link to `this.hlp`
`@cmd:args!text for link@`	displays *text for link* as link to *cmd:args*

Thus, in `rte.pkg`, note that S. Gazer coded his email address as

    d Support: email sgazer@@wemakeitupaswego.edu

The doubled at sign is of great importance if the user is to see sgazer@wemakeitupaswego.edu.

See [U] **21.11.6 Writing on-line help** for details.

Error-free file delivery

Most people transport files over the Internet and never worry about the file being corrupted in the process. They do that because corruption rarely occurs. If, however, it is of great importance to you that the files be delivered perfectly or not at all, you can include checksum files in the directory.

For instance, say that included in your package is `big.dta` and it is of great importance that `big.dta` be sent perfectly. First, use Stata to make the checksum file for `big.dta`

    . checksum big.dta, save

That creates a small file called `big.sum`; see [R] **checksum**. Then copy both `big.dta` and `big.sum` to your homepage. Whenever Stata reads *filename.whatever* over the net, it also looks for *filename.sum*. If it finds such a file, it uses the information recorded in it to verify that what was copied was copied without error.

If you do this, be cautious. If you put `big.dta` and `big.sum` on your homepage and then later change `big.dta` without changing `big.sum`, people will think there are transmission errors when they try to download `big.dta`.

Also See

Complementary:	[R] **checksum**, [R] **stb**
Related:	[R] **update**
Background:	[U] **32 Using the Internet to keep up to date**

Title

> **newey** — Regression with Newey–West standard errors

Syntax

> **newey** *depvar* [*varlist*] [*weight*] [**if** *exp*] [**in** *range*] , **lag**(*#*)
>
> [**t**(*varname$_t$*) **force** <u>**nocon**</u>**stant** <u>**l**</u>**evel**(*#*)]

aweights are allowed; see [U] **14.1.6 weight**.

newey shares the features of all estimation commands; see [U] **23 Estimation and post-estimation commands**.

Syntax for predict

> **predict** [*type*] *newvarname* [**if** *exp*] [**in** *range*] [, { **xb** | **stdp** }]

These statistics are available both in and out of sample; type **predict ... if e(sample) ...** if wanted only for the estimation sample.

Description

newey produces Newey–West standard errors for coefficients estimated by OLS regression. The error structure is assumed to be heteroscedastic and possibly autocorrelated up to some lag.

Note that if **lag(0)** is specified, the variance estimates produced by **newey** are simply the Huber/White/sandwich robust variances estimates calculated by **regress, robust**; see [R] **regress**.

Options

lag(*#*) is not optional; it specifies the maximum lag to consider in the autocorrelation structure. If you specify **lag()** > 0, then you must also specify option **t()**, described below. If you specify **lag(0)**, the output is exactly the same as **regress, robust**.

t(*varname$_t$*) specifies the variable recording the time of each observation. You must specify **t()** if **lag()** > 0. *varname$_t$* must record values indicating the observations are equally spaced in time or **newey** will refuse to estimate the model. If observations are not equally spaced but you wish to treat them as if they were, you must specify the **force** option.

You need only specify **t()** the first time you estimate a model with a particular dataset. After that, it need not be specified again except to change the variable's identity; **newey** remembers your previous **t()** option.

force specifies that estimation is to be forced even though **t()** shows the data not to be equally spaced. **newey** requires observations be equally spaced so that calculations based on lags correspond to a constant time change. If you specify a **t()** variable indicating observations are not equally spaced, **newey** will refuse to estimate the model. If you also specify **force**, **newey** will estimate the model and assume that the lags based on the data ordered by **t()** are appropriate.

noconstant specifies that the estimated regression should not include an intercept term.

level(*#*) specifies the confidence level, in percent, for confidence intervals. The default is **level(95)** or as set by **set level**; see [U] **23.5 Specifying the width of confidence intervals**.

Options for predict

xb, the default, calculates the linear prediction.

stdp calculates the standard error of the linear prediction.

Remarks

The Huber/White/sandwich robust variance estimator (see, for example, White 1980) produces consistent standard errors for OLS regression coefficient estimates in the presence of heteroscedasticity. The Newey–West (1987) variance estimator is an extension that produces the consistent estimates when there is autocorrelation in addition to possible heteroscedasticity.

The Newey–West variance estimator handles autocorrelation up to and including a lag of m, where m is specified by stipulating a lag(m) option. Thus, it assumes that any autocorrelation at lags greater than m can be ignored.

▷ Example

newey, lag(0) is equivalent to regress, robust:

```
. regress price weight displ, robust
Regression with robust standard errors          Number of obs =        74
                                                F(  2,     71) =     14.44
                                                Prob > F       =   0.0000
                                                R-squared      =   0.2909
                                                Root MSE       =   2518.4

-------------------------------------------------------------------------
             |               Robust
     price   |     Coef.   Std. Err.      t     P>|t|    [95% Conf. Interval]
-------------+-----------------------------------------------------------
    weight   |  1.823366   .7808755     2.335   0.022    .2663446    3.380387
     displ   |  2.087054   7.436967     0.281   0.780   -12.74184    16.91595
     _cons   |   247.907   1129.602     0.219   0.827   -2004.454    2500.269
-------------------------------------------------------------------------

. newey price weight displ, lag(0)
Regression with Newey-West standard errors      Number of obs  =        74
maximum lag : 0                                 F(  2,     71) =     14.44
                                                Prob > F       =   0.0000

-------------------------------------------------------------------------
             |              Newey-West
     price   |     Coef.   Std. Err.      t     P>|t|    [95% Conf. Interval]
-------------+-----------------------------------------------------------
    weight   |  1.823366   .7808755     2.335   0.022    .2663446    3.380387
     displ   |  2.087054   7.436967     0.281   0.780   -12.74184    16.91595
     _cons   |   247.907   1129.602     0.219   0.827   -2004.454    2500.269
-------------------------------------------------------------------------
```

◁

▷ Example

We have time-series measurements on variables usr and idle and now wish to estimate an OLS model, but obtain Newey–West standard errors allowing for a lag of up to 3:

```
. newey usr idle, lag(3) t(time)
Regression with Newey-West standard errors          Number of obs  =          30
maximum lag : 3                                      F(  1,    28)  =       10.90
                                                     Prob > F       =      0.0026

-----------------------------------------------------------------------------
             |             Newey-West
       usr   |    Coef.    Std. Err.      t     P>|t|     [95% Conf. Interval]
-------------+---------------------------------------------------------------
      idle   | -.2281501   .0690927    -3.302   0.003    -.3696801    -.08662
     _cons   | 23.13483    6.327031     3.657   0.001     10.17449    36.09516
-----------------------------------------------------------------------------
```

$\triangleleft$

Saved Results

newey saves in e():

Scalars

e(N)	number of observations	e(F)	F statistic
e(df_m)	model degrees of freedom	e(lag)	maximum lag
e(df_r)	residual degrees of freedom		

Macros

e(cmd)	newey	e(vcetype)	covariance estimation method
e(depvar)	name of dependent variable	e(predict)	program used to implement predict

Matrices

e(b)	coefficient vector	e(V)	variance–covariance matrix of the estimators

Functions

e(sample)	marks estimation sample

Methods and Formulas

newey is implemented as an ado-file.

newey calculates the estimates

$$\widehat{\beta}_{\mathrm{OLS}} = (\mathbf{X}'\mathbf{X})^{-1}\mathbf{X}'\mathbf{y}$$
$$\widehat{\mathrm{Var}}(\widehat{\beta}_{\mathrm{OLS}}) = (\mathbf{X}'\mathbf{X})^{-1}\mathbf{X}'\widehat{\Omega}\mathbf{X}(\mathbf{X}'\mathbf{X})^{-1}$$

That is, the coefficient estimates are simply those of OLS linear regression.

For the case of lag(0) (no autocorrelation), the variance estimates are calculated using the White formulation:

$$\mathbf{X}'\widehat{\Omega}\mathbf{X} = \mathbf{X}'\widehat{\Omega}_0\mathbf{X} = \frac{n}{n-k}\sum_i \widehat{e}_i^2 \mathbf{x}_i'\mathbf{x}_i$$

Here $\widehat{e}_i = y_i - \mathbf{x}_i\widehat{\beta}_{\mathrm{OLS}}$, where $\mathbf{x}_i$ is the ith row of the $\mathbf{X}$ matrix, n is the number of observations, and k is the number of predictors in the model, including the constant if there is one. Note that the above formula is exactly the same as that used by **regress, robust** with the regression-like formula (the default) for the multiplier q_c; see the *Methods and Formulas* section of [R] **regress**.

If `lag()` > 0, the variance estimates are calculated using the Newey–West (1987) formulation

$$\mathbf{X}'\widehat{\Omega}\mathbf{X} = \mathbf{X}'\widehat{\Omega}_0\mathbf{X} + \frac{n}{n-k} \sum_{l=1}^{m} \left(1 - \frac{l}{m+1} \right) \sum_{i=l+1}^{n} \widehat{e}_i\widehat{e}_{i-l}(\mathbf{x}_i'\mathbf{x}_{i-l} + \mathbf{x}_{i-l}'\mathbf{x}_i)$$

where m is the maximum lag.

References

Hardin, J. W. 1997. sg72: Newey–West standard errors for probit, logit, and poisson models. *Stata Technical Bulletin* 39: 32–35. Reprinted in *Stata Technical Bulletin Reprints*, vol. 7, pp. 182–186.

Newey, W. and K. West. 1987. A simple, positive semi-definite, heteroskedasticity and autocorrelation consistent covariance matrix. *Econometrica* 55: 703–708.

White, H. 1980. A heteroskedasticity-consistent covariance matrix estimator and a direct test for heteroskedasticity. *Econometrica* 50: 1–16.

Also See

Complementary:	[R] **lincom**, [R] **linktest**, [R] **test**, [R] **testnl**, [R] **vce**
Related:	[R] **regress**, [R] **svy estimators**, [R] **xtgls**
Background:	[U] **16.5 Accessing coefficients and standard errors**, [U] **23 Estimation and post-estimation commands**

Title

news — Report Stata news

Syntax

news

Description

news displays a brief listing of recent news and information of interest to Stata users. It obtains this information directly from Stata's web site.

The news command is available for Windows 98/95/NT, Power Mac, and Unix (but not Windows 3.1 or 680x0 Mac). The news command requires your computer to be connected to the Internet. An error message will be displayed if the connection to Stata's web site is unsuccessful.

Stata for Windows 98/95/NT and Stata for Power Mac users can also execute the news command by selecting **News** from the **Help** menu.

Remarks

news provides an easy way of displaying a brief list of the latest Stata news. More detail and other items of interest are available at Stata's web site; point your browser to http://www.stata.com.

Here is an example of what news produces:

```
. news
StataCorp News --- July 23, 2002
      * Intercooled Stata for Windows 2001 will be available the first day
        Windows 2001 is sold (projected release:  Aug 1, 2002)
      * STB-68 (July 2002) is now available --- use the net command to download
      * NetCourse 151: "Introduction to Stata Programming" begins next month
      * Proceedings of the 8th London User Group Meeting now available
For information on these and additional topics point your web browser to:
        http://www.stata.com
```

In this case news indicates that there is a new STB available. Windows and Mac users can click on **STB and User-written Programs** from the **Help** menu to download STB files. Alternatively, the net command (see [R] **net**) can be used directly.

Also See

Related: [R] **net**

Background: [U] **32 Using the Internet to keep up to date**

Title

> **nl** — Nonlinear least squares

Syntax

> nl *fcn* *depvar* $\left[\textit{varlist}\right]$ $\left[\textit{weight}\right]$ $\left[\texttt{if}\ \textit{exp}\right]$ $\left[\texttt{in}\ \textit{range}\right]$ $\left[,\ \underline{\texttt{level}}(\#)\ \underline{\texttt{init}}(\dots)\ \underline{\texttt{lnlsq}}(\#)\right.$
>
> $\underline{\texttt{leave}}\ \texttt{eps}(\#)\ \underline{\texttt{nolog}}\ \underline{\texttt{trace}}\ \underline{\texttt{iterate}}(\#)\ \textit{fcn\_options}\left.\right]$
>
> nlinit # *parameter_list*

aweights and fweights are allowed; see [U] **14.1.6 weight**.

nl shares the features of all estimation commands, see [U] **23 Estimation and post-estimation commands**.

Syntax for predict

> predict $\left[\textit{type}\right]$ *newvarname* $\left[\texttt{if}\ \textit{exp}\right]$ $\left[\texttt{in}\ \textit{range}\right]$ $\left[,\ \left\{\ \underline{\texttt{yhat}}\ |\ \underline{\texttt{residuals}}\ \right\}\ \right]$

These statistics are available both in and out of sample; type predict ... if e(sample) ... if wanted only for the estimation sample.

Description

nl fits an arbitrary nonlinear function to the dependent variable *depvar* by least squares. You provide the function itself in a separate program with a name of your choosing, except that the first two letters of the name must be nl. *fcn* refers to the name of the function without the first two letters. For example, you type nl nexpgr ... to estimate with the function defined in the program nlnexpgr.

nlinit is useful when writing *nlfcn*s.

Options

level(#) specifies the confidence level, in percent, for confidence intervals. The default is level(95) or as set by set level; see [U] **23.5 Specifying the width of confidence intervals**.

init(...) specifies initial values for parameters that are to be used to override the default initial values. Examples are provided below.

lnlsq(#) fits the model defined by *nlfcn* using "log least squares", defined as least squares with shifted lognormal errors. In other words, $\ln(\textit{depvar} - \#)$ is assumed normally distributed. Sums of squares and deviance are adjusted to the same scale as *depvar*.

leave leaves behind after estimation a set of new variables with the same names as the estimated parameters containing the derivative of $E(y)$ with respect to the parameter.

eps(#) specifies the convergence criterion for successive parameter estimates and for the residual sum of squares. eps(1e-5) is the default.

nolog suppresses the iteration log.

trace expands the iteration log to provide more details, including values of the parameters at each step of the process.

iterate(*#*) specifies the maximum number of iterations before giving up and defaults to 100.

fcn_options refer to any options allowed by *nlfcn*.

Options for predict

yhat, the default, calculates the predicted value of *depvar*.

residuals calculates the residuals.

Remarks

Remarks are presented under the headings

> *nlfcns*
> *Some common nlfcns*
> *Log-normal errors*
> *Weights*
> *Errors*
> *General comments on fitting nonlinear models*
> *More on nlfcns*

nl fits an arbitrary nonlinear function to the dependent variable *depvar* by least squares. The specific function is specified by writing an *nlfcn*, described below. The values to be fitted in the function are called the parameters.

The fitting process is iterative (modified Gauss–Newton). It starts with a set of initial values for the parameters (guesses as to what the values will be and which you also supply) and finds another set of values that fit the function even better. Those are then used as a starting point and another improvement is found, and the process continues until no further improvement is possible.

nlfcns

nl uses the function defined by *nlfcn*. *nlfcn* has two purposes: to identify the parameters of the problem and set default initial values, and to evaluate the function for a given set of parameter estimates.

▷ Example

You have variables y and x in your data and wish to fit a negative-exponential growth curve with parameters B_0 and B_1:

$$y = B_0 \left(1 - e^{-B_1 x}\right)$$

First, you write a program to calculate the predicted values:

```
program define nlexpgr
        version 6.0
        if "`1'" == "?" {                /* if query call ...            */
                global S_1 "B0 B1"       /*    declare parameters        */
                global B0=1              /*    and initialize them       */
                global B1=.1
                exit
        }
        replace `1'=$B0*(1-exp(-$B1*x))  /* otherwise, calculate function */
end
```

To estimate the model, you type `nl nexpgr y`. nl's first argument specifies the name of the function, although you do not type the `nl` prefix. You type `nexpgr`, meaning the function is `nlnexpgr`. nl's second argument specifies the name of the dependent variable. Replicating the example in the SAS manual (1985, 588–590):

```
. use sasxmpl1

. nl nexpgr y
(obs = 20)
Iteration 0:   residual SS =   .1999027
Iteration 1:   residual SS =   .0026142
Iteration 2:   residual SS =   .0005769
Iteration 3:   residual SS =   .0005768

    Source |       SS       df       MS                Number of obs =        20
-----------+------------------------------             F(  2,    18) = 275732.74
     Model | 17.6717234      2  8.83586172             Prob > F      =    0.0000
  Residual |   .00057681     18  .000032045            R-squared     =    1.0000
-----------+------------------------------             Adj R-squared =    1.0000
     Total | 17.6723003     20  .883615013             Root MSE      =   .0056608
                                                       Res. dev.     =  -152.317
(nexpgr)
------------------------------------------------------------------------------
         y |      Coef.   Std. Err.       t    P>|t|     [95% Conf. Interval]
-----------+------------------------------------------------------------------
        B0 |   .9961885   .0016138    617.303   0.000     .9927981    .9995789
        B1 |   .0419539   .0003983    105.346   0.000     .0411172    .0427906
------------------------------------------------------------------------------
(SE's, P values, CI's, and correlations are asymptotic approximations)
```

Notice that the initial values of the parameters were provided in the `nlnexpgr` program. You can, however, override these initial values on the `nl` command line. To estimate the model using .5 for the initial value of B0 rather than 1, you can type `nl nexpgr y, init(B0=.5)`. To also change the initial value of B1 from .1 to .2, you type `nl nexpgr y, init(B0=.5, B1=.2)`.

◁

The outline of all *nlfcn*'s is the same:

```
program define nlfcn
        version 6.0
        if "`1'" == "?" {
                global S_1 "parameter names"
                ( initialize parameters )
                exit
        }
        replace `1' = ...
end
```

On a query call, indicated by `` `1' `` being "?", the *nlfcn* is to place the names of the parameters in the global macro S_1 and initialize the parameters. Parameters are stored as macros, so if *nlfcn* declares that the parameters are A, B, and C (via `global S_1 "A B C"`), it must then place initial values in the corresponding parameter macros A, B, and C (via `global A=0`, `global B=1`, etc.). After initializing the parameter macros, it is done.

On a calculation call, `` `1' `` does not contain "?"; it instead contains the name of a variable that is to be filled in with the predicted values. The current values of the parameters are stored in the macros previously declared on the query call (e.g., $A, $B, and $C).

▷ Example

You wish to fit the CES production functions defined by

$$\ln q = B_0 + A \ln\left(D\,l^R + (1 - D)k^R\right)$$

where the parameters to be estimated are B_0, A, D, and R. q, l, and k refer to total output and labor and capital inputs. In your data, you have the variables `lnq`, `labor`, and `capital`. The *nlfcn* is

```
program define nlces
        version 6.0
        if "`1'" == "?" {
                global S_1 "BO A D R"
                global BO = 1
                global A = -1
                global D = .5
                global R = -1
                exit
        }
        replace `1'=$BO + $A*ln($D*labor^$R + (1-$D)*capital^$R)
end
```

Again using data from the SAS manual (1985, 591–592):

```
. use sasxmpl2

. nl ces lnq
(obs = 30)
Iteration 0:   residual SS =   37.09651
Iteration 1:   residual SS =   35.48615
Iteration 2:   residual SS =   22.69042
Iteration 3:   residual SS =   1.845374
  (output omitted )
Iteration 19:  residual SS =   1.761039
```

Source	SS	df	MS		
Model	59.5286148	3	19.8428716	Number of obs =	30
Residual	1.76103929	26	.06773228	F(3, 26) =	292.96
				Prob > F =	0.0000
Total	61.2896541	29	2.11343635	R-squared =	0.9713

```
                                             F(  3,    26) =     292.96
                                             Prob > F      =     0.0000
                                             R-squared     =     0.9713
                                             Adj R-squared =     0.9680
                                             Root MSE      =    .2602543
                                             Res. dev.     =    .0775148
(ces)
```

lnq	Coef.	Std. Err.	t	P>|t|	[95% Conf. Interval]	
B0*	.1244882	.0783432	1.589	0.124	-.0365486	.2855251
A	-.336291	.2721672	-1.236	0.228	-.8957387	.2231568
D	.3366743	.1361148	2.473	0.020	.0568863	.6164623
R	-3.011047	2.323489	-1.296	0.206	-7.787048	1.764954

```
* Parameter taken as constant term in model & ANOVA table
(SE's, P values, CI's, and correlations are asymptotic approximations)
```

If the nonlinear model contains a constant term, `nl` will find it and indicate its presence by placing an asterisk next to the parameter name when displaying results. In the output above, B0 is a constant. (`nl` determines that a parameter B0 is a constant term because the partial derivative $f = \partial E(y)/\partial B0$ has a coefficient of variation (s.d./mean) less than `eps()`. Usually, $f = 1$ for a constant, as it does in this case.)

◁

nl's output closely mimics that of regress; see [R] **regress**. The model F test, R-squared, sums of squares, etc., are calculated as regress calculates them, which means in this case that they are corrected for the mean. If no "constant" is present, as was the case in the negative-exponential growth example previously, the usual caveats apply to the interpretation of the F and R-squared statistics; see comments and references in Goldstein (1992).

When making its calculations, nl creates the partial derivative variables for all the parameters, giving each the same name as the corresponding parameter. Unless you specify leave, these are discarded when nl completes the estimation. Therefore, your data must not have data variables that have the same names as parameters. We recommend using uppercased names for parameters and lowercased names (as is common) for variables.

After estimating with nl, typing nl by itself will redisplay previous estimates. Typing correlate, _coef will show the asymptotic correlation matrix of the parameters, and typing predict myvar will create new variable myvar containing the predicted values. Typing predict res, resid will create res containing the residuals.

nlfcn's have a number of additional features that are described in *More on nlfcns* below.

Some common nlfcns

An important feature of nl, in addition to estimating arbitrary nonlinear regressions, is the facility for adding prewritten common *fcns*.

Three *fcns* are provided for exponential regression with one asymptote:

exp3	$Y = b_0 + b_1 b_2^X$
exp2	$Y = b_1 b_2^X$
exp2a	$Y = b_1\left(1 - b_2^X\right)$

For instance, typing nl exp3 ras dvl estimates the three-parameter exponential model (parameters b_0, b_1, and b_2) using $Y = $ ras and $X = $ dvl.

Two *fcns* are provided for the logistic function (symmetric sigmoid shape; not to be confused with logistic regression):

log4	$Y = b_0 + b_1 / \left(1 + \exp\left(-b_2(X - b_3)\right)\right)$
log3	$Y = b_1 / \left(1 + \exp\left(-b_2(X - b_3)\right)\right)$

Finally, two *fcns* are provided for the Gompertz function (asymmetric sigmoid shape):

gom4	$Y = b_0 + b_1 \exp\left(-\exp\left(-b_2(X - b_3)\right)\right)$
gom3	$Y = b_1 \exp\left(-\exp\left(-b_2(X - b_3)\right)\right)$

❑ Technical Note

You may find the functions above useful, but the important thing to note is that, if there is a nonlinear function you use often, you can package the function once and for all. Consider the function we packaged called exp2, which estimates the model $Y = b_1 b_2^X$. The code for the function is

```
program define nlexp2
        version 6.0
        if "`1'"=="?" {
                global S_2 "2-param. exp. growth curve, `e(depvar)'=b1*b2^^2'"
                global S_1 "b1 b2"
                *
                * Approximate initial values by regression of log Y on X
                *
                local exp "[`e(wtype)' `e(wexp)']"
                tempvar Y
                quietly {
                        gen `Y' = log(`e(depvar)') if e(sample)
                        regress `Y' `2' `exp' if e(sample)
                }
                global b1 = exp(_b[_cons])
                global b2 = exp(_b[`2'])
                exit
        }
        replace `1'=$b1*$b2^^2'
end
```

Because we were packaging this function for repeated use, we went to the trouble of obtaining good initial values, which in this case we could obtain by taking the log of both sides,

$$Y = b_1 b_2^X$$
$$\ln(Y) = \ln(b_1 b_2^X) = \ln(b_1) + \ln(b_2)X$$

and then using linear regression to estimate $\ln(b_1)$ and $\ln(b_2)$. If this had been a quick-and-dirty implementation, we probably would not have bothered (initializing b_1 and b_2 to 1, say) and so forced ourselves to specify better initial values with nl's initial() option when they were not good enough.

The only other thing we did to complete the packaging was store nlexp2 as an ado-file called nlexp2.ado. The alternatives would have been to type the code into Stata interactively or to place the code in a do-file. Those approaches are adequate for occasional use, but we wanted to be able to type nl exp2 without having to worry whether the program nlexp2 was defined. When nl attempts to execute nlexp2, if the program is not in Stata's memory, Stata will search the disk(s) for an ado-file of the same name and, if found, automatically load it. All we had to do was name the file with the .ado suffix and then place it in a directory where Stata could find it. In our case, we put nlexp2.ado in Stata's system directory for StataCorp-written ado-files. In your case, you should put the file in the directory Stata reserves for user-written ado-files, which is to say, c:\ado\personal (Windows), ~/ado/personal (Unix), or ~:ado:personal (Macintosh). See [U] **20 Ado-files**.

❏

Log-normal errors

A nonlinear model with identically normally distributed errors may be written

$$y_i = f(\mathbf{x}_i, \boldsymbol{\beta}) + u_i, \qquad u_i \sim \mathrm{N}(0, \sigma^2) \qquad (1)$$

for $i = 1, \ldots, n$. If the y_i are thought to have a k-shifted lognormal instead of a normal distribution, that is, $\ln(y_i - k) \sim \mathrm{N}(\zeta_i, \tau^2)$, and the systematic part $f(\mathbf{x}_i, \boldsymbol{\beta})$ of the original model is still thought appropriate, the model becomes

$$\ln(y_i - k) = \zeta_i + v_i = \ln\big(f(\mathbf{x}_i, \boldsymbol{\beta}) - k\big) + v_i, \quad v_i \sim \mathrm{N}(0, \tau^2) \qquad (2)$$

This model is estimated if `lnlsq(k)` is specified.

If model (2) is correct, the variance of $(y_i - k)$ is proportional to $(f(\mathbf{x}_i, \boldsymbol{\beta}) - k)^2$. Probably the most common case is $k = 0$, sometimes called "proportional errors" since the standard error of y_i is proportional to its expectation, $f(\mathbf{x}_i, \boldsymbol{\beta})$. Assuming the value of k is known, (2) is just another nonlinear model in $\boldsymbol{\beta}$ and it may be fitted as usual. However, we may wish to compare the fit of (1) with that of (2) using the residual sum of squares or the deviance D, $D = -2 \times$ log-likelihood, from each model. To do so, we must allow for the change in scale introduced by the log transformation.

Assuming, then, the y_i to be normally distributed, Atkinson (1985, 85–87, 184), by considering the Jacobian $\prod |\partial \ln(y_i - k)/\partial y_i|$, showed that multiplying both sides of (2) by the geometric mean of $y_i - k$, $\dot{y}$, gives residuals on the same scale as those of y_i. The geometric mean is given by

$$\dot{y} = e^{n^{-1} \sum \ln(y_i - k)}$$

which is a constant for a given dataset. The residual deviance for (1) and for (2) may be expressed as

$$D(\widehat{\boldsymbol{\beta}}) = \left(1 + \ln(2\pi\widehat{\sigma}^2)\right)n \tag{3}$$

where $\widehat{\boldsymbol{\beta}}$ is the maximum likelihood estimate (MLE) of $\boldsymbol{\beta}$ for each model and $n\widehat{\sigma}^2$ is the RSS from (1), or that from (2) multiplied by $\dot{y}^2$.

Since (1) and (2) are models with different error structures but the same functional form, the arithmetic difference in their RSS or deviances is not easily tested for statistical significance. However, if the deviance difference is "large" (> 4, say), one would naturally prefer the model with the smaller deviance. Of course, the residuals for each model should be examined for departures from assumptions (nonconstant variance, nonnormality, serial correlations, etc.) in the usual way.

Consider alternatively modeling

$$E(y_i) = 1/(C + Ae^{Bx_i}) \tag{4}$$

$$E(1/y_i) = E(y_i') = C + Ae^{Bx_i} \tag{5}$$

where C, A, and B are parameters to be estimated. We will use the data $(y, x) = (.04, 5)$, $(.06, 12)$, $(.08, 25)$, $(.1, 35)$, $(.15, 42)$, $(.2, 48)$, $(.25, 60)$, $(.3, 75)$, and $(.5, 120)$ (Danuso 1991).

Model	C	A	B	RSS	Deviance
(4)	1.781	25.74	−.03926	−.001640	−51.95
(4) with `lnlsq(0)`	1.799	25.45	−.04051	−.001431	−53.18
(5)	1.781	25.74	−.03926	8.197	24.70
(5) with `lnlsq(0)`	1.799	27.45	−.04051	3.651	17.42

There is little to choose between the two versions of the logistic model (4), whereas for the exponential model (5) the fit using `lnlsq(0)` is much better (a deviance difference of 7.28). The reciprocal transformation has introduced heteroscedasticity into y_i' which is countered by the proportional errors property of the lognormal distribution implicit in `lnlsq(0)`. The deviances are not comparable between the logistic and exponential models because the change of scale has not been allowed for, although in principle, it could be.

Weights

Weights are specified the usual way—analytic and frequency weights are supported; see [U] **23.13 Weighted estimation**. Use of analytic weights implies that the y_i have different variances. Model (1) may therefore be rewritten

$$y_i = f(\mathbf{x}_i, \boldsymbol{\beta}) + u_i, \qquad u_i \sim \mathrm{N}(0, \sigma^2/w_i) \tag{1a}$$

where w_i are (positive) weights, assumed known and normalized such that their sum equals the number of observations. The residual deviance for (1a) is

$$D(\widehat{\boldsymbol{\beta}}) = \left(1 + \ln(2\pi\widehat{\sigma}^2)\right)n - \sum \ln(w_i) \tag{3a}$$

(compare with equation 3), where

$$n\widehat{\sigma}^2 = \mathrm{RSS} = \sum w_i \left(y_i - f(\mathbf{x}_i, \widehat{\boldsymbol{\beta}})\right)^2$$

Defining and fitting a model equivalent to (2) when weights have been specified as in (1a) is not straightforward and has not been attempted. Thus, deviances using and not using the lnlsq() option may not be strictly comparable when analytic weights (other than 0 and 1) are used.

Errors

nl will stop with error 196 if an error occurs in your *nlfcn* program and it will report the error code raised by *nlfcn*.

nl is reasonably robust to the inability of *nlfcn* to calculate predicted values for certain parameter values. nl assumes that predicted values can be calculated at the initial value of the parameters. If this is not so, an error message is issued with return code 480.

Thereafter, as nl changes the parameter values, it monitors *nlfcn*'s returned predictions for unexpected missing values. If detected, nl backs up. That is, nl finds a linear combination of the previous, known-to-be-good parameter vector and the new, known-to-be-bad vector, a combination where the function can be evaluated, and continues its iterations from that point.

nl does require, however, that once a parameter vector is found where the predictions can be calculated, small changes to the parameter vector can be made in order to calculate numeric derivatives. If a boundary is encountered at this point, an error message is issued with return code 481.

When specifying lnlsq(), an attempt to take logarithms of $y_i - k$ when $y_i \leq k$ results in an error message with return code 482.

If iterate() iterations are performed and estimates still have not converged, results are presented with a warning and the return code set to 430.

General comments on fitting nonlinear models

In many cases, achieving convergence is problematic. For example, a unique maximum likelihood (minimum-RSS) solution may not exist. A large literature exists on different algorithms that have been used, on strategies for obtaining good initial parameter values, and on tricks for parameterizing the model to make its behavior as "linear-like" as possible. Selected references are Kennedy and Gentle (1980, ch. 10) for computational matters, and Ross (1990) and Ratkowsky (1983) for all three aspects. Much of Ross's considerable experience is enshrined in the computer package MLP (Ross 1987), an invaluable resource. Ratkowsky's book is particularly clear and approachable, with useful discussion on the meaning and practical implications of "intrinsic" and "parameter-effects" nonlinearity. An excellent general text, though (in places) not for the mathematically faint-hearted, is Gallant (1987). Also see Davidson and MacKinnon (1993, Chapters 2, 3, and 5).

The success of **nl** will be enhanced if care is paid to the form of the model fitted, along the lines of Ratkowsky and Ross. For example, Ratkowsky (1983, 49–59) analyses three possible 3-parameter "yield-density" models for plant growth:

$$E(y_i) = \begin{cases} (\alpha + \beta x_i)^{-1/\theta} \\ (\alpha + \beta x_i + \gamma x_i^2)^{-1} \\ (\alpha + \beta x_i^{\phi})^{-1} \end{cases}$$

All three models give similar fits. However, he shows that the second formulation is dramatically more "linear-like" than the other two and therefore has better convergence properties. In addition, the parameter estimates are virtually unbiased and normally distributed and the asymptotic approximation to the standard errors, correlations and confidence intervals is much more accurate than for the other models. Even within a given model, the way the parameters are expressed (e.g., ϕ^{x_i} or $e^{\theta x_i}$) affects the degree of linear-like behavior.

Our advice is that even if you cannot get a particular model to converge, don't give up. Experiment with different ways of writing it or with slightly different alternative models that also fit well.

More on nlfcns

Note that the syntax for **nl** is

$$\text{\textbf{nl} } fcn \; depvar \; [varlist] \; [\ldots] \; [, \; \ldots \; fcn\_options \;]$$

The syntax for an *nlfcn* is

$$nlfcn \; \{varname \mid ?\} \; [varlist] \; [, \; fcn\_options \;]$$

The *varlist*, if specified with **nl**, will be passed to *nlfcn* along with any options not intended for **nl**. Thus, it is possible to write *nlfcn*s that are quite general.

When *nlfcn* is called with a **?**, the *varlist* and *fcn_options*, if any, are still passed. In addition, **e(depvar)** contains the identity of the dependent variable; **e(sample)** contains the estimation sample according to the **if** *exp* and **in** *range* specified on the **nl** command line; and **e(wtype)** and **e(wexp)** contain the weight type and weight expression.

nlfcn is required to post the names of the parameters to **$S_1** and to provide default initial values for all the parameters. In addition, it may post up to two titles in **$S_2** and **$S_3** that will be subsequently used to title the output. The **e()** returned results provide useful information for filling in titles and generating initial parameter estimates.

When *nlfcn* is called without a **?**, it is required to calculate the predicted values conditional on the current value of the parameters. Note that *nlfcn* is not required to process **if** *exp* or **in** *range*. Restriction to the estimation sample will be handled by **nl**.

Thus, at the beginning of this insert, we gave an example for calculating a negative-exponential growth model. A better version of the *nlfcn* would have been

```
program define nlexpgr
        version 6.0
        if "`1'" == "?" {
                global S_1 "B0 B1"
                global B0=1
                global B1=.1
                global S_2 "negative-exp. growth"
                global S_3 "`e(depvar)' = B0*(1-exp(-B1*`2'))"
                exit
        }
        replace `1'=$B0*(1-exp(-$B1*`2'))
end
```

This version would title the output and allow the independent variable to be specified on the `nl` command line:

    . nl nexpgr y xval

An even more sophisticated version of `nlnexpgr` might use `e(depvar)`, `` `2´ ``, and `if e(sample)` to generate more reasonable starting values of B0 and B1.

`nlinit` is intended for use by *nlfcn*s. Its syntax is

> `nlinit # parameter_list`

`nlinit` initializes each parameter in *parameter_list* to contain `#`. For example:

    nlinit 0 A B C
    nlinit 1 D E

Saved Results

`nl` saves in `e()`:

Scalars

`e(N)`	number of observations	`e(r2_a)`	adjusted R-squared
`e(k)`	number of parameters	`e(F)`	F statistic
`e(mss)`	model sum of squares	`e(rmse)`	root mean square error
`e(tss)`	total sum of squares	`e(converge)`	0 if convergence failed; otherwise 1
`e(df_m)`	model degrees of freedom	`e(df_t)`	total degrees of freedom
`e(rss)`	residual sum of squares	`e(dev)`	residual deviance
`e(df_r)`	residual degrees of freedom	`e(lnlsq)`	1 if specified; otherwise 0
`e(mms)`	model mean square	`e(gm_2)`	geometric mean $(y-k)^2$ if
`e(msr)`	residual mean square		`lnlsq()`; otherwise, 1
`e(r2)`	R-squared		

Macros

`e(cmd)`	nl	`e(function)`	name of function
`e(depvar)`	name of dependent variable	`e(params)`	names of parameters
`e(title)`	title in estimation output	`e(predict)`	program used to implement `predict`
`e(title2)`	secondary title in estimation output		

Matrices

`e(b)`	coefficient vector	`e(V)`	variance–covariance matrix of the estimators

Functions

`e(sample)`	marks estimation sample

The final parameter estimates are available in the parameter macros defined by *nlfcn*. The standard errors of the parameters are available through `_se[parameter]`; see [U] **16.5 Accessing coefficients and standard errors**.

Methods and Formulas

`nl` is implemented as an ado-file.

Acknowledgments

nl was written by Patrick Royston of the Imperial College School of Medicine, London. The original version of this routine was published in Royston (1992). Francesco Danuso's menu-driven nonlinear regression program (1991) provided the inspiration.

References

Atkinson, A. C. 1985. *Plots, Transformations and Regression*. Oxford: Oxford Science Publications.

Danuso, F. 1991. sg1: Nonlinear regression command. *Stata Technical Bulletin* 1: 17–19. Reprinted in *Stata Technical Bulletin Reprints*, vol. 1, pp. 96–98.

Davidson, R. and J. G. MacKinnon. 1993. *Estimation and Inference in Econometrics*. New York: Oxford University Press.

Gallant, A. R. 1987. *Nonlinear Statistical Models*. New York: John Wiley & Sons.

Goldstein, R. 1992. srd7: Adjusted summary statistics for logarithmic regressions. *Stata Technical Bulletin* 5: 17–21. Reprinted in *Stata Technical Bulletin Reprints*, vol. 1, pp. 178–183.

Kennedy, W. J., Jr., and J. E. Gentle. 1980. *Statistical Computing*. New York: Marcel Dekker.

Ratkowsky, D. A. 1983. *Nonlinear Regression Modeling*. New York: Marcel Dekker.

Ross, G. J. S. 1987. *MLP User Manual, release 3.08*. Oxford: Numerical Algorithms Group.

——. 1990. *Nonlinear Estimation*. New York: Springer-Verlag.

Royston, P. 1992. sg1.2: Nonlinear regression command. *Stata Technical Bulletin* 7: 11–18. Reprinted in *Stata Technical Bulletin Reprints*, vol. 2, pp. 112–120.

——. 1993. sg1.4: Standard nonlinear curve fits. *Stata Technical Bulletin* 11: 17. Reprinted in *Stata Technical Bulletin Reprints*, vol. 2, p. 121.

SAS Institute Inc. 1985. *SAS User's Guide: Statistics, Version 5 Edition*. Cary, NC.

Also See

Complementary: [R] **ml**, [R] **vce**, [R] **xi**

Background: [U] **16.5 Accessing coefficients and standard errors**,
                [U] **23 Estimation and post-estimation commands**

Title

notes — Place notes in data

Syntax

notes [*varname*] : *text*

notes

notes [list] *evarlist* [in #[/#]]

notes drop *evarlist* [in #[/#]]

where *evarlist* is a *varlist* but may also contain the word _dta and # is a number or the letter 1.

If *text* includes the letters TS surrounded by blanks, the TS is removed and a time stamp is substituted in its place.

Description

notes attaches notes to the data in memory. These notes become a part of the data and are saved when the data is saved and retrieved when the data is used; see [R] **save**. notes can be attached to the data generically or specifically to a variable within the data.

Remarks

A note is nothing formal; it is merely a string of text—probably words in your native language—reminding you to do something or cautioning you against something or anything else you might feel like jotting down. People who work with real data invariably end up with paper notes plastered around their terminal saying things like "Send the new sales data to Bob" or "Check the income variable in salary95; I don't believe it" or "The gender dummy was significant!" It would be better if these notes were attached to the data. Attached to the terminal, they tend to fall off and get lost.

Adding a note to your data requires typing note or notes (they are synonyms), a colon (:), and whatever you feel worth remembering. The note is added to the data currently in memory.

```
. note: Send copy to Bob once verified.
```

You can replay your notes by typing notes (or note) by itself.

```
. notes
_dta:
  1.  Send copy to Bob once verified.
```

Once you resave your data, you can replay the note in the future, too. You add more notes just as you created the first:

```
. note: Mary wants a copy, too.
. notes
_dta:
  1.  Send copy to Bob once verified.
  2.  Mary wants a copy, too.
```

462

You can place time stamps on your notes by placing the word TS (in capitals) in the text of your note:

```
. note: TS merged updates from JJ&F
. notes
_dta:
  1.  Send copy to Bob once verified.
  2.  Mary wants a copy, too.
  3.  12 Aug 1998 12:46 merged updates from JJ&F
```

The notes we have added so far are attached to the data generically, which is why Stata prefixes them with _dta when it lists them. You can attach notes to variables:

```
. note mpg: is the 44 a mistake?  Ask Bob.
. note mpg: what about the two missing values?
. notes
_dta:
  1.  Send copy to Bob once verified.
  2.  Mary wants a copy, too.
  3.  12 Aug 1998 12:47 merged updates from JJ&F
mpg:
  1.  is the 44 a mistake? Ask Bob.
  2.  what about the two missing values?
```

Up to 9,999 generic notes can be attached to _dta and another 9,999 notes can be attached to each variable.

Selectively listing notes

notes by itself lists all the notes. In full syntax, notes is equivalent to typing notes _all in 1/l. Here are some variations:

notes _dta	list all generic notes
notes mpg	list all notes for variable mpg
notes _dta mpg	list all generic notes and mpg notes
notes _dta in 3	list generic note 3
notes _dta in 3/5	list generic notes 3 through 5
notes mpg in 3/5	list mpg notes 3 through 5
notes _dta in 3/l	list generic notes 3 through last

Deleting notes

notes drop works much like listing notes except that typing notes drop by itself does not delete all notes; type notes drop _all. Some variations:

notes drop _dta	delete all generic notes
notes drop _dta in 3	delete generic note 3
notes drop _dta in 3/5	delete generic notes 3 through 5
notes drop _dta in 3/l	delete generic notes 3 through last
notes drop mpg in 4	delete mpg note 4

Warnings

1. Notes are stored with the data and, as with other updates you make to the data, the additions and deletions are not permanent until you save the data; see [R] **save**.

2. The maximum length of a single note is 1,000 characters with Small Stata and 18,632 characters with Intercooled Stata.

Methods and Formulas

notes is implemented as an ado-file.

References

Gleason, J. R. 1998. dm57: A notes editor for Windows and Macintosh. *Stata Technical Bulletin* 43: 6–9.

Also See

Complementary:	[R] **describe**, [R] **save**
Related:	[R] **codebook**
Background:	[U] **15.8 Characteristics**

Title

```
nptrend — Test for trend across ordered groups
```

Syntax

nptrend *varname* [if *exp*] [in *range*], by(*groupvar*) [<u>no</u>detail <u>s</u>core(*scorevar*)]

Description

nptrend performs a nonparametric test for trend across ordered groups.

Options

by(*groupvar*) is not optional; it specifies the group on which the data is to be ordered.

nodetail suppresses the listing of group rank sums.

score(*scorevar*) defines scores for groups. When not specified, the values of *groupvar* are used for the scores.

Remarks

nptrend performs the nonparametric test for trend across ordered groups developed by Cuzick (1985), which is an extension of the Wilcoxon rank-sum test (ranksum; see [R] **signrank**). A correction for ties is incorporated into the test. nptrend is a useful adjunct to the Kruskal–Wallis test; see [R] **kwallis**.

In addition to nptrend, for nongrouped data the signtest and spearman commands can be useful; see [R] **signrank** and [R] **spearman**. The Cox and Stuart test, for instance, applies the sign test to differences between equally spaced observations of *varname*. The Daniels test calculates Spearman's rank correlation of *varname* with a time index. Under appropriate conditions, the Daniels test is more powerful than the Cox and Stuart test. See Conover (1980) for a discussion of these tests and their asymptotic relative efficiency.

▷ Example

The following data (Altman 1991, 217) shows ocular exposure to ultraviolet radiation for 32 pairs of sunglasses classified into 3 groups according to the amount of visible light transmitted.

Group	Transmission of visible light	Ocular exposure to ultraviolet radiation
1	< 25%	1.4 1.4 1.4 1.6 2.3 2.3
2	25 to 35%	0.9 1.0 1.1 1.1 1.2 1.2 1.5 1.9 2.2 2.6 2.6 2.6 2.8 2.8 3.2 3.5 4.3 5.1
3	> 35%	0.8 1.7 1.7 1.7 3.4 7.1 8.9 13.5

Entering this data into Stata, we have

```
. list
          group    exposure
     1.       1         1.4
     2.       1         1.4
     3.       1         1.4
     4.       1         1.6
     5.       1         2.3
     6.       1         2.3
     7.       2          .9
   (output omitted )
    31.       3         8.9
    32.       3        13.5
```

We use **nptrend** to test for a trend of (increasing) exposure across the 3 groups by typing

```
. nptrend exposure, by(group)
      group     score     obs    sum of ranks
          1         1       6              76
          2         2      18             290
          3         3       8             162

        z  =  1.52
   P>|z|  =  0.13
```

When the groups are given any equally spaced scores (such as -1, 0, 1), we will obtain the same answer as above. To illustrate the effect of changing scores, an analysis of these data with scores 1, 2, and 5 (admittedly not very sensible in this case) produces

```
. gen mysc = cond(group==3,5,group)
. nptrend exposure, by(group) score(mysc)
      group     score     obs    sum of ranks
          1         1       6              76
          2         2      18             290
          3         5       8             162

        z  =  1.46
   P>|z|  =  0.14
```

This example suggests that the analysis is not all that sensitive to the scores chosen.

◁

❏ Technical Note

The grouping variable may be either a string variable or a numeric variable. If it is a string variable and no score variable is specified, the natural numbers 1, 2, 3, … are assigned to the groups in the sort order of the string variable. This may not always be what you expect. For example, the sort order of the strings "one", "two", "three" is "one", "three", "two".

❏

Saved Results

nptrend saves in **r()**:

Scalars

r(N)	number of observations	r(z)	z statistic
r(p)	two-sided p-value	r(T)	test statistic

Methods and Formulas

`nptrend` is implemented as an ado-file.

`nptrend` is based on a method due to Cuzick (1985). The following description of the statistic is from Altman (1991, 215–217). We have k groups of sample sizes n_i ($i = 1, \ldots, k$). The groups are given scores, l_i, which reflect their ordering, such as 1, 2, and 3. The scores do not have to be equally spaced, but they usually are. The total set of $N = \sum n_i$ observations are ranked from 1 to N and the sums of the ranks in each group, R_i, are obtained. L, the weighted sum of all the group scores, is

$$L = \sum_{i=1}^{k} l_i n_i$$

The statistic T is calculated as

$$T = \sum_{i=1}^{k} l_i R_i$$

Under the null hypothesis, the expected value of T is $E(T) = .5(N+1)L$, and its standard error is

$$\text{se}(T) = \sqrt{\frac{n+1}{12}\left(N \sum_{i=1}^{k} l_i^2 n_i - L^2 \right)}$$

so that the test statistic, z, is given by $z = [T - E(T)]/\text{se}(T)$, which has an approximately standard Normal distribution when the null hypothesis of no trend is true.

The correction for ties affects the standard error of T. Let $\widetilde{N}$ be the number of unique values of the variable being tested ($\widetilde{N} \le N$), and let t_j be the number of times the jth unique value of the variable appears in the data. Define

$$a = \frac{\sum_{j=1}^{\widetilde{N}} t_j(t_j^2 - 1)}{N(N^2 - 1)}$$

The corrected standard error of T is $\widetilde{\text{se}}(T) = \sqrt{1-a}\ \text{se}(T)$.

Acknowledgments

`nptrend` was written by K. A. Stepniewska and D. G. Altman (1992) of the Imperial Cancer Research Fund, London.

References

Altman, D. G. 1991. *Practical Statistics for Medical Research*. London: Chapman & Hall.

Conover, W. J. 1980. *Practical Nonparametric Statistics*. 2d ed. New York: John Wiley & Sons.

Cuzick, J. 1985. A Wilcoxon-type test for trend. *Statistics in Medicine* 4: 87–90.

Sasieni, P. 1996. snp12: Stratified test for trend across ordered groups. *Stata Technical Bulletin* 33: 24–27. Reprinted in *Stata Technical Bulletin Reprints*, vol. 6, pp. 196–200.

Sasieni, P., K. A. Stepniewska, and D. G. Altman. 1996. snp11: Test for trend across ordered groups revisited. *Stata Technical Bulletin* 32: 27–29. Reprinted in *Stata Technical Bulletin Reprints*, vol. 6, pp. 193–196.

Stepniewska, K. A. and D. G. Altman. 1992. snp4: Nonparametric test for trend across ordered groups. *Stata Technical Bulletin* 9: 21–22. Reprinted in *Stata Technical Bulletin Reprints*, vol. 2, p. 169.

Also See

Related: [R] **epitab**, [R] **kwallis**, [R] **signrank**, [R] **spearman**, [R] **symmetry**

Title

numlist — Parse numeric lists

Syntax

numlist "*numlist*" [, <u>asc</u>ending <u>desc</u>ending <u>integ</u>er <u>miss</u>ingokay min(*#*) max(*#*)

<u>r</u>ange(*operator#* [*operator#*]) sort]

where *operator* is   { < | <= | > | >= };

there is no space between *operator* and *#*;

and where *numlist* consists of one or more *numlist_elements* shown below.

numlist_element	Example	Expands to	Definition
#	3.82	3.82	a number
.	.	.	a missing value
$\#_1/\#_2$	4/6 2.3/5.7	4 5 6 2.3 3.3 4.3 5.3	starting at $\#_1$ increment by 1 to $\#_2$
$\#_1(\#_2)\#_3$	2(3)10 4.8(2.1)9.9	2 5 8 4.8 6.9 9	starting at $\#_1$ increment by $\#_2$ to $\#_3$
$\#_1$ $\#_2:\#_3$	5 7:13 1.1 2.4:5.8	5 7 9 11 13 1.1 2.4 3.7 5	starting at $\#_1$ increment by $(\#_2 - \#_1)$ to $\#_3$
$\#_1$ $\#_2$ to $\#_3$	5 7 to 13 1.1 2.4 to 5.8	same	same

Description

The `numlist` command expands the numeric list supplied as a string argument and performs error checking based on the options specified. Any numeric sequence operators in the *numlist* string are evaluated and the expanded list of numbers is returned in `r(numlist)`. See [U] **14.1.8 numlist** for a discussion of numeric lists.

Options

ascending indicates that the user must give the numeric list in ascending order without repeated values. This is different from the **sort** option.

descending indicates that the numeric list must be given in descending order without repeated values.

integer specifies that the user may only give integer values in the numeric list.

missingokay indicates that missing values are allowed in the numeric list. By default missing values are not allowed.

min(#) specifies the minimum number of elements allowed in the numeric list. The default is min(1). If you want to allow empty numeric lists specify min(0).

max(#) specifies the maximum number of elements allowed in the numeric list. The default is max(1600) which is the largest allowed maximum.

range(*operator#* [*operator#*]) specifies the acceptable range for the values in the numeric list. The *operator*s are: < (less than), <= (less than or equal to), > (greater than), and >= (greater than or equal to). No space is allowed between the *operator* and the #.

sort specifies that the returned numeric list is to be sorted. This is different from the ascending option. ascending places the responsibility for providing a sorted list on the user who will not be allowed to enter a nonsorted list. sort, on the other hand, puts no restriction on the user and will take care of sorting the list. Repeated values are also allowed with sort.

Remarks

As a matter of fact, programmers rarely use the numlist command because syntax will also expand numeric lists and it will handle the rest of the parsing problem, too, at least if the command being parsed follows standard syntax. numlist is for use in expanding numeric lists when what is being parsed does not follow standard syntax.

▷ Example

We demonstrate the numlist command interactively.

```
. numlist "5.3 1.0234 3 6:18 -2.0033 5.3/7.3"
. display "`r(numlist)'"
5.3 1.0234 3 6 9 12 15 18 -2.0033 5.3 6.3 7.3
. numlist "5.3 1.0234 3 6:18 -2.0033 5.3/7.3", integer
invalid numlist has noninteger elements
r(126);
. numlist "1 5 8/12 15", integer descending
invalid numlist has elements out of order
r(124);
. numlist "1 5 8/12 15", integer ascending
. display "`r(numlist)'"
1 5 8 9 10 11 12 15
. numlist "100 1 5 8/12 15", integer ascending
invalid numlist has elements out of order
r(124);
. numlist "100 1 5 8/12 15", integer sort
. display "`r(numlist)'"
1 5 8 9 10 11 12 15 100
. numlist "3 5 . 28 -3(2)5"
invalid numlist has missing values
r(127);
. numlist "3 5 . 28 -3(2)5", missingokay min(3) max(25)
. display "`r(numlist)'"
3 5 . 28 -3 -1 1 3 5
```

```
. numlist "28 36", min(3) max(6)
invalid numlist has too few elements
r(122);
. numlist "28 36 -3 5 2.8 7 32 -8", min(3) max(6)
invalid numlist has too many elements
r(123);
. numlist "3/6 -4 -1 to 5", range(>=1)
invalid numlist has elements outside of allowed range
r(125);
. numlist "3/6", range(>=0 <30)
. display "`r(numlist)'"
3 4 5 6
```

◁

Saved Results

numlist saves in r():

Macros
    r(numlist)   the expanded numeric list

Also See

Related: [R] **syntax**

Background: [U] **14.1.8 numlist**

Title

obs — Increase number of observations in dataset

Syntax

set obs #

Description

set obs changes the number of observations in the current dataset. # must be at least as large as the current number of observations. If there are variables in memory, the values of all new observations are set to missing.

Remarks

▷ Example

set obs can be useful for concocting artificial datasets. For instance, if you wanted to graph the function $y = x^2$ over the range 1 to 100, you could

```
. drop _all
. set obs 100
obs was 0, now 100
. generate x = _n
. generate y = x^2
. graph y x
(graph not shown)
```

◁

▷ Example

If in a program you want to add an extra data point:

```
. local np1 = _N + 1
. set obs `np1'
```

◁

Also See

Related: [R] **describe**

Title

---
ologit — Maximum-likelihood ordered logit estimation

Syntax

$\big[$by *varlist*:$\big]$ <u>olog</u>it *depvar* $\big[$*varlist*$\big]$ $\big[$*weight*$\big]$ $\big[$if *exp*$\big]$ $\big[$in *range*$\big]$ $\big[$, <u>t</u>able

<u>r</u>obust <u>cl</u>uster(*varname*) <u>sco</u>re(*newvarlist*) <u>l</u>evel(*#*) <u>off</u>set(*varname*)

maximize_options $\big]$

fweights, iweights, and pweights are allowed; see [U] **14.1.6 weight**.

ologit shares the features of all estimation commands; see [U] **23 Estimation and post-estimation commands**.

ologit may be used with sw to perform stepwise estimation; see [R] **sw**.

Syntax for predict

predict $\big[$*type*$\big]$ *newvarname(s)* $\big[$if *exp*$\big]$ $\big[$in *range*$\big]$ $\big[$, $\{$ p | xb | stdp $\}$

<u>o</u>utcome(*outcome*) <u>nooff</u>set $\big]$

Note that with the p option, you specify either one or k new variables depending upon whether the outcome() option is also specified (where k is the number of categories of *depvar*). With xb and stdp, one new variable is specified.

These statistics are available both in and out of sample; type predict ... if e(sample) ... if wanted only for the estimation sample.

Description

ologit estimates ordered logit models of ordinal variable *depvar* on the independent variables *varlist*. The actual values taken on by the dependent variable are irrelevant except that larger values are assumed to correspond to "higher" outcomes. Up to 50 outcomes are allowed in Intercooled Stata; 20 outcomes in Small Stata.

See [R] **logistic** for a list of related estimation commands.

Options

table requests a table showing how the probabilities for the categories are computed from the fitted equation.

robust specifies that the Huber/White/sandwich estimator of variance is to be used in place of the traditional calculation; see [U] **23.11 Obtaining robust variance estimates**. robust combined with cluster() allows observations which are not independent within cluster (although they must be independent between clusters).

If you specify pweights, robust is implied; see [U] **23.13 Weighted estimation**.

cluster(*varname*) specifies that the observations are independent across groups (clusters) but not necessarily within groups. *varname* specifies to which group each observation belongs; e.g., cluster(personid) in data with repeated observations on individuals. cluster() affects the estimated standard errors and variance–covariance matrix of the estimators (VCE), but not the estimated coefficients; see [U] **23.11 Obtaining robust variance estimates**. cluster() can be used with pweights to produce estimates for unstratified cluster-sampled data, but see the svyolog command in [R] **svy estimators** for a command designed especially for survey data.

cluster() implies robust; specifying robust cluster() is equivalent to typing cluster() by itself.

score(*newvarlist*) creates k new variables, where k is the number of observed outcomes. The first variable contains $\partial \ln L_j / \partial(\mathbf{x}_j \mathbf{b})$; the second variable contains $\partial \ln L_j / \partial(\_\text{cut1}_j)$; the third contains $\partial \ln L_j / \partial(\_\text{cut2}_j)$; and so on. Note that if you were to specify the option score(sc*), Stata would create the appropriate number of new variables and they would be named sc0, sc1, ... sc$(k-1)$.

level(*#*) specifies the confidence level, in percent, for confidence intervals. The default is level(95) or as set by set level; see [U] **23.5 Specifying the width of confidence intervals**.

offset(*varname*) specifies that *varname* is to be included in the model with coefficient constrained to be 1.

maximize_options control the maximization process; see [R] **maximize**. You should never have to specify them.

Options for predict

p, the default, calculates the predicted probabilities. If you do not also specify the outcome() option, you must specify k new variables, where k is the number of categories of the dependent variable. Say you estimated a model by typing ologit result x1 x2, and result takes on three values. Then you could type predict p1 p2 p3, to obtain all three predicted probabilities. If you specify the outcome() option, then you specify one new variable. Say that result takes on values 1, 2, and 3. Then typing predict p1, outcome(1) would produce the same p1.

xb calculates the linear prediction. You specify one new variable; for example, predict linear, xb. The linear prediction is defined ignoring the contribution of the estimated cut points.

stdp calculates the standard error of the linear prediction. You specify one new variable; for example, predict se, stdp.

outcome(*outcome*) specifies for which outcome the predicted probabilities are to be calculated. outcome() should either contain a single value of the dependent variable, or one of #1, #2, ..., with #1 meaning the first category of the dependent variable, #2 the second category, etc.

nooffset is relevant only if you specified offset(*varname*) for ologit. It modifies the calculations made by predict so that they ignore the offset variable; the linear prediction is treated as $\mathbf{x}_j \mathbf{b}$ rather than $\mathbf{x}_j \mathbf{b} + \text{offset}_j$.

Remarks

Ordered logit models are used to estimate relationships between an ordinal dependent variable and a set of independent variables. An *ordinal* variable is a variable that is categorical and ordered, for instance, "poor", "good", and "excellent", which might be the answer to one's current health status or the repair record of one's car. If there are only two outcomes, see [R] **logistic**, [R] **logit**, and

[R] **probit**. This entry is concerned only with more than two outcomes. If the outcomes cannot be ordered (e.g., residency in the north, east, south and west), see [R] **mlogit**. This entry is concerned only with models in which the outcomes can be ordered.

In ordered logit, an underlying score is estimated as a linear function of the independent variables and a set of cut points. The probability of observing outcome i corresponds to the probability that the estimated linear function, plus random error, is within the range of the cut points estimated for the outcome:

$$\Pr(\text{outcome}_j = i) = \Pr(\kappa_{i-1} < \beta_1 x_{1j} + \beta_2 x_{2j} + \cdots + \beta_k x_{kj} + u_j \leq \kappa_i)$$

u_j is assumed to be logistically distributed in ordered logit. In either case, one estimates the coefficients β_1, β_2, ..., β_k together with the cut points κ_1, κ_2, ..., κ_{I-1}, where I is the number of possible outcomes. κ_0 is taken as $-\infty$ and κ_I is taken as $+\infty$. All of this is a direct generalization of the ordinary two-outcome logit model.

▷ Example

You wish to analyze the 1977 repair records of 66 foreign and domestic cars; a variation of the automobile data described in [U] **9 Stata's on-line tutorials and sample datasets**. The 1977 repair records, like those in 1978, take on values poor, fair, average, good, and excellent. Here is a cross-tabulation of the data:

```
. tab rep77 foreign, chi2

  Repair |
  Record |        Foreign
    1977 |  Domestic    Foreign |     Total
---------+----------------------+----------
    Poor |         2          1 |         3
    Fair |        10          1 |        11
 Average |        20          7 |        27
    Good |        13          7 |        20
     Exc |         0          5 |         5
---------+----------------------+----------
   Total |        45         21 |        66

          Pearson chi2(4) =  13.8619   Pr = 0.008
```

Although it appears that `foreign` takes on the values "`Domestic`" and "`Foreign`", it is actually a numeric variable taking on the values 0 and 1. Similarly, `rep77` takes on the values 1, 2, 3, 4, and 5, corresponding to "`Poor`", "`Fair`", and so on. The more meaningful words appear because we attached value labels to the data; see [U] **15.6.3 Value labels**.

Since the chi-squared value is significant, you could claim that there is a relationship between `foreign` and `rep77`. Literally, however, you can only claim that the distributions are different; the chi-squared test is not directional. One way to model these data is to model the categorization that took place when the data were created. Cars have a true frequency-of-repair, which we will assume is given by $S_j = \beta\, \texttt{foreign}_j + u_j$, and a car is categorized as "poor" if $S_j \leq \kappa_0$, as "fair" if $\kappa_0 < S_j \leq \kappa_1$, and so on:

```
. ologit rep77 foreign, table
Iteration 0:   log likelihood = -89.895098
Iteration 1:   log likelihood = -85.951765
Iteration 2:   log likelihood = -85.908227
Iteration 3:   log likelihood = -85.908161
Ordered logit estimates                    Number of obs   =         66
                                           LR chi2(1)      =       7.97
                                           Prob > chi2     =     0.0047
Log likelihood = -85.908161                Pseudo R2       =     0.0444
```

```
------------------------------------------------------------------------------
    rep77 |      Coef.   Std. Err.       z    P>|z|     [95% Conf. Interval]
----------+-------------------------------------------------------------------
  foreign |   1.455878    .5308946    2.742   0.006      .4153436    2.496412
----------+-------------------------------------------------------------------
    _cut1 |  -2.765562    .5988207              (Ancillary parameters)
    _cut2 |  -.9963603    .3217704
    _cut3 |   .9426153    .3136396
    _cut4 |   3.123351    .5423237
------------------------------------------------------------------------------

    rep77 |       Probability                  Observed
----------|-------------------------------------------
     Poor | Pr(       xb+u<_cut1)                0.0455
     Fair | Pr(_cut1<xb+u<_cut2)                 0.1667
  Average | Pr(_cut2<xb+u<_cut3)                 0.4091
     Good | Pr(_cut3<xb+u<_cut4)                 0.3030
      Exc | Pr(_cut4<xb+u)                       0.0758
```

Our model is $S_j = 1.46\, \texttt{foreign}_j + u_j$; the expected value for foreign cars is 1.46 and, for domestic cars, 0; foreign cars have better repair records.

The "ancillary parameters" _cut1, _cut2, _cut3, and _cut4 correspond to the κ's in our previous notation—they model the categorization. For instance, the probability that a foreign car is categorized as having a poor repair record is given by the probability that $1.46 + u_j \le -2.77$ or, equivalently, $u_j \le -4.23$.

The estimated cut points tell us how to interpret the score and the table below the estimates—produced because we specified the option table—reminds us of the interpretation. A car is estimated as having a poor repair record if the score is less than the estimated _cut1. (Actually, the table could say less than or equal, but since the logistic distribution is continuous, the probability of any particular value is zero, so it does not matter.)

For a foreign car, the probability of a poor record is the probability that $1.46 + u_j \le -2.77$ or, equivalently, $u_j \le -4.23$. Making this calculation requires familiarity with the logistic distribution: the probability is $1/(1 + e^{4.23}) = .014$. On the other hand, for domestic cars, the probability of a poor record is the probability $u_j \le -2.77$, which is .059.

This, it seems to us, is a far more reasonable prediction than we would have made based on the table alone. The table showed that 2 out of 45 domestic cars had poor records while 1 out of 21 foreign cars had poor records—corresponding to probabilities $2/45 = .044$ and $1/21 = .048$. The predictions from our model imposed a smoothness assumption—foreign cars should not, overall, have better repair records without the difference revealing itself in each category. The fact that, in our data, the fractions of foreign and domestic cars in the poor category are virtually identical is due only to the randomness associated with small samples.

Thus, if we were asked to predict the true fractions of foreign and domestic cars that would be classified in the various categories, we would choose the numbers implied by the ordered logit model:

| | tabulate | | logit | |
	Domestic	Foreign	Domestic	Foreign
Poor	.044	.048	.059	.014
Fair	.222	.048	.210	.065
Average	.444	.333	.450	.295
Good	.289	.333	.238	.467
Excellent	.000	.238	.043	.159

See *Hypothesis tests and predictions* below for a more complete explanation of how to generate predictions from an ordered logit model.

◁

❑ Technical Note

In this case, ordered logit provides an alternative to ordinary two-outcome logistic models with an arbitrary dichotomization, which might otherwise have been tempting. We could, for instance, have summarized this data by converting the 5-outcome `rep77` variable to a 2-outcome variable, combining cars in the average, fair, and poor categories to make one outcome and cars in the good and excellent categories to make the second.

Another, even less appealing alternative would have been to use ordinary regression, arbitrarily labeling "excellent" as 5, "good" as 4, and so on. The problem is that with different but equally valid labelings (say 10 for "excellent"), we would obtain different estimates. We would have no way of choosing one metric over another. That is not, however, true of `ologit`. The actual values used to label the categories make no difference other than through the order they imply.

In fact, our labeling was 5 for "excellent", 4 for "good", and so on. The words "excellent" and "good" appear in our output because we attached a value label to the variables; see [U] **15.6.3 Value labels**. If we were to now go back and type `replace rep77=10 if rep77==5`, changing all the 5s to 10s, we would still obtain exactly the same results when we reestimated our model.

❑

▷ Example

In the example above, we used ordered logit as a way to model a table. We are not, however, limited to including only a single explanatory variable nor to including only categorical variables. We can explore the relationship of `rep77` with any of the variables in our data. We might, for instance, model `rep77` not only in terms of the origin of manufacture, but also including `length` (a proxy for size) and `mpg`:

```
. ologit rep77 foreign length mpg
Iteration 0:   log likelihood = -89.895098
Iteration 1:   log likelihood = -78.775147
Iteration 2:   log likelihood = -78.256299
Iteration 3:   log likelihood = -78.250722
Iteration 4:   log likelihood = -78.250719

Ordered logit estimates                        Number of obs   =         66
                                               LR chi2(3)      =      23.29
                                               Prob > chi2     =     0.0000
Log likelihood = -78.250719                    Pseudo R2       =     0.1295

------------------------------------------------------------------------------
      rep77 |     Coef.   Std. Err.      z    P>|z|     [95% Conf. Interval]
------------+-----------------------------------------------------------------
    foreign |   2.896807   .7906411     3.664   0.000     1.347179    4.446435
     length |   .0828275     .02272     3.646   0.000     .0382972    .1273579
        mpg |   .2307677   .0704548     3.275   0.001     .0926788    .3688566
------------+-----------------------------------------------------------------
      _cut1 |   17.92748   5.551191           (Ancillary parameters)
      _cut2 |   19.86506    5.59648
      _cut3 |   22.10331   5.708935
      _cut4 |   24.69213   5.890754
------------------------------------------------------------------------------
```

foreign still plays a role, and an even larger role than previously. We find that larger cars tend to have better repair records, as do cars with better mileage ratings.

◁

Hypothesis tests and predictions

See [U] **23 Estimation and post-estimation commands** for instructions on obtaining the variance–covariance matrix of the estimators, predicted values, and hypothesis tests. Also see [R] **lrtest** for performing likelihood-ratio tests.

▷ Example

In a previous example, we estimated the model ologit rep77 foreign length mpg. The predict command can be used to obtain the predicted probabilities.

You type predict followed by the names of the new variables to hold the predicted probabilities, ordering the names from low to high. In our data, the lowest outcome is "poor" and the highest "excellent". We have five categories and so must type five names following predict; the choice of name is up to us:

```
. predict poor fair avg good exc
(option p assumed; probabilities of outcomes)

. list exc good make model rep78 if rep77==.
```

	exc	good	make	model	rep78
3.	.0033341	.0393056	AMC	Spirit	.
10.	.0098392	.1070041	Buick	Opel	.
32.	.0023406	.0279497	Ford	Fiesta	Good
44.	.015697	.1594413	Merc.	Monarch	Average
53.	.065272	.4165188	Peugeot	604	.
56.	.005187	.059727	Plym.	Horizon	Average
57.	.0261461	.2371826	Plym.	Sapporo	.
63.	.0294961	.2585825	Pont.	Phoenix	.

The eight cars listed were introduced after 1977 and so do not have 1977 repair records in our data. We predicted what their 1977 repair records might have been using the fitted equation. We see that, based on its characteristics, the Peugeot 604 had about a $41.65 + 6.53 \approx 48.2$ percent chance of a good or excellent repair record. The Ford Fiesta, which had only a 3 percent chance of a good or excellent repair record, in fact had a good record when it was introduced in the following year.

◁

❑ Technical Note

For ordered logit, predict, xb produces $S_j = x_{1j}\beta_1 + x_{2j}\beta_2 + \cdots + x_{kj}\beta_k$. The ordered-logit predictions are then the probability that $S_j + u_j$ lies between a pair of cut points κ_{i-1} and κ_i. Some handy formulas are

$$\Pr(S_j + u_j < \kappa) = 1/(1 + e^{S_j - \kappa})$$
$$\Pr(S_j + u_j > \kappa) = 1 - 1/(1 + e^{S_j - \kappa})$$
$$\Pr(\kappa_1 < S_j + u_j < \kappa_2) = 1/(1 + e^{S_j - \kappa_2}) - 1/(1 + e^{S_j - \kappa_1})$$

Rather than using `predict` directly, we could calculate the predicted probabilities by hand. If we wished to obtain the predicted probability that the repair record is excellent and the probability that it is good, we look back at `ologit`'s output to obtain the cut points. We find that "good" corresponds to the interval $\_cut3 < S_j + u < \_cut4$ and "excellent" to the interval $S_j + u > \_cut4$:

```
. predict score, xb
. gen probgood = 1/(1+exp(score-_b[_cut4])) - 1/(1+exp(score-_b[_cut3]))
. gen probexc = 1 - 1/(1+exp(score-_b[_cut4]))
```

The results of our calculation will be exactly the same as that produced in the previous example. Note that we refer to the estimated cut points just as we would any coefficient, so `_b[_cut3]` refers to the value of the `_cut3` coefficient; see [U] **16.5 Accessing coefficients and standard errors**.

❑

Saved Results

`ologit` saves in `e()`:

Scalars

e(N)	number of observations	e(ll)	log likelihood
e(k_cat)	number of categories	e(ll_0)	log likelihood, constant-only model
e(df_m)	model degrees of freedom	e(chi2)	χ^2
e(r2_p)	pseudo R-squared	e(N_clust)	number of clusters

Macros

e(cmd)	ologit	e(vcetype)	covariance estimation method
e(depvar)	name of dependent variable	e(chi2type)	Wald or LR; type of model χ^2 test
e(wtype)	weight type	e(offset)	offset
e(wexp)	weight expression	e(predict)	program used to implement predict
e(clustvar)	name of cluster variable		

Matrices

e(b)	coefficient vector	e(V)	variance–covariance matrix of the
e(cat)	category values		estimators

Functions

e(sample)	marks estimation sample

Methods and Formulas

A straightforward textbook description of the model fit by `ologit`, as well as the models fit by `oprobit`, `clogit`, and `mlogit`, can be found in Greene (1997, chapter 19). When you have a qualitative dependent variable, several estimation procedures are available. A popular choice is multinomial logistic regression (see [R] **mlogit**), but if you use this procedure when the response variable is ordinal, you are discarding information because multinomial logit ignores the ordered aspect of the outcome. Ordered logit and probit models provide a means to exploit the ordering information.

There is more than one "ordered logit" model. The model fit by `ologit`, which we will call the ordered logit model, is also known as the proportional odds model. Another popular choice, not fitted by `ologit`, is known as the stereotype model. All ordered logit models have been derived by starting with a binary logit/probit model and generalizing it to allow for more than two outcomes.

The proportional odds ordered logit model is so called because, if one considers the odds $\text{odds}(k) = P(Y \leq k)/P(Y > k)$, then $\text{odds}(k_1)$ and $\text{odds}(k_2)$ have the same ratio, for all independent variable combinations. The model is based on the principle that the only effect of combining adjoining categories in ordered categorical regression problems should be a loss of efficiency in the estimation of the regression parameters (McCullagh 1980). This model was also described by Zavoina and McKelvey (1975), and previously by Aitchison and Silvey (1957) in a different algebraic form. Brant (1990) offers a set of diagnostics for the model.

Peterson and Harrell (1990) suggest a model that allows nonproportional odds for a subset of the explanatory variables. ologit does not allow this, but a model similar to this was implemented by Fu (1998).

The stereotype model rejects the principle on which the ordered logit model is based. Anderson (1984) argues that there are two distinct types of ordered categorical variables: "grouped continuous", like income, where the "type a" model applies; and "assessed", like extent of pain relief, where the stereotype model applies. Greenland (1985) independently developed the same model. The stereotype model starts with a multinomial logistic regression model and imposes constraints on this model.

Goodness of fit for ologit can be evaluated by comparing the likelihood value with that obtained by estimating the model with mlogit. Let L_1 be the log-likelihood value reported by ologit and L_0 be the log-likelihood value reported by mlogit. If there are p independent variables (excluding the constant) and c categories, mlogit will fit $p(c-1)$ additional parameters. One can then perform a "likelihood-ratio test", i.e., calculate $-2(L_1 - L_0)$ and compare with $\chi^2\big(p(c-2)\big)$. This test is only suggestive because the ordered logit model is not nested within the multinomial logit model. A large value of $-2(L_1 - L_0)$ should, however, be taken as evidence of poorness of fit. Marginally large values, on the other hand, should not be taken too seriously.

The coefficients and cut points are estimated using maximum-likelihood as described in [R] **maximize**. In our parameterization, no constant appears as the effect is absorbed into the cut points.

ologit and oprobit begin by tabulating the dependent variable. Category $i = 1$ is defined as the minimum value of the variable, $i = 2$ as the next ordered value, and so on, for the empirically determined I categories.

The probability of observing an observation in the case of ordered logit is

$$\text{Pr(outcome} = i) = \text{Pr}\left(\kappa_{i-1} < \sum_j \beta_j x_j + u \leq \kappa_i \right)$$

$$= \frac{1}{1 + \exp(-\kappa_i + \sum \beta_j x_j)} - \frac{1}{1 + \exp(-\kappa_{i-1} + \sum \beta_j x_j)}$$

Note that κ_0 is defined as $-\infty$ and κ_I as $+\infty$.

In the case of ordered probit, the probability of observing an observation is

$$\text{Pr(outcome} = i) = \text{Pr}\left(\kappa_{i-1} < \sum_j \beta_j x_j + u \leq \kappa_i \right)$$

$$= \Phi\left(\kappa_i - \sum_j x_j \beta_j \right) - \Phi\left(\kappa_{i-1} - \sum_j x_j \beta_j \right)$$

References

Aitchison, J. and S. D. Silvey. 1957. The generalization of probit analysis to the case of multiple responses. *Biometrika* 44: 131–140.

Anderson, J. A. 1984. Regression and ordered categorical variables (with discussion). *Journal of the Royal Statistical Society*, Series B 46: 1–30.

Brant, R. 1990. Assessing proportionality in the proportional odds model for ordinal logistic regression. *Biometrics* 46: 1171–1178.

Fu, V. K. 1998. sg88: Estimating generalized ordered logit models. *Stata Technical Bulletin* 44: 27–30.

Goldstein, R. 1997. sg59: Index of ordinal variation and Neyman–Barton GOF. *Stata Technical Bulletin* 33: 10–12. Reprinted in *Stata Technical Bulletin Reprints*, vol. 6, pp. 145–147.

Greene, W. H. 1997. *Econometric Analysis*. 3d ed. Upper Saddle River, NJ: Prentice–Hall.

Greenland, S. 1985. An application of logistic models to the analysis of ordinal response. *Biometrical Journal* 27: 189–197.

Long, J. S. 1997. *Regression Models for Categorical and Limited Dependent Variables*. Thousand Oaks, CA: Sage Publications.

McCullagh, P. 1977. A logistic model for paired comparisons with ordered categorical data. *Biometrika* 64: 449–453.

——. 1980. Regression models for ordinal data (with discussion). *Journal of the Royal Statistical Society*, Series B 42: 109–142.

McCullagh, P. and J. A. Nelder. 1989. *Generalized Linear Models*. 2d ed. London: Chapman & Hall.

Peterson, B. and F. E. Harrell, Jr. 1990. Partial proportional odds models for ordinal response variables. *Applied Statistics* 39: 205–217.

Wolfe, R. 1998. sg86: Continuation-ratio models for ordinal response data. *Stata Technical Bulletin* 44: 18–21.

Wolfe, R. and W. W. Gould. 1998. sg76: An approximate likelihood-ratio test for ordinal response models. *Stata Technical Bulletin* 42: 24–27. Reprinted in *Stata Technical Bulletin Reprints*, vol. 7, pp. 199–204.

Zavoina, W. and R. D. McKelvey. 1975. A statistical model for the analysis of ordinal level dependent variables. *Journal of Mathematical Sociology* 4: 103–120.

Also See

Complementary:	[R] **lincom**, [R] **linktest**, [R] **lrtest**, [R] **predict**, [R] **sw**, [R] **test**, [R] **testnl**, [R] **vce**
Related:	[R] **logistic**, [R] **logit**, [R] **mlogit**, [R] **oprobit**, [R] **svy estimators**
Background:	[U] **16.5 Accessing coefficients and standard errors**, [U] **23 Estimation and post-estimation commands**, [U] **23.11 Obtaining robust variance estimates**, [U] **23.12 Obtaining scores**, [R] **maximize**

Title

> **oneway** — One-way analysis of variance

Syntax

$\begin{bmatrix} \text{by } varlist: \end{bmatrix}$ <u>on</u>eway *response_var factor_var* $\begin{bmatrix} weight \end{bmatrix}$ $\begin{bmatrix} \text{if } exp \end{bmatrix}$ $\begin{bmatrix} \text{in } range \end{bmatrix}$ $\begin{bmatrix} \text{, } \underline{\text{noa}}\text{nova} \end{bmatrix}$

    <u>nol</u>abel <u>mis</u>sing <u>w</u>rap <u>tab</u>ulate $\begin{bmatrix} \text{no} \end{bmatrix}$<u>me</u>ans $\begin{bmatrix} \text{no} \end{bmatrix}$<u>st</u>andard $\begin{bmatrix} \text{no} \end{bmatrix}$freq $\begin{bmatrix} \text{no} \end{bmatrix}$obs

    <u>b</u>onferroni <u>s</u>cheffe <u>si</u>dak $\big]$

aweights and fweights are allowed; see [U] **14.1.6 weight**.

Description

The oneway command reports one-way analysis-of-variance (ANOVA) models and performs multiple-comparison tests.

If you wish to estimate more complicated ANOVA layouts or wish to estimate analysis-of-covariance (ANOCOVA) models, see [R] **anova**.

See [R] **encode** for examples of estimating ANOVA models on string variables.

See [R] **loneway** for an alternative oneway command with slightly different features.

Options

noanova suppresses the display of the ANOVA table.

nolabel causes the numeric codes to be displayed rather than the value labels in the ANOVA and multiple-comparison test tables.

missing requests that missing values of *factor_var* be treated as a category rather than as observations to be omitted from the analysis.

wrap requests that Stata take no action on wide tables to make them readable. Unless wrap is specified, wide tables are broken into pieces to enhance readability.

tabulate produces a table of summary statistics of the *response_var* by levels of the *factor_var*. The table includes the mean, standard deviation, frequency, and, if the data is weighted, the number of observations. Individual elements of the table may be included or suppressed by the $\begin{bmatrix} \text{no} \end{bmatrix}$means, $\begin{bmatrix} \text{no} \end{bmatrix}$standard, $\begin{bmatrix} \text{no} \end{bmatrix}$freq, and $\begin{bmatrix} \text{no} \end{bmatrix}$obs options. For example, typing

    `oneway response factor, tabulate means standard`

would produce a summary table that contained only the means and standard deviations. You could achieve the same result by typing

    `oneway response factor, tabulate nofreq`

$\begin{bmatrix} \text{no} \end{bmatrix}$means includes only or suppresses only the means from the table produced by the tabulate option. See tabulate option above.

[no] standard includes only or suppresses only the standard deviations from the table produced by the tabulate option. See tabulate option above.

[no] freq includes only or suppresses only the frequencies from the table produced by the tabulate option. See tabulate option above.

[no] obs includes only or suppresses only the reported number of observations from the table produced by the tabulate option. If the data is not weighted, the number of observations is identical to the frequency and by default only the frequency is reported. If the data is weighted, the frequency refers to the sum of the weights. See tabulate option above.

bonferroni reports the results of a Bonferroni multiple-comparison test.

scheffe reports the results of a Scheffé multiple-comparison test.

sidak reports the results of a Šidák multiple-comparison test.

Remarks

The oneway command reports one-way analysis-of-variance (ANOVA) models. To perform a one-way layout of a variable called endog on exog, you type oneway endog exog.

▷ Example

You run an experiment varying the amount of fertilizer used in growing apple trees. You test four concentrations, using each concentration in three groves of twelve trees each. Later in the year, you measure the average weight of the fruit.

If all had gone well, you would have had three observations on the average weight for each of the four concentrations. Instead, two of the groves were mistakenly leveled by a confused man on a large bulldozer. You are left with the following data:

```
. use apple
(Apple trees)

. describe

Contains data from apple.dta
  obs:            10                          Apple trees
  vars:            2                          12 Aug 1998 13:04
  size:          140 (99.9% of memory free)
-------------------------------------------------------------------------
  1. treat       int    %8.0g                 Fertilizer
  2. wgt         double %10.0g                Average weight in grams
-------------------------------------------------------------------------
Sorted by:

. list

           treat          wgt
  1.           1        117.5
  2.           1        113.8
  3.           1        104.4
  4.           2         48.9
  5.           2         50.4
  6.           2         58.9
  7.           3         70.4
  8.           3         86.9
  9.           4         87.7
 10.           4         67.3
```

To obtain the one-way analysis-of-variance results, you type

```
. oneway wgt treat
                          Analysis of Variance
       Source            SS          df      MS             F       Prob > F
    ---------------------------------------------------------------------------
    Between groups    5295.54433      3    1765.18144      21.46     0.0013
    Within groups     493.591667      6    82.2652778
    ---------------------------------------------------------------------------
        Total         5789.136        9    643.237333
    Bartlett's test for equal variances:   chi2(3)=1.3900    Prob>chi2=0.708
```

You find significant (at better than the 1% level) differences among the four concentrations.

◁

❏ Technical Note

Rather than using the oneway command, we could have performed this analysis using anova. The first example in [R] **anova** repeats this same analysis. You may wish to compare the output.

You will find the oneway command quicker than the anova command and, as you will learn, oneway allows you to perform multiple-comparison tests. On the other hand, anova will let you generate predictions, examine the covariance matrix of the estimators, and perform more general hypothesis tests.

❏

❏ Technical Note

Although the output is a usual analysis-of-variance table, let's run through it anyway. The between-group sum of squares for the model is 5295.5 with 3 degrees of freedom. This results in a mean square of $5295.5/3 \approx 1765.2$. The corresponding F statistic is 21.46 and has a significance level of 0.0013. Thus, the model appears to be significant at the 0.13% level.

The second line summarizes the within-group (residual) variation. The within-group sum of squares is 493.59 with 6 degrees of freedom, resulting in a mean square error of 82.27.

The between- plus the residual-group variations sum to the total sum of squares, which is reported as 5789.1 in the last line of the table. This is the total sum of squares of wgt after removal of the mean. Similarly, the between plus residual degrees of freedom sum to the total degrees of freedom, 9. Remember that there are 10 observations. Subtracting 1 for the mean, we are left with 9 total degrees of freedom.

At the bottom of the table is reported Bartlett's test for equal variances. The value of the statistic is 1.39. The corresponding significance level (χ^2 with 3 degrees of freedom) is 0.708, so we cannot reject the assumption that the variances are homogeneous.

❏

Obtaining observed means

▷ Example

We typed oneway wgt treat to obtain an ANOVA table of weight of fruit by fertilizer concentration. Although we obtained the table, we did not obtain any information on which fertilizer seems to work the best. If we add the tabulate option, we obtain that additional information:

```
. oneway wgt treat, tabulate
            | Summary of Average weight in grams
 Fertilizer |       Mean   Std. Dev.      Freq.
------------+-------------------------------------
          1 |      111.9   6.7535176          3
          2 |  52.733333   5.3928966          3
          3 |      78.65   11.667262          2
          4 |       77.5   14.424978          2
------------+-------------------------------------
      Total |      80.62   25.362124         10
                    Analysis of Variance
    Source              SS         df       MS            F     Prob > F
-----------------------------------------------------------------------
Between groups     5295.54433       3   1765.18144     21.46     0.0013
Within groups      493.591667       6   82.2652778
-----------------------------------------------------------------------
    Total           5789.136        9   643.237333
Bartlett's test for equal variances:  chi2(3) =    1.3900  Prob>chi2 = 0.708
```

We find that the average weight is largest when we used fertilizer concentration 1.

◁

Multiple-comparison tests

▷ Example

oneway also has the ability to perform multiple-comparison tests, using either Bonferroni, Scheffé, or Šidák normalizations. For instance, to obtain the Bonferroni multiple-comparison test, we specify the bonferroni option:

```
. oneway wgt treat, bonferroni
                    Analysis of Variance
    Source              SS         df       MS            F     Prob > F
-----------------------------------------------------------------------
Between groups     5295.54433       3   1765.18144     21.46     0.0013
Within groups      493.591667       6   82.2652778
-----------------------------------------------------------------------
    Total           5789.136        9   643.237333
Bartlett's test for equal variances:  chi2(3) =    1.3900  Prob>chi2 = 0.708
           Comparison of Average weight in grams by Fertilizer
                            (Bonferroni)
Row Mean-|
Col Mean |         1          2          3
---------+---------------------------------
       2 |   -59.1667
         |      0.001
         |
       3 |    -33.25    25.9167
         |     0.042      0.122
         |
       4 |     -34.4    24.7667      -1.15
         |     0.036      0.146      1.000
```

The results of the Bonferroni test are presented as a matrix. The first entry, -59.17, represents the difference between fertilizer concentrations 2 and 1 (labeled "Row Mean - Col Mean" in the upper stub of the table). Remember that in the previous example we requested the tabulate option. Looking back, we find that the means of concentrations 1 and 2 are 111.90 and 52.73, respectively. Thus, $52.73 - 111.90 = -59.17$.

Underneath that number is reported "0.001". This is the Bonferroni-adjusted significance of the difference. The difference is significant at the 0.1% level. Looking down the column, we see that concentration 3 is also worse than concentration 1 (4.2% level) as is concentration 4 (3.6% level).

Based on this evidence, we would use concentration 1 if we grew apple trees.

◁

▷ Example

We can just as easily obtain the Scheffé-adjusted significance levels. Rather than specifying the bonferroni option, we specify the scheffe option.

We will also add the noanova option to prevent Stata from redisplaying the ANOVA table:

```
. oneway wgt treat, noanova scheffe
              Comparison of Average weight in grams by Fertilizer
                                    (Scheffe)
  Row Mean-|
  Col Mean |          1          2          3
  ---------+---------------------------------
         2 |   -59.1667
           |     0.001
           |
         3 |    -33.25    25.9167
           |     0.039     0.101
           |
         4 |     -34.4    24.7667      -1.15
           |     0.034     0.118      0.999
```

The differences are the same as we obtained in the Bonferroni output, but the significance levels are not. According to the Bonferroni-adjusted numbers, the significance of the difference between fertilizer concentrations 1 and 3 is 4.2%. The Scheffé-adjusted significance level is 3.9%.

We will leave it to you to decide which results are more accurate.

◁

▷ Example

Let's conclude this example by obtaining the Šidák-adjusted multiple-comparison tests. We do this to illustrate Stata's capabilities to calculate these results. It is understood that searching across adjustment methods until you find the results you want is not a valid technique for obtaining significance levels.

```
. oneway wgt treat, noanova sidak
              Comparison of Average weight in grams by Fertilizer
                                 (Sidak)
  Row Mean-|
  Col Mean |          1           2           3
  ---------|------------------------------------
         2 |   -59.1667
           |      0.001
           |
         3 |    -33.25      25.9167
           |     0.041        0.116
           |
         4 |     -34.4      24.7667       -1.15
           |     0.035        0.137       1.000
```

We find results that are similar to the Bonferroni-adjusted numbers.

◁

Weighted data

▷ Example

oneway can work with weighted data as well as unweighted data. Let's assume that you wish to perform a one-way layout of the death rate on the four Census regions of the United States using state data. Your data contains three variables, drate (the death rate), region (the region), and pop (the population of the state).

To estimate the model, you type oneway drate region [weight=pop], although one typically abbreviates weight as w. We will also add the tabulate option so that you can see how the table of summary statistics differs for weighted data:

```
. oneway drate region [w=pop], tabulate
(analytic weights assumed)
  Census |           Summary of Death Rate
  region |     Mean   Std. Dev.        Freq.        Obs.
---------+------------------------------------------------
      NE |    97.15        5.82     49135283           9
  N Cntrl |    88.10        5.58     58865670          12
   South |    87.05       10.40     74734029          16
    West |    75.65        8.23     43172490          13
---------+------------------------------------------------
   Total |    87.34       10.43    2.259e+08          50
                    Analysis of Variance
    Source            SS          df      MS            F     Prob > F
------------------------------------------------------------------------
Between groups     2360.92281      3   786.974272     12.17    0.0000
 Within groups     2974.09635     46   64.6542685
------------------------------------------------------------------------
    Total          5335.01916     49   108.877942
Bartlett's test for equal variances:  chi2(3) =   5.4971  Prob>chi2 = 0.139
```

When the data is weighted, the summary table has four rather than three columns. The column labeled "Freq." reports the sum of the weights. The overall frequency is $2.259 \cdot 10^8$, meaning that there are approximately 226 million people in the U.S.

The ANOVA table is appropriately weighted. Also see [U] **14.1.6 weight**.

◁

Saved Results

oneway saves in r():

Scalars

r(N)	number of observations	r(df_m)	between group degrees of freedom
r(F)	F statistic	r(rss)	within group sum of squares
r(df_r)	within group degrees of freedom	r(chi2bart)	Bartlett's χ^2
r(mss)	between group sum of squares	r(df_bart)	Bartlett's degrees of freedom

Methods and Formulas

The model of one-way analysis of variance is

$$y_{ij} = \mu + \alpha_i + \epsilon_{ij}$$

for levels $i = 1, \ldots, k$ and observations $j = 1, \ldots, n_i$. Define $\overline{y}_i$ as the (weighted) mean of y_{ij} over j and $\overline{y}$ as the overall (weighted) mean of y_{ij}. Define w_{ij} as the weight associated with y_{ij}, which is 1 if the data is unweighted. w_{ij} is normalized to sum to $n = \sum_i n_i$ if aweights are used and is otherwise unnormalized. w_i refers to $\sum_j w_{ij}$ and w refers to $\sum_i w_i$.

The between group sum of squares is then

$$S_1 = \sum_i w_i (\overline{y}_i - \overline{y})^2$$

The total sum of squares is

$$S = \sum_i \sum_j w_{ij} (y_{ij} - \overline{y})^2$$

The within group sum of squares is given by $S_e = S - S_1$.

The between group mean square is $s_1^2 = S_1/(k-1)$ and the within group mean square is $s_e^2 = S_e/(w-k)$. The test statistic is $F = s_1^2/s_e^2$. See, for instance, Snedecor and Cochran (1989).

Bartlett's test

Bartlett's test assumes that you have m independent, normal random samples and tests the hypothesis $\sigma_1^2 = \sigma_2^2 = \cdots = \sigma_m^2$. The test statistic, M, is defined

$$M = \frac{(T-m)\ln \widehat{\sigma}^2 - \sum (T_i - 1)\ln \widehat{\sigma}_i^2}{1 + \frac{1}{3(m-1)} \sum \frac{1}{T_i - 1} - \frac{1}{T-m}}$$

where there are T overall observations and T_i observations in the ith group and

$$(T_i - 1)\widehat{\sigma}_i^2 = \sum_{j=1}^{T_i} (y_{ij} - \overline{y}_i)^2$$

$$(T-m)\widehat{\sigma}^2 = \sum_{i=1}^{m} (T_i - 1)\widehat{\sigma}_i^2$$

An approximate test of the homogeneity of variance is based on the statistic M with critical values obtained from the χ^2 distribution of $m-1$ degrees of freedom. See Bartlett (1937) or Judge et al. (1985, 447–449).

Multiple-comparison tests

Let's begin by reviewing the logic behind these adjustments. The "standard" t statistic for the comparison of two means is

$$t = \frac{\overline{y}_i - \overline{y}_j}{s\sqrt{\frac{1}{n_i} + \frac{1}{n_j}}}$$

where s is the overall standard deviation, $\overline{y}_i$ is the measured average of y in group i, and n_i is the number of observations in the group. We perform hypothesis tests by calculating this t statistic. We simultaneously choose a critical level α and look up the t statistic corresponding to that level in a table. We reject the hypothesis if our calculated t exceeds the value we looked up. Alternatively, since we have a computer at our disposal, we calculate the significance-level e corresponding to our calculated t statistic and, if $e < \alpha$, we reject the hypothesis.

This logic works well when we are performing a *single* test. Now consider what happens when we perform a number of separate tests, say n of them. Let's assume, just for discussion, that we set α equal to 0.05 and that we will perform 6 tests. For each test we have a 0.05 probability of falsely rejecting the equality-of-means hypothesis. Overall, then, our chances of falsely rejecting *at least one* of the hypotheses is $1 - (1 - .05)^6 \approx .26$ if the tests are independent.

The idea behind multiple-comparison tests is to control for the fact that we will perform multiple tests and to hold down our overall chances of falsely rejecting each hypothesis to α rather than letting it grow with each additional test we perform. (See Miller 1981 and Hochberg and Tamhane 1987 for rather advanced texts on multiple-comparison procedures.)

The Bonferroni adjustment (see Miller 1981; also see Winer, Brown, and Michels 1991, 158–166) does this by (falsely but approximately) asserting that the critical level we should use, a, is the true critical level α divided by the number of tests n, that is, $a = \alpha/n$. For instance, if we are going to perform 6 tests each at the .05 significance level, we want to adopt a critical level of $.05/6 \approx .00833$.

We can just as easily apply this logic to e, the significance level associated with our t statistic, as to our critical level α. If a comparison has a calculated significance of e, then its "real" significance, adjusted for the fact of n comparisons, is $n \cdot e$. If a comparison has a significance level of, say, .012, and we perform 6 tests, then its "real" significance is .072. If we adopt a critical level of .05, we cannot reject the hypothesis. If we adopt a critical level of .10, we can reject.

Of course, this calculation can go above 1, but that just means that there is no $\alpha < 1$ for which we could reject the hypothesis. (This situation arises due to the crude nature of the Bonferroni adjustment.) Stata handles this case by simply calling the significance level 1. Thus, the formula for the Bonferroni significance level is

$$e_b = \min(1, en)$$

where $n = k(k - 1)/2$ is the number of comparisons.

The Šidák adjustment (Šidák 1967; also see Winer, Brown, and Michels 1991, 165–166) is slightly different and provides a tighter bound. It starts with the assertion that

$$a = 1 - (1 - \alpha)^{1/n}$$

Turning this formula around and substituting calculated significance levels, we obtain

$$e_s = \min\left(1, 1 - (1 - e)^n\right)$$

For example, if the calculated significance is 0.012 and we perform 6 tests, the "real" significance is approximately 0.07.

The Scheffé test (Scheffé 1953, 1959; also see Winer, Brown, and Michels 1991, 191–195) differs in derivation, but it attacks the same problem. Let there be k means for which we want to make all the pairwise tests. Two means are declared significantly different if

$$t \geq \sqrt{(k-1)F(\alpha; k-1, \nu)}$$

where $F(\alpha; k-1, \nu)$ is the α-critical value of the F distribution with $k-1$ numerator and ν denominator degrees of freedom. Scheffé's test has the nicety that it never declares a contrast significant if the overall F test is nonsignificant.

Turning the test around, Stata calculates a significance level

$$\widehat{e} = F\left(\frac{t^2}{k-1}, k-1, \nu\right)$$

For instance, you have a calculated t statistic of 4.0 with 50 degrees of freedom. The simple t test says the significance level is .00021. The F test equivalent, 16 with 1 and 50 degrees of freedom, says the same. If you are doing three comparisons, however, you calculate an F test of 8.0 with 2 and 50 degrees of freedom, which says the significance level is .0010.

References

Altman, D. G. 1991. *Practical Statistics for Medical Research.* London: Chapman & Hall.

Bartlett, M. S. 1937. Properties of sufficiency and statistical tests. *Proceedings of the Royal Society,* Series A 160: 268–282.

Hochberg, Y. and A. C. Tamhane. 1987. *Multiple Comparison Procedures.* New York: John Wiley & Sons.

Judge, G. G., W. E. Griffiths, R. C. Hill, H. Lütkepohl, and T.-C. Lee. 1985. *The Theory and Practice of Econometrics.* 2d ed. New York: John Wiley & Sons.

Miller, R. G., Jr. 1981. *Simultaneous Statistical Inference.* 2d ed. New York: Springer-Verlag.

Scheffé, H. 1953. A method for judging all contrasts in the analysis of variance. *Biometrika* 40: 87–104.

——. 1959. *The Analysis of Variance.* New York: John Wiley & Sons.

Šidák, Z. 1967. Rectangular confidence regions for the means of multivariate normal distributions. *Journal of the American Statistical Association* 62: 626–633.

Snedecor, G. W. and W. G. Cochran. 1989. *Statistical Methods.* 8th ed. Ames, IA: Iowa State University Press.

Winer, B. J., D. R. Brown, and K. M. Michels. 1991. *Statistical Principles in Experimental Design.* 3d ed. New York: McGraw–Hill.

Also See

Complementary:	[R] **encode**
Related:	[R] **anova**, [R] **loneway**, [R] **table**
Background:	[U] **21.8 Accessing results calculated by other programs**

Title

oprobit — Maximum-likelihood ordered probit estimation

Syntax

$\left[\text{by } \textit{varlist}:\right]$ <u>oprobit</u> *depvar* $\left[\textit{varlist}\right]$ $\left[\textit{weight}\right]$ $\left[\text{if } \textit{exp}\right]$ $\left[\text{in } \textit{range}\right]$ $\left[, \text{ } \underline{\text{t}}\text{able}\right.$

<u>robust</u> <u>cl</u>uster(*varname*) <u>sc</u>ore(*newvarlist*) <u>l</u>evel(*#*) <u>off</u>set(*varname*)

maximize_options $\left.\right]$

fweights, iweights, and pweights are allowed; see [U] **14.1.6 weight**.

oprobit shares the features of all estimation commands; see [U] **23 Estimation and post-estimation commands**.

oprobit may be used with sw to perform stepwise estimation; see [R] **sw**.

Syntax for predict

predict $\left[\textit{type}\right]$ *newvarname(s)* $\left[\text{if } \textit{exp}\right]$ $\left[\text{in } \textit{range}\right]$ $\left[, \text{ } \left\{ \text{ p } | \text{ xb } | \text{ stdp } \right\} \right.$

<u>o</u>utcome(*outcome*) <u>nooff</u>set $\left.\right]$

Note that with the p option, you specify either one or k new variables depending upon whether the outcome() option is also specified (where k is the number of categories of *depvar*). With xb and stdp, one new variable is specified.

These statistics are available both in and out of sample; type predict ... if e(sample) ... if wanted only for the estimation sample.

Description

oprobit estimates ordered probit models of ordinal variable *depvar* on the independent variables *varlist*. The actual values taken on by the dependent variable are irrelevant except that larger values are assumed to correspond to "higher" outcomes. Up to 50 outcomes are allowed in Intercooled Stata; 20 outcomes in Small Stata.

See [R] **logistic** for a list of related estimation commands.

Options

table requests a table showing how the probabilities for the categories are computed from the fitted equation.

robust specifies that the Huber/White/sandwich estimator of variance is to be used in place of the traditional calculation; see [U] **23.11 Obtaining robust variance estimates**. robust combined with cluster() allows observations which are not independent within cluster (although they must be independent between clusters).

If you specify pweights, robust is implied; see [U] **23.13 Weighted estimation**.

cluster(*varname*) specifies that the observations are independent across groups (clusters) but not necessarily within groups. *varname* specifies to which group each observation belongs; e.g., cluster(personid) in data with repeated observations on individuals. cluster() affects the estimated standard errors and variance–covariance matrix of the estimators (VCE), but not the estimated coefficients; see [U] **23.11 Obtaining robust variance estimates**. cluster() can be used with pweights to produce estimates for unstratified cluster-sampled data, but see the svyoprob command in [R] **svy estimators** for a command designed especially for survey data.

cluster() implies robust; specifying robust cluster() is equivalent to typing cluster() by itself.

score(*newvarlist*) creates k new variables, where k is the number of observed outcomes. The first variable contains $\partial \ln L_j / \partial(\mathbf{x}_j \mathbf{b})$; the second variable contains $\partial \ln L_j / \partial(\_\text{cut1}_j)$; the third contains $\partial \ln L_j / \partial(\_\text{cut2}_j)$; and so on. Note that if you were to specify the option score(sc*), Stata would create the appropriate number of new variables and they would be named sc0, sc1, ... sc$(k-1)$.

level(*#*) specifies the confidence level, in percent, for confidence intervals. The default is level(95) or as set by set level; see [U] **23.5 Specifying the width of confidence intervals**.

offset(*varname*) specifies that *varname* is to be included in the model with coefficient constrained to be 1.

maximize_options control the maximization process; see [R] **maximize**. You should never have to specify them.

Options for predict

p, the default, calculates the predicted probabilities. If you do not also specify the outcome() option, you must specify k new variables, where k is the number of categories of the dependent variable. Say you estimated a model by typing oprobit result x1 x2, and result takes on three values. Then you could type predict p1 p2 p3, to obtain all three predicted probabilities. If you specify the outcome() option, then you specify one new variable. Say that result takes on values 1, 2, and 3. Then typing predict p1, outcome(1) would produce the same p1.

xb calculates the linear prediction. You specify one new variable; for example, predict linear, xb. The linear prediction is defined ignoring the contribution of the estimated cut points.

xb calculates the linear prediction. You specify one new variable; for example, predict linear, xb. The linear prediction is defined ignoring the contribution of the estimated cut points.

stdp calculates the standard error of the linear prediction. You specify one new variable; for example, predict se, stdp.

outcome(*outcome*) specifies for which outcome the predicted probabilities are to be calculated. outcome() should either contain a single value of the dependent variable, or one of #1, #2, ..., with #1 meaning the first category of the dependent variable, #2 the second category, etc.

nooffset is relevant only if you specified offset(*varname*) for oprobit. It modifies the calculations made by predict so that they ignore the offset variable; the linear prediction is treated as $\mathbf{x}_j \mathbf{b}$ rather than $\mathbf{x}_j \mathbf{b} + \text{offset}_j$.

Remarks

An ordered probit model is used to estimate relationships between an ordinal dependent variable and a set of independent variables. An *ordinal* variable is a variable that is categorical and ordered, for instance, "poor", "good", and "excellent", which might be the answer to one's current health status or the repair record of one's car. If there are only two outcomes, see [R] **logistic**, [R] **logit**, and [R] **probit**. This entry is concerned only with more than two outcomes. If the outcomes cannot be ordered (e.g., residency in the north, east, south and west), see [R] **mlogit**. This entry is concerned only with models in which the outcomes can be ordered.

In ordered probit, an underlying score is estimated as a linear function of the independent variables and a set of cut points. The probability of observing outcome i corresponds to the probability that the estimated linear function, plus random error, is within the range of the cut points estimated for the outcome:

$$\Pr(\text{outcome}_j = i) = \Pr(\kappa_{i-1} < \beta_1 x_{1j} + \beta_2 x_{2j} + \cdots + \beta_k x_{kj} + u_j \leq \kappa_i)$$

u_j is assumed to be normally distributed. In either case, one estimates the coefficients β_1, β_2, ..., β_k together with the cut points κ_1, κ_2, ..., κ_{I-1}, where I is the number of possible outcomes. κ_0 is taken as $-\infty$ and κ_I is taken as $+\infty$. All of this is a direct generalization of the ordinary two-outcome probit model.

▷ Example

In [R] **ologit**, we use a variation of the automobile data (see [U] **9 Stata's on-line tutorials and sample datasets**) to analyze the 1977 repair records of 66 foreign and domestic cars. We use ordered logit to explore the relationship of `rep77` in terms of `foreign` (origin of manufacture), `length` (a proxy for size), and `mpg`. Here we estimate the same model using ordered probit rather than ordered logit:

```
. oprobit rep77 foreign length mpg

Iteration 0:   log likelihood = -89.895098
Iteration 1:   log likelihood = -78.141221
Iteration 2:   log likelihood = -78.020314
Iteration 3:   log likelihood = -78.020025

Ordered probit estimates                        Number of obs   =         66
                                                LR chi2(3)      =      23.75
                                                Prob > chi2     =     0.0000
Log likelihood = -78.020025                     Pseudo R2       =     0.1321

------------------------------------------------------------------------------
     rep77 |      Coef.   Std. Err.      z    P>|z|     [95% Conf. Interval]
-----------+------------------------------------------------------------------
   foreign |   1.704861   .4246786     4.014   0.000     .8725057    2.537215
    length |   .0468675    .012648     3.706   0.000     .022078     .0716571
       mpg |   .1304559   .0378627     3.445   0.001     .0562464    .2046654
-----------+------------------------------------------------------------------
     _cut1 |   10.1589    3.076749              (Ancillary parameters)
     _cut2 |   11.21003   3.107522
     _cut3 |   12.54561   3.155228
     _cut4 |   13.98059   3.218786
------------------------------------------------------------------------------
```

We find that foreign cars have better repair records, as do larger cars and cars with better mileage ratings.

◁

Hypothesis tests and predictions

See [U] **23 Estimation and post-estimation commands** for instructions on obtaining the variance–covariance matrix of the estimators, predicted values, and hypothesis tests. Also see [R] **lrtest** for performing likelihood-ratio tests.

▷ Example

In the above example, we estimated the model `oprobit rep77 foreign length mpg`. The `predict` command can be used to obtain the predicted probabilities. You type `predict` followed by the names of the new variables to hold the predicted probabilities, ordering the names from low to high. In our data, the lowest outcome is "poor" and the highest "excellent". We have five categories and so must type five names following `predict`; the choice of name is up to us:

```
. predict poor fair avg good exc
(option p assumed; probabilities of outcomes)

. list make model exc good if rep77==.
```

	make	model	exc	good
3.	AMC	Spirit	.0006044	.0351813
10.	Buick	Opel	.0043803	.1133763
32.	Ford	Fiesta	.0002927	.0222789
44.	Merc.	Monarch	.0093209	.1700846
53.	Peugeot	604	.0734199	.4202766
56.	Plym.	Horizon	.001413	.0590294
57.	Plym.	Sapporo	.0197543	.2466034
63.	Pont.	Phoenix	.0234156	.266771

◁

❏ Technical Note

For ordered probit, `predict, xb` produces $S_j = x_{1j}\beta_1 + x_{2j}\beta_2 + \cdots + x_{kj}\beta_k$. Ordered probit is identical to ordered logit except that one uses a different distribution function for calculating probabilities. The ordered-probit predictions are then the probability that $S_j + u_j$ lies between a pair of cut points κ_{i-1} and κ_i. The formulas in the case of ordered probit are

$$\Pr(S_j + u < \kappa) = \Phi(\kappa - S_j)$$
$$\Pr(S_j + u > \kappa) = 1 - \Phi(\kappa - S_j) = \Phi(S_j - \kappa)$$
$$\Pr(\kappa_1 < S_j + u < \kappa_2) = \Phi(\kappa_2 - S_j) - \Phi(\kappa_1 - S_j)$$

Rather than using `predict` directly, we could calculate the predicted probabilities by hand.

```
. predict pscore, xb
. gen probexc = normprob(pscore-_b[_cut4])
. gen probgood = normprob(_b[_cut4]-pscore) - normprob(_b[_cut3]-pscore)
```

❏

Saved Results

oprobit saves in e():

Scalars

e(N)	number of observations	e(ll)	log likelihood
e(k_cat)	number of categories	e(ll_0)	log likelihood, constant-only model
e(df_m)	model degrees of freedom	e(chi2)	χ^2
e(r2_p)	pseudo R-squared	e(N_clust)	number of clusters

Macros

e(cmd)	ologit	e(vcetype)	covariance estimation method
e(depvar)	name of dependent variable	e(chi2type)	Wald or LR; type of model χ^2 test
e(wtype)	weight type	e(offset)	offset
e(wexp)	weight expression	e(predict)	program used to implement predict
e(clustvar)	name of cluster variable		

Matrices

e(b)	coefficient vector	e(V)	variance–covariance matrix of the estimators
e(cat)	category values		

Functions

e(sample)	marks estimation sample

Methods and Formulas

Please see the *Methods and Formulas* section of [R] **ologit**.

References

Aitchison, J. and S. D. Silvey. 1957. The generalization of probit analysis to the case of multiple responses. *Biometrika* 44: 131–140.

Goldstein, R. 1997. sg59: Index of ordinal variation and Neyman–Barton GOF. *Stata Technical Bulletin* 33: 10–12. Reprinted in *Stata Technical Bulletin Reprints*, vol. 6, pp. 145–147.

Greene, W. H. 1997. *Econometric Analysis*. 3d ed. Upper Saddle River, NJ: Prentice–Hall.

Long, J. S. 1997. *Regression Models for Categorical and Limited Dependent Variables*. Thousand Oaks, CA: Sage Publications.

Wolfe, R. 1998. sg86: Continuation-ratio models for ordinal response data. *Stata Technical Bulletin* 44: 18–21.

Wolfe, R. and W. W. Gould. 1998. sg76: An approximate likelihood-ratio test for ordinal response models. *Stata Technical Bulletin* 42: 24–27. Reprinted in *Stata Technical Bulletin Reprints*, vol. 7, pp. 199–204.

Also See

Complementary:	[R] **lincom**, [R] **linktest**, [R] **lrtest**, [R] **predict**, [R] **sw**, [R] **test**, [R] **testnl**, [R] **vce**, [R] **xi**
Related:	[R] **logistic**, [R] **mlogit**, [R] **ologit**, [R] **probit**, [R] **svy estimators**
Background:	[U] **16.5 Accessing coefficients and standard errors**, [U] **23 Estimation and post-estimation commands**, [U] **23.11 Obtaining robust variance estimates**, [U] **23.12 Obtaining scores**, [R] **maximize**

Title

---

order — Reorder variables in dataset

Syntax

order *varlist*

<u>mov</u>e *varname*$_1$ *varname*$_2$

aorder [*varlist*]

Description

order changes the order of the variables in the current dataset. The variables specified in *varlist* are moved, in order, to the front of the dataset.

move also reorders variables. move relocates *varname*$_1$ to the position of *varname*$_2$ and shifts the remaining variables, including *varname*$_2$, to make room.

aorder alphabetizes the variables specified in *varlist* and moves them to the front of the dataset. If no *varlist* is specified, _all is assumed.

Remarks

▷ Example

When using order, you must specify a *varlist*, but it is not necessary to specify all the variables in the dataset. For example:

```
. describe
Contains data from auto.dta
  obs:           74                          1978 Automobile Data
  vars:           6                          9 Jul 1998 12:47
  size:        2,368 (99.7% of memory free)
-------------------------------------------------------------------------------
  1. price     int    %8.0gc               Price
  2. weight    int    %8.0gc               Weight (lbs.)
  3. mpg       int    %8.0g                Mileage (mpg)
  4. make      str18  %-18s                Make and Model
  5. length    int    %8.0g                Length (in.)
  6. rep78     int    %8.0g                Repair Record 1978
-------------------------------------------------------------------------------
Sorted by:
     Note:  dataset has changed since last saved
. order make mpg
```

(Continued on next page)

```
. describe
Contains data from auto.dta
  obs:              74                     1978 Automobile Data
  vars:              6                     9 Jul 1998 12:47
  size:          2,368 (99.7% of memory free)
-------------------------------------------------------------------------------
  1. make       str18    %-18s            Make and Model
  2. mpg        int      %8.0g            Mileage (mpg)
  3. price      int      %8.0gc           Price
  4. weight     int      %8.0gc           Weight (lbs.)
  5. length     int      %8.0g            Length (in.)
  6. rep78      int      %8.0g            Repair Record 1978
-------------------------------------------------------------------------------
Sorted by:
     Note:  dataset has changed since last saved
```

If we now wanted length to be the last variable in our dataset, we could type order make mpg price weight rep78 length but it would be easier to use move:

```
. move length rep78
. describe
Contains data from auto.dta
  obs:              74                     1978 Automobile Data
  vars:              6                     9 Jul 1998 12:47
  size:          2,368 (99.7% of memory free)
-------------------------------------------------------------------------------
  1. make       str18    %-18s            Make and Model
  2. mpg        int      %8.0g            Mileage (mpg)
  3. price      int      %8.0gc           Price
  4. weight     int      %8.0gc           Weight (lbs.)
  5. rep78      int      %8.0g            Repair Record 1978
  6. length     int      %8.0g            Length (in.)
-------------------------------------------------------------------------------
Sorted by:
     Note:  dataset has changed since last saved
```

We now change our mind and decide that we would prefer that the variables be alphabetized.

```
. aorder
. describe
Contains data from auto.dta
  obs:              74                     1978 Automobile Data
  vars:              6                     9 Jul 1998 12:47
  size:          2,368 (99.6% of memory free)
-------------------------------------------------------------------------------
  1. length     int      %8.0g            Length (in.)
  2. make       str18    %-18s            Make and Model
  3. mpg        int      %8.0g            Mileage (mpg)
  4. price      int      %8.0gc           Price
  5. rep78      int      %8.0g            Repair Record 1978
  6. weight     int      %8.0gc           Weight (lbs.)
-------------------------------------------------------------------------------
Sorted by:
     Note:  dataset has changed since last saved
```

◁

❏ Technical Note

If your dataset contains variables named `year1`, `year2`, ..., `year19`, `year20`, `aorder` will order them correctly even though to most computer programs, `year10` is alphabetically between `year1` and `year2`.

❏

Methods and Formulas

`aorder` is implemented as an ado-file.

References

Gleason, J. R. 1997. dm51: Defining and recording variable orderings. *Stata Technical Bulletin* 40: 10–12. Reprinted in *Stata Technical Bulletin Reprints*, vol. 7, pp. 49–52.

Also See

Complementary: [R] **describe**

Related: [R] **edit**, [R] **rename**

Title

orthog — Orthogonal variables and orthogonal polynomials

Syntax

orthog [*varlist*] [*weight*] [if *exp*] [in *range*] , $\underline{\text{g}}$enerate(*newvarlist*)

[$\underline{\text{matr}}$ix(*matname*)]

orthpoly *varname* [*weight*] [if *exp*] [in *range*] , $\underline{\text{g}}$enerate(*newvarlist*)

[$\underline{\text{p}}$oly(*matname*) $\underline{\text{degree}}$(#)]

iweights, fweights, pweights, and aweights are allowed, see [U] **14.1.6 weight**.

Description

orthog orthogonalizes a set of variables, creating a new set of orthogonal variables (all of type double), using a modified Gram–Schmidt procedure (Golub and Van Loan 1989). Note that the order of the variables determines the orthogonalization; hence, the "most important" variables should be listed first.

orthpoly computes orthogonal polynomials for a single variable.

Options

generate(*newvarlist*) is not optional; it creates new orthogonal variables of type double. For orthog, *newvarlist* will contain the orthogonalized *varlist*. If varlist contains d variables, then so will *newvarlist*. For orthpoly, *newvarlist* will contain orthogonal polynomials of degree 1, 2, ..., d evaluated at *varname*, where d is as specified by degree(d). *newvarlist* can be specified by giving a list of exactly d new variable names, or it can be abbreviated using the styles *newvar* 1- *newvar d* or *newvar* *. For these two styles of abbreviation, new variables *newvar* 1, *newvar* 2, ..., *newvar d* are generated.

matrix(*matname*) (orthog only) creates a $(d+1) \times (d+1)$ matrix containing the matrix R defined by $X = QR$, where X is the $N \times (d+1)$ matrix representation of *varlist* plus a column of ones, and Q is the $N \times (d+1)$ matrix representation of *newvarlist* plus a column of ones (d = number of variables in *varlist* and N = number of observations).

degree(#) (orthpoly only) specifies the highest degree polynomial to include. Orthogonal polynomials of degree 1, 2, ..., $d = \#$ are computed. Default is $d = 1$.

poly(*matname*) (orthpoly only) creates a $(d+1) \times (d+1)$ matrix called *matname* containing the coefficients of the orthogonal polynomials. The orthogonal polynomial of degree $i \le d$ is

matname[i, $d+1$] + *matname*[i, 1]**varname* + *matname*[i, 2]**varname*^{2}
+ $\cdots$ + *matname*[i, i]**varname*^{i}

Note that the coefficients corresponding to the constant term are placed in the last column of the matrix. The last row of the matrix is all zero except for the last column which corresponds to the constant term.

Remarks

Orthogonal variables are useful for two reasons. The first is numerical accuracy for highly collinear variables. Stata's `regress` and other estimation commands can face a large amount of collinearity and still produce accurate results. But, at some point, these commands will drop variables "due to collinearity". If you know with certainty that the variables are not perfectly collinear, you may want to retain all of their effects in the model. By using `orthog` or `orthpoly` to produce a set of orthogonal variables, all variables will be present in the estimation results.

Users are more likely to find orthogonal variables useful for the second reason: ease of interpreting results. `orthog` and `orthpoly` create a set of variables such that the "effect" of all the preceding variables have been removed from each variable. For example, if one issues the command

> . orthog x1 x2 x3, generate(q1 q2 q3)

then the effect of the constant is removed from `x1` to produce `q1`, then the constant and `x1` are removed from `x2` to produce `q2`, and finally the constant, `x1`, and `x2` are removed from `x3` to produce `q3`. Hence,

$$q1 = r_{01} + r_{11}\,\text{x1}$$

$$q2 = r_{02} + r_{12}\,\text{x1} + r_{22}\,\text{x2}$$

$$q3 = r_{03} + r_{13}\,\text{x1} + r_{23}\,\text{x2} + r_{33}\,\text{x3}$$

This can be generalized and written in matrix notation as

$$X = QR$$

where X is the $N \times (d+1)$ matrix representation of *varlist* plus a column of ones, and Q is the $N \times (d+1)$ matrix representation of *newvarlist* plus a column of ones ($d =$ number of variables in *varlist* and $N =$ number of observations). The $(d+1) \times (d+1)$ matrix R is a permuted upper triangular matrix; i.e., R would be upper triangular if the constant were first, but the constant is last, so the first row/column has been permuted with the last row/column. Since Stata's estimation commands list the constant term last, this allows R, obtained via the `matrix()` option, to be used to transform estimation results.

▷ Example

Consider Stata's `auto.dta` dataset. Suppose we postulate a model in which `price` depends on the car's `length`, `weight`, headroom (`hdroom`), and trunk size (`trunk`). These predictors are collinear, but not extremely so—the correlations are not that close to 1:

```
. correlate length weight hdroom trunk
(obs=74)

         |   length   weight   hdroom    trunk
---------+------------------------------------
  length |   1.0000
  weight |   0.9460   1.0000
  hdroom |   0.5163   0.4835   1.0000
   trunk |   0.7266   0.6722   0.6620   1.0000
```

`regress` certainly has no trouble estimating this model:

```
. regress price length weight hdroom trunk

      Source |       SS       df       MS              Number of obs =      74
-------------+------------------------------           F(  4,     69) =   10.20
       Model |  236016580        4  59004145.0         Prob > F       =  0.0000
    Residual |  399048816       69  5783316.17         R-squared      =  0.3716
-------------+------------------------------           Adj R-squared  =  0.3352
       Total |  635065396       73  8699525.97         Root MSE       =  2404.9

-------------------------------------------------------------------------------
       price |      Coef.   Std. Err.       t    P>|t|     [95% Conf. Interval]
-------------+-----------------------------------------------------------------
      length |  -101.7092   42.12534    -2.414   0.018    -185.747   -17.67148
      weight |   4.753066   1.120054     4.244   0.000     2.51862    6.987512
      hdroom |  -711.5679   445.0204    -1.599   0.114   -1599.359    176.2235
       trunk |   114.0859   109.9488     1.038   0.303   -105.2559    333.4277
       _cons |   11488.47   4543.902     2.528   0.014    2423.638    20553.31
-------------------------------------------------------------------------------
```

However, we may believe *a priori* that `length` is the most important predictor, followed by `weight`, followed by `hdroom`, followed by `trunk`. Hence, we would like to remove the "effect" of `length` from all the other predictors; remove `weight` from `hdroom` and `trunk`; and remove `hdroom` from `trunk`. We can do this by running `orthog`. Then we estimate the model again using the orthogonal variables:

```
. orthog length weight hdroom trunk, gen(olength oweight ohdroom otrunk) matrix(R)

. regress price olength oweight ohdroom otrunk

      Source |       SS       df       MS              Number of obs =      74
-------------+------------------------------           F(  4,     69) =   10.20
       Model |  236016580        4  59004145.0         Prob > F       =  0.0000
    Residual |  399048816       69  5783316.17         R-squared      =  0.3716
-------------+------------------------------           Adj R-squared  =  0.3352
       Total |  635065396       73  8699525.97         Root MSE       =  2404.9

-------------------------------------------------------------------------------
       price |      Coef.   Std. Err.       t    P>|t|     [95% Conf. Interval]
-------------+-----------------------------------------------------------------
     olength |   1265.049   279.5584     4.525   0.000    707.3454    1822.753
     oweight |   1175.765   279.5584     4.206   0.000    618.0617    1733.469
     ohdroom |  -349.9916   279.5584    -1.252   0.215   -907.6954    207.7122
      otrunk |   290.0776   279.5584     1.038   0.303   -267.6262    847.7814
       _cons |   6165.257   279.5584    22.054   0.000    5607.553    6722.961
-------------------------------------------------------------------------------
```

Using the matrix R, we can transform the results obtained using the orthogonal predictors back to the metric of original predictors:

```
. matrix b = e(b)*inv(R)´
. matrix list b

b[1,5]
        length      weight     hdroom       trunk       _cons
y1  -101.70924   4.7530659  -711.56789   114.08591   11488.475
```

◁

◻ Technical Note

The matrix R obtained using the `matrix()` option with `orthog` can also be used to recover X (the original *varlist*) from Q (the orthogonalized *newvarlist*) one variable at a time. Continuing with the previous example, we illustrate how to recover the `trunk` variable:

```
. matrix C = R[1...,"trunk"]´
. matrix score double rtrunk = C
```

```
. compare rtrunk trunk
```

	count	--------- difference ----------		
	count	minimum	average	maximum
rtrunk>trunk	74	8.88e-15	1.91e-14	3.55e-14
jointly defined	74	8.88e-15	1.91e-14	3.55e-14
total	74			

In this example, the recovered variable `rtrunk` is almost exactly the same as the original `trunk`. When orthogonalizing many variables, this procedure can be performed as a check of the numerical soundness of the orthogonalization. Because of the ordering of the orthogonalization procedure, the last variable and ones near the end of the *varlist* are the most important ones to check.

❏

The `orthpoly` command effectively does for polynomial terms what the `orthog` command does for an arbitrary set of variables.

▷ Example

Again, consider the `auto.dta` dataset. Suppose we wish to fit the model

$$\mathtt{mpg} = \beta_0 + \beta_1\, \mathtt{weight} + \beta_2\, \mathtt{weight}^2 + \beta_3\, \mathtt{weight}^3 + \beta_4\, \mathtt{weight}^4 + \epsilon$$

We will first compute the regression with natural polynomials:

```
. gen double w1 = weight
. gen double w2 = w1*w1
. gen double w3 = w2*w1
. gen double w4 = w3*w1
. correlate w1-w4
(obs=74)
```

	w1	w2	w3	w4
w1	1.0000			
w2	0.9915	1.0000		
w3	0.9665	0.9916	1.0000	
w4	0.9279	0.9679	0.9922	1.0000

```
. regress mpg w1-w4
```

Source	SS	df	MS
Model	1652.73666	4	413.184164
Residual	790.722803	69	11.4597508
Total	2443.45946	73	33.4720474

```
Number of obs =      74
F( 4,    69) =   36.06
Prob > F      =  0.0000
R-squared     =  0.6764
Adj R-squared =  0.6576
Root MSE      =  3.3852
```

mpg	Coef.	Std. Err.	t	P>|t|	[95% Conf. Interval]	
w1	.0289302	.1161939	0.249	0.804	-.2028704	.2607307
w2	-.0000229	.0000566	-0.404	0.687	-.0001359	.0000901
w3	5.74e-09	1.19e-08	0.482	0.631	-1.80e-08	2.95e-08
w4	-4.86e-13	9.14e-13	-0.532	0.596	-2.31e-12	1.34e-12
_cons	23.94421	86.60667	0.276	0.783	-148.8314	196.7198

Some of the correlations among the powers of `weight` are very large, but this does not create any problems for `regress`. However, we may wish to look at the quadratic trend with the constant removed, the cubic trend with the quadratic and constant removed, etc. `orthpoly` will generate polynomial terms with this property:

```
. orthpoly weight, generate(pw*) deg(4) poly(P)
. regress mpg pw1-pw4
```

Source	SS	df	MS
Model	1652.73666	4	413.184164
Residual	790.722803	69	11.4597508
Total	2443.45946	73	33.4720474

Number of obs = 74
F(4, 69) = 36.06
Prob > F = 0.0000
R-squared = 0.6764
Adj R-squared = 0.6576
Root MSE = 3.3852

mpg	Coef.	Std. Err.	t	P>|t|	[95% Conf. Interval]
pw1	-4.638252	.3935245	-11.786	0.000	-5.423312 -3.853192
pw2	.8263545	.3935245	2.100	0.039	.0412947 1.611414
pw3	-.3068616	.3935245	-0.780	0.438	-1.091921 .4781982
pw4	-.209457	.3935245	-0.532	0.596	-.9945168 .5756027
_cons	21.2973	.3935245	54.119	0.000	20.51224 22.08236

Compare the p-values of the terms in the natural-polynomial regression with those in the orthogonal-polynomial regression. With orthogonal polynomials, it is easy to see that the pure cubic and quartic trends are nonsignificant and that the constant, linear, and quadratic terms each have $p < 0.05$.

The matrix P obtained with the `poly()` option can be used to transform coefficients for orthogonal polynomials to coefficients for natural polynomials:

```
. orthpoly weight, poly(P) deg(4)
. matrix b = e(b)*P
. matrix list b
b[1,5]
          deg1       deg2       deg3       deg4      _cons
y1    .02893016  -.00002291  5.745e-09  -4.862e-13  23.944212
```

◁

Methods and Formulas

`orthog` and `orthpoly` are implemented as ado-files.

`orthog`'s orthogonalization can be written in matrix notation as

$$X = QR$$

where X is the $N \times (d + 1)$ matrix representation of *varlist* plus a column of ones, and Q is the $N \times (d + 1)$ matrix representation of *newvarlist* plus a column of ones (d = number of variables in *varlist* and N = number of observations). The $(d + 1) \times (d + 1)$ matrix R is a permuted upper triangular matrix; i.e., R would be upper triangular if the constant were first, but the constant is last, so the first row/column has been permuted with the last row/column.

Q and R are obtained using a modified Gram–Schmidt procedure; see Golub and Van Loan (1989) for details. Note that the traditional Gram–Schmidt procedure is notoriously unsound, but the modified procedure is quite good. `orthog` performs two passes of this procedure.

`orthpoly` uses the Christoffel–Darboux recurrence formula (Abramowitz and Stegun 1968).

Both `orthog` and `orthpoly` normalize the orthogonal variables such that

$$Q'WQ = MI$$

where $W = \text{diag}(w_1, w_2, \ldots, w_N)$ with $w_1, w_2, \ldots, w_N$ the weights (all 1 if weights are not specified), and M is the sum of the weights (the number of observations if weights are not specified).

References

Abramowitz, M. and I. A. Stegun, ed. 1968. *Handbook of Mathematical Functions*, 7th printing. Washington, DC: National Bureau of Standards.

Golub, G. H. and C. F. Van Loan. 1989. *Matrix Computations*, 2nd ed. Baltimore: Johns Hopkins University Press, pp. 218–219.

Sribney, W. M. 1995. sg37: Orthogonal polynomials. *Stata Technical Bulletin* 25: 17–18. Reprinted in *Stata Technical Bulletin Reprints*, vol. 5, pp. 96–98.

Also See

Complementary:	[R] **matrix**
Related:	[R] **regress**
Background:	[U] **23 Estimation and post-estimation commands**

Title

outfile — Write ASCII-format dataset

Syntax

<u>ou</u>tfile [*varlist*] using *filename* [if *exp*] [in *range*] [, <u>c</u>omma <u>d</u>ictionary

    <u>nol</u>abel <u>noq</u>uote replace <u>w</u>ide]

Description

outfile writes data to a disk file in ASCII format, a format that can be read by other programs. The new file is *not* in Stata format; see [R] **save** for instructions on saving data for subsequent use in Stata.

The data saved by outfile can be read back by infile; see [R] **infile**. If *filename* is specified without an extension, '.raw' is assumed unless the dictionary option is specified, in which case '.dct' is assumed.

Options

comma causes Stata to write the file in comma-separated-value format. In this format, values are separated by commas rather than blanks. Missing values are written as two consecutive commas.

dictionary writes the file in Stata's data dictionary format. See [R] **infile (fixed format)** for a description of dictionaries. comma may not be specified with dictionary.

nolabel causes Stata to write the numeric values of labeled variables. The default is to write the labels enclosed in double quotes.

noquote prevents Stata from placing double quotes around the contents of string variables.

replace permits outfile to overwrite an existing dataset. replace may not be abbreviated.

wide causes Stata to write the data with one observation per line. The default is to split observations into lines of 80 characters or less.

Remarks

outfile enables data to be sent to a disk file for processing by a non-Stata program. Each observation is written as one or more records—records that will not exceed 80 characters unless you specify the wide option. The values of the variables are written using their current display formats, and unless the comma option is specified, each is prefixed with two blanks.

If you specify the dictionary option, the data is written in the same way, but in front of the data outfile writes a data dictionary describing the contents of the file.

▷ Example

You have entered into Stata data on seven employees in your firm. The data contains employee name, employee identification number, salary, and sex:

```
. list
        name            empno    salary  sex
 1. Carl Marks          57213    24,000  male
 2. Irene Adler         47229    27,000  female
 3. Adam Smith          57323    24,000  male
 4. David Wallis        57401    24,500  male
 5. Mary Rogers         57802    27,000  female
 6. Carolyn Frank       57805    24,000  female
 7. Robert Lawson       57824    22,500  male
```

If you now wish to use a program other than Stata with this data, you must somehow get the data over to that other program. The standard Stata-format dataset created by **save** will not do the job—it is written in a special format that only Stata understands. Most programs, however, understand ASCII datasets—standard text datasets that are like those produced by a text editor. You can tell Stata to produce such a dataset using **outfile**. Typing **outfile using employee** creates a dataset called **employee.raw** that contains all the data. We can use the Stata **type** command to review the resulting file:

```
. outfile using employee
. type employee.raw
     "Carl Marks"       57213      24000      "male"
     "Irene Adler"      47229      27000    "female"
      "Adam Smith"      57323      24000      "male"
    "David Wallis"      57401      24500      "male"
     "Mary Rogers"      57802      27000    "female"
   "Carolyn Frank"      57805      24000    "female"
   "Robert Lawson"      57824      22500      "male"
```

We see that the file contains the four variables and that Stata has surrounded the string variables with double quotes.

◁

❑ Technical Note

outfile is careful to columnize the data in case you want to read it using formatted input. In the example above, the first string has a %-16s display format. Stata wrote two leading blanks and then placed the string in a 16-character field. **outfile** always right-justifies string variables even when the display format requests left-justification.

The first number has a %9.0g format. The number is written as two blanks followed by the number, right-justified in a 9-character field. The second number has a %9.0gc format. **outfile** ignores the comma part of the format and also writes this number as two blanks followed by the number, right-justified in a 9-character field.

The last entry is really a numeric variable, but it has an associated value label. Its format is %-9.0g, so Stata wrote two blanks and then right-justified the value label in a 9-character field. Again, **outfile** right-justifies value labels even when the display format specifies left-justification.

❑

❏ Technical Note

The `nolabel` option prevents Stata from substituting value label strings for the underlying numeric value; see [U] **15.6.3 Value labels**. As we just said, the last variable in our data is really a numeric variable:

```
. outfile using employ2, nolabel
. type employ2.raw
      "Carl Marks"     57213        24000           0
      "Irene Adler"     47229        27000           1
      "Adam Smith"     57323        24000           0
    "David Wallis"     57401        24500           0
     "Mary Rogers"     57802        27000           1
   "Carolyn Frank"     57805        24000           1
   "Robert Lawson"     57824        22500           0
```

❏

❏ Technical Note

If you do not want Stata to place double quotes around the contents of string variables, specify the `noquote` option:

```
. outfile using employ3, noquote
. type employ3.raw
       Carl Marks     57213        24000        male
       Irene Adler     47229        27000      female
       Adam Smith     57323        24000        male
     David Wallis     57401        24500        male
      Mary Rogers     57802        27000      female
    Carolyn Frank     57805        24000      female
     Robert Lawson     57824        22500        male
```

❏

▷ Example

Stata never writes over an existing file unless told to do so explicitly. For instance, if the file `employee.raw` already exists and you attempted to overwrite it by typing `outfile using employee`, here is what would happen:

```
. outfile using employee
file employee.raw already exists
r(602);
```

You can tell Stata that it is okay to overwrite a file by specifying the `replace` option: `outfile using employee, replace`.

◁

(Continued on next page)

❏ Technical Note

Some programs prefer data that is separated by commas rather than by blanks. Stata will produce such a dataset if you specify the `comma` option:

```
. outfile using employee, comma

. type employee.raw
"Carl Marks",57213,24000,"male"
"Irene Adler",47229,27000,"female"
"Adam Smith",57323,24000,"male"
"David Wallis",57401,24500,"male"
"Mary Rogers",57802,27000,"female"
"Carolyn Frank",57805,24000,"female"
"Robert Lawson",57824,22500,"male"
```

❏

▷ Example

Finally, `outfile` can create data dictionaries that `infile` can read. Dictionaries are perhaps the best way to organize your raw data. A dictionary describes your data so that you do not have to remember the order of the variables, the number of variables, the variable names, or anything else. The file in which you store your data becomes self-documenting so that when you come back to it at some future date, you can understand what it is. See [R] **infile (fixed format)** for a full description of data dictionaries.

When you specify the `dictionary`, Stata writes a `.dct` file:

```
. outfile using employee, dict

. type employee.dct
dictionary {
        str15  name                "Employee name"
        float  empno               "Employee number"
        float  salary              "Annual salary"
        float  sex     :sexlbl     "Sex"
}
    "Carl Marks"        57213       24000       "male"
    "Irene Adler"       47229       27000       "female"
    "Adam Smith"        57323       24000       "male"
  "David Wallis"        57401       24500       "male"
   "Mary Rogers"        57802       27000       "female"
  "Carolyn Frank"       57805       24000       "female"
  "Robert Lawson"       57824       22500       "male"
```

◁

Also See

Complementary:	[R] **infile**
Related:	[R] **outsheet**
Background:	[U] **24 Commands to input data**

Title

> **outsheet** — Write spreadsheet-style dataset

Syntax

> <u>out</u>sheet [*varlist*] using *filename* [if *exp*] [in *range*] [, <u>non</u>ames <u>nol</u>abel <u>noq</u>uote
>
> <u>c</u>omma replace]

If *filename* is specified without a suffix, .out is assumed.

Description

outsheet writes data in tab- or comma-separated ASCII format into a file. This is the format that most spreadsheet programs prefer.

Options

nonames specifies that variable names are not to be written in the first line of the file; the file is to contain data values only.

nolabel specifies that the numeric values of labeled variables are to be written into the file rather than the label associated with each value.

noquote specifies that string variables are not to be enclosed in double quotes.

comma specifies comma-separated format rather than the default tab-separated format.

replace specifies that it is okay to overwrite *filename* if it already exists.

Remarks

If you wish to move your data into another program, you have the following alternatives:

1. The use of an external data-transfer program; see [U] **24.4 Transfer programs**.

2. Cutting and pasting from Stata's data editor if you use Stata for Windows or Stata for Macintosh; see [GSW] **A. Starting and stopping Stata for Windows 98/95/NT**.

3. Using outsheet.

4. Using outfile; see [R] **outfile**.

Concerning alternatives 3 and 4, outsheet is typically preferred if you are moving the data to a spreadsheet and outfile is probably better if you are moving data to another statistical program.

If your goal is to send data to another Stata user, you could use outsheet or outfile, but easiest is simply to send the .dta dataset. This will work even if you use Stata for Windows and your cohort uses Stata for Macintosh. All Statas can read each other's .dta files.

▷ Example

outsheet copies the data currently loaded in memory into the specified file. About all that can go wrong is the file you specify already exists:

```
. outsheet using tosend
file tosend.out already exists
r(602);
```

In that case, you can erase the file (see [R] **erase**), specify outsheet's replace option, or use a different filename. When all goes well, outsheet is silent:

```
. outsheet using tosend, replace
. _
```

If you are copying the data to a program other than a spreadsheet, remember to specify the nonames option:

```
. outsheet using foral, nonames
. _
```

◁

Also See

Complementary:	[R] **insheet**
Related:	[R] **outfile**
Background:	[U] **24 Commands to input data**

Author Index

This is the combined author index for the *Stata Reference Manual* and the *Stata User's Guide*.

Francia, R. S., [R] **swilk**

Frankel, M. R., [U] **23 Estimation and post-estimation commands**, [R] **_robust**, [R] **svy estimators**

Freeman, D. H., Jr., [R] **svytab**

Freeman, J., [R] **epitab**

Freeman, J. L., [R] **svytab**

Frison, L., [R] **sampsi**

Frome, E. L., [R] **qreg**

Fu, V. K., [R] **ologit**

Fuller, W. A., [U] **23 Estimation and post-estimation commands**, [R] **dfuller**, [R] **pperron**, [R] **regress**, [R] **_robust**, [R] **svy estimators**, [R] **svytab**

Fyler, D. C., [R] **epitab**

G

Gail, M. H., [U] **23 Estimation and post-estimation commands**, [R] **_robust**

Galbraith, R. F., [R] **meta**

Gall, J. R., Le, [R] **logistic**

Gallant, A. R., [R] **nl**

Galton, F., [R] **correlate**, [R] **cumul**

Gan, F. F., [R] **diagplots**

Gange, S. J., [R] **xtclog**, [R] **xtgee**, [R] **xtintreg**, [R] **xtlogit**, [R] **xtprobit**, [R] **xttobit**

Garrett, J. M., [R] **adjust**, [R] **logistic**, [R] **st stcox**, [R] **st stphplot**

Gauvreau, K., [U] **2 Resources for learning and using Stata**, [R] **dstdize**, [R] **logistic**, [R] **ltable**, [R] **sampsi**, [R] **sdtest**, [R] **st sts**

Geisser, S., [R] **anova**

Gentle, J. E., [R] **anova**, [R] **nl**

Gerkins, V. R., [R] **symmetry**

Gibbons, J. D., [R] **ksmirnov**, [R] **spearman**

Glass, R. I., [R] **epitab**

Gleason, J. R., [R] **bstrap**, [R] **cf**, [R] **correlate**, [R] **describe**, [R] **generate**, [R] **infile (fixed format)**, [R] **label**, [R] **loneway**, [R] **notes**, [R] **order**, [R] **summarize**

Gnanadesikan, R., [R] **cumul**, [R] **diagplots**

Godambe, V. P., [R] **svy estimators**

Goeden, G. B., [R] **kdensity**

Goldberger, A. S., [R] **tobit**

Goldblatt, A., [R] **epitab**

Goldstein, R., [R] **boxcox**, [R] **brier**, [R] **correlate**, [R] **impute**, [R] **nl**, [R] **ologit**, [R] **oprobit**, [R] **regression diagnostics**, [R] **signrank**, [R] **xtreg**

Golub, G. H., [R] **orthog**

Gonzalez, J. F., Jr., [R] **svy estimators**, [R] **svymean**

Goodall, C., [R] **ksm**, [R] **rreg**

Goodman, L. A., [R] **tabulate**

Gorman, J. W., [R] **sw**

Gosset, W. S., [R] **ttest**

Gould, W. W., [U] **21 Programming Stata**, [R] **bstrap**, [R] **collapse**, [R] **encode**, [R] **grmeanby**, [R] **hadimvo**, [R] **infile (fixed format)**,

[R] **kappa**, [R] **matrix mkmat**, [R] **mkspline**, [R] **ml**, [R] **ologit**, [R] **oprobit**, [R] **postfile**, [R] **qreg**, [R] **range**, [R] **reshape**, [R] **_robust**, [R] **rreg**, [R] **simul**, [R] **sktest**, [R] **smooth**, [R] **swilk**, [R] **testnl**

Gourieroux, C., [R] **arch**, [R] **arima**, [R] **hausman**

Govindarajulu, Z., [U] **16 Functions and expressions**

Grambsch, P. M., [R] **st stcox**

Graubard, B. I., [R] **svy estimators**, [R] **svylc**, [R] **svymean**, [R] **svytab**, [R] **svytest**

Graybill, F. A., [R] **centile**

Green, D. M., [R] **logistic**

Greene, W. H., [R] **biprobit**, [R] **clogit**, [R] **eivreg**, [R] **heckman**, [R] **heckprob**, [R] **mkspline**, [R] **mlogit**, [R] **ologit**, [R] **oprobit**, [R] **sureg**, [R] **testnl**, [R] **xtgls**, [R] **xtnbreg**, [R] **xtpois**, [R] **xtrchh**, [R] **xtreg**, [R] **zip**

Greenfield, S., [R] **alpha**, [R] **factor**, [R] **lincom**, [R] **mlogit**

Greenhouse, S., [R] **anova**

Greenland, S., [R] **ci**, [R] **epitab**, [R] **glogit**, [R] **ologit**, [R] **poisson**

Greenwood, M., [R] **ltable**, [R] **st sts**

Gregoire, A., [R] **kappa**

Griffith, J. L., [R] **brier**

Griffiths, W. E., [R] **boxcox**, [R] **glogit**, [R] **logit**, [R] **lrtest**, [R] **maximize**, [R] **mlogit**, [R] **oneway**, [R] **prais**, [R] **probit**, [R] **test**, [R] **xtgls**, [R] **xtreg**

Griliches, Z., [R] **xtgls**, [R] **xtrchh**

Grizzle, J. E., [R] **vwls**

Gronau, R., [R] **heckman**

Gross, A. J., [R] **ltable**

Grunfeld, Y., [R] **xtgls**, [R] **xtrchh**

Guilkey, D. K., [R] **xtprobit**

H

Hadi, A. S., [U] **21 Programming Stata**, [R] **eivreg**, [R] **hadimvo**, [R] **regression diagnostics**

Hadorn, D., [R] **brier**

Haenszel, W., [R] **epitab**, [R] **st sts test**

Hakkio, C. S., [R] **egen**

Halley, E., [R] **ltable**

Halvorsen, K., [R] **tabulate**

Hamerle, A., [R] **clogit**

Hamilton, J. D., [R] **arch**, [R] **arima**, [R] **corrgram**, [R] **dfuller**, [R] **pergram**, [R] **pperron**, [R] **xcorr**

Hamilton, L. C., [U] **2 Resources for learning and using Stata**, [U] **16 Functions and expressions**, [R] **anova**, [R] **bstrap**, [R] **ci**, [R] **diagplots**, [R] **factor**, [R] **ladder**, [R] **logit**, [R] **lv**, [R] **mlogit**, [R] **probit**, [R] **regress**, [R] **regression diagnostics**, [R] **rreg**, [R] **simul**, [R] **summarize**

Hampel, F. R., [R] **ml**, [R] **rreg**

Rao, J. N. K., [R] **svytab**
Ratkowsky, D. A., [R] **nl**
Rawlings, J. O., [R] **regress**
Redelmeier, D. A., [R] **brier**
Reinsch, C., [R] **matrix symeigen**
Relles, D. A., [R] **rreg**
Richardson, M. W., [R] **alpha**
Riley, A. R., [R] **list**
Roberson, P. K., [R] **logistic**
Robins, J. M., [R] **epitab**
Robyn, D. L., [R] **cumul**
Rodríguez, G., [R] **nbreg**, [R] **poisson**
Rogers, W. H., [U] **23 Estimation and post-estimation**
      commands, [R] **brier**, [R] **glm**, [R] **heckman**,
      [R] **lincom**, [R] **ml**, [R] **mlogit**, [R] **nbreg**,
      [R] **poisson**, [R] **qreg**, [R] **regress**, [R] **_robust**,
      [R] **rreg**, [R] **sktest**, [R] **st stcox**
Ronning, G., [R] **clogit**
Rosner, B., [R] **sampsi**
Ross, G. J. S., [R] **nl**
Rothman, K. J., [R] **ci**, [R] **dstdize**, [R] **epitab**,
      [R] **glogit**, [R] **poisson**
Rousseeuw, P. J., [R] **hadimvo**, [R] **qreg**,
      [R] **regression diagnostics**, [R] **rreg**
Royall, R. M., [U] **23 Estimation and post-estimation**
      commands, [R] **_robust**
Royston, P., [R] **boxcox**, [R] **by**, [R] **centile**,
      [R] **cusum**, [R] **diagplots**, [R] **dotplot**, [R] **for**,
      [R] **fracpoly**, [R] **glm**, [R] **ksm**, [R] **list**,
      [R] **lnskew0**, [R] **nl**, [R] **range**, [R] **regress**,
      [R] **sktest**, [R] **swilk**
Rubin, D. B., [R] **impute**
Rubinfeld, D., [R] **biprobit**, [R] **heckprob**
Ruppert, D., [R] **rreg**
Rush, M., [R] **egen**
Rutherford, E., [R] **poisson**
Ryan, P., [R] **pctile**
Ryan, T. P., [R] **qc**, [R] **regression diagnostics**

S

Salgado-Ugarte, I., [R] **kdensity**, [R] **ksm**, [R] **smooth**
Sanders, R., [R] **brier**
Sargan, J. D., [R] **prais**
Särndal, C.-E., [R] **svy**, [R] **svy estimators**
Sasieni, P., [R] **dotplot**, [R] **ksm**, [R] **list**, [R] **nptrend**,
      [R] **smooth**, [R] **st stcox**
Satterthwaite, F. E., [R] **svymean**, [R] **ttest**
Savage, I. R., [R] **st sts test**
Saw, S. L. C., [R] **qc**
Scheaffer, R. L., [R] **svy**
Scheffé, H., [R] **anova**, [R] **oneway**
Schlesselman, J. J., [R] **epitab**
Schmid, C. H., [R] **brier**
Schmidt, P., [R] **regression diagnostics**
Schmidt, T. J., [R] **egen**, [R] **window dialog**
Schneider, W., [R] **meta**

Schnell, D., [R] **regress**, [R] **_robust**, [R] **svytab**
Schoenfeld, D., [R] **st stcox**, [R] **st streg**
Scott, A. J., [R] **svymean**, [R] **svytab**
Scott, C., [R] **svy estimators**, [R] **svymean**
Scotto, M. G., [R] **st streg**
Seed, P., [R] **sampsi**
Selvin, S., [R] **anova**, [R] **factor**, [R] **ltable**,
      [R] **poisson**, [R] **st stcox**, [R] **tabulate**
Sempos, C. T., [R] **dstdize**, [R] **ltable**, [R] **st stcox**
Shah, B. V., [R] **svytab**
Shao, J., [R] **svy estimators**
Shapiro, S., [R] **epitab**
Shapiro, S. S., [R] **swilk**
Sharp, S., [R] **meta**
Shewhart, W. A., [R] **qc**
Shimizu, M., [R] **kdensity**, [R] **ksm**
Šidák, Z., [R] **oneway**
Silverman, B. W., [R] **kdensity**
Silvey, S. D., [R] **ologit**, [R] **oprobit**
Simonoff, J. S., [R] **hadimvo**
Simor, I. S., [R] **kappa**
Skinner, C. J., [R] **svy**, [R] **svy estimators**,
      [R] **svymean**
Slone, D., [R] **epitab**
Smirnov, N. V., [R] **ksmirnov**
Smith, B. T., [R] **matrix symeigen**
Smith, G. D., [R] **meta**
Smith, H., [R] **regress**, [R] **sw**
Smith, J. M., [R] **fracpoly**
Smith, R. L., [R] **st streg**
Smith, T. M. F., [R] **svy**
Snedecor, G. W., [R] **anova**, [R] **correlate**, [R] **means**,
      [R] **oneway**, [R] **signrank**
Snell, E. J., [R] **st stcox**, [R] **st streg**
Soon, T. W., [R] **qc**
Spearman, C., [R] **factor**, [R] **spearman**
Spieldman, R. S., [R] **symmetry**
Spiegelhalter, D. J., [R] **brier**
Spitzer, J. J., [R] **boxcox**
Sprent, P., [R] **signrank**
Sribney, W. M., [R] **matrix mkmat**, [R] **ml**,
      [R] **orthog**, [R] **_robust**, [R] **signrank**, [R] **svy**,
      [R] **svy estimators**, [R] **svydes**, [R] **svylc**,
      [R] **svymean**, [R] **svytab**, [R] **svytest**
Starmer, C. F., [R] **vwls**
Steel, R. G. D., [R] **anova**
Stegun, I. A., [U] **16 Functions and expressions**,
      [R] **orthog**
Steichen, T. J., [R] **kappa**, [R] **meta**
Steiger, W., [R] **qreg**
Stein, C., [R] **bstrap**
Stepniewska, K. A., [R] **nptrend**
Sterne, J., [R] **meta**
Stewart, J., [R] **ltable**
Stewart, M. B., [R] **tobit**
Stigler, S. M., [R] **correlate**, [R] **qreg**
Stine, R., [R] **bstrap**

Stoll, B. J., [R] **epitab**

Stolley, P. D., [R] **epitab**

Stoto, M. A., [R] **lv**

Street, J. O., [R] **rreg**

Stuart, A., [R] **centile**, [R] **qreg**, [R] **summarize**,
  [R] **svy**, [R] **symmetry**, [R] **tobit**

Sullivan, G., [R] **regress**, [R] **_robust**, [R] **svytab**

Svennerholm, A. M., [R] **epitab**

Swagel, P., [U] **24 Commands to input data**

Swamy, P., [R] **xtrchh**

Swed, F. S., [R] **runtest**

Sweeting, T. J., [R] **st streg**

Swensson, B., [R] **svy**, [R] **svy estimators**

Swets, J. A., [R] **logistic**

T

Tamhane, A. C., [R] **oneway**

Tan, W. Y., [U] **23 Estimation and post-estimation commands**, [R] **_robust**

Taniuchi, T., [R] **kdensity**

Tanner, W. P., Jr., [R] **logistic**

Tapia, R. A., [R] **kdensity**

Tarlov, A. R., [R] **alpha**, [R] **factor**, [R] **lincom**,
  [R] **mlogit**

Taub, A. J., [R] **xtreg**

Teukolsky, S. A., [U] **16 Functions and expressions**,
  [R] **bitest**, [R] **matrix symeigen**, [R] **range**,
  [R] **vwls**

Theil, H., [R] **ivreg**, [R] **pcorr**, [R] **prais**, [R] **reg3**

Therneau, T. M., [R] **st stcox**

Thomas, D. C., [R] **st sttocc**

Thomas, D. R., [R] **svytab**

Thompson, J. C., [R] **diagplots**

Thompson, J. R., [R] **kdensity**

Thompson, S. K., [R] **svy**

Thompson, W. D., [R] **epitab**

Thomson, G. H., [R] **factor**

Thorndike, F., [R] **poisson**

Tibshirani, R., [R] **bstrap**

Tidmarsh, C. E., [R] **fracpoly**

Tilford, J. M., [R] **logistic**

Tippett, L. H. C., [R] **st streg**

Tobias, A., [R] **logistic**, [R] **meta**, [R] **sdtest**, [R] **st streg**

Tobin, J., [R] **tobit**

Toman, R. J., [R] **sw**

Torrie, J. H., [R] **anova**

Trichopoulos, D., [R] **epitab**

Tufte, E. R., [R] **stem**

Tukey, J. W., [R] **if**, [R] **ladder**, [R] **linktest**, [R] **lv**,
  [R] **ml**, [R] **regress**, [R] **regression diagnostics**,
  [R] **rreg**, [R] **smooth**, [R] **spikeplt**, [R] **stem**

Tukey, P. A., [U] **9 Stata's on-line tutorials and sample datasets**, [R] **diagplots**, [R] **ksm**

Tyler, J. H., [R] **regress**

U

Ureta, M., [R] **xtreg**

V

Valman, H. B., [R] **fracpoly**

Van Loan, C. F., [R] **orthog**

Velleman, P. F., [R] **regression diagnostics**, [R] **smooth**

Ven, W. P. M. M. van de, [R] **biprobit**, [R] **heckprob**

Verbeek, A., [R] **tutorials**

Vetterling, W. T., [U] **16 Functions and expressions**,
  [R] **bitest**, [R] **matrix symeigen**, [R] **range**,
  [R] **vwls**

Vidmar, S., [R] **means**

W

Wagner, H. M., [R] **qreg**

Walker, A. M., [R] **epitab**

Wallis, W. A., [R] **kwallis**

Ware, J. E., Jr., [R] **alpha**, [R] **factor**, [R] **lincom**,
  [R] **mlogit**

Warren, K., [R] **epitab**

Wasserman, W., [R] **regression diagnostics**

Watson, G. S., [R] **prais**, [R] **regression diagnostics**

Webster, A. D. B., [R] **fracpoly**

Wedderburn, R. W. M., [R] **glm**, [R] **xtgee**

Weesie, J., [R] **alpha**, [R] **factor**, [R] **for**, [R] **generate**,
  [R] **hausman**, [R] **label**, [R] **logistic**, [R] **matrix define**, [R] **regress**, [R] **reshape**, [R] **sample**,
  [R] **simul**, [R] **st stsplit**, [R] **tutorials**

Wei, L. J., [U] **23 Estimation and post-estimation commands**, [R] **_robust**, [R] **st stcox**

Weibull, W., [R] **st streg**

Weisberg, H. F., [R] **summarize**

Weisberg, S., [R] **boxcox**, [R] **regress**, [R] **regression diagnostics**

Welch, B. L., [R] **ttest**

Welch, F. R., [U] **2 Resources for learning and using Stata**

Wellington, J. F., [R] **qreg**

Wells, K. E., [R] **lincom**, [R] **mlogit**

Welsch, R. E., [R] **regression diagnostics**

West, K., [R] **newey**

West, S., [R] **epitab**

White, H., [U] **23 Estimation and post-estimation commands**, [R] **ivreg**, [R] **newey**, [R] **prais**,
  [R] **regress**, [R] **_robust**

White, P. O., [R] **factor**

Whitney, D. R., [R] **kwallis**, [R] **signrank**

Wilcoxon, F., [R] **kwallis**, [R] **signrank**, [R] **st sts test**

Wilk, M. B., [R] **cumul**, [R] **diagplots**, [R] **swilk**

Wilkinson, J. H., [R] **matrix symeigen**

Wilks, D. S., [R] **brier**

Wilks, S. S., [R] **canon**, [R] **hotel**

Williams, B., [R] **svy**

Winer, B. J., [R] **anova**, [R] **loneway**, [R] **oneway**

Subject Index

This is the combined subject index for the *Stata Reference Manual* and the *Stata User's Guide*. Readers interested in graphics topics should see the index in the *Stata Graphics Manual*.

Semicolons set off the most important entries from the rest. Sometimes no entry will be set off with semicolons; this means all entries are equally important.

& (and), *see* logical operators

| (or), *see* logical operators

~ (not), *see* logical operators

! (not), *see* logical operators

!, *see* shell command

== (equality), *see* relational operators

!= (not equal), *see* relational operators

~= (not equal), *see* relational operators

< (less than), *see* relational operators

<= (less than or equal), *see* relational operators

> (greater than), *see* relational operators

>= (greater than or equal), *see* relational operators

A

Aalen–Nelson cumulative hazard, [R] **st sts**, [R] **st sts generate**, [R] **st sts graph**, [R] **st sts list**

abbreviations, [U] **14.2 Abbreviation rules**; [U] **14.1.1 varlist**, [U] **14.4 varlists**
unabbreviating variable list, [R] **syntax**, [R] **unab**

aborting command execution, [U] **12 The Break key**, [U] **13 Keyboard use**

about command, [R] **about**

abs() function, [U] **16.3.1 Mathematical functions**, [R] **functions**

absolute value function, *see* abs() function

absorption in regression, [R] **areg**

ac command, [R] **corrgram**

accelerated failure-time model, [R] **st streg**

Access, Microsoft, reading data from, [U] **24.4 Transfer programs**

accum matrix subcommand, [R] **matrix accum**

acos() function, [U] **16.3.1 Mathematical functions**, [R] **functions**

acprplot command, [R] **regression diagnostics**

actuarial tables, [R] **ltable**

added-variable plots, [R] **regression diagnostics**

addition across observations, [U] **16.3.6 Special functions**, [R] **egen**

addition across variables, [R] **egen**

addition operator, *see* arithmetic operators

adjust command, [R] **adjust**

adjusted Kaplan–Meier survivor function, [R] **st sts**

adjusted partial residual plot, [R] **regression diagnostics**

.ado filename suffix, [U] **14.6 File-naming conventions**

ado-files, [U] **2.4 The Stata Technical Bulletin**, [U] **20 Ado-files**, [U] **21.11 Ado-files**; [R] **sysdir**, [R] **version**, *also see* programs
editing, [R] **doedit**
display version of, [R] **which**
downloading, [U] **32 Using the Internet to keep up to date**
installing, [U] **20.8 How do I obtain and install STB updates?**, [R] **net**
location, [U] **20.5 Where does Stata look for ado-files?**
long lines, [U] **21.11.2 Comments and long lines in ado-files**, [R] **#delimit**
official, [U] **32 Using the Internet to keep up to date**, [R] **update**
verifying installation, [R] **which**, *also see* verinst command

adopath command, [U] **20.5 Where does Stata look for ado-files?**, [R] **sysdir**

adosize parameter, [R] **sysdir**; [U] **21.11 Ado-files**, [R] **macro**

aggregate functions, [R] **egen**

aggregate statistics, dataset of, [R] **collapse**

agreement, interrater, [R] **kappa**

algebraic expressions, functions, and operators, [U] **16 Functions and expressions**, [U] **16.3 Functions**, [R] **matrix define**

_all, [U] **14.1.1 varlist**

alpha coefficient, Cronbach's, [R] **alpha**

alpha command, [R] **alpha**

alphabetizing
observations, [R] **sort**; [R] **gsort**
variable names, [R] **order**

alphanumeric variables, *see* string variables

analysis of covariance, *see* ANCOVA

analysis of variance, *see* ANOVA

analysis-of-variance test of normality, [R] **swilk**

analytic weights, [U] **14.1.6 weight**, [U] **23.13.2 Analytic weights**

and operator, [U] **16.2.4 Logical operators**

ANCOVA, [R] **anova**

ANOVA, [R] **anova**, [R] **loneway**, [R] **oneway**
Kruskal–Wallis, [R] **kwallis**
repeated measures, [R] **anova**

anova command, [R] **anova**; *also see* estimation commands
with string variables, [R] **encode**

aorder command, [R] **order**

append command, [R] **append**; [U] **25 Commands for combining data**

_append variable, [R] **append**

appending data, [R] **append**; [U] **25 Commands for combining data**

appending files, [R] **copy**

appending rows and columns to matrix, [R] **matrix define**

AR, *see* autocorrelation

[frequency=*exp*] modifier, [U] **14.1.6 weight**,
    [U] **23.13.1 Frequency weights**
frequency weights, [U] **14.1.6 weight**,
    [U] **23.13.1 Frequency weights**
fsl command, *see Getting Started with Stata for Unix*
functions, [U] **16.3 Functions**, [R] **functions**
    aggregate, [R] **egen**
    combinatorial, [U] **16.3.1 Mathematical functions**
    creating datasets of, [R] **collapse**, [R] **obs**
    date, [U] **27.2.2 Conversion into elapsed dates**,
        [U] **27.2.4 Other date functions**; [U] **16.3.3 Date
        functions**
    graphing, [R] **range**, *also see Stata Graphics Manual*
    link, [R] **glm**
    mathematical, [U] **16.3.1 Mathematical functions**
    matrix, [U] **17.8 Matrix functions**, [R] **matrix
        define**
    piecewise linear, [R] **mkspline**
    random number, [U] **16.3.2 Statistical functions**,
        [R] **generate**
    statistical, [U] **16.3.2 Statistical functions**
    string, [U] **16.3.5 String functions**;
        [U] **26 Commands for dealing with strings**
    survivor; *see* survivor function
    time-series, [U] **16.3.4 Time-series functions**
[fweight=*exp*] modifier, [U] **14.1.6 weight**,
    [U] **23.13.1 Frequency weights**

G

g2 inverse of matrix, [R] **matrix define**, [R] **matrix svd**
gamma command, [R] **weibull**; *also see* estimation
    commands
gammap() function, [U] **16.3.2 Statistical functions**,
    [R] **functions**
GARCH, [R] **arch**
garch command, [R] **arch**; *also see* estimation
    commands
Gauss–Hermite quadrature, [R] **quadchk**
Gauss, reading data from, [U] **24.4 Transfer programs**
GEE (generalized estimating equations), [R] **xtgee**;
    [R] **xtclog**, [R] **xtintreg**, [R] **xtlogit**, [R] **xtnbreg**,
    [R] **xtpois**, [R] **xtprobit**, [R] **xttobit**
generalized autoregressive conditional heteroscedasticity,
    [R] **arch**
generalized estimating equations, *see* GEE
generalized gamma survival regression, [R] **st streg**
generalized inverse of matrix, [R] **matrix define**;
    [R] **matrix svd**
generalized least squares, *see* FGLS
generalized linear models, *see* glm command
generate command, [R] **generate**; [R] **egen**
geometric mean, [R] **means**
get() matrix function, [R] **matrix get**
getting started, [U] **1 Read this—it will help**
Getting Started with Stata manuals, [U] **1.1 Getting
    Started with Stata**
    keyword search of, [U] **8 Stata's on-line help and
        search facilities**, [R] **search**

gettoken command, [R] **gettoken**
gladder command, [R] **ladder**
glm command, [R] **glm**; *also see* estimation commands
global command, [U] **21.3.2 Global macros**,
    [U] **21.3.8 Advanced global macro
        manipulation**, [R] **macro**
glogit command, [R] **glogit**; *also see* estimation
    commands
glsaccum matrix subcommand, [R] **matrix accum**
gnbreg command, [R] **nbreg**; *also see* estimation
    commands
gompertz command, [R] **weibull**; *also see* estimation
    commands
Gompertz survival regression, [R] **st streg**
Goodman and Kruskal's gamma, [R] **tabulate**
goodness-of-fit tests, [R] **brier**, [R] **diagplots**,
    [R] **ksmirnov**, [R] **logistic**, [R] **regression
        diagnostics**, [R] **swilk**
gph command, *see Stata Graphics Manual*
.gph files, [U] **14.6 File-naming conventions**; *also see
    Stata Graphics Manual*
gphdot and gphpen commands, *see Stata Graphics
    Manual*
gphprint command, *see Stata Graphics Manual*
gprobit command, [R] **glogit**; *also see* estimation
    commands
graph command, *see Stata Graphics Manual*
graphs, *also see Stata Graphics Manual*
    added-variable plot, [R] **regression diagnostics**
    adjusted Kaplan–Meier survival curves, [R] **st sts**
    adjusted partial residual plot, [R] **regression
        diagnostics**
    augmented component-plus-residual plot,
        [R] **regression diagnostics**
    augmented partial residual plot, [R] **regression
        diagnostics**
    autocorrelations, [R] **corrgram**
    baseline hazard and survival, [R] **st stcox**, [R] **st sts**
    binary variable cumulative sum, [R] **cusum**
    component-plus-residual, [R] **regression diagnostics**
    cross-sectional time-series data, [R] **xtdata**
    cumulative distribution, [R] **cumul**
    cumulative hazard function, [R] **st streg**
    cumulative spectral density, [R] **cumsp**
    density, [R] **kdensity**
    derivatives, [R] **range**, [R] **testnl**
    diagnostic, [R] **diagplots**
    dotplot, [R] **dotplot**
    eigenvalues after factor, [R] **factor**
    error-bar charts, [R] **serrbar**
    fonts, *see* fonts
    fractional polynomial, [R] **fracpoly**
    functions, [R] **obs**, [R] **range**
    hazard function, [R] **st streg**
    highlighting points, [R] **hilite**
    histograms, [R] **hist**; [R] **kdensity**
    integrals, [R] **range**
    Kaplan–Meier survival curves, [R] **st sts**
    ladder-of-powers histograms, [R] **ladder**
Continued on next page

M

Continued on next page

R

S

sweep matrix operator, [R] **matrix define**

swilk command, [R] **swilk**

Sybase, reading data from, [U] **24.4 Transfer programs**

symbolic forms, [R] **anova**

symeigen matrix subcommand, [R] **matrix symeigen**

symmetry command, [R] **symmetry**

symmetry plots, [R] **diagplots**

symmetry, test of, [R] **symmetry**

symmi command, [R] **symmetry**

symplot command, [R] **diagplots**

syntax command, [R] **syntax**

syntax diagrams explained, [R] **intro**

syntax of Stata's language, [U] **14 Language syntax**, [R] **syntax**

sysdir command, [R] **sysdir**; [U] **20.5 Where does Stata look for ado-files?**

Systat, reading data from, [U] **24.4 Transfer programs**

system estimators, [R] **reg3**

system macros, *see* S_ macros

system parameters, [R] **query**, [R] **set**

system variables, [U] **16.4 System variables (_variables)**

T

%t formats, [U] **15.5.3 Time-series formats**, [U] **27.3.3 Time-series formats**, [R] **format**

t distribution
  cdf, [U] **16.3.2 Statistical functions**, [R] **functions**
  confidence interval for mean, [R] **ci**
  testing equality of means, [R] **ttest**; [R] **hotel**, [R] **svymean**

tab characters, show, [R] **type**

tab1 and tab2 commands, [R] **tabulate**

tabdisp command, [R] **tabdisp**

tabi command, [R] **tabulate**

table command, [R] **table**

tables
  contingency, [R] **svytab**, [R] **table**, [R] **tabulate**
  epidemiologic, [R] **epitab**
  formatting numbers in, [R] **format**
  frequency, [R] **tabulate**; [R] **svytab**, [R] **table**, [R] **tabsum**, [R] **xttab**
  life, [R] **ltable**
  N-way, [R] **table**; [R] **tabdisp**
  of means, [R] **table**, [R] **tabsum**
  of statistics, [R] **table**; [R] **tabdisp**
  printing, [U] **18 Printing and preserving output**

tabodds command, [R] **epitab**

tabulate and tabi commands, [R] **tabulate**

tan() function, [U] **16.3.1 Mathematical functions**, [R] **functions**

tangent function, [U] **16.3.1 Mathematical functions**, [R] **functions**

tau, [R] **spearman**

TDT test, [R] **symmetry**

technical support, [U] **2.8 Technical support**

tempfile command, [R] **macro**

tempname command, [R] **macro**, [R] **matrix**, [R] **scalar**

temporary files, [R] **macro**; [U] **21.7.3 Temporary files**, [R] **preserve**, [R] **scalar**

temporary names, [U] **21.7.2 Temporary scalars and matrices**, [R] **macro**, [R] **matrix**, [R] **scalar**

temporary variables, [R] **macro**; [U] **21.7.1 Temporary variables**

tempvar command, [R] **macro**

termcap(5), [U] **13 Keyboard use**

terminal
  obtaining input from, [R] **display (for programmers)**
  suppressing output, [R] **quietly**

terminfo(4), [U] **13 Keyboard use**

test command, [R] **test**; [U] **23.9 Performing hypothesis tests on the coefficients**; [R] **anova**

test-based confidence intervals, [R] **epitab**

testnl command, [R] **testnl**

testparm command, [R] **test**

tests
  association, [R] **epitab**, [R] **svytab**, [R] **tabulate**
  binomial proportion, [R] **bitest**
  Breusch–Pagan, [R] **mvreg**, [R] **sureg**
  Cox proportional hazards assumption, [R] **st stcox**, [R] **st stphplot**
  epidemiological tables, [R] **epitab**
  equality of coefficients, [R] **svytest**, [R] **test**, [R] **testnl**
  equality of distributions, [R] **ksmirnov**, [R] **kwallis**, [R] **signrank**
  equality of means, [R] **ttest**; [R] **hotel**
  equality of medians, [R] **signrank**
  equality of proportions, [R] **bitest**, [R] **prtest**
  equality of survivor functions, [R] **st sts test**
  equality of variance, [R] **sdtest**
  homogeneity, [R] **epitab**
  heterogeneity, [R] **epitab**
  heteroscedasticity, [R] **regression diagnostics**
  independence, [R] **tabulate**; [R] **epitab**, [R] **svytab**
  internal consistency, [R] **alpha**
  interrater agreement, [R] **kappa**
  likelihood ratio, [R] **lrtest**
  marginal homogeneity, [R] **symmetry**
  model coefficients, [R] **lrtest**, [R] **svytest**, [R] **test**, [R] **testnl**
  model specification, [R] **linktest**; [R] **hausman**, [R] **regression diagnostics**, [R] **xtreg**
  normality, [R] **sktest**, [R] **swilk**; [R] **boxcox**, [R] **ladder**
  serial independence, [R] **runtest**
  symmetry, [R] **symmetry**
  TDT, [R] **symmetry**
  trend, [R] **epitab**, [R] **nptrend**, [R] **symmetry**

three-stage least squares, [R] **reg3**

time of day, [U] **21.3.10 Built-in global system macros**

X

Y

Z